998

KUNDUN

KUNDUN

-

A Biography of the Family of the

DALAI LAMA

-

MARY CRAIG

COUNTERPOINT
WASHINGTON, D.C.

Front jacket photograph shows Dekyi Tsering (the Great Mother) and her children pictured in the early 1950s. From left to right: Dekyi Tsering, Tsering Dolma, Thubten Jigme Norbu, Gyalo Thondup, Lobsang Samten, HH the Dalai Lama, Jetsun Pema and Tendzin Choegyal.

Text copyright © 1997 by Mary Craig
Illustrations copyright © 1997 by Anne Jennings Brown

First published in Great Britain in 1997 by HarperCollins*Publishers*

LIBRARY OF CONGRESS CATALOGING-IN-PUBLICATION DATA
Craig, Mary.
Kundun : a biography of the family of the Dalai Lama / Mary Craig.
1. Bstan-'dzin-rgya-mtsho, Dalai Lama XIV, 1935– —xFamily.
I. Title.
BQ7935.B777C73 1997
294.3'923'0922—dc21   [B]   97–28904

ISBN 1–887178–64–3 (cloth : alk. paper)

Printed in the United States of America on acid-free paper that meets the American National Standards Institute Z39–48 Standard

JACKET DESIGN: JENNY DOSSIN

COUNTERPOINT
P.O. Box 65793
Washington, D.C. 20035–5793

Distributed by Publishers Group West

1   3   5   7   9   10   8   6   4   2

FIRST PRINTING

For Anne with love

I have always felt that if I had been born in a rich or aristocratic family, I would not have been able to appreciate the
feelings and sentiments of the humble classes of Tibetans.
But owing to my lowly birth, I can understand them and read
their minds, and that is why I feel for them so strongly and
have tried my best to improve their lot in life.

The Fourteenth Dalai Lama

I think of Tibet as a beautiful country, and so it is, but the
greatest beauty to me is that the people live a life dedicated
to religion. You know it when you meet them without being
told. There is a warmth that touches you, a power that fills
you with new strength, a peace that is gentle. I remember
such people, and I feel sad that now it is so seldom one meets
their like.

Thubten Jigme Norbu, eldest brother of the Dalai Lama

A small child running out of a burning building is powerless
to put the fire out by himself. All he can do is yell, 'Fire', in
the hope that some bigger, stronger people will listen and
take action. That's exactly what we Tibetans are doing. Our
home is disintegrating and our relatives are in there.

Tendzin Choegyal, younger brother of the Dalai Lama

Contents

Acknowledgements   XI
List of Illustrations   XIII
Foreword by His Holiness the Dalai Lama   XV
Preface   XIX
Family Tree   XXI

1   Death of a Dalai Lama   1
2   The Search   11
3   In the Land of Horses   22
4   Kumbum   41
5   The Holy Child of Amdo   54
6   Lord of the Lion Throne   68
7   City of the Gods   82
8   Inside the Potala   96
9   A Window on to the World   113
10   Twilight of the Gods 1947–50   130
11   A Flight and a Return   146
12   The Brothers   155
13   Gyalo Thondup in Lhasa 1952   164
14   In China 1954–5   174
15   The Storm Comes Closer   189
16   Buddha Jayanti 1956   198
17   Uprising and Escape 1959   212
18   Fugitives   226
19   Belonging and Not Belonging   241
20   Family Matters 1960–5   255
21   ...And 1965–70   270
22   Stones and Stars 1970s   290
23   New Dawn – or False Hope? 1979–80   305
24   A Time for Grieving   320
25   Return to Darkness   334
26   The Hazards of Democracy   347
27   A Role for the Yapshi?   356

Bibliography   371
Index   373

Acknowledgements

- I should like first of all to thank the Dalai Lama, for the many hours I was privileged to spend with him, and for his patience and good humour at all times.
- Thanks are due also to the family for their friendship and co-operation, especially to Tendzin Choegyal, Rinchen Khando Choegyal, Jetsun Pema, and Namlha Taklha in Dharamsala. And to Khando Chazotsang – whom I first knew in Dharamsala and later went to stay with at her home in Utah.
- Special thanks to Jetsun Pema who arranged for me to meet her elusive older brothers, Thubten Jigme Norbu and Gyalo Thondup, when they were in Dharamsala for the sixtieth birthday celebrations of His Holiness in July 1995. And to Gyalo Thondup for the unexpected and very welcome six-hour interview he gave me later in New Delhi.
- Still in Dharamsala, thanks are due to: His Holiness's Secretary, Tenzin Geyche Tethong, for his unfailing help and support; my old friend, Tenzin Atisha at the Department of Information; and Tashi Tsering of the Tibetan Library (and Amnye Machin Foundation) for pointing me in the direction of crucial Foreign Office papers in the British Library.
- Nearer home, I am grateful to Mrs Kesang Taklha, His Holiness's Representative in London, to Phuntsok Tashi Taklha for his reminiscences, and to Tseten Samdup at the Office of Tibet, who was always on hand (at least by telephone, fax or e-mail) to encourage and advise. Phuntsog Wangyal at the Tibet Foundation contributed much fascinating material and even more intriguing insights.
- My gratitude to Hugh Richardson for his invaluable memories of former days in Tibet, and for his kindness and courtesy in receiving me at his home in St Andrews.
- Finally, I owe a huge debt of gratitude to my friend, Anne Jennings Brown, who not only provided the illustrations for the book, but also constantly spurred me on when I showed signs of flagging. She came with me three times to Dharamsala and read the manuscript in all its

various stages. Tendzin Choegyal and Khando Chazotsang also read the completed manuscript, and I am deeply grateful to them both. It was Tendzin Choegyal's suggestion that one day I should return to Dharamsala to help him with his memoirs that sparked off the idea for this book. He has been endlessly helpful.

List of Illustrations

The Tibetan artefacts depicted on the first page of each chapter are as follows:

p. 1   Woman's hair ornament. Silver inlaid with turquoise. Eastern Tibet.

p. 11   White silk scarf presented as a formal mark of esteem, of social and religious significance.

p. 22   Silver-lined wooden bowl with engraved silver cover and jade knob, to hold *chang* (beer) or tea.

p. 41   Silver seal. Used by nobility to sign letters and official documents.

p. 54   Brass spoon, designed to hang from the waistband.

p. 68   Woman's ear-ring, with supporting cord. Silver and turquoise. Eastern Tibet.

p. 82   Brass butter-lamp. Filled with yak's butter and floating wick.

p. 96   Tinder pouch. Leather with silver mounts and jade bead, steel blade and brass ring to hang from waist. Flint and tinder are kept in the pouch.

p. 113   Ritual chopper, with curved steel blade and brass *dorje* hilt (see p. 174 below). Used by lamas in ritual ceremonies to symbolically cut through obstacles.

p. 130   Marker for a rosary. Cotton cord with ten silver beads, and ornaments at each end.

p. 146   Offering bowl. Brass lined with bell metal. Filled daily with water and placed on an altar.

p. 155   *D'zi*, barrel beads of agate or glass-like material with auspicious white patterns. Believed to be from a previous civilization.

p. 164   Incense burner. The incense sticks or juniper twigs are laid inside on a layer of sand. Painted wood and gesso.

p. 174   *Dorje*, Heavenly Thunderbolt or Diamond Sceptre. Held in the right hand by monks during religious ceremonies, it represents compassion. Brass or bronze.

p. 189 Temple horn. Conch shell encased in silver. Used in temple orchestras, also to invoke water or rain.

p. 198 Tsampa bowl. To hold salted tea mixed with yak's butter and roasted barley flour (tsampa), the staple diet of Tibetans. Dark wood encased in silver.

p. 212 Knife and sheath. Steel blade with silver hilt, and sheath hung from the belt.

p. 226 Metal soup ladle, with hanging loop for when travelling.

p. 241 One of a pair of woman's silver hair ornaments decorated with coral & turquoise, suspended either side of the face. Worn by the nobility in Lhasa and central Tibet.

p. 255 Rosary of 108 prayer beads made of human bone, inlaid with silver, brass, copper, coral and turquoise.

p. 270 Silver costume ornament to hold a chatelaine or draped string of beads.

p. 290 The cranium of a deceased high lama (or wise man), lined with silver and filled with consecrated liquid in specific rituals.

p. 305 Ceremonial silver teapot used by high lamas and the nobility.

p. 320 Reliquary box with glass window to view small image or relic. Silver and turquoise.

p. 334 Reliquary box, worn around the neck. Silver with turquoise. Central Tibet.

p. 347 Decorative belt-hanging. Brocade with silver mount and turquoise. Eastern Tibet.

p. 356 Small reliquary box to hold religious charms. Silver and turquoise. Southern and western Tibet.

Foreword

By His Holiness the Dalai Lama

In the early years of my life, Tibet was a land where people were free to live according to their own traditions. What the Tibetan way of life lacked in terms of modern amenities it more than made up for in terms of contentment. Our physical needs were adequately met and our ancient culture, strongly influenced by Buddhism, brought us peace of mind. The water was pure, the air was clean and the land was vast. Our low population had little cause for fear or anxiety. Farmers and nomadic herdspeople were amply productive and no one went hungry. Education and spiritual training were available in the monasteries and nunneries. Entry to them was unrestricted and the monks and nuns received universal respect. People could come and go as they pleased, which they regularly did, mostly on pilgrimage or trading expeditions. Even our wild animals ran free due to the long-standing prohibition on hunting. In short, Tibet was a land of peace, because there was harmony between people and animals, between sentient beings and the environment.

Unfortunately, in our natural isolation, we took this peace and harmony for granted. When the storm of the Chinese invasion broke over Tibet, it took us by surprise. The subsequent occupation has been ruthless and unrelenting. From the broken promises to respect our customs and way of life to the physical destruction of our cultural monuments, artefacts and our natural environment, the occupying forces have shown little regard for anything Tibetan. After more than forty years of upheaval, there cannot be a single Tibetan family whose lives have not been turned upside down.

In telling the story of my family members, Mary Craig reveals something of the tragedy that befell our nation. Beginning with the happy days at home as ordinary farmers, she describes the great changes that took place when I was recognized as the Dalai Lama and we moved to Lhasa. Sadly those good times were short-lived. I was barely fifteen when the Chinese invaded and there were the first signs that the way of life we had known was coming to an end. Gradually, our carefree attitudes gave way to tension and anxiety. Finally, in 1959, I and those members of my direct family who remained in Tibet escaped to India as refugees.

As the Dalai Lama, I have a special responsibility towards Tibet and its people. I do not claim to have high realizations or any other quality, but I firmly believe that there is a special karmic bond between the Tibetan people and myself. Because of this I was born at this critical juncture when we Tibetans are facing great trouble and there is a need to work hard. My predecessor, the Thirteenth Dalai Lama, felt himself to be very much alone, whereas I have had the good fortune to have received the help and support of my brothers and sisters.

Historically and according to international law Tibet is an independent country under illegal Chinese occupation. However, although we have the right to reclaim our independence, I have adopted a 'middle-way' approach of reconciliation and compromise. While it is the overwhelming desire of the Tibetan people to regain their national independence, I have repeatedly and publicly stated that I am willing to enter into negotiations on the basis of an agenda that does not include independence. The continued occupation of Tibet poses an increasing threat to the very existence of a distinct Tibetan national and cultural identity. Therefore, I consider that my primary responsibility is to take whatever steps I must to save my people and our unique cultural heritage from total annihilation.

Tibet's religious culture, its medical knowledge, peaceful outlook and respectful attitude to the environment contain much that can be of widespread benefit to others. Therefore, those of us in exile have had a responsibility to preserve what we could, not only for the benefit of our brothers and sisters who remain in Tibet, but also for the world at large. In re-establishing our religious and cultural institutions we have ensured the survival of these traditions, at least for the time being. But, in the long run, we will be able to maintain them in a dynamic way only if we return to the freedom of our own land.

No matter how successful those of us in exile have been, we are but a fraction of the entire population of six million Tibetans. They continue to live under dreadful conditions. The Chinese may have brought elements of modernization and economic improvement to Tibet, but, as the saying goes, man does not live by bread alone. People need mental freedom, a conducive atmosphere in which to exercise their creative talents, and, above all, personal responsibility, the ability to determine their own future. Unfortunately, these basic rights are absent in Chinese-occupied Tibet.

It would be easy to be pessimistic. Recently, new measures have been adopted by the Chinese authorities to tighten political control in Tibet. A new crackdown has been launched against advocates of human rights and independence. People suspected of harbouring religious and nationalistic feelings are falling victim to a new wave of political persecution. Existing monasteries have been raided by the police. The construction or rebuilding of monasteries and nunneries has been prohibited and the admission of new monks and nuns stopped. Tibetans who used to work as guides for foreign tourists have been dismissed. Tibetan children are no longer allowed to study in our institutions in exile and those already doing so have been ordered to return. At the same time, the flow of Chinese settlers into Tibet continues inexorably.

Nevertheless, it is important to be optimistic. All is not lost. We Tibetans are resilient, patient and resourceful. Ours is a just cause. We continue to be confident that truth will ultimately triumph and our land and people will once more be free. Would the Chinese consider the Tibetan question so sensitive if our cause was dead? Under difficult circumstances we have kept the Tibetan spirit and a sense of hope alive. However, it is clear that these efforts alone will not be sufficient to bring about a final positive solution. Therefore, I appeal to readers of this book to support the Tibetan people, so that ultimately they may again live in peace with dignity.

8 January 1997

Preface

While I was writing *Tears of Blood*, my book on the Chinese occupation of Tibet, I made several visits to Dharamsala, the hill station in Northern India which is the home of the Dalai Lama and his administration-in-exile. It became almost a second home to me and I made many enduring friendships there. The more I learned about Tibet and Tibetans, the more I was hooked. So much so that when Giles Semper, my then editor at HarperCollins, suggested a second book on Tibet, I jumped at the chance. It occurred to me then that, while there had been many books written about the Dalai Lama himself, no one, so far as I knew, had ever written about his immediate family, his mother, father, four brothers and two sisters. I wrote to His Holiness to see whether he would agree to a book on the family, and was delighted to find that he thought the idea a good one.

That was 1993. Since then I have made many more visits to Dharamsala, consolidating old friendships and making new ones. Those of the family who live there could not have been more co-operative, and gradually I became immersed in their very different lives. The rags-to-riches-and-back-again theme is perennially fascinating, and there were so many facets to it. How do people cope with such huge and traumatic changes? How did an ordinary peasant family adapt to having a Dalai Lama in its midst? How did they learn to turn themselves into a royal family? How did they then cope with losing everything and becoming refugees? How did people steeped in the isolationism of the most mysterious land on earth adapt to life in a modern, bustling land such as India? How easily did they survive the culture shock of exchanging their own medieval world, unchanged through the centuries, for the dislocated post-modern societies of the West? Were they able to reinvent themselves, to find a role for themselves in these very different societies? Or did they themselves experience a certain dislocation?

The thread running through all their lives is, of course, Tibet. The various members of the Dalai Lama's family are linked together by their love of and loyalty to their country – and by their devotion to the Dalai Lama, to whom they refer as His Holiness, or Kundun – the Presence – rather than brother. Their lives are woven and meshed into the fabric of the Tibetan experience, the experience of a country, rich in its beliefs and culture, which was overthrown by a ruthless and powerful invader and is now threatened with the extinction of its identity. It is not possible to tell their stories without telling the story of Tibet.

This has been an absorbing book to research and write. If I have one regret at the end of it, it is that I came on the scene too late to meet the remarkable Dekyi Tsering (Amala), mother of the family and designated Great Mother of Tibet. The more I learned about her, the more I regretted not having met her. I have walked in her garden, lived in her house, even slept in the room where she died. I have a picture of her hanging in my hallway at home. But what wouldn't I give to have actually known her? The family were well blessed to have such a truly extraordinary woman as mother.

Mary Craig 1996

THE FAMILY OF THE DALAI LAMA, KNOWN AS THE YAPSHI TAKLHA FAMILY

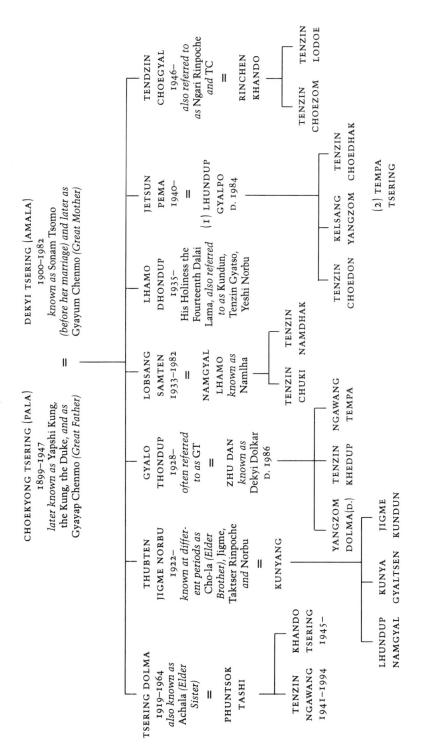

Death of a Dalai Lama

In my lifetime conditions will be as they are now, peaceful and quiet. But the future holds darkness and misery. I have warned you of these things.

The Last Political Testament of the Thirteenth Dalai Lama

On the twenty-second day of the tenth month of the Year of the Waterbird (roughly 17 December 1933 on the Western Calendar), Choekyong Tsering, a farmer from the village of Taktser in the far north-east of Tibet, rode home from market with news that would plunge his family and neighbours into deep shock. Thubten Gyatso, the Thirteenth Dalai Lama, secular and spiritual ruler of Tibet, was dead.

Arguably the greatest of all the Dalai Lamas, Thubten Gyatso had 'returned to the Heavenly Fields' at the age of fifty-eight after being ill for only twelve days with what had seemed like an ordinary cold. A strong-minded champion of his country's independence, he had ruled Tibet as a benevolent autocrat since 1895. In 1911, after a Revolution in China which had deposed the Manchu Emperor, he had lost no time in declaring Tibet's independence from China, and thereafter distanced himself steadily from the new Chinese Republic, preferring to form closer ties with the Government of Great Britain in India.[1] A political realist at the helm of a near-medieval, semi-feudal theocracy, he was aware that if Tibet was to survive, it must come into the modern age; and had forced through a number of reforms in the teeth of fierce opposition from an entrenched monastic and aristocratic Establishment. He had overhauled Tibet's anti-quated penal system and abolished capital punishment; standardized taxa-tion; extended education; introduced electricity, postal services, telegraph and telephone systems and a mint for producing currency. He had reorga-nized the small Tibetan army along British lines,[2] having its military bands play such un-Asian tunes as 'It's a Long Way to Tipperary', 'Auld Lang Syne' and 'God Save the King',[3] and adopting British words of com-mand for its drill. One way or another, the Thirteenth Dalai Lama had been determined that his country should be able to hold its own in the modern world. Had he lived a few years longer, who knows what the sub-sequent history of Tibet might have been?

In 1931, two years before his untimely death, the Great Thirteenth had published an urgent warning to his countrymen (aimed, more specifically, at the officials and the powerful monks) that preserving Tibet's indepen-dence in the modern world would require selflessness and dedication. The future lay in their hands:

> I urge you all to rise up together and work for the common good in accordance with your individual capacity...Together we can win out in the end. Avoid ri-valry and petty self-interest, and look instead to what is essential.[4]

Warning that the recent spread of revolutionary Communism to neigh-bouring Mongolia posed a threat to Tibet, and describing how monasteries (and monks) there were being destroyed, he prophesied:

> It will not be long before we find the red onslaught at our own front door. It is only a matter of time before we come into a direct confrontation with it, ei-ther from within our own ranks or else as a threat from an external (Commu-nist) nation.
>
> And when that happens we must be ready to defend ourselves. Otherwise our spiritual and cultural conditions will be completely eradicated.[5]

This prophecy, followed so closely by its author's death, struck fear into the hearts of the Tibetans. Until now, they had believed themselves pro-tected by the impregnable mountain ranges which surrounded them. If their mountains could no longer protect them, who then could save them?

But in Tibet's capital, Lhasa, the predominant emotion was grief. Losing a Dalai Lama was, for this most religious people on earth, like losing an important part of themselves. Whole families went into mourning, weep-ing openly on the streets:

the drums on the Potala Palace roof beat a sorrowful dirge, spreading the news...throughout Lhasa. Prayer flags and other house decorations were taken down, and people dressed in traditional mourning: dark colours, with no aprons and no ear-rings or other jewellery. Singing, dancing and playing music were banned; butter-lamps burned on household altars and on house-roofs; and people offered prayers in the holy Tsuglakhang Temple.[6]

When the traditional 49-day period of mourning was over and people re-sumed their normal lives, there was still, as one man wrote, 'a place in our hearts which was empty, and we prayed and hoped he would return to us soon'.[7]

Already there was speculation about where and how soon the dead leader's reincarnation would be found. In Buddhist belief, rebirth follows death: a good life merits rebirth on to a higher plane of existence, (a bad one on to a lower), until at last goodness may lead to enlightenment – the realization of things as they actually are, without delusion – and absorp-tion into the light of Ultimate Reality. Human beings who have reached the enlightened state yet choose to go on being reborn in order to help oth-ers to reach it are known as *bodhisattvas*; and every Dalai Lama is a *bod-hisattva*. Each one is a reincarnation of his predecessor, a re-embodiment of Chenrezig, the Lord of Mercy and Compassion, the patron deity of Tibet, who centuries ago vowed to continue returning to earth in human form until all sentient beings were saved.[8] Each Dalai Lama has the power to choose where and to whom he will be reborn.

What fortunate Tibetan couple would, probably in a few months' time, give birth to the boy-child in whom the spiritual consciousness of the late leader would once again be incarnated? Where and how would he be found? Every pregnant woman in the land must have prayed she might be the chosen one.

Since to the Western mind, the whole Dalai Lama business seems unut-terably exotic, it may help to look briefly at how the institution came into being and what it had come to mean. The Dalai Lamas do not stretch back into the mists of time, they have been around only since the sixteenth century; and their story is tied up with that of their country.

The Tibetans emerged with a flourish on to the world scene in the early seventh century, when their king, Songtsen Gampo, invaded the Chinese Empire and laid the foundations of what was to become one of the most powerful nations in Asia. Over the next two centuries, the Tibetan Empire came to include Nepal, Bhutan, Upper Burma, Turkestan and parts of Western China. In AD 763, showing a military genius matched only by that of Genghis Khan and his successors four centuries later, Tibetan armies marched to the gates of the Chinese capital (present-day Xian) and dictated terms of peace to the emperor, exacting from him an annual tribute of fifty thousand rolls of silk. A later peace treaty signed between the two countries in AD 821 did not, as the Chinese claim today, result in some kind of 'union' between them. On the contrary, its principal passage makes it quite clear that here were two separate, equally powerful empires:

> Tibet and China shall abide by the frontiers of which they are now in occupation. All to the east is the country of great China; and all to the west is, without question, the country of great Tibet. Henceforth, on neither side shall there be waging of war nor seizing of territory...
>
> This solemn agreement has established a great epoch when Tibetans shall be happy in the land of Tibet, and Chinese in the land of China.[9]

Long before the seventh century, wandering holy men from India had brought Mahayana Buddhism to Tibet[10] – but its impact had been slight. The real spark to Tibet's future[11] came from King Songtsen Gampo's two Buddhist wives, Wen Chang, a Chinese princess, and Bhrikuti, a Nepalese. The Chinese bride brought as part of her dowry a large bronze statue of Buddha which had originally come from India. To house it, a temple (the Jokhang, meaning House of the Lord) was built in Lhasa and became one of the most sacred sites in the whole of Asia. Having converted the king, his wives spread the Buddhist teachings wherever they went. Though still little more than a court religion, with the weight and prestige of the State behind it, Buddhism slowly and painfully absorbed and displaced Tibet's indigenous shamanism, Bön. The monastic system which would eventually give the country its political and cultural identity was established.

This golden age of Tibetan history ended in about AD 914, when a usurper king suppressed Buddhism and brought about the monarchy's collapse. For about three hundred years Tibet disintegrated into a ferment of feuding kingdoms. Yet somewhere along that chaotic road, Buddhism made a spectacular comeback, reintroduced in the eleventh century by the Indian scholar-saint, Atisha. By the twelfth century, it was universally adopted. Tibetans turned their backs on their martial past and became the sole inheritors of the peaceful Buddhist tradition, which, under Muslim pressure, had already disappeared from North-West India and Central Asia.[12]

In the early thirteenth century, Tibet came into the orbit of the legendary Genghis Khan, becoming part of the huge Mongol Empire which came to dominate most of Asia and much of Europe besides. That the Mongols did not actually invade Tibet – apart from the north-eastern area nearest to Mongolia – was mainly because the Tibetans achieved a sort of symbiotic relationship with the Khans: spiritual teaching in exchange for military protection. This Chö-Yon (priest/patron) relationship, in which neither party was considered superior to the other – suited the needs of both. When, a few decades later, the great Kubilai Khan conquered the Chinese Empire and made it the centre of his Yuan Dynasty he embraced Tibetan Buddhism for himself and his court and continued the relationship on the same mutually acceptable terms. This is the basis of China's present insistence that Tibet is part of China, yet it is a fact that no Mongol ruler ever made any attempt to impose direct rule over Tibet. 'Tibet did not even pay tax to the Mongol Empire, and it certainly was never considered part of China by the Mongol Emperors.'[13] Ten years before the end of the Mongol Dynasty in China (1386) Tibet had severed its political ties with the Empire, though the priest/patron relationship with the Mongol Khans remained.

A century passed and Tibet again relapsed into civil disorder, while in the monasteries discipline grew slack. A saviour came on the scene in the fourteenth century: Tsong-khapa (1357–1419), a monk from the north-eastern Amdo region. Tsong-khapa reasserted a long-lost monastic discipline, built the Ganden monastery outside Lhasa, and unified Buddhist doctrine by drawing up a canon of written scriptures to replace the hitherto oral tradition. Those who adopted Tsong-khapa's reforms were known as Gelugpa or Virtuous Ones – their aim being a life of simple austerity, in tune with the teachings of the Buddha.

Tsong-khapa was succeeded as head of the Gelugpa sect by one of his disciples, and it was after the latter's death in 1475 that the *tulku* system which came to be the hallmark of Tibetan Buddhism was finally established. For almost two hundred years the Tibetans had believed that the spiritual essence of holy men or great teachers (known as lamas)[14] was reincarnated in their successors who then became known as Incarnations or *tulkus*.[15] This now became an article of faith.

The *tulku* system was raised a notch higher in 1517 when the Tibetan teacher Sonam Gyatso converted Altan Khan, a descendant of the Great

Kubilai. At the court of the Khan, the warrior chieftain and the lama swore eternal friendship and bestowed magnificent titles on each other, Sonam Gyatso receiving that of Dalai Lama, a Mongolian term meaning Broad Ocean – interpreted to mean 'the teacher whose wisdom is as vast as the Ocean'.

Accepting the title not only for himself but also retrospectively for his two predecessors, Sonam Gyatso would henceforth be known as the Third Dalai Lama. The title remained a purely spiritual one until 1642 when, after a vicious civil war in Tibet, another Khan, Gushri, installed the energetic and visionary Fifth Dalai Lama as the first King of a unified Tibet, investing him with absolute secular as well as spiritual power. To consolidate his position, the new ruler made his way to Peking, where the Manchu (Ch'ing) Dynasty had recently been established. He was received as both sovereign and equal. It is recorded that the Emperor of China 'went out of his capital to meet his visitor, and that he had an inclined pathway built over the city wall so that the Dalai Lama could pass into the city without going through a gate in the wall, for pedestrians use the walls of Peking and it was felt to be unfitting that His Holiness should pass beneath a place trodden by people's feet'.[16]

The Fifth Dalai Lama – 'the Great Fifth' – was thus the first in a new line of religious kings, the first to be called His Holiness the Ruler. It was he who put Lhasa on the map and restructured the whole Tibetan system of government, ensuring that from now on all positions of importance would be filled jointly by lay officials and monks.

Few of his successors, however, lived long enough to enjoy power – for two centuries after the death of the Great Fifth in 1682, no Dalai Lama ruled Tibet for more than a few years.[17] Since they were discovered as young children, usually from peasant or middle-class families, a Regent was appointed to rule until they were old enough to take over, usually at the age of eighteen. The Regents acquired considerable power – which they were disinclined to relinquish when the time came. Could it have been coincidental that between the seventh and thirteenth holders of the office, only one ('the Great Thirteenth') reached his majority? It was generally assumed that the others were poisoned by the reigning Regent – with a little help from the Chinese who would naturally prefer a Regent who was secretly on their pay-roll to an unknown who was king, pope and incarnate god rolled into one. The Great Thirteenth himself had survived an assassination attempt shortly after his accession. In what has been described as 'the case of the accursed shoes',[18] the retiring Regent apparently attempted to regain power through black magic, preparing a powerful mantra which consisted of the figure of a man with outstretched arms and legs. Surrounding this figure were various written mantras and inside its body the words *Thubten Gyatso* and *chiwa* were written: Thubten Gyatso was the personal name of the Thirteenth Dalai Lama and *chiwa* was his birth year. This black mantra was put inside the sole of a beautiful pair of new boots.[19]

It is unclear whether the boots were actually sent to the Dalai Lama, though his British friend, Sir Charles Bell (the Government of India's Political Officer in Sikkim) believed they were.[20] At all events, the 22-year-old ruler knew there had been an attempt on his life and that his ex-Regent was implicated. The latter was placed under house-arrest and soon afterwards he too mysteriously died![21]

Given this inauspicious start to the Great Thirteenth's reign, it was hardly surprising that his sudden death should herald accusations of foul play. The young monk, Kunphela, a favourite of the late ruler, and in the running for the job of Regent, found himself arrested on suspicion of poisoning his master. Though the case against him remained unproved, he was sentenced to exile for life.

The Great Thirteenth's warnings about the future were well founded. After the overthrow of the Empire in China, the first attempt at democracy by the ruling Kuomintang (KMT, Nationalist) Party had disintegrated into civil conflict, with a number of warlords striving for power. The Chinese Communist Party had been formed in 1921, and Chiang Kai-shek, who became leader of the Kuomintang in 1926, at first supported them. But Chiang had turned on the Communists, and was now engaged in a fight to the death with them. The danger, as the Great Thirteenth well knew, was coming closer.

But the warnings went unheeded, his death in 1933 being followed by a bitter power-struggle in Tibet, with rival groups striving to have their own candidate declared Regent by the National Assembly.[22] Though it was known that the late ruler had hoped for the appointment of a Regent with some knowledge and understanding of the larger world outside, the monk die-hards in the Government insisted that Regents must continue to be incarnate lamas chosen from one of The Three Seats, the powerful Lhasa monasteries, Drepung – the largest, with 10,000 monks, Sera (about 7500), or Ganden (6000) – i.e. from men totally lacking in worldly or administrative know-how. A young, inexperienced Incarnate named Reting was selected by lottery – a choice tragic in its consequences. Under his leadership, the reforms of the Great Thirteenth would go to the wall; the economic surpluses would disappear, the ethical standards would slip and the efficient little British-style army would be left to disintegrate, with its trained officers sidelined into civil jobs.

But, in those early days after the Thirteenth Dalai Lama's death, these matters seemed of little importance beside the two urgent tasks facing the new Regent: first, to build a splendid gold mausoleum in memory of the late ruler; and then, most important of all, to undertake the search for his successor.

NOTES

1. In 1910, the Chinese had occupied Tibet's capital, Lhasa, and the Dalai Lama had fled to British India to avoid capture. While there he formed a deep and abiding friendship with the Political Officer for Sikkim, Sir Charles Bell.

2. Nobody had known which army model to choose. The Thirteenth Dalai Lama employed a few foreign instructors, and had one regiment trained by the Russian instructors, another by the Japanese and a third by the British. The British model proved to be the most viable.

3. This was also used as the Tibetan National Anthem.

4. *The Last Political Testament of the Thirteenth Dalai Lama*, trans. Glenn H. Mullin.

5. *The Last Political Testament of the Thirteenth Dalai Lama*.

6. Melvyn C. Goldstein, *A History of Modern Tibet, 1913–1951: The Demise of the Lamaist State*, University of California Press, 1989.

7. Jamyang Norbu, *Warriors of Tibet: the story of Aten and the Khampas' fight for the freedom of their country*, Wisdom Publications, 1979, repr. 1986.

8. The *Bodhisattva* prayer is as follows:
   For as long as space endures,
   And for as long as living beings remain
   Until then may I, too, abide
   To dispel the misery of the world.

9. Hugh E. Richardson, *Tibet and its History*, Appendix 1, Shambhala, 1984.

10. Mahayana Buddhism is based on unselfishness and compassion for all sentient beings, and on the belief in karma, the law of cause and effect which says that

whatever happens to us is the result of our actions in the past. Sentient beings are condemned by karma to be reborn within a world of pain and suffering until they achieve enlightenment. This comes through the practice of patience, tolerance, kindness and compassion, combined with a 'right' way of seeing things as they are.

11. Louis Magrath King, Historical Introduction to *We Tibetans* by Rinchen Lhamo, Potala Books, 1985.

12. See David Snellgrove and Hugh Richardson, *A Cultural History of Tibet*, Prajna Books, 1980.

13. *Tibet, A Source Book*, All-Party Indian Parliamentary Forum for Tibet, 1994.

14. Westerners often speak as though 'lama' is just another name for 'monk'. It is true that some lamas are monks. But not all monks are lamas, for to become a lama (teacher, spiritual guru) takes twenty to twenty-five years of study. It is a peculiarly Tibetan Buddhist belief that important lamas are reincarnated and can choose the manner of their rebirth.

15. The *tulku* system had been developed in an attempt to maintain the authority of the highest priesthood, which was celibate, and to ensure that the 'wisdom memory' of those who had been enlightened was not lost. It incorporated the belief that those who become fully realized, enlightened persons can choose to return to life again and again in order to help all living beings.

16. Magrath King.

17. See Goldstein, chapter 1.

18. W. D. Shakabpa, *Tibet: A Political History*, Potala Books, 1984, p. 195.

19. Shakabpa, p. 195.

20. Sir Charles Bell, *Portrait of the Dalai Lama*, London, 1946.

21. 'Demo Rinpoche ... is said to have been killed by being immersed in a huge copper vat until he drowned.' Goldstein, chapter 1.

22. In the Tibetan system of government, the Dalai Lama – or the Regent during his minority – was at the top of a pyramid. He was assisted by a Cabinet, known as the Kashag, consisting of four ministers, of whom three were laymen and one – the most senior – a monk. Next in importance came the National Assembly, a Parliament which was summoned by the Kashag only at times of grave national emergency. It consisted of fifty lay and monastic officials and was presided over by a Council of four senior monks. (Its deliberations were based not only on civil law but also on Buddhist moral law and so focused not only on the people's material well-being in this life but also on their spiritual welfare in the next.) Lay ministers and all Government officials were appointed from land-owning families – the latters' tenure of land being subject to their

providing at least one member of the family for unpaid Government service. Tibet was therefore ruled jointly by high lamas and the two hundred aristocratic families of Tibet, the one group providing checks and balances on the other.

The Search

The connection of every Tibetan with the Dalai Lama is a deep and inexpressible thing. To us, the Dalai Lama symbolizes the whole of Tibet: the beauty of the land, the purity of its rivers and lakes, the sanctity of its skies, the solidity of its mountains, and the strength of its people. But even more, he is the living embodiment of the eternal principles of Buddhism, and also the epitome of what every Tibetan, from the most debauched harlot in Lhasa to the saintly ascetic, is striving for – freedom, the total freedom of Nirvana.

Jamyang Norbu, Warriors of Tibet

The search for a new Dalai Lama is an undertaking without parallel anywhere else in the world. The succession is neither hereditary nor elective; with every Dalai Lama a fresh start is made. The quest begins within about a year of the former ruler's death. But it is not straightforward. It is not, as Basil Gould[1] tried to explain to a doubtless bemused British Government in 1941,

> a case of considering which of many children born at or about a certain time would be likely to make a suitable successor but of searching – as it were for a hidden treasure – for a child, exact age unknown, whose whereabouts would be indicated by divination and by signs and whose identity would be revealed by the possession of certain bodily characteristics and of marvellous mental and spiritual powers.[2]

In 1934, the Tibetan Government instructed its local authorities to look out for any remarkable boy-babies in their areas, particularly if they displayed the characteristic marks of a Dalai Lama:

> the legs' skin ought to be striped as a tiger's; the eyes wide and the brows turned outwards; the ears large; two fleshly excrescences should be found near the shoulder-blades, as a token of the two extra arms of Chenrezig, the god whose earthly embodiment the Dalai Lama is supposed to be; last, the palms should bear the pattern of a sea-shell.[3]

The late ruler had left certain clues of his own. His body was embalmed, clothed in rich gold brocades and seated cross-legged on his throne in the Norbulingka Palace, facing towards the south. All that day the people of Lhasa filed past, offering white ceremonial scarves in homage. Next morning, the attendants noticed that the head of the corpse had turned several degrees towards the north-east. Gently they returned it to its original position, and all through that second day the people continued their mournful file-past. Next morning, the head had once again slewed round towards the north-east.

Was it a sign that the reincarnation would be found in the north-east? Over the next few months, a succession of omens seemed to reinforce the message.

> The three state Oracles turned eastward in trance…a patch of snapdragons sprouted from the east end of the platform used for public sermons in Lhasa's main square; overnight a giant star-shaped fungus grew on the east side of the north-east pillar of the shrine in the Potala where the Dalai Lama's jewel-in-laid tomb was under construction. And as had frequently happened in the past when a high incarnate lama died, the people of Lhasa beheld auspicious cloud formations, now and again pierced by rainbows, rising over the barren wall of mountains ringing the north-east end of the city.[4]

In old Tibet, such signs and wonders were part of the very fabric of life.

When 1934 and part of 1935 passed without news, despondency grew in Lhasa and throughout Tibet. Then in the summer of 1935 Regent Reting and a party of high officials made a pilgrimage to the sacred lake of Lhamoi Lhatso, about ninety miles south-east of Lhasa. Mountains and lakes were held in awe in the land of mystery and magic that was Tibet, for they seemed to radiate a supernatural life of their own; they were reputed to put strange thoughts into the head and fill the ear with sounds. Some lakes were so numinous that they were consulted as oracles. Of them all, the mountain lake Lhamoi Lhatso inspired the most awe, and was always consulted about the whereabouts of the next Dalai Lama. For its guardian spirit was the goddess Palden Lhamo, who had promised the first Dalai Lama in a vision that she would watch over his successors. (Almost sixty years earlier the birthplace of the Great Thirteenth had been indicated in this same lake.)

Different people saw different things in the still blue waters – and some, it must be said, saw nothing at all. On this occasion, Regent Reting had a vision. But he kept quiet about it until the following year, by which time he had had time to reflect on what he had seen and to discuss its possible meaning with a few selected lamas and Oracles. Summoning the National Assembly, Reting announced that in the lake of Lhamoi Lhatso he had seen, clearly delineated, three Tibetan letters, *ah, ka* and *ma*; a monastery with roofs of jade-green and gold, with a twisting road leading eastwards to a bare pagoda-shaped hill and a small one-storey house with oddly-shaped guttering and turquoise tiles. He said he was now sure that the letter Ah stood for the province of Amdo in the north-east, a huge area populated mainly by Tibetans but currently ruled over by a Muslim warlord in the name of Nationalist China.

The Regent's words caused a stir. Although the earlier signs had all pointed to the possibility of the rebirth taking place in the north-east, some of the delegates were appalled at the idea of sending a search party into an area currently under the control of China. The question of the Tibetan borderlands was explosive, and some of the delegates saw no point in handing China a tailor-made excuse to meddle in Tibet's affairs. But a sacred vision was a sacred vision, and in the end the Assembly agreed that a search party must go to Amdo.

In the autumn of 1936, therefore, three teams of about forty set off for eastern Tibet, each of them led by a high lama and including both monks and lay government officials. They were despatched across the rugged Tibetan plateau, one to Amdo in the north-east, another due east and a third to the south-east, each group charged with identifying two or three likely boys and bringing them back to Lhasa for a final selection. It might well be years before any of them returned.

Over the next two years the Lhasa grapevine buzzed with reports that three, five or even more boys had been discovered in this, that or the other place. The Regent and his Government stayed silent.

Could there be many Tibetan baby boys with tiger-striped legs, long eyes, big ears, extra flesh on the shoulder-blades and a conch-shell imprint on the palm of their hand? Unlikely though it would seem, when the search party reached Amdo in the winter of 1936 they heard of several.[5] They learned from the Panchen Lama, Tibet's second highest spiritual leader, who was now in Amdo,[6] that during a public blessing ceremony at the Kumbum Monastery, he had picked out three possibles. And despite the strong suspicion that the Chinese might have been whispering in the Panchen Lama's ear, nevertheless, the advice of so august a figure could not be disregarded.

After a delay caused by heavy snowfalls, the search party, headed by Kesang Rinpoche,[7] Abbot of Lhasa's Sera Monastery, set off for Kumbum – where, to their satisfaction, they saw the three-tiered pagoda-style building with the jade-green and gold roofs of the Regent's vision. Did the *ka*, the second letter of that vision, stand for Kumbum? If so, all that was now needed was to identify a twisting road leading eastwards, a bare hill and a house with unusual tiles and guttering – and their mission might well be over.

After about six weeks they had amassed twelve names plus the three on the Panchen Lama's list. Of these three, one turned out to have died, but the other two were very serious, top-priority contenders. One was two-year-old Lhamo Dhondup, youngest son of the Amdo farmer, Choekyong Tsering, from the village of Taktser.

Taktser lay high on the Tibetan plateau, about nine thousand feet above sea-level, one of six villages under the jurisdiction of Kumbum monastery and lying on the caravan route between Siling, the seat of the Chinese administration, and Amdo's second largest monastery, Tashi Tashikiel. Along this route, in the winter of 1937, Kesang Rinpoche and his retinue slowly picked their way, having first visited Siling to pay their respects to General Ma Pu-feng, the wily Muslim warlord who ruled the area in China's name. They had decided on their plan of action: they would pose as traders, and on reaching the farmhouse where the child lived, Kesang Rinpoche's servant would pretend to be in charge, while the lama himself would dress as a servant, to gain easy access to the kitchen where the child would probably be playing.

Everything went as planned. The cavalcade approached Taktser, higher than the other villages round about, but otherwise a typical Amdo village with about thirty or so small-holdings jostling each other on a hillside, surrounded by bigger mountains and dominated by the snow- and ice-covered Mount Ami-chiri (or Kyeri). There, suddenly, was the pagoda-shaped hillock and facing it, among a group of three flat-roofed, white-washed buildings slightly higher than the rest, was the single-storey house they sought. With mounting excitement, they saw that it had turquoise tiles and strangely-shaped guttering made of gnarled juniper branches.

At the gate, decorated Tibetan-style with fluttering prayer-flags, the strangers were greeted by the farmer and his wife who offered them hospitality for the night. The 'leader', Lobsang Tsewang, was taken into the house, while his 'servant', Kesang Rinpoche, went into the kitchen. There he found two-year-old Lhamo Dhondup, who immediately ran to him and climbed onto his knee:

> The lama was disguised in a cloak lined with lambskin, but round his neck he was wearing a rosary which had belonged to the Thirteenth Dalai Lama. The little boy seemed to recognize the rosary, and he asked to be given it. The lama promised to give it to him if he could guess who he was, and the boy replied that he was Sera-aga, which meant, in the local dialect, 'a lama of Sera'. The lama asked who the 'master' was and the boy gave the name of Lobsang. He also knew the name of the real servant, which was Amdo Kesang.[8]

Gyalo Thondup, the child's nine-year-old brother, remembers the day clearly:

> With a group of about ten other boys from our village, I used to go to a Chinese school six miles away. We had a two hours' walk every morning and the same back again in the afternoon. On that day, I returned to find people and horses everywhere. I was fascinated by the sight of one tall, dark man wearing long ear-rings. Now in Amdo we did have some men who wore ear-rings, but none with long ear-rings like that. I'd never seen such a thing in my life. I dashed into the kitchen to ask my mother who all these people were. She said they were a group of travellers, businessmen, on their way to the Shartsong hermitage about fifteen miles away. They were Central Tibetans, she told me, rich traders travelling through this area via the Kumbum Monastery. There seemed to be a lot of servants and one of them stayed in the kitchen with my mother, helping her stack up logs for the stove, or carrying my little brother, Lhamo Dhondup, around the kitchen in his arms. My little brother seemed to have taken to him. My mother was busy making tea, heating water, preparing food for them all.[9]

Next morning, the 'traders' went on their way. When they returned soon afterwards, asking if they could again stay for one more night, they were greeted like old friends.

The searchers returned in triumph to their base at Kumbum Monastery and sent a coded telegram to Lhasa about their discovery. (The Panchen Lama's other remaining nominee had proved to be a nonstarter, bursting into tears and fleeing in terror at the sight of the monks – unlikely behaviour for a potential Dalai Lama!) In reply, they were told to continue their examination of the Taktser boy who sounded 'most interesting'.[10]

A few weeks later, as a stream of high lamas and dignitaries left Kumbum Monastery for phase two of the operation, three thousand monks blew a farewell on their conch-shell trumpets, a sound of good omen in Tibet. Just as they were approaching Taktser, they met a man who advised them to go by the lower road. This brought them by way of the little hermitage of Karma Rolpai Dorje on the hill above the village. Here the Thirteenth Dalai Lama had rested in 1909 on his way back to Lhasa after a four-year exile in Mongolia. He had been welcomed by the monks, and received homage from the villagers among whom had been the future farmer Choekyong Tsering, then nine years old. It was recalled that, gazing down on the village below, the Great Thirteenth had remarked on the beauty of the place. He had even left behind a pair of boots, as if intending to return.[11] It occurred to more than one of the searchers that it was not at Kumbum but here at Karma Rolpai Dorje that they had found the *ka, ma* of the Regent's vision, the place to which the Great Thirteenth wanted to return.

It was afternoon when the procession reached the farmhouse. Approaching the front entrance, they mentally registered the turquoise tiles and gnarled guttering, and asked to see the child. The farmer and his wife, awe-struck by the size and grandeur of this cavalcade, had already begun to wonder if perhaps Lhamo Dhondup, like his older brother, Jigme, might be the reincarnation of some great lama. They had always felt the child was special, but it would almost certainly not have occurred to them that he might be the most special reincarnation of them all.

'When they came back that time,' remembers Gyalo Thondup,

we noticed something very strange. The old servant wasn't a servant any more; and the young man who was supposed to be in charge was no longer in charge but seemed to be acting as assistant to the old man. It seemed as though the old man was actually in charge of the whole party. It was very puzzling – until they disclosed their real identity and purpose to my parents. They said my little brother was just possibly the reincarnation of the late Dalai Lama and they asked my parents' permission to put him to the test. Well, of course, they agreed without hesitation. They felt very privileged. The group then went into the kitchen where my little brother was delighted to see his old friend again.[12]

Everything was done according to time-honoured practice. Children considered as possible reincarnations of high lamas are generally expected to remember objects and people from their previous lives and can often recite scriptures they cannot possibly have seen or heard. In this case, the tests involved matched pairs of articles, one of which had belonged to the late Dalai Lama. 'A Living Buddha, thus returning to earth,' explains Sir Charles Bell, 'proves his identity by recognizing his rosary, bell and other religious implements, as well as servants, ponies, etc. that were with him in his previous existence.'[13] So, pairs of articles were laid out on a long trestle table in the farmhouse. They included two black and two yellow rosaries. When the boy was brought in and asked to choose, he chose the two that had belonged to the late ruler.

Next day, they offered him the late Dalai Lama's walking-stick and Kesang Rinpoche's. He looked carefully at these and started to take the fake one. The search team thought he was going to make a mistake, but the boy changed his mind, put the wrong one back and took the correct one. Later, when they thought about this near miss, they realized that the duplicate walking-stick had in fact also belonged to the Dalai Lama, who had given it to a lama, who had in turn given it to Kesang Rinpoche. So the Taktser boy had made no mistake in the three tests. The last test involved the small *damaru* drum the Thirteenth Dalai Lama had used to summon his servants. It was very plain, while the duplicate one was spectacularly beautiful, with ivory, gold and turquoise and a long, multi-coloured brocade tassel. Kheme later said he was very nervous about this test. However, the child again chose correctly, taking it immediately in his right hand and beginning to play it.[14]

His mother, in conversation with a friend, recalled the incident of the drum:

When the time came for me to take him to bed he clutched a small drum which the Thirteenth Dalai Lama had used for calling his attendants, and he beat it exactly as the monks do during prayers. He refused to be parted from it, and I was much embarrassed by the self-will shown by my usually biddable child. The lamas, however, told me to let him keep it.[15]

By now the men from Lhasa were in no doubt at all that they had found the child they were seeking. (He even had the tiger-striped legs and significantly large ears.) But when they returned a few days later to Kumbum, they dared not admit the fact, since the last thing they wanted was for the Chinese authorities in Siling to suspect the truth just yet. Unfortunately, there was only one telegraph line in Tibet, and as it was routed via the trading station, Kalimpong, in India, messages took a long time to get through. And although their telegram to Lhasa elicited the coded reply that the Taktser boy was obviously the right one and should be brought forthwith to the Holy City, they knew very well that once Ma Pu-feng got wind of this, he would demand a king's ransom before he let the boy go, and even then would insist on a huge Chinese military escort to go with him to Lhasa.

The fact was that the Chinese, whose representatives in Lhasa the Great Thirteenth had promptly expelled in 1912 when the Manchu Empire collapsed, had long been looking for an excuse to return.[16] The Kuomintang Government of General Chiang Kai-shek had already attempted to reassert Chinese influence over Tibet by sending an official condolence Mission to Lhasa after the Dalai Lama's death.[17] The Tibetan Government had wanted to refuse, but were persuaded by the senior monks that the Mission's purpose was purely religious. Such thinking was ludicrously naïve – the Mission's real objective being to find out whether, unlike the old Dalai Lama who had turfed them out, the new people in power might be intimidated or suborned back into the Chinese fold. Though General Huang Musung, the Mission's leader, was reluctantly obliged to return home after delivering his condolences, he contrived to leave behind two officials with a wireless transmitter, the only one in the whole of Tibet.

Secrecy regarding the child was vital, though it is clear that the British in India knew what was going on. A coded telegram from the Government of India External Affairs Department to the Secretary of State for India on 6 June 1938 announced that, according to a usually reliable source, 'The reincarnation of the Dalai Lama has been discovered in Amdo country... [and that] steps are being taken to recognize the child officially'. A further telegram, dated 16 August, is more specific: the child has been located in the Kokonor area of Amdo, i.e. in Chinese territory:

IT IS HOPED THAT THE CHILD MAY BE BROUGHT SECRETLY TO TIBET DUR-
ING THE WINTER. MEANWHILE, FOR FEAR OF CHINESE INTERFERENCE,
GREATEST SECRECY IS BEING MAINTAINED AND IT IS POSSIBLE THAT AS A
PRECAUTION THE TIBETAN GOVERNMENT MAY ANNOUNCE THE DISCOVERY
OF SEVERAL POSSIBLE CANDIDATES.[18]

The Tibetans did indeed take this precaution; but one by one the other candidates were ruled out. None but Lhamo Dhondup had chosen even two
items on the list right – and he had made no mistakes at all. The Tibetans
were forced to admit to Ma Pu-feng that the Taktser boy had indeed done
rather better in the tests than the others, while insisting that candidates
from other regions had still to be considered and that no definite conclusion could be reached until all the finalists had been brought to Lhasa.

Ma, being nobody's fool, took precautions of his own. 'One day,' recalls
Gyalo Thondup,

> I came home from school to find a number of armed soldiers from Siling in-
> stalled there. They said they had come to take my parents and little brother
> away. I began to howl, because it meant that I was going to be left there on my
> own, but the soldiers didn't care. My mother was trying to make arrange-
> ments for my uncle and aunt next door to look after me. She was very upset
> and frightened, and I was bawling my head off. The officer in charge merely
> said he was obeying orders from the Governor General – to take my parents
> and younger brother to Siling. There could be no arguing with that. They left
> within a day or two. Of course, when Kesang Rinpoche heard what had hap-
> pened, he dashed straight down to Siling to see Ma Pu-feng. He learned to his
> relief that my family were not in prison, they were being housed in a rather
> nice guest-house in the town. Ma asked Kesang Rinpoche if the boy really was
> the Dalai Lama, but Rinpoche said that he was only one candidate and noth-
> ing had been decided yet. He asked Ma to release the family, to let them go
> back home or at least to Kumbum Monastery.

Shortly after that, the family took their youngest child to Kumbum, and a
group of riders was despatched to bring Gyalo Thondup from Taktser to
join them. He and his parents would soon afterwards leave the monastery
and go home, but two-year-old Lhamo Dhondup would not. His brief
childhood was already over.

NOTES

1. B. J. (later Sir Basil) Gould was British India's Political Officer in Sikkim, and as such had an advisory role in Bhutan and a 'vaguely diplomatic' one in Tibet. He was in Lhasa with a small British Mission from 1936 to 1937 and returned there in 1939 for the installation of the new Dalai Lama.

2. Report by Mr B. J.Gould, C.M.G., C.I.E., On the Discovery, Recognition and Installation of the Fourteenth Dalai Lama. White Paper for official use only, 1941.

3. Giuseppe Tucci, *To Lhasa and Beyond, Diary of the Expedition to Tibet in the year 1928*, Snow Lion Publications, 1983 (first published 1956).

4. John Avedon, *In Exile from the Land of Snows*, Michael Joseph, 1984.

5. Kham is the eastern part of Tibet, Do-kham or Amdo the north-east. Both areas are inhabited by the distinctive race of Tibetans known as Khampas.

6. The Panchen Lama's monastery of Tashilhunpo near Shigatse owned huge estates. It had never been the custom for landowners and big monasteries to pay much revenue to the Government, but because of the expense of maintaining a standing army, the Thirteenth Dalai Lama had revised the taxation system to collect money from both groups. For centuries the Chinese had made a point of playing off the Panchen Lama against the Dalai Lama, and had acquired influence in the former's court. After the Dalai Lama's flight to British India in 1910 (following a Chinese occupation of Lhasa), the Tashilhunpo officials became very friendly with the Chinese. When, later, the new taxes were imposed, they saw it as a kind of revenge, possibly the thin end of the wedge. So in 1923, the pro-Chinese courtiers ran away to China, and persuaded the 40-year-old Ninth Panchen to go with them. There was great disquiet throughout Tibet at this, the Tibetans fearing that the Chinese would exploit the situation and use it as a pretext for invading Tibet.

In 1935, when it was known that the Panchen Lama wished to return home, this became a dangerous political issue, since the Chinese had obtained a large measure of control over him and his court and were insisting on his return to Tibet with a large Chinese military escort. This, of course, was seen by the Tibetans as illustrating China's determination to extend its influence over Tibet, and they were resolved to resist it. There was grave danger of a clash between the two countries, but the situation was defused both by the outbreak of the Sino-Japanese War in June 1937 and by the Ninth Panchen Lama's death while still on Chinese territory, on 1 December 1937.

7. An incarnate lama – *tulku* – is addressed as Rinpoche, or 'Precious One'.

8. Fourteenth Dalai Lama, *My Land and My People: Memoirs of the Dalai Lama of Tibet*, Potala, 1962.

9. Author interview with Gyalo Thondup, Dharamsala, July 1995.

10. Goldstein, *A History of Modern Tibet*, p. 318.

11. *My Land and My People*.

12. Author interview with Gyalo Thondup, Dharamsala, July 1995.

13. Bell, *Portrait of the Dalai Lama*.

14. Goldstein, p. 319.

15. Great Mother in conversation with Lady Gould, Isle of Wight, 1960, as reported to the author.

16. The Emperor's representatives or *ambans* had been expelled from Lhasa in 1912 after the fall of the Manchu Dynasty. The Thirteenth Dalai Lama had declared Tibet's complete independence of China.

17. The Chinese Nationalists took over the Imperial concept of an empire led by the majority Han Chinese, comprised of the Han and the four minority nationalities: Tibetans, Manchus, Mongolians and the Muslims of East Turkestan. The concept never wavered, even though Tibet, Manchuria and Outer Mongolia were functioning independently of China.

18. Oriental and India Office Collections, Political (External) Files and Collections, L/P&S/12/4178 File 15 (1). Death of the XIIIth Dalai Lama and question of successor, December 1933 – October 1940.

In the Land of Horses

For many in Tibet, material life was hard, but they were not victims of desire; and in simplicity among our mountains there was more peace of mind than there is in most of the cities of the world.

The Fourteenth Dalai Lama

Amdo in the far north-east beyond the Yangtse River, was one of the three provinces that traditionally made up Tibet: U-Tsang (Central Tibet), the land of *dharma* – the theory and practice of Buddhism; Do-toe (Kham), the land of people; and Do-may (Amdo), the land of horses. Like frontier-lands everywhere, Amdo had had a chequered history. There, where the mountains of the high plateau swept down towards the plains of western China, Tibet's borders were uncertain. It was a wild, windswept region of vast steppes from which soared some of the highest mountains in the world; a beautiful country of lush grasslands, conifer forests, giant rhododendron bushes and innumerable salt lakes, one of which was the inland sea known as Kokonor, the Blue Lake, so vast (97 km across) that a caravan would take a month to cross it. To the Chinese, Kokonor was Ching 'hai; they gave its name to the whole region and claimed it as their own.

Before the seventh century, the population had been entirely Tibetan, but since then many Chinese and Chinese Muslims had come to the area, and the indigenous Tibetans had moved up to ever higher altitudes. Since the middle of the eighteenth century, the province had been ruled by fiercely independent *gyalpos* (kings) and warlords often supported by China. (The Amdowas had not in fact been ruled as a united people by any one leader since the fall of the Tibetan Empire in the ninth century.)[1] At the time of the search for the Fourteenth Dalai Lama, the area was controlled by the Muslim warlord, Ma Pu-feng, ostensibly in the name of China, although in most respects he was answerable only to himself.

This is the area which Western scholars regard as the cradle of the Tibetan race. The majority of its people had never considered themselves Chinese, their culture and religious beliefs being unmistakably Tibetan, and their loyalty to the Dalai Lama never in doubt.

The Fourteenth Dalai Lama has a clear memory of this land of his childhood where sedge, rock jasmine, rhubarb and gentian grew on the steppes and many medicinal plants were found among the alpines that grew above the treeline:

> To the south of the village, there was a mountain that was higher than the rest. Its name was Ami-chiri, but the local people called it The Mountain Which Pierces The Sky, and it was regarded as the abode of the guardian deity of the place. Its lower slopes were covered by forests; above them a rich growth of grass could be seen; higher still, the rock was bare; and on the summit was a patch of snow which never melted. On the northern face of the mountain, there were junipers and poplars, peaches, plums and walnuts, and many kinds of berries and scented flowers. Clear springs of water fell in cascades, and the birds and wild animals – deer, wild asses, monkeys and a few leopards, bears and foxes – all wandered unafraid of man; for our people were Buddhists who would never willingly harm a living creature.[2]

Born into this earthly paradise, Lhamo Dhondup was the fifth surviving child of farmer Choekyong Tsering, whose family had lived in the area for many generations. (No one could move far away in a country without roads, where ponies and mules provided the only means of transport.) He had a sister sixteen years older than himself and three older brothers. The farmer had married seventeen-year-old Sonam Tsomo, oldest of the five daughters of Chodang Phuntsok Nima and his wife Dolma Tso from Churkha, a small village just south of Kumbum Monastery and twenty-five kilometres from Taktser. Sonam Tsomo was a good-natured, attractive girl with thick, black, glossy hair that was the envy of the other village girls. In accordance with Amdo custom, the families, both small, independent farmers, had arranged the marriage, though Sonam's grandparents were known to have protested that Taktser men worked their women too hard. Once the families had reached agreement, the astrologers were consulted, to make sure that the couple were compatible.[3] It took almost two years before they could agree on an auspicious date for the wedding. But eventually, the signs were judged to be right and on the eleventh day of the eleventh month of Fire Serpent Year (1917), Choekyong Tsering and Sonam Tsomo were married.[4]

The bride's preparations for her wedding day were laid down by tradition:

> One by one she slipped into silk blouses of red, green and white colours carefully selected to suit her complexion. Then she donned a jade-green chuba made of pure Mongolian silk and fashioned in the Amdo style. She combed her long black hair as usual into three plaits, two in the front and one in the back. From her ears she hung long ear-rings of coral, turquoise and silver. Finally, she put on a vase-shaped head-dress studded with jewels, which reached down to her waist. While she dressed, a neighbour sat cross-legged on a low, carpet-covered platform, singing traditional Amdo wedding songs in a deep, husky voice.[5]

First of all, a ceremonial engagement party took place in the altar room of the bride's house. Prayers were said, blessings invoked, and representatives of the groom's family presented a series of gifts to the bride's: tea, rice, butter, tsampa,[6] salt and lengths of silk. Most important was the *nurin* – 'breast-price' – symbolizing a payment to the bride's mother for having nourished her. The occasion was rounded off by much drinking of *chang*, the fermented barley-beer beloved of Tibetans. The guests agreed that the *chang* was so good it was in itself an auspicious sign.

That evening, a group of gaily-dressed horsemen came from Taktser to the bride's home, bringing with them a white mare on whose back the bride would be led to her new home after the wedding next day; plus a white stallion and a black heifer for her grandparents who, as senior family members, would accompany her. The leader of the group also carried the *sipaho*, an arrow-shaped banner with a painted scroll hanging from its point on which were astrological symbols depicting the stars and planets and mystical symbols for protection against evil spirits.

After a short service next day, in which a lama besought the household deity to accept the bride into her new family, the groom's representative 'touched the back of Sonam Tsomo's neck with an arrow decorated with five strips of different-coloured silk and announced to everyone present that from then on she belonged only to her husband'.[7]

The journey to the bridegroom's home, punctuated by cheerful farewell sessions with vast quantities of food and *chang* for friends and relatives along the route, took seven hours and was a very convivial occasion.

All this time, the bride, wrapped in a fur-lined cloak, kept her face covered, for the groom – whom she had not yet met – must be the first man to set eyes on her. At last the party reached Taktser and the square, single-storey farmhouse, built of stone and mud, and newly white-washed for the occasion. The door leading to the interior courtyard swung open to receive them; the bride dismounted on to a platform of barley and tea and was led across the flagstoned yard to a stack of wood, around which she walked three times in a clockwise direction:

> Moving to the kitchen door, she stood with her back to it, facing east as her horoscope had indicated, and proceeded to wash her face; then she went inside to make tea. Some of the guests tried to steal a look at her while praising the tea she had brewed, but she kept her face hidden behind one of the sleeves of her blouse, which had been cut quite full. A few mischievous older guests tugged playfully on her arm, saying, 'Let's have a look! We won't be here long, so let's see your face before we leave!' She was embarrassed but tried not to show it.[8]

Only after this, in a ceremony for family and friends in the altar room, was Sonam Tsomo placed beside her husband, and the couple set eyes on each other for the first time. She thought he was 'very handsome'; what he thought about her is not on record. Afterwards, they went up on to the roof to burn incense and offer prayers for the success of the marriage.

After three hectic days of dancing and feasting, Sonam Tsomo went back to Churkha with her family. She returned alone one month later and, on approaching the gate of her new house, was greeted by her husband's elder brother, holding a white porcelain bowl of milk:

> Into this she placed the thumb and fourth finger of her right hand, then withdrew them and flicked little droplets into the air three times. Then she went into the kitchen and brewed tea, the first steaming cup of which she placed on the altar as an offering. From that time on she was considered a regular member of the Taktser household, and the next day began to take part in the housework and other routines.[9]

The backcloth to her new life was a village like her own, mainly given over to pasturage – one village was much like another in Amdo. Since most Tibetans lived in villages separated by large distances (unlike the Chinese who tended to live in large, enclosed towns, with their farms on the outside), the people were sturdily self-reliant. The staple crops were wheat and barley; vegetables such as peas, potatoes, onions, turnips and radishes being also grown for domestic use. They drank butter-tea and *chang*, the barley beer. As in Churkha, the people of Taktser were simple peasant folk. The men all wore fur hats, high leather boots and the ubiquitous *chuba*, a voluminous outer garment belted just below the waist. The women wore long, sleeveless, woollen versions of the *chuba* with bright silk or cotton blouses.

Sonam Tsomo's new family was of pure Tibetan stock, their forefathers having reputedly come from Phenpo near Lhasa, part of the army sent by King Trisong Detsen in the middle of the eighth century to protect Tibet's frontiers against invaders. As the Amdo garrison had never been recalled, the soldiers' descendants had gone on living in the area, for centuries serving as unpaid, elected headmen of their villages. Though their speech was still peppered with words and phrases from the ancient Lhasa dialect, they spoke Tibetan in the Amdo dialect, which, since 1910 when the Chinese had reoccupied the area, now contained a strong admixture of Chinese.

The Taktser house was a large-ish farmhouse built for Sonam Tsomo's mother-in-law by her older brother, an important local *tulku* known as Taktser Rinpoche. Many years earlier, he had escaped with his life during a violent insurrection by local Chinese Muslims, in the course of which Kumbum Monastery and many of its surrounding villages had been destroyed. The farmhouse in which his family had lived for generations was burned to the ground, while he himself was hidden by a friendly Muslim butcher and enabled to escape to nearby Outer Mongolia disguised as a beggar. Discovering in himself the gifts of a natural healer, he achieved fame and fortune not only in Mongolia but in Tsarist Russia, returning eventually to Kumbum a wealthy man with a caravan load of treasures, including cuckoo clocks and musical boxes, the like of which the Tibetans had never seen. One of his first acts was to rebuild Kumbum Monastery, and then, finding his sister and her husband without a home, to restore the burned-out farmhouse.

This was now the family home. When the new bride arrived there, Taktser Rinpoche renamed her Dekyi Tsering, which means Ocean of Luck. (It was not unusual for a bride's name to be changed upon her marriage. Tibetan names can be frequently changed, usually on recovery from an illness, following the visit of a great lama, etc.) Her father-in-law, Tashi Dhondup, was a gentle, kind-hearted man, but her mother-in-law, Lhamo Dolma, a gaunt, pock-marked virago with a vile temper, was impossible to like.[10] Dekyi Tsering was scared of her and would sometimes run out of the house to escape her intolerable nagging. Within two years, however, both parents-in-law died and Choekyong Tsering became the owner of the farmhouse.

Nineteen-year-old Dekyi Tsering was used to hard work. At home, she and her sisters had worked in the fields, milked the cows, done the hundred-and-one household chores. They were a close-knit family and had shared their labours, sitting down together in the evening to sing as they sewed and mended a pile of clothes. But in Taktser, with more exhausting work and no companionship, the new bride found her grandparents' forebodings about Taktser men well justified. After a mere four hours' sleep, she would rise each morning before cock-crow to make a fire with juniper logs in the large brick stove in the kitchen. Over it she would set big copper kettles full of water for washing and for the morning tea. In Taktser, time was measured in the age-old manner, as her eldest son would write later:

> We did not need to measure time of day, but we needed to measure it for cooking. One method was to fill a special pot with water; the pot had a small hole in it, and it allowed the water to escape drop by drop. My mother would know to put in so much water to measure the time needed to cook such and such a meal. If we needed to be wakened up at such and such an hour, my mother would light a stick of incense of the right length. When it burned down to the end it would burn through a thread that held a stone above an old metal pot, and we would be awakened by the clanging and clattering as the stone fell. During the day we knew the hour by the sun, at night by the stars. Our lives in Tibet were spent without haste.[11]

Next she would go into the altar room, wash her hands, twist new wicks out of cotton, fill the containers with butter she had already melted over the stove, and light the butter-lamps. (All Tibetan families, even the very poorest, had an altar in their homes, and an image of the Buddha before which butter-lamps burned continuously.) With the rest of the household, she would perform the daily ritual of prostrating three times and saying prayers for the happiness of all sentient beings, before going outside and filling the clay incense burner in the courtyard with glowing coals and herbs such as dried Alpine roses. Only then could tea be served and the day begin.

At daybreak, Choekyong Tsering would lead his horses out to water. After breakfast, he went out to the fields, where, with the aid of three or four hired labourers and perhaps a mule or an ox, he grew barley, buckwheat, oats, jute and potatoes. His wife, meanwhile, swept and garnished the house. There were six rooms: a large kitchen, the altar room, one bedroom, a guest room, a store-room for provisions and, at the back of the house, a cow byre. Next she prepared lunch for her husband and the other men and took it out to them in a basket carried on her back or in a shoulder sling. That done, she would return home, exchange the basket for a water-carrier and fetch water from the well at the far side of the village. (In winter she would repeat this procedure more than twice a day and in summer, often in appalling heat, at least four times.) She then churned butter and cooked the evening meal. In summer they lived mainly on vegetables and salad, a particular favourite being a kind of radish pickled in a tub with sour gherkins; in colder weather there was a thick vegetable soup known as *thukpa*, potatoes, tsampa and tea. Potatoes were eaten at almost every meal, but meat – mutton or beef – was a rare luxury, except in the autumn when the sheep were slaughtered, or occasionally in summer after the wolves had killed an animal and abandoned some of the carcass. The staple food, whatever the season, was tsampa, or barley-flour. Like Tibetans everywhere, they ate it dry or mixed with liquid – milk or brick-tea specially brought from China[12] – into a kind of dough to which they added butter and salt.

The evening meal could take place only after the animals had been attended to. Whilst the farmer led the horses and mules out to drink, his wife would milk the cows in the stone-flagged byre at the back of the house. After the meal until round about midnight was the time for embroidering, mending and baking. Dekyi Tsering baked bread rolls and pastries in an old iron tin scattered with glowing coals; and her reputation as a pastrycook was second to none in the village. As to her sewing, it was said that she could have embroidered a bird on the wing.

The produce of the farmer's fields was used mainly to feed his family, the grain being ground in the mill by the village stream in nearby Balangtsa. Choekyong Tsering would take it there, pulling the mule laden with the grain sacks behind him. (As payment he would give the miller one-tenth of the ground flour.) Occasionally he would trade grain or a few sheep with passing nomads, or barter them in the nearby markets of Siling or Kumbum for Chinese brick-tea, sugar, cotton fabric and iron tools. A kitchen garden provided them with peas, mustard, potatoes, tomatoes, garlic, onions, radishes and a few green vegetables. But as crops of any kind were liable to be ruined by heavy hailstorms or severe drought, families tended to rely on animals as a source of produce: a couple of yaks,[13] cows, sheep, goats, dzomos (a cross between a yak and a cow which gave a high yield of milk), free-range chickens and pigs.

And horses. Amdo produced what were arguably the sleekest, most powerful horses in the world; in the grasslands, horses were not a luxury but a way of life. They were Choekyong Tsering's passion; and he visited the horse-markets (entailing an absence of several days) whenever occasion arose. Dekyi Tsering had soon discovered that her husband, whom she had been warned was a wild, headstrong youth, overindulged by his doting mother, cared more for the horse-markets than for labouring in the fields. The sheer drudgery of the latter he preferred, where possible, to leave to the hired help. Not that he was idle – no Tibetan peasant was ever that. In the evenings, when his hands weren't busy with such routine tasks as spinning sewing-thread and making boot-laces, he would be passing a rosary through his fingers and murmuring prayers. But it seemed to his wife that horses were all he really cared about – his knowledge of horse-flesh being wedded to a rare talent for healing – and that most of the responsibility for house and family was left to her.

The couple had a total of sixteen children, of whom only seven survived beyond infancy. The first (born in 1919) was a girl, Tsering Dolma, born, as her brothers and sisters would be, on a straw pallet on the floor of the cow byre. (In Kham and Amdo, babies were always born in the place where the animals were kept.) Lhamo Dolma, the bad-tempered mother-in-law, was still alive and when the child turned out to be a girl, her disappointment was epic: 'When my mother had a daughter,' says Gyalo Thondup, 'my grandmother was so furious that she refused to eat, she just hid herself away and wept all day long. She would not speak to my mother or look at the child.'[14] It seems that she cried herself more or less literally to death!

Three years later (1922), when his grandmother was already dead, a son was born, an occasion, as everywhere in the East, for great rejoicing. His parents called him Tashi Tsering, but he does not remember ever being called by those names. As a small boy he was known as Cho-la, an honorific meaning 'Eldest Son'. Tibetan children are frequently not given their permanent names till later on, in connection with some great occasion. Until then, they may be addressed as 'Boy', 'Girl', 'Child' – or 'Eldest Son', 'Eldest Daughter'.

Cho-la (under his later name of Thubten Jigme Norbu, given to him by the Thirteenth Dalai Lama)[15] would one day write a moving account of his childhood in Taktser. If there was a family atmosphere there, the explanation was simple, he says: there were a lot of family members around – and, as in most Tibetan villages, people thought of themselves as related to each other even when they weren't.

> The Tibetan village is spread out among the fields and meadows. Each house has a stone wall around it, with a gate leading into an inner courtyard. Inside these courtyards the great black mastiffs are allowed to roam at night. Some houses are all by themselves, but mostly they cluster together, perhaps three or four of them separated from the next cluster by open country. In [Taktser] our own family cluster was the largest, having seven or eight houses in it. A number of the men were called 'brother' by my father, but they really were not. Their mothers I called 'Grandmother'. One was blind, and whenever I went to see her she let her hands feel all over my face as she talked to me. Another 'Grandmother', who lived next door, sometimes used to fight with her son's wife, and that used to give me bad dreams. But one in particular I liked to visit...She always carried her beads in her hand and when she was doing nothing else she would murmur invocations to the gods...I liked to play with her and try to take her beads away from her. Then she would put them in a bag and I would try to take the bag. She was old and very kind to us.[16]

Tsering Dolma was the apple of her father's eye, a tomboy who shared his passion for horses – though she was more like her mother in temperament, outspoken, hard-working and kind-hearted. When Cho-la was small, she used to carry him around on her back and as he grew older, huddled together under the bedclothes in the light of a flickering oil-lamp, she would tell him the stories and folk-tales she had heard from her mother and grandmother. Stories, for example, dating back to the fourteenth century, of the heroic Prince Gesar, the legendary prince of Ling, and the many wars and battles he waged against neighbouring tribes and kingdoms. The epic of Prince Gesar was immensely popular in eastern Tibet, abounding as it did with stories of valour and daring, with the gods, titans, demons and imps that Gesar – 'Great Lion of the World' – had to do battle with. A saga which harked back to the many wars in the Amdo region between

Tibetans and Chinese. The memories of these far-off battles still survived in Amdo in a number of significant placenames, such as Gyatrag-thang, Field of Chinese Blood, and Gyadu-thang, Field of Chinese Corpses. The Amdowas, so many of whom were descended from the old Tibetan warriors, had long memories.[17]

The children spent much time with their mother: their father was often away, and in any case women play a significant role in every Tibetan household. 'At first light she went up onto the flat roof of our house taking some charcoal or yak-dung fire with her, and when I was old enough I would go too. There she lit a little fire and made offerings of cedar or juniper wood, and of a little food such as tsampa flour, dried fruits and butter. Every house in the village did the same thing, and it is done all over Tibet each morning as the sun strikes the snowy peaks of the mountains. From every roof a wavering wisp of smoke rises up to the sky, and the air is filled with sweet smells and the sound of prayers.' When that was done, they came downstairs, their mother lit the butter lamp and put it on the altar where it burned all day. The whole family would gather there, morning and evening, for prayers.

Sometimes a monk would come to the house to say prayers. 'Then he would wash my sister and me with holy water, to remove all the bad things in us. My father used to like to invite him to stay for several days so that he could read from the religious books to us and do honour to our ancestors.' But the children were not expected to sit still and listen. Nobody minded if they ran off to play.

Religion was a focal point even in the children's play. They played at building temples of clay, arranging offerings in front of them and making the prostrations that they knew instinctively how to perform. One of their favourite places was the household shrine which stood in the main courtyard. 'It was a clay tower containing various sacred images, and it was the centre of certain rites concerning the protection of the home. It was equally the centre of attraction for my friends and me, and there was no place to play that we liked better. We were not particularly conscious of its religious significance – we were simply aware that somehow this was a warm and friendly place.'

With the other village children, Cho-la and Tsering Dolma would roam far and wide through woods and meadows which were green in summer and rich with wild flowers, deep in snow during the bitterly cold winters. Cho-la's childhood hero was the village shepherd to whose hire all the villagers contributed. 'Every morning when we were at breakfast he would pass our house with the village flocks and herds. Small groups of cows and sheep joined him from every yard as he passed on his way...Our sheep and cows would all be waiting impatiently in the yard to surge out and join him.'

The villagers' cattle were taken to pasture every day of the year, except on those winter days when violent snowstorms swept the land; yet even in mid-winter there was pasture, the winds being so fierce that they drove the snow off the meadows and enabled both cattle and sheep to find roots and herbs to feed on. Although Cho-la was strictly forbidden to follow the herdsman into the mountains where the sheep and cattle were grazing, as he grew older it was one of his favourite pastimes. Especially if his father was away, he and his friends would follow the herdsman like some Pied Piper, enjoying long days, free from parental interference, playing their wildest, noisiest games, exploring the treasures and secrets of the mountains. 'We all used to steal some food from our homes, some potatoes, dry bread and some cheese, put it in string bags and tie the bags to our waists. This way our hands were free.' On good days, when they felt hungry they would pick and eat the raspberries, strawberries and bilberries which at times grew in profusion in the woods. They would stay out all day, returning only when the herdsman brought the cattle back at dusk. As afternoon approached, and Cho-la thought of the inevitable scolding awaiting him at home, he would run and gather a few particularly luscious berries 'as a propitiatory offering for my parents'. The herdsman ignored the children; he would sit on a stone, lost in thought and looking dreamily up at the sky. 'And I would sometimes think I saw his lips move as though he were talking to the clouds, the trees, the birds and the water.' It was Cho-la's first introduction to the contemplative life; and the summit of his childhood ambition was to become the next herdsman of Taktser.

But mostly the children stayed in the courtyards of their houses, playing games like hopscotch and trials of skill involving coins, coloured stones and sheep's bones.

We also had a ball of wool into which we stuck hens' feathers, and this had to be kept in the air as long as possible by kicking it up with the instep. A kind of football game we played, with a leather ball stuffed with wool, was by no means difficult. The ball was supposed to be round but it never was.[18]

In winter, when for five months the ground was covered with snow, the children would build huge snowmen, with pieces of burnt wood for eyes; and on the mountainsides, they 'slid down the slopes so often that in the end we had slides as highly polished as mirrors'. Often they would make warm burrows for themselves in the haystacks left over from the autumn grain harvest. In fact, one of Cho-la's earliest memories is of 'a day in late autumn when all the colours in the fields and on the sides of the mountains were changing. My sister and I went into the fields to play almost every day because the straw that had been cut was piled up and we had made a little house by burrowing into the pile and making little rooms. Into one room we had brought some flat stones, making a table. Other smaller stones we used as dishes. This particular day, as usual, we brought a few grains of barley and some peas, and we pretended we were having our meal. But as winter was approaching it was cold even inside our straw house, so we lit a fire to keep us warm. Of course, the whole pile of straw was soon alight, and our parents came running to beat it out with sticks and blankets. We were more frightened of the beating we might get than of the danger, but everyone was too busy putting the fire out to do more than shout at us. We were never allowed to play in the straw again and it was the last house we made together.'[19]

Cho-la was in awe of his father – who had inherited his mother's unpleasant temper. At heart, he knew him to be a good-natured man who disliked having to punish his children – 'soon afterwards he would find some opportunity for surreptitiously giving me an apricot, or he would ask me casually if I would like to go with him to the fields'. But his father's temper was legendary and Cho-la, who was frequently in trouble, used to beg his mother to intercede for him. Once, however, even his mother disowned him. He had got hold of a very fine large potato which he decided to roast over the butter-lamp in the altar room. As soon as opportunity arose, he crept into the chapel and began his illicit cookery:

It was already beginning to bake on one side and a wonderful smell tickled my nostrils, when suddenly I heard footsteps in the covered way outside, and in a panic at the thought of being caught I made a sudden grab at the potato, knocking both it and the butter-lamp onto the floor where lay the open match-box which my parents used to light the lamp. The matches caught fire, and in an instant a big sheet of flame leapt up, and the spilled butter on the wooden floor began to burn too. I shrieked in my fright, and there was my mother to the rescue again. She had been about to hang clothes in the yard to dry and instead she now used them to beat out the fire...When the job was done she turned on me with a face far more angry than I usually saw and gave me a couple of stinging clouts.[20]

Ashamed of himself and terrified of what his father would say – and do – when he came home, Cho-la fled to the neighbouring wood and stayed there until it grew dark and the night-owls started hooting. Then, even more frightened of the owls than of his father, he slunk homewards.

> When I got to the farmstead door I stood there for a while hesitating. I was afraid to knock. And then it suddenly opened, and there was my father on his way to search for his missing son. My distress didn't save me. He put me across his knee, bared my bottom, and with his hard and heavy hand he gave me a thorough drubbing. If I had set the house on fire as a result of my naughtiness I could hardly have been thrashed more thoroughly than I was because I had desecrated the sacred butter-lamp and the picture of Buddha before which it burned.

Today, 'Cho-la' is an old man and has forgotten many things. But he has never forgotten that particular night: the night-owls' screeching and the beating handed out by his father.

Though children under the age of ten were thought too young for hard labour in the fields, Tsering Dolma and Cho-la helped with such tasks as weeding, and in spring when their father ploughed the land, would follow him to gather up the sweet white tubers turned up by the ploughshare. Tsering Dolma helped her mother with the cooking and made sure the stove was adequately supplied with fuel. 'Sometimes we used yak dung, horse and sheep dung being used mainly in the fields, but we also had plenty of wood. It was not large wood, for we used to get it from the bushes that covered the hills near by, but it was good fuel and we were never without warmth.' It was a life filled with 'a hundred thousand pleasures', many of them four-legged. One of Cho-la's tasks was 'to take any food that was left over and mix it in a small bucket with some meat and bread, then take it out to our watchdog. We also used to feed the pigs, and when a sow gave birth we had to look after all the piglets to make sure they did not wander away too far.'

During the sheep-shearing season in early summer, the children had to help in earnest, holding the feet of the panicky animals as they were being shorn. 'We liked shearing time, when the wool piled up in the yard into white mountains waiting to be packed into jute sacks, work which was invariably accompanied by a good deal of shouting and jollity.'[21] Later in the year, with less outdoor work to be done, the sacks would be brought out and the wool soaked in great wooden tubs before being washed, teased and hung up to dry. When some of it had been spun, 'my mother would colour the thick ropes with dyes made from the bark of trees, earth and plants'. The favourite dye was the reddish brown obtained from the wild rhubarb growing on the mountainsides, prized not only for its colour but for the acid it contained which could be mixed with other colours.

Certain colours could be found only in the markets, and Choekyong Tsering travelling in caravan with other villagers, would set off to buy the dyes, taking with him donkeys laden with goods for barter. Each man brought grain and wool and cloth which they or their wives had woven. Naturally, Choekyong Tsering would also visit the horse-fair, where horses were taken in part-exchange, the difference being made up in sheepskins, wool or barley.

When the farmer arrived home – 'it was always good to hear my father's voice calling out as he rode back through the gate into the courtyard' – he was greeted boisterously by the family mastiff, Kyimo, 'a huge black beast with shaggy matted hair that hung down to the ground'; and more restrainedly by the cat, Shimi. (These, like the children's names, were generic, Kyimo meaning 'bitch' and Shimi simply 'cat'.) When Tsering Dolma was a baby, this cat had scratched her eyeball so badly that she had had to be fitted with a glass eye – later she always wore dark glasses. The same cat had once savaged a little musk-deer Cho-la had tended:

I loved my little musk-deer very much and I even took it to bed with me under the warm covering. In the morning it would wake me up by licking my cheek with its gentle tongue. But one morning...I woke up...and found I was cuddling its lifeless body. And then I saw that there was blood around. In the night that wretched cat had bitten through my poor musk-deer's throat.

It was a bitter experience and, though Tibetans are taught from infancy to eschew all violence against sentient beings, Cho-la's emotions got the better of him. 'For the first time in my life I felt a desire for vengeance and would have liked to see that cat suffer a similar bloody end.'

The maternal grandparents often came from Churkha, a day's journey away, and though their arrival meant the young couple having to crowd in with the children, sleeping in the kitchen on the heated platform around the stove, they were always welcome guests. At other times, the house was like a busy market, as traders and craftsmen of all kinds arrived to display their wares. Cho-la and Tsering Dolma loved the traders coming, but the door was usually locked to keep the children out. Cho-la tried his utmost to get in but 'the best I could do was to make a little tear in the cloth of the small window panels, and stare inside at all the treasures laid out there'. With the fruit-sellers they had more luck – when the traders laid the fruit on the floor for inspection, 'we usually managed to sneak a few apples away without being noticed'.

A regular visitor was the weaver, who went from farm to farm, staying for several days, setting up his loom in the yards and weaving pieces of cloth about eight inches wide and many feet in length. Dekyi Tsering made the whole family's clothes herself, using the sewing-thread spun by her husband during the long winter evenings. But for special occasions and religious festivals, a tailor would be summoned; and when these special clothes had been made, Dekyi Tsering would get out the ornaments which Taktser women saved for great occasions – long ornate head-dresses which they wore over their shoulders like a back-pack – 'for example, three red ribbons on which, silver coins, shells, corals and turquoise stones were sewn to make very colourful finery'.[22]

In summer, the family went barefoot, but in the harsh winters they wore out so many boots that the cobbler was another regular caller: he had to make several visits to sew new leather soles onto the sturdy fabric tops. Choekyong Tsering bought cow leather for the boots at the Balangtsa market and soaked and softened it ready for the cobbler to cut out. He also made the thread for tying the boots from the jute grown along the edges of his fields.

In addition, there were the carpenter and the carpet-maker, the potter (providing earthenware jars for storing water) and the itinerant glue-vendors who made their own glue from cow hooves, bones and skin, peddling it from village to village, house to house, and usually paid in food-grains. All of them – and any passing caravan driver besides – were given overnight hospitality, with their animals, in the guest-room next to the cow shed, where they slept on a broad bench against the wall. Dekyi Tsering was never known to turn anyone away. All devout Buddhists were expected to give alms to beggars, but she went far beyond the call of duty. If she met a beggar on the road, she would make sure he had adequate food and clothing.

Her one desire in life, says Phuntsok Tashi, her future son-in-law, was for people to be happy. 'My mother,' the Dalai Lama would write,

> was undoubtedly one of the kindest people I've ever known...Once, I remember being told, there was a terrible famine in nearby China. As a result, many poor Chinese people were driven over the border in search of food. One day, a couple appeared at our door, carrying in their arms a dead child. They begged my mother for food, which she readily gave them. Then she pointed at their child and asked whether they wanted help to bury it. When they had caught her meaning, they shook their heads and made it clear that they intended to eat it. My mother was horrified and at once invited them in and emptied the entire contents of her larder before regretfully sending them on their way. Even if it meant giving away the family's own food so that we ourselves went hungry, she never let any beggar go away empty-handed.[23]

Over the village brooded the awesome Kyeri, the holy mountain where lived Kye, the area's protective deity. Mountains were important in Tibetan culture: their national flag carries at its centre the image of a snow mountain and a snow lion. In Taktser, as in many villages or towns, a heap of stones (known as a *labtse*) was dedicated to the mountain deity. Here the villagers 'offered up white quartz, coins, turquoises and corals, and prayed for rain, or for sun, or for a good harvest, or for protection from bad weather'. Monks from nearby monasteries would come and conduct the ceremonies, the sonorous beating of their gongs and the ringing of their bells heightening the solemnity of the occasion.

Two days in the year were specifically devoted to the mountain-god, and then the villagers would set off on a long trek to pay their respects, present their offerings and pray to the god for peace and prosperity.

> The ride to the foot of the mountain lasted three days and went through a completely uninhabited area, so the villagers had to take everything they needed along with them. When they arrived at the end of their journey we children would be left behind in tents whilst the adults went up to the ice limit, there solemnly to burn incense.[24]

When the ceremonial was over, it was time for a huge party, with large tents and awnings worked with traditional Tibetan designs erected on the meadows; singing, dancing, plenty to eat, fresh *chang* to drink, games of dominoes and dice; and of course, in the meadows, the horse-racing and sports for which the area was famous, lassoing and shooting at moving targets – first with a rifle and then with bow and arrow – from the backs of galloping horses. Contestants would gallop past each other trying to grab the opponent's scarf from round his neck, while the villagers urged on their favourites with shouts. The winner had to provide a bowl of *chang* for the loser to drink. Though these equestrian sports were traditionally a male preserve, Tsering Dolma, truly her father's daughter, revelled in them; she could 'do anything on a horse', her daughter said many years later, 'quite amazing things, like picking up a scarf from the ground without losing speed'.[25]

It was a typically Tibetan mix of religious devotion and uninhibited fun. 'We led a happy and contented life in our remote little village,' recalled Cho-la,

> and we found it strange when the occasional travellers who passed through sometimes felt it necessary to express their sympathy with us on account of what they conceived to be our hard lot. In fact we felt that we had everything we needed for life and enjoyment. We certainly would not have changed places with any of those travellers. We lived peaceably, and on feast days even gaily; and the Buddhas listened to our prayers.[26]

Buddhism gave the people their identity. 'Everybody, rich or poor (except a few misers),' wrote the Dalai Lama, 'spent all his spare income...in building religious monuments, contributing to temples, making offerings, giving alms to the poor, and saving the lives of animals by buying them from the butchers.' Prayer-flags festooned the roof of every house; the people spun prayer-wheels as they went about their daily tasks, and constantly on their lips was the *mani* prayer, *Om Mani Padme Hum* (Hail to the Jewel in the Lotus), an invocation of the eternal compassion lying deep in the heart of all sentient beings. 'Whenever I recall my home village,' Cho-la would write,

> I always see the forest of white, weather-worn prayer-flags fluttering in the constant breeze from the mountains. I shall never forget the eerie noise they used to make when they whipped and cracked against the flagpoles when a storm was approaching from Kyeri.[27]

Before that innocent way of life vanished for ever, there was an addition to the family. A second boy had been born a year or two after Cho-la's birth, but had died in infancy. 'My mother cried a little,' he remembers, 'but we try not to cry on such occasions, and if we do, then we try to hide it. I remember being very worried and giving my mother what comfort I could, telling her that we should take my young brother to a nice place and bury him properly.'[28] But things were about to change. One day he and Tsering Dolma were awakened by the sound of lusty yelling. During the night, their mother had given birth to another 'kicking, wriggling little bundle' in the cow byre. He was given the name of Gyalo Thondup.

NOTES

1. Samten G. Karmay, 'Amdo, One of the Three Traditional Provinces of Tibet', *Lungta* 8, Amnye Machin Institute, Dharamsala.
2. Fourteenth Dalai Lama, *My Land and My People*.
3. In old Tibet, no activity of any importance was undertaken without consulting the astrologers.
4. For details of the marriage of Choekyong Tsering and Sonam Tsomo, I am indebted to chapter 3 of Michael Harris Goodman's *The Last Dalai Lama*, Shambhala, 1987.
5. Goodman, *The Last Dalai Lama*.
6. A flour made from roasted barley, the staple of Tibetan diet.
7. Goodman.
8. Goodman.
9. Goodman.
10. Tibetans, unless they belong to the aristocracy, do not have surnames or family names. For the most part, the names are given to either sex and it is often hard to decide whether one is referring to a man or a woman.
11. Thubten Jigme Norbu (with Heinrich Harrer), *Tibet Is My Country*, Wisdom, 1960.
12. Amdo people drank a tea made from dried leaves pressed into bricks which were imported from China. It was coarse and sometimes contained whole leaves and even stalks.
13. The Tibetan yak is an unbelievably useful animal. It lives on grasses and lichens, yet is a powerful beast of burden. The male gives meat while the female gives milk for butter, cheese and yoghurt. In the old days in Tibet, the yak's hide was turned into boots, saddlebags and even coracles in some parts of Tibet; its hair was used in tent-making, for blankets, ropes and clothing; its bones for building houses, its dung for fuel and insulation. Even the backbone, when crushed to powder and mixed with gold dust was put to use as a female contraceptive.

14. Author interview with Gyalo Thondup, New Delhi, July 1995.

15. Norbu, *Tibet Is My Country*.

16. Thubten Jigme Norbu (with Colin Turnbull), *Tibet*, Chatto and Windus, 1968; Pelican Books, 1972; Penguin, 1976.

17. Pema Bhum, 'Amdo: the People and their Struggle', in *The Invincible Amdo Tibetans*, by Poulius Normantas, Finland, Biokustannus Oy, 1994.

18. *Tibet Is My Country*.

19. *Tibet*.

20. *Tibet Is My Country*.

21. *Tibet Is My Country*.

22. Kim Yeshi and Emily Phipps, 'Precious Jewels of Tibet', article in *Chö Yang: The Voice of Tibetan Religious Culture* 5.

23. Fourteenth Dalai Lama, *Freedom in Exile: The Autobiography of the Dalai Lama of Tibet*, Hodder & Stoughton, 1990.

24. *Tibet Is My Country*.

25. Author interview with Khando Chazotsang (known before her marriage as Khando Tsering), Utah, February 1996.

26. *Tibet Is My Country*.

27. *Tibet Is My Country*.

28. *Tibet*.

4

Kumbum

The mountain at whose foot Tsong-khapa was born had
become a famous place of pilgrimage. Lamas came from all
parts to build their cells there, and the flourishing lamasery
whose fame spread to the furthest confines of Tartary gradually came into being. It was called Koumboum, from two
Tibetan words which mean 'Ten Thousand Pictures'. The
name refers to a tree which according to legend was born out
of the hair of Tsong-khapa and which bears a Tibetan character on each of its leaves.

*Régis-Evariste Huc, who visited Tibet in the
mid–nineteenth century*

In 1930, when Cho-la was eight, a far-reaching change took place in his
life. It is a strange story, bound up with his paternal grandmother's disappointment over the birth of Tsering Dolma. Shortly before that birth, the
old woman's brother, the Twenty-third Taktser Rinpoche, had died. As
the search for his reincarnation would soon be under way throughout the
area around Kumbum Monastery, his sister became obsessed with the
idea that the rebirth would take place in her own household. When the
child turned out to be a girl she lost all interest in life, turned her face to
the wall – and died.

The search had already begun; a list of boy candidates was drawn up and
taken to Lhasa by a party led by the two Stewards of Taktser *labrang*,[1] the

junior of whom was farmer Choekyong Tsering's elder brother. Their journey, on horseback and in caravan, took over three months. In Lhasa, the Thirteenth Dalai Lama received them very warmly: in 1904, after the Younghusband Expedition to Tibet,[2] he had fled to Outer Mongolia and on the way had spent a year in Kumbum Monastery and had come to know Taktser Rinpoche well. (Taktser had been unpopular with his monks for trying to introduce the Great Thirteenth's monastic reforms.) Dalai Lamas were said to have the gift of knowing the identity of lesser reincarnations; His Holiness scrutinized the list with interest – then handed it back saying that, alas, the right name was missing; they must return to Amdo and come back again in the following year with a new list.

Dejectedly, they made the long trek back to Kumbum, and a year later left for Lhasa with a fresh list. Same exhausting journey, same disappointing result. When the Dalai Lama again insisted that the right name was still missing, they all but wept. So demoralized were they that, on the journey back, the Senior Steward fell ill and died shortly after reaching home.

Choekyong Tsering's brother, Ngawang Changchup, now became Senior Steward and leader of the search party. Wearily, he set off yet again for Lhasa, with a list which now included the name of Dekyi Tsering's first-born son. Gyalo Thondup takes up the story, as told him by his mother:

When he arrived in Lhasa, my uncle put on his finest brocades and went to the Jokhang Temple to light butter-lamps and make offerings and prayers. When he poured the butter into the lamps, it all spilled down his front, ruining his beautiful clothes. My uncle was a very bad-tempered man and the monks who were with him were terrified he'd blame them for the accident. But to their surprise, instead of exploding with anger, he actually seemed pleased, telling them that indeed this was a very good omen for their mission. In fact, he asked for his garments to be preserved in all their buttery splendour.

Once again they were summoned to the Presence. This time, His Holiness told them to wait in Lhasa for two or three days while he prayed about the matter. On the third day, he handed my uncle a sealed letter with instructions to take it to the Abbot of Kumbum and tell him to open it in the presence of all the candidates' families.

So, back in Kumbum, a large gathering was summoned to hear the announcement. The Abbot duly opened the letter – and read out the name of my brother! My parents looked at each other and said what a pity it was my grandmother hadn't lived to see this day![3]

The monks were soon riding off towards the Taktser farmhouse bearing gifts. As Cho-la – who was about to be given the new names of Thubten (one of the Dalai Lama's own names) Jigme Norbu – relates:

> I was six or seven years old, and I remember very well how I was playing in the fields at the time, down by a little stream. My sister came running out to tell me that some monks had come to visit our home, and that they wanted to see me. She took me to the house and there in the courtyard I saw a lot of fine big horses and inside the house were the monks.[4]

Cho-la watched them through the spy-hole he had made in the thick rice paper which served as a window; then, when the monks were taken into the kitchen, he tiptoed to the wooden partition near the food-hatch and listened. Somehow, he knew, even before he heard them speak, that they had come to take him away. He could see that the head of the party was his uncle, the Steward of Taktser *labrang*, the rich and splendid establishment within Kumbum monastery which Cho-la, as the new Incarnation, would now inherit. They told him that he was the latest reincarnation of the fifteenth-century monk Taktser, and that he must leave home within a few days, to begin his studies in the little Shartsong hermitage, where the great fourteenth-century Buddhist reformer Tsong-khapa[5] had been initiated as a monk.

The boy appeared delighted and wanted to leave straight away. One of his favourite fantasies – by no means unusual among Tibetan children – had involved running away to a monastery to become a monk! Once when he was about six, he had rolled up a few belongings into a bundle and escaped through a hole in the wall. But, getting hopelessly lost, he had to be ignominiously rescued by his mother.

His parents rejoiced at the honour done to their family; and the whole village was happy, since the monks stayed for several days, handing out presents as they spread the good news around. They had brought large chests of new clothing, of finer weave and cut than Cho-la's old worsted *chuba*, and boots of top-quality leather, their uppers elaborately embroidered. Cho-la was pleased and excited by the fuss and by the unaccustomed respect which the village children were showing him. It hadn't really sunk in that he was about to say goodbye for ever to his family and his childhood.

A few days later, Cho-la (whom we shall now for a short while call by the second of his new names, Jigme) was dressed in his new clothes and told to leave behind everything that belonged to his life in the village. He managed to stow away a small bag of treasured sheep's bones and pebbles in the fold of his robe before going outside to join the waiting caravan of nine horses. His parents and sister were going too, his father carrying the infant Gyalo Thondup on the saddle in front of him.

It was only a couple of hours' ride to the Shartsong hermitage which loomed high above them as they approached, surrounded by mountains and clinging improbably to the top of a sheer 500-feet-high cliff. A welcome party waited at the base, and Jigme (Cho-la) was delighted to be treated as an important personage. But his self-confidence plummeted during the terrifying climb up the almost perpendicular reddish-brown rockface, buffeted at every step by the wind. The view from the top, however, where four white-washed houses perched on the edge of the solid rock, down into the deep gorge, more than repaid the discomfort.

Years later, in exile, he would remember this place as the most beautiful he had ever known, and, long after Shartsong had been destroyed by the Chinese, would yearn for 'its red rocks, its trees filled with birds, the deer and other wild animals', for the stream, with its 'blue, blue water', and 'the infinite peace I knew then, and the cleanness of the scents of pine and juniper and wild rose'.⁶

Each of the twenty or so monks had a modestly-furnished room in one of the houses, the only decoration being a picture portraying scenes from the lives of Buddhist saints. The monks had no personal possessions; they lived on alms donated by pious pilgrims and fed on tsampa (barley-meal) and butter sent up by relatives from the surrounding villages. For water, they made the daunting climb down to the river below, with wooden barrels strapped to their backs.

As an Incarnation, the new incumbent of the wealthy Taktser *labrang*, Jigme would not share their poverty; a beautifully-furnished room awaited him. He was inducted into his new role through ceremonies lasting three days, attended by his whole family. Though still excited, the realization was dawning that when the ceremonies were over, he would be left alone, and he clutched his little bag of coloured stones for reassurance. The parting was even more painful than he had imagined:

When I saw my parents preparing to leave, a terrible regret invaded my heart and I wept bitterly, and not all the loving encouragement and persuasions of my parents and the monks could console me. I felt a stranger in the new surroundings, I wanted to go home with my parents, and I was moved by a deep longing for my playmates and for all the things I had left behind.⁷

In vain did the kindly monks try to console him with sweets and toys and stories. They made paper dragons for him and kneaded fantastic figures out of tsampa dough; but they could not make him smile. Even when the cook brought a dish of his favourite roast mutton, he was unconsoled and refused to eat. He stared out into the dusk, shaken by uncontrollable sobs.

The gentle monk, Puntso, who was assigned to Jigme as tutor and servant, slowly put him at his ease and introduced him to his new duties, first among which was learning to write. Kumbum was the monastery where the great Tsong-khapa was born, in a tent set up by his nomad parents near a convenient watering-place. There is a famous tree growing there which is said to have grown on the exact spot where he was born. Round that hallowed place the monastery had gradually come into being, as a lasting memorial to the wonder-child who grew up to establish Buddhist rule in Tibet. Here, at Shartsong, Tsong-khapa had begun his religious studies.

> The early part of my life was spent just exactly where Tsong-khapa spent his...I was taught to write probably much as he was, for we had no pens or pencils or paper even when I was there. I used a wooden slate that was covered with chalk so that the writing showed up dark when the surface was scratched with a sharpened wooden stick.[8]

Jigme's days were filled with lessons, games and instruction, leaving little time for tears. But, though he slowly settled into the daytime routine, when night fell he was overcome with homesickness. It was, therefore, with an incredulous delight that one summer's evening he heard the sound of a horse's hooves in the courtyard below and recognized his father:

> Tears of joy and happiness rolled down my cheeks and for a moment or two I was speechless. My normally so unemotional father had to pull himself together too, and with suspiciously bright eyes he handed me a basket of my favourite pastries mother had sent me. We kissed each other on forehead and cheeks, and I made no attempt to stop my tears, forgetting the well-meant exhortations of the Abbot and of Puntso that a Rinpoche must behave like a man and not cry like a child.[9]

After two days, his father left, promising to return soon with the rest of the family. This had a galvanizing effect on Jigme; having something to look forward to spurred him on. In any case, his early longing to join a monastery had been genuine and now that he had recovered from the first shock, he was eager for his parents to be proud of him. Under Puntso's guidance, he applied himself to his lessons and made good progress. When his parents came, with Tsering Dolma and Gyalo Thondup, his bright-eyed and mischievous younger brother, he proudly showed them round his new domain, taking them to see the wide variety of birds he had made friends with on his verandah; and the tame musk-deer scampering over the rocks. In this place, where no one had ever knowingly killed anything, all wild things seemed to know instinctively that they were safe.

The visit was short, but this time the pain of parting was less acute.

Jigme was beginning to enjoy Shartsong. So he felt sad when, after three months, he had to leave for the huge parent monastery of Kumbum, home to three thousand monks, many of whom came from far-distant Mongolia to study in this ancient monastic university.[10] He was given clothes of the finest silk and the embroidery on his new boots was even more sumptuous than before. In addition, he wore a shallow, broad-brimmed hat made of gilt papier-mâché, befitting his exalted rank of incarnate lama. His horse was decked out with a new harness, a head-dress of gilt and a bushy, scarlet yak-tail springing from its halter.

Taktser, his native village, lay *en route*, and there Jigme was received like the important dignitary he now was. New prayer-flags flew from all the roof-tops and freshly-laundered sunblinds covered the doors. The incense fumes of burning alpine rose petals filled the nostrils. The whole village had turned out to express their gratitude that this brand-new Rinpoche had been chosen from amongst them, and the first to pay homage was his old hero, the herdsman.

Jigme's mother greeted him at the door with a white scarf and a ceremonial bowl of sweet cream. Only when this ritual had been observed did they drop the formalities and hug and kiss each other. Jigme looked around him, surprised to see the unfamiliar new carpets and silken hangings which had been brought by the Kumbum monks to celebrate his arrival. Before long, a crowd had assembled in the courtyard and a party was under way.

Happy and elated, oblivious both of his new silk garments and the need to keep them clean, Jigme made his way to the cowshed to cuddle a new-born calf and hug the huge black mastiff, Kyimo. Too late, he saw that he was covered with spots and stains. But it seemed there was no limit to the patience of his tutor and servant Puntso, who, without comment, produced another silk outfit for him.

Once again, the whole family came too. Neighbours lined the caravan route as they set off; and the old village headman, Pasang, urged Jigme with tears in his eyes to be sure and be a credit to Taktser village. This journey took two days and led through Churkha, his mother's old home, where he received another ecstatic welcome. Half-way between Churkha and Kumbum, five monks on horseback rode out to meet them. A brief ceremony of welcome took place in a ceremonial tent erected by the wayside, and when Jigme's party again rode on, it was with an official escort. About an hour later, from the brow of a hill, they saw Kumbum lying far below, encircled by brown hills dotted with juniper bushes and cedars, while in the valley the lush fields were edged with poplar and willow. Overcome by the size and beauty of the place, Jigme reined in his horse and stood gazing down on it. As his gaze cleared and the vision below took shape, he noticed myriad red dots at the foot of the monastery, moving 'like corn in the wind':

> And then I could hear, at first softly, and afterwards more and more clearly, the sounds of oboes and trumpets, followed a little later by the sound of the monks chanting. Was this really all for me, the incarnation of Taktser? [11]

Spurring his horse forward, Jigme was soon amongst them. Then, an umbrella of yellow silk held high over his head in token of his rank, he rode slowly through the narrow streets of the vast monastery, past the serried ranks of praying, bowing monks. Exhausted though he was, he had to be greeted by every single inmate of the Taktser *labrang*, the monastic college which he had inherited. Most of them were old and dignified monks who smiled at him with great friendliness. Jigme did his tired best to smile back, to ignore his increasing desire to slump down in his seat and sleep. But the ordeal seemed to be endless.

At last it was over and his new servants came in bearing 'a large copper dish decorated with silver and containing almost a whole stewed sheep' – just for him.[12] Only when he had eaten his fill, did the monks at last retire, leaving him alone with his family.

A few days later, his parents went home and Jigme plunged into a rigorous regime of lessons and prayer. Fortunately, there were boys of his own age to share the lighter moments, one of them a boy from Taktser who had just been initiated as a monk. 'I had a wonderful time with them; they took me all around and showed me things I had never seen or heard of before, like cuckoo clocks and music boxes.'[13] It was a revelation. To see watches and clocks for the first time and no longer need to rely on cock-crow or the position of the sun in the heavens! To his great delight, he was the proud possessor of fifteen cuckoo clocks, most of which hung on the walls of his room. His predecessor had returned from his travels in Tsarist Russia with a caravan full of treasures, including the cuckoo clocks and a number of musical boxes which Jigme found intriguing:

> When one of them, perhaps the most beautiful of all, was played, the little fig-ure of a girl appeared, and that always moved me deeply. She pirouetted gaily round and round, and in her hands she carried a box from which, to my great delight, an even smaller figure emerged. I loved this particular toy and played it again and again, and I used to imagine that the tiny figure which came out of the box carried a still tinier box from which a still tinier figure emerged – and so on, and so on.[14]

It was, he realized some years later, his first illustration of the mysterious concept of eternity!

After breakfast each day, he was free to play with the other boys. 'We used to run about the monastery and hide from each other, or else we would make statues or build houses of mud. In the summertime we were free to go out and play on the mountainside, so long as five or six of us went together.'[15]

The Taktser *labrang* possessed many fields and farms leased to peasants and farmers who must then hand over an agreed percentage of their yield as an annual rent. Out of these revenues, the *labrang* paid its own annual taxes to Governor Ma Pu-feng in Siling.

After Jigme had been a few months at Kumbum, the astrologers decreed that it was time for him to receive the monk's habit. Another boy, a six-teen-year-old called Kesang, was to be initiated with him, and three days before the ceremony the two boys' heads were shaven, apart from a small lock left on the crown. Choekyong Tsering, who visited his son about once a month, hurried to Kumbum for the great event, but Jigme himself was seized by a sudden unaccountable desire to run away.[16]

> I was afraid of the monk's habit which was now lying ready on a small table. According to the strictly prescribed ritual I was now asked whether I wished to become a monk, and to the astonishment of everyone present I remained silent. Both Puntso and my father urged me to answer, but I found it impossible to get a word out. Even the tears which finally came did not relieve my tension.[17]

As Jigme was already a *tulku*, the ceremony went on regardless, with Ke-sang firmly answering all the questions. Then the last lock of hair – the last remaining link with the world – was cut away and after being symbolically washed from head to foot in holy water, the boys were given the simple maroon woollen clothing of a monk. Henceforth their lives were to be devoted exclusively to religion.

Jigme felt confused and anxious. On the one hand, he was proud that he, a nine-year-old boy, had been accepted as a monk in the Order founded by Tsong-khapa,[18] and was now entitled to wear the same garment that the founder had worn.

> But I was still not able to talk about the reasons which had caused my strange silence during the ceremony. My father and Puntso were both deeply disturbed, and they questioned me urgently. But I could only shake my head. I wasn't even prepared to admit how deeply ashamed of myself I was.[19]

But fears and regrets had to be set aside. The training of an Incarnation involves long years of study and is far more rigorous than that of ordinary monks. From now on, however reluctantly, he had to get up each morning at four o'clock to fulfil his religious duties. Lessons became more difficult, and the prayers he had to learn by rote each day grew longer. With his new tutor, Lhagsam, he embarked on a course of studies to prepare him for the important examination which would qualify him for admission to the General Assembly of the Kumbum monks.

Not that he became a model pupil overnight. On the contrary, he often abused Lhagsam's good nature:

> Every morning and in the afternoon from four o'clock until late in the evening, [Lhagsam] had to be present at the general assembly for prayers, and whilst he was gone he relied on me to do the work he had set me. But when he left me in the early morning I would go back to bed again and have some more sleep. By the time he returned, there I was, virtuously poring over my books, the very model of zeal and industry.

For a time, the old monk was taken in, but when the truth came out,

> In holy anger he put me across his knee, raised my robes and administered a thorough slapping with the palm of his hand. I burst into loud howls of pain, with the result that the worthy man was deeply shocked at his own outburst, suspended the punishment and rather clumsily took me in his arms and tried to console me. Taken completely by surprise at this sudden change of attitude,

and feeling deeply ashamed of myself, I pressed my head to his chest and sobbed as though my heart would break.[20]

Slowly Jigme was beginning to understand what it meant to be an Incarnation. While still at Shartsong, he hadn't really taken it in, he kept asking where Taktser was and when he would be coming back. Then, at Kumbum he was puzzled when the monks pointed out certain places and objects, saying, 'This was where you used to sit', or 'You used this in your previous life'. He vaguely realized that the Taktser *labrang* with all its wealth in some way belonged to him but only now did he begin to realize that 'it was all mine not because, in some strange way, it had all been given to me as a present, but because, in a far stranger way, it had been mine even before I was born, that I actually *was* Taktser'.[21] It bothered him that he remembered nothing of his previous life.

> Nothing stirred in me except a growing realization of the responsibility that had been bestowed on me. All these people were looking up to me, an uneducated child from a peasant family, for spiritual guidance, all of them hoping secretly for some miracle. And out in the countryside, on the lands owned by my monastery, peasant folk like my own family, were depending on me to help them and guide them, using my knowledge and power and wealth for their good. It would have helped me if I had been able to recall even one event from my previous life, but I, who can often not even remember what happened yesterday, what chance is there of my remembering back to another existence?

Gradually he was absorbed into the life of the monastery. One day he stood for some minutes idly observing a group of people who had ridden into the courtyard below his window, before realizing that they were his parents, brother and sister. Then recognizing them with a rush of emotion, he dashed down the stairs to welcome them.

Someone else was with them – Phuntsok Tashi, a youth to whom Tsering Dolma had recently become betrothed and was soon to marry. The two families had long had close ties with each other. Chungtsi, Phuntsok Tashi's village, was lower down the mountain than Taktser, and whenever the Taktser crops failed, Phuntsok Tashi's family came to the rescue. They lived near some famous hot springs, and Choekyong Tsering would sometimes go and stay with them to try and cure his chronic indigestion with the waters. When the time came to look for a husband for seventeen-year-old Tsering Dolma, Phuntsok Tashi, their friends' fifteen-year-old son, was an obvious choice. But Tsering Dolma would not be leaving home. The bridegroom's parents, being gentle, unassuming folk who fully understood that their neighbours could ill afford – and indeed would be unwilling – to part with their hard-working (and much-loved) daughter, had agreed that their son should marry into his bride's family. The young man would shortly be providing an extra pair of hands in the Taktser household. Gyalo Thondup had come to Kumbum too. From the start he had been – and would remain – the wildest of all Dekyi Tsering's children. Tsering Dolma reported that as a baby he 'cried and cried and cried', and as he was in her charge, she was always accused of making him cry. Almost five now, he was a handsome boy, with large, luminous eyes, who kept his family entertained by singing a number of Tibetan folk-songs he had learned by heart. 'Altogether an agreeable child,' decided Jigme, who scarcely knew him.

In the autumn of 1932, a third son, Lobsang Samten, was born, and it was in the following year, while Choekyong Tsering was visiting Jigme in Kumbum, that news came of the Thirteenth Dalai Lama's death. As tens of thousands of butter-lamps blazed on the monastery roofs, the monks plunged into mourning for a ruler who had been both spiritual leader and king. Jigme recalls being 'so carried away by my sorrow that I couldn't conceive that things could ever be the same again, and that in time our ordinary everyday life would start up once more'.[22]

Amidst his tears, Jigme uttered a heartfelt prayer: that the Dalai Lama would soon return to live among his people. Some months later when he visited his old home in Taktser, *en route* once again for Shartsong, he found that his mother had given birth to another son, Lhamo Dhondup – 'the most delightful baby I had ever seen'. He did not know, of course, that his prayer had been answered; the Dalai Lama had returned.

It is said that one day, feeling particularly frustrated by his Ministers, the Great Thirteenth had sworn that when he was reborn it would be into a large family, with brothers and sisters who would help – not hinder – him in his work. It looked as though he had kept his word.

NOTES

1. Every large monastery in Tibet was divided into separate colleges, each of which had its own property and finances. The estate was known as a *labrang*. The amount of wealth, of course, varied. Thanks to the travels and skills of the recently deceased Taktser Rinpoche, his *labrang* was now an extremely wealthy one.

2. In 1904, the British in India feared that Tsarist Russia was about to obtain serious influence over Tibet and then might cause trouble on India's northern border. (This was the era of the Great Game, when Britain, China and Russia jockeyed for influence in Central Asia.) Accordingly, an expeditionary force was sent to Tibet under Colonel Francis Younghusband, who trounced the tiny and badly-equipped Tibetan Army. Later, however, good relations were restored between Britain and Tibet, and an Agreement was signed. The 1904 Convention with Britain, signed in the Potala Palace, made it clear that Britain was dealing with an independent Tibet over which China had no control. It arranged for British trading posts to be set up at Gyantse and Gartok in Western Tibet. (The British had since 1893 had a trading post at Dromo.)

3. Author interview, Gyalo Thondup, New Delhi, July 1995.

4. Norbu, *Tibet*.

5. See chapter 1.

6. *Tibet*.

7. Norbu, *Tibet Is My Country*.

8. *Tibet*.

9. *Tibet Is My Country*.

10. Tibetan monasteries were like complete townships, with streets, colleges, temples, etc.

11. *Tibet Is My Country*.

12. Most Westerners seem surprised to learn that Tibetan Buddhists eat meat. But vegetarianism was never a practical possibility in those parts of Tibet where few vegetables would grow. Yaks and sheep were the chief source of Tibetan food, and though some lamas and monks did refrain from meat-eating on principle, most people did not even try. However, they were never entirely easy in their minds about it and they did not lightly kill an animal. Whenever a herdsman found it necessary to slaughter for food, he would first pray for forgiveness from the animal itself and then perform rituals for its rebirth into a happier state of life. He would put holy water on the nose or mouth of the yak or sheep before killing it. In the towns, Muslims acted as butchers. Small animals and birds, which would feed only a small number of people, were taboo; and in only one area of Tibet, around the Yarlung Tsangpo river, was fishing allowed.

13. *Tibet.*
14. *Tibet Is My Country.*
15. *Tibet.*
16. Not all those who are discovered in childhood to be *tulkus* stay the course. They remain *tulkus* and are addressed as Rinpoche for the rest of their lives, but many meanwhile renounce the monastic state.
17. *Tibet Is My Country.*
18. The Buddhist Order to which most Tibetans adhere is the reformed Gelugpa Order. The others are: Nyingmapa (the old) which follows the teachings of Padmasambhava; Kagyupa (the sect of Marpa, the teacher of Milarepa); Sakyapa (the sect of Sakya Panchen, known as the Gracious Teacher). All four Orders owe their allegiance to the Dalai Lama.
19. *Tibet Is My Country.*
20. *Tibet Is My Country.*
12. *Tibet.*
22. *Tibet Is My Country.*

5

The Holy Child of Amdo

Those children wrested from their families, subjected to the strict supervision of elderly wardens...led through the endless maze of lamaistic liturgy and dogmatics and plunged forcibly into the ponderous works of their former embodiments, certainly do not know the blissful astonishment of childhood...Such strict discipline, such statue-like immobility as the dignity of that office imposes, the daily intercourse with gloomy, elderly people, look to me like a violent, ruthless suppression of childhood. That is why I actually believe there should be something exceptional in those boys, born as they are with the dreadful burden of a saintliness which must be reached and lived up to at all costs.

Giuseppe Tucci, To Lhasa and Beyond

In old Tibet, it was believed that when a high incarnate lama was about to be reborn, the place of his rebirth would first suffer a series of misfortunes. When for four successive years, the seventeen peasant families of Taktser (fifteen Tibetan, two Chinese) suffered severe crop failure, either through hailstorms when the corn was ripe or drought when it was still young, they muttered among themselves that something extraordinary must be about to happen in the village. But when disasters began to fall thick and fast on Choekyong Tsering and his wife in particular, they found a less charitable explanation: 'They were all speculating that our family had done something dreadful in a previous life and were now being punished for it,' says Gyalo Thondup.

First of all, two of the couple's babies had recently died in infancy. In spite of this, the local oracle, when consulted, told Choekyong Tsering not to worry. 'You will have many children,' he prophesied, 'and at least one of them will become famous. Through him, money will flow like water to your house.' The farmer was consoled, but, alas, his misfortunes were only just beginning, as Gyalo Thondup relates:

> For example, we had seven beautiful horses. Our valley was located at the top of a steep cliff. One day we had taken the horses to the drinking trough when suddenly all seven of them leaped in the air, ran to the cliff and jumped off it. They were all killed. We also had six mules, and at this time they caught some disease and died, one after another...Then my father became seriously ill. He could no longer walk or even get out of bed, he had become just like a skeleton. I was so frightened by his appearance that every day when I came home from school, I used to bend double when I crossed the room where he was, eyes down to avoid seeing him. So the gossips were having a fine time; they were sure there was a curse on our house. First the children dying, then the horses, then the mules and now, presumably, my father. And my poor mother was pregnant again.
>
> Before dawn on the morning of 6 July, there was a violent thunderstorm followed by torrential rain. That day, my sister, Tsering Dolma, who was not yet married, was supposed to be taking me to the market, to buy fruit and some sweets. We were both very excited at the prospect of our day out. But, during the thunderstorm, my mother went into labour and began to shout from the cow byre, calling to my sister to run and get one of our neighbours, an old lady, to come and help. I was a bit scared, my father was ill, my mother now seemed to be ill, and my sister was abandoning me. But my sister soon returned with the old lady, who was almost one of the family. She took charge of the situation and told my sister she couldn't go to market, she'd be needed at home to boil water and things like that. 'Let your brother go with the other people who are going,' she said. My sister was upset because she'd been looking forward to her treat, but the old lady told her to stop moaning and make herself useful. I was packed off.
>
> That morning, after the baby was born, my father called out, using my mother's maiden name as he always did, 'Sonam Tsomo, Sonam Tsomo, is our baby born?' 'Yes, yes, it's a boy,' she answered. He didn't hear and repeated the question. Whereupon the old lady yelled impatiently, 'IT'S A BOY!' Suddenly,

this man who'd seemed to be on the point of death got up and went to the altar-room, to light the butter-lamps in thanksgiving to our protector deities. Amazed at his sudden cure, he vowed, 'I shall make this boy a monk.''

Dekyi Tsering was understandably in two minds about her husband's miraculous recovery. 'My mother,' the Dalai Lama would write, 'remembers being annoyed...and accusing him of having stayed in bed through laziness, but he declared that he was cured.'

In Tibet, one in four boys – usually at least one in every family – was sent to a monastery, not only for pious reasons but because for poor families in a semi-feudal society it was the only way for their sons to be properly educated and have the chance of rising to the top. No farm could support too many men, whereas a monk, even from the poorest family, could aspire to very high office if he had the ability. So Choekyong Tsering's announcement would have been unremarkable, if he had not already offered two sons to the monastic life. Three-year-old Lobsang Samten was shortly to join his brother, Jigme, in Kumbum. 'I was the only layman in the family,' Gyalo Thondup says cheerfully, 'the only one who became a farmer. My father used to take me round with him, especially to the horse-fairs. He was a difficult man, with a very hot temper. When he was in a rage, he would sometimes kick me, although I must admit he didn't do so all that often. In any case, I know I was a difficult child, even my mother would get furious with me and pinch me hard. My mother could be very fierce indeed when roused, even fiercer than my father.'

Dekyi Tsering reported that she had had a number of extraordinary dreams before the birth. In one of these, two dragons came out of the ground, holding a bright jewel which they threw up into the air and watched as it fell to earth. The dragons, bowing low, picked up the jewel and presented it to her. In Tibet, dreams were important, and the fact that no one could offer an explanation of this one worried her. Still, she felt that the child she was carrying – the thirteenth to whom she would have given birth – must be someone special.

He came into the world by the light of a single mustard-oil lamp, at daybreak on the fifth day of the fifth month of Wood Hog Year (6 July 1935). Like his older siblings, he was born on a straw pallet in the cowshed amid the smell of the yak-cows and the sound of suckling calves. Neighbours told Dekyi Tsering that there was a rainbow just overhead at the time – a good omen. The baby was named Lhamo Dhondup, perhaps an odd name for a boy, since strictly speaking Lhamo was a female name, -mo being a feminine suffix. But the goddess, Palden Lhamo, was a protector deity in the Tibetan pantheon, and at times of emergency and insecurity her name was frequently given.

Though babies are usually born with their eyes closed, this child had one eye completely open. 'Maybe,' as the Dalai Lama once suggested, 'some slight indication of a clear state of mind in the womb.'[2] His sister, Tsering Dolma, however, thought that both eyes should be open and took immediate action. 'Without hesitation,' wrote the Dalai Lama, 'she put her thumb on the reluctant lid and forced it open, fortunately without ill effect.'[3]

Farming women took birth in their stride – and soon afterwards the 35-year-old mother was back at work in the barley fields with the other village women, carrying the baby on her back as she hoed and tilled the ground. She was surprised to find that whenever she paused to feed him, he would cry; but the other women reassured her:

> 'He is a special baby,' the women said. 'He doesn't like being fed in front of us. You must take him to a private place.' So after that I took him away from the field when I gave him my breast, and he was content.[4]

Then she would leave him to sleep on the ground under an umbrella tied to an upright stake. Later, when he started to walk, he would go with her when she went to milk the *dzomos*, carrying his wooden bowl for her to fill with fresh, warm milk. She sent him to the chicken coop each day to collect the eggs; one day he went missing for several hours, and was eventually found sitting in one of the nesting boxes, clucking like a contented hen.

As a baby, he slept on a bed with his mother, and later on in the kitchen with Tsering Dolma, by the stove. Once, when he was about a year old, his mother and Tsering Dolma left him asleep on the bed while they went to watch some horse-racing contest in the village. When Dekyi returned, she was relieved to find everything quiet; but relief turned to terror when the baby was nowhere to be found. She panicked, fearing the worst. Then Lhamo Dhondup crawled from underneath the bed, chortling merrily. She always felt he had been born with a fully-developed sense of humour.

He has vague memories of the family gathering in the altar-room to make offerings at the beginning of each day; and clearer ones of pulling his father's moustache 'and being hit hard for my pains'. His brother, Jigme, had already left home, and Gyalo Thondup went each day to school in a neighbouring village. Only three-year-old Lobsang Samten was still at home, the gentlest and least complicated of them all. While Gyalo Thondup, a mass of uncoordinated energy, went spinning round the room like an out-of-control top, Lobsang would pursue him anxiously, vainly trying to protect him from falling. He adored his mother and would hang on to her skirts, unwilling to lose sight of her. But at three, shortly after the arrival of Lhamo Dhondup, he was sent to Kumbum monastery.

Lhamo Dhondup, then, had to learn to play on his own. He was advanced for his years, bubbling with life, stubborn, independent and given to tantrums when he did not get his own way. To his father's disgust, he disliked horses and flatly refused to ride, but otherwise he showed little fear of anyone or anything. If he saw a group of children scrapping, he would go and join the losing side – using an imaginary rifle and shouting 'bang bang' – even if it meant getting a bloody nose. 'Even if I saw two insects fighting,' he laughs, 'I'd rush to help the one which was getting the worst of it. The desire to protect the weak seems to have been inborn in me – I suppose you could say my compassion was more than a bit partisan.'[5]

His mother observed that his play was different from that of other children. He seemed to have ideas above his station:

> He was always drawing houses in the earth. They were big houses, bigger than any in our village or any he could have seen at this time, yet he told me that soon we should live in such a house.
>
> Sometimes he touched my homespun robe, feeling the coarseness of the cloth and then pushing it away, saying it was not good and that I would soon be wearing pretty skirts which would be soft and smooth to touch. But he had never seen a silken robe in our humble dwelling.[6]

The gossip in the village had died away. It seemed clear to everyone who saw him that Lhamo Dhondup was extraordinary. A year later, Hugh Richardson of the British Mission in Lhasa would write to Basil Gould, the British Political Officer for Sikkim: 'As he grew up his parents realized that he was an exceptional child, but as they did not want to lose him, they did not bring him forward as a candidate when the party headed by [Kesang Rinpoche] came to search for the reincarnation of the Dalai Lama. It happened that while the late Panchen Lama Rinpoche was in Jyekundo he heard about the child and sent word to [Kesang Rinpoche] that he should go and see him.'[7]

By the time that letter was written, Lhamo Dhondup was already in Kumbum in the care of Jigme, now a serious young novice of fifteen who had passed his examinations and been accepted into the general monastic assembly. Earlier, he had witnessed the anguish of three-year-old Lobsang Samten's arrival at the monastery. Jigme, who was absent when his parents had left Lobsang Samten behind, had returned to find an inconsolable bundle of misery.

> On my couch sat little Lobsang Samten obviously feeling very sorry for himself. Big tears rolled down his chubby cheeks, and convulsed with sobs he was hardly able to utter a word. He just couldn't grasp the fact that his mother and father had left him behind alone in this strange place...Suddenly all the misery I had suffered when I was in his situation revived in my memory. And he was considerably younger than I had been at the time. When all my well-meant efforts to comfort him were of no avail I lost my head too and there we sat locked in each other's arms, sobbing, until in the end we were both so exhausted that we fell asleep.[8]

Jigme even sent a message to his maternal grandparents begging them to persuade his parents to take Lobsang Samten home. But the grandparents would not interfere, and Lobsang Samten settled to his new life faster than anyone had dared hope. Or at least, as he later, rather wistfully, noted, 'Time was a great healer. I adjusted to my new home and tried to make myself happy.'[9] This, in spite of the fact that he was no longer allowed to call his brother Cho-la, as he had always done. Cho-la, Jigme, as an Incarnate in training to become one of the most important lamas in the land, had another name now: he was Taktser Rinpoche, even to his family.

The nightmare was now repeating itself and the poor Rinpoche found himself with not one but two homesick little brothers to console. 'One bright and tingling winter morning' in 1938, his parents arrived at the monastery with Lhamo Dhondup; and a few days later set off again for home without him. His mother left first, telling the little boy she was going to visit her parents. When, soon afterwards, his father left too, Lhamo Dhondup was naturally upset. How could he have known – or cared – that he was to be the next Dalai Lama? All he knew was that his parents had abandoned him. As a tiny child, he had often been taken, propped up on his father's horse, to see Jigme, and had always been disappointed that Jigme could not come out and play with him. Now the positions were reversed: *he* was the one who couldn't go out to play. Jigme – Taktser Rinpoche – felt desperately sorry for him:

> Dissolved in tears he begged us to take him home. I was almost seventeen years old now, but I was still helpless in the face of such misery. Lobsang Samten was the first to join little Lhamo Dhondup in his sobs, but it was not long before I too dissolved into tears. A last attempt to distract my little brother by getting him to look at the dancing snowflakes outside the window naturally failed, and then we were all three in tears.

There were few consolations. Five-year-old Lobsang Samten, still so small that he had to be lifted over the lintels of schoolroom and assembly hall, was already attending scripture classes with other boys of his own age and was no longer available as a playmate. Lhamo Dhondup was lonely, miserable and bored. Years later he would remember 'waiting impatiently outside his classroom, and sometimes peering round the curtain in the doorway to try and attract his attention without letting his tutor see me. But the tutor was strict and Samten was helpless.'[10] Lobsang's tutor, though a strict disciplinarian who kept order with a bamboo rod, felt sorry for Lhamo Dhondup:

> Sometimes [he] used to put me on his lap and wrap me in his gown and give me dried fruits [apricots], and that is almost the only solace I remember.

Their uncle, Ngawang Changchup, was meant to be keeping an eye on the two younger boys, but they were scared of him. It was partly his appearance – pock-marked face, bristly black beard and fierce moustache – and partly his lack of patience with small boys. Once when Lhamo Dhondup, a mischievous child, had knocked over his uncle's book of loose-leaf scriptures, the latter picked him up and slapped him hard. When that sort of thing happened, the two brothers would run away and hide and though the matter usually ended with their uncle offering them sweets – 'which he never gave us when we behaved ourselves' – they never lost their fear of him. It was a wretched period of their lives.

While his own little personal tragedy was running its course, Lhamo Dhondup was the subject of some relentless power-bargaining in the world outside. Ma Pu-feng, convinced that the Taktser child was the genuine Dalai Lama, was unwilling to let the boy leave Amdo unless officially recognized as such. He was supported by the Kumbum monks, who wanted the prestige of having had the next Dalai Lama under their roof.[11] The

Tibetans wired Lhasa for the ransom money demanded – 100,000 Chinese dollars (the equivalent of 7,000 to 8,000 pounds sterling) – to be distributed partly to the authorities in Ch'inghai and partly to Kumbum. But, even when payment had been made, Ma asked for a further 300,000 Chinese dollars before he would allow the boy to leave. He would not budge, and the unfortunate search party had to spend the winter of 1938 in Kumbum monastery awaiting Lhasa's response. In the end, some sort of compromise was reached and the Tibetans agreed to pay the second instalment of the ransom. This they could only do with the help of the British Government of India.

Since 1936, the British had had a small Mission of their own in Lhasa. In the time of the Great Thirteenth, the Political Officer for Sikkim used to make fleeting visits to Lhasa if anything important had to be discussed with the Tibetan government. When a Chinese wireless station was set up in Lhasa after the funeral of the Great Thirteenth, the British, not unreasonably, were suspicious. 'We wanted to know what was going on,' says Hugh Richardson, at that time the British Trade Agent in Gyantse,[12] 'the Chinese had no treaty right to be there and we wanted to keep an eye on them.'[13] The British Mission consisted of one Officer with two clerical assistants; a Medical Officer with a small staff; and a wireless operator. 'The Tibetans were delighted to have us there, with our own radio transmitter, a much more powerful one than the Chinese had. The Chinese didn't like it. They went to the government and asked them to make us withdraw our radio transmitter. The Tibetans said they would do so if the Chinese withdrew theirs. And that was the end of that.' Within a year, the British Mission had become a semi-permanent arrangement under Basil Gould;[14] and when Gould left Lhasa in 1937, he left Hugh Richardson in charge – to keep an eye on the Chinese.

It was to Richardson that the Tibetans now turned. 'We didn't put the money up ourselves,' he says, 'but we arranged for them to have the silver without paying duty on it. The money itself was actually all raised by Muslims.' A group of rich Muslim traders going from Siling to Mecca by way of India, agreed to advance the required sum and allow the Tibetans to pay it back in Indian rupees. Thanks to the Tibetan exchange rate, the Muslim merchants would do well out of the deal, and they would also be the guarantee that Ma would not renege on the deal. Moreover, they would travel to Lhasa with the Tibetans – far more acceptable companions than the Chinese military escort that Ma was insisting on.

At last everyone was more or less satisfied and a binding document was signed by all sides, the Kumbum monks included.[15] The latter had demanded their own rake-off: a complete set of the Great Thirteenth's clothes, one of his thrones and decorations, and a 108-volume set of Buddhist Scriptures written in gold.[16] Ma Pu-feng insisted on one of the search party being left behind as a hostage – against the safe arrival of the goods from Lhasa![17]

When everything had been settled, Lhamo Dhondup was dressed in new robes and placed on a throne in Kesang Rinpoche's private quarters in Kumbum. In a brief installation ceremony, the lama uttered special ritual prayers. 'After receiving blessings from the boy, the group offered 100,000 butter-lamps at the Temple of the Golden Tree and spent the rest of the day making meritorious offerings to the monks and novices of the monastery, offering each of them a silver dollar. Then Lhamo Dhondup was taken to the Congregation Hall, where the Abbot of Kumbum offered him tea and rice followed by fruits.'[18] He dimly recalls a ceremony taking place one day at dawn. 'I remember this particularly as I was surprised to be woken and dressed before the sun had risen. I also remember being seated on a throne.'[19] He was three years old.

Lhamo Dhondup was delighted to learn that he was to go on a journey. Life seemed to be looking up. Best of all, his parents and two of his brothers, eleven-year-old Gyalo Thondup and six-year-old Lobsang Samten, were to go too. Taktser (Jigme), to his great disappointment, was to be left behind, like his sister, Tsering Dolma, now pregnant with her first child.[20]

On the first day of the sixth month of the Year of the Earth Hare (21 July 1939), two weeks after Lhamo Dhondup's fourth birthday, he and Lobsang Samten rejoined their parents and with a caravan of fifty people and three hundred and fifty horses and mules left Kumbum on a historic journey that had taken three weeks to prepare and would last for three months and thirteen days. As Lobsang Samten later recorded in a diary, 'From our village of Taktser in the region of Kokonor, from among our barley and potato fields, from our yaks and cows, from our simple peasant home, our family set out on a long, tedious journey across the endless expanse of the Tsaidam Marshes. Our destination was the Holy City of Lhasa, a city every Tibetan hopes to visit once in a lifetime to receive blessings from the seat of the Dalai Lamas.' Taktser (Jigme) has recorded his misery at the moment of departure:

The parting with my family...was very difficult. In my heart of hearts I was resentful at the decision which threatened to separate us not merely for the time being, but perhaps for ever. Together with many other monks I accompanied the great caravan for the first two hours of its journey, and my heart was heavy within me...On a little hill we all embraced each other for the last time. Secretly I still harboured the hope that at the last moment I should be asked to go with them, but nothing came of that, though my father did seem to guess my feelings and promised that he would do his best to see to it that later on I too should be called to Lhasa. Then the caravan moved off leaving me sadly staring after it.[1]

When Taktser returned to his *labrang*, it seemed empty and deserted, the children's toys still lying around as a mute reminder of the vanished past. For nights afterwards he would wake up suddenly 'with the feeling that Lobsang Samten had called out for me, or that Lhamo Dhondup had cried out in his sleep'. It was hard for him to realize he might never see either of them again.

Tsering Dolma felt equally bereft, though she was consoled by her parents' promise to send for her, should they be remaining in Lhasa. We do not know the feelings of Choekyong and Dekyi Tsering who, despite their nomadic Amdo blood, must have felt it a wrench to say goodbye to their homeland. They were leaving behind their two eldest children, their village, their house, their relations and friends, to embark on a perilous journey into the unknown. They knew that Lhamo Dhondup was in the running to be the next Dalai Lama; but although Dekyi Tsering said later that she had felt ninety per cent sure that he would be chosen, nothing had been officially decided.

As well as the family, there were the members of the search party, the Muslim pilgrims, the Chinese escort, several government officials and a large number of muleteers and scouts who, with their vast experience of the caravan routes and familiarity with the terrain, were indispensable to any long journey: only they knew where to ford the rivers and how to cross the formidable mountain passes. There were, of course, no cars, nor indeed any roads. The main party rode on horses and mules, Dekyi Tsering travelling in a separate conveyance, and Lhamo Dhondup in a specially made *treljam*: a wooden sedan-chair construction attached to two poles and fastened onto the backs of two mules. Over smooth ground he and Lobsang Samten would ride in this contraption, but when the going got rough, they had to be carried, with considerable difficulty, by the monks of the search party.

The party followed the well-worn caravan route from Amdo to the Holy City,

> through the forests of the Sandal Valley, amid scores of tiny lakes glimmering like sapphires and surrounded by lush, verdant pastures teeming with deer, antelope, wolves, bears, and large herds of *drongs* (wild yak) and *kyangs* (wild asses); on to the awesome Kokonor, its brilliant deep-blue waters reflecting the ring of snowcapped peaks along its shores...through vast steppe lands resplendent with yellow, brown, red and violet vegetation; over craggy, weather-beaten mountain passes above which eagles and vultures loomed; along the eastern edge of the marshy plains of Tsaidam, where a single mishap could cause pack animals to be swallowed up without trace; and across the eastern reaches of the windswept Chang Tang.[22]

The journey, recalled Dekyi Tsering,

> took us right across the bleak, uninhabited high plateau of Tibet. There were many dangerous rivers to cross, some with no bridges where the pack-animals had to swim across, drifting downwards with the strong current, until they could scramble ashore on the other side. We either rode our ponies and followed in their wake or were borne across in small, light coracles.[23]

Each day they travelled about ten miles, riding, as Tibetans on long journeys always did, from dawn till noon, resting in the afternoon before the winds got up, and camping in yak-hair tents at night, close to water and good grazing places, as the only dwellings on the route were a few nomad tents. In the evenings the men would sit around and chat and drink *chang*, while Dekyi Tsering busied herself with embroidery. Lobsang Samten remembers 'being wakened very early from sleep each morning and bundled into the palanquin. It was high summer and we could feel the cold wind in the air. Lhamo Dhondup and I played, teased each other and fought to the brink of tears in the palanquin.'[24]

The two boys were close, but like most small boys they wound each other up and spent much of their time sparring and punching each other. Lhamo Dhondup, the younger by two years, was usually the aggressor, and always came off best. Lobsang Samten was no weakling, but he was a peace-loving child, 'so good-natured he could not bring himself to use his superior strength against me'.[25] On this journey, the muleteers had a hard time of it, with the boys constantly scrapping in mid-palanquin. 'It was a marvellous play area,' chuckles the Dalai Lama, 'and we made the most of it.' The conveyance would lurch ominously from side to side, in danger of toppling over; and the driver would stop and summon the boys' mother. Running up to see what the matter was, she was invariably faced by a tearful Lobsang Samten, sobbing, 'The little bastard's been hitting me again.'[26] Lhamo Dhondup just sat there looking smug. 'When we'd finished fighting and had each retired to our allotted corners,' he chuckles, 'that must have been the best moment of the entire journey for the men carrying the palanquin. It was the only time it was evenly balanced. When we were quiet inside, everything was peaceful outside too. But when we started squabbling again, there was no more peace for anyone. Everyone was shouting at once. It was pandemonium.'[27]

They journeyed on, meeting no one along those vast open spaces but the occasional nomad arriving from afar to pay his respects. Even the two little boys in the *treljam* were awed by the majesty of their surroundings, the

> gargantuan mountains flanking immense flat plains which we struggled over like insects. Occasionally, we came upon the icy rush of meltwater streams that we splashed noisily across...But mostly, it was just arid, empty space with only savage dust-laden winds and angry hailstorms as reminders of Nature's living forces.[28]

And now at last the news broke in Lhasa. As autumn approached, the inhabitants were overjoyed to hear that a young boy, about whom there could be no possible doubt, had been found near Kumbum and was expected to reach Nagchuka, ten days' march north-east of Lhasa, about 20 September.

As soon as the party was over the official border with Central Tibet – and thus beyond the reach of Ma Pu-feng – the Tibetan Government dropped all pretence of uncertainty. Summoning the National Assembly in Lhasa, they formally declared the boy from Taktser to be the Fourteenth Dalai Lama. The uncommon haste was probably in order to pre-empt the Chinese official who would be coming from Peking for the enthronement ceremony, to prevent him claiming, as he was sure to – and did – that the proclamation could not be made without him.

Several days later, the travellers crossed the last high pass to arrive at the village of Bumchen, where they encamped for the night.

As the sun began to rise next morning, the parents of Lhamo Dhondup saw a crowd of standard-bearers and officials and an elaborate camp laid out in the form of a square. Here at the 'Meadow of the Four Joys', one of the monks in the search party lifted the child onto his shoulders and carried him into a yellow tent which had belonged to the Thirteenth Dalai Lama. He was dressed in new robes and seated upon a throne hurriedly constructed out of dry clods of earth. In a brief service of welcome, the child was given an official document from the Regent acknowledging him as the Dalai Lama; and presented with gifts which may only be offered to the highest Incarnation present:

> ...the Offerings to All the Gods, in the form of a butter-cake with a number of turrets; an image of Tsepame, the god of endless life; a model of a chorten; and a miniature holy book...Also gold, silver, ceremonial garments, and rolls of silk and other materials.[29]

From now on Lhamo Dhondup would ride alone in the gilded palanquin of the Dalai Lamas. The secret was a secret no longer. The parents were officially told that their son was the new god-king; they were hailed as Great Mother (Gyayum) and Great Father (Gyayap) of Tibet and presented with ceremonial robes and jewellery. They then proceeded on their way to Nagchuka, the last staging-post on the caravan route to Lhasa.

In this huge gathering-place where the routes from all over Tibet converged, the camels were left behind and the caravans reassembled for the ten-mile journey to the Holy City. Here, seated on the throne of the Dalai Lamas in the monastery which is called 'the Palace of True Peace' the four-year-old held his first official reception.

Lobsang Samten felt only relief that the long journey was almost over; he was too young to understand that it was the end of more than a journey; that from this time forward his younger brother would no longer be Lhamo Dhondup to him. Such is the mystique surrounding a Dalai Lama that even the child's own family – even his mother – would henceforth refer to him as Kundun, meaning Presence of the Buddha. It was as Kundun that Lobsang Samten would address his brother for the rest of his life.

NOTES

1. Author interview with Gyalo Thondup, New Delhi, July 1995.
2. John Avedon, *An Interview with the Dalai Lama*, Littlebird Publications, 1980.
3. Fourteenth Dalai Lama, *Freedom in Exile*.
4. Conversation of Dekyi Tsering with Lady Gould, Isle of Wight, October 1960, as reported to the author.
5. Author interview with HH the Dalai Lama, June 1994.
6. Conversation with Lady Gould, 1960.
7. Letter dated 1/10/1939, Oriental and India Office Collections, L/P&S/12/4/178. Death of the XIIIth Dalai Lama and question of successor, December 1933 – October 1940.
8. Norbu, *Tibet Is My Country*.
9. Diary in the possession of Lobsang Samten's widow, Namlha Taklha.
10. Fourteenth Dalai Lama, *My Land and My People*.
11. Cf. Richardson, *Tibet and its History*.
12. Trade Agencies, established under treaty between Britain and Tibet after the Younghusband Expedition of 1904, were Vice-Consulates in all but name.
13. Author interview, 29 September 1993.
14. The British Political Officer based in Sikkim but responsible also for relations with Bhutan and Tibet.
15. Goldstein, *A History of Modern Tibet*.
16. 108 is a sacred figure to Tibetan Buddhists.
17. Goldstein, p. 322.
18. Goodman, *The Last Dalai Lama*, chapter 1.
19. Fourteenth Dalai Lama, *Freedom in Exile*.
20. Marriages in Tibet were secular occasions, though the couple did go to the temple afterwards to seek the Buddha's blessing.
21. *Tibet Is My Country*.
22. Goodman, chapter 5.
23. Conversation of Dekyi Tsering with Lady Gould, October 1960.
24. Diary of Lobsang Samten, in the possession of his widow, Namlha Taklha.
25. *Freedom in Exile*.
26. As reported by his mother to Tendzin Choegyal.
27. Author interview, June 1994.
28. *Freedom in Exile*.
29. Report by B. J. Gould.

6

Lord of the Lion Throne

He is supposed to be the temporary embodiment of a god...called upon to lead, comfort and improve sinful, suffering mankind, and to teach the way to release. It is throughout the same being who sits on the Lhasa throne in successive embodiments. The secret person, the spiritual reality of the Dalai Lama, is immutable and only his body changes, a perishable vessel employed to reach down to the lowly human level and to make the dazzling light of the truth he embodies accessible to our limited understanding.

Giuseppe Tucci, To Lhasa and Beyond

It was almost seven years since the Thirteenth Dalai Lama had died, leaving a great void at the heart of Tibet. Now at last, he had returned. The timing was auspicious: the new ruler must enter Lhasa before the end of the eighth month of the Tibetan Year, the ninth month of the current Year of the Earth Hare being considered unlucky.

Hugh Richardson, as the *Times* Special Correspondent, shared the excitement of the people as the child drew near to the Holy City: [1]

Boy God in Lhasa

The Dalai Lama's Return

TIBETAN HOMAGE

Rigya, over two miles east of Lhasa and within sight of the soaring Potala, was the scene the day before yesterday of the first ceremony on the return of the Dalai Lama to his capital in his fourteenth reincarnation. On a plain below rocky foothills a large encampment had been set out in square formation, three lines deep around a splendid reception tent standing in a yellow walled enclosure. Its outer cover was bright yellow – a colour used only for the tents of the Dalai Lama – and decorated with blue designs; its inner roof was richly embroidered with circular patterns in blue, red and yellow; and on the roof-pole were gilded figures, including peacocks, from which it gets its name of the Peacock Tent...

The Regent went in procession with the state sedan chair up to Rigya Monastery on the hill above the camp. Before long an excited murmur told that 'the Presence' was coming and the crowd on a spur hiding the road to the east stirred expectantly as the band of the Bodyguard was heard. Soon, above clouds of dust mingled with the smoke of incense and above the mass of the people, tall banners came into sight. Deep trumpets sounded from the monastery on the hill. A reverent, silent crowd of Tibetans pressed forward to see the four-year-old child from the distant Chinese province of Siling[2] in whom their compassionate ruler Chenrezi has again become incarnate. A small troop of Chinese soldiers in dusty, quilted clothes came a little in advance, followed by a body of mounted men in bright silks and tall Mongolian hats holding banners. Behind them rode officials in ascending importance wearing magnificent brocade robes and, preceding the centre of the cavalcade, a sedan chair covered in yellow silk through the glass windows of which the small Dalai Lama could be seen looking with calm interest at the crowd. Behind rode his father and mother and his two brothers.

HOMAGE

After a short rest the Dalai Lama was carried down in the large gilded palanquin over which waved an umbrella of peacocks' feathers and one of yellow silk, to receive homage in the Peacock Tent. There he was seated on the throne. After making three prostrations before him the officials, headed by the Regent, began to file past, offering white silk scarves and receiving his blessing. The stream, which included British, Nepalese and Chinese representatives and Lhasa Moslems, poured past the throne for almost an hour, while the Dalai Lama, wearing yellow brocade and a yellow peaked fur hat, sat solemnly and with dignity holding out his hands to touch the worshippers...

The dignity and self-possession of the child impressed everyone. He looked about calmly, seeming unmoved by the magnificence and as if he were in familiar surroundings. Although appearing to grow tired towards the end of the ceremony he did not lose his composure. He never smiled, but maintained a placid, equable gaze. Much of his attention was directed to a calm inspection of members of the British Mission, as though he were trying to recall where he had seen such people before.[3]

The travellers had reached Rigya on 6 October, and the whole of Lhasa turned out to greet them. The Dalai Lama's father was resplendent in the official robes of a Cabinet Minister, but the new Great Mother still wore her simple Amdo clothes. Everyone 'was very happy to see her, and at the same time amused by her costume'.[4]

The official party spent two nights in the encampment before setting out on the last leg of the journey to Lhasa. Lobsang Samten confided his wonderment to his diary:

> The closer we got to the Holy City, more and more parties came out of Lhasa to see His Holiness. Splendidly-robed members of the Cabinet came to us amid the music of horns, cymbals, drums and gongs. Juniper branches were lit along the route, the air was full of sights and smells. The officials were so splendid, the peasants by the roadside were dressed in their best chubas and wearing all the jewellery they owned. We were dazzled. It seemed as if the whole population not only of the city but of the surrounding villages had turned out to get a first glimpse of their precious Yeshi Norbu and get his blessing. The unforgettable crowd, the music and the joy was felt by everybody, not least by the four-year-old boy for whom this great performance was being laid on.[5]

The Dalai Lama remembers only 'a sense of homecoming and endless crowds of people. I had never thought there could be so many.' Hearing the people shout 'The day of our happiness has come', he felt he was living in a dream.

Hugh Richardson watched as the procession arrived in Lhasa:

> The procession enclosing the yellow palanquin rode through streets lined
> with monks holding banners and auspicious emblems. The villagers were
> dressed in bright colours as dancers and musicians. Every window was shut
> and curtained, for no one should look from above on the Dalai Lama...
>
> As the middle of the procession reached the south entrance of the cathedral
> it was met by the Oracle of Nechung in a state of possession. A god who acts
> as guardian of religion is said to enter into him, and when he is so possessed
> he dances with convulsive movements, bending his body fiercely to the
> ground, forwards and backwards. He wears a high head-dress of white plumes
> over a golden crown and brandishes a sword and a bow. This terrible figure
> rushed to the Dalai Lama's palanquin and thrust in his head so that the spirit
> in him could do reverence. There had been some apprehension that the sight
> would frighten the child, but it is said that he was quite unperturbed.[6]

The *Times* correspondent was full of admiration for Lhamo Dhondup. 'His
calm assurance during the exacting two days of his entry into Lhasa has
been a source of wonder and delight to the people of Tibet and has confirmed their trust in the reincarnation.'[7]

Shortly after his triumphal entry into the city, the new Dalai Lama was
taken to the Jokhang Temple where he and Lobsang Samten were initiated
as monks. His hair was symbolically shorn by Reting Rinpoche, the Regent; and he was given a string of imposing new names, among them two
of the Regent's own:

> In accordance with ancient custom, I forfeited my name, Lhamo Dhondup,
> and assumed his, Jamphel Yeshe, along with several others, so that my full
> name now became Jamphel Ngawang Lobsang Yeshe Tenzin Gyatso.[8]

His names meant: Holy One, Tender Glory, Mighty in Speech, Compassionate One, Learned Defender of the Faith, Ocean of Wisdom. He would
sign himself with the last two names: Tenzin Gyatso, the Fourteenth
Dalai Lama.

The boy was then escorted to the Norbulingka Palace. Though it was already winter (past the date when the Dalai Lamas traditionally transferred to the cold and draughty Potala Palace), he was to stay in the summer palace until after his formal enthronement at the Potala. The original Norbulingka, about five kilometres west of the Potala, had been built by the Seventh Dalai Lama in the eighteenth century and successive rulers had added their own two-storey palaces and pavilions and developed the park, filling it with tame musk-deer, peacocks, pheasant and many other birds and animals. Pet fish abounded in the ponds, and on its exceptionally fertile soil grew poplars, willows, junipers, fruit trees and myriads of flowers imported from India.

The two boys were in the three-storey Kelsang Palace, largest of the smaller palaces in the inner court of the park which was surrounded by a yellow wall. It had about twenty rooms and various chapels, storage rooms for clothing, books and the writings of past Dalai Lamas.

The new ruler was happy that winter. Too young to begin his studies, he had his brother to play with, and his parents and Gyalo Thondup were lodged close by in a farmhouse known as Gyatso, about fifteen minutes' walk on the other side of the yellow wall enclosure. Life had never been so good:

> Almost every day I used to steal over, with an attendant, to spend time with them. This was not really allowed, but the Regent, who was responsible for me, chose to ignore these excursions. I particularly liked going there at mealtimes. Boys destined for the monastery were not supposed to eat pork, eggs and fish as it was believed that these foods rotted the brain. So when my parents sat down to a meal of roast pork and crackling which I loved, I would sit between them like a hungry dog with its mouth open for scraps. My mother would give in first – she was soft-hearted and couldn't stand the strain of seeing me look so longingly at what was on her plate, so she kept passing me bits surreptitiously. My father would then slip me some pieces of crackling when he thought she wasn't looking.[9]

Once a senior official caught him eating an egg. 'He was very shocked. And so was I. I shouted "Go away" in the loudest voice I could manage.'

One curious incident had startled his mother. On arrival in Lhasa, the four-year-old had mysteriously insisted that his teeth were in a certain house within the Norbulingka park. When taken there, he pointed to a box, saying that was where he'd left them. When the box was opened, it was found to contain a set of dentures which had belonged to the Thirteenth Dalai Lama![10]

Young as he was, he was already giving official audiences at the Norbulingka. Everyone was struck by his firm gaze, his personality and the extraordinary concentration and ease with which he carried out the ceremonials, granting blessings, and knotting the silk scarves to be conferred on those deemed worthy of this special honour. All who saw him were convinced that he was truly the Dalai Lama reborn. His close attendants were pleased to note his obvious affection for those with whom his predecessor had been friendly, his kindness to the Great Thirteenth's former servants and the love of flowers which he had inherited from his former manifestation.[11]

New Year 1940 – Year of the Iron Dragon – a memorable time to be in Lhasa. New Year (Lhosar) was the greatest and happiest of the annual festivals, usually located between the end of February and the beginning of March. It lasted for several weeks, being also the main season of religious observance in Tibet, the time of the first new moon, when the evil of the past year was symbolically driven out. Basil Gould[12] was among the large crowds who that year gathered to celebrate the festival – and to catch a rare glimpse of the Regent with the parents of the new Dalai Lama and his two elder brothers, Gyalo Thondup and Lobsang Samten. The brothers were, reported Gould, in a telegram to the Foreign Office in New Delhi,[13] 'aged about 11 and 8, very strong, bright, intelligent boys'.

This New Year had been chosen by the Tibetan Government for the formal return of the Dalai Lama to his Lion Throne in the Potala Palace. For six years, food had regularly been placed beside the vacant throne, as if, wrote Gould (who was to represent the British Government and the Government of India at the enthronement), 'the Dalai Lama were merely absent on a journey and might return at any time; and always those who attended ceremonies had bowed to the throne and offered a silk scarf at it, as if the Dalai Lama had been present'.[14]

Before leaving Lhasa on 4 June, Gould would advise his colleagues in New Delhi that 'in finding its Dalai Lama Tibet has also found itself and has gained enormously in confidence and hope.'[15] He had felt privileged to be an eye-witness on 21 February when the young Amdo boy made a spectacular 'return' to his palace:

Entry of the Dalai Lama into the Potala

Almost everyone who was not on duty set out at dawn to line the route. Here were assembled many ladies of the chief families in Lhasa, gay in head-dresses set with seed-pearls, coral and turquoise, over which were looped the black coils of their long hair – eight-inch ear ornaments cut flat and set in gold gem-set charm boxes – silk robes of every colour, with silk shirt-sleeves of some contrasting colour turned back over the wrist – a cascade of pearls and gems over the right shoulder – and, in the case of married women or grown-up girls, an apron in rainbow stripes of green, red, purple, green, gold, green, purple, or whatever succession of bright colours the individual weaver had chosen...

Along the route were men and women tending incense crocks, set on walls or carried on arm or shoulder, fed with artemisia or other fragrant herbs; troupes of strolling dancers, some in head-dresses like red Indians, some in masks; mummers; bands and drummers; clean-featured shepherds dressed in sheepskin, their broad-browed and plump wives wearing their hair in an hundred closely-plaited ringlets; monks of every age from four upwards in maroon robes, often tattered; beggars, farmers – thousands turning prayer-wheels of every device and size.

THE PROCESSION

First came servants, on ponies and on foot, dressed in green tunics, blue breeches and broad, red-tasselled hats, carrying the Dalai Lama's food, kitchen-ware, garments and bed-clothes; grooms to be ready for their master at the Potala; attendants carrying tall banners to ward off evil spirits; some members of the Chinese delegation; high lamas followed by the State Oracle and the Chief Secretaries; the led ponies of the Dalai Lama in gorgeous silk trappings; the head monks of the Potala monastery in claret robes fringed with gold and silver embroidery; junior lay officials in their long mantles of many colours, black shirts and white boat-shaped hats set sideways on the head and tied down under the ears; lay officers in ascending order of rank, all stiff in heavy brocade. And then through the clouds of incense which were drifting across the route, and between lines of standard-bearers, came two long double lines of men in loose green uniforms and red hats with white plumes, holding draw-ropes – which would be needed for the climb up the Potala – and men in red with yellow hats, bearing, as they moved with short, shuffling steps, the yokes which supported the poles of the Dalai Lama's great golden palanquin.

The child was invisible behind gold curtains and bright bunches of paper flowers. To his right rear was carried the tall peacock umbrella which is the privilege of the Dalai Lamas. Next came the Regent, under a gold umbrella, dressed in robes of golden silk and a yellow conical hat trimmed with black fox-skin, his horse weighed down with trappings and led by two grooms; then the Dalai Lama's father, mother and brothers; then Abbots and Tulkus from monasteries throughout Tibet, in peaked hats and wrapped in coats of gold brocade worn over maroon robes. It was seen that some Incarnate Lamas, boys as young as the Dalai Lama himself, were firmly tied to their saddles. Towards the end of the procession came more civil officials, seniors leading; more monk-officials; and finally a giant monk door-keeper of the Potala monastery who with stentorian voice kept back the dense crowd of monks, citizens and villagers who, in the manner of spectators everywhere, were closing in from the sides of the route to accompany the Dalai Lama on his progress.

As dawn broke on the great day, long before the child was due to make his entrance, the huge audience hall dominated by the Lion Throne was already full. While the officials, guests and family waited, in an anteroom attendants were laying out the splendid gifts to be presented later in the day. Among them were two magnificent horses from the Maharajah of Sikkim, and, from the British Government, 'a brick of gold, fresh from the Calcutta Mint, ten bags of silver, three rifles, six rolls of broadcloth of different colours, a gold watch and chain, field glasses, an English saddle, a picnic case, three stoves, a musical box, two pairs of budgerigars and a garden hammock'.[16] More exotic gifts had arrived from the monastery of Tashilhunpo, seat of the Panchen Lamas: golden Buddhas wrapped in coloured silks; 'holy books, sets of golden silk clothes; sets of the eight lucky signs in gold and in silver; bags of gold dust; a six-foot elephant tusk; a rhinoceros horn set in silver; silver ingots; countless rolls of silk and fine cloth; and provisions of every kind'.[17]

On that day, the Tibetan love of spectacle surpassed itself:

The Dalai Lama rode in a great golden palanquin, the draw-ropes and rear-ropes of which were held by long lines of men wearing green uniforms and red hats with white plumes. The palanquin was mounted on four long poles, each having six bearers with red dresses and yellow hats who advanced with shuffling steps. It was flanked by two great ceremonial umbrellas, one of gold and the other of peacock green. The Dalai Lama sat invisible behind the gold curtains. The palanquin was preceded by the servants of the Dalai Lama, carrying his food and clothes; they wore red hats with broad tassels, green tunics and blue breeches. Next came the carriers of the banners which are supposed to ward off evil spirits, followed by the Dalai Lama's state oracle and his chief secretaries. The ponies of the Dalai Lama were led in the procession and after them came the monks of the Potala Monastery in claret-coloured robes, the lay officers of state in order of rank, and the Cabinet Ministers. Behind the Dalai Lama's palanquin came the Regent, in gold robes with a conical yellow hat trimmed with fur; he was followed by the father, mother and two brothers of the Dalai Lama, who excited the curiosity and interest of the onlookers. The father was dressed as a *Kung* (Duke), a title bestowed on him by the Tibetan authorities. Abbots and Incarnate Lamas from monasteries throughout the country brought up the rear, wrapped in cloaks of gold brocade.[18]

To the blare of Tibetan horns and trumpets, the Dalai Lama and his retinue entered the hall and the ceremony began. The child climbed the lower steps of the Throne and was lifted on to it, wrapped in warm coverings to keep out the cold. One at a time, the monks and officials approached, prostrating their length, offering good wishes, prayers and gifts. On and on and on, for well over five hours. That ceremony represented, said Gould, 'the public and definitive acknowledgement of his people by the Dalai Lama, and of the Dalai Lama by his people'. Particularly striking was:

> the extraordinary interest of the child in the proceedings, his presence, and his infallible skill in doing the right thing to the right person at the right time. He was perhaps the only person amongst many hundreds who never fidgeted and whose attention never wavered. It was very evident that the *sitringasol* was indeed the return, in response to prayer, of the Dalai Lama to a throne which by inherent authority was already his.[19]

On the following day, 23 February, members of the small British Mission in Lhasa attended at a repeat performance of the Installation Ceremony, with Gould representing His Majesty's Government and the Government of India. The little matter of the date almost caused an international incident. The British in New Delhi, having already ascertained that the Chinese delegate, Mr Wu Chang, was 'a person of considerable importance' in China,[20] were anxious lest he be given a significant role in the ceremony. Their anxiety increased when the Associated Press of India issued – in advance of the event – a report of what they had been assured (by the Chinese) would happen at the enthronement: namely that the Regent and Mr Wu would together escort the Dalai Lama to his throne and preside over the ceremony, during which Wu would read from a golden scroll the Chinese Government's formal acknowledgement of the installation. Though this scenario turned out to be no more than Chinese wishful thinking, the British were furious! And when they heard that Wu but not Gould had been present at the ceremony on the twenty-second, Gould had a lot of explaining to do.

Telegrams winged between him and his outraged masters in New Delhi. Had the British not been invited on the twenty-second? they cabled,[21] obviously fearful that they might have been relegated to the B List. And again, a few days later,[22] 'Was there, in your opinion, ever any expectation that you would be invited to attend the ceremony on Feb. 22? Do you attribute exclusion to religious prejudice or to Regent's desire to placate Chinese by thus emphasising the special position of China *vis à vis* Tibet?' Weary of this inquisition, Gould replied firmly that there was 'NO question of religious discrimination, no question of the ceremony on 22nd being more important than on 23rd or of our being excluded from it. The question I had to consider was whether we should be present on 22 Feb. and again on another date with gifts, or make a single appearance with our gifts. I decided on the latter alternative and chose 23 Feb.'[23] Wu, he explained in a second telegram that same day,[24] 'was originally allotted the 26th for the presentation of his gifts but (apparently at the last moment) decided to attend on 22 February also. Possibly this may have been done with a view to affording some sort of foundation of truth for his false account of proceedings'. The Chinese, Gould insisted, did nothing at the ceremony which was not also done by the British and other foreigners present – i.e. Wu had merely presented a silk ceremonial scarf. 'It did not, however, perhaps suit the Chinese book to admit this and on this as on other occasions they have published a deliberately false account of what took place.'[25]

It was not true, then, that the Chinese (as they would indeed claim) played a central role in the installation of the new Dalai Lama – or that the British had been slighted.[26] Far from feeling put down, Gould was clearly ecstatic. 'As I knelt before the child,' he said later,

A long white scarf which he had blessed was placed round my neck and I felt two small firm hands on my head. Through those small hands I felt an inner strength, as though some of the strength and wisdom of many Dalai Lamas was being imparted to me.[27]

The family were there, absorbing everything with unsophisticated delight, as Gould rather touchingly commented in a letter to his superiors in New Delhi:

> It was clear that the Dalai Lama is interested in us; and constantly, before and during the installation ceremony, the parents and brothers, who were only a little way to our right across an empty space, were as smiling, and as communicative by means of smiles, as it is possible to be. I am certain that they are really nice people and that they want to be friends...

The family were entranced by the gifts the British had presented, specially chosen by Gould himself, among them 'a gold clock with a nightingale that pops out and sings, a pedal motor car and a tricycle'. The child himself could not take his eyes off them. As the audience ended, he

> was lifted down from his throne and left the hall of audience, holding the hands of two Abbots who towered on either side of him, but looking back at the things which had gripped his attention. Within a minute, his six-year-old brother was on the spot, to find out how everything worked, and additionally keen and anxious because, as he said, if he did not at once find out all about everything, his four-year-old brother would certainly beat him up...The little monk was soon going round the smooth floor of the audience chamber in the pedal car.

There was an amusing sequel to this story, when Gould came up against an unsuspected streak of stubbornness in the young god-king. As he wrote to Olaf Caroe in New Delhi:

> I have had my first tussle with the Dalai Lama...With the presents we had to submit a formal list, to be entered in the records of the Potala, and this list made mention of two pairs of budgerigars. The Lord Chamberlain had already told me that the Dalai Lama loved birds and loved his nightingale [clock], but we had wanted to keep the budgerigars with us for a time, to become acclimatized after their trying journey, and to breed. But it was no good. Messenger after messenger, each a degree more important than the last, came down from the Potala to demand the delivery of the birds, and by the time Norbhu's clerk, Pemba, was approaching the Dalai Lama's apartments with the birds, a high dignitary of the church was there to receive them.
>
> Pemba, considerably overcome, handed over the birds and tried to make himself scarce; but he was sent for by the Dalai Lama who, talking Tibetan clearly and easily, discussed the birds' food and how to keep them safe. Pemba

then noticed that the watch, nightingale clock and musical box were all on the Dalai Lama's private table, and was told that the Dalai Lama, when off duty, will hardly let them out of his sight...[28]

Before leaving Lhasa, in June, Gould would write with some satisfaction that it was 'common knowledge that the Dalai Lama refers to us [i.e. the British] as the people who gave him the presents which he likes best'.[29] He also noted that 'His Holiness has a strong will and is already learning to exercise the privileges of his position'.

'It seems clear,' scribbled the Under-Secretary in the margins of Gould's report, 'that the new Dalai Lama must be a very remarkable little boy'.[30]

Behind the glitz of public ceremonial, all was far from well in Tibet. Though Regent Reting had played a prominent role in the installation – shaving the Dalai Lama's head and bestowing his names on him – there were many who believed that he was unworthy of such honour. During his Regency, the Great Thirteenth's warnings were coming true: corruption was rife at every level of the Tibetan administration, and the social and ethical standards of the previous reign had virtually collapsed. Reting's own reputation was more than a little tarnished: his dissolute lifestyle was notorious, his greed a byword – the trading company he had set up in his *labrang* at Reting had grown into the third largest trading outfit in the whole of Tibet. The British Representative in Lhasa, Hugh Richardson, expressed the opinion that 'The Regent is governed by self-interest. He has no fixed policy and his actions are dictated by monetary considerations.'[31] Since coming to power in 1933, Reting had promoted his cronies and eliminated his critics, becoming by April 1939 effectively the sole ruler of Tibet. Opposition to him began to build up. A Lhasa street song complained that:

Yesterday's Tibetan Government
Had Tigers and Lions facing each other.
Today the wolves and the jackals
Have blown the Government to the winds.[32]

The growing public unease was heightened by the fact that in 1942 the Dalai Lama was to take his first set of monastic vows, including one of permanent celibacy. These were traditionally administered by the Regent, his Senior Tutor, a man naturally assumed to be of blameless habits. This

Reting palpably was not. Yet 'if the vows are given by someone who has broken the vows, then the vows he has given are meaningless, and the young monk has in effect taken no vows at all'.[33] The dilemma was as acute as it was unusual.

Even as the young Dalai Lama prepared to return to the Potala after his enthronement, wall-posters appeared all over Lhasa, attacking the Regent and even naming a particular Lhasa woman with whom he was said to be associated. Many declared that it was crucial for the young Dalai Lama to be tutored by a lama who was true to his own vows. For Regent Reting, the writing was quite literally on the wall.

NOTES

1. *The Times*, 4 November 1939.

2. Siling, the capital of the province of Amdo (known to the Chinese as Ching'hai).

3. *The Times*, 8 October 1939.

4. Rinchen Dolma Taring, *Daughter of Tibet*, John Murray, 1970.

5. Diary of Lobsang Samten, courtesy of his widow, Namlha Taklha. 'Yeshi Norbu' (Precious Protector) is another of the Dalai Lama's official titles.

6. *The Times*, 10 October 1939.

7. *The Times*, 8 October 1939.

8. Fourteenth Dalai Lama, *Freedom in Exile*, chapter 2.

9. Author interview with HH the Dalai Lama, Dharamsala, July 1995.

10. John Avedon, *An Interview with the Dalai Lama*.

11. Gould, *The Jewel in the Lotus*.

12. The Political Officer for Sikkim, with a 'vaguely diplomatic role' in Tibet.

13. 8 February 1940.

14. Sir Basil Gould, C.M.G., C.I.E., 'The Discovery of the Fourteenth Dalai Lama', article in the *Geographical Magazine*, October 1946.

15. Oriental and India Office Collections of the British Library, L/P&S/12/4178, File 15 (1).

16. Report by B. J. Gould.

17. Goodman, *The Last Dalai Lama*.

18. *The Times*, 23 April 1940.

19. Report by B. J. Gould.

20. Confidential letter to External Affairs Department, New Delhi, from Gould, 2 December 1939. 'The status of Mr Wu...corresponds roughly to that of a junior Minister of non-Cabinet rank. This means that in China he is a person of considerable importance and the Chinese Consul-General when writing about him refers to him as His Excellency.' Oriental and India Office Collections of the British Library, L/P&S/12/4178, File 15 (2).

21. Telegram No. 670, from External Affairs Department, New Delhi to Gould, 2 March 1940.

22. Telegram XX No. 751, 11 March 1940, External Affairs, New Delhi, to Gould.

23. Telegram XX No. 40, 14 March.

24. Telegram XX No. 39, 14 March.

25. Telegram XX No. 39 from Gould, as above, 14 March 1940.

26. Gould eventually issued a printed pamphlet on the Enthronement, 'to counter false Chinese propaganda by giving an authentic account of what actually happened'. This was later summarized for an article in the *Geographical Magazine*, October 1946.

27. Letter from Basil Gould in Lhasa to Olaf Caroe, C.I.E., Secretary to the Government of India in the External Affairs Department, New Delhi, 1 March 1940. Oriental and India Office Collections of the British Library, L/P&S/12/4178, File 15(1).

28. Letter to Olaf Caroe, Oriental and India Office Collections, as above.

29. Letter, 4 June 1940, as above.

30. L/P&S/12/4179, File 15 (2) Oriental and India Office Collections of the British Library.

31. Report of the British Mission in Lhasa, October 1938–September 1939. Quoted by Goldstein, *A History of Modern Tibet*, chapter 9.

32. K. Dhondup, *The Water Bird and Other Years*, New Delhi, Rangwang, 1986.

33. Goldstein, chapter 9.

City of the Gods

Lhasa is by no means the only city or town in Tibet, yet in Tibet, as in the world outside, to hear people talk you would think that Lhasa *was* Tibet. It is the one place that every Tibetan yearns to see at least once before he dies. Many walk over a thousand miles across snow-covered mountains and wind-swept plateaux to fulfil their desire, and many die in the attempt.

Thubten Jigme Norbu with Colin Turnbull, Tibet

Lhasa, whose name means 'abode of the gods', is twelve thousand feet above sea-level, and on roughly the same latitude as Delhi, Cairo and New Orleans. It is situated on the right bank of the Kyi Chu river, thirty miles east of where it meets the great Tsang Po, known outside Tibet as the Brahmaputra. The city was said to have been founded fourteen centuries earlier in the reign of King Songtsen Gampo (617–650) when Buddhism first flourished in Tibet. The social and commercial heart of the city which grew up around the sacred Jokhang temple was Barkhor Street, at once a pilgrimage circuit and a market-place. It was alive with people and life there had changed little over the centuries.

Apart from the numerous pilgrims swarming in and out of the city – seekers after spiritual truth used to come to this 'Mecca of High Asia' from as far away as Siberia and the southern borderlands of China – Lhasa had a resident population of forty to sixty thousand, living for the most part along narrow streets in white-washed stone houses with flat roofs and inward-sloping walls. No house was permitted to be more than two storeys high, since it was considered blasphemous to appear to compete with the Jokhang Temple or the gold-roofed Potala which crowned one of the two hills on which the city was built. The rule about height was strictly observed and applied not only to the sacred buildings but also to the person of the Dalai Lama, and by extension to the Regent.

Lhasa was to be the home of the new Royal Family. From the day the Dalai Lama arrived in Lhasa, 6 October 1939, the Tibetan Government made itself responsible for them. Although traditionally a Dalai Lama's family had no political role to play in Tibet, the change in their social position must have been unnerving to say the least. A rags-to-riches fairytale with elements of nightmare. Simple, untutored peasant-farmers from a remote mountainous province, where everybody knew everybody else and spoke the same dialect, suddenly Choekyong and Dekyi Tsering were transformed into royalty and required to live in a city which was the hub of the Tibetan universe. Like all previous Dalai Lamas' families (and almost all of them had come from similar peasant backgrounds) they were given the royal rank of Yapshi. The parents became the Gyayum and the Gyayap Chenmo, Great (Holy) Mother and Great (Holy) Father. Choekyong Tsering as head of the family became a Kung, roughly the equivalent of Royal Duke. Their male children were Sey Kusho or Prince, the females Semo Kusho, Princess. When they married, the men would also have the title Kung, while the girls would be called Lhacham Kusho, Your Ladyship. Nor was the Yapshi name restricted to mere titles; it carried with it a house in Lhasa and one or more manorial estates with attached servants.[1] As Giuseppe Tucci wrote, 'whether such families were rich or poor, as soon as they were blessed with so happy an event, they were granted an estate to be held in fee, which would secure their welfare ever after'.[2]

As landowners they needed a family name. (Only landowning families had one.) The couple first thought of adopting the name of their village, Taktser, but as it meant 'Roaring Tiger', it was felt to be unsuitable for the family of a Dalai Lama. So they chose Taklha, 'the House that Seeks Happiness', and from then on were known as the Yapshi Taklha family.

While the Kashag looked out for a suitable home for them, they were temporarily accommodated in Gyatso, an old two-storey farmhouse (four rooms down, three up) near the Norbulingka Park, about fifteen minutes walk from the enclosure where the Dalai Lama and Lobsang Samten were living. It was surrounded by fields and plentifully endowed with springs of pure, sparkling water.

Despite the rural setting, the couple missed the easy camaraderie of Amdo where every neighbour and tradesman was a relation or friend; in Lhasa their new acquaintances were aristocrats. 'They had to get by as best they could,' comments one of their sons. 'They were refugees, having to learn everything from scratch, mixing with families who had six hundred years of tradition behind them.'³ They were understandably disoriented, ignorant of the language, bemused by the strict etiquette which had pitchforked them to the lonely pinnacle of society. Dekyi Tsering was still her old, simple self, but she found the aristocratic ladies were in awe of her status as Great Mother. 'Some of the great ladies would go and call on her, but they wouldn't socialize with her,' remembers Hugh Richardson. 'It had nothing to do with snobbery. It was just that as soon as they became The Family, they were automatically treated with the deference due to royalty.'

In adapting to her new situation, Dekyi Tsering was helped by her own strength of character. She may have been raised to a dizzy social height, but she did not intend to let it turn her head. One of her future daughters-in-law said that 'when extraordinary things happened to her, she never let them make any difference. She never felt she was special.'⁴ Dekyi Tsering remained unaffected by the dazzling changes, she was and would remain a housewife, referring to herself without affectation as 'the Farmer's Wife'. She would scold her husband when he shouted at the servants; she herself treating them with the camaraderie and innate kindness which she had bestowed on the hired help or travelling artisans in Amdo, expecting them to eat with the family, for example – which they found quite shocking. When the Kashag showered her with fine silken clothes, splendid necklaces and ear-rings, she stowed them away carefully and – except on ceremonial occasions – continued to wear only the homespun clothes and traditional jewellery of Amdo. At first the city sophisticates found this hilarious; but gradually they came to understand that Dekyi Tsering was that rare phenomenon, a completely natural human being. She was as she was, and felt neither need nor desire to emulate the fine ladies of Lhasa. Always generous, welcoming and kind, Dekyi Tsering was soon as much loved in the capital as she had been in Amdo.

Her husband, the Kung, was another matter. It is not really surprising that Choekyong Tsering was thrown off-balance. Confused by the language barrier, ill-at-ease with the nobility, he let his new wealth and status go to his head. His wife might go on being the Farmer's Wife, but he had no intention of continuing to be the Farmer.

It seems that the Kashag's problems with the Kung began almost at once, when he demanded large amounts of cash for his own use. When, in June 1940, the Kashag offered him two estates – one of them the Gyatso farmhouse, the other Chayul, site of an abandoned tea plantation in southern Tibet – he accepted both, then demanded more! A confidential letter from a Tibetan official in the Government of India service dated January 1942 is quite specific about the Kung's greed.[5] (The official includes both the Dalai Lama's parents in his censure, but, in the light of all that is known of Dekyi Tsering, it seems likely that this was merely blame by association):

> As soon as the Dalai Lama's parents took over these two estates, they again demanded more fertile estates and a good living house. The Tibetan Government convened a meeting of the National Assembly and informed the parents of the decision of the meeting, that the Government cannot grant any more estates as [their] financial position is poor and they have to spend a considerable amount of money in worshipping and burning of butter-lamps. The Tibetan Government offered a living house belonging to an official...who was dismissed from service and banished on 6 June. The parents refused the offer of the house on the grounds that they [would] not feel at home in a house which the Tibetan Government had confiscated.
>
> The Dalai Lama's parents again complained that they [could] not maintain and support themselves with the two estates and they demanded three more estates, viz. Dongtse, 12 miles west of Gyantse, Seshing, about 40 miles west of Lhasa, and Jora in Lhoka (southern Tibet). They said that before they left their country with the Dalai Lama, the Tibetan Government had promised to give them everything they required and now they must get what they require. The Kashag and the National Assembly had to grant these estates and the Dalai Lama's father took charge [of them] in August 1941. [He] selected a building site in Changs[h]ep Shar in Lhasa, which is about 800 yards in length and about 500 yds in breadth. Building materials are being hurriedly collected by the Tibetan Government.[6]

All of which must have made the Kashag reflect that their new Great Father was something of a mixed blessing.

Meanwhile, the family had to settle into their new surroundings. Lhasa was no modern city; conditions were primitive. Throughout winters that were bitterly cold, houses were unheated. There was no running water for drinking, but it could be fetched from Lhasa's numerous wells.[7] Since water for washing had to be heated over yak-dung fires, washing was not a popular winter pastime. But, at a height of twelve thousand feet, washing was not of prime importance anyway, since there was little decay, and no foul smells polluted the cold, dry air. Spring was the time for washing clothes, and when the warmer weather came, women could be seen on the banks of the Kyi Chu, stamping garments with their feet or beating them against stones. The women 'would pour wet sand on the fur side of the skins; when the sand dried they would beat it out with sticks, singing all the while. The garment turned fluffy and fresh again.'[8]

Dr Regolo Moise, an Italian doctor who visited Lhasa in 1948, described sanitary conditions there as 'low but not absolutely disastrous, nor any worse than those of several better-known countries', and reported the absence of diseases such as pneumonia and pulmonary tuberculosis. 'Cold helps the Tibetans in the defence against infective illnesses, by rendering garbage innocuous and making life hard for bacteria and parasites at large.' At the same time, he points out that:

> Indoor air is usually polluted by the smell of the stables below and made sometimes unbreathable by yak-dung smoke. Acute or chronic irritation of the mucoses of the breathing channels and of the conjunctiva are the usual result.[9]

It was indoor pollution that made Tibetans particularly prone to catarrh, sinusitis, arthritis, neuritis, rheumatism and cataracts. Tibetan medicine – herbal and based on an assessment of the various humours of the body – was a mixture of the medieval and what in modern terms might be described as holistic.

With no cars, radios, theatres, cinemas, organized sports, newspapers, magazines, nor even any books apart from ancient Buddhist Scriptures, people were forced to make their own entertainments. The Tibetan historian W. D. Shakabpa, a native of Lhasa, paints an attractive portrait of life in those far-off days:

> All the residents of Lhasa, rich and poor, high and low, are peaceful. In the evenings many people walk about the Barkhor singing and playing musical instruments. Even the beggars of Lhasa have only to ply their trade for some time in the morning to get enough food for the day. In the evening they are all

nicely drunk. The people of Lhasa are physically relaxed, mentally contented and happy. The food of the city is also nutritious. No one has to strive unduly hard to make a living. Life takes care of itself, as a matter of course. Everything is splendid.[10]

With the easy-going Reting as Regent, life, at least for the nobility, was indeed pleasant. Parties were a way of life in Lhasa, particularly in the summer and early autumn when in the meadows and open spaces around the city, elaborate picnics were held in beautifully decorated tents and pavilions. 'They loved parties,' recalls Hugh Richardson:

> And their parties lasted all day...people drifted into little groups and played mahjong or bridge and then almost always you'd go for a walk with someone and have a discussion with them. In fact we got quite a lot of work done while the party was going on. If you wanted to go and write a letter, you could do that. Even if you wanted a sleep. You could idle through the whole day if you wished. A lot of Tibetan tea was served and there was a fairly prolonged lunch with those little dishes of various Chinese foods, sea-slugs, sharks' fins, fish stomachs and mushrooms of various sorts. And then bowls of excellent *thukpa* (soup). If you stayed on to dinner, you had bowls of rice and sat around the table.[11]

Spencer Chapman, who had accompanied the British Mission when it first arrived in 1936, remarked that most of these succulent delicacies seemed designed to elude the unpractised wielder of chop-sticks, 'but if one of the Shappés [Cabinet Ministers] saw us struggling with a particularly slippery slug or an intractable slice of stomach he would deftly catch the morsel with his own chop-sticks and convey it to our plates'.[12] And Basil Gould recalled the *chang* girls at the Tibetans' parties:

> Beautiful girls come round and urge each guest in turn to drink. They are said to have the right to run a long pin into a guest who hesitates.[13]

The new royal couple had to adapt as best they could to this Lhasa-style *dolce vita*. No longer were their days filled with back-breaking toil and do-it-yourself, make-do-and-mend economies. Like all the other nobles, says Richardson, 'they idled about'. Yet, says her youngest son, his mother did not actually like parties very much: 'Parties were for those who liked gambling; they were for merry-making, eating, drinking, exchanging stories and gossip. And my mother was never keen on either gambling or gossip.'[14]

In March 1940, a few days after the Dalai Lama's installation, Basil Gould wrote from the British Mission to Olaf Caroe in New Delhi,

> If, about the time when this letter is likely to reach you, I manage to get the Dalai Lama's family to a children's party with a Christmas Tree and cinema – at which the King and Queen, Charlie Chaplin and Mickey Mouse are certain to be a popular favourite – it will be because all the best children in Lhasa are anxious to come.[15]

The party did take place and over a hundred children came to it. It was a huge success:

> There was nothing wanting in the spirit in which the parents and their children [the unfortunate Dalai Lama was excluded] entered into the spirit of the party. At lunch, served on low tables in front of broad, flat cushions, all present tackled strange English foods with strange implements and good appetites and without hesitation. Then downstairs for a cinema show, at which the King and Queen's tour in Canada and the United States, and some shots of Balmoral Castle and the Gardens, were favourites, followed, in close competition, by Charlie Chaplin, Mickey Mouse, *Do You Like Monkeys?* and Kodachrome scenes of Sikkim, Tibet and Bhutan. Then tea with more strange foods faithfully dealt with, crackers and balloons – and finally a Christmas tree, presided over by two Father Christmases whose native language proved to be Tibetan, and who knew all the children. But all the time the Dalai Lama's brothers and sister, and especially the monk-brother, were wanting to save up crackers and balloons and toys for the Dalai Lama, and they went off happy with a parcel of things in the uses of which they soon instructed him when they had returned to the Potala.[16]

However popular the films about the British Royal Family, Rin Tin Tin (a weepie about a dog which had all the women sobbing with emotion) and Charlie Chaplin (who made them weep with laughter) were the undoubted favourites.

In Amdo, Taktser waited avidly for news, for the assurance that his parents had not forgotten him:

> The first news of the caravan was brought to me by a traveller who had met it crossing the high Tibetan plateaux, and he now brought me greetings from my family, together with an envelope containing ten *gormo*, and a beautiful cream-coloured pony as a riding horse.[17]

This amazing largess on the part of his father was symptomatic: the Kung was being exceedingly liberal with his new wealth. He had handed over his old farm to a cousin, Chandzo Jampa, who, leaving his wife and children in charge, had promptly set out for the installation in Lhasa.[18] Crossing the snow-covered plateaux by camel caravan, the cousin had now returned home, and arrived in Kumbum with four splendid Tibetan hounds as a present for Taktser from his father. He was also charged with buying a large number of fine horses at the Siling horse-fair – and with escorting Tsering Dolma and Phuntsok Tashi to Lhasa. (The young couple's first child had unfortunately lived for only a few months.)

When Chandzo Jampa's caravan was ready for this second journey to Lhasa, he came to say goodbye to a very disconsolate Taktser. The latter begged him to get him invited to Lhasa too, and almost wept with self-pity when, in the early summer of 1940, the caravan escorting his sister set off from Kumbum

> with thirty horses and over a hundred mules and draught animals, leaving me looking sadly after him. Apart from myself, the whole family would soon be assembled in Lhasa. How long should I still have to wait before my turn came?[19]

Taktser's longing rapidly became an obsession. He had managed to scrape through his mid-course examinations and saw no reason why he shouldn't go to Lhasa to pursue his studies at Kumbum's parent-monastery, Drepung. The argument that he had an obligation to stay in his own Taktser *labrang* cut no ice at all, and he began to work out ways of achieving his dream. In the end, his superiors, seeing that he was determined to have his own way, bowed to the inevitable and gave him permission to go to Lhasa, if and when an invitation should come. When Chandzo Jampa arrived back in Kumbum some months later with the longed-for invitation, Taktser instantly began his preparations for departure.

Most of the provisions for the journey had to be taken along, packed so as to be waterproof during river-crossings. Tsampa, stone-hard wheaten rolls, butter, dried vegetables, diced turnips, beetroots, pickled radishes, herbs and tea were all part of the necessary iron rations. Meat could be obtained along the way either by hunting or by bartering with passing nomads.

In the wild north-east, bandits were an ever-present threat and no man dared travel alone; it was always advisable to join with a larger group of travellers. In the event, Taktser found himself arranging for twenty-two people with their horses, yaks and mules. His party included an uncle, and

Chandzo Jampa, who was making the journey to Lhasa for the third time in two years. Again commissioned by the Kung to bring back some fine horses from Siling, he had taken the opportunity to buy some for himself – about one hundred and fifty horses, in fact – to sell at a handsome profit to the nobles and officials in Lhasa.

Taktser rode out of Kumbum as slowly and ceremonially as he had first entered it, 'followed by a monk carrying a large yellow umbrella behind me as the symbol of my rank, passing through long lines of monks silent and praying'. But he was no longer an impressionable boy:

> The lugubrious sound of the oboes and those four-sleeved trumpets...got on my nerves now, and I breathed with relief when we finally reached the tent where I was solemnly offered the last bowl of tea.[20]

Taktser and Chandzo Jampa left Siling in the summer of 1941, together with a group of Muslim officials and a few smaller groups of monks and nomad families who were going to the Holy City on pilgrimage. For three weeks, they wound along the shores of Lake Kokonor (the Blue Lake), that vast inland sea surrounded on three sides by craggy, snow-capped peaks. Then they pushed through uninhabited steppes and wild, mountainous terrain to the swampy plains of Tsaidam and the great nomad camp which was the last caravan assembly point. It was buzzing with activity:

> Innumerable fires were burning, and the cooks were busy preparing solid meals for their parties, something which was made easier because the nomads willingly sold us butter, meat and milk. Along the shores of the nearby salt lake some of the men were breaking up the thick salt crust and putting the pieces into sacks for the long journey. I bought a dozen sheep from the nomads for my group; they were to trot along with the yak caravan and be slaughtered for food at need.[21]

By the time the whole caravan was assembled, it included about twenty thousand animals. And though that may have improved the travellers' chances of safety, it did little for their speed.

The swamps stretching ahead for hundreds of miles would claim many victims among the pack animals. Each morning at about two, the first groups set off over the frozen ground, battling with an icy wind. After a day's march – about five or six hours in the saddle – they would pitch camp at sites where caravans had stopped since time immemorial. Hot drinks were prepared, the animals let loose to graze, fuel collected for fires.

Then, with a brief pause for enough food to dull the edge of appetite, the equipment had to be examined (and possibly repaired), the animals fed and watered. Only after all this would they take their evening meal of meat, tsampa and tea. Then the horses were covered up with saddle cloths, and the entire camp would settle to sleep and silence.

Struggling through high passes in a cold so intense that it took their breath away; crossing rivers, sometimes on horseback, sometimes walking naked into the ice-cold water, their clothes strapped to their backs in bundles, they came at last to the River Drichu, the upper reaches of that great Yangtse River which seemed to stretch ahead into infinity. It was the last great river before Lhasa and the sight of it filled Taktser with despair: how would he ever cross it? However, by dint of desperately clinging to his horse's mane, he arrived safely on the far bank and sank to the ground in exhausted relief.

Summer was already giving way to autumn and it was becoming noticeably colder in the valleys as the caravan drew near to the area which was under the political jurisdiction of the Dalai Lama. Almost immediately Taktser was made aware of his new exalted status as brother of the god-king, for the officer in charge of the frontier-post had been instructed to provide him with a military escort over the last high pass.

They began the climb in the afternoon amid a flurry of snow:

> An icy wind swept down on us from the snow and ice-covered mountain peaks ahead, but we rode on and up without pausing until by midnight we had reached the highest point of the pass, a stony desert under a glacier over which a veritable storm howled.[22]

Shivering with cold and exhaustion, they started the descent without pausing to rest; and when they reached the valley floor next morning the weather had cleared. Taktser was about to collapse into his tent when a messenger arrived from his father, bearing affectionate greetings from all the family.

Four days later they reached a nomad settlement and a safe haven at last. Giving thanks to the gods for having spared them from death by bandits, wild animals, flood, freezing or thirst, the huge caravan now split up, each group going its separate way. Two days later, almost within sight of the town of Nagchuka, Taktser and his party saw a magnificent cavalcade coming towards them. In amazement, he recognized his father at its head:[23]

He had obviously spotted me too for he now urged on his horse to greater speed. What a great change had come over the simple peasant Choekyong Tsering since I had last seen him! His upright bearing and his natural air of authority had always impressed me even from early childhood. But now, seated on a fine horse and clothed in splendid silk garments, he bore himself with the dignity of a king.[24]

They rode on together and at the last stop before Lhasa, Gyalo Thondup and Phuntsok Tashi also came out to meet them, both of them so splendidly attired that at first he hardly recognized them. They had brought sumptuous garments for him too and, best of all, a box of his mother's freshly-made pastries.

His first glimpse of the Potala, its golden roofs glowing as though aflame with the afternoon sun, filled Taktser with awe. Everything else dissolved in a haze of impressions: the crowds lining the route to greet him; the great park where the new family house was being built; and finally the Norbulingka with its stone lions guarding the gate, its sentries in British-style uniforms presenting arms as he and his father dismounted. But everything was forgotten when he caught sight of his mother – and realized that she hadn't changed at all. 'She had always been the dominant personality in the family and now even as Great Mother of the King, Dekyi Tsering behaved in a simple but modest fashion while at the same time radiating a quite impressive grandeur.'[25]

Wordlessly, the mother handed her eldest son a bowl of curdled milk and stroked his hair. In that moment the loneliness of the past was wiped out, as first Lobsang Samten ran into the room, then Tsering Dolma, holding two babies in her arms – her own son, Tenzin Ngawang, born after her arrival in Lhasa, and her nine-month-old sister, Jetsun Pema.[26]

In the afternoon, Taktser was taken to see the Dalai Lama in the Norbulingka. He prostrated himself three times before his six-year-old sibling and their conversation was at first formal and stilted. But when the ceremonial was done with,

he took me by the hand and led me out into the garden where wonderful flowers were blossoming in the shade of magnificent trees. He introduced me to all the wonders of this small paradise: the flowers, the pond, the tame animals – and the nuts, which were just ripe. Gleefully, he showed me the best way to crack them.[27]

That first evening, the whole family assembled at the Gyatso farmhouse for the last meal of the day. It was like old times: father and mother; Gyalo Thondup and Lobsang Samten; Tsering Dolma and Phuntsok Tashi. Only one was missing, the one to whom they owed their presence in this beautiful place. Would he come?

> It was already dark [wrote Taktser] when the door opened and the Dalai Lama came in and greeted us all cheerfully. We all asked him to take the seat at the head of the table, but this he refused to do, saying that it was due to his father or to me as the eldest. Finally, he sat down on a silk cushion and we all squatted on woollen cushions. After our meal the time went very rapidly with happy family chatter, and all too soon our young brother was taken away from us again.[28]

After that, the Dalai Lama managed a brief visit to Gyatso every evening.

Taktser's days were filled with visits and receptions and sightseeing, with the excitement of discovering that everything in Lhasa was so much grander than in Kumbum. Streams of visitors arrived to pay homage to him as Taktser Rinpoche and as the Dalai Lama's eldest brother. But as an Incarnate he could not remain indefinitely at home. He was destined for Drepung, the monastery which, with its ten thousand monks, was the most influential in Tibet and said to be the largest in the world. Allotted a three-room apartment on the top floor of a five-storeyed house within the monastic university, he was able to plunge at last into the studies he had so long neglected. And he did so with a zeal and enthusiasm which surprised him.

Before leaving for Drepung, he watched, a star-struck provincial, the solemn procession in which his young brother was carried in state to his winter residence, the Potala Palace. Lobsang Samten accompanied his brother. Both boys had already mastered the Lhasa dialect and used it with ease, while the rest of the family continued to speak in the patois of Amdo, able only with difficulty to make themselves understood.

NOTES

1. All land in Tibet was owned by the State, but most of it was portioned out to monasteries and to nobles in exchange for services and taxes. Except in the case of the monasteries, all land ownership involved some form of unpaid government service.

2. Tucci, *To Lhasa and Beyond*.

3. Author interview with Tendzin Choegyal, Dharamsala, 1993.

4. Author interview with Rinchen Khando, Dharamsala, June 1994.

5. Cf. also Goldstein, *A History of Modern Tibet*, chapter 10.

6. Letter from Rai Bahadur Norbhu, CBE, British Trade Agent in Dromo and assistant to the Political Officer in Sikkim, to whom the letter was addressed. The Political Officer sent it to the Foreign Secretary of the Government of India. Letter No.4 (2)–8/41 dated January 1942.

7. Today, in Chinese-occupied Lhasa, the wells have been polluted and the water is unsafe to drink.

8. *Lost Lhasa: Heinrich Harrer's Tibet*, New York, Harry N. Abrams, and Hood River, Summit Publications, 1992.

9. From Dr Regolo Moise's remarks on Medicine and the State of Health in Tibet, included in Giuseppe Tucci's *To Lhasa and Beyond*.

10. Shakabpa, *Tibet: A Political History*.

11. Author interview with Hugh Richardson, September 1993.

12. F. Spencer Chapman, *Lhasa, the Holy City*, London, 1940.

13. B. J. Gould, *The Jewel in the Lotus*, Chatto & Windus, 1957, first published in India by Oxford University Press in 1943.

14. Author interview with Tendzin Choegyal, October 1993.

15. Letter from Basil Gould in Lhasa to Olaf Caroe C.I.E., 1 March 1940, Oriental and India Office Collections of the British Library, L/P&S/12/4178, File 15 (1).

16. Report by B J. Gould.

17. Norbu, *Tibet Is My Country*.

18. This was common throughout Tibet, where the women were considered to be very much more efficient than the men.

19. *Tibet Is My Country*.

20. *Tibet Is My Country*.

21. *Tibet Is My Country*.

22. *Tibet Is My Country*.

23. Tibetans were in the habit of going two days' distance to greet their friends and family (with *chang*, tea and other refreshment) if they had come from afar.

24. *Tibet Is My Country*.

25. *Tibet Is My Country.*
26. A baby girl born in Amdo after the birth of the Dalai Lama had not lived.
27. *Tibet Is My Country.*
28. *Tibet Is My Country.*

8

Inside the Potala

And then there is the Potala Palace which must date from Tibet's days of greatness. No one today would think of erecting such a building. I once asked a stonemason why such buildings were no longer put up. He answered indignantly that the Potala was the handiwork of the gods. Men could never have achieved anything like it.

Heinrich Harrer, Seven Years in Tibet

The amazing Potala Palace would surely have been listed as one of the Wonders of the World if the Tibetans had ever admitted more than a handful of foreigners into their country to wonder at it. It is named after a mountain at the southern tip of the Indian continent, believed to be the abode of Chenrezig, the compassionate god who is embodied in the Dalai Lamas. A place of meditation built in the seventh century by King Songtsen Gampo on a hill slightly outside the city, it was enlarged a thousand years later by the Fifth Dalai Lama – the Great Fifth – at about the same time as the Taj Mahal and the Palace of Versailles were being constructed. (The Great Fifth died in 1682, but to ensure continuing popular support for the colossal building project, the Regent managed to conceal the fact for twelve years until the palace was completed.) The Potala is virtually a city in itself, a quarter of a mile long, thirteen storeys high, and entirely covering the summit of Lhasa's Red Hill.

Here were the tombs of seven Dalai Lamas, the grandest being those of the Fifth and Thirteenth, covered with gold, encrusted heavily with precious jewels, their interiors filled with gemstones, artefacts of gold and the finest porcelain. In the western wing of the palace was the monastery, home to one hundred and seventy-five monks whose exclusive duty was to assist the Dalai Lama in his spiritual practices. There were libraries, repositories of religion and culture, containing massive, heavy volumes, many of them illuminated in inks made of powdered gold, silver, iron, copper, turquoise, coral and conch shell. The eastern wing housed government offices, a school – the Tsedrung – for training monastic officials,[1] and the meeting halls of the National Assembly. Climbing ever more steeply towards the summit, past numerous chapels, audience halls and meeting rooms, one came finally to the lofty apartments of the Dalai Lamas and their attendants.

For centuries, the Dalai Lamas had come to the Potala at the start of winter – the seasons being immutably fixed, as Sir Charles Bell explained:

> On the anniversary of Tsong-khapa's death [on the twenty-fifth day of the tenth Tibetan month] winter begins; on the eighth day of the third Tibetan month it ends. This fixes winter between a date in the first half of December and another in the last half of April. Between these two dates all officials...must wear fur hats and cloaks strictly in accordance with the patterns prescribed for each grade. Outside these dates, however cold the day, they must appear only in their summer silks, gorgeous indeed in their yellow and blue, but affording cold comfort where the land is raised 12,000 feet above the ocean.[2]

Installed on the top floor of this mausoleum, the two boys were cut off from normal society. Though commanding a superb view over Lhasa and the Kyi Chu River, their quarters lacked home comforts. Lobsang Samten had a room of his own, vast, gloomy, high-ceilinged. A nervous and insecure child, he was terrified of the huge shadows; and when he asked if one of the monks could sleep in there with him, he was told to pull himself together and behave like the brother of a Dalai Lama. His brother was luckier, the only way into his room being through an ante-chamber in which an attendant always slept. In any case, he was not a nervous child, though the Potala, he admitted, was 'not a nice place to live'. As Sir Charles Bell had written:

> It is cold, this vast palace, in winter-time. I found the water in the large bowls that find place in the steps of the tombs to be frozen from top to bottom even at midday.

The bedroom allotted to the new Dalai Lama had once belonged to the Great Fifth. At one end of the room was an altar, in front of which were butter-lamps and little dishes of food and water placed in offering to the Buddhas. Every day, mice would come in search of the grain and, once he grew accustomed to their scurrying over his bed, he was glad of their lively company.

As befitted his exalted rank, he was given three other rooms, a small chapel, a room for his scriptures and commentaries, and a private bathroom, the only one in the entire palace. The bathroom, with a toilet-seat covered with fur, was reserved for the sacred personage alone: Lobsang Samten had to go outside like everyone else, down the hundreds of stone steps, even in the freezing winter weather!

The six-year-old Dalai Lama, whom we shall henceforth call Kundun – 'Presence' – knew nothing of the political dust-storm swirling around his head. He was too young to understand that his Government was corrupt; that, under Reting and his cronies, the welfare of Tibet took second place to personal greed and ambition. Kundun was fond of Reting, noting in his childish way that his Senior Tutor's 'most striking feature was a constantly blocked nose'.[3] Reting rightly regarded the discovery of the Fourteenth Dalai Lama as his finest achievement, and it was natural that he should form close ties with the boy's family. Easy-going, sociable, keen on horses, Reting had much in common with the Kung, and the two had become friends. But his moment of glory had passed. Young as he was, Kundun thinks he must have heard the rumours of misconduct, since he remembers primly telling his parents that they should not be so friendly with the Regent.[4]

In January 1941, Reting suddenly resigned both as Regent and Senior Tutor, explaining that in a dream he had been told that his life was at risk if he did not resign and pay more attention to his spiritual life! He nominated as his successor the Junior Tutor, Taktra Rinpoche, an elderly man with the reputation for moral probity that he himself so conspicuously lacked. The appointment of the austere, ultra-conservative Taktra reversed the slide into moral collapse and restored a high level of discipline and ethical standards to the Government. But it soon became apparent that Reting's withdrawal was merely tactical: he seems to have considered Taktra as a caretaker, to hold the fort until he was ready to make a comeback.

Taktra now became the Senior Tutor, his own Junior Tutor role being taken by Ling Rinpoche, a stern, rather reserved man who at first struck fear into Kundun's heart, but who came to be one of his most trusted friends. The unofficial third tutor was Kesang Rinpoche, who had led the search party into Amdo and of whom the boy was very fond. 'He was so kind that I could never take him seriously. During our lessons, instead of reciting what I was supposed to, I used to hang round his neck and say, "You read it."'[5]

In addition to his tutors, Kundun had three personal monk-attendants, the Master of the Ritual, Master of the Kitchen and Master of the Robes. For both brothers, these three were surrogate fathers. 'They looked after us as though we were their own children,' said Lobsang. The undoubted favourite was the Master of the Kitchen, Lobsang Jinpa, known as Ponpo ('the Boss') – 'a very kind and simple man, almost completely bald'. Ponpo was no good at telling stories or thinking up games, but Kundun loved him devotedly and for a long time couldn't bear to let him out of his sight. Kundun's affection for this simple monk was perhaps the deepest emotional tie of his life. 'Ponpo came into my life,' he recalls, 'when we were still a few days' journey from Lhasa on the way from Amdo. From then on, he was always there for me, he took care of me, fed me, played with me. He was my father, my mother, my whole family. I remember that he had a large brown nipple-shaped mole on his face and at the age of four, separated from my mother, I would suck at it for comfort.'[6] To the end of his days, Ponpo loved to relate how as a young boy Kundun had longed for a pair of trousers like those worn by the Westerners he had seen in magazines. Trousers being unknown in Lhasa, Ponpo solved the problem by inserting the child's legs into the arms of a voluminous Tibetan shirt and tying it round his waist with string. Kundun was delighted.

Once the boys' formal education had begun, the days were strictly mapped out. Just before sunrise large buckets of water, heated in the kitchens for Kundun, icy-cold for Lobsang, were carted up from down below for washing. After dressing, they spent an hour in meditation and prayer, while the water on the altars was changed and the butter-lamps were lit. At seven, in the middle of this prayer time, breakfast was brought in,

Tibetan butter-tea, tsampa kneaded into balls in specially-made leather bags. Sometimes a cheesecake was served, dried cheese, sugar and butter mixed into a cake and added to the tsampa.[7]

The boys would often save some of the tsampa and 'go up on the Potala roof to feed the crows; or make fantastic shapes out of the dough'.

At nine, all the monk-officials – 175 of them – gathered for soup, rice and yogurt. This was the hour for public and official audiences and, when his presence was required, the Dalai Lama would be brought in to preside in solemn state.

Then came a two-hour lesson period in the schoolroom, for which neither of the brothers felt much enthusiasm. They were kept in line, however, by the sight of two whips hanging on opposite walls, one of yellow silk, the other of leather:

> The former, we were told, was reserved for the Dalai Lama and the latter for the Dalai Lama's brother. These instruments of torture terrified us both. It took only a glance from our teacher at one or other of these whips to make me shiver with fear. Happily, the yellow one was never used, though, the leather one came off the wall once or twice.[8]

'We bullied you terribly when you were small,' Ling Rinpoche admitted to Lobsang many years later, in Dharamsala. Reluctant to take a whip to the backside of the god-king, the tutors had vented their frustration on his long-suffering brother.

The first lesson – learning four difficult Tibetan scripts on chalk-covered boards – was followed by the memorizing of texts from scripture. Religious training was the entire purpose of this education; reading, writing and grammar were no more than a means to that end.

After reciting to the Junior Tutor the passage they had memorized earlier that morning, the latter would read and explain the next one. This went on till noon when a bell sounded, a conch was blown, and the magic hour of playtime arrived. For one who was 'a very reluctant pupil' and 'disliked all subjects equally', this was the most precious time of the day.

The boys were free to roam as they pleased. With their bodyguards scurrying after them,[9] they wandered through the maze of corridors and explored the vast subterranean store-rooms of the palace, excitedly opening cupboards, chests and drawers. Dashing from one room to another, they were constantly making fresh discoveries: chests containing a large number of old wooden animals – camels, elephants, yaks, snow leopards, for example. They were fascinated by the armoury with its suits of armour, flintlock guns and antique swords; and they particularly loved rummaging among the possessions of the Great Thirteenth. In the huge cavernous store-rooms, they found an old air-rifle, complete with targets and ammunition; a telescope; and a pile of illustrated books in English about the First World War. Following the Chinese incursion into Lhasa in 1910 the Great Thirteenth had gone into exile in British India, in the hill-station of Darjeeling, where he was looked after by the Tibetan-speaking Political Officer for Sikkim, Sir Charles Bell. A deep and lasting friendship sprang up between the two men, both of whom loved Tibet and firmly believed in its right to independence. The books and maps that the brothers now stumbled on had been gifts from Bell to his friend.

Apart from the store-room treasures, there was no shortage of new toys to play with. Some (presents from abroad) were sent up from the Indian border; and visiting foreign officials would come to Lhasa laden with gifts. The Chinese tended to bring adult gifts like bolts of silk, but others understood that the intended recipient was only a child. Captain Ilia Tolstoy and Lieutenant Brooke Dolan, two American officers who came to Lhasa on a goodwill mission in 1942 presented a pair of singing birds, a model sailing ship made of silver and a gold pocket watch.[10] Favourite toys were the red pedal-car given to Kundun by the British, a wind-up clockwork train set and a large collection of lead soldiers with which the boys played at armies. Much loved too was the Meccano set presented by Sir Basil Gould at the time of the installation – and added to over the years. Kundun built cranes and railway wagons long before he had ever seen the real things. Perhaps it was his early discovery of Meccano which gave him a passion for all things mechanical. Not content with just playing, he wanted to know how everything worked. And as there was no one on hand to explain, he had to work things out for himself. He caught on quickly and soon became expert at opening up old clocks and taking them to pieces, sending the bodyguards frantic with anxiety:

> They tried to dissuade him from doing so but he was quite stubborn. If they succeeded in stopping him one day, he was certain to resume these activities the next. I don't know how he did it, nor did anyone else, but somehow he made all these things work.[11]

Lunch, the main meal of the day, brought playtime to an end at one. By two, the brief sunlight which had flooded the room at midday had already begun to fade and the Potala returned to its habitual gloom. Kundun hated this moment, feeling a shadow fall on his heart as the room sank back into shade. Afternoon lessons probably did little to lift his spirits.

At seven, he usually ate supper with his three monk-attendants – tea, broth, maybe a little meat, yoghurt and different kinds of bread sent in by his mother. Afterwards he would go down the seven flights of steps to the courtyard below, ostensibly praying and reciting scriptures as he walked, but more often making up stories in his head and anticipating the ones that his attendants might tell him before bedtime. He loved ghost stories, but they scared him and made him dread creeping back into his dark, mouse-infested bedroom at nine. 'One of the most frightening tales concerned giant owls which were supposed to snatch small boys after dark...It made me very particular about being inside by nightfall.' There were a great many night-owls around the Potala.

Few apart from the family and his personal officials and attendants were allowed to speak to Kundun directly; and even his family's access was restricted. The Great Mother had permission to visit whenever she wanted, but was not allowed to sleep at the Potala. For her, the visits to her youngest son must have been bittersweet, her relationship with him being now irrevocably changed. Now, even to her, he was Kundun. Visits to him were ceremonial occasions for which she wore her finest clothes and jewellery; and when she left she bowed before him, and he laid his hand on her in blessing. Nevertheless, she preserved some kind of normality by smuggling in some of his favourite food. Not only the bread but also little packages of chicken, eggs and sometimes even pork. She had to be careful, as these foods were frowned on. Even milk was forbidden, since its high fat content was considered bad for the liver. (The only time Kundun managed to drink any was during certain ceremonies in the Potala which called for offerings of milk. He would hide some of it to drink later.)

With the official end of winter came the annual departure to the Norbulingka, his sole excursion into the outside world. He looked forward eagerly to this escape from his gilded prison. Beginning with a two-hour ceremony which seemed like an eternity, it was followed by a formal procession. A gala day for everybody – the Regent and Cabinet Ministers marching in procession through the streets lined by crowds whose good behaviour was ensured by burly monk-police wielding clubs.

To the people's delight, the young ruler's nightingales and parrots called out from their cages while his brilliantly caparisoned horses, decked in yellow saddles, bridles and bits of gold, pranced behind their grooms; monks blew shrill, high-pitched *gyalings* or short horns and the regimental bands played 'It's a Long Way to Tipperary'. From behind the palanquin's silk-fringed windows, though, it was the sight of nature that pleased the young Dalai Lama most. 'The season was most beautiful,' he remembered. 'All the lawns were turning green, the apricot trees flowering and the birds singing. I used to love that day going from the Potala to the Norbulingka.'[12] Yet he would have given much to be allowed to walk and enjoy the natural beauties of the countryside for himself.

At the Norbulingka he could share a room with Lobsang; indeed the boys could stay in any of the smaller palaces they chose. They spent many happy hours walking through the gardens, watching the animals and birds:

> Amongst these were, at one time or another, a herd of tame musk-deer; at least six...enormous Tibetan mastiffs which acted as guard dogs; a Pekinese sent from Kumbum; a few mountain goats; a monkey; a handful of camels brought from Mongolia; two leopards and a very old and rather sad tiger...several parrots; half a dozen peacocks; some cranes; a pair of golden geese; and about thirty, very unhappy Canada geese whose wings had been clipped so that they could not fly. I felt very sorry for them.[13]

Seeing one of the parrots eating out of his Master of the Robes' hand, he eagerly held out some nuts to the bird himself. But when the parrot ignored his outstretched hand, he indignantly threatened it with a stick. 'Of course, thereafter it fled at the sight of me. This was a very good lesson in how to make friends; not by force but by compassion.'[14] He had better luck with the fish in the well-stocked lake, though even here he was not above a show of petulance:

> I used to stand at the edge and call them. If they responded, I rewarded them with small pieces of bread...However, they had a tendency to disobedience and sometimes would ignore me. If this happened, I got very angry and, rather than throw them food, I would open up with an artillery barrage of rocks and stones. But when they did come over, I was very careful to see to it that the small ones got their fair share. If necessary, I would use a stick to prod the larger ones out of the way.[15]

Once, playing at the edge, he spotted a lump of wood and tried to sink it with his stick. Unfortunately, he fell in and might have drowned had he not been rescued by one of the Norbulingka sweepers, an ex-soldier from western Tibet. The 'sweepers', whom to this day he remembers as – apart from Lobsang and Ponpo – the only real friends of his childhood, were middle-aged men, both monks and laymen, who tidied the rooms and swept and polished the floors at the Potala and the Norbulingka. (He thought they did this for his benefit, so that he could skate round the gleaming floors.) A child among grown-up children, he spent much of his leisure time with them; he loved them and they loved him.

But even in the Norbulingka, the many restrictions placed on him by Regent Taktra irked him. In the early days, he would walk with an attendant as far as a stream of the Kyi Chu river just beyond the outer wall of the Park. But in the sacred name of protocol this practice came to be forbidden and he was 'compelled to remain hidden away like an owl'.

He hated the meaningless rituals and rules by which his life was governed, and escaped whenever he could to relax with the servants at Gyatso. Most of them had come from Amdo and loved telling him stories about his native village of Taktser. They treated him just as they would any other (naughty) little boy, and sometimes joined in his pranks:

> I enjoyed their company when we went and raided my parents' food stores...The best time for these forays was in late autumn when there would always be fresh supplies of delicious dried meat, which we dipped in chilli sauce. I liked this so much that, on one occasion, I ate far too much and soon afterwards was violently sick.[16]

Every year, for the Monlam or Great Prayer Festival which immediately follows the New Year celebrations, Kundun took up temporary residence in the Jokhang Temple. He dreaded the central ceremony of Monlam more than anything else in the year. In the first place, his rooms at the Jokhang were even gloomier and colder than those at the Potala, and he almost invariably caught flu. In the second place, the ceremony lasted over four hours and at the end of it he had to recite a long passage of scripture from memory. It was an agonizing ordeal, especially as he sat high up on a throne and no one could prompt him.

> But remembering my lines was only half the problem. Because the proceedings went on for so long, I had an additional dread: I feared that my bladder might not hold out...I remember being apoplectic with fear.[17]

His worst fears were never realized, but neither did time diminish them. When the ceremony was over, his relief knew no bounds:

> Not only was the whole dreadful business over for another twelve months, but there now followed one of the best moments in the Dalai Lama's year. After the ceremony I was allowed outside to walk round the streets so that I

could see the *thorma*, the huge, gaily coloured butter sculptures traditionally offered to the Buddhas on this day. There were also puppet shows and music played by military bands and an atmosphere of tremendous happiness amongst the people.[18]

Accustomed as he was to the gloomy silence of the Potala, he was fascinated when, watching from the east window at the Jokhang, he saw little novice monks of about his own age fooling about in the courtyard below.

Quite a lot of them...spent their whole time playing. Every so often a scuffle would break out. Then they would take out their wooden bowls and crack each other over the head. The scene provoked a curious reaction in me. On the one hand, I told myself that these monks were extremely stupid. On the other, I could not help envying them. They seemed not to have a care in the world.[19]

His favourite view was from the west window, looking down on to the market place. He could only peer through a curtain, for if the people down below had spotted him, they would have rushed over to prostrate before him. On his first visit, however, his innate mischievousness got the better of him:

The sight of all those people down there was too much for me. I boldly poked my head through the curtain. But, as if this were not bad enough, I remember blowing bubbles of spit which fell on several people's heads as they threw themselves down to the ground far below.[20]

Here too there were sweepers, whose company he could enjoy. When he left the Jokhang, he missed them sorely. But one New Year, he found that all but one had been sacked after his departure. 'After I had gone last time, they let themselves into my apartment by climbing down through the ceiling skylight and made off with various items – gold butter-lamps and the like.'[21] So much for his taste in friends, he shrugs ruefully!

In Amdo, he had scarcely known his father, but circumstances now brought them together more often. The Kung frequently attended the brief morning tea-ceremony, at the Potala (in winter) or the Norbulingka (in summer). Kundun did not fail to notice that his father came more often to the Norbulingka, where the royal horses were stabled. Nor that his first visit was to the horses!

The Kung was in his element, going to the stables to feed his fine horses every day before breakfast. He rode out alone each morning towards Sera Monastery and surrounded himself with men who knew and cared about horses as he did.

But, as his son Gyalo Thondup freely acknowledges, the Kung had grown arrogant and greedy. 'People in Lhasa had shown a great deal of respect to our family because we were the Dalai Lama's family,' says GT. 'They treated us with great kindness – and my father often took advantage of them. If he saw a horse he fancied in the street, he would make the owner sell it to him then and there. He would bargain and force the price right down. The people he treated like this naturally got very upset and began to have second thoughts about the Dalai Lama's father.'[22]

The Kung refused to pay taxes on his estates; and unlawfully requisitioned free transport and labour from other people's feudal subjects without prior consultation. Yet, as Hugh Richardson points out, 'the power of landlords was not arbitrary and the subjects could appeal to the District Officer or directly to the Kashag or to the judges in Lhasa'.[23] In his letter to the Political Officer in Sikkim (see Chapter 6), Rai Bahadur Norbhu comments acidly: 'The Dalai Lama's father is interfering too much with the affairs of the Government and is taking the law into his own hands.' The Kung, he went on, was interfering in individual debt cases between creditors and debtors, and, in cases of assault, re-trying the cases himself – without acquainting himself with the true facts – and threatening the magistrates who had originally tried the case. He was making a handsome profit for himself, charging exorbitant fees, accepting bribes and even demanding protection money. His arrogance was breathtaking:

> When [the Kung] is going out to the city or returning to the Norbulingka, all mounted persons crossing [his path] must dismount and pay their respects to him regardless of their own rank. Persons who do not dismount and salute him are beaten severely in public by [his] servants.[24]

On one occasion, the scandalized Norbhu reports:

> A sick man coming to the Mission hospital for treatment came across the Dalai Lama's father as he was going out to the City. The sick man could not dismount and salute him, with the result that the [Kung] confiscated his pony.[25]

Mules and ponies were at the heart of the matter, he continues:

The Dalai Lama's father trades in ponies and mules. He calls [to the] Norbulingka Tibetan officials who like ambling ponies and mules, and makes them
purchase his mules saying, 'Don't worry about the price, it will be alright even
if you pay me after a year.' Some officials purchased ponies and mules from
[him] without even asking the price. He called them after four or five days and
made them pay [anything from] Rs 500/- to Rs 1000/- for a mule or pony.
Some of the officials tried to return the animals, but the [Kung] would not
take them back.

Often the victims would turn to Dekyi Tsering for help. 'The women-folk
of the victim would come to her and she would try and sort things out.
She exerted a really calming influence,' said an official. But very often
even she was helpless.

On another occasion, in the autumn of 1942, when several farmers from Betsang village near Lhasa went to the Tsona area in southeast Tibet to barter salt
for rice, they were met...by the headman of one of the Dalai Lama's father's
estates who wanted to buy salt. The Betsang villagers, suspecting that they
would be forced to accept an unfavourable exchange rate, refused to do business with him. The headman complained to the Yapshi Kung in Lhasa, who
summoned the Betsang headman and then imprisoned him.

Because Betsang village was an estate of Drepung monastery's Loseling college and under its protection, the Loseling Abbot went to the house where the
headman was being held and personally released him, sending him to
Drepung for safety. The Abbot then called on the Yapshi Kung, told him what
he had done, and asked him why the headman had been imprisoned. The father cursed the Abbot and threatened to shoot him with his pistol. At this
point, it is said, the Abbot coolly invited him to shoot, but he did not do so.
The Abbot filed a complaint demanding that the Yigtsang Office examine the
issue, and the Dalai Lama's father filed a counter-suit with the Kashag.[26]

Fortunately, the Kung's friends persuaded him to withdraw his complaint,
and the Abbot did likewise.

Having read Norbhu's letter, the Foreign Secretary in New Delhi wondered if Basil Gould's glowing admiration for the new royal family had not
been somewhat naïve. 'It seems to me extraordinary that the Tibetan Government should allow the Dalai Lama's family to behave in this outrageous fashion,' he commented. In a secret memo,[27] the Under-Secretary in
the Department of External Affairs referred to 'the ambition and greed of
the Dalai Lama's parents' [sic], whose position seemed 'to be not unlike

that of parents who produce child "movie-stars" and expect to bask in the fame'. Commenting on the Kung's unorthodox ways of 'getting rich quick', he added, with massive understatement: 'He may prove an annoying influence in the State'.

Indeed he would. Far from 'allowing' such behaviour, the Tibetan Government was thoroughly exasperated by it. The Kung had become an embarrassment to the new Regent – not least because he was a friend of Reting. Taktra summoned the National Assembly to discuss the situation.

In late November 1942, the Assembly recommended that any servant of the Kung who abused his position and exacted tribute either in cash or in kind from Tibetan subjects should be arrested. Regent Taktra approved the edict and, being prepared to do everything in his power to clean up the mess of the Reting years, ordered a proclamation to be exhibited on the streets of Lhasa and throughout Tibet. It revealed that ever since the arrival of the Dalai Lama's father, the Treasury had paid out a small fortune for him, over and above the cost of feeding and clothing the family and the grain-bearing estates they had bestowed on him. Yet

> The Dalai Lama's father requisitions grass, grain, butter, salt, firewood and yak-dung from poor dealers and does not pay the full cost of such articles. Moreover, he fines people heavily for minor offences without any reference to the Tibetan Government...Further, he had instructed his tenants not to obey the demands of the Tibetan Government for forced labour. Be it known to the public that henceforth the Dalai Lama's father has been ordered to behave himself in a manner similar to the other Yapshis. If any of his servants commits an offence, and if the Kashag takes no steps to try the case against the Dalai Lama's father, then the National Assembly will straightway judge the matter.
>
> The above proclamation has been passed by the National Assembly and bears the seal of the Kashag.[28]

It was clear that a line had to be drawn somewhere. Taktra would not allow anyone – not even the Dalai Lama's father – to believe himself above the law. Reting was furious at this attack on a personal friend. Perhaps it was now, when he realized the extent of Taktra's animosity towards him, that he began to regret his decision to hand over power.

In the winter of 1944–5, Reting returned to Lhasa in great pomp and style. A number of his supporters, including the Kung, rode out the traditional two days' distance to welcome him. He had come to ask Taktra to hand the Regency back to him, and it was plain that he could still count on a bedrock of support. Taktra, however, never having seen himself as a caretaker, refused to play ball and Reting retired, angry and humiliated, to his monastery. From there, as Taktra began a relentless purge of the ex-Regent's remaining supporters in the Government, Reting would plot his revenge.

Sometimes, the Kung took Lobsang Samten away with him for two or three days. They would ride on fine horses from the Norbulingka's stables into the wilderness around Lhasa, where they would pitch camp by the banks of a lake or river and make long excursions into the hills. On Lobsang's return, Kundun always wanted to know every detail of the trip. He was quite envious of his brother's freedom, although in fact neither of them liked horses and Lobsang would have preferred to stay at home. When he was a small boy in Amdo, his father had insisted on teaching him and Gyalo Thondup to ride bareback over the grasslands. Gyalo Thondup had loved every minute but poor Lobsang had fallen from his horse and been seriously concussed.

History was about to repeat itself. On one of their expeditions, the Kung, exasperated by his son's lack-lustre horsemanship, 'whacked Lobsang's mount across the hindquarters with a stick. The startled animal took off like a shot and in trying to clear an obstacle that lay in its path pitched the boy onto the ground, where he lay unconscious from a severe concussion.'[29]

The unassertive Lobsang was much put-upon, and not only by his father. Life in the Potala was very demanding, and despite their closeness the relationship with his younger brother was not an easy one. They scrapped constantly, Kundun usually being the instigator. Matters came to a head one day in the summer of 1946, as Kundun was chasing his brother with an ivory-topped swagger-stick which he had discovered in the store-rooms: 'Somehow I must have whirled it round my head and it hit Lobsang Samten who fell down, with blood gushing from his head. For a few terrible moments I thought I'd killed him...Then to my relief he stood up – in floods of tears and with a huge gash over his right eyebrow.'[30]

The wound healed, but Lobsang would retain the scar for the rest of his life. For those in charge of the two boys, however, it was the last straw. Kundun's tutors had always been nervous that Lobsang, with freer access to the outside world, might introduce his brother to dangerous modern ideas. But this latest incident made them realize that the two simply could not be left alone together. It was time for a change, time for twelve-year-old Lobsang to attend school in Lhasa. Without delay, he was enrolled in the Tharkhang school for young trainee-officials.[31]

When the moment came to say goodbye, eight-year-old Kundun knew that he was losing his last link with normal family life. He gave his brother a wooden board for writing on and a few other small parting gifts, then 'went on to the roof and watched and watched until he disappeared inside the door of the Yapshi House, my parents' house.'[32]

From now on, his daily companions would be a handful of elderly monks – and, of course, the sweepers.

But what companions they were! Despite the difference in age, these men played just like small boys themselves, with no holds barred. With them he played at war-games, running competitions to see who could mould the best tiny tanks and aeroplanes from tsampa dough, allowing them about half an hour in which to build an army and judging the results himself. He excelled at that sort of thing, using as models the pictures of actual Second World War tanks and planes he'd found in a Tibetan newspaper published in India. At this stage, he almost always won. But when actual battle was joined, it was a different story:

> Up until now, I had had everything my own way, so this was when I generally lost. For my sweepers never gave quarter in any sort of competition. I often tried to use my position as Dalai Lama to my advantage, but it was no use. I played very forcefully. Quite often I lost my temper and used my fists, but they still did not give in. Sometimes they even made me cry.[33]

Years later, in his memoirs, Kundun would recall Norbu Thondup, his favourite sweeper, 'a devoted friend and constant source of fun':

> We often came to blows during my mock battles and I remember being quite vicious towards him at times...But he gave as good as he got and never for a moment lost his great sense of humour.[34]

But there were times when he avoided even the sweepers. Once, when his mother brought him a Taktser delicacy, sausages made of minced meat and rice, he scoffed the lot, rather than share them with his friends. He paid for his greed by vomiting throughout the night. The Regent blamed the Master of the Kitchen, and poor Ponpo might have lost his job in disgrace had the illustrious culprit not owned up. Yet another lesson in the realities of life, he ruefully conceded.

Though they would not have suspected it, the sweepers were invaluable teachers for the young Dalai Lama. They groused about the difficulties of their own lives, about the injustices meted out by certain officials and high lamas; and they kept him up to date with the latest gossip on the street. His debt to them, then and later, was incalculable.

NOTES

1. Each Dalai Lama had a civil service to help him run the country. There was one branch of 175 specially-trained monk-officials (recruited from all classes of society); and another of 175 trained lay noblemen.
2. Sir Charles Bell, *The Religion of Tibet*, Oxford, 1931.
3. Fourteenth Dalai Lama, *Freedom in Exile*.
4. Author interview with HH the Dalai Lama, June 1994.
5. *Freedom in Exile*.
6. Author interview, HH the Dalai Lama, Dharamsala, July 1995.
7. From notes written by Lobsang Samten and now in the possession of his widow, Namlha Taklha.
8. *Freedom in Exile*.
9. The Dalai Lama's personal bodyguards were on average six feet tall and wore heavily-padded clothes to make them appear even larger.
10. Goodman, *The Last Dalai Lama*, chapter 7. The mission was partly a social one, to establish contact between the American and Tibetan Governments. But there was a more urgent reason. The Second World War was raging and the Americans came with a message from President Roosevelt, asking the Tibetans to allow them a land-route over which supplies might be sent from the Western Allies to China. The Tibetans, however, would not relinquish their strict neutrality.
11. Quoted by Goodman, chapter 8.
12. Avedon, *In Exile from the Land of Snows*, chapter 1.
13. *Freedom in Exile*, chapter 2.
14. *Freedom in Exile*.
15. *Freedom in Exile*.
16. *Freedom in Exile*.
17. *Freedom in Exile*, chapter 2.
18. *Freedom in Exile*, chapter 2.
19. *Freedom in Exile*, chapter 2.

20. *Freedom in Exile*, chapter 2.

21. *Freedom in Exile*, chapter 2.

22. Author interview with Gyalo Thondup, New Delhi, July 1995.

23. In a letter to the author, 12 December 1993.

24. Letter sent by Rai Bahadur Norbhu CBE, British Trade Agent in Dromo, to the Political Officer in Sikkim, and by him to the Foreign Secretary of the Government of India. Letter No.4(2)-P/41, dated January 1942.

25. See previous note.

26. Goldstein, *A History of Modern Tibet*.

27. Dated 11 April 1942.

28. Goldstein.

29. Goodman.

30. Author interview with HH the Dalai Lama, June 1994.

31. According to Rinchen Dolma Taring's *Daughter of Tibet* (John Murray, 1970), there were no public schools in Lhasa. There were just two official schools, the Tse, in the Potala itself, and the Tsikhang in Lhasa, where young monks and laymen were trained for government service.

32. Author interview with HH the Dalai Lama, June 1994.

33. *Freedom in Exile*.

34. *Freedom in Exile*.

9

A Window on to the World

When the Dalai Lama passed by me in his sedan chair and found me filming he gave me a smile. My private thought was that he was congratulating himself on his little cinema, but I am sure that no one else thought as I did; though what could be more natural for a lonely fourteen-year-old boy? Then a look at the humble and rapturous face of my attendant reminded me that for everyone else except myself, he was not a lonely boy but a god.

Heinrich Harrer, Seven Years in Tibet

1945 – Year of the Wood Bird. The Kung's grand new house in the parkland of Changseshar (Eastern Garden) was ready at last. Lying just east of the Potala, it was popularly called the Yapshi Taklha House. When Taktser first saw it, he marvelled at the strangeness of fate:

There it stood in a large garden amidst fine old poplars and willow trees, a big two-storeyed house surrounded by a high brick wall. The first time I entered it I could not help thinking of our modest old farmstead in T[akt]ser. What a difference there was![1]

The royal couple had recently suffered the loss of another son – a devout two-year-old who loved to go into the family altar-room and pay reverence to the statues. In March 1945, he had caught a fever – perhaps the smallpox which was raging in Lhasa and against which Kundun was vaccinated that year.

When it was clear that the child's death was imminent, the parents asked the Gadung Oracle to come, but he died just as the medium arrived. Gadung told the distressed parents to embalm the tiny corpse in salt, first marking it in an easily recognizable way, so that the boy could be reborn into the same house. So the servants put a smear of butter on the dead child's left buttock, before the tiny body was embalmed and taken down to the cellars.[2]

Tsering Dolma had just given birth to a daughter, Khando Tsering, in the absence of her husband, Phuntsok Tashi, who was away in Amdo at the time. The Kung had borrowed money from monasteries and from certain prominent Lhasa traders to provide loans for some of his Amdo friends; and when the latter showed no inclination to pay him back, had despatched his son-in-law to expedite the repayment. (A fruitless mission since the money had all been spent.)

Tsering Dolma was six months pregnant when Phuntsok Tashi left Lhasa. When he reached Kumbum three months later, he received a cable announcing Khando's birth. For Tsering Dolma (known to her siblings as Achala, older sister), these were fairy-tale years. She had exchanged a life of dawn-to-dusk drudgery for that of a princess in a palace; and she was revelling in her new status and freedom. Despite her Amdo accent, the older Lhasa ladies made rather a fuss of her. It was refreshing for them to meet this simple young countrywoman, frank and brave and without a streak of deviousness. She was innately artistic, and before long had become a fashion trendsetter, creating different new designs and colour-mixes for the ladies' aprons. 'For those first few years,' says Khando Tsering, Tsering Dolma's daughter, 'my mother was carried away by it all, the attention, the glamour, the comfort, the luxury. It was all new, exciting and fun, and she was happy. She joined in everything, loved the parties and became an avid mah-jong player. However, no matter what she saw, enjoyed and learnt in high society, she always remained a farmer's daughter.'[3]

It seemed to Tsering Dolma that her five-year-old sister Pema had been born with a silver spoon in her mouth. The younger girl was growing up, knowing nothing of hardship. Pema recalls an idyllic childhood at Changseshar with Khando and Tenzin and with the servants' children – playing hide-and-seek, climbing trees, swinging on homemade swings and playing at make-believe in improvised tree-houses...The boys looked for birds' nests and threw stones at them. The girls, disapproving of such wanton destruction, would go and rescue the baby birds and the eggs that were still intact. 'As there was no mother around, we used to take the fledglings to my poor aunt to look after.⁴ As if she hadn't got enough to do!'⁵

Khando's memories of Changseshar consist of isolated flashes.⁶ The huge house, a little lake, the garden surrounded by walls; four gates, each with a road leading up to the entrance; a large open roof-top where the children could play; the big staircase down which her mother once fell and ripped open her leg; her great-grandmother, a very tiny lady lost in the shadows;⁷ bone-crushing hugs from her grandfather, the Kung – 'He was very warm and loving and used to nearly smother us' – the death of Lobsang's favourite Alsatian. Having inherited her mother's (and grandfather's) passion for horses, Khando recalls insisting on having her pony in the bedroom when she had measles. As for the Kung, he had even had a special staircase built in the new house, leading down to the stables.

About two or three times a month, Amala (Dekyi Tsering, the Great Mother) and Tsering Dolma took the younger children to visit Kundun – their only forays outside the estate: 'My mother was always bustling around the kitchen,' says Pema. 'When we were going to see Kundun, she would be especially active, preparing his special foods, baking his special bread. Whenever we saw her with that bread, we knew we were going to the Potala or to the Summer Palace and we got quite excited.'⁸ Sometimes they rode but mostly they walked, and there were hundreds of steps to climb to the top of the Potala before they were ushered into the dark room where Kundun waited impatiently for them. Amala would give him the goodies she had brought, and the two of them would then be lost in conversation for a while. 'I realized later,' said Pema, 'that for my mother these moments were uniquely precious.'

Most thrilling of all was the New Year festival, Lhosar, 'when we were got out of our beds at about two in the morning and dressed in our new clothes. At that hour, all we wanted was to be back in bed again. But it was exciting too. At about four-thirty or five we went to the Potala to receive His Holiness's blessing and attend a religious ceremony.' Khando was luckier: she was so small that someone dressed her and carried her, still half-asleep, up to the Potala. After that early morning audience, they were free to enjoy themselves. 'On leaving the Potala,' remembers Khando, 'we would go and wish my grandparents Happy Lhosar and they would give us candies and money. In the evening, there would be a huge party in the courtyard, with lots of *chang* and all the servants there, singing and dancing.' Then there would be the Great Prayer (Monlam) Festival two weeks later. 'We were dressed in our new clothes again and we all had to keep very quiet,' recalls Pema. 'We didn't understand what was going on but it was fascinating. We couldn't take our eyes off all the people prostrating, lighting lamps, making offerings.'

Pema was six when Lobsang Samten left the Potala to come and live at home and go to the Tharkhang school with Gyalo Thondup and Phuntsok Tashi. She and the other little ones went to a small private school nearby. 'My mother,' she says, 'had had no formal education herself – I don't think she'd ever set foot in a school – but she was very keen that we should all be educated. At about seven or eight, we were packed off to school to learn Tibetan in a special school run by a Tibetan Government official – Khando, Tenzin, myself and four of the servants' children. We all went off each day on our ponies – a twenty-minute ride.'⁹ There were about fifty private schools in Lhasa, attended by children from all walks of life and run by Buddhists who charged no fees but taught in order to gain merit. (None of the Lhasa schools was exclusively for the children of aristocrats.) By modern secular standards, the education was very limited. 'The Tibetan child,' wrote Spencer Chapman, 'is taught to read and write, to recite prayers and long passages of the Buddhist Scriptures and the elements of arithmetic, which are taught with such elementary paraphernalia as the rosary and small pebbles or fruit-stones.'¹⁰ Religious teaching was paramount.

In his spare time, Gyalo Thondup, the only son brought up as a potential farmer, enjoyed gardening, producing 'turnips eighteen inches long, large tomatoes and fine cabbages'. He grew flowers from seeds obtained from the Norbulingka gardens and was advised and encouraged in his hobby by George Sheriff, the British representative in Lhasa, and his wife.¹¹ But his most consuming interest was in the history of the relationship between China and Tibet: he discussed the subject endlessly with his brother-in-law, Phuntsok Tashi, and with his new friends at the Chinese Mission in Lhasa. (His mother disapproved of these friendships, feeling that he was getting into bad company.) Gyalo Thondup now desperately wanted to go and study in China.

The Kung at first objected, but his friend, ex-Regent Reting, talked him round, urging that as Chinese-speaking officials were scarce in Central Tibet and those who understood the Chinese mind even scarcer, if Gyalo Thondup could learn to understand both language and people, he would be immeasurably useful to his country. Gyalo Thondup – and Phuntsok Tashi – began taking private lessons in Chinese.

Amala, meanwhile, was about to give birth again – exactly a year after the death of her last child. When another son was born, with the tell-tale butter-smear clearly visible on his left buttock, it seemed that the oracle was vindicated: everyone was satisfied that the dead child had returned.

Once again Tsering Dolma acted as midwife. There would always be a special bond between her and this her youngest brother; twenty-seven years older, she was a second mother to him. The baby was given the names Tendzin[12] (Defender of the Faith) and Choegyal (Religious King) by his brother, the Dalai Lama.

Three days after the birth, an official celebration was held. Among the guests at Changseshar was Heinrich Harrer, an Austrian mountaineer who had been interned by the British in a POW camp in northern India at the outset of the Second World War. He and another member of the mountaineering team, Peter Aufschnaiter, had made a dramatic escape from the camp, and after enduring blizzards, bandits and near-starvation, had recently arrived in Lhasa.

The two Austrians were both destined to play a key role in the life of the Dalai Lama and his family. They brought with them a breath of the outside world; and were the subject of much excited gossip and speculation. Although they had not yet received official permission to stay in Tibet, they spoke fluent Tibetan and had been adopted by Lhasa society. Harrer was already working as a gardener and Aufschnaiter as an engineer. Before long they were invited to the home of the Dalai Lama's parents. Bearing the white silk scarves which were *de rigueur* when paying social calls in Tibet, they hastened to the audience:

We soon found ourselves standing before a great gate, near which the gate-keeper was already on the look-out for us. We were led through a large garden full of vegetable plots and clusters of splendid willows till we came to the palace. We were taken up to the first floor; a door was opened and we found ourselves in the presence of the mother of the God-King, to whom we bowed in reverence. She was sitting on a small throne in a large, bright room surrounded by servants. She looked the picture of aristocratic dignity. The humble awe which the Tibetans feel for the 'Holy Mother' is something strange to us, but we found the moment a solemn one.

The 'Holy Mother' smiled at us and was visibly pleased when we handed her the scarves...Then with a beaming countenance she shook our hands, contrary to Tibetan custom. At that moment, in came the father of the Dalai

Lama, a dignified elderly man. We bowed low again and handed him scarves with due ceremony, after which he shook our hands most unaffectedly.[13]

Having thus broken the ice, they sat down to drink tea Amdo style, with milk and salt, not as the Tibetans usually make it, with butter. (The family had even learned, through visiting the British Mission, to take it the English way, with sugar!) Lobsang Samten translated from the Amdo patois into Tibetan. He was fascinated by the strangers and deluged them with questions. For their part, they were delighted to learn that his brother, the Dalai Lama, had charged him to report every detail of his meeting with them.

When they stood up to go,

> a line of servants marched up with sacks of meal and tsampa, a load of butter and some beautiful soft woollen blankets. 'By the personal desire of the Kundun,' said the "Holy Mother", smiling, and pressed into our hands a hundred-sang note. This was done so naturally and as if it was a matter of course that we felt no shame about accepting.
>
> As a final proof of friendliness, Lobsang, on behalf of his parents, laid the scarves on our necks as we bowed to him.

Next day, an excited Lobsang Samten returned the visit. For him, Harrer's arrival was miraculous. Being the Dalai Lama's brother and a monk – he was now training to be a monk-official – meant that his life was very circumscribed. Harrer, the stranger from another world, would become a life-long friend. As the Austrian wrote,

> I was soon on terms of cordial friendship with Lobsang Samten. This attractive youth was just entering upon his career as a monk. As the brother of the Dalai Lama he had brilliant prospects. One day he was to play a great part as the intermediary between his brother and the Government. But the burden of a great position was already beginning to weigh him down. He could not choose his acquaintances freely. Whatever he did and wherever he went, all sorts of inferences were drawn. When he called on a high functionary on some official occasion, his entry into the room caused an awestruck silence and everyone, even Cabinet Ministers, rose from their seats to show respect to the brother of the God-King. All this might have turned a young man's head, but Lobsang Samten never lost his modest demeanour.[14]

For Lobsang, Harrer was opening a window on to the world outside and he was hungry to know more of it.[15] One day he would introduce Harrer to his brother, the Dalai Lama, but that time was not yet.

On the eve of Gyalo Thondup's departure for China, Kesang Rinpoche invited him and Lobsang Samten to lunch. 'We went and Rinpoche was very happy to see us,' says Thondup. 'He knew I was going to China and was very encouraging. Then when lunch was over, he confessed his real motive in inviting us. "If I die suddenly," he said, "will you two conduct the search for my rebirth?" We were shocked, he looked very healthy to us and we couldn't think why he was talking like that. I don't really remember what we said, but the conversation returned to normal and we spent a pleasant afternoon with him before riding home. Three days later we heard that he had died. Lobsang and I rushed over to his *labrang* and were told, no, he hadn't been ill, just a slight headache, that was all. It was very very strange. And it remains a mystery to this day.'[16]

On 2 March 1946, Gyalo Thondup and Phuntsok Tashi[17] left Lhasa with a Tibetan delegation going to India and China, bearing congratulations to the former on the Allied victory in the Second World War, and to the latter on the successful outcome of the Sino-Japanese War. How could they guess that the end of the foreign war which had preoccupied China from 1937 to 1945 would spell disaster for Tibet? The Chinese Communists, a spent force before the Japanese invasion of Manchuria in 1931 had precipitated the war with Japan, had covered themselves in glory in that struggle. Under their new leader, Mao Tse-tung (elected in January 1935), they had steadily increased their popular support and, after the Japanese defeat, had renewed the Civil War with Chiang Kai-shek's Kuomintang Government.

The two young men spent a year visiting Indian cities while arrangements were made for their journey to China. It was not until April 1947 that they flew with the Tibetan delegation to Nanking, the capital of Kuomintang China, where they were formally received by Generalissimo Chiang Kai-shek. When Tsering Dolma also arrived in Nanking (*en route* for Kumbum to escort her grandmother, uncle and aunt, to Lhasa), the Generalissimo invited all three Tibetan royals to a meal. It was Gyalo Thondup's first meeting with the man who would become a second father to him. Meanwhile, as her husband and brother were to enter the Minorities College to study Chinese, the ever-practical Tsering Dolma asked

Lhamo Tsering, a cousin from Amdo who was already at the College, to keep a watchful eye over them.

Just before the New Year of 1947, the Kung suffered an agonizing colic and took to his bed. The family took it in turns to keep vigil by his bedside, watching helplessly as he writhed in pain. Everything was done that could be done, doctors and astrologers were called in, medicines prescribed, prayers said; but the Kung's condition grew rapidly worse. The family sent a messenger to Kundun, asking to be excused from the official New Year visit. The patient then seemed to rally, recovering sufficiently to drink a bowl of tea. Taktser, who had been staying at Changseshar, left to offer New Year's greetings to various friends. But at his very first port of call, a messenger arrived to say that his father had had a relapse:

> Of course I hurried back to the house immediately, but my father was dead when I arrived. My mother, her face a mask of sorrow, sat beside his death-bed with my youngest brother on her lap. Crouched by her side were Lobsang Samten and Jetsun Pema. It appeared that in the end my father had died a quick and painless death.[18]

A question mark hung over the 47-year-old Kung's untimely death. Some said it was food-poisoning – over-indulgence in roast pork, perhaps. Others suggested a stomach ulcer, others cancer. Inevitably, there were darker rumours: in those days it was not unusual for awkward *prominenti* to be disposed of by poison. The Kung was close to ex-Regent Reting – and to the recently-deceased Kesang Rinpoche. Could this have been a political assassination? Gyalo Thondup, for one, is in no doubt of it:

> I'm quite certain my father was murdered. He was a simple farmer who knew nothing about politics, especially about the complicated saga of the two Regencies. We were close as a family to Reting, who was especially close to my father. I was told that the Taktra clique wanted to depose His Holiness because he had been brought to Lhasa by Reting. They had plans to dispose of Reting, and they feared that if His Holiness took over the political power later he might punish them. So they wanted to remove him while there was still time and replace him with a candidate of their own, a young lama called Ditru Rinpoche. Then there was my father. If he remained alive, he would get in the way of their plans for Reting. So they poisoned him.

GT claims to have seen a document which proves his father's murder, though he admits the evidence was circumstantial. 'The crime was admitted to the Chinese after the 1959 rebellion, by the person who actually did the poisoning. *They probably interrogated him to extort a confession.* He said he had administered a Tibetan herb known as Mad Elephant to my father. I think my mother always suspected the truth, that he had been poisoned.'[19]

But as there were no post-mortem facilities in Tibetan medicine, for the time being it remained mere speculation. Before sunrise on the third day after his death, the Kung's body was carried up into the mountains and ceremonially cremated. A prescribed mourning period of forty-nine days of praying and fasting followed.[20] At the end of it, Amala, sorely in need of change and rest, went off to the family property near Gyantse, which lay on the caravan route to India. The family's finances were by now so chaotic that the Kashag appointed two senior officials to take control of them – a decision which infuriated Gyalo Thondup.

Long before the end of the mourning period, Lhasa was in the grip of a shoddy little civil war, arising from the feud between the two Regents. In early 1947, a small group of Reting's more unprincipled followers tried to assassinate Taktra by means of a hand grenade packed in a parcel. The bomb exploded before reaching its intended victim. Nobody was killed, but the near-miss convinced Taktra that he must act. Then, on 14 April, a coded telegram sent to Lhasa from the Tibetan Bureau in Nanking revealed that Reting had asked for Chinese troops, weapons, military equipment and even planes to help him overthrow Taktra; in return for accepting the Chinese claim that Tibet was part of China. The Kashag needed no further proof of Reting's treachery.[21] A small army was despatched to arrest him and bring him to Lhasa. Whereupon the monks of his college, Sera Je, rose in revolt, killed their abbot, a Taktra supporter, and stormed towards Lhasa, intent on rescuing the ex-Regent. Lhasa was in a ferment, its citizens terrified that thousands of enraged monks were about to descend on the town with murderous intent.

By the time Reting and his escort reached the confines of Sera Monastery *en route* for the Potala, the Government was ready for them. When several hundred monks swooped down from the monastery to rescue the ex-Regent, they were met with a burst of artillery fire which forced them to retreat. Reting was taken secretly to the Potala dungeons; and the Sera monks were threatened with dire consequences if they persisted in their rebellion. Ignoring the ultimatum, they declared they would fight to the last man, even if their monastery should be reduced to the condition of 'a collapsed tent'. In the fierce fighting that ensued, about two hundred monks died. Only on 26 April when Government troops surrounded the monastery and bombarded it with a few howitzers, did the rebels finally surrender.

Meanwhile, Reting and his associates were being interrogated in the Potala. It was still winter and thirteen-year-old Kundun was in the Potala when the ex-Regent was brought there:

> Some kind of committee of the National Assembly conducted the interrogations in the main hall of the Potala. Each day they brought Reting from his cell and he had to cross a big open courtyard. Once, as he passed, I was in the kitchens and some of the cooks were watching from the window. I squeezed myself in between them and watched too. I could only see him from a distance and he couldn't see me at all. I heard afterwards that he had asked to see me. I hadn't known that, but even if I had been able to see him, what could I have done? I had no official power then. He'd probably have asked for clemency, but I'd not have been in a position to grant it. I felt very sad, two Regents fighting like that and involving a whole monastery in their quarrel.[22]

Reting and his associates admitted their guilt to the National Assembly, but before sentence could be passed, Reting, suddenly and inexplicably, died in the Potala dungeons. Once again the rumour machine was busy. Heart attack or political murder? If the latter, was it poison? There are many who believe, as needless to say Gyalo Thondup does, that he too was murdered. Hugh Richardson does not rule out the possibility but is understandably cautious: 'I don't think he was physically murdered. It is certainly not true that his eyes were put out, as some have said. He may have been given the wrong medicine, perhaps deliberately, but we shall never know.'[23] When he visited the Kashag to inquire about the death, Richardson was suavely assured that 'the Regent had been so overcome by shame and remorse that he voluntarily departed this life'.[24]

The property of the rebels was confiscated and sold at public auction. Reting's houses and pavilions were demolished, his beautiful fruit trees transplanted into other gardens. Most of the Sera monks implicated in the revolt had already fled to China. As Harrer said, 'It usually happened that when there was a rising in Tibet, the Chinese had a finger in the pie.'[25] (This most recent Chinese interference was particularly disturbing since

in this year (1947) the Tibetans' traditional allies, the British, were handing over power in India to a National Government; thus severing their official links with Tibet.)

The conspirators were flogged and sentenced to life imprisonment, a
sentence which, together with Reting's mysterious death and the earlier
public humiliation of his own father, is said to have caused Kundun to distance himself from Taktra and his advisers. He contrived to send one of
his personal attendants down with food, bedding and other comforts to the
victims.[26] Despite Reting's misbehaviour, he grieved for him. But the ex-
Regent's names, Jamphel and Yeshe, which Kundun had assumed at his
enthronement, were quietly dropped.

Taktra had won, but it was a hollow victory. The rift between his supporters and Reting's was now unbridgeable, their struggle being, as one
commentator later put it, 'not between the good and the bad but between
the bad and the ugly'.[27] A present-day official in India remembers his father
talking about the situation:

> Rivalry, in-fighting, corruption, nepotism, it was decadent and horrible.
> Everything was a matter of show, ceremonial, jockeying for position. There
> were far too few people in governing circles who had any sense of service to
> the people of Tibet. And yet there were many people in Lhasa who saw the sit-
> uation clearly and knew the desperate need for reform and change.[28]

Tibet was falling apart just as its moment of greatest danger approached.
Few doubted that in the struggle against Mao Tse-tung's Communists, Chiang Kai-shek would win. But whichever side emerged victorious, it seemed
likely that China would soon be looking to consolidate – and extend – its
western borders. And that would inevitably mean trouble for Tibet.

When Kundun was twelve, Taktra decided that he should no longer make
visits home; the family's visits to him were also curtailed. He embarked
on an arduous course of education, which was, he later admitted, more
suited to the training of a medieval prince-prelate than that of a late-twen-
tieth-century ruler. Although he attended the meetings of the Government at ten each morning, he knew nothing of international events or of
the revolutionary discoveries of science and technology in the world outside Tibet. His education was in the realm of Buddhist philosophy, logic,
rhetoric and dialectics (debating), subjects in which one day he would be

expected to gain a doctorate. As that time seemed far-off, 'mostly I just worked hard enough to keep out of trouble'. Once, to jolt him out of his laziness, his tutors trapped him into a mock debating contest with the sweeper, Norbu Thondup. The latter being briefed with the answers in advance, Kundun lost. He was mortified. 'For a time I worked very hard out of sheer anger. But in the end my good intentions wore off and I slipped back into my old ways.'[29]

Secretly his tutors were pleased with his progress. Ling Rinpoche remarked that although he had 'occasionally to prod the boy with a finger or gaze thoughtfully at the whips hanging on the wall to encourage him to work more diligently, once Kundun was taught something, he never forgot it.'[30] On his first introduction to metaphysics and logic, he felt 'dazed, as though I were hit on the head by a stone', but he recovered quickly and, as other subjects were added to the curriculum, found it easier and easier to assimilate them.[31] Indeed he began to bombard his tutors with more questions than they had answers for.

Yet he hungered for knowledge of the secular world too. Eagerly he turned to a little newspaper called *Tibet Mirror*, written, edited and published by a Tibetan Christian in West Bengal; the only newspaper of any kind written in Tibetan, available in Tibet, and touching on international affairs. It appeared erratically, and its news was several weeks out of date by the time it arrived, but no matter. The Thirteenth Dalai Lama had been a subscriber, and the Regents had kept up the payments. Kundun was fascinated by this publication and devoured its contents eagerly. He was particularly keen to follow the progress of the Second World War, and loved the pictures of tanks, trucks, jeeps and aeroplanes. Learning of his enthusiasm, the British Mission sent him copies of the *Illustrated London News* and *Life*, and he had their captions translated into Tibetan by the few Lhasa nobles who had been educated in India and knew English. These men were well-travelled and well-informed, but, because of protocol, he could not speak to them directly, nor they to him, and any questions had to be put in writing and delivered by an intermediary. Kundun decided to learn English for himself and pored doggedly over crate-loads of musty text-books which he found in the Potala store-rooms.

His thirst for knowledge was not limited to books; he had always been intrigued by machines; and those magazine pictures gave him further incentive. Finding a broken generator at the Norbulingka, he became obsessed with making it work, even when it meant missing meals. (His guardians were terrified he would electrocute himself.) Then he thought about the old cars rusting away at the Norbulingka. Enlisting the help of a young Tibetan who had learned to drive in India, together they plundered one of two 1927 Baby Austins (presents to his predecessor) for spare parts and got the second one going, along with a 1931 Dodge. He was forbidden to go near the cars on his own, but one evening he crept to the shed and, having gingerly backed the Baby Austin out, drove it at speed around the garden, finally crashing it into a tree. When he saw that he'd smashed a headlight, he was apprehensive that his nocturnal joy-riding would be discovered. Managing somehow to get the car back into its shed, he fashioned a piece of replacement glass for the headlight, inexpertly fogging it with repeated applications of sugar syrup! Next day, to his undying gratitude, his driver pretended to have noticed nothing. Years earlier, he and Lobsang had discovered an old hand-cranked film projector and thirty or forty reels of film. With an old Chinese monk who knew how to operate the machine, the boys spent many fascinated hours watching Tarzan; films about the Boer War or the Jubilee of George V; one based on trick photography, showing girl dancers being hatched out of eggs; and a documentary on gold-mining. By the time the Chinese monk died, Kundun had learned to work the machine himself. But when one day the projector broke down, neither he nor anyone else knew how to repair it. Determinedly, he took it to pieces and put it together again, a dozen times and more, before he found a way to make it go – only to discover there were no bulbs:

> It was my fault. When it seemed the projector would never work again, I took out the bulbs and dropped them like bombs from the upper windows of the Potala. They made a lovely explosion when they landed.[32]

It was Kundun's passionate interest in watching films that finally brought Heinrich Harrer into his life. After two years in Lhasa, Harrer was translating foreign news and articles and photographing special events for the Tibetan government. One day, towards the end of 1948, Lobsang Samten brought a request from Kundun for him to build a cinema-room at the Norbulingka. Harrer chose a suitable site and, long before the spring exodus to the Norbulingka, had completed his task. Then the Dalai Lama sent for him. Overwhelmed by this unique honour, Harrer made his way to the cinema-room to meet the legendary ruler. The abbots with Kundun looked on disapprovingly. The young ruler, on the other hand, beamed all over his face and poured out a flood of questions. He seemed to me like a person who had for years brooded in solitude over different problems, and now that he had at last someone to talk to, wanted to know all the answers at once.[33]

Asking Harrer to put on a film about the surrender of Japan, he soon impatiently pushed him aside and began operating the machine himself. Before long, he and Harrer were engaged in animated, bantering conversation, to the shocked horror of the abbots who deplored the foreigner's disregard for protocol.

Kundun was delighted with his new acquaintance, and nicknamed the fair-haired Austrian *Gopse*, or 'yellow head'. For the next year and a half, despite the unrelenting hostility of Kundun's advisers, Harrer paid regular weekly visits to the palace, talking to Kundun about international politics, about the recent war in Europe, about the discoveries of science. In addition, he helped him with his study of English and of Western-style arithmetic.

Harrer was uniquely privileged. Other foreigners, like Hugh Richardson at the British Mission, were often received in audience but protocol did not allow them to speak to the ruler directly. Kundun, through Harrer, now tried to bridge that gap: 'We used to exchange messages through Heinrich,' says Richardson, 'exchange books, packets of seeds and so on. And we got him films. He would send us messages asking for certain ones. Most Tibetans liked the Charlie Chaplin films and an edited version of *Henry V*...The Dalai Lama borrowed *Henry V* and liked it. But he didn't want any of the comic films. He wanted films of factories and modern events. He wanted to know what was going on in the world. So we sent him the newsreels. Then he asked us to get him the book of *Henry V*, so I bought him a paperback edition in India. He was learning English then, listening to the BBC at dictation speed.'[34]

Lobsang Samten, who visited his brother twice a month, reported that 'he never complained of being either lonely or unhappy'.[35] But he *was* lonely and must often have yearned for normality. When the working day ended at five-thirty, he would climb up on to the flat roof of the Potala with his treasured telescope, looking down at the scenes below: the stallholders in the market, pilgrims prostrating; women shopping; children playing, caravans of yaks, ponies and camels arriving with brick-tea from China or cotton goods and sugar from India. He grieved in autumn when the herdsmen brought large numbers of yaks and sheep to be sold to the slaughterers: 'When I saw those poor animals, several thousand of them, on their way to be slaughtered, I felt an intolerable pain in my heart. I had to do something. I had some money, so I was able to send someone out to buy the animals for me. I could not bear to think of all those poor creatures going to their deaths.'[36]

And when he watched the prisoners walking in the yard of the Shol prison at the foot of the Potala, he could not help identifying with their plight, knowing what it was like to be deprived of freedom.

Did anyone really care about this young boy, this Presence, Wish-Fulfilling Jewel, Precious Protector, except in his role as national icon? Richardson was told by Harrer of the long hours the boy spent alone: 'He did all these ceremonials in the morning, everyone bowing and scraping in front of him. But in the afternoons he was left to himself in a dark room. That's when he virtually lost his eyesight. If he wanted anything from the market, there was nobody to get it for him. There were some idle soldiers supposed to be guarding him and he'd ask one of them or maybe the gardener. I went in one day – I'd gone to see one of his household – and I found a scruffy guard asleep on duty. I spoke to the Government about it, warned them that the Dalai Lama's life might be in danger if he wasn't looked after properly. But they didn't take kindly to criticism, they didn't like anyone interfering in their affairs.'[37]

As he left the years of his childhood behind, Kundun's religious faith gradually matured. He came to understand the importance of *dharma* – the Buddhist teachings – to his life, and felt a growing gratitude to the Buddha and to those past teachers who had brought knowledge of his teachings to Tibet. With the gratitude came a burgeoning sense of responsibility to his own high calling. Though still a high-spirited young boy, he had 'begun to realize what a destructive thing anger was and I was making a big effort to control my terrible temper'.[38] His spiritual life was awakening. Whereas in the past, during long periods of enforced mantra meditation he had waited for his tutor to fall asleep so that he could fool around, he now began to meditate seriously, at first for quite short periods, then gradually for much longer. As he made his annual spiritual retreat at the Potala, he meditated on the *dharma* and expressed his silent gratitude. And though sometimes, as he sat at his high window in the Potala, watching the boys and girls of his own age bring their animals home from pasture, he found himself wondering 'what it would be like to be happy like them', it was without any trace of self-pity.

NOTES

1. Norbu, *Tibet Is My Country*, chapter 15.

2. According to a letter sent from the British Mission in Lhasa to the Foreign Secretary in New Delhi (dated 16 April 1945, O and IO Collection, etc. File 15(2)), the boy had been treated by the Chinese doctor in Lhasa. When Pema also became ill, the parents called in Dr Terry from the British Mission. Pema thankfully recovered.

3. Author interview with Khando Chazotsang, Salt Lake City, Utah, February 1996.

4. Amala's mother and brother, together with the Kung's sister, came from Amdo in 1947 to live at Changseshar.

5. Jetsun Pema, *Tibet, Mon Histoire*, Paris, Éditions Ramsay, 1996.

6. Author interview with Khando Chazotsang, Salt Lake City, Utah, February 1996.

7. Amala's mother, brought to Lhasa in 1947 by Tsering Dolma (see 4 above).

8. Author interview with Jetsun Pema, Dharamsala, June 1994.

9. Author interview with Jetsun Pema, Dharamsala, June 1994.

10. F. Spencer Chapman, *Lhasa: The Holy City*, London, 1940; New Delhi, 1992.

11. George Sheriff died of a heart attack in 1944 and Hugh Richardson returned to Lhasa temporarily to replace him.

12. Although this name is usually spelt without a 'd', Tendzin Choegyal has always preferred to use the 'd' – the more traditional and older spelling.

13. Harrer, *Seven Years in Tibet*.

14. *Seven Years in Tibet*.

15. Interview with Namlha Taklha, October 1993.

16. Author interview with Gyalo Thondup, New Delhi, July 1995.

17. Tsering Dolma stayed at home. It was and is quite normal for Tibetan couples to be separated for longish periods.

18. *Tibet Is My Country*, chapter 15.

19. Author interview with Gyalo Thondup, New Delhi, July 1995.

20. Strict procedures were followed after a death. For seven weeks thereafter, food was served as usual in the living-room of the deceased, and prayers were offered by whichever lama was present at the death. Prayers were offered every seventh day (for a man) or every sixth day (for a woman). After forty-nine days, it was believed that reincarnation would already have taken place, and the official period of mourning came to an end.

21. See Goldstein, *A History of Modern Tibet*, chapter 14.

22. Author interview with HH the Dalai Lama, Dharamsala, July 1995.

23. Author interview with Hugh Richardson, September 1993.

24. Letter from Hugh Richardson, June 1993.

25. *Seven Years in Tibet.*

26. Goldstein, interview with Kundeling Dzasa, note at the end of chapter 14.

27. K. Dhondup, 'The Regents Reting and Tagdra', *Lungta* 7.

28. Author interview with Tenzin Geyche Tethong, Dharamsala, 1994.

29. Fourteenth Dalai Lama, *Freedom in Exile.*

30. Goodman, *The Last Dalai Lama*, chapter 8.

31. Goodman.

32. Goodman.

33. *Seven Years in Tibet.*

34. Author interview with Hugh Richardson, September 1993.

35. Goodman.

36. Author interview with HH the Dalai Lama, Dharamsala, July 1995.

37. Author interview with Hugh Richardson, September 1993.

38. Author interview with HH the Dalai Lama, October 1993.

10

Twilight of the Gods 1947–50

The Chinese People's Liberation Army must enter Tibet, lib-
erate the Tibetan people, and defend the frontiers of China.
From the Chinese Government's letters of 30 October and 16
November 1950, addressed to the Government of India

Liberate from whom?
Jawaharlal Nehru's reply

Having passed his exams with distinction, Taktser Rinpoche was about to
set off on a long pilgrimage to the Buddhist shrines of India and China,
when his father's death and the Reting riots intervened. In the event, he set
out on a very different pilgrimage, to take his father's ashes back to the
mountains of Amdo. Phuntsok Tashi, who had rushed home from Nanking
on hearing of the Kung's death, was to escort him as far as Calcutta.

Seven years had passed since Taktser had made that first perilous journey from Kumbum to Lhasa. This time the journey was easier and full of
wonders and marvels, from Hugh Richardson's farewell gift of a pair of
sunglasses to the astonishing revelations that awaited him in India –
'things I had never seen in my life before – things I should not have believed possible'. In Calcutta, he was startled to hear a train letting off
steam, 'with a tremendous hissing, stamping sound'; and later gazed in
complete disbelief at 'the monstrous silver birds' on the tarmac of the
International Airport.

Fear soon gave way to pleasure when he flew in a 'silver bird' from Calcutta to Hong Kong and Shanghai. At Shanghai he was met by Gyalo Thondup and Lhamo Tsering, and taken to Nanking where the two cousins were studying Political Science at the Central University. Though the Civil War had moved into its final stages and the Communists were sighting victory, the capital, Nanking, was still unscathed. Gyalo Thondup was enjoying life. As the Dalai Lama's brother, he had been taken up by Chiang Kai-shek and his wife:

> They couldn't have been kinder. They paid all my expenses, invited me to their home for weekends and holidays, and altogether I was very close to them. The Generalissimo was always encouraging me, telling me I must study hard to understand China. He promised that when I had finished my five years' study in China he would send me to the USA and England for more study, and only then would I return to Tibet. He said I would be very useful to the Dalai Lama and the Tibetan Government, and he himself would feel more comfortable about Tibet if I was there in a position of responsibility. He was worried about Tibet, because it was China's back door, and he didn't want the Tibetans to fall prey to foreign manipulation. But, he said repeatedly, 'If you return to work in Tibet, then I will support the idea of independence for your country.'[1]

After a few days, Taktser flew on alone to Peking. But the accelerating crisis soon forced him to cut short his visit. The Communists were coming close, he could hear their artillery, and the railway lines had already been cut.[2] Returning to Nanking, he made his slow and difficult way westwards to Amdo. At Kumbum monastery, he received a warm welcome from the monks, but found depressingly few familiar faces among them.

His first task was to take his father's ashes to the mountains above Taktser and as he said his final goodbye, he felt indescribably sad. Seven years earlier, Choekyong Tsering had left his native Amdo for power and riches beyond the imagining. Inevitably perhaps he had lost his bearings. But now he was back where he truly belonged, lying just above the village in which he and his forbears had lived for countless generations. Taktser's eyes glistened with tears as he looked down from the mountain top:

> That small village with its neat and spotless houses perched on its gentle hill looked more beautiful to me than anything I had seen on my long journey abroad; and with gratitude in my heart I turned towards Kyeri, whose snow-clad peak shone above me in the sun.[3]

In the village he greeted his old companions and Pasang, the village head-man, now stooped and white-haired. He was invited by every family in the village in turn, all of them bombarding him with questions about the Dalai Lama, the Potala, and what it was like to live in Lhasa. They were tremendously proud of having given Tibet its Dalai Lama, and proud too of this other famous son, Taktser Rinpoche, who had returned to them.

They would soon have even greater reason for pride, for at this time the Abbot of Kumbum resigned and Taktser was chosen to succeed him. Though doubting his fitness for the task (and knowing very well that he had been chosen because he was the brother of the Dalai Lama), Taktser accepted and was formally inducted just as Chiang Kai-shek's Kuomintang were facing up to the fact that they had lost the Civil War.

By the end of April 1949, the People's Liberation Army (PLA) was with-in a few days' march of Nanking. Gyalo Thondup (now twenty-one) had recently married a Chinese fellow-student, Zhu Dan, daughter of one of Chiang Kai-shek's Generals, Chu Shi-kuei.[4] 'Until then, we hadn't had any disturbances in Nanking itself, except for the student revolutionary move-ments,' he says. 'The Communists were mobilizing leftist groups among the students. But not in the school where I was, the Central Political Uni-versity. None of us took part in those demos and riots. But we were hear-ing more and more about the terrible fighting and killings in other parts of China. Then in 1949, everything changed, the Generalissimo acknowl-edged defeat, resigned and fled with his troops to the island of Taiwan.'[5]

Panic-stricken Kuomintang officials abandoned Nanking in droves. Some of them tried to persuade Gyalo Thondup to go with them to Taiwan – as the Dalai Lama's brother he would have considerable propaganda value. But, reasoning that he had gone to China solely to study Chinese, he decided to head for home.

With his wife, Lhamo Tsering, two Amdo friends and the Tibetan Gov-ernment representative and his staff, he left on a crowded train for Shang-hai, which the Communists still had not reached. From there they sailed to Hong Kong. It was a close-run thing; a few days later Shanghai was sur-rounded by the PLA and panic set in. There was a frantic run on the banks, with many people trampled underfoot in the rush; then the banks were shut down, their windows boarded up. The only way out of the city was by sea; but there were no longer any ships.

There is confusion over Gyalo Thondup's movements after this, and ac-counts vary. His own version (as told to myself)[6] is as follows:

When I finally arrived in India, I stayed first in Kalimpong with friends. Mr Nehru contacted me there and invited me to Delhi as his personal guest. He even sent his private plane for me. Nehru questioned me about China and about my own plans – was I intending to continue my studies in India or return to Tibet? He wanted me to stay in India, but I told him I hadn't decided yet. After staying as Nehru's guest for a week, I returned to Kalimpong and from there went to Calcutta in October 1949. I stayed there for seven months.

The next move came from the Communist Marshal Chu-deh who asked me to contact the Tibetan Government with a view to establishing better relations with them. Otherwise, he said, the People's Liberation Army would invade Tibet. I asked Thubten Sangbo, a Tibetan official in Kalimpong who was in telegraphic communication with the Tibetan Government, to convey this information to Lhasa as a matter of urgency. Then Nehru sent the Indian Ambassador to Peking, Mr Sardat Panikkar, to warn me that the Chinese Communists meant business and that the Tibetan Government should put itself on a war footing, start mobilizing the people immediately...He asked me to inform the Kashag, through Thubten Sangbo, that the Indian Government would help in any way it could, would even provide arms. Even the American Ambassador, Mr Anderson, asked me what help Tibet needed.

I replied that I couldn't speak for the Tibetan Government, but would pass on the messages. I passed everything to Thubten Sangbo, but months went by and there was still no response from the Tibetan Government. Nehru kept on asking if any word had come and said that the situation was growing more grave by the minute and that total mobilization by Tibet was now absolutely vital. 'Even if China invades Tibet,' he told me, 'the Tibetan Government must stand firm. If they overrun Amdo and Kham, you must move all the valuable paintings, sacred texts, statues to Central Tibet and from there to India.' India, he kept on assuring me, would provide the Tibetans with arms and ammunition and would stand four-square behind them. If necessary, they would build an airstrip outside Lhasa and send an aircraft to rescue the Dalai Lama from Lhasa.

Three times both the American Ambassador and the Indian Ambassador to Peking contacted me. But no reply ever came from Lhasa!

Why did the Tibetan Government not respond to these overtures? Gyalo Thondup puts forward several suggestions:

Well, for a start, the Tibetans had been isolated for too long, living in a world apart. They didn't know China, they didn't know India. They were far too busy quarrelling among themselves to understand the danger they were in. And no one had any control over those powerful lamas. They made an awful mess of everything. If they'd shown some political sense, things might have turned out very differently.

For another thing, they didn't trust me. In 1946, after they murdered Reting, the Tibetan Government issued a proclamation about his 'treason'. At the end of this document, they wrote that Gyalo Thondup, a protégé of his, *was now in China!* The implication was obvious. My mother knew or suspected the truth about my father's and Reting's deaths and in 1949 she wrote to me in India, advising me not to go back home. It would be too dangerous, she said. Dangerous for His Holiness too! My mother told me that His Holiness's safety depended on my not returning to Tibet where they suspected me of working for the Chinese.[7]

In those days the Tibetan Government did not keep written records, so the allegations cannot be checked. But there can be no doubt that they were suspicious of Gyalo Thondup, not only as a Reting protégé but because he had gone of his own free will to study in China. What guarantee was there that he was not a Chinese spy? They were not unaware of the danger they were in: they knew very well that Lhasa was full of Chinese agents – both Communist and Nationalist – disguised as traders or even monks. In fact, when Gyalo Thondup sent his first warnings – in 1949 – they had already taken what they thought was effective enough action. Fearing a rapid Communist take-over of the small Chinese Mission in Lhasa (the Communists had already taken over the Bank of China in Calcutta), the Kashag closed it down and expelled all Chinese officials from Tibet. When the People's Republic of China was inaugurated by Chairman Mao in Peking on 1 October 1949, the Tibetan Government believed they had asserted their independence in the nick of time. Their action, however, was interpreted as a slap in the face by Communists and Nationalists alike, and its main effect was to exacerbate the ancient quarrel between Tibet and China.

Nothing now stood between the Communists and the heartlands of Tibet but the Tibetan-populated borderlands which the Kuomintang had nominally controlled. The fate of Tibet hinged on the amount of resistance put up by those two vital frontier regions, Eastern Kham and Amdo. In the event, there was almost none. The various Kuomintang garrisons in Eastern Tibet were scattered and demoralized, lacking the revolutionary fervour of their opponents. Some of them simply went over to the Communists, some put up a token fight before quietly surrendering. In Amdo, the warlord, Ma Pu-feng, on whom the Kuomintang had pinned their hopes, commandeered two Dakota aircraft and fled with his wives and treasure before hostilities so much as began. The Communists entered Amdo unopposed.

Fugitives from the Communist onslaught and former Kuomintang soldiers with nowhere to go straggled in to Kumbum monastery, bringing reports of Communist outrages against civilian populations. 'We already knew,' wrote Taktser, 'how badly they had behaved towards our co-religionists in Mongolia and China, and we were well aware that our high dignitaries and wealthy monks in particular had every cause to fear them. Many Tibetan Buddhists in Mongolia and China had lost their lives on account of their religion, and we were sorely afraid that the Communists would persecute us and forbid us to practise our religion.'[8] In these circumstances, it was hardly surprising that many monks quietly left the monastery and went to ground in the neighbouring villages, while others joined bands of wandering nomads, in the forlorn hope that the Communists would not think of looking for them on the steppes.

With the red flag of the Chinese People's Republic hoisted over Siling, compulsory meetings aimed at the political re-education and indoctrination of the people began immediately. Taktser and a few of his senior monks went to see their new masters to find out where they stood. The PLA Commander assured them they had come as liberators, driving out the Nationalist criminals who had long persecuted the Tibetan people, and assuring a better and fairer future for all. The empty sloganizing only increased the forebodings of Taktser and his monks, who returned home in dismay.

Alarming reports began filtering through: of monasteries burned to the ground, of Communist-led mobs incited to plunder and desecrate their sacred treasures. The beautiful little cliff-top monastery of Shartsong where Taktser had begun his studies had been utterly destroyed. Fearing for Kumbum itself, Taktser went to Siling to protest to the new Governor. Once again, bland assurances were given, the Governor promising to investigate any 'irregularities' that might have taken place. Then, nothing. Instead, Taktser was formally interrogated in the offices of the new Tibet Commission in Siling:

I had to provide them with a meticulous account of my life and my career, and submit a detailed list of all the properties of the monastery and of the nobles. I was also asked searching questions about the rank, property and activities of everyone I knew.[9]

On his return, the monks heard him out with mounting anxiety. They knew by now that they were dealing with an enemy who would stop at nothing, and that among the asylum-seekers in Kumbum were many Communist spies and informers out to trap them into political discussion. Eavesdroppers were everywhere, night and day.

Villages such as Taktser, which were within the orbit of Kumbum, were already suffering not only hunger and neglect but the destruction of their centuries-old lifestyle. Taktser Rinpoche's protests fell on deaf ears, the new Governor retorting that everything was the fault of the monks and the outdated economic structure of the country. The monasteries, he said, must redistribute their lands and return their monks to the labour force. In vain did Taktser point out that there had been no hunger until the Communists arrived; that Amdo had lived in peace and harmony with its monasteries for hundreds of years; that many of the monks were skilled artisans who had learned their craft in the monasteries.

The confrontation did Taktser no good; from then on he was given two minders, with orders to 're-educate' him and never leave his side. A prisoner within his own monastery, he dared not communicate even with his closest friends. The minders argued with him round the clock, relentlessly attacking his religious beliefs, mocking his obsolete views, setting political traps for him:

> If they came upon me in prayer they would ask sarcastically whether prayer had ever filled anyone's belly. At first I tried to make them understand that prayer gave me serenity and confidence, and that a life without it was just unthinkable for me. But they mocked at our beliefs and our gods, and they insisted that it was men like Stalin and Mao Tse-tung who had put food into the bellies of the starving millions, not our Buddhas. I quickly realized that it was pointless to try and make them understand what life meant to us, and what Tibet had owed to its monasteries and its monks for many hundreds of years. Again and again they reproached me with standing in the light of progress, and declared that the monks exploited the people and wasted the national patrimony.[10]

The minders searched Taktser's possessions and censored his correspondence. Their merciless attentions brought him to the edge of breakdown; he began to wonder how much longer he could carry the responsibility for Kumbum and its monks on his shoulders. He knew, of course, that the cat-and-mouse game the Chinese were playing with him owed everything to his being the Dalai Lama's brother. Before the Communists came, this had made his appointment as Abbot eminently desirable. But he was now a terrible liability to everyone concerned.

After a number of sleepless nights, he reached a decision. During a ceremony to commemorate his first anniversary as Abbot, Taktser offered his resignation to the assembled monks and implored them to accept it. The monks listened in appalled silence. They knew what it cost him to take this step; but they knew also that he was right: they *would* be better off without him. A few weeks later, a new Abbot was installed and Taktser retired to his own *labrang*, hoping to be left in peace.

But the bulldogs stayed. In fact, now that he no longer had any official duties, it became harder than ever to shake them off. 'It was quite clear to me now that I owed their special attention to the fact that I was brother of the Dalai Lama.'[11] Taktser refused to be drawn as they constantly extolled the totalitarian State as the only way to human equality and happiness. But his depression deepened:

> Although by this time I had already heard this sort of thing often enough before, the thought of such a State never ceased to horrify me anew. It was a conception in crass opposition to everything we held dear; and as they described their paradise it sounded like hell on earth to me: a life of grey, uniform dullness, without warmth, without individual love and affection, a life not worth living, and a world not worth living in.[12]

Everything that Taktser held dear was falling apart. A ruinous system of taxation had come into force. In the days of Ma Pu-feng (which seemed in retrospect a Golden Age), the peasants had paid a fixed annual sum to the local monastery, which had then paid the required taxes to the authorities. But now payment was to be made directly to the authorities in Siling, whose demands became ever more extortionate. When the peasants protested, there were threats, increased demands and punishments, with the People's Liberation Army always on hand to back up the threats with force. Anarchy threatened:

Robbery and murder had become common in a once peaceable countryside. Dissatisfied elements banded together, and the once-feared robber bands became a reality again...and such were the topsy-turvy conditions brought about by the new rulers that the oppressed masses regarded them as heroes.[13]

About a month after Taktser had resigned, the Chairman of the Tibet Commission proposed that he should go to Lhasa to present a list of Chinese demands to the Dalai Lama. If he did this, his 'previous obstinacy and former relations with the Kuomintang and the Western Powers in Lhasa' (!) would be overlooked. If, however, he were to accept the commission, but use the opportunity to escape over the border to India, he would 'never be allowed to set foot on Tibetan soil again'. Taktser rejected the proposal outright, assuring the Chairman that, other objections apart, he would be assassinated as a traitor if he turned up in Lhasa as a messenger boy for the Communists.

They did not give up. The secretary of the Governor tried; then the Governor himself; and finally the Commanding Officer of the PLA. All without success. But, even as Taktser continued to stall, he was aware of the appalling danger he faced. If he continued to refuse, he might well be held as a hostage, a pawn with which to blackmail Lhasa. Indeed, the opportunity the Communists were offering was probably his last chance of escape. Wearily, he agreed to their suggestion, stipulating that if he was to have any credibility in Lhasa, he would need to travel with an entourage of at least twenty senior lamas. But his hopes of thus saving the lives of twenty of his colleagues were stillborn: he was allowed only two. Moreover, he was to have a Chinese escort of three: a married couple and a wireless operator with a portable transmitter. Obviously his masters were taking no chances.

Before he left, they proposed a bribe so outrageous that it winded him:

It was nothing less than a promise to make me Governor-General of Tibet if on my arrival in Lhasa I managed to persuade the Tibetan Government to welcome the entry of Chinese communist troops into Tibet as liberators, and to accept the Chinese People's Republic as an ally. As Governor-General, they pointed out, I should be in a position to assist and guide the great work of Socialist reconstruction in my country and to help replace antiquated religious beliefs with the new communist ideology. Should the Dalai Lama resist the march of progress, they indicated, ways and means would have to be found to get rid of him. At this point they even let me see quite clearly that if necessary

they would regard fratricide as justifiable in the circumstances if there remained no other way of advancing the cause of Communism.[14]

Taktser could barely restrain his disgust: 'What sort of a man did they
think I was, for heaven's sake? Did they really suppose that I was capable of
such abominations in return for the privilege of becoming their puppet?'[15]

Once again, but with a heavy heart, Taktser prepared for the journey
to Lhasa. He was given 'a large-calibre pistol and twenty-five rounds of
ammunition, three old Japanese rifles, three horses and three thousand
gormos', and told that he and his two companions should make their way
to the caravan rendezvous at Tsaidam, where their Chinese escort would
join them.

At last the bulldogs were called off, and Taktser could move around freely.
As he said goodbye to his friends, he knew it was unlikely that he would
ever see any of them again and he was in little doubt as to their probable
fate. It was with considerable mental anguish that he left the monastery.

Not even the majestic panoramas of the Tibetan plateau could raise his
spirits, their austere immensity serving only to plunge him into deeper
gloom. He sank into a state of nervous irritation, particularly as the Chinese couple seemed set on delaying the caravan as often and for as long as
possible. As time after time they insisted on stopping for rest-days, the
tensions inside Taktser threatened to boil over.

But when the party crossed the border into the Dalai Lama's territory
and the Governor of the Northern Provinces turned out to meet him, it
was the turn of the Chinese to be enraged. The Chinese writ did not run
here, and they were refused permission to enter. When the leader of the
Chinese group realized that the Tibetans were not going to let them in, he
'completely lost his head and shouted that he had just heard over his radio
that Red Chinese troops had already marched into Chamdo, the capital of
western Kham'. In spite – or perhaps because – of this horrifying announcement, the Governor confiscated the wireless transmitter and had
the three Chinese arrested and taken away under escort.

But the news was all too true. It was the twenty-third day of the ninth
month of the Year of the Iron Tiger (7 October 1950) – a year in which the
astrologers had long foretold that 'evil forces would enter Tibet'. Thirty
thousand Chinese troops had just invaded Tibet from six different directions at once. The 'peaceful liberation' had begun.

The old Imperial idea of 'barbarians' being happy to kowtow to the Son of Heaven (whether called Emperor, Generalissimo or Chairman) was ingrained in the Chinese psyche; and it implied that 'the spread of Chinese civilization into a universe of barbarian darkness was a natural process'.[16] On this matter the majority Han Chinese, whether Kuomintang or Communist, were of one mind: the national aspirations – and rights – of the minority races on their borders were completely irrelevant.

Early in 1950, the South-West China Military District was charged with invading and conquering the Kham area of Tibet. (One of the two Communist leaders who distributed instructions about the conduct of this operation was Deng Xiao-ping.) Throughout the year, the Chinese propaganda machine continued to threaten Tibet, and make wild allegations that foreign powers were arming the Tibetans for an attack on China.

It would have been laughable if it hadn't been so tragic. On 1 January 1950, Robert Ford, a Briton employed by the Tibetan Government as a radio officer in Kham's capital, Chamdo, was shocked by an announcement on Radio Peking. 'The tasks for the People's Liberation Army for 1950,' intoned the voice, 'are to liberate Formosa [Taiwan], Hainan[17] and Tibet from American and British Imperialism.'[18] Ford did a mental count: there were no Americans in Tibet, and the only Britons were Richardson (soon due to leave and hand over to his Indian counterpart), Reginald Fox, another radio operator, in Lhasa (crippled with rheumatoid arthritis), and Ford himself in Chamdo. Four 'foreign imperialists' in all, unless one included the Austrians, Harrer and Aufschnaiter. Listening to news broadcasts in both English and Tibetan, Ford regularly heard the same unvarying message. 'There was no criticism of Tibet's feudal system, no promise of land reform, no appeal to the workers to rise up and throw off their chains. It was simply a matter of getting rid of American and British Imperialism.'[19]

When the border regions succumbed to the Communists in 1949, apprehension in Lhasa turned to panic. Military training, deliberately run down since the Great Thirteenth's death because of opposition by the powerful Abbots – they had accepted supplies of arms from the Indian Government, but had declined all offers of training in their use[20] – was belatedly started. Kundun was called upon to consecrate the Army's new colours – when Chiang Kai-shek's armies were already fleeing to Taiwan. In any case, the Army amounted to only ten thousand men, and what chance would they have against the battle-hardened Communists?

Too late, the Tibetan Government realized the folly of the isolationism long imposed on it by the monks. ('The monks,' says Hugh Richardson, 'far more than the nobles, were responsible for the fall of Tibet, by failing to see that foreign contacts could have been used to safeguard their religion rather than undermine it.'[21]) Belatedly, they began broadcasting their own claims to independence – in Tibetan, Chinese and English – through Radio Lhasa, the station Robert Ford had built and opened for them. In addition, they prepared to send four separate 'goodwill missions': to India, Nepal, the United Kingdom and the USA, to try and counter the Chinese propaganda and ask for help. But Peking intervened, stating that Tibet was not an independent state but an integral part of the Chinese People's Republic, and any talks that might take place must be in Peking. They warned – with India and Nepal in their sights – that any country receiving one of these proposed 'goodwill missions' would be considered as an enemy of the Chinese People's Republic. Thus was Tibet doomed from the outset. Though ministers fired off telegrams beseeching these formerly friendly nations to receive them, the replies were, as the Dalai Lama recalls, 'terribly disheartening'.

> The British Government expressed their deepest sympathy for the people of Tibet, and regretted that owing to Tibet's geographical position, since India had been granted independence they could not offer help. The Government of the United States replied in the same sense and declined to receive our delegation. The Indian Government also made clear that they would not give us military help and advised us not to offer any armed resistance.[22]

The only remaining possibility lay in talks with the Chinese.[23] Hoping against hope for a peaceful solution, the Tibetans were prepared to hold talks – on some neutral ground, not in Peking. The go-between was Gyalo Thondup's father-in-law, Chu Shi-kuei, now a member of Communist Peking's Mongolia and Tibet Commission Office.

Chu Shi-kuei asked the new Chinese Government to arrange a meeting with a Tibetan delegation in Hong Kong. When the British authorities refused to issue visas, he suggested New Delhi as a venue, perhaps in September after the arrival of the Chinese Ambassador, General Yuan. (Jawaharlal Nehru, Prime Minister of a newly-independent India, had lost no time in recognizing the new Chinese Communist Government.)

In Lhasa, the Government was doing what came naturally to it:

All the monks in Tibet were ordered to attend public services at which the Tibetan Bible was to be read aloud. New prayer-flags and prayer-wheels were set up everywhere. Rare and powerful amulets were brought out of old chests. Offerings were doubled and on all the mountains incense-fires burned, while the winds, turning the prayer-wheels, carried supplications to the protecting deities in all the corners of heaven. The people believed with rock-like faith that the power of religion would suffice to protect their independence.[24]

When the official State Oracle[25] was consulted, he proclaimed somewhat obviously, 'A powerful force threatens our sacred land from the north and east' and 'Our religion is in danger'. Lhasa was alive with rumours, people looked to the omens for comfort. But the omens were all bad. The previous year, a comet had been seen at night and around dawn in the direction of the hills south of Lhasa. It was regarded by the Tibetans as an omen of war; the last comet having been followed by the Chinese invasion of 1910. Other fearful signs were to follow: a gilded dragon on the roof of the Jokhang Temple began dripping water, though the season was dry and no rain had fallen; freak births among domestic animals were reported; and one night the capital of an ancient stone pillar, erected at the foot of the Potala Palace to seal the peace between China and Tibet, came crashing to the ground. Fear and uncertainty crept into even the stoutest hearts.

Then on 15 August came a devastating earthquake, the fifth largest in recorded history. In the late evening, Kundun was emerging from his outside washroom at the Norbulingka when the earth shook beneath his feet. When he went back inside,

I noticed that several pictures hanging on the wall were out of alignment. Just then, there was a terrific crash in the distance. I rushed back outside, followed by several sweepers. As we looked up into the sky, there was another crash, and another. It was like an artillery barrage.[26]

A huge red glow suffused the cloudless dark sky. Next day, the inhabitants of Lhasa learned from All-India Radio that a massive earthquake had struck in the Himalaya of south-eastern Tibet and that tremors had been felt all over Tibet and India. The destruction was colossal; the face of the earth had quite literally been changed. Mountains had become valleys, valleys raised up into mountains; and the Yarlung Tsang Po (Brahmaputra) River, its course diverted by an enormous landslide, flooded hundreds of villages and claimed thousands of victims.

How could a people as superstitious as the Tibetans not see this as heralding some unspeakable disaster? Even the Dalai Lama, who set little store by popular superstition, was unconvinced by Heinrich Harrer's assurance that there must be a purely scientific explanation. This, he felt, was 'beyond science, something truly mysterious'. Whatever the cause, the citizens of Lhasa were terrified. 'People began to whisper about "Lhamak", a Tibetan *Götterdämmerung*. The gods of Tibet were doing battle with the demons of China and the frightened Lhasa folk dared not speculate on the result.'[27]

At the beginning of October 1950, as the Tibetan delegates still waited hopefully in New Delhi, the People's Liberation Army swarmed across the Upper Yangtse River and attacked the Tibetan positions in Chamdo. The Twilight of the Gods had descended.

The Tibetan Eastern Command in Chamdo was hopelessly ill-equipped to defend a 200-mile border along the west bank of the Yangtse River. Poorly-trained and outnumbered ten to one, what hope did the Tibetans have against an army equipped with the latest automatic machines and weapons – and fresh from their victory in the Civil War? The Lhasa Government, still obsessed with its own feuds, tried to gather itself together but, with conflicting reports coming out of Kham, was unable to provide any coherent leadership. Eleven days after it began, the battle for eastern Tibet was over. The Tibetan army surrendered – and the way to Lhasa lay open. Radio Peking told the Chinese people that People's Army units had been sent into Tibet 'to free three million Tibetans from imperialist oppression and to consolidate national defences on the western borders of China'.

Regent Taktra, contemptuously known as 'the old man', was widely seen as a divisive force and in this overwhelming crisis had no option but to resign.[28] The people, sick to death of all Regents, were clamouring, through street-songs and wall-posters, for the young Dalai Lama to be made Head of State, even though at fifteen he was still three years short of his majority. At such a time the country needed to unite behind its rightful ruler. A decision of such magnitude, of course, had to be referred to the State Oracle. The latter, wrote Kundun, 'tottering under the weight of his huge, ceremonial head-dress, came over to where I sat and laid a *kata*, a white silk offering-scarf, on my lap with the words *Thu-la bap* – "His time has come".'[29]

Kundun protested at first, aware of his youth and inexperience. But, in the face of the looming catastrophe, how could he not accept? The prospect was daunting but

> I could no longer refuse to take up my responsibilities. I had to shoulder them, put my boyhood behind me, and immediately prepare myself to lead my country, as well as I was able, against the vast power of Communist China.[30]

The seventeenth of November 1950 was fixed for his investiture. Before it could take place, one more shock lay in store. At the beginning of November, Taktser arrived 'in a terrible state', to stammer out the Chinese ultimatum.

Kundun was stunned. 'My brother was supposed to trick me into submission and if he didn't succeed he was to kill me. We knew that Communists committed atrocities, of course; we had heard what happened in Mongolia and we had been warned by my predecessor's Last Testament. But this was the first time it had been brought home to me, the first time it had touched me personally. And it was my own brother, someone I knew well and trusted, who was telling me these things. I was very frightened.'[31]

To this boy king, largely ignorant of the outside world with its cruel ideologies, Taktser spelled out the realities of life under Chinese Communism, urging that the only hope for Tibet was to secure foreign support and to take up arms against the Chinese. Taktser's own mind had been made up during the long journey: he would renounce his monastic vows and go abroad, to become a spokesman for Tibet. He urged his brother to leave Lhasa with all speed before the Chinese cut off the escape routes to India.

Kundun was reluctant; there was so much to be done. He had begun his reign by announcing a general amnesty for prisoners and had many other reforms in mind. Now, when he looked down with his telescope from the Potala roof, he could see nothing and no one in the prison courtyard below, 'save for a few dogs scavenging for scraps'. His isolation was complete.

During the enthronement ceremony which took place at dawn on 17 November, he was handed the Golden Wheel which symbolized his assumption of supreme secular power. His heart sank. Though the people celebrated, he knew only too well that the situation was hopeless. He was just fifteen, head of a Government that had lost all credibility, undisputed leader of a people faced with a confrontation that they did not want, that they were certain to lose, but which they could not possibly avoid.

NOTES

1. Author interview with Gyalo Thondup, New Delhi, July 1995.

2. Peking fell to the Communists on 31 January 1949.

3. Norbu, *Tibet Is My Country*, chapter 16.

4. One of the original supporters of Dr Sun Yat-sen, the revolutionary leader who had overthrown the Manchu Empire in 1912.

5. Author interview with Gyalo Thondup, New Delhi, July 1995.

6. Author interview with Gyalo Thondup, New Delhi, July 1995.

7. Author interview with Gyalo Thondup, New Delhi, July 1995.

8. *Tibet Is My Country*, chapter 17.

9. *Tibet Is My Country*, chapter 17.

10. *Tibet Is My Country*, chapter 17.

11. *Tibet Is My Country*, chapter 18.

12. *Tibet Is My Country*, chapter 18.

13. *Tibet Is My Country*, chapter 18.

14. *Tibet Is My Country*, chapter 18.

15. *Tibet Is My Country*, chapter 18.

16. Warren W. Smith, 'The Nationalities Policy of the Chinese Communist Party and the Socialist Transformation of Tibet', Robert Barnett and Shirin Akiner, eds., *Resistance and Reform in Tibet*, C. Hurst and Co., 1994.

17. On 16 April 1950, the Communists invaded Hainan and had taken it a week later.

18. Robert Ford, *Captured in Tibet*, Harrap, 1957, reissued OUP, 1990.

19. Ford, *Captured in Tibet*.

20. Letter from Hugh Richardson to the author, 12 December 1993.

21. Letter from Hugh Richardson to the author, 12 December 1993.

22. Fourteenth Dalai Lama, *My Land and My People*.

23. For a full account, see Goldstein, *A History of Modern Tibet*, chapter 18.

24. Harrer, *Seven Years in Tibet*.

25. Tibetan oracles are not soothsayers or foretellers of the future, but men and women who act as mediums between the natural and the spiritual worlds.

26. Fourteenth Dalai Lama, *Freedom in Exile*, chapter 3.

27. From an unpublished manuscript shown to the author by Jamyang Norbu.

28. He remained as Senior Tutor but died a year later.

29. *Freedom in Exile*, chapter 3.

30. *My Land and My People*.

31. Author interview with the Dalai Lama, Dharamsala, June 1994.

A Flight and a Return

The Chinese have...a profound regard for history. But history, for them, was not simply a scientific study. It had the features of a cult, akin to ancestor worship, with the ritual object of presenting the past, favourably emended and touched up, as a model for current political action. It had to conform also to the mystical view of China as the Centre of the World, the Universal Empire in which every other country had a natural urge to become a part...The Communists...were the first Chinese to have the power to convert their atavistic theories into fact. They saw their opportunity, calculated that no one was likely to oppose them, and acted.

Hugh Richardson, Tibet and its History

People in the West often wonder why the Han Chinese were so keen to annex Tibet. The answer is four-pronged: land, mineral resources, strategic position and naked power. The vast emptiness of Tibet could provide living-room for China's surplus millions; her untapped resources of mineral wealth beckoned; and, once in possession of the land which was the highest point on the planet, China would have strategic mastery over the rest of Asia.

Whatever its reasons, China was determined to claim Tibet for itself. Taktser reported in detail to the Kashag on Peking's plans to swallow up the entire country. Learning that the UN had recently mounted a rescue operation for a South Korea attacked by the Communist North, the National Assembly appealed to that Organization, pleading that the Chinese invasion of Tibet was an equally flagrant 'violation of the weak by the strong'. Tibet begged India to present its appeal to the UN, warning that the destruction of Tibet as a buffer state would imperil India's own security. But since gaining Independence in 1947, Prime Minister Nehru had rejected the old concept of Tibet as a buffer against China and the Soviet Union, in favour of a friendship with China which would bring peace and stability to Asia. Nehru would say or do nothing to displease China.

In the UN, only El Salvador sponsored a move to condemn the Chinese onslaught on Tibet. The British delegate – cravenly turning his back on Britain's long friendship with Tibet and tacit acceptance of Tibetan independence – commented weakly that Tibet's legal status was 'confusing'. Both Britain and India voted to do nothing. (To the Tibetans, Britain's betrayal was the unkindest cut of all.) The US, sympathetic but already committed to an expensive war in Korea, agreed that the question of Tibet should be shelved. 'Our friends would not even help us to present our plea for justice,' lamented the Dalai Lama. 'We felt abandoned to the hordes of the Chinese Army.' And in that grim November of 1950, that is precisely what they were.

The atmosphere in Lhasa was tense, with many of the nobles already fleeing the country. The National Assembly begged the Dalai Lama to leave immediately for Dromo, a village in the Chumbi Valley, less than three hundred miles away, just six miles from the border with India. From there he could plead his country's cause, and, if necessary, escape into India. The departure had to be a close-kept secret, because if the people came to hear of it, they might panic and try to prevent him leaving. Kundun was reluctant, but the argument that it was not he himself but the sacred person of the Dalai Lama – the very soul and essence of Tibet – which must be protected at all costs could not be denied. (The Chinese knew well that the key to a peaceful take-over of Tibet lay in their being able to take control of the Dalai Lama's person.) So Kundun resigned himself to the inevitable – 'I had to allow my people to take far more care of me than I would have thought of taking for myself.'[1]

Lobsang Samten, now a Government official, had been ill with what the doctors had diagnosed as a heart condition – but later turned out to be a nervous breakdown. 'He was so ill,' recounts his future wife, Namlha, 'that for a time people thought he was actually dead. He wouldn't speak, couldn't eat, simply stayed in bed. If Lobsang was to go with his brother – and he desperately wanted to – he would have to be carried on a stretcher as far as Dromo.'²

Taktser's problems were of a different kind. He knew it would not be long before the Chinese discovered he had double-crossed them, and therefore it was imperative for him to leave Tibet without delay. He persuaded his mother to go at once with the younger children to the family estate at Gyantse and wait for him there. Bidding farewell to the monastery of Drepung, he exchanged his monk's robes for ordinary layman's clothes and began the journey which would take him out of Tibet – and the monastic life – for ever.

Distressed though she was by this fresh upheaval, Amala knew there was no alternative if Kundun were not to fall into Chinese hands. Later, she remembered little of the journey to Dromo, except the exhaustion of long hours in the saddle. As Great Mother, she was entitled to travel in a palanquin, but she always refused the privileges of rank and elected to ride like everyone else. And as they journeyed by night and early morning to avoid the stinging sandstorms which blew by day across the open plateau, riding – often in fifty degrees of frost – was a nightmare.

Leaving Lhasa is Tendzin Choegyal's earliest memory: 'I remember the morning we left. Lobsang Samten was too ill to travel and was coming on later with His Holiness. But he had come out to the courtyard to say goodbye to Amala. It was very early in the morning, before daybreak. I could see the outline of my brother and my mother against the background of a starry sky. They were embracing, saying goodbye.'³ The five-year-old was carried on horseback by a servant, so small that the man simply tucked him in the pouch of his *chuba* – 'like a kangaroo...except that I was facing the wrong way'. He remembers that 'it was bitterly cold and my feet never warmed up'.

The Tibetan Government had already begun despatching over a thousand pack-animals, each laden with treasure, towards the border. Forty mules carried gold dust, six hundred carried bars of silver and the rest sacks of old coins⁴ – all to be concealed somewhere on the estates of the Maharajah of Sikkim.

Late in the evening of 18 December, Kundun and his officials drank a symbolic last cup of butter-tea in the Potala. That done, they refilled their cups and left them standing there, in token of their hope of a speedy return. At about 2 a.m., the young ruler, wearing layman's clothing: 'a rich coat of dark red silk lined with fur, a fur hat and woollen muffler',[5] left Lhasa with an entourage of 40 nobles, a 200-strong bodyguard and about 1500 pack animals. There was a hold-up on the outskirts of Lhasa when thousands of monks streamed onto the road to try and prevent his departure. Only with difficulty were they persuaded to let the caravan proceed. Even then, the monks threw themselves down on the track and begged Kundun to return as soon as possible.

The caravan went on its way, crossing three high passes, one of them 17,000 feet above sea level. Heinrich Harrer met them at Gyantse, horrified to see his friend, Lobsang Samten, being carried on a litter and to find that 'the doctors had used the same rough methods on him as they do on a sick horse. On the day the convoy was to leave he had lain in a swoon for several hours, so the Dalai Lama's physician recalled him to life by applying a branding-iron to his flesh.'[6]

Then on to Phari (the highest town in Tibet), before dropping down into the deep and narrow Chumbi Valley, the main channel of trade between Tibet and India, just inside Sikkim on the southern slopes of the Himalaya.[7] At the far end of the valley, squeezed in between vertical cliffs, stood Dromo, with its 'four rows of half-timbered cottages roofed with shingles, flanking two longitudinal streets of which the bigger, with its little shops, constitutes the market'.[8] The huge caravan arrived there – weary and half-frozen – on 2 January 1951, after a journey of sixteen days.

Accommodation was hard to find. For the first month, Kundun stayed in the house of the district Governor (renamed Heavenly Palace of Universal Light and Peace in his honour). Then, since hardly any light reached that house and it was piercingly cold, he moved to the small hillside monastery of Dungkhar, where Taktser was also staying. From there he could keep in touch by courier with those members of the Government who had remained in Lhasa. The rest of his family, the nobles, officials and Heinrich Harrer (who was leaving for India), were quartered in small cottages or scattered farmsteads. Some of the officials' families went directly to the Tibetan enclaves of Kalimpong or Darjeeling across the border, and, as soon as sufficient military checkpoints had been set up, the bodyguard was sent back to Lhasa.

The Chinese, meanwhile, wanting to show the world that they favoured diplomacy over force (and waiting to see how the UN would respond to Tibet's appeal), had halted their military advance about one hundred miles to the north-east of Lhasa and were offering peace talks – in Peking. The

Kashag, being in no position to argue, authorized the group of five officials still on standby in New Delhi to go to Peking and salvage whatever they could for Tibet. (The group's interpreter was Phuntsok Tashi, now an official in the Department of Foreign Affairs.)

With the Government of Tibet completely paralysed, Kundun's rigorous schedule was relaxed. When spring came, he and the now convalescent Lobsang were free to make long treks into the hills, getting rid of their pent-up energies by striding ahead of their largely overweight attendants. 'They fell behind constantly,' said Lobsang, 'but we could always tell where they were by the sound of their panting.'⁹ The brothers visited 'every monastery, shrine and temple in the entire area'.

Tendzin Choegyal was staying with his mother, Tsering Dolma, Pema, Tenzin Ngawang and Khando, in a small wooden house, so tiny that the younger children were packed off outdoors each day with a picnic lunch. 'We used to chase small birds from one bush to another. I remember the ice-cold water, crystal clear, and the masses of wild flowers. We played with pebbles. And Mr Harrer used to come. He brought us chocolate, and that was the first time I had ever tasted it. My sister, Pema, was at school in India, so she was learning English. At first I was allowed to sit in on the lessons. But I was too naughty, and they kicked me out.'¹⁰

Pema, with Tenzin Ngawang and Khando, had been sent to India a year previously. They had travelled with Tsering Dolma who was ill and had to be carried in a palanquin placed on the backs of two mules. While Tsering Dolma sought medical treatment in Calcutta, the children were sent to St Joseph's Convent in Kalimpong, transplanted suddenly into a world of school uniforms, huge dormitories and the unfamiliar English language. The change was traumatic, especially for five-year-old Khando who had never been left alone at night before. 'From the very first evening,' wrote Pema, 'the nuns decided to put her near me. I was suddenly wakened from a deep sleep by the sound of stifled sobs. My niece had just fallen out of bed. I took her in with me, consoled her, and I believe she fell asleep in my arms.'¹¹ When one day, the children heard that the family were coming to Dromo and that they were to pass the winter of 1950/1 together, they were 'mad with joy'. 'I must admit,' says Pema, 'that we did not understand the real reasons that had brought His Holiness to Dromo.'

The idyll was soon to be shattered. In Peking, the Tibetan delegation, under orders not to sign anything without reference to Lhasa, discovered that the Chinese did not intend to discuss peace terms so much as dictate them. They were insulted, abused, threatened and coerced into signing (on 23 May 1951) a Seventeen-Point Agreement, the only choice being between 'peaceful liberation' and the annihilation that would follow a renewal of the fighting. The Agreement was sealed with a replica of the Dalai Lama's personal seal, newly forged in Peking. This, the first treaty concluded between China and Tibet since AD 821, was a vaguely-worded document which promised to leave intact the Dalai Lama's authority and the political system of Tibet; and to respect the religion, language and customs of the Tibetans. No question, however, of genuine autonomy or independence, since it declared that Tibet was part of China and that henceforth all policy-making, both domestic and foreign, would be taken over by Peking. Clause One stipulated that:

> The Tibetan people shall unite and drive out imperialist aggressive forces from Tibet. The Tibetan people shall return to the big family of the Motherland – the People's Republic of China.

Kundun heard the news three days later from a Tibetan language broadcast on Peking Radio. Tuning in to a crackly old Bush radio receiver, he heard a strident voice announce the signing of a Seventeen-Point 'Agreement for the Peaceful Liberation of Tibet' by representatives of People's China and the 'local government' of Tibet. Kundun sat transfixed:

> The speaker described how 'over the last hundred years or more', aggressive imperialist forces had penetrated into Tibet and carried out 'all kinds of deceptions and provocation'. It added that 'under such conditions, the Tibetan nationality and people were plunged into the depths of enslavement and suffering'. I felt physically ill as I listened to this unbelievable mixture of lies and fanciful clichés.[12]

But, being both helpless and alone, the Tibetans had no choice but to accept their fate and hope that China would keep its side of 'this forced, one-sided bargain'.[13] Even now, they did not realize how cleverly the Chinese had played their cards. As Goldstein observes, 'This "peaceful" liberation avoided the very negative international criticism that renewed military liberation would probably have produced, and it precluded the possibility of interference from anti-Communist countries such as the United States if fighting was renewed.'[14]

Now that Tibet had been abandoned to its fate, there was a heated debate about whether or not the Dalai Lama should accept the Agreement and return to Lhasa, or 'denounce it, go into exile, and launch a political and military struggle against the Communists'.[15] The majority of his monastic advisers wanted him to return home. (It would not have crossed their minds that the Chinese would actually try to destroy Buddhism; but they foresaw trouble for themselves if Kundun did not return.) Others, including Harrer (who was already in Kalimpong), urged him to go to India and look for allies in the fight against the Chinese. Peking was putting pressure on Taktser to dissuade his brother from leaving the country. But Taktser, convinced, not least because of his own experience, that his brother was surrounded by Chinese Communist spies, begged him to go to India and from there to the United States. In this he was supported by Amala.

Taktser was now determined 'to seek that freedom abroad which I already knew from bitter experience was impossible under Communist rule'.[16] Enlisting the help of a friend who was already in the United States, he received an encouraging response. He then sought Kundun's permission to take his mother and the younger children on a pilgrimage to India, where he would arrange for a medical check-up. Kundun had been notified that the newly-appointed Commissioner and Administrator of Civil and Military Affairs in Tibet, General Chiang Chin-wu, was travelling to Lhasa via the Chumbi Valley – and was to escort him back to the capital. Taktser, knowing he must be gone when the General arrived, hastened, with much sadness, to say goodbye to his brothers.

> They knew nothing of my ultimate plans, and I could not bring myself to add to their sorrow and distress by revealing them. Would I ever see either of them again? And if so, under what circumstances?[17]

The younger children were excited at the prospect of the pilgrimage. But Taktser's heart was heavy:

> I knew that in all probability I should never again set foot on Tibetan soil, that I should never again return to my home. Voluntarily, I was now turning my back on my country for ever.'[18]

When General Chiang arrived in Dromo, Kundun was peering out of a window at Dungkar Monastery to catch a glimpse of him, half-convinced that all the Chinese would have horns and tails:

I don't know exactly what I expected, but what I saw was three men in grey suits and peaked caps who looked extremely drab and insignificant among the splendid figures of my officials in their red and golden robes. Had I but known, the drabness was the state to which China was to reduce us all before the end, and the insignificance was certainly an illusion.[19]

He left Dromo on 21 July with Lobsang Samten on horseback, though he was no lover of horses. For once, though, he was glad of the freedom of riding across the open plains and continually urged his mount forwards. (It was actually only a mule called Grey Wheels, and the Head Groom was disgusted that the Dalai Lama had been given such an inferior mount.) He arrived back in Lhasa in mid-August, after a nine-month absence. The people turned out *en masse* to welcome him. But, amid the demonstrations of public joy, he detected an undertow of hysteria. Reports had begun reaching the capital of atrocities in the eastern areas of Kham and Amdo. Fear and foreboding were in the air. Yet, quite irrationally, there was also a conviction that with Kundun's return, all would surely be well.

Hope died on 9 September when 3,000 troops of the Chinese 18th Route Army entered Lhasa, 'tubas and drums blaring, portraits of Mao and Chou En-lai held aloft, between phalanxes of China's red flag, one of whose four small orbs, circling the great yellow star at its centre, was now Tibet'.[20] Within three months two more contingents had arrived – about 20,000 soldiers, backed up by 30,000 camels and horses which they had commandeered along the way. On 24 October, after a meeting of the National Assembly, the Dalai Lama reluctantly approved the Seventeen-Point Agreement, and Tibet officially became part of the People's Republic of China. The bell had tolled for the Tibetan way of life. But as *Life* magazine mused, one crucial question hung in the air: now that the Dalai Lama had returned home, would he become merely 'one more in the succession of Moscow-pulled puppets'?[21]

NOTES

1. Quoted by Goodman, *The Last Dalai Lama*.

2. Author interview, Namlha Taklha, Dharamsala, October 1993.

3. Author interview with Tendzin Choegyal, Dharamsala, November 1993.

4. Avedon, *In Exile from the Land of Snows*, p. 91.

5. 'Flight of the Dalai Lama', *Life* magazine, 23 April 1951.

6. Harrer, *Seven Years in Tibet*.

7. Sikkim was originally an independent Buddhist Himalayan kingdom strongly linked to Tibet. In 1861, however, the British had annexed some of its southern territory, including Darjeeling. Although theoretically still a sovereign state, in practice the British administered Sikkim in much the same way as any other Himalayan state with whom they had an agreement. When they left India in 1947 the Indian Government took over the administration of these northern states, and in 1975 Indira Gandhi sent Indian troops into Sikkim to depose its ruling king and incorporate Sikkim into India proper. The issue is still a running sore in Indian politics.

8. Fosco Maraini, *Secret Tibet*, Hutchinson/Readers Union, 1954.

9. Goodman.

10. Author interview with Tendzin Choegyal, Dharamsala, November 1993.

11. Jetsun Pema, *Tibet, Mon Histoire*.

12. Fourteenth Dalai Lama, *Freedom in Exile*.

13. Fourteenth Dalai Lama, *My Land and My People*, p. 88.

14. Goldstein, *A History of Modern Tibet*, p. 772.

15. Goldstein, p. 773.

16. *Tibet Is My Country*.

17. *Tibet Is My Country*.

18. *Tibet Is My Country*.

19. *My Land and My People*.

20. *In Exile from the Land of Snows*.

21. 'Flight of the Dalai Lama', *Life* magazine, 23 April 1951.

12

The Brothers

By November 1951 it was clear that, to effect their aim of political domination, the Chinese intended to use the old form
of government as their instrument and mouthpiece to control
every aspect of Tibetan domestic affairs. The presence of the
Dalai Lama at Lhasa was an essential part of that design; but
an equally important part was the reduction of his absolute
power and divine prestige. Inroads on his authority and on
that of the monasteries, from which much of his support was
derived, began almost at once.

Hugh Richardson, Tibet and its History

Three-year-old Tendzin Choegyal had been recognized as the sixteenth
reincarnation of the former illustrious teacher, Ngari Rinpoche. 'My immediate predecessor,' he says today, 'was a fairly worldly person, interested in building houses, planting small saplings, digging springs. He was also
a skilled administrator, and with his interest in small mechanical gadgets,
you could say that, like the Thirteenth Dalai Lama, he was a man before
his time. I'm told that when he and the Great Thirteenth were studying
with the same teacher, they became good friends. And when the Fourteenth Dalai Lama arrived from Amdo, Ngari Rinpoche was among the
crowds outside Lhasa to welcome him.'[1]

When the Fifteenth Ngari Rinpoche died, the Gadung Oracle prophesied
that he would be reborn in the house of the Yapshi Taklha;[2] and so he was.

(As Hugh Richardson comments, 'the Ngari Rinpoche was not *per se* very high, but added lustre was conferred on the role by a brother of the Dalai Lama.'³) Tendzin Choegyal, already recognized as being the reincarnation of his own older brother, was now proclaimed to be the reborn Ngari Rinpoche as well. (Nobody seems to have noticed anything bizarre in this double achievement!) The fact that three of Amala's sons were now recognized *tulkus* set the seal on her reputation as the greatest of all Great Mothers: her achievement was unique in the Tibetan Buddhist tradition. Many in Lhasa believed her to be the goddess Tara reincarnated; and no one wondered that the Dalai Lama had been born to such a mother. As her friend, Rinchen Dolma Taring, recalls: 'She was unique, a truly great woman; she had no anger, no hatred, no greed, no jealousy towards anyone. She was a luminous person.'⁴

To be recognized as a *tulku* was the highest of honours. But it placed a heavy load of responsibility on young shoulders which were often ill-equipped to carry it. Tendzin Choegyal was a high-spirited child who would always find monastic discipline stifling. Now in his early fifties, he voices serious doubts about choosing young children as *tulkus*:

> I don't discount the possibility of reincarnation. We do have a past and will have a future. But choosing a particular person as a particular reincarnation of another particular person, I think that's very dicey. After all, this system developed nowhere but in Tibet and then only at quite a late stage. So, on all sorts of grounds, I have very mixed feelings.⁵

His brother, Taktser Rinpoche, who renounced the monastic state on leaving Tibet and adopted his other name, Thubten Jigme Norbu,⁶ had long had similar doubts. After all, the system was not guaranteed infallible; mistakes could be – and presumably were – made. 'I suppose it would be strange,' he wrote, 'if I did not wonder, as I do, if I really *am* Taktser's reincarnation. The Gyalwa Rinpoche [Dalai Lama] believed it; everyone else believes it; but I myself, I just do not know.'⁷

As the years passed, his attitude remained ambivalent and today the question seems to bore him: 'Well, I certainly could never remember anything about a previous life,' he says. 'But then I can't remember what I did yesterday, let alone in a previous existence. All I can say is that it's our Tibetan custom, so I go along with it. If the Tibetans think I'm a reincarnation, all right. I don't care one way or the other. Everyone still calls me Rinpoche but they could say I was a reincarnated donkey for all I'd care.'⁸

Not all *tulkus* lived up to the high ideals expected of them. In the early eighteenth century, the Sixth Dalai Lama turned out to be a libertine given to the pursuit of girls rather than sanctity.[9] But Tibetans believe that everyone is entitled to work through each of his lives in his own way, and anyway once a Rinpoche, always a Rinpoche. The monk's robes may be discarded, but one's acknowledgement as the reincarnation of a great teacher cannot be set aside. Probably neither Norbu nor Tendzin Choegyal was suited to the position assigned to them in childhood, but for many years both of them accepted it. And though both have long since renounced their vows and married, they will continue to be addressed as Rinpoche by their fellow Tibetans for as long as they live.

The Dalai Lama, saddened by their defection, believes that if history hadn't intervened his brothers would still be in their monasteries. Not surprisingly, he defends the *tulku* tradition, though with less force than one might have expected. 'There's good and bad in it, as in most traditions,' he explains. 'In our practice of choosing boys as a rebirth of some important teacher there is something positive and something negative. They do receive very special nurturing, and if that goes well it's a very positive thing. Sometimes they themselves become very special teachers. But, in cases where the young boy becomes arrogant and uses his position as a social status, manipulating other people to his own ends, then that's very bad. And yes, it does happen.'[10]

There was no sudden dramatic change in Tendzin Choegyal's life. He was not instantly taken away to the monastery but continued to live at home with his mother, with a monk from Drepung as tutor. 'I was a *tulku* but I still had to do as I was told and got into trouble if I didn't. Nevertheless, as the youngest, I suppose I *was* a bit spoilt.'[11] To Pema and Khando that is an understatement: 'He was manifestly treated in a very special way and everyone, servants, monks, friends, visitors, danced attendance on him...When we played together, we always had to obey his every whim.'[12] For instance, as Pema recounts,

My sister had a beautiful black mare which had borne a magnificent foal. As the foal got bigger, my brother decided he wanted to ride it...on the roof of our house. The servants were packed off to find the foal. Then they had to get it up the stairs...When they got the foal up to the top, the spectacle was impressive. Never before in the memory of any Tibetan had a horse been seen on a roof. On the way down, when my brother's caprice was satisfied, the servants had to hold the foal by the tail to prevent him falling.[13]

But at least Tendzin Choegyal shared the life of the family and to some extent at least was treated as an ordinary human being. It was not so with
Kundun. He addressed his mother as Amala and his younger siblings by
their names, but to them he was always the Dalai Lama and their attitude
towards him was one of the deepest respect.

When Tendzin Choegyal was four (in 1950), his mother took him to the
monastery built by the first Ngari Rinpoche at Kumulung outside Lhasa;
and there he was solemnly enthroned as the latest Incarnation of the ancient lineage. He remembers nothing about the ceremony, and he and his
mother returned home together a week later. It cannot be said, however,
that life then returned to normal, for the time exactly coincided with the
Chinese invasion and the family's flight from Lhasa.

When Amala and the younger children left Dromo with Norbu, they followed the ancient caravan route over the main range of the Himalaya by
the Nathu la Pass (14,800 feet) into Gangtok, the capital of mountainous,
jungly Sikkim, 'a toy capital, with a toy bazaar, toy gardens and toy houses, set among tree-ferns and wild orchids on a hillside among the
clouds...It is connected with the rest of the world by telegraph...it has a
post-office, a hospital and the Maharajah's palace. All the same you feel
out of the world. The whole thing is a fairy-tale.'[14]

Tendzin Choegyal has two vivid memories of this journey into fairy-
tale. The first is of being in disgrace for breaking a teapot in one of the
bungalows established by the British trade missions. 'The keeper of the
bungalow was terribly upset because he didn't know how he could account for the breakage. So my mother bought a new one when we went to
India, and we gave it him on the return journey. It was a dark brown pot,
mass-produced, probably in Stoke-on-Trent, or somewhere.'[15] The second
memory is of his first introduction to one of his abiding later passions, the
motor car. He was scared nearly out of his wits on first sighting the old
English Austin which had been sent to take them into the town:

> I was so frightened, it looked like a huge insect with two bright eyes. And the
> noise of the horn terrified me. I refused to ride in it so was allowed to contin-
> ue on horseback till we stopped for the night. Next day we were to go to Gang-
> tok, and the driver, a Nepalese, persuaded me very gently to approach the car
> and got me to touch it and stroke it and smell the leather seats. He was such a
> sensitive, understanding man. I loved it when he made the indicators flick in

and out. Later that evening, I agreed to go in the car with my mother. I was in for another shock when it got dark and they put the car lights on. The dashboard was a marvellous sight. That was the moment I fell in love with cars, and I've loved them ever since.[16]

From Gangtok they crossed the southern ridge of the Himalaya down to Kalimpong in the far north of Bengal, the traditional centre for trade (particularly in wool, musk and yak-tails) between Tibet and India, where many Tibetans had come to live. Here Norbu heard that the American Committee for Free Asia – the CIA under another name – had invited him to the USA for a year as their guest. With his immediate future thus assured, he was able at last to tell Amala and Tsering Dolma of his plans. Though naturally upset at the prospect of his departure, they understood his reasons and gave him their blessing.

Norbu left for Calcutta, to make arrangements for the journey; and from there wrote to tell Kundun that he was on his way to America. 'He wrote me this long letter,' recalls Kundun, 'saying that he saw no alternative and that therefore we might not meet again for a very long time. "Whether or not we meet again in this life, till Buddha-hood do not forget me," he wrote, using the words of our Buddhist farewell. It was a very sad moment for me.'[17]

In Calcutta, Norbu ran into the Tibetan delegates on their way back from signing the Agreement in Peking. They were all (including Phuntsok Tashi) firmly lodged in the Chinese Embassy, under the watchful eye of General Chiang Chin-wu who was on his way to Dromo to escort Kundun back to Lhasa. Norbu was urged (rather too warmly for his peace of mind) to join the party, and had to pretend to be considering the matter. At the first opportunity, however, he took his brother-in-law on one side and told him he was flying to New York that very night. Phuntsok Tashi, though alarmed, promised not to betray him.

In the USA, news that the Dalai Lama's brother was shortly to arrive had somehow leaked out, and at Idlewild Airport Norbu was greeted by 'a barrage of exploding flashlights' and surrounded by excited journalists. His host was Robert Ekvall, the son of Christian missionaries who had worked for many years in Amdo and spoke the dialect fluently. From now on it was plain sailing. As Norbu soon realized, 'Everyone's door was open to the Dalai Lama's brother.'

When at last he received the much-needed medical check-up and was found to have congestion of the lungs, Ekvall arranged treatment for him and placed a small farmstead in Fairfax, West Virginia, at his disposal. Hardly had Norbu arrived there than a telegram came from Gyalo Thondup announcing the imminent arrival of himself and family.

Before the Chinese actually invaded Tibet, Gyalo Thondup had hoped to go to Peking to resume his studies and find some way of helping his country. His decision was, he admits, irrational and naïve, but he had to do something. 'I tried to get a visa to travel via Hong Kong but the British wouldn't give me one. Then I thought, maybe I could go by way of Macao, or perhaps via the Philippines. I decided on the latter. It was an unlucky choice. There I was contacted by former Kuomintang friends who persuaded me to go to Taiwan instead.'[18] He was in Taiwan for sixteen months.

He was a welcome guest on this island where Chiang Kai-shek had re-established his Nationalist Chinese Government: 'The Generalissimo and Madame Chiang Kai-shek were very pleased to see me and tried to persuade me to settle in Taiwan, to take a job in the Tibetan Affairs section of the Government Service. But I was becoming increasingly anxious. The Communists had now begun their invasion of Tibet and I wanted to help my brother somehow. After all, I'd surely have been useful to the Tibetan Government as an interpreter. So, despite the danger, I felt I ought to go back.'

Unfortunately for Gyalo Thondup, the Kuomintang Security Department had discovered the letter which the Communist Marshal Chu-deh had written him in 1949. Naturally enough, they were suspicious.

> I suppose they had begun to think I might be a Communist spy, or at least was ripe for exploitation by the Communists...Government officials, some of whom had been my teachers at the University in Nanking, began inviting me to their houses and getting at me. They would say things like, 'Gyalo, the Chinese Communist Party is like a beautiful girl, but her beauty is skin-deep, she is riddled with disease.' Since I didn't know my letter from Marshal Chu-deh had fallen into the hands of Chinese Intelligence, I didn't know what on earth they were talking about. But I soon realized I was under virtual house-arrest. I can't claim it was uncomfortable – my wife, baby daughter and I were lodged in the Grand Hotel – but there was no doubt I was under surveillance.

The only other people staying in the hotel were American military advisers. Gyalo Thondup became friendly with one of these and used to go fishing with him. One day the American suggested that if he cared to write to President Truman, or to the Secretary of State, Dean Acheson, asking for permission to study in the USA, he would deliver the letter personally. 'My wife and I sat down and composed a letter and gave it to him, just as he was leaving for a visit to the US. Not long after, a friend of mine in the Kuomintang came rushing into the hotel, saying, 'Mr Thondup, Mr Thondup, we've had a letter from the American Secretary of State, asking us to let you go to the USA, so you're free to go.'[19]

The Generalissimo and his wife accepted defeat with a good grace, giving GT a sumptuous farewell dinner and $50,000 towards his education. But the British still would not give him a transit visa for Hong Kong. His wife, Zhu Dan, had no difficulty – since her mother was currently in Hong Kong, but Gyalo Thondup was forced to go via Japan. Zhu Dan joined him in Tokyo with their baby daughter, and they travelled together to the USA and the farmhouse where Norbu was staying.

Hardly had he arrived – in September 1951 – than he announced his intention of returning to Tibet. His new acquaintances in the State Department offered him a Scholarship to Stanford University and did their best to dissuade him from such suicidal folly. He appreciated their concern, and was indeed tempted by their offer. 'But, as I kept telling my friends, my obligation was to serve Tibet in her hour of need. My conscience wouldn't let me stay. I knew how ignorant most Tibetans were about China and Chinese Communists. Well, I didn't know the Communists, but I did know the Chinese and the way their minds worked.' His mind was made up.

His brother was furious.

Norbu said he knew what the Communists were like better than I did and I would be crazy to go back. But I knew I had to go. I told them all, 'Tibet is a huge country, the Chinese won't be able to control everybody there. In any case, if I can't handle it, then I'll escape to India.' Crazy talk, but I was young and young people are like that. They said it would be impossible to escape from Tibet, but I laughed at them. I knew the terrain well and there was a 2,000-mile border between India and Tibet. The Chinese couldn't have eyes everywhere.[20]

So in February 1952, Gyalo Thondup returned to India via Darjeeling, where he left Zhu Dan, now pregnant with their second child. Pema, Tenzin Ngawang and Khando would join her there and go to school. He had alerted his mother to wait for him in Kalimpong.

Amala, Tsering Dolma and the children had been on pilgrimage to the sacred Buddhist places of India and Nepal. But the sweltering heat of the Bengali plains had driven them to cut short the pilgrimage and return to the relative coolness of Kalimpong, where friends had been loaned them a house.

The family were in Kalimpong in October 1951 when the People's Liberation Army entered Lhasa and Tibet was swallowed up by China. Amala feared for her other two sons and for her widowed mother who had been brought from Amdo to live with the family in Lhasa. She could neither sleep nor eat and lost weight alarmingly. Since no local doctor was able to suggest a remedy, a Tibetan doctor travelled from Lhasa with a supply of herbal medicines. By early 1952 she was pronounced fit enough to travel, and as soon as Gyalo Thondup arrived, the family set out on the return journey.

Whatever their apprehension about the future, they were going home. When Amala caught sight of the Potala's golden turrets gleaming in the sunlight, she felt as though a weight had been lifted from her shoulders.[21]

NOTES

1. Author interview with Tendzin Choegyal, July 1995.
2. Families of Dalai Lamas were known as Yapshi families.
3. Letter to the author, 12 December 1993.
4. Letter to the author, 6 November 1993.
5. Author interview with Tendzin Choegyal, Dharamsala, November 1993.
6. Since this time, he has been usually known as Norbu.
7. Norbu, *Tibet.*
8. Author interview with Thubten Jigme Norbu, Dharamsala, July 1995.
9. He was also a fine lyrical poet.
10. Author interview with HH the Dalai Lama, Dharamsala, June 1994.
11. Author interview with Tendzin Choegyal, Dharamsala, June 1994.
12. Jetsun Pema, *Tibet, Mon Histoire,* my translation.
13. Jetsun Pema, *Tibet, Mon Histoire,* my translation..
14. Fosco Maraini, *Secret Tibet*162.
15. Author interview with Tendzin Choegyal, Dharamsala, June 1994.
16. Author interview with Tendzin Choegyal, Dharamsala, June 1994.
17. Author interview with HH the Dalai Lama, Dharamsala, June 1994.

18. Video recording made by Gyalo Thondup for the monks of Namgyal Monastery, Dharamsala in 1991.
19. Author interview with Gyalo Thondup, New Delhi, July 1995.
20. Author interview with Gyalo Thondup, New Delhi, July 1995.
21. Goodman, *The Last Dalai Lama*.

13

Gyalo Thondup in Lhasa 1952

How can there be laughter, how can there be pleasure, when
the whole world is burning? When you are in deep darkness,
will you not ask for a lamp?

The Dhammapada

When the Chinese 18th Army first marched into Lhasa, the inhabitants
had clapped their hands, not in applause but in the time-honoured way for
driving out evil. Children threw rocks and stones and many of the monks
were observed 'knotting the ends of their shawls and hitting the Chinese
who were riding by'.[1]

This first phase of the occupation of Lhasa was puzzling. The soldiers
were orderly and made considerable efforts to be friendly and co-operative.
Loudspeakers assured the populace that the Chinese had come in a spirit
of brotherhood to liberate the Tibetans and bring them back to the Great
Motherland; they would respect the Tibetan way of life and honour the
Seventeen-Point Agreement. But to ordinary Tibetans they were not liberators, they were the *Tenda Gyamar*, the Red Chinese Enemies of Religion.

The United Front policy – which operated until Chinese Communist
power could be properly established – required that the leaders of society
should be wooed and encouraged with new titles and fat salaries. Far from
persecuting the upper and middle classes, the Chinese openly courted them,
promising that if they studied Marxism and sent their children to the new
Chinese schools, their status in the new society would be assured.[2] There

was no talk of 'class-enemies', nor so much as a whisper of 'democratic re-forms'. The Chinese even gave money to the monasteries – and the word 'barbarians', their habitual description of the Tibetans, was firmly taboo.

Many of the nobles and Government officials seemed happy enough to accept the Chinese occupation, not all of them for self-serving reasons. Some of the more progressive and socially aware among them recognized their country's need of economic and social reform and genuinely believed that the new, radical ideas coming out of China would be Tibet's salva-tion. When the PLA marched into Lhasa, many of these progressives joined the Chinese and set to work translating Marxist texts into Tibetan. 'The Seventeen-Point Agreement was in force,' explains Phuntsok Tashi, 'and we had to make the best of it.'[3] Hugh Richardson conjectures that 'Ti-betan officialdom, both monk and noble, did as they had done at those times when the Manchu emperors sought to assert authority in Tibet – they ostensibly acquiesced in the new arrangements while constantly try-ing to obstruct and delay changes and to blunt the edge of Chinese zeal.'[4]

That wasn't the way Gyalo Thondup saw it when he returned to Lhasa in February 1952, afire with youthful zeal and intolerance. He was in-censed at the sight of 'most of the Tibetan officials busy chasing after Chi-nese silver dollars, collaborating with the Chinese, getting a few hundred silver dollars a month for very little work. They all seemed to be on the Chinese payroll, my own sister and her husband among them.'[5] Khando comes to the defence of her parents: 'I think they had a very difficult tightrope act to perform. It wasn't that they were collaborating, they really liked some of the Chinese as friends and tried to work with them, believ-ing that that was the best course. They didn't see what else they could do, and they just hoped it would work out right for Tibet.'[6]

Gyalo Thondup's own behaviour must have seemed ambivalent, to say the least. The Chinese top brass treated him as the prodigal son returned, a high-profile, Chinese-speaking fellow traveller. 'General Chiang Chin-wu, the Military Commander, General Tan Kuan-sen, the Political Commis-sar, all the senior officers and officials, were very happy that I'd decided to come back. They gave parties for me, banquets, we exchanged visits about once a week, sometimes I went to them, sometimes they visited me.'

Whatever the Tibetans may have thought about these shenanigans, Gyalo Thondup claims he was playing a double game. However much the officials were cosying up to the Chinese to preserve their jobs and positions, he knew that the ordinary people of Lhasa detested them unreservedly.

The latter were almost at breaking-point, not least because there were too many Chinese mouths to feed in Lhasa and the food was running out.

The twenty thousand Chinese troops required food, lodging and transport, all, under the terms of the Agreement, to be provided by the Tibetans. (In the absence of motorable roads or airfields, there was no way of bringing in provisions or equipment from China.) At first, the Chinese had paid their way, requisitioning, renting or even buying houses from the nobles, while building a large military camp in the pleasant picnic-meadows beyond the Norbulingka. But before long they began demanding free food and lodging as of right. Their demand for two thousand tons of barley was more than the state granaries could cope with and reserves had to be called in from the monasteries and private estates. As food got scarcer, prices first doubled, then shot sky high. When a new General with another thousand troops arrived, the fragile economy collapsed completely. For the first time in living memory, the people of Lhasa were faced with starvation. Fuel was so scarce that people were burning horns and bones, filling the city with a terrible stench.[7]

It was too much. Although new laws made any opposition to China treasonable, the people began putting up CHINESE – GO HOME posters and handing round leaflets, shouting slogans, singing ribald street-songs, spitting, throwing stones. A popular resistance movement (the *Mimang Tsongdu*) came into being, and, as tension mounted in the streets, five men presented a six-point list of grievances to the Chinese. But instead of acknowledging the people's genuine distress, General Chiang reacted angrily with talk of 'imperialists' and 'conspiracy', blaming the crisis on the Dalai Lama's two Prime Ministers, the layman, Lukhangwa, and the monk, Lobsang Tashi. Lukhangwa, who had taken no Chinese money nor deigned to collaborate in any way, had dared to point out to General Chiang that the people were hungry and the Chinese demands exorbitant. For this the General hated him: Lukhangwa, he accused, was an imperialist reactionary who did not want to improve relations between China and Tibet. He would not accept that Lukhangwa was simply an honest patriot who was not for sale.

Shortly after his arrival, Gyalo Thondup had gone to see the two Prime Ministers with a plan of his own concerning land reform: 'I knew about the terrible atrocities that had taken place in China during the land reforms. I wanted to advise His Holiness that it was imperative for them to take the decision now to redistribute Tibetan lands, and not leave it to the

Chinese. The old system of land ownership was rotten and needed reform, but if the Kashag didn't take action themselves soon, the Chinese would eventually do it much more brutally. I told them I was ready to give up all the Yapshi Taklha properties, and I painted the picture for them of what had happened in China. They must not let the same thing happen in Tibet, I said.'[8]

The two Prime Ministers, being sensible men, warned Gyalo Thondup to keep his opinions to himself. Talk to nobody, they insisted, not even to Kashag Ministers; Lhasa was full of informers. Gyalo Thondup heeded their advice. 'I had to call on those senior Ministers, but I was careful. I just told them I was glad to be home after so many years, and that it was good to see my mother and His Holiness again.' He was beginning to realize he had dropped into a hornet's nest.

Promising to keep the two Prime Ministers informed, he set about cultivating the Chinese military. He talked to the ordinary soldiers who confided that they hated Lhasa. They couldn't sleep because of the high altitude; they had no appetite and were plagued by headaches; the children threw stones at them, adults sang songs which they couldn't understand but which were obviously rude; they spat at them and hurled abuse.

Perhaps it was because they were behaving like conquerors, I suggested. They seemed surprised when I told them that was why the Tibetans disliked them. It hadn't occurred to them before. Yet every time I invited General Tan to dinner at my house, I could see soldiers posted on the roof with their rifles.

Like General Chiang, Lhasa's Political Commissar, Tan Kuan-sen, cultivated Gyalo Thondup:

They were always assuring me that the *Mimang* (People's Movement) was being masterminded by Lukhangwa and Lobsang Tashi, both of whom were reactionaries and American spies. I laughed and said they were wrong, the two Prime Ministers were good men, but so ignorant that they wouldn't even know where America was! I told them to be patient, to move slowly, otherwise they would destroy a thousand years' relationship between the Chinese and the Tibetans. We had for the most part lived in harmony all that time. I told them that to arrest – or, even worse, execute – the two Prime Ministers, would be a terrible mistake. 'You say Tibetans and Chinese are brothers. Well, Tibetans are the younger, you the elder brother. If Younger Brother is behaving badly, you must try to persuade him patiently to stop. You have the power, you have the weapons, but what you are doing will in the long run be against the true interests of China.' I said that the situation was getting worse only because of the growing Chinese presence in the city, that the Tibetans were protesting because they were afraid the Chinese were going to take away the power of the Dalai Lama and that this fear had nothing to do with the two Prime Ministers. But Tan didn't listen, he was striding furiously up and down the room, banging the table at intervals and threatening to have the two men executed straight away. Of course they were American spies, he shouted: one of the Kashag Ministers had told him so the previous night![9]

The Chinese did not execute the two Prime Ministers, but in the early spring of 1952 they 'asked' Kundun to remove them from office. As the 're-quest' was backed by the assurance that if he refused the army would be brought in, and as the Kashag begged him not to make things even worse than they already were, Kundun knew he must sacrifice his Prime Ministers to avoid a blood-bath. For the sake of appearances, they were allowed to resign. As there was no question of their being replaced, there was no longer anyone whom Kundun could whole-heartedly trust. To underline his powerlessness still further, he was made to imprison the five men who had presented the initial petition to the Chinese.

Kundun was no less keen than GT to bring about reforms and modern-ize Tibet. As a young boy, his sweepers had told him of the great injustices in his country, the imbalance in the distribution of wealth, and he knew that such inequality was out of line with Buddhist teachings. A radical re-former by instinct, he longed to be able to improve the lives of his people, but so far he had been given no chance.

Taking advantage of the brief truce which followed the removal of his Prime Ministers, Kundun set up the Reform Committee which he had had in mind ever since, on the way to the Chumbi Valley in 1950, he had seen for himself the state of deprivation in which so many of his people lived. He wanted to establish an independent judiciary, build some much-needed roads, and provide the Tibetans with decent schooling. He had no very clear idea of what constituted modern education, but he knew his country needed it.

In the short term, he agreed with Gyalo Thondup, the land-tenure sys-tem must be reformed. The large private estates ought to revert to the State, and when compensation had been paid to the owners, be redistrib-uted among the peasants who actually worked the land. After that, he would abolish the principle of hereditary debt owed by a tenant to his landlord. His sweepers had told him how unbearably the peasants suffered from this burden:

> It meant that the debt owing to a landlord by his tenants, perhaps acquired as a result of bad harvests, could be transferred from one generation to the next. As a result, many families were not able to make a decent living for themselves, let alone hope one day to be free.[10]

Given time, and if fate had been on his side, Kundun might have gone down into history as a great social reformer. But in the present context, he could not hope to succeed. In the first place, the landowners themselves stubbornly resisted reform. Even more significantly, the Chinese would never allow him to upstage them. *They* were the liberators of Tibet, the ones to whom the masses must be indebted; the Dalai Lama and his Government were cast in the class-war role of 'enemies of the people'. The Chinese were already showing their contempt for the Tibetan political system, bypassing the Kashag and dealing direct with the Dalai Lama, at once isolating and increasing their control over him.

Time was running out for Gyalo Thondup and he knew it. His insane mission to save Tibet single-handed had failed miserably:

> I had wanted to help the people of Tibet and my brother, but such a situation made it difficult for me to do anything at all...I kept urging the Tibetan Government to go along with His Holiness's land reforms, but all they could say was, 'Mr Thondup, *you* may not care about owning land, but what about your children?' I said, 'For heaven's sake, long before my children or yours are old enough to care, the land will have been taken anyway. If you don't act now, you'll be giving the Chinese a sword with which to divide us.'[11]

He resolved at least to set an example. 'I had two estates near the Indian border...The Chinese knew what I was intending to do: I had sworn to give away every inch of my land to the people who worked on it, and to set fire to generations of debts.'

Fate intervened when General Tan was directed, in a cable from Chairman Mao, to appoint GT to lead a Tibetan Youth Delegation to Peking. There he was to join the Chinese Youth Delegation going to the World Peace Conference in Vienna. In 1952, as part of a public campaign of indoctrination designed to soften up the Tibetans for Socialism, the Chinese were setting up 'patriotic' and 'cultural' groups, among the first of which was the Patriotic Youth Association (PYA). Gyalo Thondup, as the Dalai

Lama's brother, was scheduled for a starring role, like his sister, Tsering Dolma, who was to be Chairwoman of the Patriotic Association of Women (PWA). (She and Phuntsok Tashi were also destined for Peking and Vienna.) Gyalo Thondup, feigning rapturous delight, said that first he must carry out his projected land reforms. General Tan agreed to wait.

It was make or break time:

> I talked the situation over with my mother and Lobsang Samten. The Tibetans at that time seemed to have no friends anywhere, but we all felt that if I went to India, I could use the good offices of the Indian Government to persuade the Chinese to go easy on Tibet. I could also tell the outside world what was happening. My mother said I must go and see Nehru. So I contacted the Indian Representative in Lhasa and told him I wanted to escape to India, preferably to Darjeeling – to get outside help for Tibet. Next day, I was informed that Nehru had agreed to grant me asylum. So the only question now was how to get out of Tibet? [12]

The Chinese Generals gave him a farewell lunch and told him to hurry back.

Gyalo Thondup did not return. Taking with him only 700 rupees, to avoid suspicion, he hurried to his estates, divided the property among the workers, tore up the debts as promised, then, with seven companions slipped over the border into what was then still known by its British name, the North East Frontier Agency area of India (NEFA). 'We had good weapons, maps, a compass and above all good horses. As a family we were excellent judges of horse-flesh and I chose some of the finest horses from our stables, so swift that even if the Chinese had chased us, they wouldn't have caught us.' The journey, however, was not without its terrors: there were five hundred Chinese troops patrolling the area. 'It was very worrying, but fortunately we knew the terrain well and how to avoid the troops. We lay low during daylight hours and travelled only by night.'

By an irony of fate, their real troubles began when they reached Assam. After descending the Se la Pass they encountered a posse of Indian military police, who, seeing them to be armed and possessed of maps and compasses, arrested them as Chinese spies. Gyalo Thondup, confident that by now the Indian authorities must have alerted the border security forces to his expected arrival, handed over his weapons and maps and asked to be taken to HQ. Under guard, they walked for about a day and a night from the border to the town of Tawang, only to find that the CO was on leave and the Political Officer was visiting the nearby Buddhist monastery.

Above: The search for a new Dalai Lama. Original woodcuts depicting the cavalcade looking for Tibet's new spiritual leader in Amdo in 1937 and their triumphant return to Lhasa with the four-year-old Lhamo Dhondup almost two years later. (These woodcuts were presented to Sir Basil Gould by the Tibetans following the installation of the Dalai Lama in 1941, and are now in the possession of his widow, Lady Gould.)

Left: The Fourteenth Dalai Lama of Tibet as a young monk. One of his many titles is Kundun, meaning the Presence (of the Buddha).

Top: Dekyi Tsering with her husband Choekyong Tsering, the parents of the Fourteenth Dalai Lama, in the early 1940s. The children are (left to right): their granddaughter Khando Tsering, younger daughter Jetsun Pema and third son Lobsang Samten.

Above: Lobsang Samten with Professor Heinrich Harrer in 1966.

Left: The children of Tsering Dolma, Kundun's elder sister, in Cambridge, 1961 – Khando and her brother Tenzin Ngawang, on his graduation day.

Above: Tibet's capital, Lhasa. In the foreground is Changseshar, the residence of the family of the Dalai Lama (Photo: Noji).

Below: Dekyi Tsering, also known as the Great Mother and also informally as Amala, with her youngest son Tendzin Choegyal (Photo: Noji).

Right: Family gathering in Dharamsala, 1979. (Left to right) Amala, eldest son Thubten Jigme Norbu, Lobsang Samten, the Dalai Lama, Jetsun Pema, Tendzin Choegyal.

Below: Second son Gyalo Thondup (right) and his family, 1960.

Below middle: Dharamsala, the northern Indian home of the exiled Tibetans.

Top right: Amala enjoys a trip to the circus in the 1970s.

Below right: Lobsang Samten, with a nomad girl, during the first fact-finding visit to Tibet, 1979.

Clockwise from top left: The four surviving siblings of the Dalai Lama pictured in 1995, Thubten Jigme Norbu, Gyalo Thondup, Jetsun Pema, Tendzin Choegyal (Photos: Anne Jennings Brown).

Above:
A family portrait for the Dalai Lama's 60th birthday celebrations in Dharamsala in 1995.

Left: With the author in 1994.

His Holiness Tenzin Gyatso, the Fourteenth Dalai Lama of Tibet (Photo: Vijay Kranti).

They kept us in their military compound. I was very tired as I hadn't slept for four days and nights. So I asked the Indian official to leave me alone and just let me sleep, but to tell me when the Political Officer returned. At midnight, the Political Officer came back, half-drunk. He rushed into where I was sleeping, shook me awake and accused me of being a Chinese spy. I told him who I was and asked him to check his files. I wrote out my name for him. He was very angry and extremely rude. I insisted that he should go and check and he stormed off, returning within minutes to say there was nothing at all on file about me. I asked him to try again, to look further back in his files. At 2 a.m. he came back, shaking with fright. He had found the instructions, which in fact had come about a month earlier. Well, then he wanted to transfer me instantly to the best room in their guest-house, but I was too exhausted to care. I told him I'd move in the morning, but right then all I wanted was to go back to sleep. Would you believe it, next morning he brought me my breakfast in bed on a tray, still apologizing profusely?

Gyalo Thondup stayed for about a week in Tawang. News of the arrival of the Dalai Lama's brother spread, and people from neighbouring villages came to see him. 'Hundreds of them came. They brought me chickens, eggs, butter. It turned out they thought I had come to settle their future. In 1950, three years after the British had left, the Indian Government had sent troops to occupy their area, but the people were Tibetans and felt that they had really always belonged to Tibet. Had I come to solve their problem? I told them I was very sorry, but I was actually a refugee myself. I couldn't help them but I went to see them quite often – I've never eaten so many eggs in my life.'

As there was no road between Tawang and the railway terminus at Tezpur, Gyalo Thondup and his companions covered the distance on foot, walking for seven days. From Tezpur he returned at last to Darjeeling to find his pregnant wife, their daughter Yangzom and baby son, Tenzin Khedup. (A second son, Ngawang Tenpa, was born shortly after his return.) Pema was in the house and remembers the shock of his arrival. 'One morning, at dawn, Gyalo Thondup arrived in a pitiable state, gaunt, haggard and suffering from malaria. Two servants supported him, one on each side.'[13]

From Darjeeling he set about organizing help for Tibet. Making contact with the Indian Government he described the state of affairs in Lhasa, begging them to persuade the Chinese to relax the pressure on the Tibetans. 'At the same time I wrote to the President of the United States and to Chiang Kai-shek. Nehru didn't like that. In August he sent his

Political Officer, Mr B. K. Kapoor, to see me, asking me to stop writing to international leaders, and asking for copies of the letters I'd already sent. Mr Kapoor came to Darjeeling with this message and I was very angry. I said, "Before I left Tibet I informed Nehru that I was coming for this one particular purpose, to get help for Tibet. He agreed. Is he now changing his mind?" I refused to give him copies of my letters.'

Mr Kapoor 'went away and told the police superintendent in Darjeeling to keep me under surveillance. I went on writing letters to anybody I thought might help. In October I received a telephone call in Darjeeling from a Mr Kumar in the Police Security Office in Calcutta. He had been Second Secretary at the Chinese Embassy in Nanking in 1947 when I was there, so I knew him quite well. Kumar told me a high official wanted to meet me. He said he didn't know any details, but this man had travelled from Delhi to Darjeeling and wanted me to have lunch with him in a certain restaurant. I went to the restaurant – and the mystery man turned out to be the Director of Indian Intelligence. He brought an apology from Nehru, and a promise that I was free to do whatever I wanted. So from October 1952 onwards I was in constant contact with Indian Intelligence and Nehru simply turned a blind eye.'[14]

The letters abroad bore fruit. From Taiwan, the Kuomintang offered material and financial support, but as their publicly expressed view was that America and India were behind the trouble in Tibet, and that Tibet's real desire was to 'rejoin' the Chinese Motherland represented by Taiwan, GT refused to have anything to do with them. It was different with the Americans. They had been watching events in Tibet with great interest and considerable anxiety, and needed someone to monitor the situation for them. Who better than a well-informed, articulate Tibetan who, by an incredible stroke of luck, was also the Dalai Lama's brother? To the CIA, Gyalo Thondup must have seemed heaven-sent. From now on, he would play a crucial role in the accelerating saga of Tibet.

For the next two years, he lived quietly in Darjeeling, on the lower slopes of the towering Kangchenjunga, the third highest mountain in the world. They were halcyon days, in which he recovered his health and learned to relax with his family. The town had once belonged to the kingdom of Sikkim, but in 1861 the British, by agreement with the Maharajah, had annexed the heavily-forested southern Darjeeling district, turning it into a hill-station, a fashionable summer resort away from the humid heat of the plains. When the British left India in 1947, the new Indian

Government quietly took over all the Himalayan northern border states. But Darjeeling kept its special links with Tibet, based on religious allegiance, trade and ethnic affinity – after all, its very name is Tibetan, being a corruption of Dorje Ling, Place of the Thunderbolt. In the 1950s when the first Tibetan refugees from Communist China began crossing the border into India, it was natural that they should choose to settle either here or in Kalimpong.[15]

It was in Darjeeling that Gyalo Thondup would plan and scheme for the Tibetan cause. There in 1954, with two fellow exiles, he set up the Committee for Tibetan Social Welfare, which, despite its innocuous-sounding name, was in reality an intelligence-gathering organization and was destined to become the nerve-centre of the Tibetan Resistance.

NOTES

1. Rinchen Dolma Taring, *Daughter of Tibet.*

2. The Chinese were indeed building schools, but these were little more than centres for political indoctrination.

3. Author interview with Phuntsok Tashi Taklha, London, 1993.

4. Richardson, *Tibet and its History*, chapter 12.

5. Author interview with GT, New Delhi, July 1995.

6. Author interview with Khando Chazotsang, Utah, February 1996.

7. Rinchen Dolma Taring.

8. Author interview with GT, New Delhi, July 1995.

9. Author interview with GT, New Delhi, July 1995.

10. Fourteenth Dalai Lama, *Freedom in Exile*, chapter 3.

11. Author interview with GT, New Delhi, July 1995.

12. Video recording made by Gyalo Thondup for the monks of Namgyal Monastery, Dharamsala in 1991.

13. Jetsun Pema, *Tibet, Mon Histoire.*

14. Author interview with GT, New Delhi, July 1995.

15. By an agreement with Bhutan, Kalimpong also had been attached to British India in 1861.

In China 1954–5

Integration of the nationalities into the PRC political system
was a prerequisite for their socialist transformation. The socialist transition process itself was a method to increase central control over minorities...Autonomy for nationalities was
to be confined to such superficial aspects of nationality culture as song and dance which were in any case, according to
Marxist ideology, the only meaning of nationality.

Warren W. Smith, 'The Nationalities Policy of the CCP'[1]

Though Kundun had been deliberately kept in the dark about Gyalo
Thondup's flight, the Chinese suspected him of being involved. 'I think
they wondered what my game was,' he says. 'After all, a few years earlier
they had sent my eldest brother, Taktser, on a mission to me, and from
their point of view he had betrayed them. Then Gyalo Thondup came and
went – and they had had high hopes of him too. So I suppose it's not surprising that at this stage they were very suspicious of me.'[2]

The Chinese were disappointed in the Tibetans: instead of the gratitude
and admiration which they had expected, they were treated as unwelcome
aliens and shown active hostility in the streets. And they had signally
failed to win over the Dalai Lama. If they were to have any hope of controlling Tibet through him, a change of strategy was called for.

As a first step, they invited him to China, ostensibly to lead a Tibetan
delegation to the first National Assembly of People's China in Peking

where a new Constitution was about to be adopted; but in reality to step up the brainwashing process. They were fairly certain that a visit to the Motherland would do the trick. Apart from his historic journey from Amdo to Lhasa, he was untravelled, had been nowhere. At nineteen he was still an impressionable boy – and his interest in the modern world and modern technology were well known. Surely, when he saw the political, economic and cultural marvels of Mao's China, he would be eager for Tibet to share in them.

Kundun was no fool. He knew that he was being manipulated, that the Chinese intended to use his presence in Peking as proof to the world that he agreed to Tibet's being part of China, but there was not much he could do about it. Besides, as a Buddhist, he genuinely believed that patient co-existence with the enemy was better than confrontation. He accepted the invitation.

His decision caused anguish and wringing of hands among Tibetans, who were convinced that their beloved ruler would disappear forever if once he set foot in China. Delegations came from all corners of Tibet, begging him to change his mind. From Darjeeling, Gyalo Thondup's Committee for Tibetan Social Welfare 'forwarded several letters to the Dalai Lama and to Chairman Mao Tse-tung, all to the effect that the absence of His Holiness from Tibet was contrary to the wishes of the Tibetan people'.[3] Though Kundun assured them all that he was going to China of his own free will, and Tibetan officials borrowed loud-hailers to promise that he would return within a year, the people simply did not believe that he was acting as a free agent.

In the high summer of 1954, Kundun and about five hundred of his officials set off on the two thousand mile journey from Lhasa to Peking. Despite their forebodings, the citizens put on their best clothes and came in their thousands to say goodbye. There was a farewell reception in a huge tent by the river – with music played by military bands from both Tibetan and Chinese regiments. Then, as monks waved banners and the people burned incense and hoisted flags to wish him a safe journey and speedy return, Kundun walked down a white carpet to the river's edge and crossed the little Kyi Chu river in two yak-hide coracles lashed together. Attendants held a red umbrella over his sacred person. As he turned to wave goodbye to his people,

I could see that they were in an emotional state. Many were crying and it looked as if some were on the point of throwing themselves into the water, convinced that they were seeing me for the last time.[4]

Hundreds of Chinese and Tibetan troops lined the bank to discourage any such extravagant reaction; and the crowds watched mournfully as their leader disappeared from view. But, as he began his journey, riding with Lobsang Samten in the old 1931 Dodge car which had belonged to his predecessor, Kundun could not resist a feeling of exhilaration. He was, after all, setting out on a rare adventure.

Tendzin Choegyal was in the party. Two years earlier, aged six, he had been taken to the monastery of Kumulung to begin his formal education and training as a *tulku*. From then on, he had to wear a monk's garb, and though life in Kumulung was relatively easy-going, and his holidays were spent at home, he was very homesick: 'I missed my mother terribly. She used to send me homemade cookies, lollipops, chewing gum (in small quantities in case I made myself sick) all wrapped up in a scarf. I would sniff the scarf, desperately trying to recapture the smell of her.'[5] When he heard that the Dalai Lama was going to China and that his mother, Tsering Dolma (as Chair of the Patriotic Women's Association) and Lobsang Samten (as Youth Association Chairman) were to accompany him, he determined not to be left behind. He pestered his mother until she agreed to take him along.

One of the two old Austins had been repaired and he, Amala and Tsering Dolma travelled in it. Phuntsok Tashi, recently appointed Commander of Kundun's Bodyguard, rode a motorcycle: Kundun recalls that when he removed his dust mask and protective goggles some hours later his nose was bright red with sunburn![6]

After about ninety miles, they exchanged their wheeled transport for mules; and twelve days out of Lhasa, the going became extremely rough. Though the Tibetans had wanted to follow their old caravan route to Kham, the Chinese had insisted on using the new Lhasa–Chengdu road which was still under construction. Unfortunately, heavy rains had washed away whole sections of it, there was flooding from mountain streams, bridges had collapsed, and as rocks and heavy boulders crashed down, the way was frequently blocked by landslides. Three people were killed and several mules fell over precipices onto the rocks below. The rest trudged on painfully, up to the knees in mud, wretched in the rain and fog. 'I had never in my life seen so much fog,' remembers Tendzin Choegyal.

Even more distressing to him was the sight of large numbers of Chinese workers, 'literally hewing out the road from rocks. I discovered later that they were either prisoners of war or people who had been arrested during the land reforms in China. They had been "liquidated".'

General Chiang, the Military Commander escorting Kundun, gloomily predicted that conditions would soon get even worse and they would have to proceed on foot:

> Therefore, in his capacity as representative of the Central People's Republic, he would personally link arms and escort me along the way...It occurred to me that the General was under the impression that not only could he exert his power over my two Prime Ministers, but he could also bully Nature!'

A month after leaving Lhasa they reached a motorable road and piled into Russian jeeps and trucks for the journey to Chamdo, which had been under Chinese occupation since 1950. The further they travelled from Lhasa, the more obvious were the signs of Chinese domination: loud-speakers blaring forth canned Chinese music, and at every stopping-place a welcome committee, a formal banquet and a guard of honour. But nothing could have prevented the Tibetans from turning out in force to greet their beloved Kundun. He gave them his blessing before crossing the ancient border between Tibet and China and proceeding to Chengdu, the first town in China proper.

From there a short plane ride (his first ever) took Kundun to Xian where a special train waited to carry him on the twelve-hour journey to Peking. At the railway station, the clapping and cheering of the rent-a-crowd students and youth groups disturbed him; he knew they would just as readily have booed and jeered, if so ordered. Yet, by and large, he was enjoying the lack of formality in China – enamel mugs instead of jade cups, friendly waves and handshakes in place of prostrations and reverently lowered eyes. It was refreshing to be treated like an ordinary human being rather than a god-king. And the brand-new spotlessly clean train waiting in the station could not fail to excite one who had never so much as seen a train before. 'The train really stunned us both,' recalls Tendzin Choegyal. 'It was purpose-built, a show-piece, ordinary people didn't travel in that sort of style. There were sleeping cars, dining cars, proper sitting-rooms. Marvellous food in the dining-car.'8

The Panchen Lama had been brought along. The Chinese lost no opportunity of showing that the two most important Lamas of Tibet were equal in status. Throughout history, they had always tried to play off one against the other and although the Panchen Lamas had no claim to political power at all, the Chinese chose to disregard that fact. The Ninth Panchen had died in Amdo in 1937, still waiting to return home to his monastery in Shigatse. Within the next few years, two boys were discovered as possible reincarnations, one in Amdo, the other in Kham. Though neither had been submitted to the religious tests, in 1944, the Chinese Kuomintang Government declared the eight-year-old Amdo boy to be the true reincarnation and enthroned him forthwith, thus acquiring a convenient figurehead for their own purposes. When the Communists won the Civil War in 1949, it did not take them long to see what a prize had fallen into their laps – and without delay (or any inconvenient sense of irony) they pronounced the boy to be spiritual and temporal leader of Tibet. Making him Chairman of a 'Provisional Government of Tibet', they proclaimed on Peking Radio that the Panchen Lama had invited Mao to 'liberate Tibet'. Mao graciously replied that 'The People's Liberation Army can surely satisfy the yearnings of the Tibetan people.' To the Tibetans, the Amdo boy was merely one of two candidates – but as part of the Seventeen-Point Agreement in 1951 they were forced to acknowledge him. Ever since, the Chinese had been building up their man as a counterweight to the Dalai Lama, conferring powers on him which the Panchen Lamas had never traditionally enjoyed. Now, in Peking, the two young men were equals; where one went, the other went too.

Kundun fell under the spell of Mao Tse-tung. When he first shook hands with him, he felt himself to be 'in the presence of a strong magnetic force'. Mao 'did not have the aura of a particularly intelligent man', but he had an air of dignity and decisiveness that was impressive. He was shabby and down-at-heel, but 'his mere presence commanded respect'.

In the course of their first meeting, Mao expressed disappointment that the Tibetans were so ungrateful to their Chinese benefactors. The Dalai Lama explained that patience was needed; social reforms could not be imposed instantly or by force. Mao said he had abandoned his original intention of governing Tibet directly from Peking, in favour of a degree of self-government. A Preparatory Committee for the Autonomous Region of Tibet (PCART), consisting mainly of Tibetans, would prepare Tibet – by which he meant only that area which had been under the Dalai Lama's direct authority at the time of the invasion in 1950 – to take its place as a constituent part of the People's Republic of China.

Kundun was relieved to hear that Tibet would retain at least some control over its internal affairs. Mao's proposal seemed reasonable, particularly as the Chairman assured him that the pace of reform would be dictated by the wishes of the Tibetan people themselves.

With Mao assuring his guest that China's whole purpose was to help Tibet, Kundun began to relish the idea of co-operating with such a man. His hosts' efforts were already paying off, he was finding Marxism attractive:

> A senior official at the Minorities Office was appointed to indoctrinate me. He was a very nice man, he used to come to my room and lecture me on the history of the Chinese Revolution and on Marxist philosophy...Here was a system based, like Buddhism, on equality and justice for everyone. I couldn't accept its materialistic view of human existence, but I felt sure that it ought to be possible to work out a synthesis between Marxism and Buddhist doctrine. I still believe that some of those original Marxist ideas were excellent.
>
> Then I had many meetings with the veterans of the Long March – and with a few good Tibetan Communists. They seemed selfless in their service to others, I admired them and they had a big influence on me. At that time I really had faith in Chairman Mao and I had a genuine respect and admiration for the Communist Party. I even expressed a wish to become a Party member![9]

After ten weeks of official meetings, interminable rambling speeches and endless banquets, Kundun and his officials were taken on an orchestrated tour of northern China to see the marvels of industrial progress at first hand: factories, co-operative farms, workers' organizations, schools, universities and museums. Unlike his officials, most of whom were bored rigid, Kundun was awed by the new technology and dazzled by the Communist achievements. He longed for some of that efficiency and progress to rub off on Tibet.

But Communism's darker side did not escape him. He was disappointed, for example, that he was not allowed to speak to the ordinary people and was given no chance to step outside of his official programme or visit unscheduled places. The excuse was always that they dared not put his safety at risk. 'Yet it was not only I who was kept isolated from the common people, so were all the Chinese from Peking. They too were forbidden to do anything independently.'[10]

As time went by, he saw that the Chinese people were like programmed robots. Oppressed by 'a grey fog of humourless uniformity', remorselessly organized and processed, they had lost all trace of spontaneity and individuality. The human cost of all this progress, he concluded regretfully, was too high. Attractive though Marxism might be as a theory, Kundun could only pray that his own people would never be subjected to this fanatical interpretation of it. He knew now what he was up against.

Amala and Tsering Dolma had been busy in Peking. Apart from the mandatory political lectures, there was sightseeing, shopping, official banquets and receptions, even a visit to the zoo. As Chair of the PWA, Tsering Dolma had meetings to attend; she was also learning Chinese and continuing the study of Tibetan begun when she had first arrived in Lhasa. Then there was Tendzin Choegyal to supervise. This *enfant terrible* was in his element. Always a sociable child, he found the Chinese friendly and kind. 'They kept enthusing, "Look how good things are in today's China, so much better than under the Kuomintang. Isn't everything splendid?" I knew they were just trying to impress us but I didn't in the least mind playing along with them, paying them all the compliments they wanted. In any case, I meant many of them. For example, I thought the Chinese soldiers, their weapons, their drill, everything about them, *were* wonderful.'

The child learned to speak fluent Mandarin in a matter of months, a skill of which the official party made good use when they returned to Peking in January 1955. 'I was easier to deal with than the official interpreters,' he says, 'so after a bit I became the translator for the whole entourage, particularly if anyone wanted to see a doctor. I loved it, I was glad to have something to do – and they gave me cookies and sweets.'

But, as Kundun noted, his brother's linguistic prowess had its drawbacks:

> If ever my mother or anyone made a disparaging remark about one of our hosts, my little brother would pass it on without hesitation. We all had to be very careful of what we said in front of him. Even then, he could always sense when someone was being vague or evasive.

Tendzin Choegyal was 'a constant source of delight and terror to everyone, including the Chinese', remarks Kundun. Affectionately regarded as a kind of mascot, in the guest-house where the family stayed he spent his time 'mainly fooling around', sometimes with calamitous results. Once he threw cold water over the head of a steward who was snoozing just outside the kitchen. 'He woke up with a start and banged his head on the shelf above his head. I saw the blood flowing and ran for my life.'

Kundun alone, it seems, was prepared to discipline his wilful young brother. As Tendzin Choegyal ruefully recalls, 'There was an ornamental pond full of goldfish in the garden where we were staying. I was very taken with it. I once took a badminton racquet and scooped the fish out onto the grass. They were leaping around. I put them back after a time, but some-one told His Holiness what I'd done and he came down, gave me a ticking off and boxed my ears hard.'[11]

Just before Kundun's return to Lhasa, Mao summoned him to a last meeting. After a spate of fatherly suggestions about their future co-operation, he said abruptly:

> Your attitude is good, you know. Religion is poison. Firstly, it reduces the population, because monks and nuns stay celibate, and secondly it neglects material progress.[12]

'Religion is poison!' The words fell on Kundun like hammer-blows, but he had the self-control not to betray his shock: 'How could he have misjudged me so? How could he have thought that I was not religious to the core of my being?'[13] He could only suppose that Mao, aware of his new enthusiasm for Marxism, had presumed 'that my religious practices were nothing more to me than a prop or a convention'. Kundun's faith in Mao was shattered. He would continue to believe that Mao was a great leader, a sincere person even, without guile or deceit; but never again would he allow admiration to cloud his judgement.

The new road was now finished,[14] so when they left the train at Chengdu, Kundun's party was able to proceed by jeep and truck. Not that the return journey was without peril. There were still a number of landslides and at one river crossing where 'the terrible waters [looked] absolutely black, [and] one could not hear anything else above the terrific noise of water falling down and pushing boulder against boulder',[15] a bridge collapsed and was washed away moments after Kundun's jeep had crossed it.

Kundun's reservations about Maoism were reinforced on the three-month journey back to Lhasa. The good intentions professed by Mao did not seem to have filtered down to his provincial subordinates. Wherever Kundun stopped in eastern Tibet, he sensed 'a heavy air of foreboding', a mounting hatred and resentment of the Chinese. For the first few years of occupation, while the new roads linking eastern Tibet with Lhasa were still under construction, the Chinese had soft-pedalled on social change. But by the end of 1954 when the roads were finally completed, the need for conciliation passed and the mask of tolerance could be dropped. Marxism was to replace Buddhism, anti-religious propaganda was to be stepped up and the 'democratic reforms' implemented. By which was meant the forcible introduction of collective farming in which the people would be relieved of their meagre possessions without any regard for their customs, wishes or needs. Worse, Tibetan children were being forcibly abducted for education in China.

That the Chinese were now the masters in Kham and Amdo was brought home to Kundun during a visit with his mother to Kumbum and their native Taktser. (He had received invitations to towns and monasteries all over Kham, but was allowed to visit only those which actually lay on his route.) At Kumbum, only eight hundred monks remained, living in a state of wretched poverty. The longed-for visit to Taktser was not a happy one. For one thing, many of their friends had been deported or had died in unexplained circumstances. 'The visit to my old home was terribly upsetting for my mother,' recalls Kundun. 'Whenever she inquired about their living conditions, our relatives always answered like parrots, "Oh, thanks to Chairman Mao Tse-tung and the People's Republic of China, we are very happy." But they were crying as they said the words.'[16]

In this place, where he was surrounded by relatives and old friends, the Chinese paranoia about his security descended into absurdity and caused great distress, especially to his mother:

My mother was deeply disturbed. I remember her crying because there in my own birthplace I was not allowed to eat food prepared for me by the villagers, not even when they were members of my own family. The Chinese forbade me to eat anything that had not been prepared by themselves. My mother simply did not know how to explain this to her Taktser friends...There was another thing that my mother pointed out with real regret: even the bread they put on the table was smaller than it used to be. They used to bake these enormous round loaves, so big that a mule could carry only two of them. When you had that bread with mutton, it was so delicious. Or with tea, with some cream. Wonderful![17]

At a monastery in Kham, thousands of people had turned out to pay their respects; but, as Kundun later discovered, the Chinese authorities had spread the disinformation that his visit would take place the following week. 'They lied about the date in order to prevent people from seeing me. As a result, thousands turned up after I had left.'

In the crowd was an eight-year-old Khampa girl, Rinchen Khando Tasotsang, from a village near the monastery. Many years later, in another country, she would become the wife of Tendzin Choegyal. This was her first sight of him:

> We went to a public audience, and one of our servants hoisted me onto his back so that I could see. There were many many people, a huge crush. I remember there was this little boy of my own age, and people kept telling me that he was His Holiness's brother and a Rinpoche. I also remember that I lost one of my shoes in the crush. When we'd all left the monastery, I discovered my left shoe had gone. I had to be carried all the way back to our tent because I couldn't walk.[18]

Kundun's visit was a small oasis of joy in the desert to which life in this once happy land was rapidly being reduced. The local lamas and chieftains to whom Kundun spoke were all fearful; they reported that the peasants were bitter over the growing threat to their way of life and to their religion; tensions were mounting and all the signs suggested that the Chinese would stop at nothing to enforce their will. A spiral of violence was in the making. The Khampas[19] presented a petition to Kundun begging him to persuade the Chinese to reverse their policies in these rural areas before it was too late.

Their belief in his power to change the course of history was touching; to them he was the Dalai Lama, the all-powerful god-king. But, as Kundun followed the road back to Lhasa in that summer of 1955, he must have reflected sadly that he was every bit as powerless as they were.

His arrival back in Lhasa in May 1955 was greeted with relief, and a huge gathering of Government officials, incarnate lamas, monks and ordinary citizens turned out to welcome him. Prayers of thanksgiving for his safe return were offered at the Norbulingka Palace.

But, with the opening of the two new roads from China (from Siling in the north and Chengdu in the east), Lhasa itself had undergone a sea change, its narrow streets suddenly choked with the noise and stench of Chinese cars and military trucks. The Chinese were still practising a degree of restraint, still trying to be liked. But with their lines of communication and supply assured, they were now free to consolidate their power. They had already stepped up their anti-religious propaganda and taken political indoctrination into the schools.

Nevertheless, for a time, Kundun remained optimistic. Now that he had openly shown his admiration for the Communist achievement in China, the authorities in Lhasa were more inclined to trust him. 'They thought,' he laughs, 'that I had the makings of a good Marxist after all.'[20]

Lobsang Samten had been appointed Lord Chamberlain – the head of the Dalai Lama's household and treasury, and his official personal representative on the Kashag. Lobsang was an honest, decent, but somewhat naïve young man. The Chinese, among whom he had many friends, used him as a liaison between themselves and the Dalai Lama; and many Tibetans, noting his frequent visits to the Chinese Office, accused him of fraternizing rather too freely with the enemy. 'But they were wrong,' protests Kundun. 'It was just in Lobsang's nature to like everyone. He was very uncomplicated, but he was also steadfast and loyal.'[21] 'The thing was,' adds Namgyal Lhamo (Namlha), his future wife:

> Lobsang was one of those in favour of radical change. He had come from a peasant home where there was a lot of freedom. He was open, frank, down-to-earth, not at all rigid or formal. He hated any kind of restriction. He wanted change for Tibet, to get away from the old rigid conservatism. So, yes, he was friendly with the Chinese, because he thought at first that that was what they wanted too. They knew what he was like and how idealistic he was; and they set out to exploit him.[22]

When Gyalo Thondup had escaped them in 1952, the Chinese had made Lobsang the Chairman of the Youth Association – one Dalai Lama's brother presumably being interchangeable with another. Like the Patriotic Women's Association, the Youth Association was a key part of the Chinese Communist system and all Tibetan children were at first encouraged – later on, ordered – to join. 'Under the age of fourteen we were called Pioneers and wore red scarves,' recalls Namlha (herself a fourteen-year-old schoolgirl at the time):

> When we passed fourteen we became members of the Youth Organization. Actually, although our parents were not very keen, many of us were really enthusiastic for this new order of things...In fact, we did do a lot of good work, social work, planting trees, cleaning the main street outside our (Chinese) school. It was fun too, there were lots of social gatherings and dances. We enjoyed the

freedom of going to dances and parties, a freedom we'd never had before the Chinese came. But there were also meetings where they quizzed us about our families, what property or land they had. They were busy collecting information for future use. They also used us to talk to people at certain events – if there was a big occasion, they would get us to explain to the Tibetans what it was about. We were well and truly brain-washed. Behind all their planning was the idea that we young people would become sympathetic to Communism and then we would be useful tools for them. But they were quite subtle about it and we didn't realize then that they were merely moulding us to their requirements.[23]

Namlha belonged to the important Tsarong family. In 1951 when many of the old noble families were sending their children away to be educated in British schools, she and her younger sister had been sent to school in India; but in 1954 many parents bowed to Chinese pressure to bring their children back to Tibet. Namlha returned to Lhasa in 1954, entered a Chinese school and became a flag-waving Pioneer. Lobsang Samten was then a remote figure, seen from afar on the occasion of important meetings.

By autumn of 1955 rumours of increasing Chinese brutality in the East began to reach Lhasa. Traders from places like Siling brought alarming stories of persecution. Far from relaxing their pressure, as the Dalai Lama had asked, the Chinese were ruthlessly implementing the democratic reforms, imposing huge taxes, confiscating estates, arraigning and executing landowners for 'crimes against the people', even rounding up thousands of the nomad farmers who roamed the steppes of Amdo and Kham. They were forcibly indoctrinating the people against religion, harassing, beating and publicly humiliating lamas, monks and nuns. In every village, the Khampas responded with active resistance, for which the Chinese were exacting a terrible revenge. They were forcing children to abuse or even execute their own parents, were seizing and deporting others to China, and had introduced the infamous practice of *thamzing* (class struggle sessions), in which men and women were shamefully humiliated, spat on, beaten, kicked, in order to make them confess to reactionary thoughts or behaviour. Attendance at these sessions was compulsory; participation had to be enthusiastic and positive, on pain of imprisonment or death.

As the first refugees arrived in Lhasa with their tales of indescribable horror, hostility to the Chinese rose to fever pitch. Leaflets were distributed on the streets and public meetings were held. When the Chinese arrested three men for 'inciting anti-democratic crimes', the people's rage merely intensified.

Would the establishment of the new Preparatory Committee for the Autonomous Region of Tibet solve anything? It was being hyped by the Chinese as a great step forward for Tibet, and in April 1956 was launched with a huge fanfare in a purpose-built municipal hall in Lhasa. Marshal Chen-yi, China's Foreign Minister, came from Peking for the occasion. Military bands played, rousing Communist ballads such as 'The East is Red' were sung, and scarlet flags and banners depicting Chairman Mao and his colleagues fluttered triumphantly in the breeze. Congratulatory speeches praising Socialism, the Party and even the Chinese activities in Tibet, were made. ('I even had to make one myself,' admits the Dalai Lama in embarrassment, '[I said hopefully] I was sure that the Chinese would honour all their undertakings to introduce reform at the pace the people wanted and to permit freedom of worship.'[24]) There were banquets and all sorts of lavish entertainments. (It was at a committee meeting to plan the Youth Organization dinner that Namlha first met Lobsang Samten: 'People were coming from all over China. We were told that the Dalai Lama's older brother would be coming to the dinner and they wanted a couple of Tibetan girls to sit on his table. I was one of the two chosen. I was about fourteen, we were generations apart, he was a monk and an important official; and we had nothing whatever to say to each other.'[25])

The new Committee was, Kundun knew, 'the last hope for the peaceful evolution of our country'. On the surface, his optimism seemed justified; the Committee must surely be preferable to direct military rule. After all, the word 'autonomous' was in the title, and it included representatives of all parts of Tibet under a single administration. Kundun was to be Chairman, the Panchen Lama Vice-Chairman, and out of fifty-six members, fifty-one were to be Tibetan.

In reality it was a shameless confidence trick, intended to propagate the lie that Tibet had chosen the Socialist path. Amdo and Eastern Kham, despite their largely Tibetan populations, had been integrated into China proper, and were no longer considered part of Tibet; and of the fifty-one Tibetan delegates on the Committee, not one was elected and all but fifteen (one of these being Kundun himself) had been hand-picked by the Chinese. 'Allowed,' said Kundun with some bitterness, 'to keep their power and property so long as they did not voice any opposition.'[26] And though the Kashag and the National Assembly continued to exist, they no longer had any power; they could be outvoted by a two-thirds majority on any and every issue. In any case, all real power lay with the Committee of the Chinese Communist Party of Tibet and no Tibetan was eligible to belong to that. The Dalai Lama's authority had vanished. He understood now that the Chinese needed him only as a figure-head, as a name to lend their schemes a spurious appearance of Tibetan approval.

Lobsang Samten found himself appointed to the newly-created Security Department. If Kundun was taken aback at the news, Lobsang himself was aghast:

> Being such a kind and gentle person, there can have been no one less suited to the job than he. I shall never forget the look on his face when he returned from a meeting with his Chinese opposite number. All had gone well until the man turned to Lobsang Samten (who spoke some Chinese) and asked him what was the Tibetan for 'Kill him'. Up to that moment my brother had thought this new official to be quite pleasant and straightforward, but this question left him dumbfounded. The idea of killing even an insect was so far from his mind that he was lost for words. When he arrived at the Norbulingka that same evening, his face was full of bewilderment. 'What *am* I to do,' he asked.[27]

To Lobsang his appointment must have seemed like a sick joke calculated to undermine still further his shaky reputation among ordinary Tibetans. It undoubtedly increased the stress and tension from which he was suffering. Yet, whatever the pressures on him, he remained, Kundun insists, 'remarkably serene. Lobsang was never in any doubt as to where his loyalties lay.'[28]

The Chinese had what they wanted now: all power was securely in their hands. So much for the Seventeen-Point Agreement, which had guaranteed to leave Tibet's political system intact and the status, functions and powers of the Dalai Lama unchanged.

NOTES

1. Barnett & Akiner, eds., *Resistance and Reform in Tibet*, p. 57.
2. Author interview with HH the Dalai Lama, Dharamsala, June 1994.
3. Shakabpa, *Tibet: a Political History*, chapter 18.
4. Fourteenth Dalai Lama, *Freedom in Exile*.
5. Author interview with Tendzin Choegyal, July 1995.
6. Goodman, *The Last Dalai Lama*.

7. *Freedom in Exile.*

8. Author interview with Tendzin Choegyal, Dharamsala, October 1993.

9. Author interview with HH the Dalai Lama, Dharamsala, June 1994.

10. *Freedom in Exile.*

11. Author interview with Tendzin Choegyal, Dharamsala, October 1993.

12. *Freedom in Exile.*

13. *Freedom in Exile.*

14. The much-vaunted building of this road and that from Siling to Lhasa benefited only the Chinese who were now able to move their armoured vehicles and military equipment into Tibet and secure their occupation of the country. Moreover, once the roads linking Tibet with China were completed, the Chinese moved to alter the age-old trading patterns of the Tibetans, ordering them to cease trading with India and to trade with China instead. Gradually Tibet's outdoor markets were closed down.

15. Rinchen Dolma Taring, *Daughter of Tibet.*

16. Author interview with HH the Dalai Lama, Dharamsala, June 1994.

17. Author interview with HH the Dalai Lama, Dharamsala, June 1994.

18. Author interview with Rinchen Khando, Dharamsala, October 1993.

19. People of Kham are called Khampas – those of Amdo are Amdowas.

20. Author interview with HH the Dalai Lama, Dharamsala, June 1994.

21. Author interview with HH the Dalai Lama, Dharamsala, June 1994.

22. Author interview with Namlha Taklha, Dharamsala, October 1993.

23. Author interview with Namlha Taklha, Dharamsala, October 1993.

24. *Freedom in Exile.*

25. Author interview with Namlha Taklha, Dharamsala, October 1993.

26. *Freedom in Exile.*

27. *Freedom in Exile.*

28. Author interview with HH the Dalai Lama, Dharamsala, June 1994.

15

The Storm Comes Closer

[In the summer of 1956] I was given a copy of a newspaper published by the Chinese authorities at Karze in Kham. In disbelief, I saw that it contained a photograph of a row of severed heads. The caption said something to the effect that they had belonged to 'reactionary criminals'. This was the first concrete evidence of Chinese atrocity that I had seen. Thereafter, I knew that every terrible thing I heard about our new masters' behaviour was true...I began to wonder if there could be any hope for the future. My predecessor's prophecy was beginning to be proved entirely accurate.

The Fourteenth Dalai Lama, Freedom in Exile

After six months of treatment, the American doctors declared Norbu cured of his lung congestion. He took a crash course in English at Berkeley University in California, then set off for the 1952 World Buddhist Congress in Tokyo.

Unfortunately, during his stay in Japan, his Indian identity papers lapsed, so he was unable either to visit India or return to the United States. He had to stay in Japan for almost three years, making the most of his time by learning Japanese and making many Japanese friends. It was a pleasant life, marred only by 'the bitterness, the frustrated hopes and the nagging anxieties of the emigrant who has to wage a seemingly hopeless nerve-racking struggle with a vast anonymous bureaucracy'.[1]

When his documents arrived (early in 1955), he returned to the USA via India and Europe, in order to meet Gyalo Thondup in Calcutta.

In his house in residential upper Darjeeling, Gyalo Thondup was father to a fairly rumbustious extended family. In addition to three children of his own – his daughter Yangzom, and two sons (Tenzin) Khedup and (Ngawang) Tenpa – during holidays and every fourth weekend, Pema, Tenzin (Ngawang) and Khando joined the family. With some help from the Indian Government, GT sent the boys to St Joseph's College, North Point, a celebrated boarding school run by Canadian Jesuits for about three hundred boys from Burma, Thailand, Sikkim, Bhutan, Nepal, as well as European children whose parents were working in India. The girls were at a Convent run by Loreto nuns from Ireland.

'It was a wonderful life with the Thondups,' says Khando. 'We weren't short of money, we belonged to the Gymkhana Club, we went skating and riding, Uncle and Auntie used to play tennis – in fact, they were the local champions. Auntie was a very kind person. We never thought of her as Chinese, we just loved her. She cooked our favourite dishes for us and looked after us well.' Though Gyalo Thondup was kind also, he was a strict disciplinarian of whom the children were very much in awe. 'At meal-times, we had to be in our places on time, with faces washed and hands and finger-nails scrubbed. And we weren't allowed to leave the table until everyone had finished. I was so small that I used to fall asleep at the table, and then would have to be carried up to bed. Pema and I shared a room. Uncle Thondup would come to say goodnight to us, then he would turn off the light and we didn't dare put it back on again when he'd gone.'

Khando was a bright, intelligent child who spent all her monthly pocket-money on books (sometimes, she admits, comics) and, having learned English almost from infancy, was completely bilingual and would read everything she could lay hands on. This passion for reading used to get her in trouble at school, where she was often found reading after lights-out. 'The nuns would confiscate the books, and, even worse, bring them down to show Uncle Thondup when he and Auntie brought us tuck at weekends. My heart used to sink, I knew I'd get a spanking when I went home at the end of the month.' Uncle Thondup would scold Pema for a different reason. She had always found study difficult, especially in English. While Tenzin Ngawang, a brilliant student, was winning almost every prize on offer and Khando the ones for the subjects which interested her, Pema was usually awarded the application or needlework prize. Uncle Thondup was mortified!

In that spring of 1955 when Norbu came from Japan to see his brother, they heard that their elder sister was due to arrive in India, on her way back from China. Tsering Dolma was to attend a Trade Show in Calcutta and then go on to New Delhi for a meeting of the Tibetan Women's Delegation. Phuntsok Tashi was also coming, so Tenzin Ngawang and Khando would be reunited with their parents.

Khando has good reason to remember that time. The thrill of a trip to Calcutta and then to the Chinese Embassy in New Delhi – where she watched the Chinese staff doing their morning exercises to music over the tannoy – was overshadowed by an unpleasant incident which marked the end of her political innocence.

> Wherever our group went we were escorted by a Tibetan-speaking Chinese officer. I couldn't stand the man – he was arrogant and never left us alone. One morning we were in our sitting-room, and he just walked in without knocking. He strolled over to the table where there was a big bowl of assorted fruits and picked one up. 'May I?' he asked casually. I saw red. 'NO, YOU CAN'T,' I shouted furiously. There was a dead silence. Then after a while, someone rather nervously broke the silence and relaxed the tension. My mother signalled me to follow her into the bedroom: and never before or later did she whack me as hard as she did that morning. 'Don't you understand anything?' she asked, angrily. 'Don't you realize the danger you are putting us all in?' Well, of course I didn't, it would never have occurred to me to think that a ten year old's hostility could be taken as a political statement. But I never forgot the lesson. I suddenly realized the seriousness of the situation for my parents and indeed for our whole family. From then on I was aware of fear.

She had more reason than she knew to be afraid, for her parents were under considerable pressure to bring the children back to Tibet. 'Uncle Thondup told us that the Chinese wanted to send all of us children to be educated in the Soviet Union.' He told us not to go, that it would ruin our lives. We didn't really understand what it was all about, but, at Uncle Thondup's prompting, every time our parents brought up the subject, we would shout, "WE DON'T WANT TO GO, WE DON'T WANT TO GO."' The brothers too were under pressure, and their joy at seeing their sister again was blended with irritation, since they knew she was under orders to bring them back with her. From her own point of view, there was nothing Tsering Dolma would have liked better. Besides, as she angrily assured her brothers, if they went on refusing to return, the Chinese would take it out on Kundun.

Neither Norbu nor Gyalo Thondup had any illusions about what going back would mean; and neither of them had the least intention of doing so. But they knew their sister was apprehensive about returning to Lhasa empty-handed: 'We both made it clear to her that so long as the Chinese Communists were in power in Tibet there could be no return for us, much as we longed to see our native land again. But because she urged us so persistently we did go to see the Chinese consul in Calcutta, and he too did his utmost to persuade us to go back to Lhasa. But we remained firm and gave him a number of ostensibly good reasons which would prevent our return to Tibet for an indefinite period.'³

Norbu flew back to New York to resume his studies, while Tsering Dolma and Phuntsok Tashi prepared to return to Tibet. 'We could tell they were afraid, and it made us anxious,' says Khando. The parting was difficult for all of them. 'We drove by car to Gangtok, and stayed there for a day or two with the Sikkimese royal family before going by jeep to the Nathu la Pass, where about twenty horses and mules stood waiting. We had a picnic meal and then it was time to say goodbye. I remember my mother getting on to her horse and we watched from the top as they rode down the side of the Nathu la towards Dromo. We felt so sad watching them go down the hill and out of sight.'⁴ But Tsering Dolma had no choice but to return to Lhasa, where she would blame her failure on the stubbornness of her two brothers.

She continued to study Tibetan with Rinchen Dolma Taring. (Tendzin Choegyal remembers her working at it far into the night.) But it was an uphill struggle and her heart was never quite in it. She had begun to chafe at the role the Chinese had imposed on her as the Dalai Lama's sister. 'She was a patriot, devoted to the cause of Tibet,' says Tendzin Choegyal. 'The work she did for the Chinese made her very uneasy.'⁵

At nine, Tendzin Choegyal was still too young to be aware of the political situation and remembers carefree summer holidays at Gyatso, riding, learning to fish in the pond in front of the house, wearing ordinary clothes like a normal little boy, playing with friends:

We experimented a lot, we had to make our own toys and games and were fairly inventive. We'd make bows from the bamboo which was meant for making pens – we had better uses for it. For arrows, we'd wade knee-deep in mud to get reeds and then dry them. To make a sharp tip, we'd cut biscuit tins and shape them into arrowheads with a stone, then fix them to the reed. Then we'd add a feather to stabilize the arrow in flight. We used to take the feathers from the roosters' tails. Soon the poor roosters' tails were completely bald. My mother kept wondering why and we looked innocent and said we'd no idea. We confessed eventually and I don't suppose she was surprised.

The adults often joined in the fun: 'We used to jump from the upper storey into the place where the hay was stored. Some of the grown-ups would jump so vigorously they almost dislocated their shoulders...There were a few accidents, but nothing really serious.'

Tendzin Choegyal was at the monastery of Drepung, though with all his heart he would have preferred being at home. 'I was never cut out to be a monk,' he admits. On returning from China in the summer of 1955, he had lived at home for a while, before being formally inducted into Drepung monastery the following winter. Drepung, the biggest and richest of Lhasa's monasteries, had been founded at the beginning of the fifteenth century by a poor herdsman from Eastern Tibet, a disciple of the great Tsong-khapa. It owed its name (which means 'Rice Heap') to its tiers of white-washed buildings, one behind the other on a sloping site at the edge of a wedge-shaped valley. It was said to be the largest monastery in the world; and from a distance looked just like a fortified city. Its sheer immensity came as a shock to Tendzin Choegyal:[6] 'I think that going to Drepung for the first time I lost a lot of freedom. For a start, it was so big. I had to grow up when I went there. I found it extremely difficult to get used to the robe: the shape was the same, the style was the same, but it had to be made of coarse wool cloth rather than the cotton I was used to. It was rough and scratchy, I used to itch all over. I had a high fever when I first went to Drepung, yet I couldn't escape all the endless induction ceremonies. I felt terribly lonely.'[7]

It was the start of what, had history not intervened so dramatically, would have been an eleven-year course of arduous study. Despite his obvious lack of vocation, he would probably have survived somehow. Apart from the all-important rituals, there are no dogmatic rules in Buddhist monasteries. As Spencer Chapman wrote, 'As long as [the Tibetan monk] attends the service in the monastery temple and is subject to the lay discipline of the proctors, he can pursue any spiritual goal and can endeavour to reach it by whatever means he chooses.'[8] Tendzin Choegyal's memories of those years are those of any mischievous ten-year-old, characterized more by horseplay than piety.

I used always to carry a needle and thread in my shirt. When we sat down in Assembly, sometimes I would sew together the robes of the two people in front of me. My friends and I were *tulkus*, so we occupied important seats among the grown-ups. While those solemn monks were chanting or meditating, I used to stitch them together down the whole length of their cloaks. When the session was over and they stood up, it was quite a sight – both pulling in different directions and discovering they were joined together. I used to make myself scarce and watch the fun from a distance. Sometimes, for a change, I'd sew the monk's cloak to the cushion he was sitting on. Novice-monks always got up to tricks of that sort, it was traditional; we thought it was great fun and the older monks didn't seem to mind. We must have sorely tried their patience, though.

The boys cut the ropes that were used in dark places as handrails; and put homemade catapults to unorthodox uses: 'In the evenings there'd be long, dreary sessions of prayer and debating. During the prayer session, we would be sitting on some raised ground near a pavilion surrounded by butter-lamps. I used to organize my friends to use their catapults to knock off the butter-lamps when it got dark. I directed the fire and it sounded like an artillery barrage – they were actually quite good shots.'

Later on, he managed to smuggle air pistols into the monastery. He had a passion for guns and knew how to handle them – having been given his first air rifle at the age of six by a Tibetan trader, he had persuaded the Royal Bodyguard to teach him to use it. He later acquired a Webley air pistol which he took to Drepung with him and which afforded him plenty of scope for mischief: 'There were some bells in front of the hostel where I lived, and when the wind blew they used to make a terrible din. So whenever the wind got up, it was a marvellous opportunity to use the bells as target practice. Everyone was very puzzled, but nobody ever found me out.'

Despite Buddhist teaching about the sanctity of all sentient life, he enjoyed taking pot shots at birds. Until, that is, one day he shot a sparrow and watched in horror as it died, blood oozing from its wounds. Full of remorse, he vowed never again to take a life. From then on, he restricted his targets to inanimate objects.

He would organize the making of bows and arrows from the reeds that were used for making the monastery's sweeping-brooms and his ingenuity devised ever more dangerous games: 'I had seen the film of *Henry V* and noticed that in the battle scenes, the English longbow was shot very high into the air, with the French cavalry at the receiving end. I thought that was marvellous, arrows coming down from the sky like rain. So when we got out the bows and arrows, I would tell my gang to split into two groups and fire the arrows in the air at each other. Then we'd all dodge the arrows as they fell...It was very exciting.'

If only Kundun's existence could have been as carefree! Though, superficially, life pursued its even course – he prayed and meditated with growing seriousness, studied, gave and received teachings as usual – the background to these daily activities was growing ever more threatening. Public unrest in Lhasa was reaching danger level and, as the Chinese would tolerate no opposition, they made him issue a proclamation banning public gatherings and asking his people 'to refrain from anything that would impair the good relations between Tibet and China'.[9]

The full horror of the tragedy in Eastern Tibet had not yet come to light in Lhasa. Armed resistance had broken out in Kham and Amdo at the end of 1955 and became an organized guerrilla movement in the summer of 1956 after most of the nomad chiefs and village headmen had taken to the hills in protest at the punitive 'democratic reforms'. These Khampa warriors successfully attacked the new roads and bridges, army posts, military camps and supply columns but Chinese retaliation with superior firepower was devastatingly swift and merciless.

With the aerial bombardment of Lithang Monastery in Kham in June 1956, the struggle entered a new phase. The Chinese knew that the monastery had given refuge to resistance fighters from the local village and had ordered the monks to hand the rebels over or face being bombed. As most of the monks had never even seen an aeroplane let alone a bomb, they did not understand the significance of the threat. Until, that is, the bombs actually fell, killing the majority of those inside the monastery. 'When I heard of it, I cried,' said Kundun. 'I could not believe that human beings were capable of such cruelty to each other.' But even worse was to follow. The bombardment was followed by most sadistic reprisals: sexual abuse of celibate monks and nuns; and the torture and execution of the women and children whose husbands had dared to join the resistance.

Details of the Chinese atrocities in Kham were later supplied to the International Commission of Jurists and were published in August 1960. Eye-witnesses described how monks and laymen were tortured and many killed, often in barbarous ways; women raped and others publicly humiliated; venerated Lamas subjected to brutal and disgusting degradations; other monks and Lamas compelled to break their religious vows; men and boys deported or put to forced labour in harsh conditions; boys and girls taken from their homes, ostensibly for education in China; children incited to abuse and beat their parents; private property seized; monasteries damaged by gunfire; and sacred images, books and relics carried off or publicly destroyed.[10]

In vain did Kundun protest to General Chiang. The latter replied unblinkingly that any Tibetan who opposed the necessary reform of his country must expect to be punished![11] Still believing that these horrors were being perpetrated by over-zealous local functionaries out of step with the Chinese leadership, Kundun wrote to Mao. He received no reply, either to that letter or the next, or the one after that. It was difficult to go on believing in the Chairman's good faith.

Despite all his efforts, a peaceful resolution of Tibet's problems seemed further away than ever; the Preparatory Committee was an empty sham within which he and his ministers had been deprived of power; the stand-off between the guerrillas and the Chinese looked set to continue indefinitely, with neither side victorious, and women, children and the elderly being made to suffer the consequences. He felt he was losing the moral control of his people in Lhasa: how much longer could he hold out against their understandable desire to retaliate? He longed to be able to renounce the political leadership; yet he could only do that if he left the country. And that he was still unwilling to do.

NOTES

1. Norbu, *Tibet Is My Country*.
2. This was, of course, before the break in relations between China and the USSR.
3. *Tibet Is My Country*.
4. Author interview, Khando Chazotsang, Utah, February 1996.
5. Author interview with Tendzin Choegyal, Dharamsala, June 1994.
6. Drepung was divided into four colleges, each housing monks from a different locality. As Ngari Rinpoche, Tendzin Choegyal was a member of Gomang College.

7. Author interview with Tendzin Choegyal, Dharamsala, June 1994.

8. F. Spencer Chapman, *Lhasa, the Holy City.*

9. Gompo Tashi Andrugtsang, *Four Rivers, Six Ranges: A True Account of Khampa Resistance to the Chinese in Tibet*, Dharamsala, 1973.

10. Hugh Richardson, *Tibet and its History*, chapter 12.

11. This was an article of faith with the Chinese. Since the Han Chinese were the spearhead of the socialist revolution, the national minorities should strive to learn from them and emulate them. Any attempt to thwart the plans of the Han Chinese was a crime and must be vigorously opposed. See *Resistance and Reform in Tibet*, p. 57.

16

Buddha Jayanti 1956

Though all we see may seem to be eternal
It will soon fall to pieces and disappear.
Yesterday perhaps one had enough or more:
All today is gone and nothing left.

Milarepa, eleventh-century Tibetan poet and saint

Towards the end of 1956, the 2,500th anniversary of the Buddha's birth –
the Buddha Jayanti – was to be celebrated in India. As Nehru was eager
for the Dalai Lama to attend, he consulted Gyalo Thondup and W. D.
Shakabpa, co-founders of the Committee for Tibetan Social Welfare. 'Mr
Shakabpa and I,' says GT,

> told Mr Nehru and the Indian Government that it would be tragic for His
> Holiness to come and then have to return to Tibet. The Indian Government
> said that if they found a way of persuading the Chinese and if we could per-
> suade His Holiness to accept, they would offer him asylum in India. They
> said he could live in any of the Maharajahs' Palaces in India, and that then
> they would help him negotiate with the Chinese. We were pleased with the
> offer. So in the spring of 1956 Nehru sent the Maharajah of Sikkim who was
> President of the Mahabodhi Association of India with an invitation to His
> Holiness to attend the Buddha Jayanti. Through different channels we con-
> tacted His Holiness and urged him to accept their invitation, whatever the
> Chinese said.'

Kundun says of the secret discussions that followed: 'Even Lobsang Samten was kept in the dark. Mr Phala who was now my Lord Chancellor had felt compelled to distance himself from him because he was thought to be too close to the Chinese. Mr Phala was in secret communication with the Indian Mission in Lhasa, trying to decide whether or not I should take part. From time to time he would tell me what was going on, but he said nothing whatever to Lobsang Samten.'²

Kundun had made it clear he wished to attend the celebrations, but the Chinese insisted that his presence was necessary in Lhasa, what with all the Preparatory Committee work, the trouble in the East and so on. Everybody else in Lhasa felt he should go to India, and Nehru even hinted that Sino-Indian relations might suffer if the Dalai Lama were prevented from attending the Jayanti.

The Chinese continued to stall – until an eleventh hour telegram from Nehru persuaded them to relent – on condition that the Panchen Lama went too! When told the good news, Kundun rushed off, 'smiling as if my mouth would reach my ears', to tell his two tutors and three council ministers to prepare for the journey. The Chinese controlled their anger, but with hindsight, Kundun came to understand that it was this decision in 1956 to go to India against their wishes that turned their latent mistrust of him into outright hostility.³

Kundun left Lhasa in late November with his speeches pre-prepared by the Chinese – and to the tune of a solemn lecture from General Chiang about what he was to say and not say whilst in India. 'Of course, the Chinese suspected him,' admits Tendzin Choegyal. 'After all, my mother already had two sons out of the country, both of them well known for their anti-Chinese sentiments.'

Amala and Tsering Dolma, believing there was little chance of Kundun being allowed to attend the Jayanti, had already left for India. Many Tibetans were doing likewise, some of them seizing the opportunity to get out for good. (Among the latter were the Tsarongs. 'My parents were very unhappy with the Chinese occupation of our country,' says Namlha, 'and they foresaw worse problems ahead. So my mother insisted on our going back to India, especially as they were coming under increasing pressure to send my sister and me to China for our studies. She just took us away for the Buddha Jayanti pilgrimage and we never went back.') Norbu also made his way to India, hoping against hope that Kundun would be allowed to come. When Gyalo Thondup's wife met him at Calcutta airport with the news that his mother and sister had already reached Kalimpong, he hastened there to meet them. They told him about the massacres in Eastern Tibet and about the growing tension in Lhasa, where the refugees were multiplying rapidly.

When news came that Kundun was actually on his way to India, both brothers set off for the border without delay.

Lobsang Samten was to join the party and once again Tendzin Choegyal was determined not be left out:

> I heard that all the family was going to India. So early next morning, I walked all the way from Drepung to the Norbulingka to find Lobsang Samten. He was in the middle of washing. I told him I didn't want to be left behind, and he suggested that I should talk to His Holiness. I did so straight away. Kundun sighed and said, 'Don't you think you should stay behind and study?' I started to cry and after a bit he relented, as I knew he would.[4]

For Tendzin Choegyal, going to India was a great jaunt, combining the pleasures of being with his mother, taking part in a special pilgrimage, seeing Pema, Tenzin Ngawang and Khando again, and escaping from the monastery. But for Lobsang Samten, it was a different matter. He was under enormous pressure from the Chinese, and his official job as a liaison between them and what remained of the Tibetan Government meant that he was trusted by neither side. He was very depressed.

The travellers followed almost the same route as in 1951, when they had fled to the Chumbi Valley, but this time, the new road allowed them to go as far as Dromo by car, the journey taking two days instead of twenty-one. At the last settlement before the border, they mounted ponies, and with Chinese exhortations ringing in their ears – to beware of foreign imperialists and spies and to remember the glorious benefits the Chinese had brought to Tibet – the Dalai Lama's caravan began the long trek upwards into the mists and cold of the Nathu la Pass which marked the frontier with India. At the top of the pass stood a large mound of stones festooned with the prayer-flags which the Tibetans called *lung ta* – 'wind-horses' – which carry the prayers of the people into the unseen spiritual realm. In accordance with time-honoured practice, each of them added a stone to

the mound and shouted out, *Lha Gyal Lo* (Victory to the Gods) before beginning the descent to the wooded, snow-encrusted gorges of Sikkim and
the steaming plains of India beyond.

In a bungalow just beneath the pass, Norbu and Gyalo Thondup were
waiting impatiently. 'At last, late one evening, we heard the bells of a large
caravan coming down from the pass, and despite the heavy falls of snow
we hurried up to meet it.'[5]

Tendzin Choegyal rode ahead of the main party, his horse descending
the hill at speed. 'I have a vivid memory of suddenly catching sight of Taktser Rinpoche and Gyalo Thondup, and they both started laughing and
running towards me. We hugged each other, we were so happy.'

Kundun rode forward to exchange more formal greetings, then gave the
signal for the caravan to proceed towards the bungalow. He recalls the
breathless urgency with which his two older brothers greeted him:

> I really hadn't made up my mind about whether I would be returning to Tibet.
> But as soon as I reached the Sikkim border I was met by my brothers and the
> very first words they said, before even hello, how are you, nice to see you, were
> '*You must not go back.*' Their urgency really shook me. I knew that the situa-
> tion in Lhasa had deteriorated beyond recall, and I knew there was good reason
> for me to stay in India. But it was a very difficult decision to make. I couldn't
> be a hundred per cent certain that I would be doing the right thing if I stayed.[6]

That night, 'for the first time in our lives, we five brothers were assembled
round the same table. It was a solemn moment', wrote Norbu. The discussions went on until well past midnight. Norbu reported to Kundun that
the outside world was showing an interest in the fate of Tibet and that
help might be forthcoming. (A guarded reference, perhaps, to the fact that
he – and, through him, Gyalo Thondup – had already approached the CIA
for help, but if so, it was lost on his brother. The unworldly Kundun had
no suspicion that his brothers might be up to something.) Tendzin Choegyal was unaware of the political undercurrents, 'but I knew the conversation was about very serious matters. Some Tibetans who'd lived in India
for years had come along and they were very agitated.'

Norbu and Gyalo Thondup, sharing a tent on that bitterly cold night,
found sleep elusive. Next day, the brothers went their separate ways. Kundun was taken to Bagdogra on the Indian plain, where he boarded a specially chartered plane for New Delhi. His three brothers made their own way
there via Calcutta, where they found their mother and Tsering Dolma at

the airport. Pema, Tenzin Ngawang and Khando, on holiday from school, also joined them.

Kundun was welcomed by Prime Minister Nehru and by a huge crowd of Tibetans, spinning prayer wheels, offering khatas, prostrating, showing their love and respect in every way they knew. Journalists present were baffled by so spontaneous an outpouring of love. One of them described the scene as 'strange and different, a blend of reverence, esteem and affection...This is something no reporter can demonstrate quantitatively, or even prove at all, but can only report as something he knew existed.'[7]

Next morning Kundun made a special pilgrimage to the Rajghat, to venerate the ashes of his hero, Mahatma Gandhi:

> I was deeply moved as I prayed there on the green lawns which slope down to the Jamuna River. I felt I was in the presence of a noble soul...a true disciple of Lord Buddha and a true believer in peace and harmony among all men. As I stood there, I wondered what wise counsel the Mahatma would have given me if he had been alive. I felt sure he would have thrown all his strength of will and character into a peaceful campaign for the freedom of the people of Tibet...I made up my mind...to follow his lead whatever difficulties might confront me. I determined more strongly than ever that I could never associate myself with acts of violence.[8]

At a UNESCO meeting in Delhi, held to coincide with the Buddha Jayanti, Kundun threw away the prepared speeches given him by the Chinese and, though careful not to abandon caution altogether, told his audience that while all the world was preaching peace, vulnerable small nations were being swallowed up by large powerful ones. This, he said simply, should not pass unnoticed.[9]

As the Indian Government had placed a train at Kundun's disposal, the whole family travelled with him across India, visiting the sacred Buddhist sites. Amala immediately made friends with the Indian cooks on the train and they sometimes allowed her to prepare Tibetan meals for them all. The only irritant was the inescapable presence of Chinese functionaries, most of whom understood Tibetan. When Pema showed her displeasure, one of them commented to Amala, 'Your daughter obviously doesn't like us.' Fortunately he took no action.

Sixteen now, Pema felt that it was on this journey that she began to know Kundun for the first time. While the younger children were running all over the train, she had the opportunity of long, serious talks with her brother. He showed an interest in her life in India and seemed to approve of the education she was receiving from the nuns. (Nevertheless, she longed to return to Tibet, and asked Amala if it might be possible. Aware of the ever-listening Chinese, Amala replied quietly that perhaps it might be better for her to remain in Darjeeling.)

Whenever Kundun had to stay several days in the same place, a house was put at the family's disposal. For Pema it was a dream come true. 'We all took our meals together. For the first time I saw His Holiness as an ordinary human being. Even though I continued to respect him enormously as the Dalai Lama, I realized at that time that he was also a wonderful man. There was no longer that distance between us symbolized by all those steps at the Potala.'[10]

In Calcutta the family were lodged at the Grand Hotel. 'It was an eye-opener,' recalls Pema. 'For the first time I was learning the true story of what was going on in Tibet. It brought it all so much closer and made me long to be able to do something positive for my country.'[11] In this close family atmosphere, Norbu was swept by a wave of nostalgia for the past:

> When my mother made tea for her assembled brood in the old familiar way, it seemed to me almost that the dull and typical hotel room began to look like our old kitchen in Taktser. We older ones reminisced, and told the younger ones...of the happy days we had spent in the uplands of Amdo as children. And later on in the evenings, when they had gone to bed, we talked with the Dalai Lama and my mother of the future outlook, and I did not conceal my opinion that their days in Tibet were numbered too.[12]

Throughout, Amala preserved a calm common sense. Her principal concerns were Pema and Tendzin Choegyal. As the latter hurtled about the train playing with the Indian servants, she wondered about his future. He was the last of her children: Norbu was settled in the States, GT in India, and Lobsang Samten (who had undergone an appendectomy and tonsillectomy in Nangal in mid-journey) had decided against returning to Tibet. Should she perhaps arrange for Tendzin Choegyal to stay behind in India for his education? She consulted her older sons, they advised against it. As an Incarnate, they said, his place was in Tibet – for as long as it remained possible.

In the three months he spent travelling around India, Kundun found the freedom exhilarating – so different from his experience of China two years earlier. It was wonderful to be able to talk about the teachings of Buddha to scholars from many countries, and he tried to imagine what it would be like to be free, as they were, to proclaim and discuss Buddhist ideas! When he thought about how his hands were tied, how powerless he was to help his people, he wondered about staying in India, from where he could tell the world what was happening in Tibet. Abruptly he made up his mind to ask Nehru for political asylum.

The illusion that the choice was down to him was understandable but it ignored the political realities. Whatever Nehru might have assured Gyalo Thondup, he still held passionately to his belief that the peace of Asia depended on the friendship between India and China. (Regardless of the fact that the only danger to the peace of Asia was posed by China itself.) Much as he revered and sympathized with the Dalai Lama, Nehru would not permit him to endanger his dream. When the Tibetan leader broached the subject of political asylum, Nehru urged him to return to Tibet and work with the Chinese within the Seventeen-Point Agreement. In vain did Kundun protest that he had tried for seven years to do just that, while the Chinese had broken every single term of the Agreement. 'You must realize,' Nehru retorted, 'India cannot support you.' The most he would promise was to speak to the Chinese Prime Minister, Chou En-lai, due to arrive in Delhi next day.

In the event, Kundun saw Chou En-lai (Chew and Lie, as one Indian newspaper called him) before Nehru did, and voiced his concern over what was happening in Tibet. Chou lived up to his reputation as a silken-tongued charmer, but his words held an undertow of menace. 'He said that he had heard a rumour that I was considering staying in India. It would be a mistake, he warned. My country needed me.'[13] Chou was well aware that the situation all over Tibet was getting out of hand and, while professing sympathy for the Tibetans, he made it quite clear that the Chinese would use force in the event of trouble.

Kundun understood that he had no option but to return to Tibet. He went first to Calcutta to rejoin the family for a few days. Norbu and Gyalo Thondup had also met with Chou En-lai. They had resisted his blandishments to return to Tibet, Taktser telling Chou that everything he had heard about Chinese behaviour in Lhasa, coupled with his own experiences as Abbot of Kumbum, convinced him that 'the Chinese Communists were deliberately out to destroy everything that was holy and dear to us'.[14] Chou oozed charm to both brothers, but when he realized he was getting nowhere with them, insisted that at least they should persuade the

Dalai Lama to return home with all speed. Norbu and Gyalo Thondup replied that though they themselves preferred to live in freedom they had no authority over their brother.

In fact they, especially Gyalo Thondup, were furious at the way Nehru, under pressure from Chou En-lai, had reneged on his promises. 'Nehru betrayed us,' says GT angrily. 'I told the Indian Government officials at the time, "You are murdering His Holiness, you are murdering the people of Tibet. Look at how he has exposed his real feelings while he has been in India, and now you're pushing him back into the jaws of death." I was absolutely livid and even today [1995] I still feel we were betrayed.'[15]

Both brothers were still doing their utmost to persuade Kundun not to go back, to seek asylum elsewhere, if not in India. 'We felt there would be some terrible, unthinkable disaster if he returned.' They were baffled by his obstinacy:

> When I explained that, although I could see the logic of their arguments, I could not accept them, Gyalo Thondup began to show signs of agitation. He was – and still is – the most fiercely patriotic of my brothers. He has a very strong character and a tendency to be single-minded to the point of stubbornness...Taktser Rinpoche is milder-mannered than Gyalo Thondup...but on this occasion he too showed signs of exasperation.[16]

When Amala urged Kundun to stay, he replied gently, 'What good would remaining here in safety be, while all the people of Tibet are left at the mercy of the Chinese?'[17]

Bad weather delayed his departure for almost a month, but towards the end of March 1957, when the snow began to clear from the Nathu la, he began the depressing journey back to Lhasa. First came the parting with Lobsang Samten. 'It was a very sad goodbye,' he recalls. 'Lobsang Samten was weeping, despite the fact that his cheeks had so often borne the mark of my nails when we were children together.'[18] Amala understood that from his own point of view Lobsang's decision not to go back was a wise one; but she was anxious for Kundun who would be losing his best friend and most loyal supporter. Moreover, the Chinese would probably hold him responsible for the defection of yet another of his brothers!

Gloomily, Norbu (who was returning to the USA) and Gyalo Thondup accompanied Kundun to the frontier where his caravan waited. The last snows of winter were still falling, as they joined the weeping crowds of Tibetans and Indians at the top of the Nathu la. Kundun must have shuddered when he saw, overpowering the Tibetan *lung ta* fluttering prayerfully over the pass, the blood-red banners of the People's Republic of China.

The Lhasa to which he returned on 1 April 1957 was in turmoil. Chou Enlai had indeed ordered a few cosmetic changes: the Chinese had removed some troops and some of the blue-uniformed political officers responsible for introducing the more unwelcome reforms; work had been stopped on a new army barracks and on a controversial hydro-electric plant; and there was much ostentatious breast-beating in the local papers about the excessive zeal shown by the Han Chinese, their lamentable failure to respect local customs, etc. But by and large, this belated sensitivity to Tibetan feelings was the usual hogwash, for in reality the situation was deteriorating fast. That the invaders were settling in for the duration was obvious – a whole new district had sprung up in Lhasa to accommodate the Chinese officials and their families. (It was the beginning of a ruthless take-over, which within a few years would transform Lhasa into a featureless concrete jungle indistinguishable from any other Chinese city.) The Provisional Committee continued to discuss meaningless policies, while relentlessly whittling down Kundun's authority and stifling any voice of protest.

The spiralling violence in eastern Tibet – attack followed by brutal military reprisals – had turned the region into a wasteland. Throughout the preceding year the proud and independent Khampa chieftains had overcome their ancient tribal animosities – and the vast distances that separated them from each other – to form a loose-knit alliance to protect their traditional Buddhist values. Called first 'The Volunteer Army to Defend Buddhism', it became known as Chushi Gangdrug ('Four Rivers, Six Ranges'), the old name for Eastern Tibet.

The rebels made contact with Gyalo Thondup in India, asking him for help with weapons and training. From now on, GT's Committee for Tibetan Social Welfare would become the power-house of the Tibetan Resistance. He had all the right connections. With the help of his Chinese-born wife, he enlisted the aid of the Nationalists in Taiwan in parachuting a limited number of arms and supplies to the guerrillas. And as these requests were always filtered through the CIA, the Americans suggested that perhaps he should deal directly with them.

In Darjeeling, Pema, Tenzin Ngawang and Khando had at least a glimmering of their Uncle Thondup's other life. 'He was always very political, very wrapped up in the Tibetan cause,' says Pema. 'He encouraged us to be patriots like himself, told us how important freedom was for a nation.'[19] He was 'always in and out, we were never quite sure where he was,' echoes Khando. 'He often used to come home and ask us to cyclostyle leaflets. We would spend the whole weekend doing them. Much later, he told us that they were being dropped over Tibet.'

When the CIA offered to train a number of Tibetans in guerrilla warfare, Gyalo Thondup did not hesitate. 'We chose a small group of Khampas and in 1956 we started a border crossing,' he says. 'I used to take the men from the Tibetan border to Darjeeling and Kalimpong, then to the Pakistan border where the Americans were waiting to collect them.' They were flown to an unidentified island in the North Pacific (possibly Guam) to be taught about modern weaponry and commando techniques. One of them was Gyalo Thondup's cousin, Lhamo Tsering.

A year later they were parachuted into Tibet, to help organize the Resistance more efficiently. Each of them carried 'a pistol, a small machine-gun, an old Japanese radio, $132 in Tibetan currency, and a bracelet containing vials of poison to be taken in the event of capture.'[20] There was also, and this later became a very contentious issue, a 'yellow parachute', allegedly containing gold, dollars, Tibetan and Indian money.

But, even with CIA help, the Tibetan freedom fighters were still hopelessly ill-equipped. Air-drops of weapons made by the Americans often did more harm to the Tibetans than to the Chinese. The Americans were anxious that their assistance should not be attributable, the Dalai Lama later wrote, so 'they dropped only a few badly made bazookas and some ancient British rifles which had once been in general service throughout India and Pakistan and thus could not be traced to source in the event of capture. But the mishandling they received whilst being air-dropped rendered them almost useless.'[21] Occasionally the CIA would delay too long and by the time help arrived it was already too late.

The Chinese response was savage. They not only shelled the villages which were giving support to the guerrillas, but let loose a campaign of atrocities against the people of eastern Tibet:

> The obliteration of entire villages was compounded by hundreds of public executions, carried out to intimidate the surviving population. The methods employed included crucifixion, dismemberment, vivisection, beheading,

burying, burning and scalding alive, dragging the victims to death behind galloping horses and pushing them from air-planes; children were forced to shoot their parents, disciples their religious teachers. Everywhere monasteries were prime targets. Monks were compelled to publicly copulate with nuns and desecrate sacred images before being sent to a growing string of labour camps.[22]

Survivors, monks and laypeople from the villages, began a long and arduous trek towards Lhasa and by 1958 almost ten thousand were camped all around the city. The people of Lhasa grew more and more inflamed by the refugees' stories. As the Resistance Movement acquired a new headquarters in Lhoka, a region to the south-east of Lhasa, and thousands of angry volunteers rushed to join it, it was suddenly clear that the focus of revolt had shifted from the East to Central Tibet. Co-operation with the Chinese was at an end. Hatred of the invaders was – temporarily, at least – uniting all Tibetans. Under the leadership of a trader from Lithang, Gompo Tashi Andrugtsang, the guerrilla force was reorganized and became the National Volunteer Defence Army. As the rebels edged ever closer to Lhasa, notching up an impressive number of successes, the Chinese military commander, General Chiang, began pressuring the Dalai Lama to bring in the Tibetan Army against them.

Kundun was in a Catch-22 situation. On the one hand, the rebels believed that he and his Kashag were in league with the Chinese since they would not countenance the use of violence against them. On the other, the Political Commissar, General Tan, made his life a misery, coming every day to the Norbulingka, 'to urge, cajole and abuse me', until eventually the mere sight of the audience room in the palace began to fill him with dread. Furious at Kundun's refusal to bring in his troops (on the grounds that the Tibetan Army was too small, too ill-trained, and in any case likely to defect and join the rebels), General Tan changed tack, denouncing Norbu, Gyalo Thondup and the Committee for Tibetan Social Welfare as traitors and demanding that they be stripped of their Tibetan citizenship. Kundun, reckoning his brothers were safely out of harm's way, agreed to excommunicate them. His main concern was how to prevent the fighting from reaching Lhasa itself – which would make catastrophe certain.

'My classmates in Drepung were all talking about resisting the Chinese. We knew there was going to be a fight, and we were sure we'd win.'[23] Tendzin Choegyal at twelve was aware at last of the political realities.

Like all the monks at Drepung, he had gradually been drawn into the Chinese net: 'The Chinese used everyone, even me. I was paid a salary of thirteen Chinese dollars a year, with which I could buy toys. I was made a member of the Department of Religious Affairs while I was in Drepung. All the high lamas were paid a salary and given a job description. You hadn't got to do anything; just attend meetings whenever you were told to. Actually, they thought I was a good Communist. I was quite good at deceiving them.'[24]

As the Chinese began arming their own civilians and setting up barricades, tension escalated. 'No one dared speak openly because someone might be listening,' Amala later told a friend:

> Many people, especially those known to hold anti-Chinese views, disappeared never to be seen again...I visited His Holiness every week and brought him a loaf of the Amdo bread he liked so much. He kept reassuring me that everything would be all right and that I should not worry. I asked him why I shouldn't worry. 'What could happen?' he asked me. 'They will kill you,' I replied. 'What good would *that* do them?' he said, laughing. 'And if they try to take me to China against my will, I won't go.'[25]

With the family, the Chinese were still playing cat-and-mouse. 'On the surface,' says Phuntsok Tashi, 'things were all right, but in a subtle way we knew everything had changed.' The officials were still friendly, dropping in regularly to see Amala or Tsering Dolma. 'But when they came, they were really trying to feel the pulse of the family, trying to discover what they felt about things.'[26] Amala, suspected of engineering the escape of her three sons, was under strict surveillance; and it did not help that Pema, Tenzin Ngawang and Khando were still at school in India. As Pema later explained, the Chinese had forbidden the family to leave Tibet and contact with them had almost dried up:

> My mother and sister couldn't write to us, because the Chinese were always breathing down their necks, asking why their children were in India. They didn't even dare have our pictures in the house. They had to hide them away, because the Chinese kept insisting that we should be brought back to Lhasa and sent to Peking for our education. So they had to keep a low profile and we didn't hear from them very often. It was hard for us children to understand that.[27]

One day, a distant relative of Kundun's late father who worked in the Chinese Security Service let slip a warning while drunk. 'The Chinese mean you no good,' he blurted out after attending a meeting where plans to 'make sure of catching the old woman' had been discussed. And at an official Patriotic Women's meeting, Tsering Dolma was horrified to hear General Tan say that where you had a piece of fly-blown meat, you had to destroy the meat before you could get rid of the flies. His audience was left in no doubt that the polluted meat was the Dalai Lama and his Kashag. But, frightened though she was, Amala hid her fear and did her best to rally the spirits of her family. 'It doesn't matter what happens to any of us individually,' she told her youngest son firmly. 'Our whole country is being persecuted. Why should we bother about our family being singled out?'[28]

The long, cold winter months of 1958–9 passed with agonizing slowness. Amid daily reports of Chinese outrages against civilians in the East, Kundun forced himself to study in preparation for his final examinations scheduled for March. It was hard not to hate the Chinese, yet Buddhist faith forbade hatred: 'I reminded myself constantly of the Buddha's teaching that our enemy is in a sense our greatest teacher. And if this was sometimes hard to do, I never really doubted that it was so.'[29]

As tension rose, Kundun heard of a memo sent by the PLA to Mao. The prisons were all full of rebellious Tibetans, it said. What did Mao advise? Mao replied that Tibetan discontent was immaterial and if necessary they could gaol the whole population. Kundun thought of the old days when he had recognized and empathized with every prisoner in the Potala. He often wondered what his hero, Gandhi, would have done in this present situation. Would he have continued to advocate non-violence?

Time was running out. Even before the New Year of 1959 – Earth Hog Year – had dawned, Kundun had 'definite information that the Chinese were fully prepared to attack us. It was only a question of the day and the hour.'[30]

NOTES

1. Author interview with Gyalo Thondup, New Delhi, July 1995.
2. Author interview with HH the Dalai Lama, Dharamsala, June 1994.
3. Author interview with HH the Dalai Lama, Dharamsala, June 1994.
4. Author interview with Tendzin Choegyal, Dharamsala, October 1993.
5. Norbu, *Tibet Is My Country*.
6. Author interview with HH the Dalai Lama, Dharamsala, June 1994.

7. Goodman, *The Last Dalai Lama*.

8. Fourteenth Dalai Lama, *My Land and My People*, chapter 8.

9. Shakabpa, *Tibet: A Political History*, chapter 18.

10. Pema, *Tibet, Mon Histoire*.

11. Author interview with Jetsun Pema, Dharamsala, June 1994.

12. *Tibet Is My Country*.

13. Fourteenth Dalai Lama, *Freedom in Exile*.

14. *Tibet Is My Country*.

15. Author interview with Gyalo Thondup, New Delhi, July 1995.

16. Fourteenth Dalai Lama, *Freedom in Exile*.

17. Goodman, interview with the Gyayum Chenmo (Amala), Dharamsala, May 1980, quoted in *The Last Dalai Lama*.

18. Author interview with HH the Dalai Lama, Dharamsala, June 1994.

19. Author interview with Jetsun Pema, Dharamsala, June 1994.

20. Goodman.

21. *Freedom in Exile*.

22. Avedon, *In Exile from the Land of Snows*.

23. Author interview with Tendzin Choegyal, Dharamsala, June 1994.

24. Author interview with Tendzin Choegyal, June 1994.

25. Goodman, interview with the Gyayum Chenmo (Amala), Dharamsala, May 1980, quoted in *The Last Dalai Lama*.

26. Author interview with Phuntsok Tashi Taklha, London 1993.

27. Author interview with Jetsun Pema, Dharamsala, June 1994.

28. Author interview with Tendzin Choegyal, October 1994.

29. *Freedom in Exile*.

30. Avedon, *An Interview with the Dalai Lama*.

17

Uprising and Escape 1959

The only published figure we have for Tibetans killed in the
Lhasa uprising and its aftermath is from official sources. A
booklet marked 'secret' and published in Lhasa on October 1,
1960 by the political department of the Tibetan Military District, says...'From last March up to now we have already
wiped out over 87,000 of the enemy.'

Jamyang Norbu, 'The Tibetan Resistance Movement'[1]

Yet Earth Hog Year started like any other, with festivities in the streets
followed by a three-week prayer festival. The tragedy began in quite a low
key with an invitation to the Dalai Lama and his family to attend a
performance by a new dance troupe from China at the military HQ in Lhasa
early in March; and with a statement on Radio Peking that the Tibetan ruler
would be attending the National People's Congress in Peking in April.

Kundun had accepted neither invitation, being entirely preoccupied
with thoughts of the looming final examinations for his Doctorate in
Metaphysics, the goal towards which his many years of study had been
leading him. It involved intensive debating on a wide range of subjects in
which he must pit his wits against the finest minds in Tibet. The course
usually took twenty years to complete, yet he had taken only half that
time. For the last two years he had been studying hard and had already
passed the preliminary bouts – dialectical debates in front of the combined
colleges of all Three Seats: Drepung, Sera and Ganden. The all-important

final would take place in the Jokhang temple, and now that the time had come he was nervous. 'The field of study was so vast, there were so many texts and commentaries, you simply had no idea from which area the debaters would choose their questions.'[2]

The Chinese had their own agenda and no mere religious examination would be allowed to interfere with it. On the evening before the examination, when Kundun had already taken up residence in the Jokhang, the Political Commissar, General Tang, despatched two junior officials to his quarters to insist on his fixing a date for the entertainment. Nothing could have been further from Kundun's thoughts at that moment and he managed to persuade the officials to wait at least until next day's examination was over. But however much he tried to concentrate on the work in hand, he could not fail to notice the signs of mounting tension outside. 'The examination hall was just opposite a house which the Chinese had bought from a noble family. It was sandbagged on the top of the roofs and round all the windows like all the other houses the Chinese occupied in Lhasa.'[3]

Next day, 2 March, he performed brilliantly and achieved a distinguished doctorate. Three days later he returned to the Norbulingka in the traditional glittering procession. It would, in fact, be the last parade, the swansong of Old Tibet. And from it, for the first time since the occupation, the Chinese were notably absent.

Having no excuse for further stalling, Kundun agreed on a date – 10 March – for the dance-troupe performance. On the ninth, his brother-in-law, Commander of the Bodyguard, Phuntsok Tashi, was summoned from his breakfast to discuss the arrangements. He was stunned to be handed a list of impossible conditions: that the visit should be kept secret (as if Kundun's movements could ever be kept secret from the Lhasa populace!); that Kundun was to go to Chinese headquarters unaccompanied by either ministers or bodyguard; and that no Tibetan troops were to be stationed beyond the bridge which marked the boundaries of the military camp.

With his customary cool, Kundun found the provisos merely 'a little strange and unusual', whereas to his ministers they seemed utterly bizarre. As for what the Tibetans would say when the news leaked out – as it assuredly would – of that there was absolutely no doubt. They would conclude that the Chinese intended to abduct the Dalai Lama to Peking and they simply would not allow it.

The news did leak out and Lhasa, overflowing with New Year revellers, monks attending the Great Prayer Festival, and refugees from the East –

reacted with predictable passion. Whatever scenario the Chinese had in mind, they had almost certainly underestimated the devotion of the Tibetans to their leader, their determination to protect him from harm at all costs. From now on, it would be the people who dictated the course of events. By sunset on 9 March, thousands of them had streamed out of Lhasa to camp – with cooking pots, knives and blankets – outside the Norbulingka gates, ready to defend Kundun to the death. Rinchen Dolma Taring recalls a young man running into her office with the news that everybody in Lhasa was off to the Norbulingka:

> Everybody knew that the Chinese had already invited some lamas in eastern Tibet to their theatres and then kidnapped them, so now thousands were around the Norbulingka, begging His Holiness not to go into such danger. The young man said he was on his way to join the crowd...⁴

By dawn on the tenth, their numbers were swollen to about fifteen thousand; the mood was ugly and uncompromising. When a junior official suspected of being a Chinese spy put in an appearance he was dragged from his bicycle and stoned to death. The people were serving notice on the Chinese that they had had enough.

Alarmed by this turn of events, Kundun cancelled his attendance at the entertainment. The crowds were told but they had already passed the point of no return – they had made themselves the guardians of his safety and would do whatever the situation demanded. For Kundun, it was like being trapped between two erupting volcanoes.

> On the one hand there was the vehement, unequivocal, unanimous protest of my people against the Chinese regime; on the other, there was the armed might of an aggressive occupation force. If there was a clash between the two, the result was a foregone conclusion. The Lhasan people would be ruthlessly massacred in their thousands; and Lhasa – and the rest of Tibet – would see a full-scale military rule with all its persecutions and tyranny.⁵

Until that day, Kundun had felt little anxiety on his own behalf. But now, he realized, everything had suddenly changed, the situation had assumed a relentless momentum of its own. Though perhaps neither side would in cold blood have chosen this particular place and time for a showdown, long-repressed resentments were rising to the surface, and could no longer be contained. He sensed that this 10 March 1959 was a date he would remember for ever:

I remember it with vivid clearness. I was upstairs with my Lord Chamberlain, Mr Phala, who was trying to explain what was happening and what we ought or ought not to do next. It was about ten in the morning. The sky was unusually blue, the sun very bright. I remember saying very slowly to Mr Phala that perhaps this day, 10 March, would be a landmark in Tibetan history. I didn't know then how right I was![6]

At roughly the same moment, his younger brother, Tendzin Choegyal, was being collected from Drepung in a Soviet-made car for the three-mile trip to the Chinese camp. With no sense that history was about to be made, the boy was looking forward to an interesting day out, away from the restrictions of Drepung. But on arriving at the camp he knew instantly that something was wrong:

For a start, they were all armed, all the Chinese and all the pro-Chinese Tibetans. An old friend of my brother Lobsang Samten came up to me. I made to embrace him and could feel the pistol inside his gown. They knew something was about to happen all right, and they knew how they were going to respond...General Tan was furious that His Holiness wasn't coming. His face was crimson and he kept thumping the table with his fist, saying it was all the fault of a bunch of reactionaries. He would liquidate them, he shouted, if they didn't come to heel. I had never seen him so angry. They went ahead with the performance, though, or at least a shortened form of it.[7]

With hindsight, Tendzin Choegyal recognizes he was lucky to escape with his life that day. His mother certainly feared the worst. A former Amdo neighbour had burst in on her early that morning, with the news that everyone was heading for the Norbulingka. The Great Mother did not rush to the palace, but neither did she go to the theatrical performance. When the Chinese drivers came to collect her, her servants told them she was unwell – and after a brief scuffle threw them off the premises. From behind a curtain in her bedroom she watched them drive away in a fury. All that day she had feared for the life of her youngest son; even imagining she could hear his terrified cries. Without much hope, she posted a servant at the crossroads where the road from the camp forked off towards Drepung. When the man saw a car approaching with Tendzin Choegyal inside, he beckoned the Chinese driver to stop, telling him that the young man's mother was ill and he was to go home rather than to the monastery. 'I got out of the car and walked the remaining distance. The gate was – most unusually – closed, but when the gatekeeper saw it was me he opened it. My mother was watching from an upstairs window and when she saw me she was so relieved she clapped her hands, then burst into tears.'[8]

It was as though her son had returned from the dead.

Before going to bed that night, the boy looked out his old .22 rifle. Disappointed to find only one bullet left, he nevertheless loaded the rifle and slept with it by his side. All over Lhasa, people were doing likewise, determined to fight with what few resources they had, naïvely convinced that they would win.

Next morning, Tendzin Choegyal and his mother breakfasted on butter-tea and tsampa, talking of everyday matters, as though nothing untoward had happened. The charade ended at 7.30 when a driver arrived in one of Kundun's personal jeeps to take them to the Norbulingka. 'The Great Mother was quite calm,' Phuntsok Tashi recalls. 'She kept telling us not to worry. She was mainly concerned with making the proper arrangements for her seventy-year-old mother to be looked after.'[9] In fact, contingency plans for a possible escape had already been carefully drawn up, but all involved in the planning were sworn to the utmost secrecy. Phuntsok Tashi had made Tsering Dolma swear on oath that she would give no hint, not even to her closest friends, of what was afoot. She was to pack a few things, but discreetly, so that nobody might suspect that an escape was in the offing.

The pace of events began to accelerate. The Tibetan National Assembly in emergency session unanimously declared the 1951 Seventeen-Point Agreement to be null and void – the Chinese having breached almost every one of its clauses. Tibetan Army units which had been incorporated into the People's Liberation Army exchanged their Chinese uniforms for the old Tibetan khaki and distributed their surplus weapons to the crowds outside the Norbulingka.

Nervous householders were building stockades, covering their flat roofs with barbed wire, barricading themselves in with sandbags and sacks of salt; and though Kundun continued to plead for calm, everyone knew that the showdown was at hand. That evening, 'loudspeakers appeared on the roofs of buildings controlled by the Chinese. They announced that everyone should understand that all resistance to the Chinese occupation of Lhasa was futile. "You are like ants scratching at the elephant's feet," they said, "China is as mighty as the sun and wherever there is sun, there the Chinese are also."'[10] Over one hundred Chinese trucks converged on Lhasa from the west and east.

Next day, Kundun consulted the State Oracle:

To my astonishment, he shouted, 'Go! Go! Tonight!' The medium, still in his
trance, then staggered forward and, snatching up some paper and a pen, wrote
down, quite clearly and explicitly, the route that I should take out of the Norbulingka, down to the last Tibetan town on the Indian border...That done, the
medium, a young monk named Lobsang Jigme, collapsed in a faint, signifying
that [the god] had left his body. Just then, as if to reinforce the oracle's instructions, two mortar shells exploded...outside.[11]

'Until that morning, we had been in two minds about leaving,' recalls
Phuntsok Tashi, 'but after the bombs exploded, we had no choice. I sent
some people ahead to alert the guerrillas south of the river Kyi Chu.'[12] 'I
think the final decision to go was taken only hours before we left,' says
Tendzin Choegyal. 'It was very hush-hush, and only a very few crucial
people were in the secret. There were spies in the crowd who would have
informed the Chinese about anything suspicious. In any case, if the Tibetans had known His Holiness was leaving, they'd all have tried to follow
him and then there'd have been a bloodbath.'[13]

The sun was still shining, and they knew that if they were to have any
hope of success, they must wait for darkness. That evening, one of the
monk-officials on guard over the weapons store in the Norbulingka, noticed a man waiting beside an open-topped truck. 'This was very unusual.
I asked what he was doing and he said vaguely he was just waiting for
someone. I went back to the Norbulingka to collect some weapons and
when I returned, the vehicle was no longer there. Then suddenly it re-ap-
peared, with the cover down. I gaped as I saw His Holiness's tutors, the
Gadung Oracle and various Kashag officials getting inside. They were leaving Lhasa, in a truck, hidden underneath a tarpaulin. I decided then and
there it was time for me to go too.'[14]

It had been agreed that the party should split into small groups of three
or four which would join up only after they had crossed the river Kyi Chu.
Amala, Tsering Dolma and Tendzin Choegyal followed close behind,
Amala wearing the green, fur-lined *chuba* of a Khampa man and a maroon
hat with gold stitching. Tendzin Choegyal, who had found an old Luger
pistol and managed to collect several bullets for it, had changed out of his
monk's robes into a simple *chuba* and covered his shorn head with a
woollen cap. When he saw his mother and sister dressed as Khampas, he
burst out laughing.

The soldiers came, giving them the all-clear. It was, he remembers, about nine o'clock in the evening:

> We went out into the cold March air and started to walk towards one of the gates which faced south. We just prayed that we wouldn't be seen as we crossed the courtyard. I have to say, we were very, very lucky. My mother, who had an arthritic knee, was offered a mule to ride on, but the rest of us walked until we came to the south bank of the river Kyi Chu. It was dark, with just a sliver of moon. When our eyes got used to the darkness, we could see the lights of the Chinese camp ahead of us. Fortunately, there was a wind blowing from the direction of the camp and I hoped it would muffle whatever noise we might be making.[15]

The 'wind' was one of those sandstorms by which Lhasa was habitually plagued. That night it probably saved their lives. The blinding sandstorm, wrote the usually sceptical Heinrich Harrer in *Life* magazine,[16] was 'so providentially timed that I found myself believing in a miraculous divine intervention'. Harrer, to whom Kundun told his story later, wrote that 'these sandstorms in Lhasa obliterate everything. You must close your eyes to avoid being blinded. You close your lips tight shut, yet still the sand gets into your teeth. When you are caught in such a storm you must just wrap your mantle right round you, covering your face and head and wait for it to pass.' This, suggests Harrer, is what the Chinese soldiers, in their garrison a mere two hundred yards to the south of the Norbulingka, must have done that night 'as the god-king moved invisibly through them'.

Small units of his personal bodyguard guarded the way to the river, with orders to draw off the Chinese fire in the event of an attack. 'It seemed like an eternity,' says Phuntsok Tashi. 'We kept mistaking the branches of trees for men. Fortunately the moon was not very bright and we had cloud cover. But we were so frightened, every time the clouds cleared we simply prayed for them to return.'[17] But the Chinese noticed nothing, as one after another, the small groups of Tibetans arrived at the far side of the river Kyi Chu. 'There was a stretch of sand and our feet sank into it as we walked, making progress terribly difficult,' remembers Tendzin Choegyal.

> When we reached the river, we crossed it by the wooden ferry. You couldn't see anybody's face, but you could make out a lot of silhouettes moving up and down – and lots of horses. I walked by myself along the river bank until I could see the outline of my monastery, Drepung, in the distance, towards the north-west...I prostrated three times and prayed that I would see Drepung

again before I died. Then I turned round and went back. A group of about thirty Khampa guerrilla fighters were waiting there with ponies for us all. Before we rode off, there was a tremendous commotion. I could hear voices shouting, 'He's come, here he is.' Then a figure rode up on horseback, wishing us all *Tashi Delek*, the greeting we generally reserve for New Year. I recognized the voice as that of Mr Phala, His Holiness's Chamberlain; and I knew then that His Holiness was safe and had gone ahead of us.'[18]

Kundun was in an agony of spirit. Once the decision to go had been taken, he went to his chapel to pray before returning to his room and replacing his monk's robes with a soldier's uniform and fur cap. Exhausted and drained, he slung a rifle over his shoulder and removed his glasses to complete the disguise. Then, going out into the dark garden, he passed unnoticed through the Norbulingka gate. Throughout the ferry crossing he feared 'that every splash of the oars would draw machine-gun fire down on us', but he arrived safely on the opposite shore. The escape from Lhasa, one of the great epic stories of the twentieth century, was under way.

There are still those who argue that it should never have taken place, that the Dalai Lama was deserting his people in their hour of need. That argument, forceful enough to the Western mind, is meaningless to a Tibetan: it misunderstands the Dalai Lama's role, the fact that to Tibetans he is not just the ruler of Tibet but *is* Tibet; that if harm comes to him Tibet itself is finished. Given a choice, Kundun might well have chosen to stay and share his people's fate, but he too was reared in that tradition and had to bow to its logic. 'If I'd stayed in Lhasa, I don't suppose I'd have been left alive,' he says, 'the Chinese would have considered me expendable. But even if they had kept me alive, Tibet would have been finished.'[19]

The frequent criticisms infuriate Tendzin Choegyal: 'Those who say – or even think – such things have no idea what they're talking about. His Holiness could have done nothing for Tibet by staying. The Chinese would have increased their stranglehold just the same, all Tibetans would have been subjected to their power; we'd all have been slaves. They would have used His Holiness just as the Japanese used poor Pu Yi. That's what he would have become, another Pu Yi[20].'[21]

All that night and most of the next day, they rode towards the Brahmaputra River, which in Tibet is called the Tsang Po. Avoiding the well-worn south-westerly routes to India for fear of Chinese patrols, they headed south-east, to a vast area of pathless mountains, beyond which lay the main Himalayan range and India. By daybreak on the next morning they had reached the foot of the Che la, a 16,000-feet high Himalayan pass, which lay between them and the river. Ten hours after leaving the Norbulingka, they stopped for a first cup of steaming hot butter-tea before tackling the rigours of the high pass.

The climb to 16,000 feet over rocks and on horseback was exhausting and perilous. At the top, they dismounted and stood in the snow and ice to take a last sad farewell of Lhasa, before descending the steep sandy slopes on the other side. There is a saying in Tibet that if your horse will not carry you uphill, it is no horse, while if a man will not walk downhill to rest his horse he is no man.[22] Struggling through soft sand dunes blown up by storms from the river was particularly hard for Amala, says Tendzin Choegyal:

> Our horses would take one step up and slide back four. My mother was the worst sufferer. Her arthritic leg was hurting and she wasn't dressed very warmly. It wasn't too bad on the way up, but coming down at daybreak – on slippery, sandy slopes – we all had to dismount and walk, which was awful for her, with her arthritic knees. Two of our escort supported her between them one holding her left arm, the other her right, half lifting her off the ground, half dragging her along.

But however hard the going, his mother never lost her sense of humour and never complained:

> When we were negotiating those sandy slopes, for example, the going was very slippery. One of the members of our party was very fat and his saddle was almost sliding off his horse's back. He was hanging on to the mane for dear life, and my mother was convulsed with laughter.[23]

When finally they reached the level ground of the valley, another violent dust-storm blew up and almost blinded them.

Ten miles to the east was the Pentsha ferry, the only means of crossing the river – they could but pray the Chinese had not reached it first. Luck was with them and early in the morning on the second day they were rowed across in yak-hide coracles. Despite their exhaustion, they rode on, and the sun was already setting when for the first time in twenty-four hours they were able to stop and eat the tsampa, dried meat and dried cheese they had brought with them. There on the far side of the Tsang Po, they were at last in the territory held by the Chushi Gangdrug, the Tibetan guerrillas. Phase One of the escape had been well handled by the Palace party,[24] but from here on, the guerrillas would take charge. Reinforcements were waiting; the party swelled to one hundred, with an escort of three hundred and fifty Tibetan soldiers and at least fifty guerrillas. 'We had a radio link with our people in Lhasa, so we knew what was happening,' says Gyalo Thondup. 'At that time, the Resistance had more or less stitched up the southern part of the country; no Chinese troops dared go there. So as soon as His Holiness had crossed the river, our people were there to meet him. I was the first to be informed that they had linked up. I was very relieved when the message came through.'[25]

At the monastery of Rame, the travellers had their first night's rest. Kundun had already been there for several hours when the rest of the family arrived. 'We went in,' says Tendzin Choegyal, 'and saw Kundun watching from a window facing the courtyard. I went straight up to see him. At first he just stood there, wearing those unfamiliar layman's clothes, staring silently out of the window. Then he turned round and looked at me and asked if I was tired. I said no. He turned to the window again and said slowly, "Tendzin, do you realize we're free now?"'[26]

Breaking into separate groups to avoid detection from the air, and watched over by relays of devoted guerrillas, they left Rame next morning to cross the Sabo Pass. Kundun took Tendzin Choegyal under his wing, believing that his mother and sister would make better speed without him. The boy was proud to be travelling with his brother; his Luger pistol was pressing painfully into his hip-bone, but he would not remove it from its place of honour on his belt. Thus armed – with a dagger in his belt for good measure – he believed himself a match for any would-be attacker. Unfortunately for his romantic self-image, the aspiring hero was given Kundun's umbrella to carry!

Each day small bands of guerrillas, many of them tough Khampa giants, festooned with pistols, swords, daggers and charm-boxes, would appear from nowhere to protect their advance. At this stage, the plan was for Kundun to establish a temporary base at the hill-top fort of Lhuntse Dzong, sixty miles north of the Indian border, from where he could negotiate with the Chinese about the future of Tibet. So far, they had heard no news on the battery-operated radio receiver they carried with them: Radio Lhasa had gone dead. At one stopping-place, they picked up a Voice of America bulletin which spoke of unrest in Lhasa and indicated that the

Dalai Lama's whereabouts were uncertain; but that was all. They continued to push forward to Lhuntse Dzong, battling with fierce blizzards, crossing high passes every day, some as high as 19,000 feet and encrusted with ice and snow. On 24 March, a broadcast confirmed Kundun's worst fears: two days after they had left Lhasa, the Chinese had shelled the Norbulingka – and opened fire on the crowds milling around it; then had turned their heavy artillery on the city, the Potala, the Jokhang and the main monasteries. Only later would they learn the terrible truth that, after three days of bitter fighting, Lhasa had been reduced to a smoking ruin, with thousands of dead and wounded lying in its wreckage; and thousands more on their way to years of imprisonment in the Chinese Gulag. They heard then that the Chinese still did not know the Dalai Lama had left, and were frantically searching for him among the dead round the Norbulingka. (Whether to kill or capture him was unclear.) Ploughing their way through the piled-up corpses outside the palace, the Chinese soldiers had examined each one, calling out 'Dalai Lama, Dalai Lama' as they did so.

Kundun heard all this in a daze of disbelief and horror. Why, he wondered, had the Chinese responded with such mindless ferocity to the people's heart-felt protest? He could think of only one possible reason:

> Our people – not especially our rich or ruling classes, but our ordinary people – had finally, eight years after the invasion began, convinced the Chinese that they would never willingly accept their alien rule. So the Chinese were trying now to terrify them, by merciless slaughter, to accept this rule against their will.[27]

What he did not know until years later was that when Mao was told that order had been restored in Lhasa, the Chairman had asked: 'And what of the Dalai Lama?' Told that Kundun had escaped, he sighed heavily and said, 'In that case we have lost the battle.'[28]

Tendzin Choegyal was horror-struck by the news from Lhasa. 'I had never for one moment doubted we would win,' he says, 'but when we heard that the Norbulingka had been bombarded and that so many Chinese troops were involved, it came as a terrible shock. It was impossible to absorb.'[29]

On the twenty-eighth, Chou En-lai announced the dissolution of the Tibetan Government and its replacement by the Provisional Committee. The old Tibet was thus officially declared dead.

Further negotiation with the Chinese was clearly out of the question, and nowhere, not even Lhuntse Dzong, would afford them a safe haven. The Chinese, realizing at last that Kundun had escaped, had already crossed the Tsang Po in force, and PLA troops had been ordered to find and block off all escape-routes from southern Tibet to India. It was time for quick thinking. With his options running out, Kundun, in a brief ceremony at Lhuntse Dzong, formally re-established his Government – then sent a small group of the fittest men ahead to India with an urgent request to Prime Minister Nehru for political asylum.

When they set off again next day, two of the highest, most inaccessible passes had still to be faced. It would take them many days more in diabolical weather. On the summit of the Lagoe la Pass, a violent snowstorm hit them; their fingers and hands were numb with cold; their eyebrows and moustaches froze to their faces. They did not have enough warm clothing and the only way to keep their blood from freezing was to dismount and lead their ponies with hands that nearly froze to the reins. As an additional worry, there was very little food left for the exhausted pack animals.

By midday, they had crossed the Pass and after a brief stop for bread, hot water and condensed milk, found their way to the village of Jhora where they rejoined Amala and Tsering Dolma who had travelled by another route. Next day, on the Karpo la, the last high pass before India, they were first buffeted by snow and wind, then, when the sun came out, almost blinded by snow-glare. They protected their faces from the glare with strips of cloth or with their long braided hair. Then, just when they thought the worst was over and sat down with relief to eat their midday meal, a fierce dust-storm whirled over their heads. As they neared the highest point of the Karpo la, out of the blue, a plane appeared directly above them. 'We didn't know whether it was Chinese or from another country,' says Tendzin Choegyal, 'but it flew directly overhead and it couldn't fail to have seen us, hundreds of men and horses on the pure white snow.' Badly shaken, the Tibetans scattered, fearing that the Chinese now exactly knew where they were and would soon be in hot pursuit. 'The mountain was covered with snow and we knew we could all be seen very clearly,' said a monk-official. 'We got down from our ponies. Too late we realized that the horse-blankets were red and would be all too visible from the air. His Holiness told us to reverse the blankets and keep going.'[30]

They journeyed on for two more days, convinced that all was lost. They endured another dust-storm, another exposure to the blinding glare of the snow, before beginning their slow descent, down to the steaming rain-forests that covered the lower approaches to India. On the way, Kundun received the welcome news that the Indian Government was willing to grant him asylum.

In the tiny village of Mangmang, the last outpost of Tibet, the weather chose to wreak its final fury on them. The rain fell in stair-rods, forcing the exhausted Tibetans to erect tents for shelter. Kundun's tent leaked and, as the night wore on, his flimsy bedding got more and more sodden, no matter where he tried to move it. Tendzin Choegyal was with him: 'The water ran in rivulets down the inside of the tent. The fever he'd been fighting off for days developed into a chill and then into dysentery. I watched him become weak and ill.'[31]

By morning he was too ill to go on, so his friends moved him to a small house nearby. This provided scarcely more protection than the tent; it was dirty and black with smoke, and beneath him, all night long, the cattle lowed incessantly. All that day and the next night he tossed in fever. But the following day brought news that Chinese troops were converging on a village nearby, and the need to move on became urgent. This last day in Tibet, knowing that by next morning he would have crossed the border into exile was, says Kundun, one of the unhappiest times of his life. The time for goodbyes had come: 'With a heavy heart, I said goodbye to the group of people who had acted as my escort: my personal bodyguard, soldiers, officials, including some quite important ones. They were staying behind to face the Chinese forces. In other words, they were returning to face almost certain death. They expressed such unselfish devotion. They said they could not serve me in India, where they did not know the language or the way of life, but what they could and must do was stay and fight the Chinese. They said that next day the Dalai Lama would enter India safely and that therefore they had fulfilled their responsibility. Now they must go back. That was an inexpressibly sad moment. I had known some of them for many years, others for just a few years, some for only a few weeks. But they had all become like old friends. Now not only were they leaving, but we all knew in our hearts that many of them would be killed. I was filled with admiration for their courage and their loyalty.'[32]

As he was too ill to ride a horse, his companions placed him on the broad back of a *dzo*[33] and on this lowly beast of burden, 'in a daze of sickness and weariness and unhappiness deeper than I can express', on 31 March 1959 he was carried out of Tibet – and into an uncertain future.

NOTES

1. Jamyang Norbu, 'The Tibetan Resistance Movement', *Resistance and Reform in Tibet*, ed. Barnett & Akiner.
2. Author interview with HH the Dalai Lama, Dharamsala, July 1995.
3. Author interview with HH the Dalai Lama, Dharamsala, July 1995.
4. Rinchen Dolma Taring, *Daughter of Tibet*.
5. Goodman, *The Last Dalai Lama*, p. 286.
6. Author interview with HH the Dalai Lama, Dharamsala, June 1994.
7. Author interview with Tendzin Choegyal, Dharamsala, June 1994.
8. Author interview with Tendzin Choegyal, Dharamsala, June 1994.
9. From the Memoirs of Phuntsok Tashi Taklha (published in Tibetan only).
10. Philippa Russell and Sonam Lhamo Singeri, 'The Tibetan Women's Uprising', in the journal *Cho Yang: The Voice of Tibetan Religion and Culture* 5.
11. Fourteenth Dalai Lama, *Freedom in Exile*, chapter 7.
12. Author interview with Phuntsok Tashi Taklha, London, 1993.
13. Author interview with Tendzin Choegyal, October 1993.
14. Author interview with monk-official, Dharamsala, June 1994.
15. Author interview with Tendzin Choegyal, Dharamsala, June 1994.
16. Heinrich Harrer, 'The Miraculous Escape of the Dalai Lama', *Life*, 4 May 1959.
17. Author interview with Phuntsok Tashi, London 1993.
18. Author interview with Tendzin Choegyal, Dharamsala, June 1994.
19. Author interview with HH the Dalai Lama, Dharamsala, June 1994.
20. Pu Yi. The last (child) Emperor of Imperial China. Deposed in 1912 and was later used by the invading Japanese as puppet leader of the newly-formed state of Manchukuo. He was later imprisoned by the Communist Chinese and died a broken man.
21. Author interview with Tendzin Choegyal, Dharamsala, June 1994.
22. Heinrich Harrer, 'The Miraculous Escape of the Dalai Lama'.
23. Author interviews with Tendzin Choegyal, Dharamsala, 1990, 1993.
24. Mr Ghadrang; the Lord Chamberlain, Mr Phala; and Phuntsok Tashi.
25. Author interview with Gyalo Thondup, New Delhi, July 1995.
26. Author interview with Tendzin Choegyal, Dharamsala, June 1994.
27. Fourteenth Dalai Lama, *My Land and My People*, chapter 11.
28. *Freedom in Exile*, chapter 13.
29. Author interview with Tendzin Choegyal, October 1993.
30. Author interview with monk-official, Dharamsala, October 1993.
31. Author interview with Tendzin Choegyal, May 1991.
32. Author interview with HH the Dalai Lama, Dharamsala, June 1994.
33. Animal rather like an ox.

18

Fugitives

Now, where a society has existed for hundreds and hundreds
of years – it may have outlasted its utility but the fact is – uprooting it is a terribly painful process. It can be uprooted slowly, it can be changed even with rapidity, but with a measure of
co-operation. But any kind of forcible uprooting must neces-
sarily be painful, whether it is a good society or a bad society.

Nehru speaking on Tibet in the Indian Parliament,

27 April 1959

Amala, Tsering Dolma and Tendzin Choegyal went on ahead of Kundun,
with an escort of Gurkhas, down through the dripping jungles of Assam.
The contrast with the dry, light air of the Tibetan plateau underlined
with cruel force that they were exiles without a home. Choegyal has
often reflected that in those first days he was a typical refugee – 'all I
had were the clothes I stood up in, my drinking-bowl, my gun, and Kundun's umbrella'.

For the moment, his main emotion was bitter disappointment: 'I had
had two beautiful torches which I treasured. They even had new batteries
in them. That first night in India, I took them out and put them between
cushions so that they'd be easily accessible. But next morning, we were in
such a hurry to pack up and leave that I forgot them. I was devastated.'[1]

Such minor troubles were forgotten, however, five days later, when they
reached Tawang, in the North-East Frontier Agency territory (NEFA).[2]

Here, at India's largest Buddhist Monastery, they were welcomed by three hundred monks and a vast crowd of tribesmen.

Indian Air Force planes flew in low over a large meadow outside the town and dropped supplies: 'The Indians were extremely efficient and there was nothing half-hearted about their reception of us,' applauds Choegyal.

> All sorts of things were provided, food, clothing, medical supplies. We were wearing fur hats and fur-lined chubas in that terrible damp heat, so we needed lighter clothes. I remember our officials asking the Indian Government for more suitable head-gear and they air-lifted crates of trilbies for us. Sometimes the parachute didn't open and you could see the black shape hurtling down to the ground. When it was oil-drums that were dropped they exploded with the force of a bomb, it made a horrible mess – I used to love watching it.[3]

The planes flew in every third day. Choegyal discarded his fur-lined Tibetan *chuba* and, even more reluctantly, his pistol. He liked Tawang, 'it was beautiful, on a hill, undulating rather than rugged, surrounded by meadows and evergreen forests'. The weather was pleasant and every day he would stroll around to see how everyone was getting on and catch up on the latest gossip. He had brought five Tibetan silver coins from Lhasa, and exchanging these for twenty-five Indian rupees, 'went into the military canteen and bought a jar of jam, a packet of cream crackers, a packet of butter, and started having a feast'.

From Tawang, they travelled by pony along a bridle path towards the formidable 14,500-feet high Se la Pass, skirting the pass at 9,600 feet above Bomdila, the administrative centre of the area. Here Kundun joined them and was greeted by high officials and by thousands of tribesmen who came in their best finery and danced in his honour. Bomdila, says Choegyal, was 'ugly and full of dust'; but it was there that Kundun received a formal telegram of welcome from Mr Nehru:

> MY COLLEAGUES AND I WELCOME YOU AND SEND GREETINGS ON YOUR SAFE ARRIVAL IN INDIA. WE SHALL BE HAPPY TO AFFORD THE NECESSARY FACILITIES TO YOU, YOUR FAMILY AND ENTOURAGE TO RESIDE IN INDIA. THE PEOPLE OF INDIA, WHO HOLD YOU IN GREAT VENERATION, WILL NO DOUBT ACCORD THEIR TRADITIONAL RESPECT TO YOUR PERSONAGE. KIND REGARDS. NEHRU[4]

Choegyal recalls a splendid high tea at the home of the District Commissioner: 'They gave us *rasgulas*, a very sweet and spongy cheese; and they sang Indian songs.' Encouraged by this warm reception, Kundun lingered in Bomdila for a few days, before continuing on his journey. On 18 April the party drove in a cavalcade of jeeps through the forests which shelter Bomdila from the plains. At the road-camp of Foothills, the Indian public caught their first glimpse of the exiled ruler as he alighted from his jeep, followed by his mother, sister, brother, and about seventy Tibetans, among whom were all that remained of his Government. With Indian soldiers providing a guard of honour, he walked across a makeshift carpet of tarpaulins to the camp overseer's cottage where he breakfasted on cornflakes, poached eggs, toast, and fresh bananas.

Much excitement was caused by the arrival of Gyalo Thondup. The latter, says Choegyal, 'wept for joy when he caught sight of us. It was a very moving reunion, and we were all very happy.'[5] Gyalo Thondup accompanied them to Tezpur, a railway junction thirty miles away. Choegyal loved Tezpur – 'the lush green foliage, Indian bearers in their white uniforms, fans whirring. There was plenty to eat. It had everything, colour, sound, smell, excitement. It really raised our spirits.'

Among the waiting crowds was Heinrich Harrer, apprehensive lest Kundun might not recognize him: it had been eight years since they met. 'I need not have worried,' he reported.[6]

> As the jeep reached me, he waved and smiled in delighted recognition. Then, as he dismounted, my anxiety turned to astonishment. He had grown so tall. And when he greeted me as *trogpo*, friend, his voice, which was just beginning a boyish break when I left Lhasa, was rich and deep. I was surprised, too, at seeing him with spectacles in public, although I had myself suggested that he get them when he was fifteen. In those days he had disliked wearing them, for in Tibet wearing spectacles [was] thought to be a foreign affectation.

Kundun received hundreds of messages, telegrams, letters and cards in Tezpur. Heartened by all the expressions of good will, he felt he must lose no time in telling the world about Tibet. Accordingly he composed a third-person statement to be read out jointly by an Indian and a Tibetan official, summarizing the key events: that the 1951 Seventeen-Point Agreement with the Chinese had been signed under duress; that his Government had been stripped of all power; that broken promises and religious persecution had finally forced him to flee; and that – despite Chinese claims that he had been abducted by rampaging Khampa tribesmen – he had left Lhasa entirely of his own free will. He voiced his unhappiness over the fate of

Tibet, while allowing himself to hope that the situation could be saved without further bloodshed.

A few hours later, Kundun boarded a special Indian Railways steam train for a three-day journey to Dehra Dun, eighteen miles from the former British hill station of Mussoorie, where the Indian Government had provided a house for him.

When Lobsang Samten had chosen not to return to Tibet in 1957, he had convalesced for a while in India, before joining Norbu in New York. 'He felt a bit insecure at first, but he soon settled down,' says Norbu, who had obtained an invitation for Lobsang to enter Georgetown University in Washington. Norbu himself was shortly afterwards invited to the 1958 World Congress of Buddhists in Bangkok, and was able, *en route*, to satisfy an old longing to visit the Buddhist shrines of Thailand, Burma and Ceylon. On his way back home, in early 1959, he visited Gyalo Thondup in Darjeeling – and discovered at last the vocation his restless spirit had been seeking. Ever since his return from Tibet in 1952, Gyalo Thondup and his wife (now called by a Tibetan name, Dekyi Dolkar), had been watching events in Tibet closely, and through the Tibetan Welfare Commitee had helped care for the many refugees from Chinese rule. There were so many of them in Darjeeling and Kalimpong that by the end of the Fifties they had become a serious problem: the Welfare Commitee could no longer meet even their most basic needs. Worse still, because of its identification with the Tibetan guerrillas after 1956, the Commitee was an embarrassment to a nation determined on friendship with Communist China. Gyalo Thondup needed to look elsewhere for funds.

Norbu was just the man he needed, and his brother responded eagerly. Returning to the US via Europe, in both continents he approached powerful institutions and welfare organizations to persuade them to help the refugees. The timing was opportune – 1959 was World Refugee Year – and before long, the first consignments of tents, blankets and tinned foods had been despatched by World Church Services to the destitute Tibetans in Kalimpong.

Norbu found willing helpers at every turn and was grateful to be able at last to help his compatriots. One evening in mid-March 1959 he was in the kitchen of his New York apartment, preparing a Tibetan soup for supper and idly listening to the radio, when suddenly he was transfixed by the announcement of an uprising in Tibet. Leaving the soup to boil over, he heard reports of violent disturbances in Lhasa, of thousands of people surrounding the Norbulingka Palace to prevent the Chinese from kidnapping His Holiness. Norbu was shaken to the core. 'I stood there with my mind in a whirl. What I had most feared for many years had come about at last.' A few days earlier he had been alarmed by an article in *Time* magazine, prophesying an imminent showdown between Tibetans and Chinese. Since then he had been praying that Kundun and the rest of his family would be safe. But now the worst seemed to have happened.

> What was going to happen now? The lives of my relatives were obviously in the greatest danger. Would they be able to escape? The Dalai Lama, I knew, was young, vigorous and in good health, he would be quite capable of the fatigues of any journey. On the other hand, the Chinese would clearly move heaven and earth to prevent his escape? Was he even still at liberty? My mother was already sixty years old, and Tendzin Choegyal...was still a child. All in all, I was worried by the most disagreeable imaginings, and there was no question of sleep for me that night.[7]

He rang Lobsang Samten in Washington. He too was frantic at the news and arranged to join his brother in New York that very night. To calm his nerves, Norbu tried telephoning various friends, but couldn't handle their well-meant sympathy. Rejecting sundry offers of a meal or a bed for the night, he sat by the radio set in nail-biting silence, waiting for each and every news bulletin. When Lobsang Samten arrived, the brothers tried to calm each other's fears but succeeded only in making them worse – the sense of events lurching out of control induced panic. At about midnight, when the newsboys began to shout special editions of the newspapers in the streets, Norbu 'rushed out and bought every newspaper I could get hold of in the hope of obtaining further news'. But though they devoured every single line, they learned nothing more.

As the days went by, they nearly suffocated with anxiety, the sporadic news bulletins – vague, confused and contradictory – offering no relief at all. Bombarded by conflicting rumours, they swung wildly between hope and despair. Only after days of unendurable suspense did news reach them that Kundun and his entourage had crossed safely into India. The brothers collapsed with relief. 'We were just so happy,' says Norbu simply. They sent a telegram to Kundun, via Gyalo Thondup in Darjeeling; and Norbu determined to go to India as soon as possible.

Kundun was a hero to the Indian people. His journey by train to Dehra Dun was a triumphal progress, with enormous crowds thronging the route, blocking the track, shouting greetings. It was, reported *Life*, 'a procession through adoring throngs, caught between joy at his safety and anger at his enemies. Indians as well as expatriate Tibetans honoured him with smoking incense, fanfares of horns and thousands of traditional homespun scarves thrown in his path.'[8]

What a dramatic contrast to the anguished weeks he had recently spent as a fugitive! Three times, at Siliguri, Benares and Lucknow, Kundun left his carriage to address 'huge, impromptu meetings of flower-throwing well-wishers'. Siliguri was packed with Tibetan exiles from Kalimpong and Darjeeling, among them Gyalo Thondup's wife, Dekyi Dolkar, with Pema, Tenzin Ngawang and Khando, all of them weeping for joy. They had known for some time that the situation in Tibet was grave. 'At Gyalo Thondup's house,' says Pema, then nineteen and in her last year at school, 'we had been aware of an unusual amount of activity. Everyone looked scared. They tried to reassure us, but we became very frightened for Amala, for my sister and her husband, for Tendzin Choegyal and for His Holiness. I trembled at the thought that their lives were in danger.' The Loreto nuns had rounded up all the newspapers they could find for Pema and Khando and morning and evening had the whole school praying 'for Pema's family'. 'The whole school was involved in our anxiety,' Pema remembers,[9] 'Khando and I were so worried, we couldn't sleep, couldn't eat.' 'One day,' adds Khando, 'the nuns told us we were leaving immediately, a car was coming to pick us up and take us home. At home, Uncle Thondup warned us there would be a lot of newspaper people asking questions and we weren't to tell them anything. Well, what could we have told them, we knew nothing ourselves? I remember that Uncle Thondup was very nervous, he had no idea whether our family would succeed in escaping. Then came the wonderful news that they had escaped into India. The relief was overwhelming.'[10] Gyalo Thondup had set off immediately to meet his brother.

As Kundun's train drew into Siliguri station, a shout of joy went up. 'The carriage door opened,' writes Pema, 'the bodyguard got out, and suddenly there was His Holiness, thin and haggard. He looked exhausted and care-worn. The few steps dividing me from him seemed endless. I offered him a *kata*, received his blessing, and then I was literally thrown into the train by the bodyguard. At last I could embrace Amala, my sister and my brothers. For the first time in three years we were together.'[11] The practical

Dekyi Dolkar had brought along a change of clothing for them all, and food, both fresh and canned. 'We had lost everything,' wrote Pema, 'but I was so happy they were all alive that nothing else mattered. Nevertheless, it was at that moment that I realized that for us a new life was beginning, a life of exiles and political refugees.'

Two hours later, despite their protests, Pema, Tenzin Ngawang and Khando, were packed off back to school in Darjeeling. They had, after all, been given only one day's leave.

Mussoorie was about an hour's drive from Dehra Dun. There, at Birla House, the home of a multi-millionaire Indian industrialist, Kundun's epic 1,500-mile journey at last came to an end.

But he was not to be left in peace. The Chinese were incandescent with outrage over his Tezpur statement. A New China News Agency report, referring to it as 'a crude document, lame in reasoning, full of lies and loopholes' insisted that it had been fabricated 'by foreign imperialists', since 'everyone knew' the revolt was the work of an 'upper strata reactionary clique' by whom the Dalai Lama had been abducted. A lengthy editorial in the Peking *People's Daily*[12] claimed that the Chinese military action was justified in order to liberate the Tibetan people from the horrors of their old feudal society, and that the Tibetans had longed for the kind of 'peaceful revolution' that the Chinese had brought. Asserting that the aforementioned 'reactionary clique' had murdered Regent Reting by strangling him in prison, they rather intriguingly went on to claim the Dalai Lama's father as another innocent martyr for their cause. 'The father of the present Fourteenth Dalai Lama, now in Mussoorie,' continued the editorial, darkly, 'because of his patriotic ideas, was poisoned by reactionaries who had connections with foreign countries, in order to facilitate their control over the Dalai Lama.' Both these 'notorious crimes', apparently, had been 'committed by stooges of foreign interventionists within the ruling clique'.[13] (According to a young Tibetan then studying at the Peking Institute of National Minorities, the students were assured that 'the chief trouble-maker' was Gyalo Thondup, who was 'colluding with American Imperialists and foreign reactionaries'.)[14]

Whether or not Kundun had yet seen the Peking *People's Daily*, he was certainly stung by the News Agency report and promptly issued another statement – in the first person this time – in which he stood by his earlier words. 'It astonished me yet again,' he wrote in his memoirs, 'to see how the Chinese blamed everyone they could think of for the revolt – like an injured dog which snaps at everybody...They could not allow themselves to recognize the truth: that it was the people themselves, whom the Chinese claimed to be liberating, who had revolted spontaneously against their liberation, and that the ruling class of Tibet had been far more willing than the people to come to agreement.'[15]

The Chinese reaction put Nehru on the spot. His decision to offer political asylum to the Dalai Lama had been well-received at home: when he told the Indian Parliament of the Dalai Lama's safe arrival, they stood up and cheered. Given the popular mood, Nehru could scarcely have acted otherwise. The snag was that he was still obsessed with the idea of friendship with China, even though the Chinese conquest of Tibet had laid the northern areas of India itself open to Chinese attack. Already embarrassed by the Tibetan Welfare groups in Darjeeling and Kalimpong, he now felt threatened by the fall-out from his decision to stand by a friend in need. In a debate on the Tibetan situation in the Indian Parliament in April, he tried to have it both ways, deploring on the one hand the Chinese predilection for clichés such as 'upper strata reactionary clique' – 'The attempt to explain a situation by the use of rather worn-out words, phrases and slogans is seldom helpful,' he observed.[16] On the other hand, he anxiously reassured the Chinese that his support for the Dalai Lama was a purely humanitarian act, and that the Tibetan leader would not be allowed to make political capital out of the situation.

As soon as Kundun was installed at Birla House – it did not take long, since all his belongings were in four trunks – Nehru came to call. He was affable enough and the two 'old friends' posed smiling for a photograph; but he told his guest bluntly that India would never recognize his Government, nor support the cause of Tibetan independence. Kundun was dismayed, but, not wishing to antagonize Nehru, agreed to be discreet in his public utterances.

For two months he kept the low profile demanded of him. Until, that is, a second wave of refugees started pouring in, thousands of men, women and children, streaming over the Himalaya to Bhutan, Sikkim, Nepal and India, bringing with them tales of horror to curdle the blood. Not only of forced collectivization, class warfare, political re-education, but of mass imprisonments, executions and inhuman atrocities carried out by the new Military Control Commissions which now ruled Tibet. The Chinese had consolidated their position throughout Tibet, replacing the Dalai Lama with their own tame puppet, the Panchen Lama, and warning the rebellious Lhasans to surrender or die. As Kundun would later testify to the International Commission of Jurists:

> Tens of thousands of our people have been killed, not only in military actions, but individually and deliberately. They have been killed, without trial, on suspicion of opposing communism, or of hoarding money, or for no reason at all. But mainly and fundamentally they have been killed because they would not renounce their religion. They have not only been shot, but beaten to death, crucified, burned alive, drowned, vivisected, starved, strangled, hanged, scalded, buried alive, disembowelled and beheaded.[17]

This was the 'peaceful liberation' brought by the Chinese. By the end of June, nearly 20,000 ragged, destitute refugees had arrived, driven from Tibet by starvation and terror. For the most part they were the landless peasants, nomads and yeoman farmers the Chinese claimed to have liberated but whose lives they had instead destroyed. They had braved the terrors of the high uncharted peaks and the ever-vigilant Chinese patrols; and many of those who had set out had died in the attempt. The escape routes were littered with corpses, bullet-ridden, wounded, snow-blinded, starved or frozen to death. The survivors were now on the low-lying plains of India at the start of the hottest season of the year; and the injections given them by the Indian authorities against cholera and typhoid served only to increase their miseries.

This fresh evidence that the Chinese intended to wipe out every trace of the old Tibet was the last straw for Kundun. Anguish for his tortured country overrode his promise to Nehru, made him break his silence and beseech the outside world for help. On 20 June, with obvious emotion he addressed a crowd of international journalists. Once more declaring the Seventeen-Point Agreement to be null and void, he told them of the attempted extermination of his people, their religion and their culture, and he pleaded for an international commission to investigate the atrocities so consistently reported by all the refugees.

That evening, the Indian Government formally refused recognition to the Dalai Lama's Government-in-Exile.

But Kundun's appeal for a commission of inquiry was heard. The International Commission of Jurists – a respected body of lawyers – launched an investigation in July 1959 and a year later concluded that Tibet had

indeed been a sovereign and independent nation before the Chinese invasion; and that the atrocity accounts were true. China, the lawyers accused,
was guilty of 'the gravest crime of which any person or nation can be accused – the intent to destroy, in whole or in part, a national, ethnic, racial
or religious group as such'.[18] Guilty, in other words, of genocide.

Emboldened by the Jurists' report, Kundun tried again with the United
Nations. His efforts were partially rewarded: Ireland and Malaya co-spon-
sored the Tibetan case which was debated at length at the fourteenth session of the UN General Assembly in October 1959. But, predictably, the
monolithic Soviet bloc insisted that Tibet was nobody's business but
China's and accused Tibet's sponsors of fabricating a 'non-existent Tibetan
question' in order to stir the pot of the Cold War. As stirring the pot was
something that Britain and the USA would go to any lengths to avoid, the
issue of Tibet's sovereignty was cravenly shelved. Tibet's cause foundered
on the impotence and moral cowardice of the West. A resolution was
adopted, however, expressing grave concern at the forcible denial of basic
human rights and freedoms in Tibet and called for these rights – and the
distinctive Tibetan way of life – to be respected.

It was better than nothing, perhaps, but it was hardly likely to make
China tremble.

In June, Kundun received a visit from Norbu and Gyalo Thondup. Norbu,
attending a conference on Tibet in Tokyo, had been drumming up support
for the Tibetan cause. A few days later, Gyalo Thondup met him at Delhi
airport and drove him to Mussoorie. The brothers arrived early one morning, but were held up for several hours outside the town by a road block
set up by the Indian authorities to keep 'undesirable elements' away from
Kundun's weekly audiences. When their identity was established, they set
off for Birla House, amazed by the crowds:

> The closer we came to Birla House, the bigger the crowds grew until in the
> end they were so dense we had to leave the car and make our way forward on
> foot. We were met in the garden of Birla House by Tendzin Choegyal who ran
> up to us excitedly and embraced us warmly. He then accompanied us indoors
> where the Dalai Lama was waiting for us on the staircase to take us into his
> private apartments. I was about to prostrate myself before him, as I had al-
> ways been accustomed to do, and to present the usual *kata*, when with a ges-
> ture of the hand he indicated that I should not do so here. Wordlessly he

pointed to a *thangka* with a picture of the Buddha Shakyamuni; and deeply moved I laid my good-luck scarf over it. Henceforth our reverential greetings were to honour the Buddhas alone; from now on the Dalai Lama regarded himself only as the first fugitive among his oppressed people.[19]

When it was time for Kundun to show himself to the crowds outside, Norbu went in search of his mother. He knew she would be grieving for Tibet, and for her old mother who had been left in Lhasa with one of his aunts. He found her standing at the window, looking out at the crowds, and as Norbu went to her side she quietly took his hand:

My mother was the first to break the silence: 'Jigme-la,' she said in a low voice, using my childhood name for the first time in many years, 'Jigme-la, from now on we are refugees too.'

I led her back into the room and sat down beside her. The consoling words I wanted to say did not come so easily. Yes, of course, we were all in safety; and we could rely on a certain amount of assistance; but we had lost our country. The enemies of our religion and our way of life had the upper hand there now, and they were intent on destroying everything that we held dear. Our people were forced to bow their backs to the oppressors, and those who refused to do so, lost their lives or were carried off to forced labour. How many of our friends had already suffered so harsh a fate! Many of them had been killed, and others had disappeared, never to be heard of again.[20]

Unable to find words of comfort, mother and son lapsed into silence.

Kundun, however, was a little consoled by Norbu's assurance that people everywhere were anxious to help the Tibetan refugees. In the weeks that followed, he sent his brother to visit the transit camps in Northern India and report back on the condition of the refugees. Together they worked out a plan of campaign, and Norbu was glad to have Kundun's backing for his work. Both of them realized that the stream of refugees would soon become a deluge. And then what would the Indian Government do? Anxiety gave them sleepless nights.

August found Norbu in Vienna, to put Kundun's case at an International Youth Congress. There he sought out Heinrich Harrer, and, in view of the great interest all over the world in the Dalai Lama and the Tibetan refugees, the two old friends decided to collaborate on a book about Norbu's own experiences.[21] But work on it would have to wait, as Norbu must first of all go to Switzerland, to meet a Swiss industrialist, Dr Charles Aeschimann, who was already implementing a plan to bring Tibetan children to the

Pestalozzi Children's Village near St Gallen, founded during World War II to care for war orphans. And as similar children's Homes existed in Germany, Britain and France, Norbu doggedly set off to rustle up support there too. Tibetan children were to be selected in India and sent to these Children's Villages in Europe.

The last visitor to Mussoorie was perhaps the most longed for: Lobsang Samten, the companion of his childhood. Kundun was overcome by emotion: 'When I learned that Lobsang was to come next day, I felt tremendously excited. When he actually came, we just stood and looked at each other for some moments without words. I shed no tears, but my eyes must have betrayed the depth of my emotion. As for Lobsang, the tears were rolling freely down his face.'[22]

As the refugees continued to pour in, Kundun could only mourn his powerlessness to help them. They were being accommodated in primitive conditions in two transit camps, Missamari in the steamy heat of Assam, and Buxa Duar, a former British POW camp further west, in Bengal. Hugh Richardson who visited all the refugee areas between February and April 1960, admired the patience and good humour of the Tibetans in Missamari, twelve thousand of them, living in three hundred bamboo huts. 'It was a horrible place,' he says, 'dusty, no decent water, and they were living in makeshift bamboo shanties.' Richardson had taken a number of statements from the refugees. 'Many of them were people I'd actually known in Tibet and knew to be honest. Their statements were utterly consistent, but the Press refused to believe them.' Most of the cynical Western journalists dismissed the atrocity stories as the whinings of a dispossessed privileged class. To the refugees, this scepticism on the part of the newspapermen (and intellectuals) was a crushing blow, compounding their bewilderment and shock. They had lost their homes, their families and everything they held dear in the most violent of circumstances; they were suffering from humidity, heat-stroke, lack of sanitation and from an unfamiliar diet, as a result of which an outbreak of amoebic dysentery was carrying them off in droves. And journalists, either indifferent or unwilling to believe ill of China's revolutionary social experiment, would not even listen to what they had to say.

The monks and lamas, most of whom were in Buxa Duar camp, were the worst off, housed in thirty concrete barracks, surrounded by high barbed-wire fences. 'It was very unhealthy there, and lots of the monks died of cholera, malaria, dysentery and hepatitis,' says Tendzin Choegyal. 'Apart from the health hazards, they had no electricity, no lamps. Some of them bought kerosene and made wicks, so that they'd have some kind of lamp to read the Scriptures by. But the lamps gave out poisonous smoke and the monks breathed in the fumes. As a result, many of them died from TB – the death-rate was extremely high.' Yet from the survivors of Buxa Duar came many of the scholar-monks who would one day spread a knowledge of Tibetan Buddhism throughout the West.

In Darjeeling, on the site of the house where the Great Thirteenth had passed his exile, Gyalo Thondup's wife Dekyi Dolkar set up a Self-Help Centre, where the refugees could help preserve the traditional arts and crafts of Tibet, while providing employment for themselves either as craftsmen or retail salesmen. With the help of foreign relief organizations, this provided a model for a series of centres which sprang up in the hill-districts of northern India, supporting traditional handicrafts dominated by carpet-weaving.

This kind of self-help programme would eventually be the salvation of the Tibetans. Most of them were illiterate and for the present were glad to be paid a few rupees a day for working on the new military roads being built by the Indian Government in the relatively cooler Himalayan areas to the north. The work was hard but at least the high-altitude climate was more bearable than the torrid heat of the plains; and in earning their own keep they were able to regain some of their lost self-respect.

In Tibet itself, the mainly Khampa guerrillas of the National Volunteer Defence Army did not immediately give up the struggle. But with the Chinese pouring troops and equipment into the area and sealing off the borders, the odds were hopelessly unequal. Three weeks and many deaths later, their field commander, Gompo Tashi Andrugtsang, shut down his HQ in the mountains of Southern Tibet and crossed into India to continue the fight from there. He went to see Gyalo Thondup in Darjeeling, and the two men sought ways of directing Tibetan resistance into more effective channels.

Kundun, realistically accepting that there would be no early return to Tibet, had somehow to assure the survival of his country in exile. He knew that democracy was the only key to survival in the modern world. But introducing it to the Tibetans would not be easy. He had already made some changes, ridding himself of much of the suffocating protocol which he had always hated. His officials were for the most part appalled. They thought of the democratic process as being only a short step away from Communism.

But Kundun persisted, knowing that change was ultimately inevitable and that his Government-in-Exile must have a modern constitution, even if no other nation in the world was prepared as yet to acknowledge its existence.

In December 1959 Kundun went to the Buddhist shrines to give teachings. In the Deer Park at Sarnath where the Buddha had preached his first sermon, he addressed two thousand tearful pilgrims – from all three provinces of old Tibet: Amdo, Kham and Central Tibet. He did not mince matters. 'Tibet's sun and moon have suffered an eclipse,' he told them bleakly, and while one day they would undoubtedly go home it would not be for the foreseeable future. Meanwhile, if they were to survive, they must lay aside their traditional regional antipathies, to unite to preserve what was worthwhile in their culture. Afterwards, pilgrims from all three provinces of old Tibet, gathering together (a unique occurrence) for a traditional prayer service to wish long life to His Holiness, vowed to work together in the future. Then, most of them returned to hard labour in the road gangs of Sikkim.

NOTES

1. Author interview with Tendzin Choegyal, Dharamsala, June 1994.
2. One of the Himalayan hill-states which the British had acquired by local agreements, and which the Indian Government had inherited in 1947 after Independence. Today this area is known as Arunachal Pradesh.
3. Author interview with Tendzin Choegyal, Dharamsala, June 1994.
4. Fourteenth Dalai Lama, *Freedom in Exile*, chapter 8.
5. Author interview with Tendzin Choegyal, Dharamsala, October 1993.
6. 'Miraculous Escape of the Dalai Lama', *Life*, 4 May 1959.
7. Norbu, *Tibet Is My Country*, p. 249.
8. 'Miraculous Escape of the Dalai Lama', *Life*, 4 May 1959.
9. Author interview with Jetsun Pema, Dharamsala, June 1994.
10. Author interview, Khando Chazotsang, Utah, USA, February 1996.
11. Jetsun Pema, *Tibet, Mon Histoire*.

12. 6 May 1959.

13. *Concerning the question of Tibet. Collection of documents, speeches, news dispatches, editorials, commentaries and background material concerning the Tibetan question.* Foreign Language Press, Peking, 1959. From Oriental and India Office Collections of the British Library.

14. Tsering Dorje Gashi, *Ten Years in Communist China and Tibet...1956–1966*, Dharamsala, 1977.

15. Fourteenth Dalai Lama, *My Land and My People*, chapter 13.

16. Nehru, Statement in the Lok Sabha on The Situation in Tibet, 27 May 1959.

17. *My Land and My People*, chapter 13.

18. Avedon, *In Exile from the Land of Snows*, p. 80.

19. *Tibet Is My Country*, chapter 21.

20. *Tibet Is My Country*, chapter 21.

21. *Tibet Is My Country*.

22. Author interview with HH the Dalai Lama, Dharamsala, June 1994.

Belonging and Not Belonging

Here we see a strange thing, a society which had been isolated completely for hundreds of years suddenly coming out into the open, events throwing it into this mad world of ours, cold wars and all kinds of things happening...Imagine the contrast in these two. It is a vast gulf. It is inevitable that painful consequences flow from this type of thing. You cannot simply wish it away.

Nehru speaking on Tibet in the Indian Parliament, 8 May 1959

Kundun had known from the start that his stay in Mussoorie would be temporary. He was nevertheless surprised when, within a year, Nehru offered him permanent settlement in Dharamsala, in the Himalayan foothills on the northern edges of the Punjab. Never having heard of the place, he looked it up on the map. It seemed to be in the middle of nowhere, 450 miles north-west of – and a day's journey from – New Delhi. He was dismayed. 'We felt we were being pushed out of sight,' he recalls.[1]

Indeed they were. Mussoorie was a popular refuge from the heat of the Indian plains, and while Kundun was there, visitors from India and all over the world flocked to see him. The Chinese did not conceal their displeasure at this, nor at his continued presence so near to the Indo-Tibetan border. 'Nehru's Government made the excuse that the Birla family wanted to reclaim their house,' says Gyalo Thondup. 'Then they suggested Dharamsala, very remote and cut off from everywhere. I think Nehru hoped that if we were shunted out there we might disappear. If so, he must have been disappointed.'

In the 1860s, British officers had set up a hill-station at McLeod Ganj just above Dharamsala – perched on a ridge of the Dhauladhar spur of the Himalaya. They built over a hundred large bungalows and an Anglican church – St John-in-the-Wilderness – complete with spire and country churchyard. (A former Viceroy, Lord Elgin, was buried in a great Gothic tomb there in 1863.) But, popular though McLeod was, the British abandoned it as a summer resort in 1905 after an earthquake levelled many of the bungalows and destroyed the church steeple.

Their departure spelt disaster to the Nowrojee family, Parsees from Bombay who had set up a canteen in 1860 to serve the British and seen it expand into a flourishing General Store selling 'everything from a pin to an elephant'. By 1960, Nauzer Nowrojee, a descendant of the founder, was wondering how to make ends meet. Having failed to persuade government agencies, businesses, religious organizations, to move to Dharamsala, Mr Nowrojee approached Nehru with the proposal that the Dalai Lama and his refugees should be housed there. Nehru was delighted at this simple solution to his dilemma. Surely the Chinese would be mollified by his shunting the Dalai Lama out of sight to this 'forgotten ghost-town wasting in the woods'?

Kundun was less enthusiastic, but he could nevertheless see that Dharamsala had possibilities. It was a mountainous area with woods and streams, not unlike Tibet. In April he sent one of his Ministers to look the place over. Dharamsala is at its best in spring, and when the Minister reported with enthusiasm that 'the water of Dharamsala is sweeter than the milk of Mussoorie', Kundun's reluctance evaporated. What if it *was* a long way from Delhi, making communication with the outside world difficult – at least there would be room for expansion. In Dharamsala perhaps he and the remnant of his people could make a fresh start.

Accompanied by his mother, Tsering Dolma and about eighty officials, Kundun left Mussoorie on 29 April 1960, travelling by overnight train and motorcade. (Khando had been left behind at the Convent of Jesus and Mary in Mussoorie, as her parents were reluctant to change her school yet again.) Past crowds of cheering, flower-strewing Indians, they drove up steep hills to McLeod Ganj where a floral arch with WELCOME in big golden letters had been erected. The last stage of the journey – by jeep – led them up a hillside covered with pine, larch, rhododendron and Himalayan oak, round a series of frightening hairpin bends to their new home in the clouds, appropriately known as Swarg Ashram, the House of Freedom.[2] Consisting of four colonial-style bungalows perched precipitously on the edge of the mountainside, Swarg Ashram commanded a breathtaking view over the lower slopes of the Dhauladhar mountains and the sweeping valley below.

Kundun's spartan bedroom, his chapel and private office took up the front section, while to the rear lived his mother, Tsering Dolma and Phuntsok Tashi, the Lord Chamberlain and various secretaries and translators. Most of the officials were housed in the remaining three bungalows in the compound, while other Tibetans were scattered through the forests, in small wooden huts, derelict shacks and even cowsheds.

Although the Swarg Ashram compound was surrounded by barbed-wire fencing and patrolled by Tibetan and Indian guards, Kundun none the less knew an unaccustomed freedom there. He could play a little badminton and go trekking in the mountains immediately above the bungalow. But such leisurely activities were mainly crowded out by more pressing concerns for the refugees. 'We were confused and disturbed in those days', he says, 'demoralized by the destruction of Lhasa and the news of so many thousands of dead. When we discovered that the Government of India could do nothing to help us regain our independence, we felt a kind of hopelessness, realizing how powerless we were. So for the next few years, all we could do was concentrate on the present and try to rehabilitate our people in India.'[3]

He was not entirely without resources: various international voluntary agencies offered aid and although the Indian Government refused to give political support, it was generous with grants for educating and resettling the Tibetans. In addition, each refugee paid a voluntary tax of two rupees per month and salaried workers accepted an income tax of two per cent. But those amounts came nowhere near meeting the actual expenses.

It was now that the treasure in gold dust and silver bars which had been sent to Sikkim should have come into its own. But disaster had struck. In 1950, three men had been put in charge of the bullion, none of whom knew anything about business. As the Kashag planned to make the gold and silver work for the possible future benefit of Tibetan exiles, they invited the help of one of the most successful businessmen in Tibet, the Khampa trader, Yarphel Padatsang. The latter came to India to take charge of the treasure, but the three Tibetans, suspecting him of being a Chinese agent, refused to hand it over. Instead, the three asked Gyalo Thondup to advise them. When Kundun and his officials fled to India in 1959, they expected to find that the bullion had been securely invested. Too late, the three trustees realized what they had done. 'Then the trouble started,' says Phuntsog Wangyal, a prominent Tibetan exile in London, 'Everything had already passed under the control of Gyalo Thondup.'[4]

The latter explains that in 1959 he delegated responsibility to others who duly exchanged the bullion for cash.[5] Unwisely, they invested two or three crore rupees (about two or three hundred million) in the stock markets of Calcutta and Bombay. Then, because they were busy with other problems, they gave the share certificates into the care of Indian stockbroker friends – who promptly sold them. The Tibetans invested the rest of the money in some steel-pipe business – which went bankrupt. 'It was terrible,' mourns Gyalo Thondup, 'we lost eighty per cent of His Holiness's money. When we realized what had happened, we tried to chase the money up, but it was too late. It was all lost.' If only, he laments, 'we had bought property in Delhi instead of investing all that money in the stock market! Land at that time was very cheap and it would have been an excellent investment.'

Whatever the true facts of the matter – and they are almost impossible to establish – when Kundun and his officials came to set up a trust to cater for the needs of the refugees, only twenty per cent of the money remained. The Kashag was deeply suspicious of Gyalo Thondup's explanations – it was the beginning of a deadly feud between them.

The Tibetans worked hard to re-establish the Kashag and various departments. Food was basic and eaten 'on the run between jobs'. Everyone was working out of a single room, with two or three portfolios being dealt with by one person. In these conditions, Kundun reformed his Government; set up a Bureau in New Delhi to link the Indian Government with the various foreign relief agencies; established four unofficial embassies, in New York, Tokyo, Geneva and Kathmandu; and created ten civil service ranks. Determined to preserve the best elements of Tibetan culture, he established an Institute of Tibetan Performing Arts, to keep the traditional folk-dances and operas alive; a Tibetan Medical Centre, to preserve and dispense the traditional herbal remedies; and a Library of Tibetan Works and Archives to store what had been salvaged of Tibet's sacred literature and scriptures. Finally, he drafted a new democratic constitution for a future in which there would be free elections to a National Assembly of People's Deputies

– managing to insert a clause whereby he himself could be removed as Head of State if there was a two-thirds majority in the National Assembly in favour. The idea that the Dalai Lama could ever be pushed out, no matter what the circumstances, nearly gave the more conservative ministers heart-failure, but Kundun stood firm and the clause stayed.

There were by now about 30,000 refugees in the road-camps and few of them could be found homes in Dharamsala. Concerned for their poverty, homelessness and vulnerability to disease, Kundun turned to Nehru – who asked the less populous Indian states in the south for suggestions. When Karnataka offered an uninhabited stretch of jungle at Byllakuppe to the west of Mysore, Kundun accepted with gratitude. By December 1960, a contingent of 660 Tibetan refugees was despatched to Byllakuppe, to create the first of what eventually became 57 thriving Tibetan communities in India. But, for these early pioneers, the task seemed utterly hopeless. When they felt the tropical heat and caught sight of the barren wilderness, many of the former nomadic herders and agricultural labourers from the Land of Snows broke down and wept, beseeching Kundun to send them somewhere – anywhere – else. But there was nowhere else to go. In those first terrible years before the survivors learned to adapt, hundreds died of sunstroke, heat exhaustion and despair.

It was the children Kundun worried about most. During frequent visits to the road camps, he had been appalled: 'Children, women and men were all working side by side in gangs...They had to endure a full day's hard physical toil under a mighty sun, followed by nights crammed into tiny tents.'⁶ Kundun fretted that the Tibetans were in danger of losing an entire generation. In Tibet itself, children were being deported wholesale to China for brainwashing; while in India orphans and semi-orphans roamed the camps in search of food or family, and died of starvation and disease. Nehru again came to the rescue. 'The children are your most precious resource,' he sympathized. When Hugh Richardson visited Kundun in Mussoorie in early 1960, he reported that two or three houses had been set up, with 'children clean and bright, in white tops and blue shorts or skirts'.⁷ These houses would provide the nucleus for the Mussoorie Homes Foundation set up by Rinchen Dolma and Jigme Taring, two of the first Tibetans to have been educated in India. In March 1960, fifty ragged and hungry young men, former monks, Khampa warriors and Government officials aged from eighteen to twenty-five were sent to Mussoorie where, under the guidance of the Tarings, a Tibetan school had been set up in an old house bought cheap from an Indian Army officer. Other residential schools followed, one in Simla, and a school-cum-craft-centre organized by Gyalo Thondup's wife in Darjeeling.

Kundun had been in Dharamsala only two weeks when he heard that a group of refugees being transferred from the Missamari camp to work on the new military roads in Ladakh had been trapped by blizzards and that young children in the group were dying. There was no time to lose. Fifty-one sick and near-starving children, aged between four and fifteen, were rescued and brought to Dharamsala, in so pitiful a condition that Kundun wept when he saw them. They were temporarily housed in the officials' bungalows. But a few days later, on 17 May 1960, Kundun took over two large, derelict British bungalows and, with the Government of India providing the basic rations and international voluntary agencies helping in various other ways, opened a nursery and small infirmary with his sister Tsering Dolma in charge, and nothing but her maternal instinct to guide her.

Conditions were far worse than in Mussoorie. The place, said Hugh Richardson, was 'squalid and muddy and the latrines were terrible'.⁸ There was scarcely room even for the original 51, but by the end of the year, their numbers had increased tenfold, and within two years there were over 1500 children. (At one point, 120 were sharing a single bedroom, sleeping five or six to a bed!) They were orphans or children whose parents were unable to support them; they came from different camps all over India, hungry, dirty, ragged and often seriously ill. Overcrowding was aggravated by lack of food, clothing, medicines – and adequate staff. In fact, as Tsering Dolma noted in her first Report from the Nursery in 1962, in those early years there was 'a shortage of everything except children'. When Pema, having left school, came to Dharamsala to help her sister for a while, her first sight of McLeod Ganj filled her with despair: 'Three buildings, just one shop, and nothing but canvas tents everywhere, with Tibetans in rags, children weeping and shivering with cold, women crushed by the weight of their misery. I could not help but wonder how much suffering they had endured in order to reach this wretched village?'

Gyalo Thondup was potentially the Tibetans' trump card, the man best equipped to steer Kundun through his present difficulties. Unlike the Tibetan officials still mired in their medieval past, GT was urbane and articulate; a successful businessman who spoke several languages, knew his way around the international scene and had powerful contacts all over the world. Among the Tibetans, he alone had the capacity to think globally.

He now looked around for allies. The Americans offered help. Before 1959, they had given only perfunctory support to the rebels, but after the exodus their enthusiasm had increased: supporting the freedom struggle in Tibet was, in their view, a good way to destabilize Communist China. But Gyalo Thondup was not sure. As a student of history, he considered that the countries nearest to Tibet – India, Pakistan and the USSR – would be more useful than far-away ones like the United States.[9] A 'man from Moscow' came to see him in Delhi, assuring him that the Russians alone could be trusted to help the Tibetans, the Americans would sell them out to China. GT toyed with the idea of an operation involving India and the USSR, but when he told Indian Intelligence what he had in mind, their reaction, he said was 'furious and frightened'. Disconcerted by this, then remembering that the Chinese now hated the Russians and would never in the future take him seriously if he accepted help from them, he backed off. A tentative approach to British Intelligence (both MI5 and MI6) elicited nothing more helpful than a recommendation to stay close to the Americans. Gyalo Thondup then re-established contact with the CIA – who offered the Tibetans training, arms and money. His Tibetan Welfare Committee became an office for co-ordinating the activities of the CIA with those of the Resistance – with his cousin Lhamo Tsering in charge. A new fighting force was to be formed from the ranks of the former Chushi Gangdrug warriors working as coolies in the road-gangs of Sikkim. 'We planned,' says Lhamo Tsering,[10] 'to send them back in groups to resume guerrilla operations in areas of Western Tibet where Chinese troop concentrations were not overwhelmingly high.'

A base was chosen – Mustang, a remote area in Northern Nepal which was ethnically and culturally Tibetan and lay close to the edge of the Tibetan plateau. Fifteen thousand feet above sea level, Mustang perched on a spur jutting out over western Tibet. Over a month's trek from Kathmandu, the 750-square-mile territory could only be approached by a deep and narrow gorge to the south, but it had the strategic advantage of being close to the new Chinese road which ran from Kham, along the northern Himalaya, to Ladakh in the west, and from there to the Sino-Soviet border. It would be an ideal launching-pad for raids on Chinese army posts and a fall-back position for the isolated guerrilla units still active in the south and east of Tibet.

Leaders of the Resistance were instructed to recruit the first batch of three hundred volunteers for CIA combat training, bearing in mind that as nobody was quite sure about the operation's legality, the need for secrecy was paramount. Gyalo Thondup went to Kalimpong and addressed the Khampas there. 'We are,' he told them, 'fighters, not farmers, not settlers of the land. We are fighting for the independence of Tibet.' Everyone cheered him. And the exodus began.

'Quietly,' says GT, 'we began sending groups of young men from Sikkim to Nepal.'[11] 'Quietly' was perhaps not the right word. As virtually all the Khampas in the road-camps were itching to take on the Chinese, they exploded with a sort of spontaneous combustion. Suddenly Indian contractors found their workforce was disappearing. On 1 August 1960, the Calcutta Statesman reported: 'Mysterious Exit from Sikkim: Khampas Leaving in Hundreds', and alleged that more than seven or eight hundred workers had already left.

'There were too many people arriving, more than we could handle,' says Lhamo Tsering. 'The Americans got very alarmed about this and about the newspaper report, and they temporarily abandoned the whole operation. But that didn't prevent the volunteers from coming.'

Through the second half of 1960, Chushi Gangdrug fighters trekked through the dense jungles of southern Nepal to reach their new operations base on the windswept plateau of Mustang. Though the Americans recovered from their fright and returned, in that first year there were many difficulties, little money and less food. Nobody actually died of starvation, but all came close to it. Some froze to death in the snow. 'Before sufficient supplies could be parachuted in,' wrote John Avedon, 'most of the initial four thousand men were reduced to boiling their boots and saddles for food, with some, according to one account, carrying out raids across the border into Tibet, not to attack the Chinese, but to steal livestock for their own survival.'[12] But, as they slowly built up a network of interconnecting bases, their single-minded enthusiasm was astonishing. 'Even the CIA were amazed by it,' says Gyalo Thondup. 'The Americans who did the parachute training said they'd never seen such spirit. "Your people are really something else," they told me, "they actually laugh as they jump out of the plane."'[13]

Gyalo Thondup came to Dharamsala to recruit. His undoubted charisma was matched by a singular talent for making enemies. (Even Kundun complains of his brother's stubbornness – 'He creates controversy and is

difficult to control,' he says. 'Once he's made up his mind about something, no one can change it. Certainly, I can't.'¹⁴) In Dharamsala, GT was
disgusted to find that the old officials were still around – and, moreover,
suspicious of his handling of the bullion affair. Smarting from this and
from the recollection of 'those years when I was sending all those messages from Mr Nehru to Lhasa, and being ignored', Gyalo Thondup made
no secret of his contempt. 'They didn't seem able to understand that times
had changed,' he fumes. 'Facing an enemy like the Chinese, we should
have been using all the bright intelligent young people we could find for
the Government, no matter what their background, even if they were from
beggar families. But I couldn't get that through to those corrupt, feudalis-
tic, superstitious old men. We didn't need people like them, we needed
people dedicated to change, not lackeys and time-servers from the past.
During the Uprising, when His Holiness escaped from Lhasa, I had sent
groups of people into Lhasa to find out what the Chinese were up to. None
of those officials would have taken the kind of risk those men took. It was
because we used people from all strata of society that we were able to get
His Holiness out.'¹⁵

The dislike being entirely mutual, battle was joined. The opening shots
were fired by what was generally supposed to be the Kashag's own creation, the Reform Party, formed in an attempt at national unity after Kundun's Bodh Gaya appeal. Its Committee of six front men, representing all
three provinces of old Tibet, produced a nine-point manifesto, two of them
calculated to put the cat among the pigeons. What exactly, they demanded
to know, had happened to the fortune in gold and silver from Sikkim? (The
pathetic amount realized had been published in an Indian newspaper.) And
what about the yellow parachute full of American, Indian and Tibetan
money, which had been dropped in 1958 in Tibet by the CIA? (Before the
contents of the parachute could be put to use, the Chinese attack had intensified and the guerrillas had fled.) The loot, alleged the Committee, had
been brought out of Tibet by Chushi Gangdrug and had until recently been
stashed in a hut in the Missamari camp. It had now disappeared. Where
was it? And who was the guilty party? They demanded explanations and
pointed an accusing finger at – Gyalo Thondup.

Gyalo Thondup, Machiavellian to his fingertips, would not stoop to a
public slanging match. But it was a sticky situation and he knew that if
there was to be a showdown with the Reform Party and its Kashag back-
ers, he needed a power base of his own. He had no actual political status,

though already the refugees, seeing him under attack from the important Kashag ministers, were putting him on a par with them, giving him the courtesy title of *Tsawang Chenmo*, Mr Senior Minister. He needed a bedrock of reliable support. And he knew just where to find it: Chushi Gangdrug was tailor-made for his purpose. Had not the Khampas always resisted rule from Lhasa? Had they not always fiercely protected their independence? Here, precisely, was their opportunity. In those days, the Khampas were riding high in world opinion, even people who knew almost nothing about Tibet had heard of these warrior tribesmen who had stood alone against the might of the Chinese Army. In exile and no longer paying taxes to a hated Lhasa, they were every man's equal and determined to prove it. They and Gyalo Thondup needed each other.

One by one, the supporters of the Reform Party were winkled out of the road-gangs to join the guerrillas in Mustang, until finally, none but the six leaders remained. 'They had nobody to represent, they were in touch with nobody,' says an observer. 'Their followers were stuck in Mustang with no access to the outside world.'[16] Indian security then stepped in and put the six potential trouble-makers on a train to Calcutta, ordering them to stay there. Well aware that they were finished, there was one last task they wished to fulfil. On the way to Calcutta, one of the six was deputed to return to Dharamsala to explain their failure to the Kashag and to return to Kundun the two thousand rupees which he had initially advanced them. Arriving in Dharamsala with the money in a folder, the man put up in a small hotel. No sooner had he arrived than the rumour-machine got busy, accusing him of being a Chinese spy. A group of thugs went to his hotel and demanded everything he had. Ignoring his plea that at least they should leave him the folder meant for His Holiness, they beat him up, took him outside and lashed him to a large tree. It was two hours before the Indian police arrived and found him. They cut him down, and after taking him to hospital for emergency treatment, put him on the next train for Calcutta. He did not even meet Kundun, and the latter probably heard nothing about his visit either then or later.[17]

It was the end of the Old Guard. They never recovered from the Reform Party's collapse and one by one they resigned from office and emigrated. Soon, there was no one left from the old Kashag. Some still believe that their departure was a sad loss for the Tibetans, for they were for the most part men of experience and wisdom, and in the end would have come to terms with the necessity for change. At the very least, they provided a counter-weight to the ambitious Khampas. But it was not to be. Whether or not the removal of his old enemies had been Gyalo Thondup's intention – and he swears that it had not – now that they were out of the way, he was without a doubt the most powerful man on the Tibetan refugee scene. And there were many who believed that he would stop at nothing to make himself the *de facto* leader of Tibet-in-exile.

Before the Chinese occupied Tibet, the 2,000 mile border with India caused few problems and no defensive measures were considered necessary on either side of it. For over a thousand years, Tibet was a peaceful and friendly buffer state which presented no threat to its neighbours. When the Communists over-ran Tibet, India recognized the dangers, yet Nehru trusted that, in the interests of Asian brotherhood, China would respect his territorial integrity. But China's mounting fury over the Dalai Lama and the Tibetan refugees had led to increased tension. The Chinese huffed that the frontier needed to be redefined, Nehru retorting that the mountains of the Himalaya were clearly India's frontier, according to both treaty, custom and geography.

At 5 a.m. on 20 October 1962, using Tibet as a launching-pad, 20,000 troops of the Chinese People's Liberation Army swept over the border into the North-East Frontier Area of India and into Ladakh 1,500 miles away to the north-west. The strength of the attack winded Nehru; he simply did not have the resources – or the men – to fight a high-altitude war. The Himalaya, his unassailable first line of defence, had turned into his Achilles' heel. Several of the Tibetan work-camps near the border were shut down, Tibetans once again became homeless refugees.

As the Chinese army pushed its way into Indian territory with the ease of a knife through butter, panic set in throughout India. But, having rammed home the point that what they did in Tibet was their business and India could do nothing about it, the Chinese declared a cease-fire and contemptuously withdrew.

Kundun was saddened at this humiliation of his Indian friends. Nehru was devastated – the friendship with China had been the cornerstone of his foreign policy. Admitting that he had been living in a fool's paradise of his own making, he lost all zest for life, became a shadow of his former self – and within two years was dead.

In that time, however, his foreign policy underwent a sea change.

Gyalo Thondup claims that three weeks before the attack, Chushi Gangdrug had warned the Indian Prime Minister that the Chinese intended to attack, 'but at that time he wouldn't listen'. After the invasion, a chastened Nehru abandoned his cherished policy of non-alignment in the Cold War and turned to America for support. He also recalled Gyalo Thondup's persistent request for him to provide some kind of military training for the young, able-bodied (non-Khampa) Tibetans still working in the Sikkim road-camps. As long as Nehru had his dream, he would not risk upsetting China; the road-building programme was all he would offer. 'But as soon as the war started,' claims Gyalo Thondup, 'Mr Nehru came looking for me. His attitude towards us had changed overnight. Suddenly he was a man in a hurry, in search of men who would be able to withstand the cold and fight at high altitudes without getting sick. "Now," he said briskly, "about training those Tibetans of yours. We'll do it, if you can provide the men." "Of course," I said. "How many do you have?" he asked. "Five thousand," I said. "Right," he replied, "will you work with the Defence Ministry or with Indian Intelligence?" I chose Intelligence. I knew the CIA would prefer them, and anyway I'd been in contact with Indian Intelligence ever since 1952.'[18]

Thus was born the Special Frontier Force (known as SFF or, more usually, Establishment 22[19]), a high-altitude army of paratroop commandos which would be trained by the CIA to defend India's Himalayan border against further Chinese attack; and to be ready to parachute into Tibet, to make contact with the underground and disrupt the PLA, should fighting break out again. It was formed in November 1962 under the auspices of Indian Intelligence, and it consisted entirely of Tibetans. Informed that a new unit was being formed, independent of the Khampa guerrillas, Tibetan refugees left the road-gangs in droves to join it. After six months basic commando training not far from Dehra Dun, an embryo Tibetan Army of 10,500 men and its own officer corps was operational. Thanks to them, India was able to build up a network of bases from Assam to Ladakh. But China did not invade again.

In Mustang, the Khampas' morale had soared when the Americans made their first arms drop – just inside Tibet, on the mountainous border between Tibet and Mustang. There were arms and ammunition enough to equip four companies of soldiers; and plans were instantly made for raids on seven different sites inside Tibet. The raids were carried out successfully, and caused much disruption to the Chinese military and civil administration in all seven places. On another occasion, the guerrillas isolated a Chinese truck from its convoy, killed everyone in it and seized the contents of the vehicle. 'The truck happened to have been carrying a regimental commander bearing many confidential documents – complete sets of Party directives to area commanders, political manuals and so on. The documents were of great importance. Among them was one which gave the disposition of army groups in Tibet – and revealed the entire system of information-gathering by various spy networks on the Tibetan borders.'[20]

Every year after that, in winter when the rivers were frozen and could be crossed, Chushi Gangdrug sent raiding teams inside Tibet. By 1963–4 the Xinjiang–Shigatse section of the road to Lhasa became virtually unusable by the Chinese. But inside Tibet itself resistance had been crushed. Though the last remaining guerrilla units had held out until 1962, the CIA had already written them off a year before that and were concentrating on the secret underground activities which might have more chance of success. At Camp Hale in Colorado Springs they were secretly training about 500 Tibetans, to be parachuted into their native areas to organize a network of resistance groups throughout the country.

Gyalo Thondup's office in Darjeeling worked round the clock to co-ordinate the various activities, setting up spy networks from Ngari in the west to Kongpo in the south-east, eight networks along the borders and others operating further inside the country, even in Lhasa. Small teams were sent in to carry out reconnaissance, establish safe houses, find food supplies and so on. They had to travel over the mountains and over land, and their assignments were difficult and dangerous. One by one, the teams were blown by Chinese Intelligence. The Chinese would later claim that they had captured fifty-two foreign agents in Tibet to most of whom they had awarded life-sentences. The price of resistance was very high.

But in Dharamsala, Tibet-in-Exile was painfully coming to birth. Kundun had democracy firmly in his sights when in March 1963 he managed to push through a new draft constitution. In the National People's Assembly elections which followed, Tibetans were introduced for the first time to the mysteries of the ballot box. The changes did not as yet go far – how could they? – and democracy was still a long way off. But the first tentative steps towards it had been taken.

NOTES

1. Author interview with HH the Dalai Lama, Dharamsala, June 1994.

2. To the British it was Highcroft House, the seat of the District Commissioner; and today it has become a Mountaineering Centre.

3. Author interview with HH the Dalai Lama, Dharamsala, October 1994.

4. Author interview with Phuntsog Wangyal, London, February 1996.

5. Author interview with Gyalo Thondup, New Delhi, July 1995.

6. Fourteenth Dalai Lama, *Freedom in Exile.*

7. Letter to the author, 12 December 1993.

8. Letter to the author, 12 December 1993.

9. Video interview with Gyalo Thondup by a monk of the Namgyal Monastery, Dharamsala.

10. Author interview with Lhamo Tsering, Dharamsala, October 1993.

11. Author interview with Gyalo Thondup, New Delhi, July 1995.

12. Avedon, *In Exile from the Land of Snows.*

13. Author interview with Gyalo Thondup, New Delhi, July 1995.

14. Author interview with HH the Dalai Lama, Dharamsala, June 1994.

15. Author interview with Gyalo Thondup, New Delhi, July 1995.

16. Author interview with Phuntsog Wangyal, London, February 1996.

17. This account was given to the author by Phuntsog Wangyal (see note 4 above).

18. Author interview with Gyalo Thondup, New Delhi, July 1995.

19. Gyalo Thondup provided the first five thousand men within six weeks and soon exceeded the target.

20. From an unpublished manuscript shown to the author by Jamyang Norbu.

Family Matters 1960–5

Cast from Tibet while most countries stayed mute
all those who fled tasted the bitter fruit –
of exile, and the deep, heart-searing pain,
that they might never see their homes again.

Dr Louella Lobo Prabhu, an Indian journalist
and social worker in Karnataka[1]

From now on, the family had lost its central focus – Lhasa. They were
scattered, and would become even more so, throughout the Tibetan diaspora, united only by their loyalty to Kundun and their devotion to Amala.

Amala herself, nearing sixty at the time of the hazardous escape, was
having problems with her health. Since her arrival in Dharamsala, she had
suffered from a blockage in the throat. A doctor in Delhi discovered a
polyp but, assuring her it was benign, arranged for its removal at St Mary's
Hospital in London. On the journey back from Delhi, the car was hit by a
speeding vehicle just outside Pathankot. Anyone who has travelled the
road between Delhi and Dharamsala knows only too well what a death-
trap it is, the proof lying everywhere along the roadside – vehicles burned
out, crushed, overturned, mangled. Amala's injuries, fortunately, amounted to no more than a whiplash neck and a dislocated arm.

Rinchen Dolma Taring, who was to accompany Amala to England as
companion and interpreter, began teaching her some basic conversational

English and how to write her name in English script. The two friends stayed first in a small boarding-house in Welwyn Garden City, then, after the operation, crossed to the Isle of Wight, where Sir Basil Gould's widow, Cecily, lived. 'I had a phone call from the Tibet Society one day,' says Lady Gould, 'asking me to arrange for two weeks' convalescence, nothing too expensive. I booked them into a small guest-house in Freshwater, insisting that the ladies should be incognito. I was told that the Great Mother's son, Jigme Norbu, would come down and see if the place was auspicious, but in the end he gave his consent without actually visiting it. He said he would trust me.'

The two ladies stayed on the island for six weeks: they had the homely guest-house to themselves, and the weather was glorious. Cecily Gould found them both delightful: Mrs Taring, the highly-educated aristocrat who spoke perfect English, and the Great Mother, 'a peasant woman with the grace of a queen, so very composed, with a gracious, lovely demeanour. She just radiated warmth and peace.' Lady Gould drove them around the island, took them for pub lunches and arranged sightseeing trips, though what they liked best was to stay indoors playing draughts. Occasionally, they would prepare trays of the Tibetan dumplings known as momos and invite Lady Gould and the doctor – a daily visitor who made no charge for his services – to supper. Amala, her bad arm supported in a sling, supervised Mrs Taring in the cooking. Amala loved momos. 'Once or twice,' says Mrs Taring, 'I used to suggest that she should eat a bit less as she was putting on weight and complained of pains in her legs. She joked that everyone else told her to be sure and eat well to stay healthy, and here was I telling her the reverse.'[2]

One day they spotted a couple of local police constables at the door. With police-state memories still uppermost in their minds, Mrs Taring bravely insisted that Amala should lock herself in her bedroom, while she confronted the unwelcome callers. Luckily, the constables were just searching for a missing cat!

Amala fretted constantly about her old mother who, for reasons of security, had had to be left behind in Lhasa. 'My mother must really have suffered over leaving my grandmother behind,' says Kundun. 'They were very close – they even looked alike. When we left Lhasa, one of my uncles and my mother's youngest sister went to live in the family house and look after the old lady.'[3] Amala was almost sick with anxiety, saying over and over to Mrs Taring, 'If only we could go back to Lhasa to see my mother and your children.'⁴ (Mrs Taring herself had been stranded on the far side of Lhasa during the Uprising, unable to make her way home, and had had no news of her husband, his mother, four small grandchildren and two other daughters and their babies.) But in spite of all the terrible things that had happened, says Mrs Taring, 'the Great Mother believed that everything was taken care of, and there was no real point in worrying. She would say that politics was not our concern, our task was to pray and watch our own minds so that we committed no sin.'

Nevertheless, Amala went on worrying, not least about Tendzin Choegyal who was at boarding school in India. Within six weeks of his arrival in exile, he was on his way to St Joseph's College, North Point, Darjeeling. 'Gyalo Thondup drove us to Delhi, which was terribly hot and I couldn't sleep,' he remembers. 'My sister, Pema, was with us. She was going back to the Loreto Convent in Darjeeling, after being allowed to come and visit us in Mussoorie.'⁵

In Darjeeling, he was taken to meet the Rector of North Point, Fr Maurice Standford. His uniform was assembled in two days and on 6 June he began school. 'I had to wear short grey trousers, long socks, shirt, tie, pullover, all very British public school, not at all what I was used to. I couldn't communicate with anybody, I only knew a few words of English. It was very frustrating. I used to lock myself in the urinals and cry my heart out.'

There was nothing for it, however, but to buckle down. Though at first his English and Maths were way down at kindergarten level, he learned fast. Within six months, he had made good progress in English, and was soon being pointed out to beginners as an example of what was possible. Initially placed with much younger children in the Primary Division, before long he was holding his own with boys nearer his own age, not only in Tibetan and English but in French, Scripture, Arithmetic, General Science, Elocution, Spelling and Art. (Art was his favourite.) It was a far cry from the life of an incarnate lama at Drepung, but Tendzin Choegyal adapted to his new life with the natural ease of a chameleon. And he was comforted by the presence of Tsering Dolma's son, Tenzin Ngawang, the nephew six years older than himself who was already studying for his Senior Cambridge Certificate. 'Tenzin Ngawang used to give me reading lists and urge me to read as much as I could, and study hard. He loved literature and music, especially Bach, and he conveyed something of that love to me as a child.'⁶

Earlier that year, in January 1960, Norbu had moved from New York to Seattle University, to take up a one-year assignment in the Tibetan Studies Department, where another eminent Tibetan was also in residence: the Head of the Buddhist Sakyapa sect, the direct descendant of the lama whom the great Kubilai Khan had adopted as spiritual adviser and to whom he had handed the overlordship of Tibet. Throughout the thirteenth and fourteenth centuries, the Sakyapa ruled as priest-kings in Tibet. But eventually the sect lost out, in a civil war, to the reforming Gelugpa sect, to which the Dalai Lamas have all belonged. Nevertheless, the Sakyapa still command a large following. They preserve their hereditary priesthood, not by the celibate *tulku* system of the Gelugpa but by insisting that the eldest son of the sect's head – the 'Holder of the Throne' – must marry and produce an heir, the rest of the family embracing celibacy as monks or nuns of the Sakya order.

The current 'Holder of the Throne' was married, his younger brother was already a monk, and his young sister, Kunyang, was about to enter a nunnery. Then Norbu arrived in Seattle. When he had first met seventeen-year-old Kunyang a year earlier in Darjeeling, he had dismissed her as 'a little wisp of a girl', merely the sister of an important lama. Now he fell in love with her. Kunyang, for her part, abandoned all thoughts of a nunnery, and within three months they were married. A year later they returned to New York, where a friend of Norbu's had found him a job as assistant curator of the Tibetan collection at the Museum of Natural History. Cataloguing Tibetan artefacts and works of art, Norbu slowly began to appreciate the value of the ordinary, everyday objects which at home in Tibet he had taken for granted.

Norbu's marriage, which made newspaper headlines in the USA, where the activities of the Dalai Lama's brother were hot news – was unsettling for Amala. Upset that her Rinpoche son should have forsaken his vows and decided to marry, her anxiety was all the more acute since Lobsang Samten too had renounced his monastic vows and was with Norbu in New York. He was known to have a Japanese girlfriend – what if he were to marry her, or, even worse, an American girl? At the time in question, most Tibetans had still not emerged from their cocoon of isolation, and the idea was horrific. Amala and Tsering Dolma decided that Lobsang must marry a Tibetan girl without delay. And who better than Pema's friend, Namlha Tsarong?[7]

Namlha and her sister Norzin had attended a Protestant school in Darjeeling, while Pema and Khando were at the Loreto Convent. Their paths did not cross until some mutual friends brought them together in Calcutta after the Buddha Jayanti of 1956. (Gyalo Thondup had persuaded his mother to return to Calcutta for a holiday with the rest of the family, after Kundun returned to Lhasa.) After that the four girls began exchanging letters during term-time and occasionally met at weekends at Gyalo Thondup's house.

It was during winter holidays in Calcutta that the friendship really took off. 'Darjeeling was so terribly cold in winter,' remembers Namlha, 'we used to go to Calcutta for two weeks to escape being frozen.' Amala would be there with Tsering Dolma and Tendzin Choegyal. 'She was always very warm and welcoming, very motherly. Whenever my sister and I went to see Pema and Khando, she would take sweets or chocolates out of a cupboard for us. Sometimes she would come with the four of us when we went shopping or to the movies – and then she'd buy us tea and cakes in a café afterwards. We loved films, especially English-language ones; and we loved rock 'n' roll dancing. Actually, Pema didn't do rock'n roll, she would just stand and watch us – though I remember she danced the Charleston really well. She and I were rather shy and reserved, unlike Khando and Norzin who were far more extrovert. They liked to wear print dresses with big flowers and laughed at us for being old-fashioned and boring. They nicknamed us Grandmother One (Pema) and Grandmother Two (me).'

One day in 1961, Namlha received a letter from Pema, asking what she would think about marrying Lobsang Samten. She was taken aback. 'I'd known Lobsang from a distance, I'd met him once at an official dinner in Lhasa, but then he was a very important monk, and, besides, he was ten years older than me. I had seen him only once since those days, in Calcutta when he and Norbu had briefly joined the rest of the family. They didn't waste any attention on us girls, they were so much older; and in any case they had had to look after Tendzin Choegyal, such a bright, intelligent little boy, but unbelievably naughty.'

Pema enclosed a photograph of Lobsang taken outside the UN building in New York. Namlha thought him attractive, but laughed off Pema's idea as 'girl-talk', such as they'd often indulged in. She had her own plans for the future: she had just taken the Senior Cambridge Examination and was doing a secretarial course with French, after which she intended to go to the States. 'A friend of my grandfather's, Ilia Tolstoy, had come to India to see how the refugees were coping. He asked me what I wanted to do, but I didn't know: Tibetan girls at that time didn't really think about a career, we simply got married and looked after the house. But when he found that I was quite good at Art, he invited me to New York to study at an Institute owned by a friend of his. I jumped at the chance, it seemed almost too good to be true.'

But Pema did not let the matter drop. One day Gyalo Thondup came to see the Tsarongs, with a formal request that their daughter might marry Lobsang Samten. 'My parents asked me what I thought,' says Namlha. 'My father said it was entirely up to me, but marrying into a Dalai Lama's family would not be easy. There would be a lot of pressures, over-exposure to limelight and so on. At that point, my mother broke in and said they mustn't interfere, it was my life and I had to make my own decision. I said that at least I ought to meet Lobsang before deciding.'

Lobsang was persuaded to return to India. Arriving in Madras, he rang Namlha to arrange a meeting. She recalls that he was as nervous as she was, they 'just talked a bit awkwardly about Pema' and arranged to meet some time later in Calcutta. The second meeting went much better: they liked each other instantly, the ten-year age gap seeming not to matter at all. 'What I liked about Lobsang was his wonderful sense of fun,' says Namlha. 'He was utterly straightforward and very kind. We spent just over a week getting to know each other, and then he went to Dharamsala to see His Holiness. We were already writing to each other by then, and I had de-cided to stay in India and marry him.'

Though he did not tell Namlha, Lobsang's encounter with Kundun was not easy. The latter was angry that first Norbu and now Lobsang had aban-doned the celibate state for marriage. Perhaps because he had always been so close to Lobsang, his anger against him was the greater. 'I didn't really speak to either of my brothers for some time,' he says wryly, uncomfortable now at the recollection,[8] 'but I was particularly mad with Lobsang Samten. I remember shouting at him, "Even a dog doesn't copulate while it's actual-ly being beaten." It really did seem to me at that time that Tibet was like a dog being viciously whipped and that all our efforts ought to be directed to saving it. But later, when I thought about what I'd said to Lobsang, I realized that if my comments were to be taken literally, there would be no more Ti-betans born inside or outside Tibet. I understood that I'd been illogical as well as unfair, I'd allowed my emotions to run out of control. I was sorry for that. But,' he adds feelingly, 'at the time I was very angry indeed.'

Lobsang and Namlha met again in August 1962 and decided to marry as soon as possible. Amala and Tsering Dolma disapproved of their impatience.

'That year was said to be inauspicious for us,' says Namlha, 'it was a bad-luck year! Neither Lobsang nor I was superstitious, we were very much in love and we didn't care, but Lobsang had a hard job persuading his mother. But in the end she withdrew her objection and we were married that same month.'

After a traditional wedding ceremony in Gyalo Thondup's house in Darjeeling, the young couple went on a honeymoon trip to Srinagar in Kashmir, a wedding present from Gyalo Thondup.

There was some political trouble there, and we were subjected to curfews. We didn't really mind that. But Srinagar was so very like Tibet, so like Lhasa itself, that it made me terribly homesick for my family and sad about those we'd left behind. During the Lhasa Rebellion, my 74-year-old grandfather, the one known as the Great Tsarong, had been chosen as a People's Representative, to negotiate with the Chinese. We heard later that when the Chinese had stopped shelling Lhasa they came to our house – Tsarong House – and took my grandfather and youngest uncle away. They were both imprisoned in the Potala and made to do hard labour. A fellow-prisoner who escaped to India afterwards told us what happened to my grandfather. One day the Chinese ordered his former servants to humiliate and beat him up at a *thamzing* session next morning. When morning came, my grandfather was found dead. He'd apparently just had a heart-attack! Then there was my youngest brother, an Incarnate Lama who'd been left behind in Tibet, I kept wondering if he was still alive. So, even though it was my honeymoon, it was a sad time.

On their return to Dharamsala, Lobsang took Namlha to Swarg Ashram to present her to Kundun. She was terribly nervous. 'I'd only seen him twice before in my life, once when I was a small child and once when I was at the Chinese school in Lhasa. When he left for the Buddha Jayanti, we schoolchildren all lined up to wish him goodbye. And now here he was, my husband's brother. I don't even remember what he said to us, I was shaking so much. But he was very kind and gave us several wedding presents. There was a lovely charm-box with a Buddhist picture in it, a set of seven silver bowls and a length of beautiful dress material.'

Lobsang who was working in the Refugee Rehabilitation Department in Dharamsala, was awaiting transfer to the Tibet Office in Delhi, where Namlha also had found work. Kundun had appealed to young, educated Tibetans to forget self-interest and put their talents to work for the refugees – 'We are not just one big family,' he had reminded them, 'we are trying to rebuild a nation.' Namlha had responded to the call. 'There were so few of us who spoke good English, and English-speakers were desperately needed. So I had agreed to go to Delhi as a secretary/interpreter.'

While waiting for his transfer, Lobsang stayed at home and did the cooking, while Namlha went to work. He was an excellent cook – 'The only fights we ever had were over cooking,' says Namlha, admitting that preparing food was not really her forte. At first she went home each day for lunch, but as the journey by auto-rickshaw cost her more than a month's wages, she soon stopped. When Lobsang was appointed Assistant to Kundun's Representative in Delhi, they acquired a bed-sitting room, bathroom and shared communal kitchen above the Tibet Office. 'It wasn't much, but we were happy. Whenever Lobsang wanted to cook something special, we went into the bathroom where we had a tiny stove. Lobsang was always a realist. He never put on airs. When the others left the kitchen dirty, as they often did, he would come down on Sundays in his shorts and clean it up.'

Even after their daughter, Choekyi, was born (1963), they continued living in their one room above the office. 'There was just one cupboard for our clothes, another for the baby's things. We were terribly cramped. I was so stressed that I didn't have enough milk for the baby and had to supplement it with a bottle. But Lobsang was a fantastic father. He would often get up to give the baby her bottle during the night when I was sleeping so heavily I didn't know anything about it till morning.'

Their son, Tenzin Namdhak, was born two years later. Between the refugees and their own children, life became a constant struggle against exhaustion, their social life limited to an occasional visit to the cinema – where Lobsang invariably fell asleep.

On returning to Dharamsala, Amala found it swarming with orphaned and sick children. She would go down to the Nursery every day, helping with the laundry, showing the ayahs how to handle the children and so on. But, with fifty or sixty new children crossing the border into India every day, conditions in the Nursery were inevitably, as Tsering Dolma admitted, 'shocking to some visitors whose imagination was not vivid enough to realize that it was an emergency, in fact a war situation'.

One of these visitors was an Irish writer, Dervla Murphy, who arrived in 1963 to do voluntary service at the Nursery and was indeed shocked by what she found:

...bronchitis, pneumonia, TB, whooping-cough, chicken-pox, measles, mumps, amoebic and bacillary dysentery, round-hook, tape- and wire-worms, scabies, septic headsores from lice, septic bed-bug bites, boils, abscesses of incredible size, rickets, bleeding gums, weak hearts, asthma, conjunctivitis, trachoma and otitis media. The majority suffer from calcium and Vitamin C deficiency and a heart-breaking number, no matter what is done for them now, will probably be partially blind or deaf or both in maturity...Many of the children are so covered with festering, open sores that you couldn't find room for a sixpence on a clear bit of skin. And when put to bed – six children lie across each bed – the heat so aggravates the itch and pain that they often lie awake whimpering quietly for hours.[9]

At their first meeting in early August 1963, Ms Murphy took an instant dislike to Tsering Dolma. The Principal welcomed her warmly, was 'very sweet and charming and apparently deeply concerned about my comfort while in the camp; she was effusive in her expression of sympathy for the children and of gratitude to all Western helpers'. But even on such scant acquaintance, the new volunteer decided that Tsering Dolma was too 'enjoyably aware of being the Dalai Lama's sister'. The more the Irishwoman grew to love the Tibetan children (Tiblets, she affectionately called them), the more hostile she became to Tsering Dolma, dismissing her as 'a completely uneducated peasant woman who just happens to be His Holiness's sister', a high-handed authoritarian 'with a genius for alienating even those who are best disposed towards Tibetan officialdom'.

The temperaments of the two women made battle inevitable. By November Dervla Murphy's tolerance was wearing thin. In her book *Tibetan Foothold* she writes that 'Tsering Dolma is becoming more and more difficult to deal with', and speaks of 'flaming rows' which have resulted from 'her incomprehensible attitudes'.[10] When the Principal refuses to allow a sick orphan child to leave the Nursery for a camp with a better standard of living in Simla, Ms Murphy accuses her of using the Nursery as a power-base. 'Undoubtedly,' she writes, 'she has compensated herself for the loss of the nationwide power she enjoyed in Tibet by asserting her authority here beyond all reasonable limits.'

The gloves were off and all pretence at politeness was dropped. Suspecting that the interpreters were toning down her own pungent comments when reporting back to Tsering Dolma, Dervla Murphy shrugged, 'I don't blame them. If *I* were constantly in Mrs Tsering Dolma's company I'd be very careful indeed not to translate anything that might worsen her temper during the next twenty-four hours.'

Kundun was not aware of the unpleasantness at the time, but acknowledges that his elder sister may have been difficult to work with. 'My sister, like the rest of us, had a very short temper,' he says. 'I think it was probably true that she was over-conscious of being the Dalai Lama's sister and it may have gone to her head. Don't forget she was an uneducated peasant girl and she was already grown-up and married when her life was turned upside down. She was expected to handle situations and jobs which would ordinarily never have come her way.'[11]

Khando defends her mother more robustly. 'She had the will and the heart for the job, but she knew nothing about management. She cared deeply about those children, some of whom were only babies. She wept because so many died and because she didn't have the means to save them. When my brother and I came to Swarg Ashram for the summer and winter holidays,[12] she had no time to look after us – we had a roof over our heads, we had food to eat, we could look after ourselves, we didn't need her as those poor children in the Nursery needed her. She used to bring some of them to Swarg Ashram, and we'd all try to look after them. To her, those children were not just a job, she was totally involved in them.' Khando feels that Dervla Murphy was unfair. 'She made a lot of petty accusations, such as that my mother wore dark glasses so that nobody could see where she was looking. That was quite unjustified. My mother wore dark glasses on orders from her doctor – to protect her one good eye, as she was blind in the other one. All these personal attacks on my mother, in my view were more demeaning to Ms Murphy than to her. Actually, had my mother spoken English or had a better translator, they might have communicated more successfully.'[13]

Volunteers from other foreign organizations – among them the Swiss Red Cross, the French Service Civil International and the British Save the Children Fund – worked well enough with Tsering Dolma. In fact it was a woman doctor with the Swiss group who first alerted Tsering Dolma to the fact that she was ill. 'Dr Anderhof said she could tell from the texture of my mother's hands, and she begged her to go to the hospital for treatment. But at that stage she was not feeling any physical pain, so she ignored the advice – and we were all too busy to notice.'

By the time Tsering Dolma went to the hospital in Calcutta for a medical check-up, it was too late. Told that she had cancer of the lung and womb, she battled on valiantly. 'No matter how ill she was,' says Kundun, 'she still put her entire self into what she did. She had an enormous capacity for hard work and a deep sense of responsibility.' Though in considerable pain, she got up early every morning for the long walk to the Nursery. As late as 1964, only six months before her death on 21 November, she joined in ball games with the helpers and the bigger girls during the Nursery's fourth anniversary celebrations.

When Pema took her back to Calcutta in June, her doctor, an expatriate Englishman, recommended major surgery at the Westminster Hospital in London. Tendzin Choegyal telephoned her in Calcutta before she left for England. 'I can still hear her voice,' he says sadly. 'She said, "Don't worry about me. I'm not in much pain." The way she said it, I felt she was at peace, but I think she knew she wasn't going to make it. That phone call was our goodbye. When she got to England, she was told they could do nothing.'[14]

Khando had finished school in 1962 and after an eighteen-month period with a Swiss family in Neuchâtel to learn French was studying in England at the House of Citizenship, an international school for young women in Aylesbury. ('We were taught to read newspapers properly, research certain issues, debate them in class, make intelligent conversation on every subject under the sun. We learned how to entertain and how to deal with conflict situations. It was wonderful and the teaching was first-class. But for the life of me, I couldn't think how any of it was relevant to my own life. Later, of course, it turned out to be incredibly useful.') When news came of her mother's illness, she dropped everything and went to London. 'We talked and talked,' she says. 'After she'd had the surgery, my mother was full of plans for the future. She didn't really believe she was going to die.'

One day Khando received a letter from an old school friend of her brother's, Rapten Chazotsang, who, after a period of working in the Dalai Lama's Private Office in Dharamsala, had won a scholarship to the United States to study Political Science. They had known each other on and off for years, had lent each other books and records. 'But he thought I was a fat, ugly school-girl,' says Khando, 'I just wasn't his type.' Since going to the States, however, he had kept in touch occasionally, and, hearing of Tsering Dolma's illness, wrote again to offer sympathy.

'When I saw my mother in hospital and told her about Rapten's message,' says Khando, 'she got very excited and said she had always felt sure we liked each other...My mother said I must write back to him, that he was a wonderful young man, very steady and likeable. Sadly, it was then when she was dying that my mother began to weave plans for the future. "When I get better," she told me, "I shall take life more easily. I'd like a little home of my own where you, Tenzin Ngawang, your spouses and children, can come and I can be a real grandmother." It made me weep, it was so sad. When I thought about it later, I realized she'd never had a family life. She had lived her life in the shadow of my grandmother, always, as the eldest daughter, at her beck and call. She didn't resent that and she knew she would go on doing it. But she still had her dreams. She longed to have her own home, just like other women. She even knew the house she wanted, she'd picked it out, a tiny little cottage in Dharamsala. She thought it was the most beautiful place she'd ever seen, and she dreamed about it. But the dream didn't come true.'

Tsering Dolma died on 21 November 1964, aged forty-five, in the Westminster Hospital, with Phuntsok Tashi, Khando and Tenzin Ngawang at her bedside. 'My father,' says Khando, 'went to pieces and wept. It was heart-rending.' Norbu who flew in from the States, arrived just too late.

The body was cremated in England and the ashes taken to Dharamsala for disposal in accordance with Buddhist ritual. Kundun himself moulded them with clay and imprinted them with images of the gods, the clay images being then enclosed in the casket. Describing himself as 'I, Tenzin Gyatso, Buddhist *bikkhu*' (which is to say, 'a simple monk'), he prayed that her rebirth would be a good one. 'Beloved sister,' he said, 'who was here a moment ago, smiling, talking and telling of her joys and sorrows, is just a memory. She is afar from the field of our vision and hearing. My heart is heavy with grief.'[15]

Whatever the criticisms of her, Kundun has never doubted that Tsering Dolma was the right person in the right place: 'My sister...never gave in to despair,' he wrote in his memoirs.[16] 'She was a powerful woman and quite strict, having inherited the family temper in full measure. At heart, though, she was a very kind person with a good sense of humour. Her contribution in those difficult times was invaluable.' Khando agrees, insisting that her mother was never 'Dervla's devious and scheming harpy', but a simple, warm-hearted woman with no airs and graces, a woman who was inadequately prepared for some of what life threw at her. 'I'm proud to have been her daughter. She had no education, yet she acquitted herself as well as could be expected in the positions she was thrust into. She looked after her mother, had an unquestioning love and devotion for His Holiness, and was a good sister to all her brothers – one of her greatest regrets at the end was that Gyalo Thondup had caused His Holiness such difficulties in Dharamsala – and the other was that she had let down a few very close friends in Tibet by being unable to let them know of the secret plans to flee Tibet. I'm just sorry she died so young, before my brother and I had families of our own and might have been able to make her life a lot happier.'[17]

Tsering Dolma was succeeded at the Nursery by her 23-year-old sister, Pema. Pema's schooldays in Darjeeling, amid nuns who 'instilled high principles into us', had on the whole been happy. 'We were taught to be kind and compassionate above all, and that, of course, was also the basic teaching of Buddhism.'[18] Leaving school, she had gone to La Pelouse, a finishing school in Switzerland, and then to Mrs Hoster's College for Young Ladies in London for a combined Secretarial and Office Administration course. She intended then to return to India and work in the Private Office, recently set up to handle Kundun's income and expenditure (including his daily twenty-rupee allowance from the Indian Government[19]). But on reaching Dharamsala in March 1964, she realized that her sister, Tsering Dolma, was ill and needed her help.

Pema admired her sister's courage and what she had achieved in the face of enormous difficulty. 'She did a great deal for the children in the Nursery,'[20] she said, 'at a time when we had almost no facilities. She was the original moving spirit behind what eventually became the Tibetan Children's Village, with almost a thousand children to take care of and precious little to do it with.' Pema, in common with many others, believes there was a deeper reason for the feud with Dervla Murphy. 'I felt hurt by Dervla's criticisms of my sister, but then Dervla had been hurt too. She actually wanted to adopt a Tibetan child and my sister would not allow it. That was why Dervla felt resentment; and where there is resentment, people overreact. It was all rather sad.'

Younger, educated, energetic and flexible, Pema was more in tune with the foreign volunteer workers than her sister – though she too had inherited the family temper. While waiting to go to Switzerland, she had been roped in to teach English to Kundun's two personal monk-attendants. The two monks were slow learners, and Pema was as impatient as the rest of her siblings. 'She used to pinch their hands and dig her nails into their knuckles as a punishment for being so slow,' recounts her brother,

Tendzin Choegyal. 'In the end, they went on strike and said they didn't want to learn English any more.'[21]

When Pema talks about the early days, she can barely resist a shudder. 'Shortage of staff, shortage of funds, shortage of facilities, shortage of food, clothing, space, shortage of just about everything. The children just came flooding in, and we had to devote our energies to keeping them alive, finding enough for them to eat. Everyone was very dedicated, the house mothers, the cooks, the office workers, but we were desperately short of trained teachers. With so many of our teachers unqualified, the children's basic general education left a lot to be desired.' But, against all the odds, they survived, and under Pema's careful guidance the Nursery grew and flourished. In September 1964, Dervla Murphy received an enthusiastic letter from Judy Pullen, a Canadian volunteer teacher at the Nursery:

Lois and I have seen a lot of Pema (younger sister of His Holiness, who has replaced Mrs Tsering Dolma) and the more we see her the more we like her. She's a wonderful gal and is working like a dog at the Nursery. She's there from 9 a.m. to 8 p.m. seven days a week. She was sick with tonsillitis one week and Thomas [the doctor] ordered her to bed but she refused to go and came to work every day. Everyone is just thrilled with her, and things at the Nursery have improved 100 per cent…You can rest assured the Nursery is in good hands.[22]

When, in April 1965, Dervla Murphy returned briefly to Dharamsala, she could scarcely believe her eyes. Her diary for 23 April records:

Hard to believe that the miserable children among whom I worked less than a year and a half ago have been transformed into these bouncing, bright-eyed, rosy-cheeked Tiblets. Had I been dropped into the compound by helicopter I would never have recognized the place; there are now twice the number of buildings – and half the number of children…the present policy is to keep numbers down to a maximum of 500, and Pema-la very wisely refuses to admit any but orphans from the road-camps.

It was to Pema, her 'intelligence, common-sense and flair for leadership' that she attributed the transformation. 'Young people like Pema,' she wrote, 'gave one hope for the future of their country.'

NOTES

1. Published in the *Tibetan Bulletin*, March–April 1995.
2. Letter to the author from Rinchen Dolma Taring, 1993.
3. Author interview with HH the Dalai Lama, 1993.
4. Letter to author from Rinchen Dolma Taring, 1993.
5. Tenzin Ngawang and Khando were to pursue their studies in Mussoorie.
6. Author interview with Tendzin Choegyal, UK, 1996.
7. All the information that follows is the result of various conversations with Namlha Taklha in Dharamsala, 1993, 1994 and 1995.
8. Author interview with HH the Dalai Lama, Dharamsala, June 1994.
9. Dervla Murphy, *Tibetan Foothold*, John Murray, 1966; Pan 1969.
10. Murphy, *Tibetan Foothold*.
11. Author interview with HH the Dalai Lama, Dharamsala, July 1995.
12. Khando was still at school, but Tenzin Ngawang was studying at St John's College, Cambridge.
13. Author interview with Khando Chazotsang, Utah, February 1996.
14. Author interview with Tendzin Choegyal, Dharamsala, June 1994.
15. In Buddhism, death is followed by rebirth either as human or animal. A good life which has built up meritorious karma earns rebirth onto a higher plane until at last goodness leads to Enlightenment or Buddha-hood.
16. Fourteenth Dalai Lama, *Freedom in Exile*.
17. Author interview with Khando Chazotsang, Utah, February 1996.
18. Author interview with Jetsun Pema, Dharamsala, June 1994.
19. Slightly more than a dollar, rather less than a pound sterling.
20. Author interview with Jetsun Pema, Dharamsala, June 1994.
21. Author interview with Tendzin Choegyal, Dharamsala, 1993.
22. *Tibetan Foothold*.

...And 1965–70

A nation is a soul or spiritual principle. These are but two aspects of the same thing. One is in the past, the other in the
present. One is the common possession of a rich legacy of
memories; the other is the present consent, the desire to live
together, the wish to continue to assert the undivided heritage that has been handed down. A nation is therefore a huge
solidarity, constituted by the feeling of sacrifices that have
been made, and which will continue to be made. It supposes a
past, but it nevertheless comes down to the present in a tan-
gible fact: the consent, the clearly expressed desire to continue living together.

Ernest Renan, Discours et Conférences

'Springtime has come to Tibet...serfdom is finished...the moment the people have waited for has come,' a Chinese propaganda film burbled joyously. But the Lhasa Uprising had brought home to the Chinese that they
could never govern the Tibetan people by consent. With the entire country
now at their mercy, they divided Tibet into eight military zones and imposed a reign of terror. By the end of July 1960, sixty thousand refugees had
fled Tibet for India. Over the next few years, as forced collectivization
brought about a constantly repeated cycle of starvation, resistance and repression, the number would increase to more than one hundred thousand.
It was partly anger at this continuing haemorrhage that drove the Chinese

to invade India in 1962; since when they had used different tactics to try and staunch the flow. In 1964 hoardings in major towns offered tempting incentives to any Tibetans who might return to the new 'socialist paradise' – accompanied by unmistakable threats to the families of those rash enough to refuse. Few responded.

In 1965, when Tibet officially became the Tibet Autonomous Region, the same old puppet 'leaders' were still in place. With, however, one surprising exception: the Panchen Lama. Ordered in 1962 to move to the Potala, denounce the Dalai Lama and take his place as Chairman of the PCART, 'Mao's Panchen' had refused, advising the Tibetans instead to preserve their cultural heritage at all costs. For two years, he was banned from appearing in public. Then, one day in 1964, he was given a last chance to redeem himself by denouncing his predecessor. On that day he earned his place in Tibetan history and in Tibetan hearts when, in front of ten thousand people, he affirmed that the Dalai Lama's survival was a sign of hope for Tibet; and proclaimed his belief 'that Tibet will soon regain her independence and that His Holiness the Dalai Lama will return to the Golden Throne'.[1] The Tibetans wept at his brave words, and knew he would have to pay for them. Arrested and subjected to horrific *thamzings*, he was taken to Peking and was now in solitary confinement in China's top security prison. With their two religious leaders gone, most Tibetans were in a state of shock and grief, far removed from the determined Chinese portrayal of a happy people whose dream had just come true.

Just under a year later in 1966, Chairman Mao, in a crazed attempt to restore his flagging personal power, let loose his young Red Guards in the barbaric Cultural Revolution. Its aim was to erase the past by destroying 'the Four Olds' – old culture, old customs, old habits, old ways of thinking; the definition of 'old' being left to the Red Guards who were allowed to rampage at whim. For Tibet, last bastion of 'the old', that period of collective insanity meant an orgy of undiluted horror. Buddhism was the main target. Most of the remaining monasteries – they had once numbered over six thousand – were destroyed; sacred scriptures were burned or used as paper for the latrines; statues – stripped of their gold and silver – were mutilated and beheaded. Tibetans were forced to throw their prayer-wheels into the river and replace their mantras with the Thoughts of Chairman Mao. Even to be seen moving one's lips in prayer was a crime punishable by death. Celibate monks were made to copulate in public, abbots of great monasteries were crowned with dunce caps and ritually humiliated before being murdered or sent to the gulags in the far north to be worked and starved to death. Anyone remotely connected with the Dalai Lama or the old system was thrown into prison and subjected to *thamzings*. 'The word Hell,' wrote one observer, 'is too soft to describe what happened in those years.'² The British writer Bernard Levin has described it as nothing less than genocide.³

The Cultural Revolution was even more brutal and lasted longer in Tibet than anywhere else in the People's Republic of China. For well over a decade, Tibet disappeared into the darkness of total night. 'We heard very little,' says Kundun, 'just occasionally, from Nepalese traders who had crossed the borders, and their news was always long out-of-date. We knew the Cultural Revolution had begun and that there was immense destruction. But we had so often been overwhelmed by negative events that this seemed like just one more terrible chapter to be added to all the others. We didn't yet realize that it eclipsed in horror everything that had happened before.'⁴ What he did know was that the Chinese leaders in Peking had launched a character-assassination campaign against him, denouncing him as 'that wolf in monk's clothing', hypocrite, thief and even rapist, the Number One Enemy of the Tibetan People!

Mercifully unaware of the events which were crucifying their homeland, by the mid-Sixties the Tibetan exiles in India and Nepal were experiencing a kind of rebirth. In southern India they were fast becoming skilled agricultural workers in a tropical climate; in the north and in Nepal they had established handicraft centres, set up market-stalls, ramshackle shops, tea-houses and even small hotels. Dharamsala continued to be the home of the Tibetan Government-in-Exile, and here Kundun was preserving elements of the old Tibet while coaxing his people politically into the twentieth century.

Nehru's successor, Lal Bahadur Shastri, not only sympathized with the Tibetans but, unlike Nehru, was prepared to uphold their cause in public. In autumn 1965 when the UN once again discussed Tibet, Shastri's India actually voted in Tibet's favour. Though the UN again contented itself with pious exhortation, calling for 'respect for the fundamental rights of the Tibetan people', Kundun felt hopeful that India at least might be near to recognizing his Government-in-Exile. Alas, on 1 September 1965, war broke out between India and Pakistan and, although the fighting was over in six months, within a few hours of signing the peace treaty Mr Shastri was dead. It was a cruel blow. Not only, grieved Kundun, had India lost one of her finest statesmen and the world an enlightened leader – but Tibet had lost one of its few friends in high places.

Since Dharamsala was less than one hundred miles from the Pakistan border, when Kundun left to visit the Tibetan settlements in the south later that year, a total blackout was in force. His driver had to make the dangerous descent to the station at Pathankot without headlights. From the station, they could hear shells exploding over the airport nearby.

At Byllakuppe, the progress made by the settlers was heart-warming. The land had been cleared and, thanks to the International Red Cross and others, most of the refugees at least had access to medical care. 'No longer,' he wrote, 'did I have to confront people who were on the edge of despair.'[5] Because of the war, his visit to the south was extended: two bombs had already fallen on Dharamsala and the Kashag insisted on his staying in South India until the trouble was over. So from Karnataka, he travelled to Mysore, Madras and Kerala, to give teachings.

In Kerala he decided to become a vegetarian. As noted earlier, the assumption in the West that Tibetan Buddhists are all vegetarians is a fallacy. Nevertheless Kundun, though an enthusiastic meat-eater all his life, believed in vegetarianism as an ideal for monks and nuns. When, in Kerala, he saw a chicken being strangled for his lunch, he decided the time had come to put the ideal into practice!

Two months later, when the war ended, he returned to Dharamsala with all the fervour of a new convert. For the next eighteen months he ate 'no eggs, no fish – and, of course, no chicken'. Following the advice of Indian friends, he supplemented his diet with plenty of milk and different kinds of nuts. His mother was appalled, protesting to her friends that 'he'd been fed on meat all his life and if he didn't have it he'd die.'[6] But he persisted – until, one day in the autumn of 1967, he collapsed with a severe dose of Hepatitis B. Nauseous and without appetite, he lay for several weeks in a state of total exhaustion. When, after a long course of Tibetan medicine, the doctors pronounced him cured, they scolded him for being foolhardy. 'They insisted that not only must I eat less greasy food, cut out nuts and reduce my milk consumption, but I must start having meat again instantly. They feared that the illness had caused permanent damage to my liver and had probably shortened my life.'[7] As several Indian doctors agreed, Kundun reluctantly resumed his meat-eating. Amala breathed again.

Lobsang had been posted to Geneva as Assistant to Kundun's Representative. The Swiss Red Cross had already found homes for hundreds of Tibetan orphans, having them adopted into Swiss families while encouraging them to preserve their Tibetan culture and identity. More recently they had undertaken to resettle a thousand Tibetan adult refugees, providing food, clothing and medical assistance as well as accommodation. 'They were bringing the Tibetan adults over from India, and some of them arrived looking very tidy and neatly dressed,' recalls Namlha. 'When they stepped off the plane, the press were waiting and of course their pictures were in the papers. There was an outcry, people protested that they were supposed to be helping poor Tibetans, not well-dressed ones. The Swiss were very upset about it, they felt they were getting the wrong kind of people. They turned to Lobsang and asked if he would go to India and personally select the refugees for resettlement. So he went back and made his way to the road-gangs in Kulu, gathered the workers together and told them to pick out the very poorest among them. The Red Cross then brought these people to Switzerland and everyone was happy.'[8]

Lobsang travelled all over Europe, wherever there were Tibetan refugees. Namlha worked as interpreter and secretary, but both of them spent most of their time just listening to the problems of the refugees and co-ordinating the efforts of the various international agencies. They were expected to attend the usual round of diplomatic functions, but being 'simple people who like fresh air, walking and simple pleasures', they cared little for these formal occasions. Their budget did not allow of elaborate entertaining: when it was their turn to invite guests to their sixth-floor apartment, they cooked the meal themselves. 'The diplomats seemed to love our informality,' says Namlha.

When Amala came to Geneva to spend a year with them, 'we insisted she was to have a rest and not do any work,' says Namlha. 'We thought we were being kind, but she absolutely hated it; she wanted to help and we wouldn't let her. One day I went to her room and found her sewing up the hem of her dress, looking very depressed. When I asked her what on earth she was doing, she said, "Sitting around waiting for death. You two won't let me do anything, and I can't stand being idle. So I've unpicked this hem and am sewing it up again." Well, naturally, we were very upset, and after that we let her help as much as she wanted. She joined me in the kitchen and taught me how to bake that wonderful yeasty Amdo bread sprinkled with turmeric and fenugreek. "You young girls don't know how lucky you are," she would scold me if I ever dared grumble. "When I was young, as soon as the cock had crowed, I had to get up and make bread, clean the house, prepare the altars. And in the evenings I'd still be embroidering and mending clothes till after midnight. I never got more than four hours' sleep. Girls today don't know they're born."'

Khando also came to Geneva to recover from a serious illness. After four and a half years of study in England she had returned to India. 'His Holiness and my father had decided I needed to be brought down to earth and experience a bit of real life.' Phuntsok Tashi took her to Mustang, where he had some business with the guerrillas. 'There I was, in my best clothes, fresh from England, suddenly looking round for walking shoes and borrowing my father's jacket to go into the wilderness. The experience did me a lot of good, but unfortunately I caught some rare stomach bug in Kathmandu and became very ill.' She was packed off to Zurich for treatment in a clinic run by a Swiss doctor friend.

Convalescing in Geneva was a rare opportunity for her to get to know her grandmother better. 'I remember she used to say extremely long prayers, and as she was very self-disciplined, she'd get up at the crack of dawn and get them all over with at once. When breakfast time came, she would say cheerfully, "Well, the prayers are said, so I'm free for the rest of the day." Then we used to go out for walks or go shopping together.' Khando's brother, Tenzin Ngawang, had come fifteenth in all Bengal in the Higher Cambridge examinations, and had gone on to study Sociology at King's College, Cambridge. On his way back to India, he fell in love with Dr Charles Aeschimann's daughter, Danielle, and decided to marry her. When his father protested that they were temperamentally unsuited to each other, Tenzin enlisted Kundun's help, and Phuntsok Tashi was persuaded to withdraw his objections. Tenzin then went to work in the Education department in New Delhi, before moving to Darjeeling to be editor of the Government's *Tibetan Review*. He and Danielle were married in 1964.

His schoolfriend, Rapten Chazotsang, who had acquired a Sociology degree in the USA, wrote to Khando to say that he was passing through Geneva on his way home to India! On his first evening, the pair went out to the cinema and did not return until the small hours. Amala was shocked. 'My grandmother was cross with me next day. She said I'd spent far too long with him and if we went out together again I was to come home earlier. But I know she liked Rapten really.'

When Khando returned to New Delhi and moved in with her father, she and Rapten had already decided to marry. To her relief, her father approved the match. Maybe Phuntsok Tashi was relieved too, since, though he had not yet told his daughter, he was planning to get married again, to Kesang, a young Tibetan woman many years his junior, who was working at the Nursery in Dharamsala. When Khando first found out, she was furious. But as time went by she relented and grew quite close to Kesang. Amala, however, found it difficult to forgive her son-in-law for remarrying.

Norbu, as Assistant to Kundun's Representative in New York, divided his day between the Tibet Office and the Museum. He and Kunyang had moved out of their tiny apartment to a larger flat near Central Park in 1962 when their first son, Lhundrup Namgyal, was born. A second son, Kunga, arrived in 1963, followed by a third, Jigme, in 1965. By this time Norbu was engaged on a six-month lecture tour about Tibet, visiting colleges and universities in almost every state of the US and Canada. Towards the end of the tour, he was invited to join the staff of Indiana University in Bloomington. Having spoken on the campuses of a number of colleges, many of them quite small, he formed a mental image of the university in question as a small insignificant rural outfit 'surrounded by a vast number of cornfields' – though, with three young sons, and a dog, there was something to be said for moving from New York to a place where 'grass and trees grew around houses' and where they would have space to run around. He decided to take a look at Bloomington.

He was in for a surprise. 'Instead of a small college in a sleepy town with perhaps a thousand students, I was astonished to discover a beautiful sprawling campus bustling with activity and with a student population of almost thirty thousand.' After talking the matter over with Kunyang, he accepted the offer and the family moved to Bloomington in time for the beginning of the 1965 academic year. The university provided him with a two-bedroomed house which, though small, was palatial compared to their New York apartment. The boys were delighted to be in the country – seeing, for the first time in their urban lives, real fruit growing on real trees. They settled into Bloomington life with ease.

In his first semester, Norbu, with only one language course – in elementary Tibetan – and only three students, had time on his hands. He spent it getting to know the place and making new friends. In the years that followed he was given more demanding language work, as well as courses on Tibetan oral literature, religion, the monastic orders and the political system in Old Tibet.

In 1967, to Norbu's great delight, Amala came to visit. He had been eight years old when he left home for Kumbum. After that, though he had sometimes visited his family in Taktser, and had had a room in his parents' home in Lhasa, the monastery had been his real home. Following his flight from Tibet in 1951, he did not see his mother again until the Buddha Jayanti in 1956, and after that not until she reached India as a refugee in 1959.

He was overjoyed at the prospect of seeing her. 'I felt that my mother's presence under my roof would bring us some degree of the home life and family atmosphere of Amdo that I had sorely missed since my childhood, and especially throughout my life of exile.' The boys were thrilled to realize that, like all their American friends, they would have a real 'Grandma' with them for Thanksgiving and Christmas. As Amala spoke no English, they would have to polish up their own Tibetan.

Norbu went to meet Amala in New York, and showed her the big city before bringing her home in triumph to Bloomington. She immediately took the whole family under her wing. 'She helped organize our household, taught my wife special Amdo dishes, constantly fussed over the children, and behaved in every way like an adoring grandmother.' Fortunately Amala and Kunyang took an instant liking to each other. Kunyang, an orphan from early childhood, was soon telling her friends that Amala was a real mother to her. Norbu – perhaps realizing more than ever how much he himself had been deprived – loved to see her playing with the boys. 'She had a wonderful way with children,' he wrote. 'My boys all adored their Mo-la and even the neighbours' children would gather round her calling her Mo-la.'

Throughout that year, Norbu marvelled that his mother had retained her unassuming simplicity, despite the high station to which she had been elevated. 'She had a natural dignity that sprang from her inner strength of character and self-reliance; she never assumed the airs of a grand lady.'

Planting and replanting – 'every morning she was in the garden watering the flowers' – mending the family's clothes, rearranging furniture, playing with the children, Amala's year passed all too quickly. When it was time for her to leave, the parting was difficult for them all. 'She had,' said her son, 'immeasurably enriched our household with love and care and with the peace and serenity that she inspired in all of us.'

Tendzin Choegyal was still at school in Darjeeling. Though two of his elder brothers had abandoned the monastic state, it was taken for granted that he at least would continue to be a monk. He was Ngari Rinpoche, an important Incarnation, destined to take charge of a number of monasteries in Ladakh and Zanskar. At the same time, he was an adolescent who had been torn, at the formative age of thirteen, from a Tibetan Buddhist monastery and transplanted into a Roman Catholic, English-speaking boarding school. Somehow, he had survived. In the higher forms now, he was studying Scripture, Moral Science (i.e. Religion), History, Geography, Chemistry, Physics, Biology, Maths, PE, Arts and Crafts, English Language and Literature – and Tibetan. It was a general education such as Kundun might have envied.

In the lower school, Religion had been just another lesson, involving little more than the mechanical repetition of scriptural texts, a routine which reminded him of home. As he grew older, the lessons became more challenging and controversial. 'Some of the non-Christian boys became quite hostile towards Christianity,' he remembers, 'they asked snide, aggressive questions in class. But I never wanted to mock. I think that in spite of appearances I had always been drawn to the spiritual life, and these Christian teachings began to rekindle the flame. Having been brought up in a monastery, and in a national culture dominated by religious beliefs and spirituality, I was quite open to learning what I could from Christianity.'

Studying the Gospels, he was happy to find them close in spirit to Mahayana Buddhism, the Beatitudes and the Sermon on the Mount in particular sounding a familiar note. 'The Christian message of altruism and love just reinforced my Buddhist beliefs. The Mahayana ideal is also love: we search for enlightenment in order to help other sentient beings along the path. Christianity and Buddhism both worked in me, the one feeding the other, and for me the synthesis of the two was something positive.'[9] Sometimes, when all was quiet, he used to go to the chapel – to meditate in silence or recite his Buddhist prayers. There he was at peace.

That the Christians he met seemed to live their beliefs impressed him. 'With our monks, it was so often just a matter of lip-service...But here it was different...Priests were doing all kinds of social service, becoming teachers and so on. I liked that and made a lot of friends among them.'

At the end of that year – his last but one at the College – Tendzin Choegyal, to everyone's surprise, failed his exams. Unable to face repeating the year, he decided on impulse to pick up his monastic studies in Dharamsala. Joining the rest of the family at Swarg Ashram, he enrolled in Buddhist philosophy classes given by the Abbot of Namgyal Monastery.

One of his fellow-students was a young monk working in the Private Office, Tenzin Geyche Tethong. Tenzin Geyche, from an old aristocratic family, had been sent to a Methodist school in Darjeeling from an early age. He and Tendzin Choegyal had met only after the latter came to India as a refugee. 'I'd already been out of the country for about ten years and his Tibetan was so much better and more fluent than mine,' says Tenzin Geyche. 'I was very impressed.'

When they met again in Dharamsala, Tenzin Geyche was impressed in a different way. 'As Ngari Rinpoche, he was responsible for all those monasteries in Ladakh. I used to tease him about it, calling him King of Ladakh. It really was a small kingdom that he had inherited.' When studies were over for the day, the two boys would escape to the hills. 'Up there in the mountains we used to let off steam, yelling and shouting our heads off for the sheer joy of it,' says Tenzin Geyche. 'Sometimes we would recite Shakespeare at the tops of our voices. Or make paper gliders which used to fly very well if you made them properly.'

Tendzin Choegyal did not find the transition altogether easy. 'Rinpoche had a brilliant mind and an excellent memory, but he was terribly impatient,' remembers his friend. 'The philosophy lessons given by the Abbot were really quite short, only about an hour. But Rinpoche had a wrist watch with an alarm on it, and as the lesson began he used to set the alarm to go off in exactly one hour's time. He had no intention of staying any longer than he had to.'[10] Fortunately, the Abbot was a tolerant man.

While in Dharamsala, Tendzin Choegyal was ordained as a monk.

In the summer of 1966, the monks of Rangzom in Ladakh, the chief monastery associated with the Ngari Rinpoches, requested a formal visitation: as Tenzin Geyche had teased, he *was* virtually king of Ladakh. 'Well,' he explains – with some embarrassment – 'Ladakh and Zanskar are my territory, rather like a bishop and his diocese.' As Kundun was making an official visit to that extreme north-west area of India, they travelled together. Choegyal visited all seven of his monasteries and stayed on for a month after Kundun had left. He was miserable: 'It was difficult to sleep at such a high altitude, the food was terrible, everything was dirty and the people were appallingly superstitious. I felt I had travelled backwards in time into a medieval world.' The solemn ceremonial with which he was received unnerved him and on at least one occasion embarrassment pushed him into behaving outrageously. 'They were very solemn, but I wasn't,' he explains. 'At Karsha monastery, one of the biggest in Zanskar, they had set up a formal welcome, banners everywhere, the Abbot in attendance, horns, trumpets and all that. We rode in solemn procession, and our progress was dismally slow. I ran out of patience and said to the Ladakhi official who was riding next to me, "Oh, come on, let's gallop!" He took his whip out from under the saddle and slapped the rumps of the monks' horses in front of us. So the whole procession galloped the last five kilometres, straight through the crowd and up to the monastery. I really enjoyed myself and the villagers laughed their heads off, it was the first time they'd ever seen an Abbot gallop. Nobody minded; we are, don't forget, a fun-loving people. But I must admit it was unusual.' What the Abbot felt – or said – he does not reveal.

Choegyal's inability to take his prestigious role seriously may have been symptomatic of a larger confusion already making itself felt. With hindsight, he thinks that, despite his so recent ordination, he was already doubting his vocation as a monk. 'You either have it or you don't, and I don't think I ever had it.' He didn't mind the studying, nor even the rigours of the life. But somehow he could not identify with what Buddhist monks were meant to be about. 'We spent our time assimilating knowledge. But what good was all that learning without practice? Philosophy should hold the key to the meaning of life, but here it did not.' Knowledge on its own was of little use in confronting one's personal demons. 'Our one real aim in life should be the practice of *dharma*, any act, word or thought aimed at eradicating the three afflictive emotions of hatred, greed and ignorance.[11] But it seemed to me that most of the monks concentrated on learning for its own sake, not on putting that learning to good use, nor on trying to grow in happiness and holiness. I really felt they were missing the whole point.'[12]

Helping Tibet in some way was the point for him. Answering Kundun's appeal to young Tibetans – to rebuild their nation in exile. That, in Tendzin Choegyal's book, was the true practice of *dharma*.

Towards the end of the Sixties, things began to go wrong for Gyalo Thondup. Acting on complaints from some of the younger, CIA-trained officers in Mustang, he had sacked the Commander of the National Volunteer

Defence Army, the Khampa General Baba Yeshi, replacing him by General Gyatso Wangdu, sole survivor of the first group of Tibetans trained by the CIA.[13] Baba Yeshi retired to Dharamsala to lick his wounds, before returning to Mustang, publicly breaking with the NVDA, and accusing Gyalo Thondup of misappropriating the contents of the famous yellow parachute. Then, with about two hundred disgruntled Khampas, he set up a private army. A dangerous stand-off resulted, not only in Mustang where the two groups actually came to blows, but also throughout the Tibetan settlements, where the refugees lined up on either side of the old tribal fault-lines: Khampas versus the rest. Refusing to join any of the regular Tibetan settlements such as Byllakuppe, Khampa leaders set up thirteen breakaway settlements of their own. Like Baba Yeshi they believed that Gyalo Thondup had betrayed them and that he was part of a sinister Dharamsala (i.e. old Lhasa) plot to keep them down.

Gyalo Thondup had belatedly realized the danger of depending solely on the powerful Khampas for his support, and had been slowly distancing himself from them. When he actually formed a new political group, the United Party, culled from all three of the former provinces of Tibet, the Khampas turned against him, regarding him from that time forward as the arch-betrayer. The situation got so out of hand, Tibetan loyalties became so polarized, that the fragile unity of the refugees in Dharamsala seemed about to collapse.

The CIA chose this of all times to announce that they were closing down the Tibetan operation. They sugared the pill somewhat by offering a three-year programme which would supposedly enable the Tibetan SFF to become self-sufficient, but it was no more than a face-saver. Gyalo Thondup's right-hand man, Lhamo Tsering, is still bitter. 'It was just a ploy to keep us from making too much of a fuss,' he accuses. 'They had us completely fooled.' By the time American aid was cut in 1970, Gyalo Thondup had had enough of Dharamsala and had retired in disgust to Hong Kong. (Without, however, breaking his ties with the Indian Secret Service.) The Tibetans would not see him again for almost a decade.

Many of the younger Tibetan refugees had idolized Gyalo Thondup and, like him, wanted radical change. Chafing at their elders' reluctance to move with the times, they talked incessantly about how to harness the energy of Tibetan youth in the cause of their country's independence. Four young men[14] came up with the idea of a Youth Congress, with leaders who would be forward-looking and accountable to the members. 'We needed some kind of youth forum where people could come together and pool their ideas. We all felt the voice of Tibetan youth had to make itself heard; their energies had somehow to be channelled to help Tibet,' says Tendzin Choegyal.

Kundun gave the youngsters his blessing, and offered to meet the costs of an inaugural meeting, with the one proviso that it must represent refugees from *all* three regions. On 7 October 1970, three hundred eager young Tibetans gathered in Dharamsala to ask some pointed questions of their elders. Why, they wanted to know, had the Chinese been able to walk into Tibet so effortlessly in 1950; what had the Kashag been doing to let it happen; and why hadn't the army in the east put up a credible fight? It was obvious that a vibrant new political opposition party was in the making, one that might eventually replace GT's United Party. The more conservative Tibetans were unhappy about it, but, like it or not, half-way through that week of tough talking and debate, the Tibetan Youth Congress was officially inaugurated by Kundun.

Tenzin Geyche was elected first President of what was, in those early days, a pretty chaotic organization. 'We didn't have an office,' says Tendzin Choegyal, 'just a tin trunk in which we kept all the documents and papers. Sometimes we held our meetings in empty rooms with no furniture, so the tin trunk had to act as table as well.'[15] But what they lacked in comforts, they more than made up for in enthusiasm. Their aims were unambiguous: to preserve their Tibetan identity and culture; to stay united under the leadership of the Dalai Lama; and, last and most aggressively, to regain Tibet. 'For the first time since the exile,' claimed Jamyang Norbu, a member of the first Central Executive Committee, 'we had an organization which knew what it wanted to do; which was not a court organization, not regional, not sectarian. It was something new: it was national.'[16] The Kashag viewed them sourly as the thin end of a highly undesirable wedge. The Youth Congress saw itself as a loyal opposition, but, as Jamyang Norbu put it, 'the Kashag did not want *any* opposition, loyal or otherwise'. As over half of the Youth Congress members were actually employed within the Government service, squalls could safely be predicted.

The founders of the new movement all belonged to that new breed of young Tibetans who had received a modern Western-style education outside of Tibet. They spoke English and Hindi along with Tibetan. They were not emotionally bound to their old outdated system; and they could clearly see the problems which their society faced as it struggled to join the modern world. They recognized that there were now two kinds of young Tibetans: those born inside Tibet, under a Chinese military dictatorship, with no experience of freedom, no knowledge of their own traditions or of the Dalai Lama; and those others who had been born as refugees in exile, affected by Western values, knowing nothing of the Chinese, nor of Communism.

The central executive (CENTREX) of the Youth Congress was to be in Dharamsala, with branches set up wherever there were young Tibetans. Darjeeling, for example. For no particular reason that he can think of, Tendzin Choegyal had gone there for a holiday in the summer of 1969, after revisiting his monasteries in Ladakh. (This time, with his social conscience working overtime, he had applied himself to introducing democratic principles, making radical changes in the distribution of his monastic wealth. 'There were certain monasteries which had accumulated wealth but were not putting it to good use. Their excuse was that this wealth was mine, intended for me personally. So I sent out letters to all the monasteries, insisting that whatever money there was belonged to them and was to be used for the benefit of all, not just for certain monasteries and certainly not for me. In the end I just renounced my personal claim to any of it.'[17]) Meeting his old Headmaster, Fr Maurice Standford, he was persuaded to return to St Joseph's College and finish his interrupted studies. He enrolled as a day boy, living in Gyalo Thondup's house until the last month of the school year when he once again became a boarder. By dint of working hard, at the end of the year he 'managed to scrape through' his leaving examinations. 'My results were just about good enough,' he shrugs. In the circumstances, he had expected no better.

Accepting belatedly that he had no vocation to the monastic state, he announced that he was abandoning it. It is said that his mother was deeply distressed by his decision, but if so she hid the fact from him. 'You're not the first high lama to disrobe,' she consoled him, 'it's happening more and more now, in exile.' Kundun admits that for a while he felt disappointed that yet another brother had reneged on his calling. But he too was a realist and soon accepted the situation. Rinchen Khando, whom Choegyal would later marry, believes that his decision to abandon the monastic state took a great deal of courage. 'He was desperately anxious to lead a good life without hypocrisy and I think that his being an Incarnation and a monk set up a terrible conflict within him. The very fact that he was able to stand up and say he could no longer be a monk, well, it took a lot of guts. Many men in that position couldn't have done it.'[18]

For a few months Choegyal continued to study at St Joseph's, underlining his new lay status by outlandish behaviour and a style of dressing which can only be called bizarre. 'There was a Humphrey Bogart-style trench-coat which I loved...teamed with a broad, pale blue tie with polka dots. I'd stick a pipe in my mouth and wear sideburns plastered in place with egg-white.' He swears that as a technique for attracting the attention of girls, it worked, 'if only because no one else looked quite so odd'.

At their first meeting since Tendzin Choegyal had disrobed, Kundun treated him gently. 'You've been passing through a wild phase,' he said, 'but, even if you're no longer a monk, you're still a follower of the *dharma*. Hold on to that. Get married,' he went on to advise, then, mindful of his younger brother's impulsiveness, 'but don't rush. Take your time. Find a really suitable girl.'

In September, at a Youth Congress meeting, Choegyal met Rinchen Khando Tasotsang, a student at the Loreto College in Darjeeling. He remembers thinking quite dispassionately, when he first set eyes on her, 'If I ever marry, that will be the girl.' Their meeting impressed Rinchen Khando too, for a quite different reason. Since childhood, she had been devoted to the Great Mother. 'In my mind I always felt very close to her. I was sure she was the reincarnation of the Goddess Tara, not because I knew much about her but because she had given birth to someone as outstanding as His Holiness. In college I had a picture of her on my desk. But it was past its best, so one day after a Youth Congress meeting, I plucked up courage to ask her son for a new one. That was my first meeting with Rinpoche. [Like most people, even his closest friends, Rinchen Khando still refers to her husband as Rinpoche.] He asked me why I wanted it and seemed a bit surprised when I told him. But he found a photograph for me, so I was quite content.'

The Tasotsangs were a family of prosperous Khampa traders who had lived very simply in Kham. 'We all used to eat together in a big room, the village children, the servants, ourselves, sometimes about thirty-five of us. There were no differences between us. People were happy then.' She was about four when the Chinese came and tore everything apart. 'They started dividing people into ranks and setting them against each other, interfering in the way the village was run. They used to watch our every movement, everything we did, how we behaved towards each other.' In 1956, when Rinchen was seven, the family moved to the apparent safety of Lhasa. There for a while she attended a Tibetan school until her parents decided to follow the example of several other families and send their children to schools in India. Enrolled as a boarder at St Joseph's Convent in Kalimpong, Rinchen dreaded being parted from her parents, and when she found herself actually in Kalimpong, with her school uniform already packed, and her parents preparing to return to Tibet, she was inconsolable. Fate then took a hand, in a way that at the time she was too young to understand. 'Suddenly my parents had a letter from my uncle telling them not to go back to Tibet. I was so happy that they were not going to abandon me that I didn't really bother about the reasons.' It was March 1959!

Unable to return home, Rinchen's parents stayed in Kalimpong for a year and then moved to Darjeeling. But when China invaded the border territories of India in 1962, the Tasotsangs like many other Tibetans abandoned the town which was so uncomfortably near to the war zone, and settled instead in Mussoorie.

The Tibetan school in Mussoorie had an excellent reputation. It had been opened in 1960 for fifty young men from the Missamari transit camp, and, at Kundun's request, Rinchen Dolma Taring and her husband Jigme had taken charge. The young men were in rags and permanently hungry, there were no toilet facilities – but no one complained. Gradually, as individuals and charitable organizations came to the rescue, (and eventually the Government of India took over the school) things improved. By the time the young men had finished their education and dispersed to train as teachers themselves, the school was already a recognized High School, with Jigme Taring as Principal. Those first students were replaced by about six hundred boys and girls, of whom Rinchen Khando was one. Later she was admitted to a Protestant school in Mussoorie, where she obtained her Senior Cambridge Certificate.

From Mussoorie, Rinchen moved to Darjeeling to train as a teacher at the Loreto College for Girls – just at the time when delegates were being chosen for the inaugural meeting of the Tibetan Youth Congress in Dharamsala. She and Tendzin Choegyal were both selected. Afterwards, they both worked enthusiastically to set up a Darjeeling branch, devoting all their Sundays to the task. 'We worked together and got to know each other very well,' says Choegyal.

Choegyal, however, went off to the USA to pursue his studies. He applied to do student counselling at Seattle University, but unfortunately his qualifications were not good enough and he was despatched to a Junior College to acquire the necessary credits. It was demoralizing for a young man of twenty-three, beset by confusion and low self-esteem. As his sense of inadequacy deepened, so did his depression. Then, filled with a sharp longing 'to go back to India and help the refugee community', he left Seattle and returned to Dharamsala.

It was the onset of a long period of clinical depression. Tenzin Geyche was alarmed at the change in his friend: 'Rinpoche found life almost unendurable at this period,' he recalls. 'He was staying with Jetsun Pema at the TCV. At one point he would stay in his room all day long, refusing to get dressed or to eat, unwilling to talk to anybody. As I was one of the few he would see, I used to go and visit him, doing anything I could think of to drag him out of his misery. Once I even resorted to standing on my head – in my monk's robes – just to make him laugh. Sometimes I'd stay with him all night. He couldn't sleep, and he wouldn't let me sleep either.'[19]

Gyalo Thondup stepped in with a practical suggestion: if his brother really wanted to help his fellow exiles, he should go to Nepal and work in one of the Handicraft Centres. Still in a state of shock, Choegyal bowed to GT's wishes. 'I wasn't keen on the idea of exporting carpets and things like that. But, as GT wanted it, that was what I did. It was no good, though. I could work up no enthusiasm for what I was doing and after six weeks I gave up.' But he had resolved to pull himself together and make something of his life. His sister Pema found him a job at the Nursery which, thanks to continuing aid from international voluntary organizations had become the Tibetan Children's Village, modelled on the Pestalozzi Villages in Switzerland. (They had moved to a house (originally called Egerton Hall) further up the mountainside and were busily expanding all over it. The TCV was beginning to resemble a small city, with over one thousand destitute children ranging from six months to eighteen years.)

Pema charged him with finding sponsors for the children of Tibetans working in the road-gangs. 'We were supposed to go and take photographs of the children to be sponsored and write up their case histories,' he says. 'It was my first real job of work. I went off with two companions to find the children. As we had to pass through the Kulu Valley on the way to the road camps, we saw a lot of marijuana growing wild. I'd never had anything to do with drugs before, but it seemed a good time to try. Every time we reached our destination for the day, we used to cut some grass, rub it, roll the resin into small balls, dry it off and try and smoke it. We would get stoned out of our minds and go to sleep. It was certainly effective, it changes your consciousness, lifts you onto a different level. But I didn't like it, it made me sick – possibly because we were so eager to smoke the grass we had cut that we didn't dry it properly, we just heated it in a fry-ing-pan like tsampa. This first experience with drugs wasn't exactly a plea-sure and I never touched the things again.'[20]

He 'found over one hundred children, took their photographs, gave them all numbers and wrote brief case histories of them all'. When the job was done, Pema offered him a teaching job at the TCV. 'They were very short of teachers, and anyone who knew English and had a little Maths was good enough,' he says. He taught most subjects in the lower forms, and PE as far as Class 5, and feels immense pride that 'his' Class 2C all went on to gain university degrees.

Amala was as anxious as Kundun for Tendzin Choegyal to settle down. She was relieved to learn that he already had a Tibetan girl in mind – Rinchen Khando Tasotsang. Arrangements went ahead and in 1972 Norbu accompanied him to Mussoorie where he and Rinchen were married with a simple ceremony in her parents' house. 'Everyone expected us to have a very traditional ceremony with a big party to follow,' says Rinchen. 'But neither of us liked a lot of fuss. All we wanted was a blessing from His Ho-liness and from His mother.'[21] 'Besides,' adds Choegyal, 'we didn't have money to throw around. After all, we were refugees.' They went straight back to Dharamsala.

Since 1968, Kundun had been living in his new quarters, aptly renamed Thekchen Choeling, the Island of Mahayana Buddhism. In these surround-ings, he was more relaxed, free at last to indulge his talent for gardening. He had planted many new fruit trees and flowers, and, delighting in the numerous small animals and birds which came to visit, had constructed a bird-table just outside his study window, surrounding it with netting to keep out the huge circling birds of prey. Occasionally the netting was not sufficient deterrent and then he had recourse to his air-pistol. 'Having spent a great deal of time as a child at the Norbulingka practising with the Thirteenth's air-rifle, I am quite a good shot,' he chuckles, hastening to ex-plain that the air-pistol is for scaring the birds, not killing them.'[22]

He was pursuing other old hobbies too, like photography and mending watches, and as his new residence had rooms to spare, he had acquired a set of tools and converted one of the rooms into a workshop. He had lost none of his taste for taking things apart and putting them together again. At the same time, he was trying to learn something of Western thought, particularly in the fields of science, astronomy and philosophy. Even more seriously, he was 'putting more effort into meditation and study. At long last I found the enthusiasm and determination to meditate properly on Compassion and Emptiness. These two practices really did change my life. I began to understand something about the possibility of salvation, the permanent cessation of all negative emotions. Once you're convinced that salvation is possible, you work towards it steadily and your faith becomes much stronger. The more I concentrated on Compassion in the late Sixties and early Seventies, the more patient I became, the less prone to anger. Anger still comes but it's more like a lightning flash now, it doesn't last.'[23]

NOTES

1. Avedon, *In Exile from the Land of Snows*, p. 274.

2. Harrison E. Salisbury, 'Hell – and Hope – in Shangri-La', article in *From Liberation to Liberalisation: Views on Liberalised Tibet*, Dharamsala, 1982.

3. *The Times*, 7 September 1990.

4. Author interview with HH the Dalai Lama, Dharamsala, June 1994.

5. Fourteenth Dalai Lama, *Freedom in Exile*, p. 195.

6. Letter from Rinchen Dolma Taring to the author, 1991.

7. Author interview with HH the Dalai Lama, Dharamsala, 1993.

8. Author interview with Namlha Taklha, Dharamsala, 1993.

9. Author interview with Tendzin Choegyal, Dharamsala, October 1993.

10. Author interview with Tenzin Geyche Tethong, Thekchen Choeling, October 1993.

11. Known in Buddhism as 'the three afflictive emotions'.

12. Author interview with Tendzin Choegyal, October 1993.

13. *In Exile from the Land of Snows*, chapter 5.

14. Tenzin Geyche and his brother, Tenzin Namgyal Tethong, Lodi Gyari and Sonam Topgyal.

15. Author interview with Tendzin Choegyal, October 1993.

16. Author interview with Jamyang Norbu, Dharamsala, September 1991.

17. Author interview with Tendzin Choegyal, October 1993.

18. Author interview with Rinchen Khando Choegyal, June 1994.

19. Author interview with Tenzin Geyche Tethong, Thekchen Choeling, October 1993.

20. Author interview with Tendzin Choegyal, October 1993.

21. Author interview with Rinchen Khando Choegyal, October 1993.

22. *Freedom in Exile*, p. 203.

23. Author interview with HH the Dalai Lama, Dharamsala, July 1995.

Stones and Stars 1970s

...your own life, timid and standing high and growing,
so that, sometimes blocked in, sometimes reaching out,
one moment your life is a stone in you, and the next, a star.
Rainer Maria Rilke, 'Sunset'

After six years in Geneva, Lobsang Samten was restive. Though life there
was enjoyable and the children were well settled in school, Switzerland
was an expensive country, especially on the sort of pittance he earned
from the Government-in-Exile. Besides, Lobsang felt he was existing in a
goldfish bowl. As the brother of the Dalai Lama, he was too exposed, his
every action was watched. Part of him – the private self who longed for
freedom and anonymity – wanted to go back to the United States and become an American citizen. He loved America, with its rich racial mix, its
hotch-potch of cultures. In America he could wear what he chose, go
where he wanted, lead his own life, instead of being placed on a pedestal as
the Dalai Lama's brother. He and Namlha both had the Green Card that
would allow them to work in the US. In 1971, they packed up and went.
'We started life all over again,' Namlha says cheerfully.

Staying first with Tibetan friends in New York, they helped set up a Tibetan Arts and Crafts Centre on Madison Avenue. Five Tibetan families
put up the money and Gyalo Thondup and his wife (who were sharehold-
ers) sent handicrafts made by the refugees in Darjeeling. A Tibetan ac-
countant worked the till, Namlha did the window display, and she and

Lobsang 'worked as cleaners, sellers, packers and as an information centre about Tibet for the many people who came to ask.'

When the venture collapsed, Namlha found work in the New York offices of 'The Board Room', an executive lunch-and-dining club in Park Avenue, 'replacing all five girls in the office in turn, when they went on holiday, and doing the payroll for the telephone switch-board operators.' Lobsang, on the other hand, was jobless. He and a few friends wanted to open a small Tibetan café, but as they could afford neither the initial overheads nor the insurance premiums, the idea was a non-starter. Lobsang then vainly searched for casual work as a cook. 'You have to remember,' says Namlha, 'he had no qualifications, no degrees or certificates, he hadn't even been to a modern school. It was difficult to think what he could do.''

Their first priority, however, was to find a suitable school for their children, Chuki (13) and Tenzin Namdhak (11). They could not afford private school fees and wanted to avoid inner-city schools with their reputation for violence and drugs. When a real estate man from New Jersey told Lobsang of a good school in Scotch Plains, they moved there, even though it meant Namlha commuting daily by bus to New York. With the help of friends and a 25-year mortgage from the bank, they bought a small shingled four-roomed house in Scotch Plains. And as Namlha did not arrive home before seven and the children could not be left alone in the evenings, Lobsang looked around for a day job. One day, a neighbour told them that the local school needed a night caretaker, and he decided to apply for the job. It was better than nothing.

So Lobsang Samten, who once had been Lord Chamberlain of Tibet and head of the Dalai Lama's Household and Treasury, became a night-shift school janitor in Scotch Plains, New Jersey. 'It worked all right,' says Namlha, 'though we scarcely saw each other except at weekends. By the time I got home, Lobsang was ready to leave for work, and in the mornings I had to go off straight after breakfast. But at least we ensured that one of us was always there for the children.'

Some of the Tibetan exiles were scandalized to hear that His Holiness's brother was doing such menial work. But Kundun took a more realistic view. 'Lobsang didn't mind being a caretaker,' he says. 'In fact I think he enjoyed it. He was a very happy person with a natural humility. He had no false pride. It was very endearing.'

For the next two years, Lobsang and Namlha lived in Scotch Plains, with little money but many friends. When they wanted to get away or simply to be reminded of their Tibetan mountains, they climbed in the nearby Watchungs, which boasted a somewhat less exalted elevation of 400–500 feet. Chuki and Tenzin enjoyed school and found nothing strange in their father's being janitor. Their parents were anxious for them to have as normal a childhood as possible and hardly ever mentioned Lobsang's past. 'Our children had no sense of coming from a privileged or famous background,' says Namlha, 'we brought them up to respect people whoever they were or wherever they came from, so it would not have occurred to them to boast about the Dalai Lama being their uncle.'

Lobsang declared the work 'wonderful'; and as the teaching staff swore they had never before had such a conscientious janitor, everyone was happy. 'They called him Sam,' smiles Namlha. 'He was very popular. Whenever we went shopping in the market on Saturdays, there were people shouting "Hi, Sam!" He kept the school so clean that some of the parents tried to talk him into cleaning their apartments too. But he wouldn't do that. He said the school was quite enough.'

After two years of janitoring, however, he began to feel the lack of mental stimulus. He was 44 and life seemed to be passing him by. But however ready he was for a change, he was unprepared for what happened next.

His story came to the attention of Morris Kaplan, a *New York Times* reporter who asked for an interview. Lobsang ignored the request. 'He was a very private person, didn't want any publicity. He told the man he was an ordinary middle-class American and wanted to be left alone.' But Kaplan knew a good story when he saw one. Having failed to persuade Lobsang, he went to the school. And then, of course, the cat was out of the bag. 'People just didn't know what to think,' says Namlha. 'They were stunned when they first found out that the school janitor wasn't what he seemed to be. Then they started urging him to tell his story to the newspaper.'

Thus did Kaplan gain access to the little house in Scotch Plains, and thus was Lobsang's precious anonymity shattered. On Monday 19 July 1976, the *New York Times* carried the article on its front page: DALAI LAMA'S BROTHER, NOW A JERSEYAN, ENJOYS HIS JOB AS A SCHOOL JANITOR. The headline was scarcely pithy, but the story could not fail to attract attention. Lobsang was pictured shaven-headed like a Tibetan monk; and then with an all-American crew-cut and summer shirt, polishing chairs in the school cafeteria, grinning self-consciously at the camera. 'In Peking, he dined with Mao Tse-tung and Chou En-lai,' readers were breathlessly told:

In his native Tibet he dealt familiarly with Sir Edmund Hillary and Tenzin Norkay, conquerors of Mount Everest...Lobsang Samten is now a $8,100-a-year custodian at the Scotch Plains-Fanwood High School in central New Jersey. To fellow-workers, neighbours and students, the 44-year-old copper-skinned Tibetan is known as 'Sam'.

'Until he got a haircut a few days ago, we also called him 'Kung-Fu,' said Louis Santacross, the head custodian...

'He's well-mannered, well-respected, a damn good worker and he's learning a lot,' Mr Santacross volunteered. 'He's my right-hand man, a wonderful guy.'

The 'wonderful guy' modestly explained to the reporter why he was doing such work. 'I never went to school, except in the monastery where I studied Buddhism. I did some social work with Tibetan exiles in India, but I have no truly modern skills.'

His brother, Norbu, 'professor of Tibetan language, culture and history at Indiana University' rated a mention, Namlha too, though the fact that her family was one of the most historic in old Tibet did not emerge. A single sentence in Kaplan's article referred to 'Mrs Samten, an alert, well-spoken office employee' who 'learned English at a Methodist mission school in Darjeeling, where she was married in 1962'.

Such nation-wide exposure put paid to their anonymity. 'After the article appeared,' says Namlha, 'we were no longer just Sam and Namlha. Suddenly Lobsang was the most famous man in Scotch Plains. People used to drive over in their cars just to look at the house and gawp at us. It was terrible. We absolutely hated it.'

Ruefully they decided to return to India, not only for their own but for the children's sake. It was time for Chuki and Tenzin Namdhak to rediscover their Tibetan roots. 'We worried about them becoming so Americanized,' Namlha says. 'Their lifestyle was a little too free and unrestrained. Scotch Plains was a small town and the school was good, but some of the children there were quite violent, and drugs were beginning to be a problem. It was what we had always dreaded.'

Thirteen-year-old Chuki was actually relieved. 'She told us she didn't want to go to High School. She was a very attractive girl and was beginning to be hassled by boys who wanted to date her. She wouldn't go with them. Her friends thought she was mad, but she just didn't want that kind of life.'

In the winter of 1976, the news that Amala had had a stroke clinched the matter. They sold up and prepared to uproot themselves yet again. 'I knew Lobsang would always regret it if he didn't see his mother before she died,' says Namlha.

When Kundun had set up a Library of Tibetan Works and Archives in Dharamsala, to preserve Tibet's written treasures for the exile community, he invited his brother, Norbu, to be its first Director. It was 1972, and Norbu was due for a sabbatical. And though it meant his sons missing a year's schooling in America, he reckoned 'they would more than make up for it by learning Tibetan and living in a Tibetan community'. So, renting out his house in Bloomington for the academic year of 1972–3, he moved his family to Dharamsala.

In his own book,[2] Norbu writes that he found a small cottage in Dharamsala which he renovated and furnished. Kashmir Cottage, later to be known and loved by many overseas visitors to Dharamsala, was, in fact, a large-ish bungalow built by the British at the turn of the century. Since then, it had come down in the world. When Kundun first opened the Nursery, the Indian Government loaned the place to him as a sort of halfway house for sick and undernourished children. A few years later, in 1966, Kundun's Private Office managed to buy it to use as a Guest House for foreign visitors. Unfortunately, the venture misfired. 'The person in charge was misusing the income,' explains Tendzin Choegyal, 'and Kashmir Cottage was getting a bad name. There was a lot of argument about what was to be done with it.'[3] Norbu's arrival was timely. He bought Kashmir Cottage from the Private Office and installed his mother there with his own family.

After his long exile from Tibet, 'it was a wonderful change to be surrounded by the sights, sounds and smells of Tibet,' to be free to spend his days collecting folklore and oral literature from exiles of all classes and occupations and from every region of Tibet. And for the leisure hours, it was a joy to have Pema, Tendzin Choegyal, and various other relatives living nearby. 'My boys soon found themselves swimming in a sea of assorted cousins, uncles, aunts, nieces, nephews, and so on.'

When Norbu was ready to return to Bloomington, in the autumn of 1973, Amala decided to sell her Lhasa jewellery and buy Kashmir Cottage from him. In those days, property was still relatively cheap.

To everybody's satisfaction, Tendzin Choegyal and Rinchen Khando were to move in with her. After their marriage in 1972, Choegyal had returned to his teaching job at the TCV and Rinchen, seeing that they 'were short of staff, had few resources and the health of the children was deplorable', volunteered for secretarial work in the Sponsorship office. The young couple were found 'very restricted accommodation' within the TCV precincts. A few months later, Choegyal was transferred to work for his friend Tenzin Geyche in Kundun's Private Office as 'one of the minions who dealt with things in English' and Rinchen – by now pregnant – continued working until just before their daughter, Choezom, was born in October 1973.

She intended to find someone to look after the baby while she returned to work. But Amala intervened and asked her if that was what she really wanted. 'She made it clear that if she were me she would want to look after the baby herself, but she would fully understand if I decided otherwise. When I thought about it, I realized she was right. Then, when she suggested that we should move in with her at Kashmir Cottage, we were delighted. Not only would it be easier for Rinpoche to get to his job at the Private Office from there, but Amala herself would have company. Staying with her and my baby would have much more meaning than continuing with a job that required no special skill.'⁴

Rinchen's relationship with her mother-in-law was unique, both women feeling sure they had known each other in a previous life. 'I called her Amala,' says Rinchen. 'It came naturally to me to call her mother, but some found it lacking in respect. All the other daughters-in-law called her Gyayum, Great Mother, but I couldn't bring myself to call her anything so formal. She was a real mother to me. We shared so much, she was so kind to me, and I loved her – not just because she was the mother of His Holiness, but for the sort of person she was.'

'Amala loved gardening and looked after all the flowers herself,' remembers Rinchen. 'We'd be walking in the garden and she'd say, "Gather the seed of this or that plant and we'll take it back to Tibet with us when we go." There was one particular tree that she was quite sure she would one day replant in Tibet. I felt quite sad, because I knew that she'd never see Tibet again. But she was always an optimist. She planted these orange trees in the garden. People kept saying they would never bear fruit, but she said it didn't matter. "Look," she'd say, when the blossoms came, "there may not be any fruit, but aren't the blossoms beautiful?" Then one day, the fruit did come, and the oranges gradually grew bigger. So then she said, "You see, if you do things with hope, something is sure to happen. But if you do nothing at all, then nothing will happen." She was a person who lived in the present moment.'

Amala didn't waste time grieving for past grandeurs. She had always taken responsibility for her life – as she once told Rinchen, with a husband like hers she had had to take a double share. Exile was no different. She had her health and strength, and that was as much as anyone could ask. 'So many things had happened to her,' reflects Tendzin Choegyal, 'that she had come to have a very clear idea of the meaning of life. She knew that suffering was important because it increased a person's compassion for others. To her dying day, my mother was unfailingly kind to any who sought her help.'

In 1974, Rinchen gave birth to a son, Tenzin Lodoe. And in August of that year, Tendzin Choegyal enlisted in the Special Frontier Force of the Indian Army.

The SFF was now the only fighting force that the Tibetans had, for the guerilla army no longer existed. It had finally fallen victim to American President Nixon's determination to seek better relations with China. The guerrillas received their last instalment of American aid in 1973. Lhamo Tsering (whom GT had left in overall charge) was bitter. 'There was no getting away from it,' he said, 'It was no longer in America's interest to support Tibet.'

Pursuing its advantage, in 1974, China asked the Nepalese Government – threatening attack if the request was ignored – to ensure that all arms held by Tibetans were handed over. The new King of Nepal, anxious not to antagonize China, offered to re-settle the Tibetans in Nepal if they surrendered their arms. The Khampas refused outright. Nepal issued an ultimatum, calling on the Tibetans to leave Mustang by 30 July – or be driven out. The guerrillas were unconcerned – the Nepalese Army did not exactly scare them.

Kundun now faced an agonizing dilemma. He could never accept the guerrillas' use of violence, but he had always admired their courage and determination, and knew how much the Tibetan people – and he himself – owed them. But the present situation in Nepal – with its implicit threat of huge loss of life – could not be allowed to continue, and he alone had the power to stop it. So he sent Phuntsok Tashi, his Head of Security, with a taped message in which he 'said that it would be senseless to fight the Nepalese, not least because there were several thousand Tibetan refugees settled in Nepal who would also suffer if they did. Instead they ought to be grateful to the Nepalese Government. They should therefore lay down their arms.'[5]

The guerrillas listened to the tape in incredulous dismay. 'How can I surrender to the Nepalese when I have never even surrendered to the Chinese?' cried one of the leaders, in horror. 'We should all return to Tibet this minute and die there fighting rather than live in shame.'[6] When the other leaders decided – reluctantly – that the Dalai Lama must be obeyed, this man went outside and cut his throat. Another jumped into a river and was drowned. Phuntsok Tashi returned home with his thoughts in a turmoil, his heart going out to the guerrillas, knowing that 'they were right, they could have handled the Nepalese, they commanded the heights'. It was one of the most difficult things he ever had to do, he says, 'and it still chokes me to remember it'.[7]

No sooner had the Khampas started to disarm than the Nepalese reneged on their promises. Entering Mustang, they seized Tibetan property and arrested those guerrillas who had already surrendered their weapons. With about forty of his men, General Wangdu fled, to continue the fight elsewhere. But just before the Indian border, they fell into a Nepalese ambush, and most of them, Wangdu included, were killed. The sacked Commander, Baba Yeshi, in exchange for protection and political asylum, had handed over to Nepal details of the guerrillas' troop strength, supplies, weaponry and positions, together with information about resistance networks in Tibet. The Nepalese gave them to the Chinese and the whole Resistance operation was finally blown. Such was the tragic end of a struggle which the Khampas had waged with outstanding courage for almost two decades.

So only the SFF remained. The Tibetan Youth Congress (which, with forty branches, had become the community's largest opposition party) believed that responsibility for the Tibetan struggle had now passed to them, and decided to develop a freedom-fighting wing. All graduates of Tibetan schools were urged to support the SFF for a period of six or twelve months. Tendzin Choegyal, who had recently succeeded Tenzin Geyche as President of the Youth Congress, resigned his position and volunteered. 'Most people said I was only a rubber-stamp for the Committee anyway,' he shrugs.[8]

The HQ of the Special Frontier Force, codenamed Establishment 22, was in New Delhi, but active units were scattered around the Himalayan border areas, wherever there was danger of Chinese attack. One was at Chakrata, just north of Dehra Dun. Rinchen and the children moved in with her parents in Mussoorie, though later she joined her husband at Chakrata where she taught English (unpaid) and acted as general counsellor to about a hundred Tibetan girl soldiers in the Girls' Company. Choegyal was plunged in at the deep end of a new way of life – and revelled in it. 'We were a crack body of Paratroop Commandos, trained in infantry tactics and guerrilla warfare,' he says. 'We did map-reading, field-craft, demolition, weaponry, parachuting, survival techniques, and the arts of ambush and sabotage.' It seemed possible, even likely, that his restless spirit had at last come home.

After six months basic training – during which he proved himself a crack shot – he was urged to stay on. Though Indian officers filled the highest ranks, nevertheless there was a Tibetan officer corps. He was made a Deputy Leader – equivalent to the rank of Captain in the British Army – and put in charge of a platoon. Within a further six months he was promoted to Company Leader and volunteered to run one of the special centres for the training of new recruits – a posting he enjoyed greatly. The prospects looked good, and when he was again promoted, to Political Leader (equivalent to a British Colonel), it seemed that he had truly found his niche.

But it didn't work out – largely because of Tendzin Choegyal's impossible idealism. For a start, he was disillusioned by the lack-lustre attitude of the Tibetans: 'It was a Force made up of Tibetan refugees for the sake of Tibet,' he argues passionately, 'yet many of the Tibetan officers seemed to have lost sight of that. They were behaving as though they weren't Tibetans at all. Our situation needed real dedication and commitment, yet the majority were merely concerned with pleasing the Indians and not rocking the boat. There were many Judases.' When he told his compatriots that they ought to be speaking Tibetan not Hindi, his Indian superiors took it as a declaration of war. Many of the latter, he believes, hated him because of his education and because of who he was. His own *bête noire* was the most senior officer in the Force who, he says, showed public contempt for the Dalai Lama, when the latter visited the station one day. 'How could they have put such a boor in charge of men who, whatever their shortcomings, were undeniably devoted to His Holiness? I really hated that man.'

The SFF was meant to be a crack force of Tibetans trained to defend the Himalayan borders and if necessary fight inside Tibet itself. 'The potential was there,' Choegyal insists bitterly. 'Even if we were never called on to fight the Chinese, we could have formed the nucleus of a fighting-force for a future Tibet. We could have created a body of first-rate troops if all the officers had been prepared to pull their weight. But many of the Indian officers were only concerned with lining their own pockets; they had only volunteered for the SFF because their own Indian Army regiments threw them out. Far from being willing to give a proper training to the Tibetan troops, they were just bullies who thought they could trample all over them.'

The fur flew in all directions, but in the nature of things Choegyal was bound to lose. 'The Security Office in Dharamsala had hoped I would be put in overall charge of training in the Force. Instead I was side-lined into a school for soldiers' children. It was all very sordid,' he complains. The experience was traumatic. Not only did it pitchfork him into a second bout of clinical depression, even worse than the first; it also developed in him a cynicism about authority which has never left him. 'I saw that power always went hand in hand with corruption; people who had power would always abuse it.' Overwhelmed once again by a despairing sense of failure, in May 1977 he resigned from the Special Frontier Force. 'A few people understood what had happened, though they didn't know how to help. But most of them thought I was a spoiled brat. They said I was depressed because I couldn't get my own way. That still rankles.'[9]

'Rinpoche went through a terribly difficult period,' says Rinchen loyally.[10] 'The trouble is that he can see much more clearly than most when things are not as they should be. He is sensitive and intelligent, and feels things very deeply. I believe he had to go through what he did because of these characteristics. He's a perfectionist in everything he does...He expects too much of people, and when reality falls short of expectations, he gets very upset and depressed.'

Rinchen needed all her powers of understanding and sympathy. 'What gave me strength was being able to see what was happening. Here was a man who was honest, crystal-pure in his motives, longing to do something for other people, for the cause of Tibet, for His Holiness himself. And when it proved to be impossible, he became miserable and angry. It wasn't *him* getting angry, it was all these factors driving him. When I understood that, it was easier for me to walk the path with him wherever it might lead.'

During the absence of her son and daughter-in-law, Amala had lived on at Kashmir Cottage, with three servants to help in the house and garden. One of these, 17-year-old Lodoe, spent seven of the happiest years of his life in her service.[11] She had saved his life when as a child he had epileptic fits and his parents believed he was possessed by evil spirits. Amala had no time for such superstitious nonsense and whisked him off to a Western doctor for treatment. Lodoe adored her. 'She was like a mother to me, she cared about me. We used to work together in the garden and she'd tell me about her life in Amdo, the cooking, the farm-work, the sewing and so on. She was always patient if I made mistakes, never got cross, always ex-plained things. She taught me to cook. His Holiness used to come and see her and we all helped to get the lunch and tea ready. We didn't do anything special, but we always cleaned the house thoroughly. When he came, there was no ceremonial, his mother just used to go out and greet him at the car, then they'd go in and have lunch together in the dining-room.'

The Tibetans, says Lodoe, regarded Amala as an Incarnation of the god-dess, Green Tara, because she'd given birth to three high *tulkus*. They revered Kashmir Cottage as highly as His Holiness's residence. 'Some peo-ple came to ask for her cast-off clothes, believing they could cure sickness. She didn't believe that, but she would never turn anyone away. If anyone came to her door, she would give them some tea first, then food or shelter or clothes, just as she had done all her life. She had real compassion.'

Khando was back in Dharamsala. She and Rapten, with their three young daughters – Youdon (7), Diki (5) and baby Dolkar – had spent three years in Bhopal (Central India), where Rapten had managed a paper mill that the Tibetan Government had bought. But the mill had to be sold, and they returned to Dharamsala. The Kashag sent for Khando and asked her to take over from Mrs Taring who was retiring from the Mussoorie Homes Foundation.[12] She protested that she wasn't up to such a demanding job and would need time to think it over. (The Foundation, which was run on similar lines to the Tibetan Children's Village in Dharamsala, had six hun-dred Tibetan orphans in twenty-five family groups staffed by live-in house-parents). Then Kundun summoned her. 'Normally, I would go in and prostrate myself before him, and then he would greet me affectionate-ly. On that particular day, he didn't even allow me to finish my prostra-tion. "What is there to think about?" he asked furiously. "You've been lucky enough to receive a first-class education, which not many of our people have received. And now you must give something back, no matter how difficult it may be." He really made me see things quite clearly, and I knew he was right. I was silly to have been so cautious and afraid.' She and Rapten, who was to replace Jigme Taring as Rector of the Tibetan School, duly went off to Mussoorie, where Rapten remained for six years (before being appointed as General Secretary to the Council for Education in Dharamsala) and Khando stayed for almost thirteen.

As Phuntsok Tashi had predicted, Tenzin Ngawang's marriage had ended in divorce.[13] Though the Tibetan Government asked him to return to Dharamsala to work for them, he refused. Disenchanted with the slowness of change within the Tibetan community, he was turning his back on his past. Somewhere along the way, he had lost his Buddhist beliefs, though Tendzin Choegyal, the younger-than-himself uncle to whom he had always been part elder brother, part spiritual mentor, insists that he was a deeply spiritual man who could not tolerate the way spirituality was expressed in his own society. 'He was much misunderstood,' claims Choegyal. 'He rejected rituals and superstition, and he wanted to go and live in China. He even talked to His Holiness about it, and the latter asked him to wait a bit before making up his mind. But from then on the Tibetans labelled him as a Marxist. Well, perhaps he was. But I would rather call him a humanist of the best sort.' Tenzin Ngawang bowed out. He had diabetes, but, in spite of all urging, refused to take proper care of himself. He retired to lead an almost spartan life in America, earning his living as a freelance teacher of computer science.

In the winter of 1976, Amala suffered a stroke, and it was a matter of general concern that none of her children was with her when it happened. Kundun's personal attendants came regularly to Kashmir Cottage to see how she was, as did Pema when the demands of the TCV allowed. But the old lady was fretting for her youngest son. Again and again she would ask when Tendzin Choegyal was coming home, when his next leave might be. She did not know of his breakdown, so when he came home in May 1977 her joy knew no bounds.

But the truth could not be hidden. For eight months Tendzin Choegyal remained in a state of chronic depression and anxiety, rarely sleeping more than one hour a night. His mother buried her own pain in his, trying to reassure him that the darkness would pass, while Rinchen and his friends did everything they could to help. Once, to goad him into some sort of response, Tenzin Geyche picked him up bodily and dropped him into a tub of cold water. But he remained alienated and hopeless. Only when he at last agreed to accept some kind of treatment did the nightmare begin to recede. To aid his recovery, Tenzin Geyche, with Rinchen and Pema, took him to the Kangra River some miles away for a swim. 'He wasn't keen, but we insisted. Unfortunately, when he came out of the river, he discovered he'd lost his wedding ring. I was terrified that all our good work would be undone, but fortunately Rinchen dived into the water and found it.'[14]

The worst was over, but with his army career blighted and its memories still raw, there was little now to motivate him. He was found employment in the Security Department of the Tibetan Administration, and worked there diligently but without enthusiasm until December 1979, when Tenzin Geyche asked him to help in his office for a week or two. 'He didn't explain and I had no idea that I was actually being tried out for his job,' says Choegyal. 'Then after about ten days, he told me he was being transferred to Education and I was to take over.' So Choegyal became one of Kundun's Private Secretaries, dealing with English correspondence and acting as interpreter during the audiences with English-speaking visitors. 'It was a job I loved. I had daily contact with His Holiness, and though he was quite strict and not above giving me a rocket when I forgot things or made mistakes, mostly we had a very warm secretary/boss relationship.' It could also have been that Kundun was keeping a watchful eye on his mercurial younger brother.

Before 1977 was out, Lobsang Samten and Namlha had returned to Dharamsala. Lobsang was relieved to see his mother again, and Namlha too had cause for rejoicing: her younger brother, Drikung Chetsang Rinpoche, whom the whole family had believed to be dead, was alive and in Dharamsala. He was a 10-year-old *tulku* when the Chinese came to his monastery in 1959, arrested all the older monks, but sent home those under the age of twelve. 'They just told them to go, though they'd nowhere to go to,' says Namlha. 'My brother walked all the way to Lhasa and came to Tsarong House, but of course there was nobody there. He had to beg for food, and live as best he could.' Seventeen years later, he managed to escape, the first Tibetan from a prominent family to do so since the start of the Cultural Revolution. To Namlha his escape was little short of a miracle, 'We were convinced he was dead. At least, all of us except my mother. I remember her coming to see us in America and saying she knew she would see him again. I told her, "No, no, you mustn't even think it, it's all over, we'll never see him again, we just have to pray for him, that's all." Then one day my father got a telegram saying, "Rinpoche has arrived in Kathmandu". We couldn't believe it. My father took some photographs out of the album so as to be able to be sure it was him, and he came up to Dharamsala and recognized his son.' Not surprisingly, when the young man turned up in Dharamsala, the Tibetan Government suspected him of being a Chinese spy, for how otherwise could he have escaped? The Chinese must surely have had him under surveillance! 'They refused to receive him officially,' Namlha says. 'It was awful for him. He walked up the hill towards the TCV, and to get to our brother Jigme's house, he had to pass Pema's. He looked up to see my mother-in-law standing on the verandah, looking at him and smiling. She shouted down, "I don't care what they're all saying about you, you just come right in here and have something to eat." He almost wept, it was the first time since he had arrived in India that anyone had made him feel welcome.'

To leave behind the everyday luxuries of America and settle for a couple of rooms and a kerosene stove at the Tibetan Children's Village could not have been easy. 'It was an interesting time, though,' Namlha insists, 'especially for the children, because there were so many new things for them to discover.' Namlha soon discovered that the American love of making a fast buck had rubbed off on her son. 'One day, he came home from school and said he'd made a lot of money. When I asked him how, he said he'd taken some packets of Wrigley's Chewing Gum that friends of ours had sent from the States, and had sold them to the other children. Just what an American schoolkid would do! I had to explain to him that most of the children at the TCV were very poor, and he must give the money back to them. He wasn't keen, but he did it.'

While Namlha studied Buddhist philosophy with a lama, Lobsang went walking in the mountains above Dharamsala. Often he would call on Kundun and the two brothers would enjoy a simple meal together. 'Lobsang was good company. He was a very happy person, always telling jokes, most of them, I'm afraid, rather bawdy,' laughs Kundun. Tenzin Geyche was impressed by Lobsang's incredible humility. 'He'd held top positions and, as His Holiness's brother, was held in great esteem among Tibetans. Yet, whenever His Holiness was leaving Dharamsala on a journey, Lobsang would line up with the rest of the public to see him off. It was very touching the way he simply mingled with the crowds waiting to say goodbye – and later to welcome him back. I don't think Rinpoche [Tendzin

Choegyal] would have done that. Nor would I. But Lobsang Samten was completely without self-importance.'[15]

Every Sunday, Lobsang, Namlha and their children came to spend the day at Kashmir Cottage. 'We'd arrive very early and would all be milling around in the kitchen, helping my mother-in-law to prepare lunch, ourselves, Pema and her two children, Rinpoche and his family. There was a lot of teasing and laughter.' These gatherings are among Choegyal's son Tenzin Lodoe's earliest memories. He was a small, round-faced boy, and his uncles and aunts teased him about his Mongolian features. 'Uncle Lobsang used to greet me in the Mongolian language, and ask me where my camel was. I would say that I'd left it down the hill at the Tibetan hospital. I didn't mind being teased, I loved Uncle Lobsang. He was kind and played lots of games with me.'

When evening came, they would set off on the long uphill walk back home to the TCV. 'We didn't even notice,' says Namlha, smiling, 'those were wonderful days.'

They were among the last they would ever know.

NOTES

1. Author interview with Namlha Taklha, Dharamsala, October 1993.

2. Norbu, *Tibet Is My Country*.

3. Author interview with Tendzin Choegyal, Dharamsala, October 1993.

4. Author interview with Rinchen Khando, Dharamsala, June 1994.

5. Fourteenth Dalai Lama, *Freedom in Exile*, chapter 10.

6. Avedon, *In Exile from the Land of Snows*, chapter 5, p. 127.

7. Author interview with Phuntsok Tashi, London, 1993.

8. Author interview with Tendzin Choegyal, Dharamsala, October 1993.

9. From author interviews with Tendzin Choegyal in 1993, 1994 and 1995.

10. Author interview with Rinchen Khando, June 1994.

11. Author interview with Lodoe, October 1994.

12. At that time, such appointments were made by the Dalai Lama in consultation with the Kashag and his Private Secretaries.

13. There were two daughters from the marriage.

14. Conversation with Tenzin Geyche, Dharamsala, 1993.

15. Conversation with Tenzin Geyche, Dharamsala, 1993.

23

New Dawn – or False Hope? 1979–80

I feel that the struggle of the Tibetan people is not only for freedom but also for survival as a race. Our country is being ransacked, our temples and monasteries have been destroyed and our people face the danger of extermination.

Jetsun Pema, 1980

Mao died in September 1976, his death being followed by the arrest of his wife, Chiang Ching, and the other members of the 'Gang of Four', evil geniuses of the Cultural Revolution – and handy scapegoats for every crime committed in China before, during or since. Very senior voices were heard admitting that the Cultural Revolution had been a disaster. Was this just another swing of the pendulum which in nearly thirty years of Communism had so often sent China lurching from left to right and back again? Or might there be hope of a lasting improvement? The Tibetans held their breath.

After Mao's death, Peking's attitude to Tibet appeared to soften. As one cynical Tibetan intellectual remarked, there was 'a moulting of the Peking Duck'.[1] A few of the more draconian rules concerning religious practice were relaxed, the Panchen Lama was released after fourteen years in prison, and Peking declared that the Dalai Lama and his followers would be welcome to return to Tibet whenever they wished! Towards the end of 1978, Deng Xiao-ping emerged as the new leader of China. One of the earliest and most committed of the Communist hierarchs, Deng bore a fair share of responsibility for the repressions, murders and massacres which had long predated the Gang of Four, but – thanks to his hounding by the latter – he was currently being hailed as a moderate. At any rate, Deng, while leaving the political situation intact – and whatever criticisms were permitted about the Cultural Revolution no one had dared speak against the system itself – introduced a flurry of economic reforms which would propel China into the international market and earn him plaudits in the West as the Great Liberalizer. His popularity – and the continuation of his draconian regime – were alike assured. Deng was an astute politician.

Events began to move fast. In November 1978, thirty-four Tibetan prisoners (mostly elderly members of Kundun's administration in Lhasa, in prison since the 1959 Uprising) were released – and allowed to emigrate, if they so wished. Then the Panchen Lama made his first public appearance for fourteen years, calling for the Dalai Lama to visit his homeland – 'I can guarantee,' he urged, 'that the present standard of living of the Tibetan people in Tibet is many times better than that of the "old society".' (If the Panchen Lama had once again become the mouthpiece of Peking, after so many years of imprisonment and torture, who could blame him?)

In Dharamsala, hopes soared. Did this mean the exiles could now return home? Few seemed to notice that in effect little had changed, that in April Deng had banned all criticism of the regime, and warned that a Western-style human rights movement would not be tolerated.[2] 'The totalitarian regime still stands,' commented a Tibetan critic, 'and is, maybe, further strengthened by its decision to provide its cowed populace with the latter-day equivalent of bread and circuses – Coca Cola and foreign movies.'[3]

Out of the blue, Gyalo Thondup turned up from Hong Kong – with the news that Deng Xiao-ping had invited him to Peking for talks. 'I was expecting it,' he says airily. 'I knew that if the Chinese wanted to take things forward, they would contact me. The director of the Xinhua News Agency, which represents the Central Government of China in Hong Kong, came and asked me to go to Peking. He said, "It won't take long, you can go there and back in a day." I reminded him I was just a hard-working businessman with no authority to talk to anyone in Peking. But he wouldn't take no for an answer.'[4]

Insisting that he must first consult the Dalai Lama, Gyalo Thondup set off in search of his brother, whom he found giving religious teachings somewhere in Central India. Kundun was initially doubtful – 'as the ancient Indian saying goes, "When you've once been bitten by a snake, you are cautious even of rope".'⁵ All his experience suggested that the Chinese leadership did not know what it was to tell the truth or keep a promise. But in the end he felt he owed it to his people to investigate this latest opening. With Kundun's cautious blessing, therefore, Gyalo Thondup flew to Peking, only to find that in the meantime war had broken out between China and Vietnam and Deng was somewhere on the border 'directing the war personally and talking about giving the Vietnamese a lesson they would not forget'. (Of course, gloats GT, 'what happened was that it was the Vietnamese who taught *him* a lesson, not the other way round.'⁶)

GT was no admirer of Deng Xiao-ping, whom he referred to as 'the dwarf' and regarded as an unreconstructed Maoist at heart. 'After all, in 1949, it was Deng who directed the South-West Military Bureau, charged with destroying Tibet's monasteries. He blames all that on the Gang of Four now [1995] but most of the monasteries were destroyed while he was in control, long before the Cultural Revolution. I actually saw some 1962 documents in which the military authorities asked Deng's permission to dismantle the monasteries in Tibet. He replied, be careful with the monasteries on the border because the border is sensitive internationally, but do whatever you want in the interior of the country. All the looting and killing, all the massacres in Central Tibet and in Kham were all directed by Deng. But in 1978 he was doing his utmost to conceal his own part in the tragedy of Tibet and was claiming to be very concerned about its future.'

It was three weeks before Deng returned from the war zone. The two men greeted each other warily. 'Deng asked me why I hadn't been back to China in all those years – 29 years in fact – and asked me if I was surprised at all the changes. I said no, I was a China-watcher in Hong Kong and everything was more or less as I'd expected. Deng then said he wanted to meet the Dalai Lama for discussions, and that everything would be negotiable – except Tibetan Independence. No Chinese leadership could ever agree to that, he said. On behalf of His Holiness I asked if he proposed doing anything about the way Tibetans in India and those in Tibet had been cut off from each other for twenty years. And as we'd heard that in a number of Tibetan areas there were neither schools nor teachers, I also asked if we could send some of our young people from India who had been newly-trained as teachers. Thirdly, I asked if we could send teams of representatives to see for themselves what "New Tibet" was like. To my surprise, he agreed on all three counts – and was especially enthusiastic about the teachers, saying they weren't just needed in Tibet, but even in the Minority Colleges in Peking. When I suggested fifty for a start, he said "no good, we need at least one thousand"!'

Kundun was heartened by his brother's report and asked him to continue as 'bridge-builder'. Deng agreed to an official fact-finding delegation from Dharamsala visiting Tibet to examine conditions there. It seemed a reasonable arrangement, though Kundun knew that a number of the exiles – particularly the younger ones – would consider any *rapprochement* with China which ruled out the possibility of independence to be a sell-out. The thirteen (Khampa) settlements were loud in their accusations that Gyalo Thondup was up to his old tricks again.

Plans for the first fact-finding visit to Tibet went ahead in such secrecy that news only leaked out the day before the group's departure. Kundun had chosen as delegates men who were familiar not only with old Tibet but with the modern world as well. He had included Lobsang Samten in this five-man group, despite initial misgivings: '[Lobsang] was going through a very modern phase in terms of dress and appearance. He wore his hair long and had a thick, droopy moustache. His clothes were very casual too. I was a little worried that he might not be recognized by those in Tibet who should remember him.'[7] Lobsang had no such qualms. Since returning from America, he had again been suffering from the 'goldfish bowl' syndrome: that careful deference, mixed with envy and mistrust, accorded to a brother of the Dalai Lama. He missed America, the free and easy life, the fast food and standards of hygiene, but beyond everything he missed Tibet. When Kundun asked him to join the first delegation, 'he felt he was going home,' says Namlha. 'He had always talked about Tibet, wherever we went, whoever he was with. Going back there was his dream.'

On 2 August 1979, the group flew to Hong Kong.[8] At an official lunch in the Xinhua News Agency offices, their Chinese host proposed a 'Welcome' toast and bluntly told them exactly where they stood. 'We are the great land of China and you are a minority people. For too long you have been separated from your motherland. We two peoples, the Han and the Tibetans – one of the most important minority groups – should never be apart. Now we are very happy that you have come back to visit...You must understand that you have such a good opportunity only because of the enlightened policy and excellent qualities of the Communist Party leadership.' The Tibetans nearly choked on their drinks, but apart from pointedly ignoring the toast, there was little they could do.

In Hong Kong they met Gyalo Thondup. 'Don't talk politics,' he advised, 'simply tell the people His Holiness has sent you with his best wishes for the people of Tibet. That's enough. All we want is to restore the thread that has been broken for twenty years. Talk to people, find out about their lives. But no politics.'⁹

At the Canton airport terminal, Lobsang Samten had a moment of panic when he and his friends stood, surrounded by Red Army guards, under a life-size portrait of Mao Tse-tung. Had they walked straight into a trap? The feeling resurfaced in Peking, when they were lodged in an army guesthouse with hundreds of high-ranking PLA soldiers. Lobsang was in no doubt that the place had been deliberately chosen to show the Tibetans where the real power lay.

After two weeks in Peking, working out a 2,500 miles itinerary, they set off on the morning of 28 August, in two white Toyota minibuses and accompanied by a Chinese escort. Driving due west, they headed towards Amdo, where Lobsang Samten had been born. At an altitude of ten thousand feet,¹⁰ Lobsang spotted a yak, and, overcome with emotion, insisted on leaving the minibus for a photograph. 'We didn't care what the Chinese thought,' he said afterwards, 'You can't imagine how it felt just to see a yak after all those years.'

A single moment of pure pleasure, to be followed by a thousand unpleasant surprises. As they approached the town of Tashikiel, once renowned for the glories of its monastery, news of their arrival had spread and a crowd of 6,000 had gathered. Since freedom of assembly had been denied to the Tibetans for twenty years, the Chinese were terrified. Having swallowed their own propaganda that the Tibetans hated the Dalai Lama and all he stood for, they warned the visitors to keep the doors and windows of the minibus shut, for fear of being lynched by the mob! This, however, was no angry mob, but a crowd of famished Tibetans, weeping for joy that their exiled countrymen, among them a brother of their beloved leader, had come at last. 'We opened our windows,' reported Lobsang Samten. 'It was unbelievable. Everywhere people were shouting, throwing scarves, apples and flowers...They broke the windows of all the cars. They climbed on the roofs and pushed inside, stretching out their hands to touch us. The Chinese were screaming, "Don't go out! They'll kill you! They'll kill you!" All of the Tibetans were weeping, calling, "How is the Dalai Lama? How is His Holiness?" We yelled back, "He's fine. How are you?" Then, when we saw how poor they were it was so sad, we all started crying too.'

The people would not go away. Hundreds camped all night outside the locked gates of the military guest-house where the delegates stayed. By next morning, the crowd had swelled to ten thousand, and they surged around the visitors as they left, no matter how hard the police strove to keep them apart. 'Everyone rushed at us, weeping and calling for His Holiness,' said Lobsang Samten. 'People were crying hysterically. There were some who just collapsed in tears on the ground. The others pulled our hair and tore our clothes for mementos – blessings, in fact. From that time on, I lost so much hair, my hands were always cut and my voice was constantly hoarse from shouting. Altogether one overcoat, a raincoat, two shirts and a cap were torn off [me] during the trip.'

The few hundred small pictures of the Dalai Lama they'd brought with them had disappeared long before they reached the entrance to the Tashikiel monastery, which Lobsang had last visited in 1955 on returning with Kundun from China. Outside the monastery, which had been razed almost to the ground by the Chinese, a few hundred elderly Tibetans stood in a long row, weeping as the visitors passed by. 'God! They were crying so much,' recounted Lobsang. 'We have nothing left,' they kept saying. 'Everything has been destroyed.'" Though the Chinese enthusiastically blamed the Gang of Four, Lobsang learned from an old monk that the monastery had actually been destroyed before 1959.

A new Chinese town had grown up round the old Tashikiel, and the old Tibetan section was 'little better than an open grave,' commented Lobsang. 'Its buildings were in total disrepair, its streets muddy and impassable. The people lived in dark, decaying rooms with barely any furniture or utensils and no running water and only intermittent electricity. On the other hand, the Chinese quarter, though itself showing signs of neglect, was newly built, its inhabitants far better fed and clothed than the Tibetans.' Yet their Chinese minders kept up an incessant chorus of praise for the benefits showered on the Tibetans by China. Were they blind, brain-washed, or just stupid, the visitors wondered?

For four days, they were besieged by visitors begging to be allowed to see them, to touch them. 'Whenever we asked people what had happened since the revolt,' related Lobsang Samten, 'they would just start crying. Then, after composing themselves, they'd reply, "Our country has nothing now. Everything is finished. But...our spirit is strong. As long as His Holiness is not in the hands of the Chinese we have hope."' Lobsang felt crushed by so much misery, his shock and outrage compounded by the sight of an old Amdo friend, a former village headman released only a few days earlier after twenty years in prison. Lobsang was stunned. 'He had been such a strong, heavily-built man. Now I could barely recognize him. The fellow was just broken. He said everything he owned, his land, his home and possessions, were taken. His family had been separated. He had never seen them again. He had just heard that his son had died in prison. "Look at me, Lobsang," he said. "I have nothing left except this one suit of clothes they gave me."'

Over the next three weeks, criss-crossing the desolate landscapes of Amdo, visiting towns and villages, communes and nomad encampments, their despair increased as the tales of suffering and death unfolded. They heard of 'years of famine, mass starvation, public execution and gross and disgusting violations of human rights'.[12]

In Lhasa, the authorities, forewarned, were taking no chances. At the obligatory political assembly each evening the citizens were given their orders: Lhasa's streets and buildings were to be scrubbed and tidied, the people were to wear their best clothes and look cheerful at all times; if spoken to by the visitors – by definition, 'counter-revolutionaries' – in a firm, convincing tone they should relate how good life was under the new order. Families likely to be visited by the delegation were given coupons for new work suits and gaudy pink and blue ribbons for the women's hair. Thermoses, blankets and quilts were handed out and rooms inspected to make sure that portraits of Mao and Party Chairman Hua Guo-feng were prominently displayed on the walls.[13]

A few days before the delegates were due to arrive, the people were given a politically correct version of the facts. The delegates, they were told, were coming from Amdo where the people had been so incapable of restraining their hatred of counter-revolutionaries that they had attacked them on every possible occasion. Hundreds apparently had turned out to throw dirt and stones and denounce and spit on the visitors. Such inhospitable behaviour would not be allowed in Lhasa, the officials threatened piously.

On 26 September, the group reached Lhasa and as Lobsang caught his first glimpse of the Potala's golden roof-tops, he was overcome by nostalgia. 'My whole childhood, living with His Holiness in that beautiful building, came into my mind. Then it was full of life; people worked in the offices, prayed in the chapels, walked on the outside stairways and on the rooftops, and at night its windows were always lit by hundreds of butter-lamps. But now it looked completely dead – empty and cold. All of its dignity was gone.'[14]

Despite their protests, they were driven to a guest-house outside the city. When Lobsang suggested his family's house as an alternative, the Chinese informed him that the house now 'belonged to the public'. 'What public?' Lobsang could not help asking. 'Tibetans or Chinese?' 'Oh, just the public,' they said, and changed the subject. A few days later, the delegates were quietly removed to a guest-house inside the city.

Order had already broken down. On the first morning, the delegates had gone to the Jokhang Temple, parts of which had been turned by the Red Guards into a pig-sty and slaughter-house during the Cultural Revolution. It had recently been reopened in a modest revival of at least the external forms of religion. (Of Buddhist teaching there was none. Religion was still officially viewed as counter-revolutionary poison, and in any case nearly all the teachers were in prison, in exile or dead.) That morning, seventeen thousand Tibetans trampled the security police underfoot in the rush to greet their compatriots. It was Amdo all over again. Stern warnings were given at that night's political meeting. But, though hundreds bowed to official pressure to remain indoors next day, thousands took to the streets, on the off-chance of speaking to – or just touching – the visitors.

There was a moment of pure farce when the delegates were conducted round the Norbulingka and its (sadly untended) gardens where Lobsang Samten and Kundun had played as children. When they came to the two-storied palace built in 1956 for Kundun under Lobsang's supervision, the guides burbled on: This is where the Dalai slept, where he ate, where he met his mother, and so forth. Lobsang reminded them that he'd built the place himself and worked in it every day, and that *he* would be happy to give *them* a guided tour if they wished, but irony was wasted on them. Lobsang's irritation turned to distress when, through the broken glass panes of the larger Kelsang Palace where he and Kundun had stayed when first they came to Lhasa, he saw the heaped-up shards of broken statuary. It was too much, and though he had promised the Chinese not to speak in public, he stormed out to the front steps of the palace and began to address the large crowd assembled on the flagstones. 'Long live the Dalai Lama,' chanted the crowd as soon as he appeared, and a man offered him a white scarf draped over the end of a long stick. 'His Holiness misses you,' shouted Lobsang, accepting the proffered scarf, 'and he knows how you have suffered. We hope that one day he will come to see you...When we return we will report the truth.'

As he turned to walk back inside towards the glowering Chinese, hundreds broke through the police cordon and followed him. Ignoring the protests of the officials, he whipped around again and plunged into their midst. As John Avedon recounts: 'Ten young men linked arms to protect him from the commotion. In their midst he spent the next five hours walking back and forth across the Jewel Park. Several times, the whole group was inadvertently pushed over, once waist-deep into a pond. 'It was so chaotic that I only managed to sit down and picnic with people in a few spots...When I did, after only a few minutes of polite conversation, the people's real feelings would pour out and they would start to cry uncontrollably. I'd try to get up to move on, and they would beg me to stay. Then they'd insist that we all have just one dance. So, for a little while, everyone, old men, women and children would join arms and try to do a few of our own Tibetan steps, laughing, singing, crying and dancing all at once.'[15] One of the delegates overheard a high-ranking Chinese cadre remark bitterly to a colleague, 'The efforts of the last twenty years have been undone in a single day!'[16]

There was a tragic footnote to these extraordinary events. Tsering Lhamo, the 56-year-old wife of one of the Norbulingka gardeners, was so carried away by the excitement of the moment that she cried out, 'Tibet is independent!' She was taken away for interrogation and three days later was brought before her 600-strong neighbourhood committee and given *thamzing* to the accompaniment of severe beatings. Protesting her innocence, she was returned to prison and tortured with electric shocks. When news of this reached the delegates, and they realized the danger to which their presence was exposing their compatriots, they told their Chinese hosts that they would cancel all further engagements and return home. Hastily, the Chinese released the woman. How could the Tibetans have guessed that as soon as they had gone, she would be rearrested and subjected to electric shocks so violent that she was reduced to a permanent vegetable state?[17]

By late December, the group was back in Dharamsala, with audio recordings, hundreds of rolls of film, more than seven thousand letters from Tibetans to their relatives; and countless requests for prayers.

Why did the Chinese get it so wrong? They had planned to show the visitors that the new Tibet was now an earthly paradise. So convinced were they by their own official propaganda they had even invited forty-four Peking-based journalists to Lhasa. It did not seem to have occurred to anyone that the visit would instead reveal the Tibetans to be in mourning for the destruction of their ancient culture and for the exile of their leader, the Dalai Lama. Peking had been woefully misled by the local Government of Tibet. (Heads inevitably rolled, the local Party leaders being sacked and replaced by more moderate men.) The question now was, would the Tibetan Government-in-Exile present this evidence of Chinese failure to the outside world, thus wrecking all chance of dialogue and risking further misery to their compatriots inside Tibet? The Chinese had impressed on Lobsang Samten that negative criticism would not be tolerated. The unspoken threat hung in the air. So, although Lobsang and his colleagues drew up a detailed report of their findings, the Dalai Lama reluctantly decided not to release them to the outside world. A small item appeared in Dharamsala's official *Tibetan Bulletin*, thanking the Chinese for making the visit possible! The dialogue with China was set to continue.

Critics angrily pointed to this evidence of a sell-out. Where now was the talk of Tibetan independence, they asked bitterly? It had become a bargaining chip, pushed out of sight by the human rights issue.[18] Tibetan officials denied the charge, claiming that the way of dialogue was the only way forward. The Chinese had already agreed to accept a second delegation, and after that a third and a fourth. There was much to be hoped for from such continuing contact.

The story of the second delegation cannot be reported in detail here, since no member of the family was a member of it. Yet neither can it be completely ignored, for it set the pattern for what was to follow. To demonstrate that the younger generation of Tibetan exiles was educated and articulate, it was made up of young men in their early thirties. They travelled through southern Amdo and Kham to reach Lhasa, where the Chinese had already taken steps to prevent a repetition of previous events, warning that nobody was to have any contact, whether by word or by gesture, with the visitors. They made it ominously clear that the names of those who had greeted the first delegation were on file, and that if any of them dared put in an appearance this time, they could expect to share the fate of the unfortunate Tsering Lhamo. But their warnings fell on deaf ears. Everywhere, the delegates were mobbed by desperate crowds, and cries of Tibet is Independent rent the air. In Lhasa, the young delegates' patience snapped and they launched into passionate – and very public – denunciation. They were accused of deliberately inciting the Tibetans to break with the motherland and were expelled from the country in disgrace.

In the light of this débâcle, if the third delegation, led by Kundun's sister, Pema, and composed of six educationists – one of them Khando's husband, Rapten Chazotsang, now General Secretary to the Council for Education – had not already been in Tibet, it might never have got off the ground.

Pema had reluctantly agreed to lead the third delegation, calming her fears with the knowledge that the first had returned unharmed. (Had she known what was to befall the second, she might have been even more apprehensive.) She had a fright when they arrived in Hong Kong and the Chinese took the group's passports away. 'That was a bad moment,' she says. There would be many bad moments, for the hosts' bonhomie had quite evaporated.

The itinerary itself was a problem. Pema's brief was to visit as many schools as possible and to see what kind of education Tibetan children were receiving; she planned to visit those areas of Tibet not covered by the first and second groups. But the Chinese would not hear of it. In Peking, she was told that the plan was impracticable: too many places on the list, not enough time, no motorable roads, not enough money. They were ordered to provide an alternative plan – with Chinese assistance. When they reached Tibet, this revised journey-plan would be followed to the letter; there would be no unscheduled stops, even where – or perhaps especially where – thousands of people lined the roadsides in the hope of speaking to them.

Pema at first seethed in silence. 'We visited fifty different towns and villages and everywhere we went it was the same old story. They wouldn't allow the people to come and see us. Even when we went into our guest-house for the night, they would lock the gates so that the people couldn't get near us.' But the legendary family temper was rising: 'I let it pass for four or five days. But on the fifth or sixth day, I really blew my top. I flatly refused to go any further if they didn't allow us to meet the people. We might as well go home, I said. After that, they allowed the people to come and talk to us. People would crowd round us, wanting to touch us – especially me, because I was His Holiness's sister. Everyone was wanting to talk about His Holiness, to have a picture of him. When they found that we had lamas in the group, everyone wanted a blessing. Of course, it was one horror story after another. They all spoke of terrible suffering, of torture, of death, of starvation. The commune system was still in existence and most of them didn't have enough to eat, the rations given them for a month being scarcely enough for two weeks. We wept to see how poor they all were, they were dressed in rags and so very unhappy.'[19]

Everything was so much worse than they had anticipated, says Rapten. 'Wherever we went, the Chinese organized meetings of public dignitaries – who, despite their titles were no more than mouth-pieces. They would spout statistics and make propaganda points, but they were quite incapable of answering our questions, and they would look at the Chinese for permission to speak before they dared open their mouths. The Chinese who had accompanied us from Peking were obviously trying to set us against each other, enjoying seeing us at each other's throats. After a time, we realized what their game was and stopped provoking arguments. Why should we argue with our own countrymen when they were not free agents anyway?'[20]

Almost every experience in the 105 days they spent in Tibet was disturbing. It was partly the constant wrestling with Chinese bureaucracy and the systematic lack of co-operation from the local authorities; partly the surreal experience of reconciling Chinese lies and fantasies with the reality they found – 'The Chinese have absolutely no shame,' wrote Pema afterwards in a personal account that pulled no punches. 'They can tell you one thing at one time and the very next moment either deny having said it or tell you something quite different...Time and again they would give us elaborate figures when they knew that only hours later we would find out the truth.'[21] There was also the crushing sadness of reality itself. The once flourishing monasteries, for example, now no more than hastily rebuilt show-pieces from which the gods had fled. Throughout Tibet, 6,254 monasteries had been destroyed (their contents mutilated or sent to Peking to be sold); only 37 remained more or less intact. 'Our monasteries,' mourned Pema, 'were places of worship where anyone could come anytime to pray and to seek spiritual guidance. They were also places of learning and religious practice – where prayer, meditation, the practice of good and the avoidance of evil had become a way of life. The Chinese have turned them into sterile museums with false exhibits [intended] to show what a luxurious life the monks led in the old society and how cruel and ruthless they were.'

After her return, Pema agonized over the impossibility of finding words to convey Tibet's tragedy to the outside world. She was stricken by the horror of all she had seen and heard: 'Parents had to witness their sons being murdered and if they failed to smile and clap and thank the Chinese for killing their own children they too would be condemned.' She spoke to a mother who had made soup from her own blood to keep her children from starvation, and such cases were not unique. It was far worse even than they had expected. 'When I saw their emaciated bodies and heard their tales of suffering, there was no way to hold back my tears. Throughout our stay in Tibet most of us were crying at one time or another.'

As for the education they had come to investigate, they were constantly told of the unprecedented progress being made. Impressive statistics about students and teachers and government expenditure were always to hand. But the statistics could never be verified. 'What we did find out,' complained Pema, 'was that it was extremely difficult to arrange a visit to a school. We were not demanding to see hundreds and thousands of schools. All that we requested was to see one or two.' But somehow, wherever they went, the schools were 'closed for the summer holidays,' the excuse offered on every one of the 105 days, from 10 June until 23 September. Strange, in a country which practically came to a standstill during the paralysingly cold winters and could be expected to spend the summer months making up for lost time. 'At first we insisted that we should visit the school just to see the empty building. Later I realized that "the school is closed for summer vacations" was their way of saying "there is no school" or "we don't want you to see this school".' 'The Chinese,' commented Rapten Chazotsang, 'must have been incredibly naïve to think we'd swallow all the propaganda they threw at us.'

In one place where a school was 'closed for lunch' – at ten in the morning – closer investigation revealed the classrooms to be stacked ceiling-high with timber. Elsewhere, they were shown a nomad 'tent school' in which everything was brand new 'from the tent to the children's clothes, the tables, the mats and the blackboard, even the grass was fresh and green inside the tent and a classroom where intricate Tibetan grammar was being taught to children who did not even know the alphabets'. Pema was speechless with indignation, and even their Chinese escort had the grace to look embarrassed.

In spite of these *opéra bouffe* attempts to fob them off, the delegates visited seventy primary, middle and high schools and found the overall standard abysmally low, with a seventy per cent illiteracy rate among Tibetans. 'Where we found Tibetan teachers,' says Rapten, 'we were astounded to find that their basic qualification was their social background: if they were poor farmers or had collaborated with the Chinese, they would have been given a reasonable education. After reaching about the third grade, they were then sent for teacher-training.' But almost all the teachers were Chinese, the Tibetan language was almost a thing of the past and few children spoke it correctly. Tibetan children were being taught to despise their own culture, while absorbing the alien ideology of Marxism-Leninism. When the group returned to Dharamsala, they report-ed that while there had undeniably been an improvement in the standard of education over the past twenty years, 'to the Chinese, the real value of reading was to enable children to study the Thoughts of Chairman Mao, and of writing to enable them to produce "confessions"'.[22]

How could one come to terms with such a harrowing of the soul? 'When I came back from Tibet, I was terribly emotional,' Pema shudders. 'I could feel only hatred, bitterness and disgust, and I could not stop crying. I kept seeing the faces of the people we had met, and I could not for one moment shake off the memory of their terrible sufferings.'[23] Rapten, too, had been mentally scarred by the encounters with his compatriots. 'They'd all been shunted around the country. Those from Lhasa had been sent to outlying parts, while the Tibetans in Lhasa itself all seemed to come from other parts of Tibet. Once, when we were coming down from the ruins of Gan-den Monastery, a lot of Tibetans had gathered on the roadside waiting for us. I heard someone calling my name, saying, Rapten, Rapten, don't you know me? It was an old friend, from my own district of Kham. He was about the same age as myself, but his face was that of an old, old man. He couldn't really speak, the tears were just coursing down his cheeks. When I came back, I kept on having nightmares about that face. Memories like that stay with you, they affect you for the rest of your life.'

Between them, the three delegations drew up a devastating indictment of the Chinese record in their country: One-fifth of the population had been murdered or had died of starvation; 6,254 monasteries and nunneries had been destroyed, their contents looted, melted down or sold on foreign markets; sixty per cent of Tibet's sacred literature had been incinerated; Amdo had become the world's biggest gulag, with the capacity for holding ten million prisoners; one in every ten Tibetans was in prison; one hun-dred thousand had disappeared into labour camps; mountains had been shorn of their forests and the abundant wildlife of Tibet had almost be-come extinct.

And in all those who had revisited their homeland, something had died.

NOTES

1. Jamyang Norbu, article with that title in *Illusion and Reality: Essays on the Tibetan and Chinese Political Scene from 1978 to 1989*, Tibetan Youth Congress Books, 1989.

2. Noted by Jamyang Norbu, writing in the *Tibetan Review*, April 1989.

3. Jamyang Norbu, 'A Moulting of the Peking Duck', article in *Illusion and Reality*.

4. Author interview with Gyalo Thondup, New Delhi, July 1995.

5. Fourteenth Dalai Lama, *Freedom in Exile*, chapter 13.

6. Author interview with Gyalo Thondup, New Delhi, July 1995.

7. *Freedom in Exile*, p. 253.

8. For the following account of the first delegation's visit to Tibet, I am indebted to Avedon's *In Exile from the Land of Snows*, chapter 11.

9. Author interview with Gyalo Thondup, New Delhi, July 1995.

10. Yaks cannot survive at a lower altitude than this.

11. This quotation, like most of those concerning the delegation's visit, are from *In Exile from the Land of Snows*.

12. *Freedom in Exile*, p. 256.

13. *In Exile from the Land of Snows*.

14. *In Exile from the Land of Snows*.

15. *In Exile from the Land of Snows*.

16. *Freedom in Exile*, p. 254.

17. Amnesty International Report 1983.

18. Jamyang Norbu, 'There and Back Again', article in *Illusion and Reality*.

19. Author interview with Jetsun Pema, October 1994.

20. Author interview with Rapten Chazotsang, Utah, February 1996.

21. *Three Months in Tibet: a personal viewpoint*, pamphlet by Jetsun Pema published by the Tibetan Children's Village, Dharamsala.

22. *Freedom in Exile*, p. 263.

23. Author interview with Jetsun Pema, October 1994.

24

A Time for Grieving

Neither in the sky, nor deep in the ocean, nor in a mountain-cave, nor anywhere, can a man be free from the power of death.
The Dhammapada

'After Amala had the stroke, I felt the need to be with her more than ever before,' declared Rinchen. 'There were so many things that I could do for her that no one else could. Like sitting with her for hours on end and changing her clothes. There was a big change in her after the stroke. She hated not being able to do many of the things she liked doing. Most of all that she couldn't do things for other people, they had to do things for her instead. She thought she was being a burden – yet everyone felt it was a privilege to be able to help her.'

Kundun was relieved that his mother was in such caring hands, but feared that the strain would be too much for Rinchen. 'One day, His Holiness came to Kashmir Cottage and he suggested that if I wanted to go back to work, he might be able to find someone to look after Amala. I was astounded. After all, I'd not complained. I knew I was in the right place and there was no better thing I could be doing. So I answered, "For me, serving His Holiness's Mother and serving His people are one and the same thing. I'm happy and proud to look after Your mother."'[1]

Khando made a fourteen-hour journey from Mussoorie to see her grandmother, and was shocked at the change in her. 'She had been so full of a zest for life and suddenly she was helpless and frail. I felt quite frightened.

All I could do was sit with her and hold her hands'. But, with her indomitable will and with treatment both Tibetan and Western, Amala rallied. One evening, while helping her into her nightdress, Rinchen was moved to exclaim, 'Amala, what a lot of muscle you still have!' 'What's surprising about that?' came the reply. 'After all, I *am* a farmer's wife!' But Rinchen noted that 'she no longer talked about taking seeds back to Tibet'.

Her capacity for laughter remained strong. 'After she had the stroke,' says Rinchen, 'we begged her not to laugh so much. She would try, but not always successfully. One afternoon, when the children were small, I was rubbing ointment into her leg as we watched TV together. (She had rheumatism in her legs every autumn when the house got damp.) Suddenly there was an earthquake tremor. I panicked: she couldn't walk, what on earth was I to do?...I got the children outside and tried to lift her, but she was so heavy, I couldn't move her. I was so frightened. But she wasn't, she thought it was hilarious, she just laughed and laughed.'

But the laughter died when first Lobsang then Pema returned from Tibet to report the destruction they had seen. Norbu too. In 1979, he had spent his second sabbatical as a visiting scholar at the Institute for Studies of Languages and Cultures of Asia and Africa in Tokyo. From there he was invited to the USSR, and after visiting the Oriental Institute in Leningrad with its large collection of Tibetiana, he had flown to Moscow and on to Ulan Ude. There, in the heart of Soviet Siberia, he attended a service at a Tibetan-style monastery:

> Soon there came the familiar sounds of chanting, the deep tones of the Tibetan long trumpet, the piercing cries of the Tibetan shawm, the booming sounds of the drum, the clashing of cymbals, the tinkling of bells, the smell of incense, the flickering of butter-lamps, and the rows of sacred images and *thangkas*. These were sights, sounds and smells so familiar to me from my early childhood, youth and young manhood, worlds away from my daily life in Bloomington, and yet always and ever a part of me. I was swept away in nostalgia, and tears brimmed in my eyes. I wanted to remain there as long as I could.[2]

To his surprise, he was granted a visa for Mongolia and took off almost immediately for Ulan Bator. As the plane flew over Lake Baikal, the Kokonor of his childhood, nostalgia increased a hundredfold. The closer they approached the hills and grasslands of the Mongolian steppes, the more he was reminded of Amdo, and visiting Mongolia's most famous monastery, he could almost believe himself back in Tibet.

In fact, he was to go there. In Tokyo, he had been invited by Peking to visit Tibet, and now embarked on a nostalgic journey to Kumbum, the monastery which had been his home for so many years and whose Abbot he had once been. He was depressed to find that, though a few temples were in use as tourist attractions, of the once-thriving monastic town of over three thousand monks there was no sign.

In his home village of Taktser he was overcome with grief. Not only were the Tibetans now a tiny minority in the village but more than twenty of his relatives were dead:

> Only one cousin was still living, and I visited her home and met her child. When I asked her what happened to her father, she replied, 'He is dead.' When I asked her how and where, she did not know. Their farm had been taken, and their house torn down. Many of the people I talked with had such sad stories. When I asked them about their life now, they would just cry, they had no words. Others told me how their families and friends were killed, imprisoned, sent to labour camps, maimed and crippled. Some were beaten so severely over and over again with clubs and boards, that they lost their hearing or sight. Others had bodies that were bent and twisted from being forced to pull heavy carts, like animals...They told me that in 1959 or 60 all men were rounded up, put in trucks and sent away to labour camps; that the only people you saw then were women, children and the aged.[3]

Whatever grief these revelations caused Amala was compounded later in 1980 when her youngest sister arrived from Tibet.[4] It was the first time the two had seen each other for twenty years. 'This aunt was the one who had looked after my grandmother when we left,' explains Kundun. 'My grandmother, fortunately, had died before the Cultural Revolution started, but my poor aunt suffered greatly, was forced to undergo *thamzing* and was imprisoned. She had dreadful digestive problems afterwards and her husband was semi-paralysed. After she was released from prison, she earned some money by dress-making.'[5]

The sisters laughed and wept in turn over their reunion, but its net effect on Amala was catastrophic. 'Her sister was a sweet woman,' says Rinchen, 'but not very subtle. She told everything exactly as it had happened, all the awful things the Chinese had done to their family and friends, down to the last terrible detail. So-and-so died, so-and-so starved to death, so-and-so's house was burned down, so-and-so was in prison. On and on, each story more depressing than the last.' 'My aunt,' agrees

Tendzin Choegyal, 'spent the whole time relating horror-stories. Most of our relatives had either died of starvation or been liquidated – just like almost everyone else's relatives, really. The constant repetition took its toll of my mother and she became terribly depressed.'[6]

Rinchen noted that from then on 'Amala finally understood that the Tibet she had known and loved had gone for ever, and the realization killed her.' When her sister returned home (where she died a few months later), Amala had lost the will to live.

In the winter of 1980, Tendzin Choegyal accompanied Kundun to Bodh Gaya where the latter was to give teachings. Amala had always gone to Thekchen Choeling to say goodbye to him. But this time she could not. The cold, damp Dharamsala winters were increasingly hard for her, in spite of Rinchen's struggles to keep the house warm. Amala had a chill. Kundun therefore came to Kashmir Cottage to say goodbye.

For Rinchen, this last meeting between the two is an unforgettable memory. 'His Holiness sat by her bed and talked to her, just like a little boy coming home to see his mother. It was very beautiful. "So," he asked in a matter-of-fact way, "is there anything you want to tell me?" I can hear her so clearly saying, "No, nothing at all." He told her gently not to be afraid of dying, but to concentrate on the *thangkas* (sacred scrolls) and say the *mani* prayers. He asked her, "Are you afraid?" and she answered confidently, "No, I'm not afraid." It was a lesson in how to die. He said goodbye to her then, adding "Who knows, we may perhaps see each other again." But I think both of them knew it was goodbye.'

Khando came again to Dharamsala, *en route* for a family backpacking holiday in Goa. Rapten was still suffering nightmares and was profoundly depressed (his father had died while he was in Tibet) and she had been advised by friends to get the family away for a break. 'I came to Dharamsala and Mo-la (Grandma) asked me to stay with her for a few days before going to see my father. She kept giving me dresses, old photographs, and other things. As I left her, she hugged me so tight and for so long that I wept for a long time afterwards. I knew in my heart that we both knew this would be the last time we'd ever meet. We were right: on the day I reached Bombay, I heard that Mo-la had passed away. It was one of the saddest times of my life.'[7]

Lobsang Samten scarcely left his mother's side. Perhaps because he was the gentlest and most vulnerable of her seven children, he had always been her special favourite, a fact she admitted towards the end of her life.

Kundun recounts with distinct glee that Tendzin Choegyal had asked her point blank which of them was her favourite, expecting it to be himself. He was devastated when, after a brief pause, she said 'Lobsang Samten'. Kundun admits that he too felt a stab of disappointment, but is consoled by the knowledge that it was Lobsang Samten who was with his mother at the end.

Amala had come to terms with death. Often now she was quiet for long periods, but sometimes she would talk. 'Once,' says Rinchen, 'when we were discussing the death of one of the lamas from Amdo, she said, "We have all these wonderful teachers around us and we feel sad when they leave us. But the important thing to remember is that they *never* leave us; their teachings are always with us. If we have really loved them, we should follow their teachings so that they become part of us." I have never forgotten her words. I have always tried to live as she would have wanted me to live.'

She died of pneumonia within two months of her eighty-first birthday, on 12 January, 1981. 'The day before,' says Rinchen, 'she called all of us in – Lobsang Samten, Namlha, myself, the children, the doctor, the servants. She said, 'You've all been so good to me, thank you for your kindness, and I'm sorry to have been such a nuisance.' She was quite matter-of-fact about it; there were no tears, it was as though she was about to set off for England on a holiday or something. She was completely unafraid, she had detached herself from earthly things, and now she was saying goodbye. Late that night, she told me to unroll the *thangka* in her room. She didn't want to lie down, she wanted to sit up and meditate on the *thangka*, just as His Holiness had told her.'

'It was a cold winter's morning,' remembers Tenzin Lodoe, who was then about eight. 'Normally I slept late. But that day I got up just before the sun had risen and went to my grandmother's room. I sat with her for a bit, she patted my head and said, "Tenzin Lodoe, when you grow up, you must remember to be a good man." Then I massaged her feet and rubbed her hands a little because they were so cold. I stayed about two hours, then went away and got myself some breakfast.'

'Amala was still looking at the *thangka*,' said Rinchen, 'when the end came. She died in my arms. She was the very first person I had ever seen die, and it was a wonderful example of what death can be like.'[8]

Tenzin Lodoe returned to his grandmother's room at about ten, in search of the sticky sweets she kept in a wall cupboard – 'My grandmother would always give me some when my mother wasn't looking.' That morning, hoping his mother was busy elsewhere, he slipped into the room. 'Then I saw my grandmother on the bed, covered up to her neck with a white sheet. Her eyes were closed. In the right-hand corner of the room an old monk, a hermit from the mountain, was murmuring prayers. In front of him were two big bowls filled with saffron water. As I moved towards the bed, he saw me, and got very agitated. "Get out, get out," he shouted. I ran out, very confused, not knowing what to think. I ran into my mother and Auntie Namlha, and asked them what was happening. Auntie Namlha turned to my mother. "Didn't you tell the kids?" When my mother said no, Auntie Namlha said, 'Well, you'll have to tell them now.' Then my mother told me very gently that my grandmother had passed away. It came as a great shock, because nobody close to me had ever died before. I started crying. My mother said, "Don't cry. Just keep in mind your grandmother's last words to you." But I couldn't stop crying, and rushed out of the room to find my sister, Chozoem, and tell her. She just wouldn't believe it.'

'Both children were terribly upset,' says Rinchen. 'I could only tell them "If you really loved your granny, let's all remember what she wanted us to be, and do the things that would make her happy. She will always be with us."'

The death of Dekyi Tsering, Amala, the Gyayum or Great Mother who had given birth to three *tulkus*, was, of course, an occasion for deep mourning. Immediately the Tibetan Administration Offices in Dharamsala were closed, one thousand lamps were lit and prayers were started at the Tsuglakhang Temple. The Minister for Religious Affairs and his staff all came round to Kashmir Cottage to pay their respects, and, accompanied by a crowd of several hundred, to recite the Great Mantra, *Om mani padme hum* (All Hail to the Jewel in the Lotus).

The Kashag worried about how to break the news to Kundun in Bodh Gaya, feeling that to telephone or send a telegram would be insensitive. Instead, says Kundun (and one can imagine that Dekyi Tsering would have enjoyed the joke), 'they sent a letter to my Senior Tutor, Ling Rinpoche, asking him to convey their condolences to me. But as Ling Rinpoche was teaching at the time, the letter was handed directly to me. I opened it, read its contents, and handed it to Ling Rinpoche who had then formally to tell me of my mother's death.'[9] At the end of his teachings that day, Kundun asked the pilgrims to pray for his mother beneath the Bodhi tree where the Buddha had received Enlightenment.

At daybreak on 14 January, the wooden casket containing Amala's body was carried by a group of monks to the old palace of Swarg Ashram. Prayers were offered by the abbot of the Dalai Lama's own Namgyal monastery – and the body was placed on its funeral pyre. Lighting one end of a stick wrapped in a paraffin-soaked white scarf, Lobsang Samten performed the last rites for his mother. The mourners circled round the pyre, placing scarves and incense sticks on it as they chanted prayers. Pema, returning from TCV business in Amsterdam next day, too late for the funeral rites, found an immense crowd still massed on the hillside. She joined her tears to theirs, acknowledging that Amala had been 'more than a mother, she was the very soul of our family'.

Rinchen Khando feels uniquely privileged to have shared those last months with her beloved Amala. 'I benefited so much from being with her,' she says, 'she was an education in herself. As the mother of the Dalai Lama, she could have gone anywhere, done anything, acted like a queen. But right from the first, she rejected the trappings of power. She never forgot her roots. And she never forgot the poor or those who were in any kind of pain.'

They do not forget her either. While she lived, Kashmir Cottage was accorded the reverence that always accrues to a holy place. That aura still clings to it. Though since her death it has reverted to being a guest-house, her spirit lingers on. As one old man said to Rinchen, five years or more after Amala had died, 'We always felt Kashmir Cottage was special because of her, and that it would cease to be so when she had gone. But, young lady, I have to tell you you're a very lucky woman, because nothing has changed. She's still here.'[10]

Later that same year, Kundun lost the surrogate 'mother' of his childhood, the head of his household, Lobsang Jinpa, always known as Ponpo, the Boss. This kindly monk had taken care of him from the day when, as a small, bewildered boy, he had come to Lhasa to take possession of the Lion Throne. 'He fed me,' says Kundun simply. 'Most mammals consider the creature that feeds them as the most important in their lives. That was the way I felt about Ponpo. I knew my teachers were more important than my cook, but emotionally the strongest bond was with him. He was my mother, my father, my entire family. When my mother died I was sad, but I didn't cry. But when Ponpo died and I looked down on his dead body, I wept.'[11]

Next it was Pema's turn to weep. In February 1984, she had gone to southern India for the official inauguration of a new Tibetan Children's Village in Byllakuppe and had spent the rest of the winter holiday in Bangalore where her husband, Lhundup Gyalpo, having run a successful Tibetan restaurant for eleven years, had just opened a second. In March she returned with the three children (now 17, 15 and 11) to Dharamsala in time for the opening of the new school term. At about two o'clock one morning, early in May, she was wakened from sleep by shouts and a loud knocking on the window. It was Gyalo Thondup's wife, Dekyi Dolkar, announcing that Lhundup Gyalpo's body had been discovered in a burned-out car in Bangalore. In a state of shock, Pema woke the children and told them, struggling to stay calm for their sakes. Gyalo Thondup drove them to Bangalore, and took Pema straight to the police station to see her husband's remains. Rumours were already rife about the death: nobody being sure whether it was accident, murder or suicide. Lhundup Gyalpo had set out at night in his car and that was all anybody knew until next morning when the burned-out car was identified by his assistant. When the funeral rites had been performed, and all the prayers were said, Gyalo Thondup and his wife suggested that Pema should hire a detective to investigate. But Kundun advised that the desire for revenge could only be destructive, and in the end she decided not to proceed. Many people criticized her decision, 'few of them understanding,' she wrote, 'my desire to protect the children and avoid any unsavoury publicity for our family.'[12] Instead, she returned to Dharamsala and to the demanding work of the TCV.

Lobsang Samten's personality had undergone a sea change. 'When he came back from Tibet,' says Namlha, 'all his enthusiasm, life, energy, jokiness had gone. He was like a zombie.' While Namlha watched helplessly, he lapsed into a permanent depression. 'We Tibetans talk about a disturbance of the wind energy,' she says, 'when both mind and body are in the grip of stress.' For about a year after his return, people would seek him out for news of their families. When these people came, the information he gave was always sad, their relatives were in prison, murdered or dead of starvation; this or that monastery had been destroyed. He used to talk about it and we all sat there and wept. It seems to me that we never stopped crying that first year. It was difficult for all of us; but Lobsang it destroyed: he began to drink heavily and to suffer from violent mood swings.'[13]

In 1980, a Director was needed for the Tibetan Medical Institute in McLeod Ganj, with its Medical College in Dharamsala and clinics all over India and Nepal. There was no one with the required qualifications to run this combination of hospital, pharmacy and medical school for traditional Tibetan medicine, but as Lobsang had had some experience of administration, had worked for the Tibetan Government and done some fundraising in the USA, he was appointed Director, with Namlha as his English secretary and interpreter and eventually as Assistant Director in the foreign department. They moved from the Tibetan Children's Village to a small café/guest-house in McLeod. Lobsang, however, was a shadow of his former self and 'all his bubbly energy had gone.' 'He had been such a happy person,' adds Kundun, 'always telling jokes. But after going to Tibet, he just fell into an almost chronic depression.'[14]

Lobsang immersed himself in the work of the Medical Institute, trying to ward off the terrible nightmares. But in 1984, even as he was drawing up plans for a new Medical Institute in Delhi, he warned Namlha that he did not have long to live. Tibetans often have astrology charts made, to ascertain their lifespans. Namlha had had one done for herself and for the children, but Lobsang 'didn't hold with that kind of thing, he said it was weird'. Nevertheless, he knew his time was up.

In April 1985, they were offered a three-roomed apartment to rent in the Namgyal Monastery in McLeod. Lobsang, recovering from a gastric attack, took no interest in the move, not caring which room was which, nor even about where he would sleep. But one day in May, on impulse, he suggested inviting the family to a party: Pema and her three children came, Khando and Rapten. 'A friend happened to drop by and took a photograph of us all – it was the very last time we would be together.' 'It was a wonderful evening,' Khando remembers. 'Lobsang seemed to be his old self, cheerful, teasing us all, cracking his terrible dirty jokes. We were doubled up with laughter.'

Soon afterwards, Lobsang and Namlha began commuting to Delhi to set up a clinic and look for land on which to build a new Medical Institute. (Both of their children were in Delhi, Tenzin reading Political Science at St Stephen's College, and Chuki, who had graduated in Psychology at Chandigarh University, at secretarial school.) They spent two months setting up an exhibition of Tibetan Medicine at Tibet House in Delhi, trudging around in the sweltering heat of the city for eight or nine hours each day in search of a suitable place for a clinic. Eventually they found a house, bought furniture, appointed staff and opened for business: on the very first day, about two or three hundred Indians came for treatment. Lobsang's work in Delhi was almost done, though he still had to finalize an arrangement with the Indian Government concerning the purchase of land for the Institute. At this juncture, Kundun arrived in Delhi, on his way to Switzerland.

'I had decided to take Lobsang along,' he says. 'He wanted to come, but at the last minute told me he ought to stay in Delhi to clinch the business about the land. When I came back, he was still waiting for the man to turn up. I was returning to Dharamsala by overnight train and asked him if he'd like to travel with me.' Lobsang and Namlha had already decided to go back to Dharamsala and catch up with the backlog of work, before returning to Delhi. They were booked on to next day's bus. Kundun's offer was a godsend. 'I was delighted,' says Namlha, 'Lobsang was very tired and stressed-out, and travelling up in His Holiness's special coach would at least ensure he had somewhere to lie down. I left on the bus next morning, and they were due to leave that evening.'

But Lobsang didn't arrive. Just before leaving, he had discovered that the man dealing with the land business was due in Delhi in ten days' time. He decided to wait for him.

Namlha attacked the daunting backlog of work at the Institute. When Inge, a German friend visiting Dharamsala, suggested they should travel down to Delhi together for Lobsang's birthday on 1 September, she reluctantly refused. 'Besides, as I told Inge, I needed to be on my own for a while. Lobsang and I had never once been apart in our entire married life (except when he went to Tibet) and for some unexplained reason I felt I must experience what it was like to live alone. Inge told me not to be morbid, but my mind was made up.'

Lobsang wrote to say he would be coming home soon, but couldn't say when. At first Namlha was unconcerned. Only after a week had gone by did she begin to worry. On Monday she phoned Chuki in Delhi. 'I asked her how [Lobsang] was, and she told me he was getting over some kind of flu virus. He had been to see a doctor and was now staying with Gyalo Thondup's wife in Delhi. I was shocked but relieved. My sister-in-law was very motherly and practical, so he'd be in good hands. I asked Chuki to go and see her father and call me if necessary. But I could no longer concentrate on work. I was not in the habit of making personal calls from the office, but next day I rang Dekyi Dolkar...who told me Lobsang had developed jaundice. I dropped everything and ran.'

According to Kundun, one of Lobsang's friends misguidedly 'gave him rum or brandy or something to treat the flu, and that made everything worse, turned the 'flu to fever and then to jaundice. From then on, his condition began to deteriorate rapidly.'

Catching the night bus from Dharamsala that same day (Tuesday), Namlha went straight to her sister-in-law's apartment. 'I found Lobsang in the dining-room, wearing a white kurta pyjama and reading the newspaper. He looked terribly thin and exhausted, almost lifeless. When he saw me, he dropped his paper, came and hugged me and burst into tears. I hugged him back, stammering out through my own tears that he was ill and ought to be in bed. He went to bed, but each day insisted on coming down to meals because – like his mother – he didn't want to be a bother to anyone. On Sunday afternoon, he was unable to get off the toilet and called me to help. I cleaned him up and called for my brother who was in the house. Together we wrestled him back to bed, he was a dead weight. Later that evening, when I tried to get him to take his medicine, he became violent. He'd always had a temper, but it was never more than a momentary thing. This time, he pushed me away – hard. Something was terribly wrong. My sister-in-law and I went for a doctor. There was a Tibetan one nearby, but Lobsang refused to see him. We looked for the Indian doctor, but it was Sunday and he was out for the day. There was nothing for it but to return home and wait.'

The Indian doctor came at about eight and ordered Lobsang to hospital. But where to take him on a Sunday evening? They took him to the only hospital Namlha knew, the Catholic Holy Family Hospital. When they arrived, Lobsang was delirious and uncontrollably violent. 'There were three young doctors and two nurses, but none of them could handle him. He had lapsed into a coma, from which hour after hour he would wake up and cry aloud in pain – but he wouldn't let the doctors come near. I went and whispered prayers in his ear. When he relapsed into coma, I would go out and help the nurses with five or six terminal cases who were constantly crying for water. In the room that night, I lay down on a shawl, but I couldn't sleep.'

Next morning, the Bureau of Tibet in Delhi informed the Indian Government of Lobsang's condition and he was transferred to the All-India Medical Centre. There he lapsed into a final deep coma – which lasted for thirteen days. Kundun still reproaches himself for not being with him at the end. 'I sent my own physician, Wangyal, to him,' he says sadly, 'but there was nothing he could do. I couldn't stop myself thinking, over and over again, if only Lobsang had come to Switzerland with me, none of this would have happened. If I'd insisted on his getting the train with me from Delhi, it wouldn't have happened. There was so much negligence. Lobsang was alone and exhausted when he got sick, and he didn't take steps to look after himself until it was too late.'

Pema had arrived in Delhi to be with Namlha – and Chuki. Lobsang's son, Tenzin, was so distressed that he had not been seen at his university hostel for two days. Tempa (Gyalo Thondup's younger son, a doctor) had come from Darjeeling to be with the family.

In the early afternoon of 28 September 1985, Pema was out shopping, Chuki was with her mother, Tenzin was still incommunicado. Namlha was resting, intending to go as usual to the hospital at five. At three o'clock, she became unaccountably agitated and knew she must go to Lobsang without delay. Tempa drove her and Chuki to the hospital. 'As I walked into the hospital, I saw Pema queuing for the telephone. She said, "Something has happened to Lobsang, I was trying to ring you." My son, Tenzin, had just arrived too. We went up together, and there we were, Pema, the children, me – and Lobsang. It was as though he had known I would come and had waited for me. As I got to his side, he breathed his last.'

The doctors wanted the body removed immediately, as they needed the bed. But the family wished the Buddhist after-death ritual to be followed. 'His Holiness had sent two people to help. Rinpoche [Tendzin Choegyal] had come with them, but he was so upset that we felt he should not stay and sent him back to Dharamsala with one of the secretaries. With the help of one of His Holiness's helpers, I washed Lobsang's body all over with the remains of some holy water which he had sent. Then we dressed him in a white kurta pyjama that I had bought for him in Bombay two years earlier. A Rinpoche from Tibet House said the last rites. It was stiflingly hot in Delhi. My mother suggested that we should have the body cremated there. But when I rang His Holiness, I was given the message that I must take the body to Dharamsala that very night.'

Lobsang Samten was cremated in Dharamsala. It was, Kundun says today, 'one of the very saddest times of my life. I think it is no exaggeration to say that Lobsang died of a broken heart. He simply couldn't understand how the Chinese could be so indifferent to the sufferings they had caused in Tibet.'[15]

For Namlha, there was overwhelming grief. She and Lobsang had been married for twenty-three years and in that time had scarcely ever been apart. 'Ours was a love-match,' she says, 'and we were the best of friends as well as lovers. When he died, a part of me died too.'

In October, she was asked to take over Lobsang's post as Director of the Medical Institute. Appalled at the suggestion, she refused, protesting that she was quite unequal to such a heavy responsibility, but offering to help the new Director all she could. The physicians from the Institute said they had already written to His Holiness and to the Kashag, and, if she continued to refuse, the entire staff of the Medical Institute would stage a sit-in in her apartment. Namlha was petrified. 'I asked them to wait a few days, as I didn't want to make a big issue of it. I went to see His Holiness's Private Secretary to ask him if a divination could be done, to determine whether or not I would be suitable for the job.'

She then left, with Chuki and her uncle, Jigme Taring, for Bodh Gaya. 'I went there to pray for Lobsang. I felt completely empty. My uncle said he thought I should not live alone, because I'd never been used to it, but I told him I should simply have to learn.'

Namlha was still in Bodh Gaya when news of her appointment as Director of the Medical Institute came through. 'When I received that letter, I went to the main temple with Chuki, and there, in front of the statue of the Buddha I promised to do my best and prayed for blessings on the work.'

She took up the appointment on 1 January 1986. 'It was difficult and strange,' she says, 'but the very worst thing of all was sitting in the chair that had been Lobsang's.'

NOTES
1. Author interview with Rinchen Khando, 1993.
2. Norbu, *Tibet Is My Country*, p. 269.
3. *Tibet Is My Country*, p. 274.
4. Tibetans were being allowed out of Tibet to visit relatives in India, but only on condition that they left a son, daughter, husband, parent behind as hostage.
5. Author interview with HH the Dalai Lama, 1994.
6. Conversation with Tendzin Choegyal and Rinchen Khando, 1994.
7. Author interview with Khando Chazotsang, Utah, February 1996.

8. Conversation with Rinchen Khando, October 1994, in the room where the Great Mother died.

9. Author interview with HH the Dalai Lama, October 1994.

10. Author interview with Rinchen Khando, 1993.

11. Author interview with HH the Dalai Lama, 1994.

12. Jetsun Pema, *Tibet, Mon Histoire*.

13. Author interview with Namlha Taklha, Dharamsala, 1993.

14. Author interview with HH the Dalai Lama, 1994.

15. Author interview with HH the Dalai Lama, June 1994.

25

Return to Darkness

On the whole, the...switch of policy in Tibet is just the crunchy end of the time-honoured stick-and-carrot treatment which China has, with a fair rate of success, applied to its Tibetan problem. What it has gained through force and terror it now hopes to consolidate by coercion and bribes.

Jamyang Norbu, 1980

Gyalo Thondup was a disappointed man. By 1983, he had visited Peking twelve times as Kundun's personal emissary. 'The Chinese wanted to trick us, giving us sweets as if we were three-year-old children. They were sure they could persuade us of the advantages of going back to Tibet.' As Deng was already back-tracking on the promises he had made (cancelling the request for teachers, for example), and as he was tired of being a hate-figure in Dharamsala, GT once again retired hurt to Hong Kong. 'I told the Chinese it was a thankless task being a go-between. I said, "You kick me like a ball to Dharamsala and Dharamsala kicks me right back again. Both of you suspect me and I can't take any more." They tried to persuade me to carry on, saying things would get worse if I gave up. But I'd had enough. I told His Holiness that in future he could send his officials to Peking, not me.'¹

Kundun hoped to visit Tibet in 1985. To this end, he sent a delegation of three senior ministers – among them his Minister of Security, Phuntsok Tashi Taklha – to Peking to open a dialogue. It was a waste of time. The Chinese wanted one thing only – to get the Dalai Lama back. (They needed his help to develop Tibet. As they had told GT, 'One word from him would be worth a thousand from us.') Accordingly, they set their own agenda, refusing to discuss anything except the Dalai Lama's future political status, whether he would reside in Peking or Lhasa, by what route he would return, and so on. No amount of argument would persuade them that these were side-issues, says Phuntsok Tashi, 'far less important than improving the well-being and happiness of the Tibetan people. To them, there was no such thing as "a Tibet problem".'

Chinese immigrants began flooding into Tibet in 1983, raising for the first time the spectre of what the Dalai Lama called 'a final solution by stealth' in which Tibetans would be edged out in their own land. Chinese nationals, mainly the young and poorly-educated, were being encouraged – with irresistible incentives in pay, housing, special privileges and holidays – to leave their own over-populated areas and assist in 'developing the Tibetan Autonomous Republic'. For them there were rich pickings to be had. For the Tibetans it spelled disaster. In Lhasa, prices soared and thousands found themselves out of work, as even their traditional trades and crafts were taken over by the Chinese. Before long only the most unskilled, underpaid jobs were available for the Tibetans and most of them had to resort to street-hawking and begging. Kundun dropped his plans for a visit.

By May 1984, sixty thousand skilled and unskilled Chinese workers had arrived in Tibet. Many others followed as private individuals, and the new invasion showed every sign of gathering force. As active resistance to the intruders grew, so did a new wave of repression, arrests and public executions.

In September, a second attempt at dialogue with Peking had as little success as the first. Unsurprisingly, perhaps, since China was being asked to accept 'the historical status of Tibet and its right to self-determination, the right to reunification of the three traditional provinces of Tibet, the need for a relationship or alliance with China on an equal footing and the transformation of Tibet into a zone of peace'.[2]

In 1986, a year after Tibet had officially 'celebrated' twenty years as the Tibet Autonomous Region, Kundun's brother, Norbu, who made no secret of his loathing for Chinese colonialism, was refused a visa to visit friends and relatives in Tibet. An official at the Chinese Consulate General in New York cited Norbu's aggressive support for Tibetan Independence and the 'many things' he had said against China.

In this stalemate, the Kashag swallowed its pride and turned again, cap in hand, to Gyalo Thondup. 'For three years,' says GT virtuously, 'I had kept a very low profile. I didn't go near China. Then the Kashag began writing to me, asking me to come to Dharamsala. I said I had nothing to say to them. They replied that if I wouldn't come to them, they'd come to me in Delhi. They came and confessed that their relationship with China was at breaking-point. The Chinese had told them not to come back any more unless they were prepared to travel as "overseas Chinese", which of course they weren't. So, please would I try again. I agreed to see the Chinese Ambassador in Delhi about reopening the discussions. Peking replied "Gyalo Thondup is an old friend and, like any other member of the Yapshi family, will be welcome in China,"[3] so then I resumed my visits.'

During this period, GT's wife, Dekyi Dolkar, died. Many felt she had never recovered from the death of her daughter, Yangzom, in a motor-car accident in the Sahara four years earlier. Yangzom, who was married to Namlha's brother Jigme Tsarong, left a young son, and after her death Dekyi Dolkar took the boy home with her and brought him up as her own. But her health was already declining and in 1986 she was diagnosed as having cancer of the pancreas. Though her sons flew her to New York for surgery, it was too late, and she died on the operating table. Despite her Chinese birth, she was mourned by the Tibetans as a true Tibetan who devoted her life to their cause. For Tendzin Choegyal, she had been a truly formative influence. 'I miss her still,' he says, 'she was warm, understanding, and utterly honest. When you talked to her, you felt you'd talked with a real human being. There was no deviousness in her.'

Over the next three years, GT resumed his visits to Peking. He claims that he told the Chinese repeatedly that their policies were morally and politically wrong. 'They accused Tibetan exiles of being splittists, but they were the real splittists – they had split off huge chunks of Tibet and absorbed them into China; they'd destroyed our culture and sucked up Tibet like a giant vacuum cleaner; they claimed to have liberated us, but Tibet was in chains. "You are worse than the Manchus," I said. "Mao wanted all the minorities to love each other and be happy within the Motherland. But look at the Tibetans, they're very unhappy and they hate you."'[4]

Indeed, many Tibetans were still braving the terrors of the high Himalaya to reach India or Nepal. All of them yearned to see the Dalai Lama, and as they had no option but to go to Dharamsala for screening (the Chinese being known to plant spies among them), their wish was usually granted. Kundun saw them in groups or individually, listened to them, wept with them, and grieved that he could help them so little. There were so many shortages, of accommodation, of water, of electricity – of money. As a guest of the Indian Government, he couldn't levy taxes, and was dependent on what he received from the host country, from donor agencies, private benefactors and donations made to him personally through his teachings and lectures. Among the refugees, salary earners contributed two per cent of their salaries, business men ten per cent of their takings and everybody else at least one rupee a month.

Dharamsala had flourished. The Government-in-Exile ran small hotels, guest-houses, restaurants, travel agencies, handicraft centres and an import/export business. The place was awash now with market-stalls offering anything from fine bronze Buddhas, Tibetan antiques and jewellery through to fluorescent socks and tawdry cotton T-shirts. The Tibetan Medical Centre offered traditional remedies, while the Delek Hospital, staffed by volunteer doctors from all over the world, provided more modern, Western treatments. In South India, Nepal, Bhutan, Switzerland, the USA and the UK also, Tibetan refugees were proving themselves to be survivors rather than victims.

Though much remained to be done, their achievements were remarkable. The eighty-two schools, for example, in the Indian sub-continent alone, thirty of them supported by the Government of India, forty-three entirely by the Tibetan Administration. The nine Tibetan Children's Villages, overseen by Pema, fed and clothed about eight thousand refugee children, two thousand of whom were in Dharamsala. They were arriving at the rate of about two hundred each year and the Homes were stretched to breaking point. Pema would never turn any child away – even if they had to be housed in makeshift shacks, they would manage somehow. Things were changing, though, not least in the attitude of the TCV's supporters. The old days when donors gave money without being much concerned about the overall picture disappeared when Kundun began travelling and making personal contacts. People had become more interested in Tibet itself. Pema was finding that helpers were no longer concerned just for the immediate needs of the children, but also for 'our culture, our religion, our Tibetan identity. People seem to have realized that we have something to offer the world'.[5]

For six years Khando had successfully run the Tibetan Homes Foundation, Mussoorie, and all its branch programmes scattered around in India. Her predecessor, Mrs Taring, had adopted an old-fashioned, authoritarian approach, but Khando was different: 'Mine was a management style geared to consensus and an open-door policy. I was determined to hold open meetings with house-parents and older students, but I'm afraid that some of the house-parents really did not approve of the freedom with which the older students expressed their views on behalf of all the children. Initially when we had meetings, they all sat with their heads bowed, waiting for me to address them. One day I said, "Look, I don't think this kind of meeting is getting us anywhere. Frankly, it's a waste of time. For me, a meeting is about identifying difficulties, you telling me what you need, setting our priorities, and then all of us putting our heads together to see if we have the necessary resources and money. I'm learning too, you know."'

It was hard-going. But Kundun supported her. 'He kept telling me that difficulties and problems were inevitable and didn't matter as long as we did our best with a good conscience...His encouragement and the hard teamwork of the rest of the staff paid off, as slowly we developed the capacity to provide quality care and education for our children. Donations began to pour in, and with help from many different organizations and from the Government of India, we put up more buildings and made improvements to the existing ones. I really thrived in the new atmosphere.'⁶

One day in 1986 Pema walked down the mountainside to McLeod Ganj, and called on a cousin who lived near the Temple. The atmosphere was ominously still. Suddenly, a thunderous boom from the mountain reverberated through the valley. Within seconds, the earth began to shake and noise exploded all around them. 'I huddled against the door, my thoughts full of the children up at the Village. My cousin began praying aloud, and we could hear people shrieking outside.'⁷ The quake (with a force of seven or eight on the Richter scale) lasted only a few seconds and when it was over Pema rushed to Kundun's residence from where she could telephone to see if the children were all right. In fact, three or four of the makeshift houses in the Village had collapsed, covering the children's beds with rubble. But to her intense relief, the children were all outside and there were no casualties.

Kundun had been reading when the earthquake hit. His house, built by the British at least eighty years earlier and only partially renovated, did not withstand the seismic shocks. Stones were dislodged from the space between the roof and the ceiling, and some of them fell inside the house. Huge cracks appeared in several of the walls. It was clear that something would have to be done. As news of the earthquake spread throughout the world, letters and donations poured in. Work began almost immediately on a new, shock-resistant residence for Kundun on the site of the old.

For Pema, there was an unforeseen outcome. During this period, she came into frequent contact with one of Kundun's Private Secretaries, Tempa Tsering, who in the late Seventies had been a firebrand President of the Tibetan Youth Congress, outspoken advocate of a greater militancy against the Chinese. Independence, he had proclaimed, 'wouldn't come on a plate. It had to be fought for and won.'[8] Under Tempa's embattled leadership The TYC had briefly flirted with the idea of terrorism – against Chinese embassies and personnel abroad. Some training got under way, the TYC expanded its contacts with underground groups inside Tibet, but in the end, its vow of loyalty to the Dalai Lama – and the more hopeful climate of the early 1980s – had caused Tempa Tsering to shelve his plans. Invited to become Secretary of the foreign section of the Private Office, with the prospect of travelling the world with Kundun, he became convinced instead that 'Tibet's unique hope lay not where the guerrillas had failed, but in the strength of the traditional society, now rebuilt and entering the world at large.'[9]

Pema had long been a pillar of that traditional society when she and Tempa Tsering decided to marry. Her decision exploded like a bombshell in Dharamsala, since Tempa Tsering was, to put it mildly, not liked either by the community in general or by the Yapshi family in particular. In her autobiography, Pema writes that the Tibetans did not expect the Dalai Lama's widowed sister to remarry, they would have preferred her to become a nun. But 'I did not attach too much importance to the opinion of others. Honesty is what counts; one must be true to oneself and not pretend to be other than one is.'[10] When she consulted her children, they told her it was her life and she must make her own decision. The marriage took place in New Delhi, with Gyalo Thondup giving the blessing. Shortly afterwards Tempa Tsering was transferred to Bangalore and Pema was separated from her new husband for months on end. Both of them accepted the situation as normal. The Tibetan cause had to come first.

In 1980, Tendzin Choegyal had accompanied Kundun on his first visit to Zanskar and Ladakh in the mountainous north-west of India. This was the area in which the monasteries of Ngari Rinpoche lay and though he had

long since handed over control to the monks themselves, he was still ultimately responsible for them. Kundun, learning that the monasteries were
in a state of neglect, now told his brother in no uncertain terms to do
something about them. Tendzin Choegyal thereupon sent out a letter to
all his monasteries, informing them that he was resuming a degree of control. For the next few years, he sent a friend and colleague from army days
to keep an eye on the monasteries' affairs. 'He was full of ideas. He built
tourist hostels to generate income and set up co-operatives. Thanks to
him, the monasteries in the Leh area bought some land, built houses on it,
and rented them out. The arrangement worked quite well. The abbots
thought I was eccentric but at least they knew I wasn't a crook.'[11]

After Amala's death, he and Rinchen had decided to support their family
by reconverting Kashmir Cottage into a guest house. Rinchen pawned
some of the family valuables to finance the renovation and the building of
a new house close by for themselves. With Amala gone and the children
growing up, she took up (unpaid) social work among Tibetan women with
large families, and fundraising for nuns who were finding it difficult to
survive. When the Tibetan Women's Association was revived in 1984, she
was elected as its first President. The Association commemorated the
courageous women who had risen against the Chinese during the Lhasa
Uprising, many of whom were arrested and died in prison. In exile, small
local groups of – mainly illiterate – women had gathered together to keep
their memory alive. They had started small handicraft centres, but had
few resources and no cohesion. The new Association was both national
and international, with a network of representatives from twelve different
regions of India and Nepal and with influential contacts in the USA, UK,
Norway, Sweden and India. It aimed to keep alive the sense of belonging to
a unified Tibet, and to preserve the Tibetan language and culture in an
alien environment. 'Our women were in a strong position to do this,' avers
Rinchen, 'because they were the ones who bring up the children. They
needed to be made aware of their potential and the value of their own contribution. But we had a wider aim too: to make contact with women all
over the world, so that we could tell them about what had been done to
Tibet and work with them to bring peace to the world.'

To Rinchen's delight, Kundun asked if nuns could be included. 'I'd always been interested in the lives of nuns, partly because when I was a
child in Kham, I had a very kind and loving aunt who lived in a hermitage
in a beautiful valley with a stream running by...But nuns had never

received a proper education like the monks: that's why there isn't a single nun *geshe*[12] today. It really was high time we provided a decent system of education for them.' So, with a gift of money from the Council for Religious Affairs and from the refugees' fund, the Tibetan Women's Association incorporated a special Nuns' Project. A year or two later, when Tibet was again in turmoil and monks and nuns were at the forefront of resistance, the full force of Chinese revenge was directed against them. Many of them were tortured almost to the point of death; hundreds of survivors took the difficult and dangerous route to India and freedom. When sixty-four refugee nuns arrived on one day in Dharamsala with nowhere to put them, Rinchen sent an SOS to friends in the West for money for beds, then rented a large house behind Kashmir Cottage, and started planning a permanent nunnery and an Institute for Higher Studies. She was offered some land in the beautiful Kangra Valley and a friend donated the money with which to build on it. 'Our real hope,' explains Rinchen, 'is that when the nuns get their degrees, they will be able to return to Tibet and teach. And not only teach. Some of them will train as health workers and nurses. If all goes according to plan, they will be able to play a really useful role in our community.'[13]

Kundun had become a popular ambassador for his country, not least in the USA where during visits in 1979, 1981 and 1984, he had received many offers of support. In July 1985 the US Congress wrote to the President of the Chinese People's Assembly in Peking, approving the negotiations taking place between China and the Dalai Lama's representatives and asking for the Tibetans' requests to be given due consideration. That the Chinese would ignore the missive was a foregone conclusion. Nevertheless, Congress had served notice that it both recognized and upheld the Dalai Lama's cause. Other countries followed suit.

Early in 1987, Kundun was again in Washington, to address a Congressional sub-committee on Human Rights. Friends suggested that he might like to put forward a list of aims with which supporters of Tibet round the world might identify. Accordingly, on Capitol Hill on 21 September, Kundun proposed what came to be known as his Five-Point Peace Plan – a Buddhist Charter for Tibet:

1 Tibet should be designated a Zone of Peace, the entire plateau to be an area without weapons of destruction. Even the peaceful use of nuclear energy would be banned, because of the pollution it would cause. Tibet would become the world's biggest nature reserve, in which plant and animal life would be protected, the environment guarded from exploitation, and social development attuned to the needs and potential of the people. With peace actively promoted, Indian troops could abandon their defensive positions along the Himalayan borders and trust could be re-established. But the precondition of such trust would be the withdrawal of Chinese troops from Tibet. 'After the holocaust of the last three decades...only a withdrawal of Chinese troops could start a genuine process of reconciliation.'

2 China should abandon its population transfer – its Final Solution by stealth – which was threatening the very existence of Tibet. If this did not happen, Tibetans would 'soon be no more than a tourist attraction and a relic of a noble past'.

3 Human rights and democratic freedoms should be respected. Tibetans had become second-class citizens in their own country under a system of outright *apartheid*.

4 The environment should be restored. The wildlife of Tibet had been almost totally wiped out and irreparable damage done to what had once been an unspoiled wilderness sanctuary.

5 Serious negotiations should take place with the Chinese, concerning not only the future of Tibet but the relationship between the Tibetan and Chinese peoples.

This last proposal the Chinese interpreted as a call to 'independence in disguise'. Their fury found expression three days later in a mass political rally in Lhasa at which fifteen thousand people were compelled to watch the sentencing of eight Tibetan dissidents, three of them to death.

This reversion to terror tactics served only to push the Tibetans over the edge. On 27 September 1987, the first of more than eighty spontaneous non-violent uprisings erupted, spear-headed by monks and nuns and all demanding Tibetan independence. It was, as one woman who took part told the author, 'an absolutely universal rejection of the regime'. At first the authorities were caught off guard, but they soon recovered, introducing specially-trained riot squads who would shoot to kill, and beat people up without mercy. Over the next three years, there followed a savage programme of murder, torture and intimidation unequalled since the Cultural Revolution and to which even the Chinese gave the name of 'merciless repression'.[14] The difference was that this time both the protests and their suppression were witnessed by foreign tourists[15] and by the world's press. No longer could anyone plead ignorance of the human-rights abuses being perpetrated in Tibet.

With more and more Tibetans being killed, wounded or arrested every day, the policy of non-violent resistance hung by a thread. Knowing that at any moment the Tibetans might resort to violence, Kundun intensified his search for a solution. While Western leaders called on China to resume talks with the Tibetans, on 15 June 1988 he stood before the European Parliament in Strasbourg and enlarged on the theme of his Five-Point Peace Plan. Reaching for the bottom line of what he was prepared to offer, he declared himself ready to abandon claims for full Tibetan independence and to be willing to leave foreign policy and defence matters in the hands of the Chinese. In effect, he was offering China 'suzerainty' in exchange for the Tibetans' right to conduct their own internal affairs. It was an attempt in good faith to find out what China was willing to concede.

Kundun made it clear that the final decision would be left to the Tibetan people themselves. But the fall-out from Strasbourg was enormous and the shock-waves are still reverberating today. The Chinese predictably denounced it as 'splittist'. But their reaction was nothing to the fury of young (and some not-so-young) Tibetans in Dharamsala and the exile communities world-wide. Individuals and groups protested openly, defying the Dalai Lama to an unprecedented degree, wondering how such a spectacular sell-out could ever have been contemplated. By what right could Tibetans in Dharamsala hand over the very independence for which their fellow countrymen in Tibet were daily paying with their lives? Phuntsog Wangyal, a prominent Tibetan in London, spoke for many. 'History has always believed that Tibet was independent,' he said bitterly. 'His Holiness had always talked about Independence. But with Strasbourg, suddenly a new chapter on Tibet began: "not-Independence". Was that in his own best interests? Or in the interests of history? To exchange Independence for whatever is on offer now, at this moment?'[16] Kundun was blamed for wishful thinking, the Kashag and various foreign advisers for giving him bad advice, and Gyalo Thondup – for still carrying on his unofficial talks with the Chinese.

GT was indeed still talking to the Chinese, though to scant effect: 'They kept on about our being splittists, even when I told them they were being paranoid. They were suspicious of their own shadows, I said. They thought His Holiness was being exploited by the Americans and I couldn't convince them it wasn't true. Of course, what they really wanted was for His Holiness to say openly that Tibet was part of China. I told them that was impossible, because historically it wasn't true. Tibet had never been ruled by the Chinese.'[17] Norbu did not share the views of either GT or Kundun. 'My eldest brother disagrees with me fundamentally on this issue,' says Kundun.[18] 'He expresses his feelings quite forcefully and is very critical of my approach.'

'I don't believe in violence but I certainly don't think His Holiness is being tough enough,' agrees Norbu. 'China has absolutely no excuse for being in Tibet. We're not Chinese, we're Tibetans. If a thief comes to your house, you must drive him out, and China should get out of Tibet. We owe nothing to China, we have our own language, our own culture – if we talk, we have to talk as equals and not with China dictating the terms.'[19]

The killing did not stop for Strasbourg. The force of Tibetan resistance would be broken only by the brutal imposition of martial law after the last big riot in March 1989, less than three months before the more famous massacre on Peking's own Tiananmen Square. 'The idea of China imposing martial law in Lhasa was terrifying,' wrote Kundun.[20] 'It looked as if the Chinese must be about to turn the place into a slaughter-house, a Himalayan killing-fields. Two days later, on the thirtieth anniversary of the Tibetan People's Uprising, I therefore sent an appeal to Deng Xiao-ping, asking that he intervene personally to lift martial law and end the repression of innocent Tibetans. He did not reply.'

Martial law failed to crush the Tibetan spirit – calls for violent action were increasingly heard. When the Tibetan Youth Congress assembled in Dharamsala in the September after Strasbourg, the delegates were breathing fire. Kundun opened their deliberations, arguing that violence would only beget worse violence and the use of force would forfeit the sympathy of the outside world; but they were unwilling to listen. I saw him in the afternoon, when he was still bruised from the encounter. 'There they all were this morning,' he sighed, 'wanting to take up arms and fight the Chinese. It's very easy for them to talk, but when you come down to the practical details, it's impossible. For one thing, India wouldn't tolerate it. Nor America, Russia, France – nobody would help or supply weapons. And there's one more thing – if Tibetans turned to violence, they would no longer be special. Many countries now support us because we are fighting for our freedom through non-violence. That's something quite new on this planet and it is unique.'[21]

In the end, the young Tibetans did not make a call to arms, though they agonized over the decision. 'Every nation has the right to defend itself from annihilation,' the new President, Lhasang Tsering, told me emotionally as the Congress ended. 'We are talking about our very survival.' Later, he and many others would note that Strasbourg, in compromising on Independence, had opened up a tragic fault line in Tibetan society. 'We are traditionally divided over religion, provinces and many other issues, but we never before had two opinions on Independence. The Strasbourg Proposal divided us.'[22]

The world, however, approved Kundun's judgement, for in December of that year he was awarded the Nobel Prize for Peace. The Award cited his unwavering non-violence and tireless search for 'peaceful solutions based upon tolerance and mutual respect in order to preserve the historical and cultural heritage of his people'. Here was an implicit condemnation of China – which in June had dealt with its own people's aspirations by leaving them dead and dying on Tiananmen Square. China was stung and, protesting that the Nobel Committee's decision had 'hurt the Chinese people's feelings', imposed even more draconian restrictions on Tibet. Kundun saw the Award differently, as signifying the world's recognition of the value of compassion, love, and forgiveness even of one's enemies. In his acceptance speech on 10 December 1989, speaking as 'a simple monk from far-away Tibet', he drew the world's attention to his country's tragic fate and to its continuing non-violent resistance. The prize money (3 million kroner, $469,000, about £281,000) was used to set up a Foundation for Universal Responsibility: for needy people everywhere, particularly in his host-country, India; and for a number of peace projects throughout the world. The Chinese, for their part, ended this infamous year with another mandatory public rally in Lhasa at which eleven monks received jail sentences of up to nineteen years for the crime of campaigning for Tibetan Independence.

As for Gyalo Thondup, he had decided that discretion was the better part of valour. What was the point of bothering, he asked himself. 'No matter what I said to the Chinese, they didn't listen. And no matter what I said to the Tibetans, they did not listen either.' It was an impossible situation. From now on, he determined to 'emulate the three monkeys: hear all, see all, say nothing'.

NOTES

1. Author interview with Gyalo Thondup, New Delhi, July 1996.

2. 'Sino-Tibetan Negotiations since 1959', *Resistance and Reform in Tibet.*

3. In other words, no Cabinet Ministers. By underlining that the Yapshi family was welcome in China at any time, the Chinese may have intended to cause discord in Dharamsala.

4. Author interview with Gyalo Thondup, New Delhi, July 1996.

5. Author interview with Jetsun Pema, June 1994.

6. Author interview with Khando Chazotsang, Utah, February 1996.

7. Jetsun Pema.

8. Avedon, *In Exile from the Land of Snows*, chapter 5.

9. Author interview with Gyalo Thondup, New Delhi, July 1996.

10. Jetsun Pema, *Tibet, Mon Histoire.*

11. Author interview with Tendzin Choegyal, Dharamsala, October 1993.

12. Buddhist Doctor of Philosophy and teacher.

13. Author interview with Khando Chazotsang, Utah, February 1996.

14. For details of this period, see, among many other sources, my own *Tears of Blood*, HarperCollins, 1992.

15. Tourists had been allowed into Tibet after 1980.

16. Author interview with Phuntsog Wangyal, London, February 1996.

17. Author interview with Gyalo Thondup, Delhi, July 1995.

18. Author interview with HH the Dalai Lama, October 1994.

19. Author interview with Thubten Jigme Norbu, Dharamsala, July 1995.

20. Fourteenth Dalai Lama, *Freedom in Exile*, p. 288.

21. Author interview with HH the Dalai Lama, September 1989.

22. 'Talks with Lhasang Tsering', *Lungta* 7, 1993.

26

The Hazards of Democracy

A wise man calmly considers what is right and what is wrong, and faces different opinions with truth, non-violence and peace.

The Dhammapada

Tendzin Choegyal felt he was going mad. Beset alternately by depressions and panic attacks, his self-esteem was at an all-time low. It was while accompanying Kundun on his second visit to Zanskar and Ladakh in 1988 that he 'went from full-blown depression to full-blown mania'. As Kundun's Private Secretary, he was in charge of arrangements for the visit. 'In Zanskar,' comments His Holiness, 'many meetings had been organized. Tendzin Choegyal is a perfectionist and expected everything to go exactly according to plan, but, of course, things don't always turn out the way we want them to, and this was no exception. One major factor in what happened was his terrible temper, another was his extreme anxiety. When things went wrong, he lost control.'[1]

'I really hallucinated,' admits Choegyal. 'Usually your reason exercises some sort of control and makes you aware that part of you is fantasizing, but when you enter a manic phase, rationality is completely over-shadowed. There was one incident...without going into details, I behaved outrageously. I can only describe it by saying I was 'on a trip', without having taken any hallucinogens. It cost me no money, but I certainly paid with my reputation. After that, people used to shy away from me, as if I was possessed.'

Total nervous collapse ensued. 'It was his very worst period, when we were in Zanskar together,' reflects Kundun. 'He seemed to be completely out of control. I felt a kind of desperation and worried endlessly about what I could do to help. I tried telling him that many people suffer from that condition and that it could be treated, but it was no use.' Doctors confirmed that Choegyal was suffering from manic depression, and prescribed a course of Lithium tablets. The cure was effective, but in one sense came too late: his position as Private Secretary to Kundun had been fatally compromised. 'I resigned,' he says heavily, 'I felt it would be completely irresponsible of me to hang on to a job of such importance...I discussed it with His Holiness, and he told me to do as I saw fit.' It's all water under the bridge now, he shrugs.

'Resigning was a hard decision, but I think it was best for his peace of mind,' says the long-suffering Rinchen. 'The most important thing was that he should be happy. I never really despaired, but I must admit that it was difficult not to be depressed. At times I used to wonder if there would ever be an end to it, but I tried not to show him those feelings. In marriage you make promises for life, for the bad times as well as the good, and this was a time for hanging on and waiting.'

Choegyal himself made heroic efforts to control the destructive rage – the all-consuming wild-fire as the Buddhist texts describe it – which periodically possessed him and came near to destroying him. Rinchen worried about the children – 'I had to make them understand that their father loved them, that when he was angry and impatient he needed help not blame. The important thing was for us to work through these difficult times together, to discuss everything, share all the problems. And in fact he does deserve a lot of credit – he worked terribly hard on overcoming his problem after he resigned.'[2]

In January 1989 the Tenth Panchen Lama died. Since his release from prison in 1978 the Panchen had abandoned celibacy, married a Chinese woman in Peking and had a daughter by her. Publicly, he toed the party line, but the Chinese no longer trusted him. In 1985 they allowed him to visit Lhasa for the twentieth anniversary celebrations of the Tibet Autonomous Region, but though they did their best to hide the true state of affairs from him, the Panchen was not deceived. Seeing the sufferings of the Tibetans, he took up their cause with Peking: protesting about the degradation of the environment, the destruction of Tibetan culture and the devastating effect of large-scale immigration by the Han Chinese. When misery exploded into protest in 1987, he deplored the torture and the killings, and as the Chinese introduced ever more repressive measures to keep the Tibetans down, he insisted that such policies would invite catastrophe. He warned other Tibetans to be wary. When Gyalo Thondup, for example, met him in Peking, 'He was circumspect when the Chinese were present, but when we were alone, do you know what he advised me? "Gyalo-la," he said, "think very hard before you agree to let the Dalai Lama return. You mustn't let him go back to Tibet." He was warning me not to fall into the Chinese trap.'[3]

When the Panchen Lama returned to Tibet in January 1989 for a special ceremony at his home monastery of Tashilhunpo, it was known that before leaving Peking he had had a showdown with the Communist leaders. What benefits had the Chinese ever brought to Tibet, he had demanded to know at a high-level meeting, hitting the table hard with his clenched fist? 'Take away my chair [i.e. in the Chinese National People's Congress],' he taunted the officials. 'It doesn't matter. My real position has nothing to do with you. It is not yours to take or give.'[4] In Tibet itself, at a meeting attended by Chinese officials, he went further – and probably sealed his death warrant. Whatever benefits the Chinese may have brought, he said, were not worth the terrible price the Tibetans had had to pay. A week later, seemingly in excellent health, he was at Tashilhunpo to consecrate a new *stupa* to the memory of past Panchen Lamas. After a party that evening for the workers who had built it, he retired early to bed. Next morning, as the assembled monks waited for him to perform the consecration, news came that he had died during the night. A heart attack, commiserated the Chinese. Nobody believed them.

Kundun was invited to attend the funeral in Peking, but refused. He knew that now the Panchen Lama had gone, the Chinese would be more intractable than ever. He also foresaw trouble ahead, when the time came to seek the reincarnation of the dead Panchen. How could the Chinese fail to exploit that situation for their own political ends?

In May 1990, as martial law in Lhasa was replaced by an even more punitive civilian regime, Kundun took another small step towards democracy for his people in exile. History was made when forty-six elected members of the Tibetan Assembly from all over the Tibetan diaspora came to Dharamsala to elect a new Kashag – the very first time that it had not been chosen by Kundun himself. He was impatient that the changes were still only skin-deep. 'We should be drawing up a document about electing the People's Deputies themselves more democratically, as well as allowing them to appoint the Cabinet,' he told me on that historic day, adding his long-felt hope that one day the Tibetans would accept that he himself is dispensable. 'The Tibetans,' he said ruefully, 'conceive of the Dalai Lama as the ultimate and necessary ruler of Tibet, but they will have to stop thinking like that. Otherwise we shall never have a truly democratic system. I have told them that I will remain as their leader as long as we are in exile, but when we have achieved our freedom, then I will no longer participate in Government. They must learn to do without me.'⁵ (In the following year, the Deputies reluctantly agreed to accept that one day their Supreme Ruler might be edged out. 'We actually took the clause out,' admits Tendzin Choegyal, who had emerged from his hibernation to be elected to the Assembly, 'but he made us put it back in, insisting that without it there would never be any democracy.')

One of those elected to the Kashag was Pema. It was an honour that she would have preferred to forego. She rushed up to the Private Office to explain that she did not want to be a Kalon, and had no aptitude for officialdom. It was explained to her that for the first time in the history of Tibet a woman had been elected to the Kashag, and she must rise to the occasion. In a panic, she rang her husband, Tempa Tsering, in Bangalore, and he counselled her to accept. She could always resign later if it didn't work out, he suggested.

On 12 May, Pema, with two other elected ministers, took the oath as the new Minister of Education. 'To be honest, I was very tense and unhappy,' she said. 'I had to read a text in Tibetan, and that terrified me. I wasn't familiar enough with the Tibetan script – I read English much more easily – and I made lots of mistakes.' Outside, a huge crowd waited to congratulate her and festoon her with white felicitation scarves. 'But I felt more like crying. I wanted to tell them that they'd made a bad choice, just when Tibet was facing such terrible problems. I knew nothing about politics, my skills were all in the field.' Though many of her former pupils wrote to say how happy they were about her election, she herself was wretched.

Matters went from bad to worse. On her first day in the Kashag office, she was horrified to find that all the documents were in Tibetan script, and she needed help to read them. Once they had been translated for her, she was able to reflect carefully on their contents, but she knew very well that she was a misfit. Instead of the hands-on work she excelled in at the TCV, she now had administrative responsibility for the education of all the children in exile, for the TCV itself, the Tibetan Homes Foundation, and the schools run jointly with the Indian Government.

A year later, she offered her resignation, but Kundun refused it, saying: 'We need you.'

In May 1991, Pema contacted Gyalo Thondup and asked him to break his three-year silence and advise Kundun on how things stood with China. The Assembly, meanwhile, celebrated its new freedom by electing GT to the Kashag. 'For some years,' says Kundun, 'the Assembly had been wanting my brother to be given more responsibility, to be given Cabinet rank, but I did not respond.'[6] Now, however, the decision was theirs to make. As Phuntsog Wangyal, one of the delegates, explains, 'It seemed that whenever something important was happening, like negotiations with China, suddenly GT would be on the scene – appearing out of nowhere. We never quite understood how it happened, he was supposed to be just a businessman in Hong Kong. None of us dared ask too many questions, but it was obvious he had important political connections. Within the Assembly, when things went wrong with China, everyone blamed GT, but if things went well, the Tibetan Government took the credit. Some of us decided it was time to stop using GT as a convenient whipping-boy. We should either ignore him altogether or give him a responsible position within the Government. So we brought him into the Kashag.'

Gyalo Thondup felt trapped. He was aware that he knew very little about the affairs of Tibet-in-exile, that in fact he did not really know many individual Tibetans. At first he thought of refusing the Kashag position, but he realized that if he did so many people would be upset. So he came to Dharamsala to test the waters – and decided to accept.

From the outset, he had many enemies in the Assembly. Over the years of negotiations, the Chinese had made not a single concession to Tibet, yet here he was, still advocating making a deal with them, at the expense of Tibetan independence. He had actually urged Tibetans to give up all claims to independence and return to Tibet to work things out. The trouble was that many, possibly most, of the ordinary Tibetans in exile still almost worshipped GT, both because of his past work for the Resistance and as His Holiness's older brother, the secular head of the Yapshi Taklha family. These people found it hard to believe that GT was not the authentic mouthpiece of Kundun, so anyone daring to oppose him must automatically be 'against the Dalai Lama'. While GT was fighting his corner in the Kashag, a rent-a-mob of students from the school for new arrivals from Tibet at Bir in the Kangra Valley was trucked in to Dharamsala, carrying placards and banners, and wearing head-bands proclaiming 'WE LOVE GYALO'. At the same time, there was an outbreak of fighting at Bir, with pro- and anti-Gyalo Thondup factions slogging it out with knives, rocks, sticks and even axes. The school had to be closed down for several months.

In 1992, while visiting the USA, Gyalo Thondup infuriated Tibetan exiles there by publicly berating them for their boycotts of Chinese goods and their campaign to have China's Most Favoured Nation status cancelled. If China lost its MFN status, said GT, forty thousand Chinese would lose their jobs in Guangdong Province alone. Since he believed Tibetan Independence to be a mere pipe-dream, he urged that a deal should be worked out as quickly as possible with the present Chinese administration. The resulting furore was predictable, but the Tibetans in the USA and Canada whose letters of protest were published in the Tibetan press, were threatened with violence and arson by those who supported GT.

A Commission was set up in Dharamsala to investigate GT's outrageous statements, but no one really believed it would get anywhere. The dangers of opposing GT were underlined when Pema Bhum, a writer recently arrived from Amdo, was accused of 'opposing the *dharma*' and received serious death threats. He had urged the students at Bir to stay out of factional politics, and at a public meeting of Amdowas had been the sole dissenter to a decision to withdraw from the democratic process altogether if the commission investigating GT were not called off. (When the present author asked GT about his supporters' tactics, he replied soothingly, 'Some of them behave quite badly, I agree. Our people don't always understand how complicated everything is, and besides there will always be some people determined to use a situation for their own ends.'[7]) In the end, the investigating commission crawled out of its responsibilities, clearing GT unreservedly, claiming that his remarks (which certainly did not represent Tibetan Government policy) were simply 'personal opinions'. 'Gyalo Thondup,' reflects a critic, 'affects a somewhat Olympian attitude in matters of statecraft, coolly making public statements absolutely contrary to Tibetan Government policies – and getting away with it.'[8]

In his last few months in office, Gyalo Thondup arranged talks with the Chinese leadership in both Taipei and Peking. He took two officials with him to Taipei and three to Peking. Incredibly, none of them spoke Chinese, the language in which the negotiations were conducted. 'This,' wrote Jamyang Norbu at the time, 'has raised the suspicion among many, including, I understand, the aides themselves, that the participation of these three officials was nothing more than window-dressing for Tibetan public opinion, behind which GT once again did exactly as he pleased.'[9]

Kundun admits that he has frequently been embarrassed by the behaviour of his maverick elder brother. By 1993, he had come to accept that his efforts to initiate a dialogue with the Chinese had been misplaced. Speaking at the Tibetan Institute of Performing Arts in April 1993, he admitted that absolutely no headway had been made. That on the contrary Chinese overtures actually concealed an insidious long-term plan for ensuring the end of Tibetans as a distinct nation and people. Tibet now faced its greatest danger in the ever-increasing immigration of Chinese into Tibet, and he called on all Tibetans to do everything they could to combat this threat.[10]

In the end, GT had to go. 'He did some good things, but he also made many mistakes. He is stubborn and he creates controversy wherever he goes,' says Kundun wearily. 'He ended by offering his resignation and I accepted it.'[11] 'He'd failed and knew he'd failed,' says Tendzin Choegyal. 'The game was up for him. I think he was manipulated by the Chinese. He took their bait, without even knowing that it was a bait.'

He resigned. Yet his brief reign in the Kashag was not all loss, claims Phuntsog Wangyal. 'It worked in a way, because for the first time in his life GT had to explain himself, had to be accountable. That was one of our achievements. He had to face parliamentary criticisms and we made him justify his actions. Previously he'd always got away with everything.'[12] By this time, Pema too had gone. In 1992 she had tried again to resign, again in vain. But in the following July she took matters into her own hands and sent a written letter of resignation to Kundun – 'in English, the language I know best'. Kundun accepted defeat and she returned with gratitude to her own world of the TCV. She was succeeded as Minister of Education by Tendzin Choegyal's wife, Rinchen Khando, who, as Minister of Health, had been the second woman to be elected to the Kashag.

Gyalo Thondup still believes he was much misunderstood. His two years in office in Dharamsala were blighted, he claims, by the feuding within the Tibetan community, by the regional divisions which both the Chinese and certain Indian politicians were all too ready to exploit. 'The Chinese do exploit the rivalry,' he says, 'they send funds to certain groups. And the Indians also have a finger in the pie. You see, neither China nor

India wants to see a strong set-up in Dharamsala, because then the Dalai Lama would be difficult for them to manipulate. They prefer to keep us semi-conscious rather than fully awake.' He is adamant that he resigned for health reasons – he has diabetes – and because he was exhausted. At the same time, he admits to having been 'very fed up. We're supposed to be here for a purpose, we're meant to be thinking about going back to Tibet. People in Tibet have a terribly low standard of living and we should be thinking of how to improve it when we go back. We give little thought to the education of Tibetans in Tibet. We are just wasting time.' His voice, already animated, rises dramatically. 'For the last few years I've been telling them, His Holiness is getting old, I'm getting old, our days are numbered and the Chinese are waiting for us to die. We must achieve something solid before His Holiness dies. If we don't, we shall become like the hundreds and thousands of Tibetans on the south side of the Himalayas, most of whom are by now hybrids, half-Indian, half-Tibetan. Our younger people here are going the same way. We must persuade some of them to return to Tibet, to make a contribution towards educating their fellow Tibetans. And we *must* try and deal with China. Even if we don't want to, we have to. But when I say this kind of thing, they accuse me of being pro-Chinese. It's a no-win situation – the trouble is the Chinese think I don't see their point of view at all.'[13]

GT, it may be surmised, has not yet spoken his last word on the subject. Meanwhile the stalemate continues.

NOTES
1. Author interview with HH the Dalai Lama, June 1994.
2. Author interview with Rinchen Khando, October 1993.
3. Author interview with Gyalo Thondup, New Delhi, July 1995.
4. Article in the *Far Eastern Review*, 1 June 1995, 'Designation of Panchen Lama stirs a storm', by Lincoln Kaye in Peking and Vijay Kranti in New Delhi.
5. Author interview with HH the Dalai Lama, May 1990.
6. Author interview with HH the Dalai Lama, June 1994.
7. Author interview with Gyalo Thondup, Delhi, July 1995.
8. Jamyang Norbu, 'Some Observations on the Independence Controversy' in *Lungta* 7. This article is the source of the above information.
9. Author interview with HH the Dalai Lama, June 1994.

10. HH the Dalai Lama speaking to TIPA, April 1993.
11. Author interview with HH the Dalai Lama, June 1994.
12. Author interview with Phuntsog Wangyal, February 1996.
13. Author interview with Gyalo Thondup, July 1995.

27

A Role for the Yapshi?

It appears the Chinese have won now
But the Dalai Lama still waits
in Time's vast momentariness
and in its infiniteness
for truth to triumph
From a poem by Professor
U. R. Ananthamurthy[1]

Tibetans do not set much store by birthdays, few of them being sure of when exactly they were born. But on 6 July 1995, wherever they were in the diaspora, they celebrated the sixtieth birthday of the Dalai Lama. The Yapshi were no exception: the whole family, brothers, sister, nephews, nieces, cousins and their spouses met in Dharamsala to celebrate the occasion with a special Long Life liturgy in Kundun's private temple. (There were, sadly, a few missing faces: Tsering Dolma, Lobsang Samten, GT's wife and daughter, and, most recently, Tenzin Ngawang. The latter, living in the States, had neglected his health to a degree that suggested he was weary of living, and early in 1994 his condition had worsened. Phuntsok Tashi brought him back home to Dharamsala, where he died a few months later.)

There was a larger shadow over the birthday celebrations that July. Relations with China had recently taken a nose-dive over what can only be called the Case of the Two Panchen Lamas. Briefly, what happened was this. Since the death of the Tenth Panchen Lama in 1989, all help offered by Kundun in the search for the next reincarnation had been rejected by the Chinese as 'outside interference'. Gyalo Thondup, as usual, was on the scene. 'I had kept on raising this issue with various Ministers,' he says,[2] 'requesting them to advise the Chinese leadership about the right procedures to be followed. These procedures, I told the Chinese, must be undertaken with the knowledge of His Holiness, otherwise there would be a lot of misunderstandings.' In 1993, the action accelerated. 'In July, Chatral Rinpoche, the Abbot of Tashilhunpo Monastery and Chairman of the Chinese Government's Selection Committee, came to Beijing to see me and gave me a letter for His Holiness. I brought the letter to India. In the letter, Chatral Rinpoche asked His Holiness for prayers and help in the search for the new Panchen Lama. The signs, he said, indicated that the reincarnation had already taken place – in Tibet. His Holiness immediately asked the Chinese to allow Chatral Rinpoche to come to India for discussions. I handed that letter personally to the Chinese Ambassador in Delhi. It was ignored.'

Over the next two years, Kundun made several attempts to discuss the matter with the Chinese, but in vain.

Meanwhile the search went on, with around thirty names of possible candidates being submitted from inside and outside Tibet. After a number of tests, oracles and divinations, Kundun finally chose six-year-old Gendun Choekyi Nyima as the authentic reincarnation. And on 13 May 1995, it was decided to go public with the recognition. Gyalo Thondup takes up the story:

On 13 May, His Holiness's Secretary telephoned me about the decision to make the announcement on the 14th. I was instructed to tell the Chinese. It was Saturday, and the 14th therefore was a Sunday. This presented me with a very big problem, since on the Sunday all the offices would be closed, and although I had a hot line to various Ministers, I didn't have their home telephone numbers. It took me hours to find the numbers and get through to them. When I did, they were all absolutely furious. They shouted at me, saying that His Holiness had not consulted the Chinese Government and was playing politics. They insisted he was breaking the rule whereby in former times the Emperor (and now the Chinese Government) had the final say in the selection. And so on. I told them to calm down – we'd tried to consult them at every step of the way, I said, but they'd always ignored us. I said it was unfair of them to suggest that His Holiness was playing politics – he was under a lot of pressure from the lamas in both Tibet and India, pushing him to make a decision, and if he was really playing politics, wouldn't he have selected a boy from India, instead of one from Nagchuka with whom he could have no contact?...'Anyway,' I said, 'you're all atheists, you don't believe in any of this, so why should you care about selecting the Panchen Lama?' They went on being angry, but they were worried men. They knew they'd got themselves into a mess and didn't know how to get out of it. I warned them to be very careful how they handled the situation. 'If you handle this badly,' I said, 'you'll become a laughing stock in the eyes of the world. People have heard about the search for the Panchen Lama, they're watching you.' They didn't take any notice, of course. On 17 May, they began reviling His Holiness and blackening his name.³

On 18 May, Chatral Rinpoche was arrested and flown to Peking, charged with having been in contact with the Dalai Lama over the matter. A new wave of repression and intimidation hit Tibet, with a ban on gatherings of more than three or four people and another on any discussion about the Panchen Lama's reincarnation. Over fifty monks and laypeople were detained in custody.⁴ Monks and nuns were confined to their monasteries, and religious leaders were forced to prepare written and oral statements denouncing the Dalai Lama and Chatral Rinpoche. The six-year-old reincarnation and his parents were taken from their home to Peking, and have not been heard of since.

In November, the Chinese men-in-suits chose another six-year-old, Gyaltsen Norbu, whose parents just happened to be Communist cadres. He was selected by the Golden Urn method at the Jokhang Temple in Lhasa and installed as the Eleventh Panchen at Tashilhunpo monastery in the presence of monks who had been coerced into attending. He too was then spirited away to Peking. Doubtless, the Chinese will take no chances with him – they will not risk a repetition of what happened with his predecessor. Given the fact that the Dalai and Panchen Lamas have to recognize each other's reincarnations – a tradition the Chinese were quite happy to ignore in the present instance – he is their passport to the future, a watertight guarantee that, when the present Dalai Lama dies, Tibet will become truly theirs. If this Fourteenth Dalai Lama finally declares, as he well may, that he is the last of his line, then, if all goes to plan, the Chinese puppet Panchen will be the undisputed – if captive – ruler of the land they call the Western Treasure House.

In Dharamsala for the birthday celebrations in July, GT aired his general sense of frustration. 'There are too many people here who think they're somebody,' he accuses. 'I'm always telling them we're nobodies, vagabonds, beggars, who need one day to go back to Tibet and must be ready.' He recalls the words of an old Chinese friend, a businessman from Shanghai and close friend of Jiang Ze-min, the Chinese Premier. 'This old man said to me, "You Tibetans are very naïve. The Chinese Communists are just waiting, counting the days till the Dalai Lama dies. When he does, the Tibetans are finished. Whatever has to be done must be done *now*, while he is still alive. Gyalo-la, don't miss the opportunity.' Gyalo Thondup takes the warning seriously. Tibet is always on his mind, but the conclusion he arrives at is that its future is bound up with China. He has obviously discussed the question at the highest levels in the Chinese leadership, in a way that must surely alarm the Tibetans. 'I told them, if I come back to China, I will participate in the Government, but I will not be a rubber-stamp. There have been enough puppets in our history – don't expect His Holiness and myself to be rubber-stamps for you. If you want Tibet to remain part of China you must treat us as equals. For a start, we want the whole Tibetan-speaking area – Amdo, Kham and Central Tibet – to be reunified.'

It is this sort of talk, off-the-top-of-his-head, over-confident, arrogant, bombastic, that maddens the Tibetans and not only those who hold to the idea of independence-or-nothing. To them, particularly the younger ones, it illustrates that Gyalo Thondup is out of touch with his own people, that he thinks like a Chinese and to all intents and purposes *is* Chinese. The criticisms sadden his sister, Pema, for whom GT has always been both fa-ther-figure and friend. 'He had so much to offer the Tibetan cause, and at the time when we most needed help, we had much cause to be grateful to him,' she sighs. But she cannot deny that GT, with his high-handedness and craving for power, has always been his own worst enemy. 'He's so stubborn, he won't listen to anybody else. So of course, he's made many enemies.' 'He thinks,' says a normally placid observer, 'that he's the only person who can solve the Tibetan problem and that he must solve it before he dies.'

GT, sixty-eight now and disillusioned with Tibetans and Chinese alike, has put himself on the back-burner once again – resuming his role of mys-tery man and 'China-watcher' in Hong Kong. 'I've told the Chinese Minis-ters I'm not going back to Beijing unless they can come up with some

positive suggestions.' He did not hesitate to lay the blame for the continuing stalemate on Deng Xiao-ping and his closest cronies, though he knew
well that one day he might pay for such outspokenness. 'If Deng is still
alive when the Chinese take over Honk Kong,' he said cheerfully, 'he'll
probably have my head.'

Two years later, Deng is dead – and the situation in China is wide open.
GT may be in less danger of losing his head, but he is tired and has once
again 'categorically retired'. Then, lest anyone should think that is his
final word, he hastens to qualify it. 'Of course,' he says, 'if His Holiness
were to ask me to come back again, how could I refuse?'[5]

Norbu takes a more long-term view of the situation than his brother. 'If
we talk to the Chinese,' he says, 'it should be as equals, not with China
dictating the terms. I know what the Chinese are like. We Tibetans
shouldn't yield an inch on regaining our independence. We have to have
the hope of returning one day, but who knows when? Maybe in ten years
time, maybe a hundred, maybe not for several generations.'[6] Tibetans who
share this viewpoint must prepare themselves for a long struggle, the outcome of which they will not live to see. 'I'm retired now,' Norbu shrugs
patiently, as if to underline his attitude. 'I just pull up the weeds. Well, I
pull them up one day and next day they're back.' It is true that most of his
life is now spent quietly. He lives on the premises of a Centre for Religious
Studies which he started after his retirement in 1987. 'He is a very spiritual person and very simple,' comments Tendzin Choegyal. 'The very fact
that he hasn't come up with some fancy Dharma Centre in the States
speaks volumes. He could have commanded a huge following, but he was
strong-minded enough to resist the temptation.'

Certainly Norbu is too honest and blunt to be a politician, and he too
makes enemies among the Tibetans. 'They think I'm a reactionary,' he
says, 'I come on a bit too strong for their tastes.' But he has the courage of
his convictions. On 16 March 1995, this 75-year-old patriot with a pace-
maker completed a 'Trek for Tibet', walking 75 miles through rural Indiana to draw attention to his country's plight. Addressing a press
conference afterwards, he did not pull his punches. 'The time for negotiat-
ing with the thief, that is the Chinese Government, has passed,' he asserted. 'We Tibetans must stand up and loudly state, CHINA, GET OUT OF
TIBET. We must also shout TIBET MUST BE INDEPENDENT. He professed

his solidarity with Kundun. 'I do not advocate violence,' he said, while emphasizing the need for a tough approach. 'I speak for justice that is grounded in compassion. We must be more aggressive when fighting the Chinese Government – not with military weapons of destruction, but with political, legal and economic weapons.' Announcing the formation of a new International Tibetan Independence Movement with himself as Chairman, Norbu promised that in the following year he would march from Washington DC to the UN Building in New York. 'Until then,' he pleaded, 'I call upon all Tibetans to speak up and listen to their teacher, the Great Compassionate One, His Holiness, the Fourteenth Dalai Lama. Tell my brother what you think. Take more personal responsibility for Tibet's future. Our greatest danger is that we Tibetans will become too comfortable in exile, and will forget that we ever had our own country. Our strength lies in our wisdom, our generosity, our ability to act. Fight for justice with compassion in your heart, and Tibet will be independent once again.'[7]

Exactly a year later, 76-year-old Norbu completed the 25-day march from Washington to New York. Before leaving Washington, he stood outside the city's Chinese Embassy to address a large crowd:

> I am very pleased to speak to you today where the diplomats and agents of the People's Republic of China can hear us and see us. It is important that we speak up here, so that people inside the Chinese Embassy can know that no matter what methods they use to suppress the desires of the Tibetan people, the Tibetan struggle for independence will always continue. It will not end until the legitimate hopes and desires, that is, their inalienable right to independence, not some sort of 'autonomy' within China, is eventually realized.

He ended with a passionate peroration:

> We cannot and will not fly half of the Tibetan flag. Our entire flag must be flown all over the world, including at the United Nations. We will not occupy one-half of a seat at the United Nations. We have the right to a full seat.[8]

'The important thing for Norbu,' says Phuntsog Wangyal, who himself holds this view and believes that His Holiness secretly does too, 'is that this Dalai Lama should not put his seal of approval on anything less than total independence. He must not go down in history as the Dalai Lama who gave away Tibet. Norbu loves him too much to let that happen, and so do I.'[9]

As might be expected, the women of the Yapshi family are involved less with rhetoric than with the day-to-day business of nurture and survival. Pema, having completed over thirty years service in the Tibetan Children's Villages, still lives in Dharamsala in a school that is literally the size of a village, with twelve hundred residential pupils and about one hundred day scholars; and caring for ten thousand more Tibetan children throughout the diaspora. To mark her thirty year achievement, in 1994 the National Assembly gave her the official title of Amala, Mother of Tibet. She often thinks back to those early days when there was no money, no staff, no equipment, no food, no clothing, no shelter – and realizes that the threat now is of a different order. 'Nowadays our problem is how to educate our young, how to bring them up as true Tibetans, what values we should be trying to instil into their minds. We *must* maintain our culture, our identity as Tibetans must not be lost and it is the children who will preserve it. They are the seed-grains of the future. But how to preserve our identity in the face of outside pressures and influences? It's not a question of whether we have slanty eyes or wear Tibetan dress, our Tibetan-ness has to be interior. We have a special culture: we take whatever happens, however awful, in our stride – and we go on smiling. How do we get our children to understand that?'[10]

Khando has temporarily left the scene – partly to prevent burn-out and partly to provide herself and her family with a breathing-space (and a College education for their daughters). She and Rapten are in America, in Utah. She had returned to Dharamsala in 1987, knowing in her heart that she would never make it there. 'When I returned I was asked to work at the Council for Home Affairs as Additional General Secretary, and I plunged into it headlong, determined to make a go of it. But I was up against a lot of male chauvinists – small-time politicians who stay alive by manipulating the weaknesses of a society – and an enormous amount of prejudice. I was too independent, too outspoken, too impatient with their out-dated Anglo-Indian bureaucracy, too Western in my attitudes – and, worst of all, a WOMAN! Then I became General Secretary of Information and International Relations and when that didn't work out, certain people were so keen to take over my job that I did not even get the chance to clear my desk! I'd had enough. The fight had gone out of me.'

Rapten's parents had died, their children were growing up. Working in the Government service for all those years, they had made no money and had no independent means. Kundun had occasionally stepped in to help with the children's education, but both she and Rapten felt that the time had come to move on, to emigrate. 'We agonized over the decision,' says Khando, 'alone, together, with relatives and friends. But when Rapten filled in the immigration forms, I knew His Holiness would know that I too was leaving. When I went to break the news to him I felt very sad, as though I was letting him and the family down by breaking away from all the things I had worked so hard for in the last thirty odd years. If he was disappointed, he did not show it, but I know he understood and felt my unhappiness, as he used the intimate form of address he has always used with me and said "Yes, I know, and I understand completely." I had to struggle not to cry, it was a very emotional moment. Later on, of course, when I was already in the States and went to meet him, he joked about it. "Well," he teased, "the consumer society obviously agrees with you. You've put on a lot of weight."

Khando and Rapten both have found jobs in the Utah Valley State College, advising American and foreign students, working with the faculty and staff to internationalize the campus. There are about sixty Tibetans in the Salt Lake City area – 'all the immigrants keep in touch and help and support each other'. Their own house is always full of people, their own and the children's many friends, and a constant stream of relatives and visiting friends. Khando swears that they come in the first place out of simple curiosity as to why the Chazotsangs chose to come to Utah!

'Life's odd, isn't it?' she muses. 'Here was this Tibetan girl, whose parents were born into a farming family in Amdo, then were elevated to become the highest family in the land, surrounded by every luxury and privilege. Then she was sent away from home and put into an Irish Roman Catholic convent...A refugee in India, despatched to England to lead another kind of privileged life. Then back again among the Tibetans, the hard, hard work, the traumas of learning about the torture and death in Tibet, the frustration and the anger. And finally, fetching up in Salt Lake with many more friends, some of whom are wonderful Mormons. Everything in that Tibetan girl's life has enlarged her horizons and added depth to her experience.'

What has belonging to the Yapshi family meant to her? 'Well, it's a privilege, of course. A privilege and a great joy to be related to such a great, compassionate and marvellous person as the Dalai Lama. But it's also a responsibility and sometimes a heartache. If I hadn't been a Yapshi, I might not have had the opportunities I was given, but then people can sometimes accuse you of being too much of a Yapshi, when that is simply not true...I used to be embarrassed by the adulation, I used to plead with people not to prostrate to me. That sort of thing somehow seemed demeaning to everybody concerned, although I know it was done out of respect for His Holiness. The latter is always reminding us to practise compassion in our lives at every moment, and to try and put others before self. I'm trying very hard to do that – because it makes a lot of sense to me.'

And what of Tendzin Choegyal, still known to most of his compatriots as Ngari Rinpoche and venerated accordingly? The veneration irritates and unsettles him. 'Sooner or later,' he says, 'people will find out it was all a mistake.' He really does not believe in the *tulku* system, and finds the present mania for creating new ones distasteful. 'I think it appeals to people who don't really know what Buddhism is about,' he complains. 'It's a kind of spiritual materialism. Real Buddhism means interior change, but no one wants to be bothered with that.'

On Kundun's insistence, he has been back again to Ladakh, since his breakdown eight years ago. 'His Holiness says I am Ngari Rinpoche whether I like it or not, whether I believe it or not, and I must accept that. He tells me, "Forget about the religious side of things if you must, just go and advise them on practical matters. And if they ask you about the spiritual life, just tell them what you can." The trouble is, I can't be what they want me to be: a colourful personality dressed in exotic robes, sitting on an ornate throne and mouthing a lot of nothings. When I go there, I feel I'm expected to be some kind of Moses, even if they see me driving a Land Rover rather than a camel. But I can't be. They think themselves blessed because I'm Ngari Rinpoche and I'm there with them, but they don't really understand a word I say. It's what I said earlier: true Buddhism has nothing to do with blind faith, it is about transforming the mind.'

Even Kundun is surprised by the intensity of his younger brother's search for the spiritual life these days. Seeking a deeper meaning in life is, he claims, all that really matters; he has no other ambition. Sometimes he thinks he would like to look after the mentally ill or mentally handicapped or the depressed, but most of all he would like to be some kind of contemplative. With his love of people, his capacity to immerse himself in their lives, he would have to be an extremely mobile contemplative, with time off for stimulating conversation. One writer on Tibet commented that 'many who have been fortunate enough to have long conversations with him are convinced that he is actually one of the best teachers that they have ever encountered'.[11] Many friends would echo that, but, with few exceptions, they would probably be Westerners. Tendzin Choegyal is a born-again Westerner, fully convinced that in no previous life could he have been Tibetan.

With his own people, he is frequently at odds. Partly it is the old goldfish bowl syndrome, the constantly being in the public eye, the object of envy and sometimes of malice. Partly it is his own inability to suffer fools gladly, his intolerable desire for things to be as they should be and manifestly are not. Nowhere were these two strands more in evidence than during the five years he served as a member of the National Assembly. 'His impatience and high-handedness earn him many enemies,' reflects his friend, Tenzin Geyche. 'He loses his temper easily and people get hurt. Then, of course, they think he's arrogant and spoiled. Those who remember his father in Lhasa think that Tendzin Choegyal inherited even more of his bad temper than the others.'[12] Tendzin Choegyal did not enjoy his five years in the Assembly and will not be standing for re-election. He is scathing about the experience: 'It's chaotic,' he says, 'they fight over small issues and disregard the more important ones. Essentially they do nothing at all.'

Because he cares so deeply about the *dharma*, it angers him that many of the monks and nuns in the Tibetan community seem not to care about it at all. There are far too many monks, he claims – adding that His Holiness has said so too. 'The majority of monks and nuns in our community seem to do nothing but wear the robes. They don't seem to have the faintest idea that a monk is supposed to be on the path to becoming a realized being.' Tenzin Geyche tries to soften the tirade, though by and large he too agrees. 'Some of the younger ones are a disgrace,' he admits. 'They don't understand the vocation they have chosen and some of them behave very badly indeed. When you see monks going out to watch videos, riding motorbikes, standing around on street corners and going with women, that's very bad. But the picture isn't quite as black as Rinpoche makes out. There are still many very holy and excellent monks about.'

Though Tendzin Choegyal is frequently depressed, three things save him from total despair. One is an impish sense of humour that endears him to his many friends and rarely deserts him, except perhaps in the darkest moments. The second is his closeness to Kundun, the brother he resembles in so many ways, and whom he loves, admires and respects above all other human beings. To some extent, Choegyal is Kundun's right-hand man, or as the latter describes him, his 'man of action', practical and talented in many directions, an engineer or perhaps an inventor *manqué*. It is said that before he died, the Great Thirteenth wrote to his friend and fellow-student, the Fifteenth Ngari Rinpoche, 'In our next incarnations, we shall be very much closer to each other.' There is no denying the special relationship between the two brothers, alike in their ideas, their interests and in their engaging capacity for laughter. ('Kundun is many people in one person,' says Choegyal typically, 'someone from whom I receive great teachings, political guidance, personal encouragement, and occasionally a few rockets.')

The third and most important saving grace is his increasing dependence on the *dharma*. This is reflected in a poem he has written:

He [the Buddha] gave us the gift
of the path called *dharma*
that opens our eyes
to perceive the world with joy.[13]

And lastly to Kundun himself. In his sixties now, he seems to have the energy and dynamism of one half his age. He is a seemingly inexhaustible ambassador for his country, jetting across the world with breathtaking frequency, yet emerging from these marathons with his famous smile, plunging instantly into the talks and teachings demanded of him. These days in the West, he has become almost a cult figure, taken up by a host of famous actors, directors and politicians. Yet, although the Western media like occasionally to debunk him as a fashionable, trendy guru, those who come to scoff often stay to admire. In a *Sunday Times* article featuring the Dalai Lama in a gallery of men with 'allure', its author's conclusions were less glib than might have been expected. 'I once heard him give a talk on "The Virtues of Compassion",' wrote the journalist,[14] 'and, although I had come with a sceptical attitude, I found myself getting more and more wise and compassionate by the minute.' Here, she decided, was 'one of the saintliest men in the world'.

Kundun is hopeful that the democracy he has tried so hard to introduce to his people in exile has at last taken root, though he knows that the real test will come if and when he and his people return to Tibet. The idea that in that event he himself will bow out of any political role is hard for the Tibetans to swallow. They don't quite believe him, but he is determined. 'I have my reasons,' he says, 'and they have nothing to do with any loss of interest in Tibetan affairs.' Meanwhile, he remains the undisputed leader of his people, though, as Tendzin Choegyal says, 'one hundred per cent of our Tibetans hero-worship His Holiness, yet only about ten per cent listen to what he is saying.' Some say that people only tell him what they think he wants to hear and that he does not really know what they are thinking. This is not for want of encouragement on his part, but, as Phuntsog Wangyal says, 'If people speak their minds, they will immediately be cast out by the community, *in his name*. They won't take the risk of that happening.' Kundun agrees that 'very few are willing to speak out against me on certain issues', but claims that 'on most matters they're only too ready to complain'. Meanwhile, he sees many of the young people in exile adopting Western, consumer-orientated values, and worries that what made Tibetans special is fast disappearing.

In spite of everything they have done, he firmly refuses to hate the Chinese – though he admits it's quite a struggle. 'I can curse and rave in private but I do not allow hatred to rise in my heart. I tell myself constantly that whatever the Chinese have done, maybe it is not their fault. If I ever allow myself to believe that such and such a person does not deserve happiness, then my *bodhisattva* vow would be broken.'[15] He tells a story which has moved him deeply, of a monk who came to Dharamsala in 1980 after twenty years in a Chinese prison. In all those years, he told Kundun, the greatest danger he faced was that he might lose his compassion for the Chinese. 'Now, I think that's wonderful,' exclaims Kundun. 'I have the feeling that in his place I'd have let rage engulf me. Either that, or' – and here he bursts into the familiar, sometimes disconcerting gales of laughter – 'I might have done a Yes, Minister, saying yes, yes, of course, oh sure, to whatever the Chinese suggested.' He believes that had he been put to the test he would have been nowhere near as brave as the last Panchen Lama, whom he describes lovingly as 'a true freedom fighter'.

Optimism is strong in him, and he is confident of returning to Tibet within a few years. 'The present totalitarian system cannot last much longer. There will be change, either total collapse or evolutionary change. I hope it will be evolutionary – it'll be less chaotic. If there were to be conflict in that huge country, the bloodshed would be enormous.' His astrological chart tells him that he will live to the age of 122, but his dreams suggest the figure 113. 'I know that's highly unscientific,' he chuckles, adding that he himself thinks he'll live to be ninety. (Which may be some consolation to his bodyguard and to the security personnel provided by the Indian Government to protect a life which is constantly under threat.)

If Kundun does end his days in Tibet, he knows exactly where he will go: the Reting Monastery, home of the disgraced Regent who first discovered him to be the Fourteenth Dalai Lama. 'We passed through there when I was coming from Amdo,' he reminisces, 'and again as we returned from China in 1954. In the main temple, standing in front of the principal statue, I was overcome with a sense of the great teacher who had founded this monastery over one thousand years ago, Drom, disciple of the Indian scholar-saint, Atisha. With that feeling came tears – I cried and cried as though I would never stop. It was one of the most powerful emotional experiences of my whole life, and after it was over I knew I would spend my last days in the little forest surrounding that holy place. I still believe I shall do that.'

It may be that he is too optimistic. Since 1994, when the West stopped putting pressure on China to improve its human rights record, the Chinese have tightened their control over Tibet and declared all-out war on the Dalai Lama. The Tibetan People's Congress openly admits it. 'Let everyone in the Tibetan Autonomous Region understand clearly,' they announced in the spring of 1996, 'that the struggle against the Dalai Lama group is a long-term, bitter, complex, you-die-I-live political battle with no possibility of compromise.'[16] They couldn't say clearer than that. In probably the severest crackdown since the Cultural Revolution, officials throughout Tibet have been ordered 'to fight tooth and nail', against the Dalai Lama, the 'Number One criminal' who is bent on splitting the Chinese Motherland. The Tibetan independence movement is described as a snake, and the Dalai Lama as 'the serpent's head', which must be cut off.[17] Once again all photographic representations of him – and of the authentic Panchen Lama – have been banned. Not only from Government offices and public places, but from monasteries, temples, schools and private homes. From Lhasa come reports of monks and nuns being beaten up – and shot – in struggles with the police over the ban. House-to-house and school-to-school searches have been taking place – and resistance is growing. Fresh waves of unrest threaten to engulf Tibet.

Perhaps even more dangerous in the long term, China's new Tibet policy[18] calls for greater indoctrination of Tibetan children in schools, while urging ever more Chinese to come to Tibet. Tibetan children studying in India and elsewhere have been ordered home. The prognosis is hardly hopeful. But then, the same could have been said of the situation in the Soviet Union and Eastern Europe in 1989. Miracles still do happen. Political change must come to China – and one can only pray that it will not be too late to save Tibet. Must one then agree with Gyalo Thondup that it is better to be pragmatic and seek a serious accommodation with China, making a return from exile possible and assuring some kind of normality for Tibet in the near future? Or should one, like Norbu, insist on nothing less than total liberation, even if it takes ten, twenty, a hundred, even a thousand years? Caught between the polarized views of his elder brothers, the Fourteenth Dalai Lama still seeks the middle way of dialogue and non-violence. Which of them is right will be for history alone to judge.

The Great Thirteenth expressed the hope that in his next incarnation he would have brothers and sisters to help him in his work. His successor has seen that hope richly fulfilled. His siblings – like siblings in any family – may not always see eye to eye with him, and may even differ quite forcefully. But his goals are always their goals and their lives, like his, are dedicated to achieving them. He knows that, whatever the disagreements, the love and the loyalty of his Yapshi family will always be beyond question.

NOTES

1. Published in *Tibetan Bulletin*, January–February 1995.
2. Author interview with GT, New Delhi, July 1995.
3. Author interview with GT, July 1995.
4. See: 'The Panchen Lama: Politics intruding on a religious discovery', DIIR Publications, Dharamsala; and Amnesty International report, 18 January 1996, which used earlier documents: 'Three detained in Panchen Lama controversy', ASA 17/40/95 and 'Crackdown on Tibetan dissent continues', ASA 17/74/95.
5. All the above from author interview with Gyalo Thondup in New Delhi (1995) and Jetsun Pema in Dharamsala (1994).
6. Author interview with Thubten Jigme Norbu, Dharamsala, July 1995.
7. *Today* Press Conference, 16 March 1995, Indianopolis.
8. Reported in *Tibetan Bulletin*, March–April 1996.
9. Author interview with Phuntsog Wangyal, London, 1996.
10. Author interview with Jetsun Pema, Dharamsala, June 1994.

11. Roger Hicks, *Hidden Tibet*, Element Books, 1988.

12. Author interview with Tenzin Geyche Tethong, 1993.

13. Tendzin Choegyal, unpublished poem, 'The New Path', September 1995.

14. Rhoda Koenig, 'Allure Boys', *The Sunday Times*, 12 May 1996.

15. Author interview with HH the Dalai Lama, 1995.

16. Sunanda K. Datta-Ray, 'Diplomacy Key to Beijing's 'war' with Dalai Lama', *The Straits Times* (Singapore) 7 June, 1996.

17. See: 'Cutting off the Serpent's Head: Tightening Control in Tibet 1994–95', Tibet Information Network (London) and Human Rights Watch/Asia (USA), 1996.

18. The Third National Forum for Work on Tibet, held in Peking, July 1994.

Bibliography

Avedon, John, *An Interview with the Dalai Lama*, Littlebird
 Publications, 1980.
——, *In Exile from the Land of Snows*, Michael Joseph, 1984.
Barnett, Robert, & Akiner, Shirin, eds., *Resistance and Reform in Tibet*,
 Hurst, 1994.
Chapman, F. Spencer, *Lhasa the Holy City*, New Delhi, Bodhi Leaves,
 1992 (First published London, 1940).
Craig, Mary, *Tears of Blood: A Cry for Tibet*, HarperCollins 1992; Fount
 Paperbacks 1993.
'Cutting off the Serpent's Head: Tightening Control in Tibet, 1994–95',
 Tibet Information Network and Human Rights
 Watch/Asia, 1996.
Dalai Lama, His Holiness the, *My Land and My People*, New York,
 Potala, 1962.
——, *Freedom in Exile: The Autobiography of the Dalai Lama of Tibet*,
 Hodder & Stoughton, 1990.
——, *HH the Dalai Lama: Speeches, Statements, Articles and Interviews
 1987–95*, Dharamsala, DIIR, 1995.
Dhondup, K., *The Water Bird and Other Years*, New Delhi,
 Rangwang, 1986.
Ford, Robert, *Captured in Tibet*, OUP 1990 (First published by Harrap, 1957).
Goldstein, Melvyn C., *A History of Modern Tibet, 1913–1951: The
 Demise of the Lamaist State*, University of California Press, 1989.
Goodman, Michael Harris, *The Last Dalai Lama*, Shambhala, 1987.
Harrer, Heinrich, *Seven Years in Tibet*, Paladin/Grafton, 1988
 (First published Rupert Hart-Davis, 1953).
Jetsun Pema, *Tibet, Mon Histoire*, Paris, Éditions Ramsay, 1996.
Murphy, Dervla, *Tibetan Foothold*, John Murray, 1966; Pan, 1969.
Norbu, Jamyang, *Warriors of Tibet*, Wisdom, 1979.
——, *Illusion and Reality: Essays on the Tibetan and Chinese Political
 Scene from 1978 to 1989*, Tibetan Youth Congress Books, 1989.

Norbu, Thubten Jigme, with Harrer, Heinrich, *Tibet Is My Country*, Wisdom, 1986.

Norbu, Thubten Jigme, with Turnbull, Colin, *Tibet*, Chatto & Windus, 1969; Penguin, 1976.

Ra, Raghu (photographs), & Perkins, Jane (text), *Tibet in Exile*, Cassell, 1990.

Richardson, Hugh E., *Tibet and its History*, Shambhala, 1984.

Shakabpa, W. D., *Tibet: A Political History*, Potala Books, 1984.

Taring, Rinchen Dolma, *Daughter of Tibet*, John Murray, 1970.

Tucci, Giuseppe, *To Lhasa and Beyond: Diary of the Expedition to Tibet in the year 1928*, Snow Lion Publications, 1983 (first published 1956).

Index

Although Taklha is the Yapshi family name, few of its members actually use it. I have also had a general problem over the use of Tibetan surnames. Some use their second or third given names as a surname, e.g. Choegyal, Norbu, Taklha, Taring; others – even within the same branch of the family – do not use a surname at all. (And among those whose first name is Tenzin, some prefer to spell it thus, others with a 'd'.) I have tried to be consistent, but it is never easy and not always possible, and if in some cases I have made the wrong decision, I can only apologize.

Aeschimann, Dr Charles 236–7
Aeschimann, Danielle, m. Tenzin
    Ngawang, 244, 275
Amala – see Dekyi Tsering, mother
    of Fourteenth Dalai Lama
Amdo (province) 5, 13, 14, 15,
    chapter 3 passim, 60, 64, 84,
    88, 134, 135, 136; fact-finding
    delegations in 309–11, 314;
    under Chinese Communist
    occupation (1949) 135–6, 138,
    182, 185, 186, 195, 322–3;
    world's biggest gulag 318. See
    also Taktser (Amdo), birthplace
    of Fourteenth Dalai Lama
Amdowas in Dharamsala 352
Ami-chiri (Kyeri), Mt 15, 37, 131
Andrugtsang, Gompo Tashi 206,
    208, 238
anti-religious measures in Tibet
    182, 184, 185

Assembly of Tibetan People's
    Deputies 244–5, 253, 349–50,
    362
Atisha (eleventh-century Indian
    holy man) 4, 368
atrocities in Chinese-occupied
    Tibet 185, 195–6, 207–8, 222,
    233–4, 237, 270–2, 322–3,
    342–3
Aufschnaiter, Peter 117, 140
Autonomous Region of Tibet
    (TAR) 186

Baba Yeshi, General 280–1, 297
Barkhor, the 82
Beijing – see Peking
Bell, (Sir) Charles, Political Officer
    in Sikkim, 7, 8n, 97, 101;
    and the Thirteenth Dalai
    Lama 101
Betsang village 107

Bhrikuti, Queen (Nepalese wife of King Songtsen Gampo) 4
Bir 352
Birla House (Mussoorie) 232, 233, 235
Bloomington (Indiana) 245, 276–7, 294
Bodh Gaya 239, 249, 323, 325, 332
bodhisattva 3, 8n, 367
Bomdila (Assam) 227, 228
British India (Government of Great Britain in India) 1, 11, 18, 20, 52n, 61, 67n, 73, 75, 76–7, 107–8, 123, 154n, 172; after 1947 173n
British (later Indian) Trade Mission in Lhasa 61, 70, 76, 81n, 87, 88, 101, 118, 124, 126, 158
Buddha Jayanti (1956) chapter 16 *passim*
Buddhism in Tibet – *see* Mahayana Buddhism
Buxa Duar camp (Bengal) 237–8
Byllakuppe (S. India), refugee settlement 245, 273, 281

Calcutta 130, 133, 134, 150, 159, 172, 190, 191, 192, 201, 202, 204, 250, 259, 265
Caroe, Olaf 78, 81n, 88
Central Intelligence Agency (CIA): and Norbu 159, 201; and Gyalo Thondup 172, 201, 206; and the Tibetan guerrillas 207, 248, 249, 252, 253, 281; and the SFF 252
Chakrata 298
Chamdo 139, 140, 143, 152, 177

Chandzo Jampa, 89, 90
Changseshar (Yapshi house in Lhasa) 85, 113, 114–15, 120
Chapman, F. Spencer 87, 116, 193
Chatral Rinpoche 357, 358
Chazotsang, Khando Tsering (daughter of Tsering Dolma and Phuntsok Tashi): childhood in Lhasa 114–16, 157; and Tsering Dolma 165, 192, 264, 265–7; and Phuntsok Tashi 276; at school in India 150, 161, 190–1, 231, 232, 252; with the Thondups in Darjeeling 190–1, 207, 231; incident at Chinese Embassy, New Delhi (1955) 191; at Buddha Jayanti (1956) 202; greets her refugee family (1959) 231; and further education 265; in Geneva 275; and Kundun 300–1, 338, 363; and Amala 275, 323; and the Mussoorie Homes Foundation 300–1, 337–8; in Dharamsala (1987) 362; in Utah 362–4
Chazotsang, Rapten (m. Khando Tsering) 265, 275, 276, 300, 301, 315, 316, 317, 318, 323, 362, 363
Che la Pass 220
Chenrezig, patron deity of Tibet 3, 69, 96
Chen-yi, Marshal 186
Chiang Chin-wu, General 152, 165, 166–8, 177, 196, 199, 208
Chiang Kai-shek, General 7, 18; and Chinese Communist Party 7, 119; and the Civil War in

China 119, 123, 132, 140; and
Gyalo Thondup 119, 131,
160-1

China, Civil War in 119, 131, 132,
178

China, Imperial 1, 3, 4, 7, 8n, 18,
52n, 140, 165

China, Nationalist (Kuomintang)
13, 14, 18, 20nn, 21n; and
enthronement of Fourteenth
Dalai Lama 76-7, 119, 140

China, People's Republic of (PRC)
134, 135, 138, 140, 141, 146,
151, 153, 175, 206, 341; and
Tenth Panchen Lama 178,
348-9; first National Assembly
in Peking 174; and Tibet 178,
233-4; and the minority races
197n, 336; and the Cultural
Revolution 272, 305; and the
Dalai Lama 155, 272, 305, 343,
344, 368-9; and the Seventeen-
Point Agreement 150-1, 153,
164, 165, 166, 178, 187, 204,
216, 228; and the Lhasa
Uprising chapter 17 passim,
232; and repression in Tibet
during 1980s and 1990s 342-3,
349, 358, 368-9; declared guilty
of genocide 235, 272; and
invasion of India (1962) 251;
after death of Mao 305, 306;
and the fact-finding delegations
to Tibet 308-18; and talks with
Dharamsala 334, 343, 351-4;
and Tibetan Independence 335,
368; and Tiananmen Square
344, 345; and Most Favoured
Nation status 352, 368; and
search for Eleventh Panchen
Lama 356-8

Chinese Communist Party (CCP)
7, 119, 308

Chinese immigrants into Tibet
335, 349, 353, 368

Chinese Mission in Lhasa 18, 116,
134

Chinese People's Liberation Army
(PLA) 130, 132, 135, 137, 138,
139, 140, 143, 153, 162, 164,
166, 207-8, 210, 216, 223, 251

Chodang Phuntsok Nima
(maternal grandfather of
Fourteenth Dalai Lama) 23

Choegyal, Rinchen Khando (m.
Tendzin Choegyal) 183; and
Tendzin Choegyal 283, 285,
294-5, 299, 302; at TCV 295;
and Amala 295-6, 320-1,
322-5; and the Tibetan
Women's Association 340; in
Kashag 353

Choegyal, Tenzin Lodoe (son of
Rinchen Khando and TC) 296,
304, 324-5

Choegyal, Tendzin Choezom
(daughter of Rinchen Khando
and TC) 295, 325

Choekyong Tsering (father of the
Fourteenth Dalai Lama, aka
Gyayap Chenmo, Great Father
and the Kung) 1, 14, 15-19,
23-5, 28-9, 33-5, 36, 45, 48, 50,
54-6, 63, 66, 73, 76, 109,
chapter 7 passim, 115, 117-18;
enters Lhasa 69-71; relations

with the Kashag 106–9, 131; and Reting Rinpoche 98, 108, 116, 120; National Assembly proclamation against 108; at Changseshar 113–15; unexplained death of 120–1, 232

Chou En-lai, Prime Minister of PRC 204, 205, 206, 222

Chö-Yon (priest/patron) relationship 5

Chu Shi-kuei, General 111, 120

Chu-deh, Marshal 132, 141

Chumbi Valley 147, 149

Chungtsi 50

Churkha 23, 25, 26, 35, 47

Chushi Gangdrug (Khampa Resistance Organization) 206, 207, 247–8, 249; and Gyalo Thondup 206, 208, 247–8, 250, 252, 253, 280–1. See also National Volunteer Defence Army

Committee for Tibetan Social Welfare 175, 198, 206–7, 208, 233, 247, 253

Cultural Revolution: in China 305; in Tibet 271–2, 302, 312, 322

Dalai Lama (in general) 54, 68; physical signs of 11, 12, 14, 17, 18; title of (first bestowed by Altan Khan) 5–6; institution of 3–7, 11; 'Great Fifth' restores Potala 96; meaning of the Dalai Lama to Tibetans 3, 11, 147, 219, 350; power struggle after death of Thirteenth 7–8

Dalai Lama, Fourteenth (Lhamo Dhondup, later Tenzin Gyatso, aka Gyalwa Rinpoche and Kundun): search for 3, 11–19; birth and infancy of chapter 5 passim; in Kumbum Monastery 59–62; ransom paid for 61–2; travels from Amdo to Lhasa 62–6; formal acknowledgement of Lhamo Dhondup as Dalai Lama 65–6; enters Lhasa and is installed as Dalai Lama 69–77; initiated as monk 71; in the Norbulingka 72–3, 102–4; enthronement of 74–7; in the Potala 74–9, chapter 8 passim, 124; education programme 100, 123–4, 212; and Regent Taktra 104, 123; and the Kung 105; and the trial of Reting 122–3; and Heinrich Harrer 125–6, 143, 149, 152; and arrival of Taktser Rinpoche in Lhasa 144; enthronement as Head of State 143–4; flight to Chumbi Valley 147–53; and the 1951 Agreement with China 151–2, 187; returns to Lhasa (1952) 153; and the two Prime Ministers 168; in China (1954) 174–83; and Chairman Mao in Peking 178–81; returns to Lhasa via Amdo (1955) 181–3; and the PCART 186–7; attends Buddha Jayanti (1956) 198–205; returns from India to Lhasa (1957) 205; and the Chinese in

Lhasa 199, 208, 210; and the
Lhasa Uprising (1959) 212–17;
and the escape from Lhasa
217–24; welcomed to India
(1959) 227–9, 231–2, 233;
makes statements re Tibet 228,
232, 233, 234; in Mussoorie
232–7, 245; and Nehru
(post-1959) 227, 233, 234; and
his Government-in-Exile 234,
244, 314, 337, 352; and the
refugees in India and Nepal
236–9, 243, 245–6, 261, 273,
336–7; moves to Dharamsala
241–3; and the Nursery 246; at
Thekchen Choeling (from
1968) 287–8; and the guerrillas
196, 208, 296–7; and the fact-
finding delegations to Tibet
308, 314; in USA 341–2; and
the Strasbourg Declaration
343; and the Five-Point Peace
Plan 341–3; wins Nobel Peace
Prize (1989) 345; and the search
for Eleventh Panchen Lama
349, 356–8; and reform 168–9;
and relationship with China
(post-1959) 232, 306–7, 314,
342, 343, 344–5, 353–4, 356–8,
367, 368;
and Amala chapter 5 passim,
115, 205, 273, 320, 323, 325
and democracy 238–9, 244–5,
253, 349–50, 366–7
and Deng Xiao-ping 344
and dharma 127, 210, 288, 367
and future of Tibet 367–8
and Gyalo Thondup 170, 205,
248–9, 306–8, 351, 353, 369
and Jetsun Pema 158, 202–3, 327,
338, 351, 353
and Khando 300–1, 338, 362–3
and Lobsang Samten chapter 8
passim, 109–10, 184, 205, 237,
260, 303–304, 328, 329, 330–1
and non-violence 196, 208, 210,
296–7, 342, 343, 345, 367
and Norbu (Taktser Rinpoche)
159, 205, 235–6, 260, 344, 361,
369
and 'Ponpo' 99, 110, 326
and Tendzin Choegyal, (Ngari
Rinpoche) 180–1, 283, 284,
302, 340, 347, 348, 364, 365–6
and the Tenth Panchen Lama 367
and the tulku system 157
and Tibetan Independence 342,
343, 344–5, 361, 369
and Tsering Dolma 57, 264, 265,
266
and vegetarianism 273
Dalai Lama, Third: Sonam Gyatso
is given title of 5–6
Dalai Lama, Fifth 6, 96, 97, 98
Dalai Lama, Sixth 157
Dalai Lama, Seventh 72
Dalai Lama, Thirteenth
(1876–1933) 1–2, 6–7, 12, 13,
16, 17, 18, 20nn, 30, 42, 51, 61,
62, 68, 73, 97, 100, 101, 124;
and Fifteenth Ngari Rinpoche
155
Darjeeling (India) 101, 149, 154n,
161, 171, 172–3, 190, 207, 229,
238, 246, 253, 259, 283, 285,
Dehra Dun 229, 231, 252, 298

Dekyi Tsering (mother of
Fourteenth Dalai Lama, aka
Gyayum Chenmo, Great
Mother, and Amala) 26, 27, 28,
31, 36–7, 66, 102, 106, 121,
134, 159, 242, 259, 274;
marries Choekyong Tsering
23–5; and birth and childhood
of Lhamo Dhondup 55–8;
journeys from Amdo to Lhasa
63–6; enters Lhasa 69–71; at
the Enthronement 76; as Great
Mother in Lhasa 73, chapter 7
passim, 117; and birth of
Tendzin Choegyal 117; and
three sons as tulkus 156, 283,
300; returns to Lhasa (1952)
162; in Peking (1954) 176, 180;
in India (1956) 199, 201, 202–3,
204; in Chinese-occupied
Lhasa 209–10; and the Lhasa
Uprising 215–16; and the
escape from Lhasa 217–24; first
days as refugees 226–9, 231–2;
in Mussoorie (1959) 236; in
Dharamsala 243, 260, 261, 262;
in England (1960) 255–7; in
Geneva 274–5; in USA 277; at
Kashmir Cottage 294–6, 300,
303; last illness and death
293, 301;
and Gyalo Thondup 19, 56, 58,
134
and Kundun chapter 5 passim,
115, 205, 273, 300
and Lobsang Samten 58,
258–61, 274–5, 294, 302, 323–4,
326

and Norbu chapter 3 passim, 92,
236, 258, 277
and Rinchen Khando 295–6, 293,
301
and Tendzin Choegyal 156, 176,
203, 257, 287, 294, 301, 324
Delek Hospital, Dharamsala 337
'Democratic Reforms' 185. See also
atrocities in Chinese-occupied
Tibet; Amdo (province); Kham
(province); Eastern Tibet
(Kham and Amdo)
Deng Xiao-ping 305–6, 334; and
Gyalo Thondup 307–8, 360;
part in the destruction of
Tibetan monasteries 307
Dharamsala (India) 241, 242–3,
253, 272, 273, 306, 334, 337,
343, 349–50, 352, 354
Dolan, Brooke 101, 111n
Dolma Tso (maternal grandmother
of Fourteenth Dalai Lama) 23
Drepung Monastery 7, 93, 107,
148, 193–5, 196n, 212
Drikung Chetsang Rinpoche 302–3
Dromo (in Chumbi Valley) 147,
148, 149, 150, 152, 153, 158,
159
Dungkhar Monastery 149, 152

earthquakes (1950) 142–3; (1986)
338
Eastern Tibet (Kham and Amdo):
Chinese atrocities in 185,
195–6, 200, 207–8, 322–3;
Khampas organize resistance in
206; turned into wasteland
(1957) 206; refugees from flood

into Lhasa (1958) 195–6, 208.
See also International
Commission of Jurists
education: in old Tibet 45, 56,
112n, 116; in India and Nepal
245; in Chinese-occupied Tibet
315–18
Ekvall, Robert 159

Five-Point Peace Plan 341–2
Foothills 228
Ford, Robert, 140, 141
Fox, Reginald 140

Gadung Oracle 114, 155, 217
Ganden Monastery, 5, 7, 212, 318
Gandhi, Indira 154n
Gandhi, Mahatma 202, 210
'Gang of Four' 305, 307, 310
Gangtok (capital of Sikkim) 158,
159
Gelugpa (dominant sect in Tibetan
Buddhism) 5, 53n, 258
Gendun Choekyi Nyima, the
Eleventh Panchen Lama 356–8,
368
genocide, China declared guilty of
234–5, 272
Gesar of Ling, saga of 30–1
Gompo Tashi Andrugtsang
(founder of National Volunteer
Defence Army) – see
Andrugtsang
Gould, (Sir) Basil (Political
Officer for Sikkim) 11, 20n, 58,
61, 73, 76–7, 79, 81n, 87, 88,
101, 107
Gould, Cecily (Lady) 256

guerrillas 195, 206, 207–8, 219,
221–4, 296–7. See also Chushi
Gangdrug, Central Intelligence
Agency (CIA), Gyalo Thondup,
Lhamo Tsering, Mustang,
National Volunteer Defence
Army; 'yellow parachute'
Great Game, the 52n
Gyalo Thondup (older brother of
Fourteenth Dalai Lama) 15,
16–17, 19, 39, 42, 44, 46, 51,
57–8, 72, 73, 92, 93, 106, 109,
260, 290; and birth of Dalai
Lama 55–6; shows early
interest in China 116; and
Kesang Rinpoche 119; at
school in Lhasa 116; and his
father's death 120–1; and
Regent Reting 116, 122; leaves
Lhasa for India and China
(1946) 119; and Chiang Kai-
shek 119, 171; in Nanking 131,
132; escapes from Shanghai
(1949) 132; in India 133; in
Taiwan 160–1; relations with
Kuomintang (after 1952) 172;
and the Kashag (1949) 133–4;
returns to Tibet via USA (1952)
160–1; and land reform in Tibet
166–7; in Lhasa (1952) and
escape 165–71; seeks help for
Tibet 171–3; in Darjeeling
172–3; and the Committee for
Social Welfare 175, 198, 206–7,
208, 229; and the CIA 172, 247;
and Indian Intelligence 172,
247, 252; and the Resistance
173, 206, 238, 248–9; and the

escape from Lhasa 221, 228;
and Nehru 133, 170, 172, 198,
205, 252; and Buddha Jayanti
(1956) 198, 201, 204–5; and
Dharamsala 248; and the
Sikkim treasure 244, 249; and
the Kashag (in India) 121, 244,
249; and the Khampas (in
India, post–1959) 250, 281, 308;
and the NVDA 280–1; and the
SFF 252, 254n; leaves
Dharamsala for Hong Kong
281; and Deng Xiao-ping
306–8; and the delegations to
Tibet 309; and talks with
China 232, 334, 335–6, 343,
345, 351–4, 359–60; elected to
Kashag 351–4; in USA 352; and
the search for Eleventh
Panchen Lama 349, 356–8;
and Jetsun Pema 327, 339, 351,
359
and Kundun 205, 208, 228, 235,
248–9
and Tibetan Independence 351,
352, 369
Gyaltsen Norbu (Chinese choice
for Eleventh Panchen Lama)
358
Gyatso 72, 83, 85, 93, 104, 192–3
Gyayap Chenmo – see Choekyong
Tsering
Gyayum Chenmo – see Dekyi
Tsering

Harrer, Heinrich 113, 117, 140,
150, 218, 228, 236; and
Lobsang Samten 118–19, 149;

and Kundun 125–6, 143, 149,
152; leaves Tibet (1950) 149
Huang Mu-sung, General 18

incarnate lamas – see tulkus and
tulku system
India: becomes independent (1947)
123; recognizes PRC 141; and
NEFA 171; refuses to support
Tibet at UN (1950) 147;
receives Kundun and family as
refugees 224, 227–9, 233; and
Sikkim 172–3; Tibetan refugees
in 233–4, 243, 272, 285, 294,
336, 337, 351; and the Tibetan
guerrillas 250; invaded by
China (1962) 251, 270–1; war
with Pakistan (1965) 272; votes
in Tibet's favour at UN (1965)
272; and the SFF 252, 254n
Indian Intelligence: and Gyalo
Thondup 172, 252, 281
Indian Mission in Lhasa (after
1947) 170, 199
International Commission of
Jurists: reports on Chinese
atrocities in Tibet (1960)
195–6, 234–5

Jamyang Norbu 8n, 11, 212, 282,
334, 352
Jetsun Pema (younger sister of
Fourteenth Dalai Lama):
childhood in Lhasa 114–16,
120, 128n, 157; at school in
India 150, 161, 190–1, 209, 231,
257, 267; at Buddha Jayanti
(1956) 202–3; further education

267; and the Nursery (later the TCV) 267, 268, 337, 351, 353, 362; and the third fact-finding delegation 305, 315–18; and Amala 326; and death of Lhundup Gyalpo 327; and the earthquake 338–9; marries Tempa Tsering 339; as a Kalon 350–1, 353; given title 'Mother of Tibet' 362;
and Kundun 202–3, 231, 232, 351, 353
and Tsering Dolma 265
and Gyalo Thondup 171, 207, 327, 351, 359
and Tendzin Choegyal 286
and Namlha 259, 331
Jhora 223
Jokhang Temple 71, 82, 83, 104, 105, 213, 312, 358

Kalimpong (India) 18, 133, 149, 150, 159, 173, 207, 229, 248
Kaplan, Morris 292–3
Kapoor, B. K. 172
Karma Rolpai Dorje hermitage 16
Karnataka State (India) 245, 273
Karpo la Pass 223
Kashag, the 12, 19, 65; in the Tibetan system of government 9–10n; and the ransom 61; corruption in 79, 98, 123; and the new Yapshi family 83–5; and the Kung 85, 106–9; and Reting 98, 108–9, 120, 121–2; and Taktra 98, 108–9, 120; and Gyalo Thondup 121, 133–4, 167, 244, 249, 250, 335,

351–354; closes Chinese Mission (1949) 134; and talks with Chinese 150, 335–6; and the Chinese invasion 167–8; sends goodwill missions (1950) 141; and Taktser Rinpoche 146; and the treasure in Sikkim 148, 243; and the Chinese in Lhasa 167–8, 186, 208, 210; dissolved by Chou En-lai (1959) 222; in Dharamsala 244, 249, 250, 350; and the Youth Congress 282
Kashmir Cottage, Dharamsala 294, 295–6, 300, 301, 304, 320, 323, 325, 326, 340, 341
Kelsang Palace (Norbulingka) 72, 312
Kerala 273
Kesang Rinpoche 62, 99; and the search for the Fourteenth Dalai Lama 14–19; death of 119, 120
Kham (province) 20n, 139, 140, 143, 182; Chinese atrocities in 185, 186, 189, 195–6, 206, 207–8
Khampas: present petition to Kundun (1955) 183; actively resist Chinese 185, 195–6, 206; persecution of 185 195–6; and Chushi Gangdrug 206, 219, 221–4, 248–9; and Gyalo Thondup 207, 248, 250, 251; in Mustang 247–8, 281, 296–7; and the Thirteen Settlements 281, 308
Kokonor, Lake 18, 22, 64, 90, 321
Kumbum monastery 14, 15, 16, 18, 19, 26, 41–60, 61, 62, 89, 90,

131, 135, 182; Taktser Rinpoche returns to 131, 135–9, 322

Kumulung monastery 135, 176

Kundun – *see* Dalai Lama, Fourteenth

Kung, the – *see* Choekyong Tsering

Kunyang (m. Thubten Jigme Norbu) 228, 258, 276, 277

Kuomintang (former Nationalist Government of China) 7, 18, 119, 132, 134, 135; and Gyalo Thondup 160–1, 172, 206; and the Panchen Lama 178. *See also* Taiwan

Kyeri, Mt – *see* Ami-chiri

Kyi Chu river 86, 217, 218

Ladakh and Zanskar 251, 252, 339–40, 347–9

Lagoe la Pass 223

land ownership and reform in Tibet 94n, 166–7

Levin, Bernard 272

Lhamo Dhondup – *see* Dalai Lama, Fourteenth

Lhamo Dolma (paternal grandmother of Fourteenth Dalai Lama) 27, 29, 41

Lhamoi Lhatso, lake 12–13

Lhamo Tsering: in Nanking 120, 131, 132; and the CIA 207, 246, 281; and the guerrillas 246, 248, 281, 296

Lhasa 62, 82, chapter 7 *passim*, 101; and death of Thirteenth Dalai Lama 2–3, 12, 13; receives news of Fourteenth Dalai Lama's arrival 65; Fourteenth Dalai Lama's entry into 69–71; schools in 116; civil war in (1947) 121–2; corruption in 79, 98, 123; panic in (1950) 140–4; Chinese occupation of 153, 162, 164–9, 184–5, 209, 210; and Mimang Tsongdu 166, 167; Dalai Lama returns from China to (1955) 183; and the new roads (1955) 176–7, 181, 182, 183–4, 188n; and the refugees from Eastern Tibet 185, 195–6, 208; and the PCART 186, 187, 195, 196, 206; Kundun returns (1957) from India to 206; Uprising (1959) and its aftermath chapter 17 *passim*, 233–4; and the fact-finding delegations 311–13, 314; and the Chinese immigrants 335; pro-independence riots (1987–9) 342–3; repression in 335, 342, 343, 344, 345, 349; unrest in (post-1995) 368–9

Lhasa Uprising – *see* Lhasa

Lhasang Tsering 345

Lhoka 208

Lhosar (Tibetan New Year festival) 73, 115

Lhundup Gyalpo (Jetsun Pema's first husband) 327

Lhuntse Dzong 221, 223

Library of Tibetan Works and Archives 214, 294

Ling Rinpoche 100, 124, 325

Lobsang Jinpa, aka 'Ponpo' 99, 110, 326

Lobsang Samten (older brother of Fourteenth Dalai Lama) 51, 56, 57–8, 66, 71, 73, 78, 92, 93, 119, 120, 170; in Kumbum Monastery 58–60; travels from Amdo to Lhasa 62–6, 70; in the Potala 97–104, 109–10; and the Kung 109; at school in Lhasa 110, 116; and Heinrich Harrer 118–19, 125; and the flight to Chumbi Valley 147–50, 153; with Kundun in China (1954) 176; and need for radical change 184; appointed Chairman of Tibetan Youth Association (1952) 184; and the Chinese Communists 187; appointed Lord Chamberlain (1955) 184; and the Buddha Jayanti 199, 200; decides not to return to Tibet (1956) 203, 205; in USA (1959) 229, 258; receives news of Lhasa Uprising 229–30; in Geneva 274–5, 290; in USA (1971) 290–4; returns to Dharamsala (1977) 294, 302–4; and the first fact-finding delegation to Tibet (1979) 308–14, 327; performs funeral rites for his mother 326; and the Tibetan Medical Centre 328–9; illness and death 329–31;

and Kundun chapter 8 *passim*, 109–10, 176, 184, 205, 237, 260, 303–4, 328, 329, 330–1

and Namlha 184, 186, 259, 260–1, 262, 327–32

and Amala 274, 294, 323–4, 326

Lobsang Tashi (monk Prime Minister in Lhasa) 166–8

Lobsang Tsewang 15

Lodoe 300

Loreto Convent (Darjeeling) 190, 231, 257

Loseling, Abbot of: and the Kung 107

Lukhangwa (lay prime minister in Lhasa) 166–8

lung ta 200, 206

Mahabodhi Association of India 198

Ma Pu-feng, General 18, 19, 23, 48, 60–2, 65, 135, 137

Maharajah of Sikkim – *see* Sikkim, Maharajah of

Mahayana Buddhism 3, 4–6, 8–9nn, 27, 36, 38, 53n, 128n, 175, 210, 238, 269n, 278, 312

Mangmang 224

Mao Tse-tung (Chairman Mao) 123, 136, 169, 175, 178, 336; becomes leader of CCP (1935) 119; inaugurates PRC (1949) 134; and Kundun 178–81, 196, 222; memo to PLA *re* Tibetans (1958) 210; death of (1976) 305

marriage ceremony in Amdo 24–5

Marxism 164, 165, 174, 179, 180, 181, 182, 318

McLeod Ganj 242, 246

Milarepa (Tibetan poet and saint) 198

Mimang Tsongdu 166, 167
Missamari camp (Assam) 237, 246, 249, 285
Moise, Dr Regolo 86
monks and monasteries 1–2, 4, 5, 9n, 44–51, 52n, 56, 93, 136, 149, 152, 271, 307, 310, 316, 321, 322, 368; in India 237–8, 365, 367
Monlam (Great Prayer Festival) 104, 115–16
Murphy, Dervla 263–4, 267, 268
Mussoorie (India): Kundun in 229, 232–7, 241, 245; Tibetan schools in – *see* Mussoorie Homes Foundation
Mussoorie Homes Foundation 245–6, 285, 300–1, 337–8, 351. *See also* Chazotsang, Khando Tsering; Taring, Rinchen Dolma
Mustang (Nepal) 247, 252–3, 281, 296–7
Nagchuka 65, 66, 91, 358

Nanking 119, 121, 132, 160
Nathu la Pass 158, 192, 200, 205, 206
National Assembly of Tibet 7–8, 9–10n, 97; summoned by Regent Reting (1936) 13; declares Lhamo Dhondup to be the new Dalai Lama 65; and the Kung 85, 108; and Reting Rinpoche 8, 122; appeals to UN (1950) 146–7; persuades Dalai Lama to leave Lhasa (1950) 147; and the Seventeen-Point Agreement 153, 216; under Chinese rule 186–7
National Volunteer Defence Army (NVDA) 208, 221–4, 238. *See also* Andrugtsang; Central Intelligence Agency (CIA); Chushi Gangdrug; Gyalo Thondup; Lhamo Tsering; Mustang (Nepal)
Nechung Oracle 71
Nehru, Jawaharlal, Prime Minister of India 1947–1964 130, 241; recognizes People's Republic of China 141; and Gyalo Thondup 133, 170, 171, 198, 204, 205, 252; and relationship with China 147, 199, 204, 229, 233, 241, 242, 251; and the Buddha Jayanti (1956) 198, 202, 204; and Kundun as refugee (1959) 226, 227, 234, 242; and the Tibetan refugees 234, 245; and the border war with China (1962) 251, 252; and formation of SFF 252
Nepal: and the Tibetan guerrillas 247, 248, 296–7; and the refugees 272, 286, 296
New China News Agency – *see* Xinhua
New York Times 292–3
Ngari Rinpoche (general) 156, 158
Ngari Rinpoche, Fifteenth 155, 366
Ngari Rinpoche, Sixteenth – *see* Tendzin Choegyal (younger brother of Fourteenth Dalai Lama)

Ngawang Changchup 42, 43, 60
Nobel Peace Prize (1989) 345
Norbu – see Taktser Rinpoche
    (eldest brother of Fourteenth
    Dalai Lama)
Norbu, Lhundrup Namgyal 276
Norbu, Kunga Gyaltsen 276
Norbu, Jigme Kunden 276
Norbu Thondup 110, 124
Norbulingka (Summer) Palace
    (Lhasa) 12, 72, 92, 102–4, 105,
    125, 213, 312–13; and Lhasa
    Uprising 213–16, 222
North East Frontier Agency
    (NEFA) 170, 226, 239n, 251
Nowrojee, Nauzer 242
Nursery for Tibetan refugee
    children, Dharamsala 294; and
    Tsering Dolma 262–5; and
    Jetsun Pema 267–8
Oracles, State 12, 13, 71, 74, 76,
    114, 117, 142, 143, 145n,
    155, 217

Pakistan, war with India (1965) 272
Palden Lhamo 13, 57
Panchen Lama, Ninth 14, 20n, 58
Panchen Lama, Tenth (1938–1989);
    recognized by Kuomintang
    Government (1944) 178;
    invites Mao to 'liberate' Tibet
    (1949); in China (1954) 177;
    and the PCART 186, 271; as
    Chinese puppet leader 234;
    imprisoned by Chinese (1964)
    271; after Mao's death 305,
    306; and the Tibetans 271,
    348–9; death of (1989) 348–9;

search for the reincarnation of
    356–8
Panikkar, Sardat 133
Patriotic Women's Association
    170, 176, 191, 210
Patriotic Youth Association
    169–70, 184–5, 186
Peace Treaty with China (AD 821)
    4, 151
Peking 145n, 151, 307, 308, 309,
    315, 334, 344, 348, 358;
    Kundun's visit (1954) 174–83;
    and Tiananmen Square 344,
    345
Peking People's Daily 232
Peking Radio 140, 143, 178, 212
Pema Bhum 352
People's Liberation Army (PLA) –
    see Chinese People's Liberation
    Army
People's Republic of China
    (PRC) – see China, People's
    Republic of
Phala (Dronyerchemmo), Lord
    Chamberlain at time of the
    Uprising and escape 199, 215,
    219, 225n
Phuntsog Wangyal 244, 343, 351,
    353, 361, 367
Phuntsok Tashi – see Taklha,
    Phuntsok Tashi
Pioneers (junior branch of Tibetan
    Youth Association in Lhasa)
    184–5
Ponpo – see Lobsang Jinpa
Potala Palace (Lhasa) 3, 12, 52n, 72,
    83, 92, 93, chapter 8 passim,
    115, 122

Preparatory Committee for the Autonomous Region of Tibet, (PCART) 178, 186, 196, 199, 206
Pullen, Judy 268
Pu Yi, the 'Last Emperor' of imperial China 219, 225n

Radio Lhasa 141, 221, 222
Rai Bahadur Norbhu 16, 85, 106–7
Rame monastery 221
Rangzom Monastery, Ladakh: and Ngari Rinpoche (Tendzin Choegyal) 279
Reform Party, the 249, 251
reforms in Tibet 1–2, 166–7, 168–9
Reting monastery 368
Reting Rinpoche (Regent of Tibet) 87, 232; elected Regent after death of Thirteenth Dalai Lama 8; and Fourteenth Dalai Lama 12–13, 71; and the Kung 116, 120; and Gyalo Thondup 116; growing opposition to, and resignation 79–80, 98; and Taktra 98, 108–9, 121; arrest and death in Potala prison 121–2, 232
Richardson, Hugh (official representative of British and Indian Governments in Lhasa, 1936–1950) 58, 68, 71, 84, 87, 106, 126, 127, 128n, 130, 140, 141, 146, 155, 156, 165, 237; and the Dalai Lama's ransom 61; and the death of Reting 122; in charge of British Mission in Lhasa (1937) 79, 128n

Rigya 69, 70
roads (built by Chinese in Tibet) 176–7, 181, 182, 183–4, 188n, 247, 253

Sabo Pass 221
St Joseph's College, Darjeeling 190, 257, 283
St Joseph's Convent, Kalimpong 150, 285
Sakyapa sect 258
Scotch Plains (New Jersey) 291–3
Seattle University 258, 286
Se la Pass 170
Self-Help Centres in India and Nepal 238, 246, 272, 286, 290, 340
Sera Je College 121–2
Sera monastery 7, 15, 121
Seventeen-Point Agreement with China (1951) 150–1, 153, 164, 165, 166, 178, 187, 204, 216, 228, 234
Shakabpa, W. D. 86, 198
Shanghai 131, 132
Shartsong hermitage 15, 43, 44, 46, 50, 51, 135
Shastri, Lal Bahadur 272, 273
Sheriff, George 116, 128n
Sikkim 154n, 158, 172–3, 192, 201, 233–4, 239, 247, 248, 252; treasure in 243–4, 249
Sikkim, Maharajah of 75, 148, 158, 172, 198
Siliguri 231
Siling (capital of Amdo) 18, 19, 28, 48, 61, 69, 89, 90, 185; and the Chinese Communists 135, 137, 185

Sino-Indian border war (1962) 251, 271

Sino-Japanese War (1937–1945) 20n, 119

Sonam Gyatso – see Dalai Lama, Third

Sonam Tsomo – See Dekyi Tsering (mother of Fourteenth Dalai Lama)

Songtsen Gampo, seventh-century king of Tibet 3, 82, 96

Special Frontier Force (SFF) 252, 254n, 281; and Tendzin Choegyal 296, 297–9

Standford, Maurice, SJ 257, 283

Strasbourg Declaration 343, 345

Sun Yat-sen, Dr 145n

Swarg Ashram 243, 261, 264, 279, 326

sweepers, the 103–4, 105, 110, 111, 124, 142

Switzerland, Tibetan refugees in 236–7

Taiwan 206. See also Chiang Kai-shek, Gyalo Thondup, Kuomintang

Taklha (family name of the present Yapshi family) 83

Taklha, Chuki 262, 291, 293, 328, 329, 331, 332

Taklha, Kesang 276

Taklha, Namlha (Namgyal Lhamo, formerly Tsarong, m. Lobsang Samten): at school in India 184, 199, 258–9; and Lobsang Samten 184, 186, 259, 260–1, 290–4, 327–32; and the

Pioneers in Lhasa 184–5; in Delhi 262; in Geneva 274–5; in USA (1971) 290–4; in Dharamsala (after 1977) 294, 302–3, 308, 324, 325, 327; and the Medical Centre 328–9, 332

Taklha, Phuntsok Tashi, General 37, 89, 92, 191, 209, 243; and Tsering Dolma 50–1, 266; at school in Lhasa 116; leaves Lhasa for India and China (1946) 119, 130; interpreter in talks with China (1950) 150, 159; in Lhasa (1952) 165; Commander of Kundun's Bodyguard 176, 213; and the escape from Lhasa 216, 217–8; and Tenzin Ngawang 275, 356; and Khando 275; marries Kesang 276; and the guerrillas (1974) 296–7

Taklha, Tenzin Namdhak 262, 291, 293, 303

Taktra Rinpoche: as Regent and Senior Tutor (1941) 98, 104, 123; summons National Assembly to discuss Kung's behaviour 108; and Reting 98, 108–9, 120, 121; resigns as Regent (1950) 143, 145n

Taktser (Amdo), birthplace of Fourteenth Dalai Lama 14–19, chapter 3 passim, 43, 51, 54, 113, 131, 136, 182, 203, 322–3

Taktser labrang 43, 44, 47, 48–50, 52n, 63

Taktser Rinpoche, Twenty-Third 26, 41, 42, 48, 52n

Taktser Rinpoche, Twenty-Fourth (eldest brother of Fourteenth Dalai Lama), aka Cho-la, Jigme, Thubten Jigme Norbu, Norbu 62–3, 120; childhood of 29–39; Cho-la/Jigme becomes 41–60; and his younger brothers in Kumbum monastery 59–60; leaves Kumbum for Lhasa 88–93; returns to Amdo via Shanghai (1947) 130–2; scatters his father's ashes 131–2; as Abbot of Kumbum 132, 135–9; and the Chinese Communists 135–9; makes second journey to Lhasa (1950) 139; arrives in Lhasa with Chinese ultimatum (1950) 144; prepares to leave Tibet (1951) 148, 149, 152; and the USA 159; in Japan 189; and Gyalo Thondup 161, 190–2, 229; in India for Buddha Jayanti (1956) 199–200, 201, 202, 203–5; receives news of Lhasa Uprising and visits Mussoorie 229–30, 235–6; at Seattle University 258; marries Kunyang 258; in New York 276; in Indiana 276–7, 293, 360; takes sabbatical in Dharamsala (1972) 294; and in USSR and Tibet (1979) 321–2; and the Chinese 335, 360; and Kundun 159, 205, 208, 344, 361, 369 and Tibetan Independence 335, 344, 360–1, 369

and the Tibetan refugees 229, 235, 236–7 and tulku system 44, 46, 48–49, 50, 156–157
Tan Kuan-sen, General (Political Commissar in Lhasa after 1952) 165, 167, 168, 169, 170, 208, 210, 213
Taring, Jigme 245, 301, 332
Taring, Rinchen Dolma 156, 192, 214, 245, 255–7, 285, 300, 337
Tashi Dhondup (paternal grandfather of Fourteenth Dalai Lama) 27
Tashikiel town and monastery 14, 309–10
Tashilhunpo monastery (seat of the Panchen Lamas) 20n, 349, 357, 358
Tasotsang family 284–5. See also Choegyal, Rinchen Khando
Tawang 170, 171, 226, 227
Tempa Tsering 339
Tendzin Choegyal (younger brother of Fourteenth Dalai Lama), aka Ngari Rinpoche: birth 114, 117; recognized as Sixteenth Ngari Rinpoche 155–6; at Changseshar 157–8; earliest memories 148, 158–9; in India (1952) 158–9; as a tulku 176, 193–5, 203, 279, 280, 364; in China (1954) 176–7, 180–1; and Drepung 193–5, 196n, 208–9, 218; in India for Buddha Jayanti (1956) 200, 201, 259; and the Uprising and escape 215–16, 217–24; arrives in India (1959)

227–9, 231–2, 235; at school in Darjeeling 257, 278–9, 283, 284; in Dharamsala 279; in Ladakh and Zanskar (1966) 279–80; (1969) 283; (1980) 339–40; (1988) 347–8; (1994) 364; and the TYC 282, 284, 297; in USA 286; and the TCV 286–7, 295; in SFF (1975) 296, 297–9; as Private Secretary to Kundun 302, 323, 347–8; moves to Kashmir Cottage 294, 340; and the Assembly of Tibetan People's Deputies 350, 365;

and Amala 156, 176, 203, 257, 287, 294, 301–302, 324
and Dekyi Dolkar 336
and depression 286, 299, 301–302, (manic) 347–348
and Gyalo Thondup 286, 353
and Kundun 180–181, 284, 302, 303–304, 340, 347, 348, 364, 365–366, 367
and Norbu 360
and Rinchen Khando (Tasotsang) 183, 284, 285, 287, 294–5, 340, 348
and spirituality and dharma 278, 280, 364–6
and Tenzin Ngawang 257, 301
and Tibetan monks in India 280, 365
and Tsering Dolma 117, 192, 265
Tenzin Geyche Tethong 129n, 279, 282, 286, 295, 302, 303, 365
Tenzin Gyatso – see Dalai Lama, Fourteenth

Tenzin Ngawang (son of Tsering Dolma) 92, 114–15, 150, 202, 207, 231, 232, 266; education of 190, 257, 269n, 275; and Danielle Aeschimann 275, 301; in Darjeeling 164, 275; and Tendzin Choegyal 257, 301; death of 356
Tezpur 171, 228
thamzing (class struggle session) 185, 261, 271, 272, 322. See also atrocities in Chinese-occupied Tibet; Panchen Lama, Tenth
Tharkhang school 110, 116
Thekchen Choeling 287, 323
The Sunday Times 366
The Times 68–71
Thirteen Settlements, the 281, 308
Thondup, Dekyi Dolkar (Tibetan name of Zhu Dan, m. Gyalo Thondup) 132, 161, 190, 200, 206–7, 229, 231, 232, 238, 246, 327, 329, 336
Thondup, Tenzin Khedup 190
Thondup, Ngawang Tempa 190, 331
Thondup, Yangzom 190, 336
Thubten Gyatso – see Dalai Lama, Thirteenth
Thubten Jigme Norbu – see Taktser Rinpoche
Thubten Sangbo 133
Tibet: early history 1–7; and the Dalai Lamas 219; and Younghusband Expedition 52n; signs Agreement with Britain 52n; system of government

9–10, 111n; and education 112n; fall of Amdo and Kham (1949) 134–5; and the Seventeen-Point Agreement 150–1, 153, 164, 165, 166, 178, 187; and the Communist system 184–5, 196, 197n, 204, 210; and the PCART 178, 186, 196, 199, 206; Lhasa Uprising and aftermath 212, chapter 17 *passim*, 233, 270, 271; Chou En-lai announces end of Government of (1959) 222; becomes TAR (1965) 271; and the Cultural Revolution 271–2; post-Cultural Revolution 306; Chinese immigrants flood into (1983 onwards) 335, 349, 353; and the fact-finding delegations (1979) 308–18; as 'zone of peace' 335, 342; Chinese record in 318; Chinese repression (from 1987) 342–3, 344, 345, 358, 368–9; and China after death of Tenth Panchen Lama 358

Tibet Autonomous Region (TAR) 271, 335, 368

Tibet Mirror 124

Tibetan Army 2, 8, 8n, 20n, 175, 216; overwhelmed in Chamdo (1950) 143; revived (1950) 140

Tibetan Children's Village(s) (TCV) 267, 286–7, 300, 303, 327, 337, 338, 351, 362. *See also* – Jetsun Pema; Nursery; Tibetan refugees: children

Tibetan delegations and goodwill missions 119, 141, 308–18

Tibetan Government-in-Exile 244, 314, 337, 352. *See also* Kashag

Tibetan Homes Foundation (Mussoorie) – *see* Mussoorie Homes Foundation. *See also* Taring, Rinchen Dolma, and Chazotsang, Khando Tsering

Tibetan Independence 1, 20n, 52n, 101, 131, 233, 307, 314, 335, 339, 342, 343, 344, 345, 351, 352, 359, 361, 368–9; and Norbu 344, 360–1, 368–9

Tibetan Institute of Performing Arts (TIPA) 244, 253

Tibetan Medical Institute 244, 328–9, 337

Tibetan monasteries – *see* Drepung; Ganden; Kumbum; Sera, etc. *See also* monks and monasteries; *tulkus* and *tulku* system

Tibetan nuns 340–1

Tibetan Nursery – *see* Nursery; Jetsun Pema; Tibetan Children's Village(s)

Tibetan refugees:
children 245, 246, 262–5, 286–7, 337. *See also* Nursery; Tibetan Children's Village(s)
in Bhutan 337
in India 173, 229, 233–234, 238, 245, 251, 270–271, 272, 281, 285, 336–7. *See also* Mussoorie Homes Foundation; Nursery; Self-Help Programmes; Tibetan Children's Village(s)
in Lhasa 185, 195–6, 208, 213
in Nepal 272, 286, 296, 336, 337

in Switzerland 236–7, 274
in UK 337
in USA 337, 352, 363
self-help programmes 238, 246,
    272, 286, 290
Tibetan Review: Tenzin Ngawang
    editor of 275
Tibetan settlements in southern
    India 245, 273
Tibetan Women's Association 340,
    341. *See also* Patriotic
    Women's Association
Tibetan Youth Congress 282–3,
    297; and the issue of violence
    339, 344–5; and the SFF 297;
    and Tempa Tsering 339
Tolstoy, Ilia 101, 111n, 259
'Trek for Tibet' 360
Trisong Detsen (eighth-century
    Tibetan king) 26
Tsang Po (Brahmaputra) River: and
    the 1950 earthquake 142–3
Tsarong family 185, 199, 258, 260,
    261, 302–3. *See also* Taklha,
    Namlha
Tsedrung (school in Potala) 97
Tsering Dolma (elder sister of
    Fourteenth Dalai Lama) 46, 62,
    63, 89, 92, 93, 119, 150, 159,
    162, 242; childhood in Amdo
    29–39; betrothal to Phuntsok
    Tashi 50–1; and birth of Dalai
    Lama 54–7; early days in Lhasa
    114–16; and Tendzin Choegyal
    117, 180, 192, 265; in Chinese-
    occupied Lhasa (1952) 165, 170,
    209–10; in Peking (1954) 176,
    180; visits India on way back

from China (1955) 191–2; at
    Buddha Jayanti 199, 201; and
    the escape from Lhasa 216–24,
    227–9, 231–2; in Dharamsala
    243; and the Nursery 246, 262,
    264; and Dervla Murphy 262–4,
    267; and Gyalo Thondup 267;
    illness and death of 264–7
Tsering Lhamo 313, 314
Tsong-khapa (1357–1419) 5, 41, 45,
    49, 97
Tsuglakhang Temple – *see* Jokhang
    Temple
tulkus and *tulku* system 5–6, 9n,
    10n, 20n, 52n, 53n, 156–7, 176,
    194, 203, 302–3; and Taktser
    Rinpoche 44, 46, 48–9, 50, 156;
    and Tendzin Choegyal 156

United Front policy in Lhasa 164
United Nations Organization 146,
    147, 235, 272
United Party, the 281, 282
United States of America 147, 151,
    160–1, 171, 172, 247, 252, 296.
    See also Central Intelligence
    Agency (CIA);
    Amala in 277
    Gyalo Thondup in 161, 352
    Khando in 362–4
    Kundun in 341–2
    Lobsang Samten in 229–30, 258,
        290–4
    Norbu in 159, 229–30, 258, 276,
        360–1
    Tendzin Choegyal in 286
    Tibetan refugees in 337

vegetarianism among the Tibetans
52n, 159; and Kundun 273
Volunteer Army to Defend
Buddhism – *see* Chushi
Gangdrug

Wangdu, General Gyatso 281, 297
war between India and Pakistan
(1965) 272
Wen Chang, Queen (Chinese wife
of King Songtsen Gampo) 4
Wu Chang 65, 76–7, 80–1n

Xinhua, New China News Agency
232, 306, 308

Yangtse River 91, 143
Yapshi Taklha family 83, 167,
209–10, 212, 255, 290, 298,
303, 304, 308, 328, 336, 339,
346n, 351, 356, 362, 363–4,
365; and Khando 363–4
Yarphel Padatsang 243
'yellow parachute' 207, 249, 281
Younghusband, Colonel (Sir)
Francis 42, 52n

Zhu Dan – *see* Thondup, Dekyi
Dolkar

Where Beauty, Truth, and Love......321
Where Cross the Crowded Ways.....383
Where Restless Crowds...........373
Where Wilt Thou Put Thy Trust?.....148
While Humble Shepherds..........236
Who Will Go Forth and Serve.......499
With a Steadfast Faith............497
With Eyes of Faith...............122
With Happy Voices Ringing........29
With My Substance I Will Honor.....460

With Thankful Hearts We Meet........3
Within the Shelter of Our Walls........9
Word of God, Come Down on Earth..227
World Around Us, Sky Above Us.....135
Would You Bless Our Homes........447

Yesu, Yesu, Fill Us with Your Love...407
You May Sing of the Beauty..........8
You Satisfy the Hungry Heart.......345
Your Cause Be Mine..............420

FIRST LINES

Ride on, Ride on in Majesty 268
Rise Up, O Saints of God 378

Savior, Like a Shepherd Lead Us 162
Savior, Thy Dying Love 442
Send Forth Thy Light, O Zion 317
Send Me Forth, O Blessed Master 424
Sent Forth by God's Blessing 493
Shout the Tidings of Salvation 469
Silent Night! Holy Night! 244
Silvery Star, Precious Star 239
Sing Praise to God 40
Sing Songs of Joy 241
Sing to the Lord a Joyful Song 55
Sing to the Lord of Harvest 46
Soldiers of Christ, Arise 393
Sometimes a Light (Springtime) 154
Sometimes a Light (Surprise) 155
Sound Over All Waters 261
Source of All Gifts 400
Sovereign and Transforming Grace 12
Spirit Divine, Attend Our Prayer 288
Spirit, Now Live in Me 285
Spirit of God, Descend 181
Spirit of Truth, of Life, of Power 426
Standing at the Portal 144
Still Other Sheep I Have 479
Sweet Hour of Prayer 87
Sweet the Time, Exceeding Sweet 4

Take My Life and Let It Be 408
Take Time to be Holy 180
Teach Me, God, to Wonder 176
Teach Me, My God and King 439
Teach Us, O Lord, True
   Thankfulness 440
Tell It! Tell It Out with Gladness 470
Tell Me the Story of Jesus 215
Tenderly, Tenderly, Lead Thou Me
   On 146
Thank You for Giving Me the
   Morning 74
The Bread that Giveth Strength 423
The Cause of Zion Summons Us 314
The Church's Life Is Built Upon 297
The Church's One Foundation 294
The City Is Alive, O God 375
The First Nowell 246
The Living Word of Scripture 299
The Lord Almighty Spoke the Word . . . 195
The Lord Bless You and Keep You 483
The Lord Jehovah Reigns 25
The Lord Our God Alone Is Strong . . . 196
The Lord's My Shepherd 124
The Love of God 107
The Spirit of God Like a Fire 33

The Strife Is O'er 276
The Vision of a Life to Be 349
The Voice of God Is Calling 394
The Weight of Past 118
There Is a Balm in Gilead 147
There's a Church Within Us 290
There's a Spirit in the Air 214
There's an Old, Old Path 158
These Things Shall Be 323
They'll Know We Are Christians 466
This God Is the God We Adore 481
This Is My Father's World 52
This Is My Song 315
Thou Must Be True Thyself 379
Thou Whose Purpose Is to Kindle 111
Though Anxious and Disheartened . . . 380
Thy Kingdom Come, O Lord 320
Thy Love, O God 163
'Tis Midnight, and on Olive's Brow . . . 264
'Tis the Blessed Hour of Prayer 83
Touch Me, Lord, with Thy Spirit 409
'Twas on that Dark, that Solemn 337

Unmoved by Fear, My Praise Is Due . . 131
Unto God, Who Knows 472
Unto the Calmly Gathered Thought . . . 450

Walk in the Light 303
We Are Living, We Are Dwelling 376
We Are One in the Spirit 466
We Bring Our Children, Lord 348
We Come, Aware of Sin 334
We Gather Together 11
We Give Thee But Thine Own 401
We Limit Not the Truth of God 309
We Plow the Fields and Scatter 76
We Thank Thee, God, for Eyes 465
We Thank Thee, O God, for a
   Prophet 307
We Thank You, Lord, for Strength 78
We Would See Jesus (Cushman) 217
We Would See Jesus (Mora Proctor) . . 218
Were You There 267
We've a Story to Tell 477
What a Friend We Have (Blaenwern) . . . 85
What a Friend We Have (Erie) 86
What Child Is This 257
What Wondrous Love Is This 216
When God Created Human Life 434
When His Salvation Bringing 225
When Holy Ghost Shall Come 471
When I Survey the Wondrous Cross . . . 265
When Jesus Wept, the Falling Tear . . . 270
When Kindled by Thy Spirit's Light . . . 282
When Morning Gilds the Skies 35
When the Church of Jesus 445

More Love to Thee, O Christ 411
Morning Has Broken 22
My Children, "Hear Ye Him" 205
My Faith Looks Up to Thee 143
My God, How Wonderful Thou Art . . . 193
My Jesus, I Love Thee 204
My Life Flows On in Endless Song 157
My Lord, I Come This Hour to Make . . 357
My Lord, I Know that All My Life 457
My Shepherd Will Supply My Need . . . 125
My Song Is Love Unknown 202
My Soul, Praise the Lord 61
My Times Are in Thy Hand 137
Mysterious Presence, Source of All 169

Nearer, My God (Bethany) 138
Nearer, My God (Wilmington) 139
Newborn of God, His Glory Manifest . . 247
Now in This Moment 58
Now Let Our Hearts Within Us Burn . . 495
Now Let Us from This Table Rise 327
Now, on Land and Sea Descending . . . 501
Now Thank We All Our God 60
Now the Green Blade Rises 280

O Christ, My Lord, Create in Me 174
O Church of God, Arise 451
O Come, All Ye Faithful 238
O Come, O Come, Emmanuel 211
O Day of God Draw Nigh 319
Oh, for a Closer Walk with God 117
Oh, for a Faith 159
Oh, for a Thousand Tongues 19
O God, from Whom Mankind Derives . 367
O God in Heaven, We Believe 356
O God, in Restless Living 177
O God of Every Nation 175
O God, Our Help in Ages Past 200
O God, Our Source (Festal Song) 302
O God, Our Source (Vineyard Haven) . 301
O God, Send Heralds 429
O God, the Eternal Father 335
O God, to Us Be Present Here 358
O God, Whose Presence Glows in All . . 14
O Help Us, Lord, to Keep This Day 90
O Holy Dove of God Descending 285
O How Blessed Are the Poor 322
O Jesus Christ, to Thee 224
O Jesus, I Have Promised 463
O Jesus, Master, When Today 422
O Jesus, Our Lord 229
O Jesus, the Giver 64
O Jesus, Thou Art Standing 385
O Little Town of Bethlehem 248
O Lord, Around Thine Altar Now 7
O Lord, Grace Our Communion 1

O Lord, How Can It Be 332
O Lord of Heaven (Thanksgiving) 77
O Lord of Heaven (Stewardship) 396
O Lord of Light, and Love 435
O Lord, Thy Benediction Give 486
O Lord, Thy People Gathered Here . . . 352
O Lord, We Come as Children All 360
O Lord, We Come in Gratitude 455
O Love of God (De Tar) 189
O Love of God (Dedicare) 188
O Love That Wilt Not Let Me Go 132
O Master, Let Me Walk with Thee . . . 462
O Master, to All Children Dear 347
O Master Workman of the Race 219
O May Thy Church Build Bridges 431
O My People, Saith the Spirit 387
O Perfect Love 368
O Sacred Head, Now Wounded 262
O Sing the Mighty Power of God 42
O Son of God, Thou Madest Known . . . 222
O Thou God, Who Hearest Prayer . . . 105
O Thou Joyful, O Thou Wonderful . . . 235
O Thou Who Hearest 16
O Thou, Whose Youthful Years 207
O Word of God Incarnate 305
O Worship the King (Hanover) 28
O Worship the King (Lyons) 27
O Worship the Lord 15
O Young and Fearless Prophet 210
O Zion, Haste 476
Obedient, Lord, to Thy Command . . . 359
Of the Father's Love Begotten 220
On This Day Earth Shall Ring 245
Once in Royal David's City 240
Once More Before We Part 500
One Hour with Jesus 82
Onward to Zion 316
Open My Eyes, O Lord 454
Our Father, Who in Heaven 80

Pass Me Not, O Gentle Savior 149
Pour Down Thy Spirit from Above . . . 165
Praise God from Whom 43
Praise Him, Praise Him 68
Praise, My Soul, the King 41
Praise the Lord, Ye Heavens 66
Praise to the Living God 47
Praise to the Lord, the Almighty 67
Praise Ye the Lord (Praise) 62
Praise Ye the Lord (Rimington) 63
Prophetic Church, the Future Waits . . 293

Redeemer of Israel 313
Redeeming Grace Has Touched 351
Rejoice, Ye Saints of Latter Days 36
Remembering Thy Son, O God 341

FIRST LINES

Here at Thy Table, Lord, We Meet....338
Here, O My Lord, I See Thee.......328
Here We Have Come, Dear Lord.....109
Holy, Holy, Holy Is the Lord.........57
Holy, Holy, Holy! Lord God.........56
Holy Spirit, Come with Power.......287
Holy Spirit, Truth Divine...........281
Hope of the World (Ancient of Days)..208
Hope of the World (Vicar).........209
Hosanna to the Lamb...............34
How Can Creation's Voice Be Still....300
How Firm a Foundation...........136
How Gentle God's Command.......130
How Shall We Come Before You Now.106

I Am Trusting Thee, Lord Jesus......127
I Heard the Bells on Christmas Day...250
I Heard the Voice of Jesus Say......134
I Know Not What the Future Hath....126
I Know that My Redeemer Lives.....212
I Know that My Redeemer Lives; What
   Joy (Lasst uns erfreuen)...........273
I Know that My Redeemer Lives; What
   Joy (Truro)...................274
I Lift My Soul to Thee, Lord.........110
I Love to Tell the Story.............473
I Need Thee Every Hour...........129
I Sought the Lord.................213
I Wonder as I Wander.............251
I Would Be True..................404
If by Your Grace I Choose to Be.....432
If Suddenly upon the Street........389
Immortal, Invisible, God Only Wise...32
In Christ There Is (McKee)..........448
In Christ There Is (St. Peter).......449
In God's Most Holy Presence.........5
In Heavenly Love Abiding..........120
In Memory of the Savior's Love.....330
In Nature's Voice We Hear You......441
In the Cross of Christ I Glory.......203
Infant Holy, Infant Lowly.........242
It Came upon the Midnight Clear....256

Jesus Calls Us O'er the Tumult......371
Jesus Christ Is Risen Today........278
Jesus, Good Above All Other.......259
Jesus' Hands Were Kind Hands.....443
Jesus Is Calling.................391
Jesus Loves the Little Children.....223
Jesus, Mighty King in Zion........353
Jesus, Priceless Treasure...........121
Jesus, Savior, Pilot Me.............145
Jesus, the Very Thought of Thee.....167
Join with Us in Sweet Accord.......475
Joseph, Kind Joseph...............234
Joy to the World..................258

Joyful, Joyful, We Adore Thee.......20
Just as I Am, Thine Own to Be......421
Just as I Am, Without One Plea.....119

Lead On, O King Eternal...........374
Leave We Now the Table of Our Lord.326
Let All the World in Every Corner.....30
Let God Be God..................197
Let the Words of My Mouth.......461
Let Us Break Bread Together......342
Let Us Breathe One Fervent Prayer...482
Let Us, Brothers, Let Us Gladly.....403
Let Us Give Praise to the God.......398
Let Us Pray for One Another.......312
Let Us Sing a Worldwide Anthem....468
Let Us Sing of Easter Gladness......279
Let Your Heart Be Broken..........377
Life of Ages, Richly Poured.........304
Lift High the Cross...............263
Lift Your Glad Voices.............271
Lo, How a Rose E'er Blooming......255
Look at This Man................230
Look for the Beautiful............437
Lord, as We Rise to Leave.........491
Lord God of Hosts...............446
Lord God, We Meet in Jesus' Name...365
Lord, Here Amidst the Poor........427
Lord, I Want to Be a Christian......464
Lord, I Was Blind................178
Lord, in This Hour...............150
Lord, Lead Me by Your Spirit......183
Lord, Let Thy Blessing Rest........490
Lord, Let Thy Holy Spirit Come....346
Lord, May Our Hearts.............26
Lord, May Thy Will Be Done.......92
Lord of All Hopefulness...........185
Lord of All Nations...............467
Lord of the Bronze-green Prairies.....456
Lord, Pour Thy Spirit.............364
Lord, Save Your World............310
Lord, Speak to Me................412
Lord, Thank You for This Hour......93
Lord, Thou Hast Brought Us..........6
Lord, Thy Church on Earth........438
Lord, Thy Mercy Now Entreating....114
Lord, We Come Before Thee Now.....10
Lord, Who Views All People.......459
Lord, Whose Love Through Humble...17
Love Divine, All Loves Excelling.....170

Make Room Within My Heart, O God.182
Make Us, O God, a Church........484
Master, Speak! Thy Servant Heareth!..410
May Thy Presence Be Ours.........102
May We Who Know the Joyful Sound.416
Met in Thy Sacred Name, O Lord......2

Come, Ye Disconsolate............166
Come, Ye Thankful People
(Benevento)....................37
Come, Ye Thankful People
(St. George's Windsor)............38
Come Ye Yourselves Apart.........84
Creation Flows Unceasingly........69
Creator God, Creating Still........190
Creator of Sunrises..............186
Crown Him with Many Crowns......228

Day Is Dying in the West...........45
Dear Lord and God of Humankind...115
Dear Master, in Whose Life I See.....113
Declare, O Heavens...............21
Deep Were His Wounds, and Red....269
Descend, O Spirit, Purging Flame....355
Doxology.......................43
Draw Thou My Soul, O Christ......168

Earth and All Stars...............49
Earth with Her Ten Thousand
Flowers.....................194
Eternal God, Whose Power Upholds..370
Eternal Ruler of the Ceaseless Round..458
Every Good and Perfect Gift.......151

Fairest Lord Jesus................226
Faith of Our Fathers.............433
Father Almighty, Grant to Us........81
Father, Bless Thy Word to All......474
Father, Hear the Prayer We Offer....453
Father, in Heaven, We Believe......356
Father, in Thy Mysterious Presence...141
Father, When in Love to Thee......116
Father, Who in Jesus Found Us.....331
For All the Saints................480
For Bread Before Us Broken........340
For the Beauty of the Earth.........75
For the Book of Mormon's Witness...221
For the Fruits of All Creation........73
For the Healing of the Nations......452
Forgive Our Sins as We Forgive......108
Forgive Us, Lord................103
Forth in Thy Name, O Lord, We Go..498
Fountain of All Revelation........298
Freely, Freely..................382
From All That Dwell Below the Skies...50
From Isles and Continents (Belsize
Square).....................418
From Isles and Continents (Dedicare)..417
From Thee All Skill and Science.....89

Go Make of All Disciples..........392
Go Now Forth into the World.......436
Go, Tell It on the Mountain........249

Go to Dark Gethsemane..........266
God Be with You (God be with you)...488
God Be with You (Randolph).......489
God Forgave My Sin in Jesus' Name..382
God Has Spoken Through the Ages...306
God Himself Is with Us............39
God in His Love for Us............402
God Is My Strong Salvation
(Aurelia).....................160
God Is My Strong Salvation
(Wedlock)....................161
God Is Working His Purpose Out.....324
God of Creation................395
God of Earth and Planets.........198
God of Eternity................192
God of Grace and God of Glory......419
God of Our Fathers..............191
God of Smallness, God of Greatness...164
God of the Earth, the Sky, the Sea.....65
God Send Us Saints..............425
God, the Source of Light and Beauty..406
God Who Gives to Life Its Goodness..184
God Who Spoke in the Beginning.....308
God, Who Touchest Earth with
Beauty......................172
Good Christian Friends, Rejoice and
Sing........................275
Good Christian Friends, Rejoice.....260
Good News! Great Joy............243
Gracious Spirit, Dwell with Me......284
Grant Us, Lord, the Grace of Giving..413
Great and Marvelous Are Thy Works...48
Great God, as Followers of Thy Son....13
Great God, Attend While Zion Sings...59
Great God of All the Earth..........91
Great God Our Source............444
Great Hills May Tremble.........153
Great Is Thy Faithfulness.........187
Guide Us, O Thou Great Jehovah....311

Hail to the Brightness.............318
Hallelujah! Hallelujah!............53
Hark, the Herald Angels Sing.......252
Hark! The Voice of Jesus Calling....381
Hast Thou Heard It, O My Brother...390
He Leadeth Me.................123
He Lives in Us! Immortal King!......199
Hear Our Prayer, O Lord..........94
Heaven and Earth and Sea and Air....51
Heavenly Father, Grant Thy Blessing.496
Heavenly Father, We Adore Thee....112
Heir of All the Waiting Ages........253
Help Us Accept Each Other........171
Help Us Express Your Love........415
Here at the Water's Brink We Stand...354
Here at Thy Table, Lord...........333

Look for the beautiful. . . . 437
Lord of all nations. 467
Lord, who views all. 459
O church of God arise. . . . 451
O Son of God, thou. 222
O young and fearless. 210
The cause of Zion. 314
We bring our children, . . . 348
When God created human. 434
World around us, sky. . . . 135

Youth (*see also* **Children, Family, Parents**)
Just as I am. 421
We are living, we are. 376
Zion (*see also* **Community, Kingdom of God, Peace—National and World, Unity**)
See numbers 310-324
All things are thine. 397
Awake! Ye saints of God. . 140

By thy redeeming cross. . . 292
Come now, sound the call. 386
God has spoken through. . 306
Hast thou heard it, O. . . . 390
O my people, saith the. . . 387
O Zion, haste. 476
Unto God, who knows our. 472
We are living, we are. 376
When, his salvation. 225
When Holy Ghost shall. . . 471

First Lines Index

Italicized listings are alternate names by which some hymns are known.

A Charge to Keep I have. 399
A Diligent and Grateful Heart. 362
A Mighty Fortress Is Our God. 142
Abide with Me. 128
According to the Gifts That God. . . . 363
According to Thy Gracious Word. . . . 325
Admonition 387
Afar in Old Judea. 296
Again, Dear Savior. 494
All Creatures of Our God and King. . . 72
All Glory, Laud, and Honor. 23
All Hail the Power (Coronation). 71
All Hail the Power (Diadem). 70
All Things Are Thine. 397
All Things Bright and Beautiful. 18
All to Jesus I Surrender. 430
Almighty Father, Hear Our Prayer. . . 88
Amazing Grace. 104
Amen (Dresden). 95
Amen (Fourfold). 98
Amen (Sevenfold). 100
Amen (Sixfold). 99
Amen (Threefold, Danish). 96
Amen (Threefold, Houston). 101
Amen (Twofold). 97
An Upper Room Did Our Lord Prepare 343
Angels from the Realms of Glory. . . . 231
Angels, Roll the Rock Away. 277
Angels We Have Heard on High. 237
As Saints of Old. 405
As with Gladness Men of Old. 254
Awake! Ye Saints of God, Awake. . . . 140
Away in a Manger (Mueller). 232
Away in a Manger (Cradle Song). 233

Baptized in Water. 350
Be Present at Our Table, Lord. 336
Be with Me, Lord, Where'er I Go. . . . 487

Bear Each Other's Burdens. 369
Behold the Savior at Your Door. 372
Behold Thy Sons and Daughters. 361
Beloved Community of God. 414
Beneath the Cross of Jesus. 428
Beneath the Forms of Outward Rite. . 339
Beyond the Mist and Doubt. 152
Blest Be the Tie that Binds. 485
Blest Be Thou, O God of Israel. 24
Bread of the World, in Mercy Broken. 329
Break Thou the Bread of Life. 173
Breathe on Me, Breath of God. 179
Brethren, Breathe One Fervent Prayer. 482
Brothers and Sisters of Mine. 388
Brothers, Sisters, Let Us Gladly. 403
By Revelation Called of God. 366
By Thy Redeeming Cross. 292

Cast Thy Burden upon the Lord. 133
Children of the Heavenly Father. 156
Christ for the World We Sing. 478
Christ Is Alive. 272
Christ Is the Foundation. 295
Church of Christ, in Latter Days. 291
Come Down, O Love Divine. 289
Come, Gracious Lord. 492
Come, Holy Ghost, Our Hearts
  Inspire. 286
Come, Labor On. 384
Come Now, Sound the Call of Zion. . . 386
Come, O Creator Spirit. 283
Come, Rejoice Before Your Maker. . . . 44
Come, Risen Lord. 344
Come, Thou Almighty King. 54
Come Thou Fount of Every Blessing. . 31
Come, Thou Long-expected Jesus. . . . 201
Come, Thou, O King of Kings. 206
Come Ye Apart. 79

Jesus, priceless treasure . . . 121
Joy to the world! 258
Lead on, O King Eternal . . 374
Lift high the cross 263
Lord God of Hosts 446
O Church of God, arise . . . 451
O come, all ye faithful . . . 238
Oh, for a thousand 19
Praise the Lord, ye 66
Redeemer of Israel 313
Ride on, ride on in 268
Soldiers of Christ, arise . . . 393
The cause of Zion 314
The Lord Jehovah 25
We gather together 11
We've a story to tell to 477

Vocations (see also **Service**)
See numbers 375-379
Come, labor on 384
From thee all skill and 89
"Go, make of all 392
Hark! The voice of Jesus . 381
In Nature's voice we hear . 441
Just as I am, thine own to . 421
Just as I am 119
Let us give praise to the . . . 398
Lord, whose love through . . 17
My Lord, I know that all . . 457
O Jesus, the giver of all . . . 64
O Son of God, thou 222
Sent forth by God's 493
Take my life and let it be . . 408
The voice of God is 394
There's a church within . . . 290
There's a spirit in the air . 214
When the church of Jesus . 445
Your cause be mine 420

War (see **Peace, Victory**)

Way, The (see **Christ the Way**)

Whitsuntide (see **Pentecost**)

Wholeness (see **Health & Healing, Salvation**)

Wisdom (see also **Knowledge, Teacher**)
God of grace and God of . . 419
O Lord, thy benediction . . 486
O Word of God incarnate . 305
The Lord Jehovah reigns . . 25
The Lord our God alone is . 196

Witness (see also **Commission, Convey, Mission**)
See numbers 432-438, 468-479
By thy redeeming cross . . . 292
Church of Christ, in latter . 291
Come now, sound the call . 386
Eternal God, whose 370
Father, who in Jesus 331

Forgive our sins as we 108
From all that dwell below . . 50
Go, tell it on the 249
God forgave my sin in . . . 382
God has spoken through . . 306
God is working his 324
Help us express your 415
In Nature's voice we hear . 441
Let your heart be broken . . 377
Lift high the cross 263
Make room within my 182
Make us, O God, a church . 484
Now let our hearts within . 495
Now let us from this table . 327
O Church of God, arise . . . 451
O Jesus, the giver of all we . 64
O Master, let me walk 462
O my people, saith the . . . 387
O Word of God incarnate . 305
Oh, for a thousand 19
Praise him, praise him! . . . 68
Redeeming Grace has 351
Rise up O saints of God! . . 378
Send forth thy light, O . . . 317
Send me forth, O blessed . . 424
Sent forth by God's 493
Silent night 244
Sound over all waters 261
Spirit divine, attend our . . 288
Tell me the story of Jesus . 215
The living Word of 299
The Lord almighty spoke . 195
There is a balm in Gilead . 147
There's a spirit in the air . 214
Thou must be true thyself . 379
Thy love, O God, has all . . 163
We are one in the Spirit . . . 466
We give thee but thine 401
When, his salvation 225
Where beauty, truth, and . 321
With a steadfast faith 497
With my substance I will . . 460

Word of God (see **Christ the Word, Scriptures**)

Work (see also **Service, Vocations**)
According to the gifts that . 363
Come, labor on 384
Forth in thy name, O 498
Let God be God 197
Lord God, we meet in 365
Lord of all hopefulness . . . 185
O Lord of light and love . . 435
O Master, let me walk 462
O Master Workman of the . 219
O Son of God, thou 222

World (see also **Earth, Nations**)
Christ for the world we . . . 478
Come now, sound the call . 386
Draw thou my soul 168

Eternal God, whose 370
Father, bless thy word to . . 474
For all the saints 480
From all that dwell below . . 50
From isles and 417, 418
Hope of the world . . 208, 209
In Christ there is no . . 448, 449
Jesus loves the little 223
Joy to the world! 258
Let all the world in every . . 30
Let us pray for one 312
Let us sing a world-wide . . 468
Lord, save your world 310
O God of every nation . . . 175
O Lord of light and love . . 435
Shout the tidings of 469
Teach me, God, to 176
The city is alive, O God . . 375
This is my song 315
Thy love, O God, has all . . 163
When Holy Ghost shall . . . 471
When the church of Jesus . 445

Worship
See numbers 1-5, 13-17, 27-31
All creatures of our God . . 72
All hail the power of . . 70, 71
Christ is the foundation . . . 295
Come, thou Almighty 54
Earth and all stars 49
Fairest Lord Jesus 226
Father, when in love to . . . 116
God himself is with us 39
Good Christian friends . . . 275
Heavenly Father, we 112
Holy, holy, holy 68
Jesus, the very thought of . . 167
Joyful, joyful, we adore 20
Lord, as we rise to leave . . . 491
Lord, thank you for this 93
Mysterious Presence, ... 169
Now let our hearts within . 495
O sing the mighty power . . 42
Oh, for a thousand 19
Sent forth by God's 493
The Lord almighty spoke . . 195
This is my Father's 52
Unto the calmly gathered . 450
When the church of Jesus . 445
Word of God, come down . 227

Worth (see also **Humanity and Humanness**)
He lives in us! 199
Help us accept each other . 171
How shall we come before . 106
I lift my soul to thee, ... 110
If by your grace 432
In Christ there is no . . 448, 449
In Nature's voice we hear . 441
Just as I am, without one . . 119
Let us give praise to the . . . 398

Teacher & Teaching (see also Convey, Intellect, Knowledge, Wisdom)

Heavenly Father, grant . . . 496
Lord, speak to me 412
O Lord, thy benediction . . 486
Teach me, God, to 176
Thou must be true thyself . 379
Would you bless our 447

Temptation (see also Sin)

Go to dark Gethsemane . . . 266
I need thee every hour 129
What a friend we have . . 85, 86
With eyes of faith 122
World around us, sky 135

Testimony (see Witness)

Thanks, Thanksgiving (see also Harvest, Praise)

See numbers 73-78
A diligent and grateful . . . 362
Brothers, sisters, let us 403
Come, rejoice before your . . 44
Come, ye thankful 37, 38
Father, who in Jesus 331
For bread before us 340
For the Book of Mormon's . 221
Forgive us, Lord, for 103
God in his love for us 402
God of the earth, the sky, . . 65
Lord, thank you for this 93
Now thank we all our God . 60
O Jesus, the giver of all 64
O Lord, we come in 455
O Sacred Head, now 262
Sent forth by God's 493
Sing to the Lord a joyful . . . 55
Sing to the Lord of 46
Standing at the portal 144
Teach us, O Lord, true 440
Unmoved by fear, my 131
We thank thee, God, for . . 465
We thank thee, O God, for . 307
You satisfy the hungry 345

Tithing (see Stewardship)

Tolerance (see Fellowship, Love)

Tranquillity (see Peace-Inner)

Trinity

All creatures of our God . . . 72
Come, O Creator Spirit . . . 283
Creator God, creating 190
For all the saints 480
Heavenly Father, grant . . . 496
Holy, holy, holy 56
Now thank we all our 60
Praise God, from whom . . 43
The Lord almighty spoke . . 195
We are one in the 466

Word of God, come down . 227

Trust (see also Faith, Hope)

See numbers 120-162
All to Jesus I 430
An upper room 343
Away in a manger . . . 232, 233
Be with me, Lord, ... 487
Come, rejoice before your . . 44
Day is dying in the West . . . 45
Dear Lord and God of 115
"Go, make of all, ... 392
God is working his 324
Great God, attend while . . . 59
Great God our source 444
Hast thou heard it, O my . . 390
Heavenly Father, we 112
I lift my soul to thee, ... 110
I would be true 404
Let us breathe one 482
Lord of all hopefulness . . . 185
More love to thee, O 411
My Lord, I know that all . . 457
Now, on land and sea 501
O God, whose presence 14
O how blessed are the 322
O Jesus, I have promised . . 463
O Master, let me walk 462
O perfect love 368
O thou God, who hearest . . 105
O worship the King 27, 28
One hour with Jesus 82
Open my eyes, O Lord 454
Praise the Lord, ye 66
Praise to the living God! . . . 47
Praise to the Lord, the 67
Praise ye the Lord! 62, 63
Prophetic Church, the 293
Sent forth by God's 493
Sweet hour of prayer 87
Take time to be holy 180
This God is the God we . . . 481
This is my Father's 52
'Tis the blessed hour of 83
Unto God, who knows our . 472
We give thee but thine 401
Would you bless our 447

Truth (see also Light, Revelation)

See numbers 301-306
Break thou the bread of . . . 173
Come, Holy Ghost, our . . . 286
Declare, O heavens, the 21
Earth and all stars 49
Eternal God, whose 370
Fountain of all 298
Gracious Spirit, dwell 284
Heavenly Father, we 112
Holy Spirit, truth 281
Let us give praise to the . . . 398
Look for the beautiful 437

My life flows on in endless . 157
My Lord, I know that all . . 457
O God, whose presence 14
Open my eyes, O Lord 454
Spirit divine, attend our . . 288
The church's life is built . . 297
Thou must be true 379
Thy love, O God, has all . . 163
Unto the calmly gathered . 450
We limit not the truth of . . 309
Where beauty, truth, and . 321
Word of God, come down . 227

Understanding (see Knowledge)

Unity (see also Community, Fellowship, Kingdom of God, Peace—National and World, Zion)

See numbers 465-468
All things are thine 397
Awake! Ye saints of God . . 140
Breathe on me, breath of . . 179
Church of Christ, in latter . 291
Come, risen Lord 344
Eternal Ruler of the 458
Father, who in Jesus 331
For the healing of the 452
Forth in thy name, O 498
Great God of all the 91
He lives in us! Immortal . . 199
Heavenly Father, grant . . . 496
Help us accept each other . 171
In Christ there is no . . 448, 449
Leave we now the table of . 326
Let all the world in every . . . 30
Lord God of Hosts 446
O come, O come, ... 211
O God to us be present . . . 358
O may thy church build . . 431
Pour down thy Spirit from . 165
Rejoice, ye Saints of latter . . 36
Sent forth by God's 493
The Church's one 294
There's a church within . . . 290
These things shall be: a . . . 323
Thy love, O God, has all . . 163
With a steadfast faith 497
You satisfy the hungry 345

Victory

See numbers 271-279
A mighty fortress 142
Blest be thou, O God of 24
Come, thou long-expected . 201
Come ye yourselves apart . . 84
Crown him with many . . . 228
God is working his 324
God of eternity 192
Hail to the Brightness of . . 318
Hope of the world . . . 208, 209
How can creation's voice . 300
I heard the bells on 250

Sharing (see also **Gifts, Offering**)

A diligent and grateful . . . 362
Come ye yourselves apart . . 84
Creator of sunrises 186
For the healing of the 452
God forgave my sin in 382
God of creation 395
If by Your grace I choose . . 432
Let us pray for one 312
Sent forth by God's 493
We thank you, Lord, for . . . 78

Sick, The (see **Health**)

Sin (see also **Repentance, Temptation**)

Bear each other's burdens . 369
Come, thou long-expected . 201
Deep were his wounds, . . . 269
For the healing of the 452
Forgive our sins as we 108
Heavenly Father, grant . . . 496
Hope of the world . . . 208, 209
I heard the bells on 250
Let God be God 197
Lord, I was blind 178
Lord, save your world 310
Lord, who views all 459
My God, how wonderful . . 193
O Christ, my Lord, create . 174
O God of every nation 175
O Jesus, thou art 385
O Lord, how can it be 332
O Sacred Head, now 262
O thou God, who hearest . . 105
Pour down thy Spirit from . 165
Redeemer of Israel 313
The city is alive, O God . . . 375
The love of God is broad . . 107
The weight of past and . . . 118
Thou whose purpose is to . 111
Unto the calmly gathered . 450
We come, aware of sin 334
When I survey the 265
Where restless crowds are . 373
Where wilt thou put thy . . 148
With eyes of faith 122
World around us, sky 135

Singing (see **Music**)

Sisterhood (see **Children of God, Community, Fellowship, Unity**)

Sorrow (see **Grief**)

Spirit, Holy (see **Holy Spirit**)

Spiritual Baptism (see **Confirmation**)

Spiritual Gifts (see also **Gifts, Holy Spirit**)

According to the gifts that . 363
Every good and perfect . . . 151
If by your grace I choose . . 432
Let us give praise to the . . . 398
Lord God, we meet in 365
O God to us be present . . . 358

Steadfastness (see **Trust**)

Stewardship

See numbers 395-402
A diligent and grateful . . . 362
As saints of old 405
Brothers and sisters of . . . 388
For the fruits of all 73
Let us pray for one 312
Lord, lead me by your 183
O help us, Lord, to keep . . . 90
Take my life and let it be . . 408
The city is alive, O God . . . 375
Thou must be true thyself . 379
We thank you, Lord, for . . . 78
With my substance I will . . 460
Would you bless our 447

Strength (see also **Courage**)

A mighty fortress 142
Behold thy sons and 361
"Come ye apart" 79
Father, hear the prayer . . . 453
Father in thy mysterious . . 141
God of grace and God of . . 419
God, who touchest earth . . 172
Great hills may tremble . . . 153
How firm a foundation . . . 136
I would be true 404
Jesus good above all 259
Lead on, O King 374
Lord of all hopefulness . . . 185
Lord of the bronze-green . . 456
My Lord, I know that all . . 457
O God to us be present . . . 358
O Jesus Christ, to thee . . . 224
Oh, for a faith that will . . . 159
Praise to the living God! . . . 47
Soldiers of Christ, arise . . . 393
Standing at the portal 144
Touch me, Lord, with thy . 409
We are living, we are 376
We come, aware of sin 334

Striving (see **Perseverance**)

Submission (see **Obedience, Resignation**)

Suffering (see also **Comfort, Health, Hope**)

Go to dark Gethsemane . . . 266
Lord, here amidst the 427

Lord, whose love through . . 17
O Love that wilt not let . . . 132
Oh, for a faith that will . . . 159
The voice of God is 394
'Tis midnight, and on 264
Where cross the crowded . 383

Supplication (see also **Prayer**)

Abide with me 128
Almighty Father, hear our . . 88
Be with me, Lord, ... 487
Christ is the foundation . . . 295
Come down, O Love 289
Come, gracious Lord 492
Come, thou Almighty 54
Declare, O heavens, the . . . 21
Father, bless thy word to . . 474
Father hear the prayer we . 453
Father in thy mysterious . . 141
Father when in love to 116
From thee all skill and 89
God of grace and God of . . 419
God of smallness, God of . . 164
God send us saints whose . . 425
God, the source of light . . . 406
God, who touchest earth . . 172
Great God our source 444
Heavenly Father, we 112
Hope of the world . . . 208, 209
I lift my soul to thee, Lord . 110
Let the words of my 461
Lord, let thy blessing rest . . 490
Lord, let thy Holy Spirit . . 346
Lord, may thy will be 92
Lord, pour thy Spirit from . 364
Lord, save your world 310
Lord, thy mercy now 114
Love divine, all loves 170
Master, speak! Thy 410
My faith looks up to thee . . 143
O Jesus, I have promised . . 463
O Lord, around thine altar . . 7
O Lord, grace our 1
O Lord, thy benediction . . 486
O Lord, we come in 455
O young and fearless 210
Oh, for a faith that will . . . 159
Pass me not, O gentle 149
Pour down thy Spirit from . 165
Redeemer of Israel 313
Spirit divine, attend our . . 288
Teach me, my God and . . . 439
Thou whose purpose is to . 111
Touch me, Lord, with thy . 409
Word of God, come down . 227
World around us, sky 135
Yesu, Yesu, fill us with . . . 407

Talents (see **Gifts, Creativity, Stewardship**)

TOPICAL

Salvation (*see also* **Eternal Life, Grace, Reconciliation**)

As with gladness men of . . 254
Come, thou long-expected . 201
From all that dwell below . . 50
Go now forth into the 436
God is my strong 160, 161
Good Christian friends, . . . 260
Heir of all the waiting 253
I know that my Redeemer . 212
I lift my soul to thee, ... 110
I love to tell the story 473
Jesus, mighty king in Zion . 353
Let us give praise to the . . . 398
Lo, how a rose e'er 255
Lord, save your world 310
Love divine, all loves 170
Praise the Lord, ye 66
Redeemer of Israel 313
Tell it! Tell it out with 470
Unto the calmly gathered . 450

Schools and Colleges (*see* **Knowledge, Intellect, Teaching**)

Science (*see also* **God the Creator, Knowledge, Nature**)

Beyond the mist and 152
Eternal God, whose 370
From Thee all skill and 89
God of earth and planets . . 198
Great God our source 444
Lord, save your world 310
The Lord our God alone is . 196
We limit not the truth of . . 309

Scriptures (*see also* **Book of Mormon, Doctrine and Covenants, Restoration, Revelation**)

See numbers 305-309
Afar in old Judea 296
For the Book of Mormon's . 221
"Go, make of all 392
In the cross of Christ I 203
My children, "hear ye . . . 205
Mysterious Presence, ... 169
Praise to the living God 47
"Still other sheep I have" . 479
Tell it! Tell it out with 470
The living Word of 299

Second Coming

Come, thou long-expected . 201
Come thou, O King of 206
God is working his 324
Guide us, O Thou great . . . 311
I know that my Redeemer . 212
O come, O come, ... 211
O day of God, draw nigh . . 319
Onward to Zion, faithful . . 316
Redeemer of Israel 313

Security (*see* **Protection, Refuge**)

Self-reliance (*see* **Courage, Strength**)

Sending Forth (*see also* **Benediction**)

See numbers 491-499
An upper room 343
Eternal God, whose 370
Go now forth into the 436
God of grace and God of . . 419
Hark! The voice of 381
Hast thou heard it, O my . . 390
Leave we now the table of . 326
Make us, O God, a church . 484
O God, send Heralds 429
O Lord of light and love . . 435
Send forth thy light, O 317
Send me forth, O blessed . . 424
The Lord bless you and . . . 483
The voice of God is 394
This is my song 315
Though anxious and 380
When Holy Ghost shall . . . 471

Separation (*see* **Reconciliation, Sin, Unity**)

Servanthood

A charge to keep I have . . . 399
According to the gifts 363
Beloved community of . . . 414
Brothers and sisters of 388
By revelation called of 366
For all the saints 480
Forth in thy name, O 498
Great God, as followers 13
In God's most holy 5
Just as I am, thine own to . 421
Look for the beautiful 437
Lord God, we meet in 365
Lord, here amidst the 427
Lord of all nations grant . . 467
Lord, speak to me 412
Lord, who views all 459
Lord, whose love through . . 17
May we who know the 416
O God in heaven, we 356
O God, send Heralds 429
O God to us be present . . . 358
O how blessed are the 322
O Jesus, I have promised . . 463
O Jesus, the giver of all we . 64
O Lord, we come as 360
O Master, let me walk 462
Take my life and let it be . . 408
The bread that giveth 423
The city is alive, O God . . . 375
The voice of God is 394
There's a church within . . 290
With happy voices ringing . 29
You satisfy the hungry 345
Your cause be mine 420

Service (*see also* **Ministry, Servanthood, Vocation, Work**)

See numbers 403-467
A charge to keep I have . . . 399
A diligent and grateful . . . 362
All things are thine 397
An upper room 343
Christ for the world we . . . 478
Church of Christ in latter . 291
Come, Holy Ghost, our . . . 286
Come now, sound the call . 386
Creator God, creating still . 190
Declare, O heavens, the 21
Father, who in Jesus 331
For all the saints 480
Forgive us, Lord, for 103
God who spoke in the 308
Good news! Great joy to . . 243
Hark! The voice of Jesus . 381
Help us accept each other . 171
Here we have come, dear . . 109
Holy Spirit, come with . . . 287
Hope of the world . . . 208, 209
If suddenly upon the 389
In God's most holy 5
Jesus calls us o'er the 371
Jesus is calling 391
Lead on, O King Eternal . 374
Let your heart be broken . . 377
Lift high the cross 263
Lord, as we rise to leave . . 491
Lord, lead me by your 183
Lord, let thy Holy Spirit . 346
Lord, whose love through . . 17
Make us, O God, a church . 484
My children, "hear ye . . . 205
My Lord, I come this hour . 357
Now let our hearts within . 495
O Jesus Christ, to thee . . . 224
O Jesus, thou art standing . 385
O worship the Lord 15
O young and fearless 210
Onward to Zion, faithful . . 316
Rise up O saints of God! . . 378
Send forth thy light, O . . . 317
Sent forth by God's 493
Source of all gifts 400
Take time to be holy 180
Teach me, God, to 176
The love of God is broad . . 107
There's a spirit in the air . . 214
Thou whose purpose is to . 111
Though anxious and 380
Thy kingdom come, O 320
Unto God, who knows our . 472
We are living, we are 376
We thank you, Lord, for . . . 78
We would see Jesus . . 217, 218
Who will go forth and 499
With a steadfast faith 497
With happy voices ringing . 29

My shepherd will supply . . 125
"My times are in thy 137
O Master, to all children . . 347
O worship the King 27, 28
Praise to the living God! . . . 47
Praise to the Lord, the 67
Praise ye the Lord! 62, 63
Savior, like a shepherd . . . 162
Standing at the portal 144
The Lord's my shepherd . . 124
This God is the God we . . . 481
Unmoved by fear, my 131
We gather together 11
With thankful hearts we 3

Providence (*see* **God the Sustainer**)

Purity and Piety

Again, dear Savior 494
Breathe on me, breath of . . 179
Dear Lord and God of 115
Descend, O Spirit 355
God, who touchest earth . . 172
I need thee every hour 129
Look for the beautiful 437
Lord, I want to be a 464
Lord of the bronze-green . . 456
Lord, speak to me 412
O how blessed are the 322
Take time to be holy 180
Within the shelter of our 9

Radiance (*see* **Light**)

Rebellion (*see* **Sin, Repentance**)

Reconciliation (*see also* **Forgiveness, Grace, Repentance, Salvation**)

Bear each other's burdens . 369
Christ for the world we . . . 478
Christ is alive! Let 272
Come, Holy Ghost, our . . . 286
Come, thou, O King of . . . 206
Deep were his wounds, . . . 269
Eternal Ruler of the 458
Father, bless thy word to . . 474
Father, when in love to . . . 116
Father, who in Jesus 331
Forgive our sins as we 108
Gracious Spirit, dwell 284
Great God of all the 91
Hark the herald angels . . . 252
Heavenly Father, grant . . . 496
Help us accept each other . 171
Here, O my Lord, I see . . . 328
Hope of the world . . . 208, 209
Let us give praise to the . . . 398
Lord, thy church on earth . 438
O God of every nation 175
O Jesus, thou art standing . 385
O little town of Bethlehem . 248

O Lord, how can it be 332
O may thy church build . . 431
Oh, for a thousand 19
Pour down thy Spirit from . 165
The cause of Zion 314
The Lord's my shepherd . . 124
There is a balm in Gilead . 147
Unto the calmly gathered . 450
We come, aware of sin . . . 334

Redemption (*see* **Grace, Reconciliation, Salvation**)

Refuge (*see also* **Protection**)

A mighty fortress 142
Abide with me 128
Beneath the cross of Jesus . 428
Children of the heavenly . . 156
Come ye yourselves apart . . 84
Great God, attend while . . . 59
Guide us, O thou great . . . 311
How firm a foundation . . . 136
How gentle God's 130
I heard the voice of 134
In God's most holy 5
In heavenly love abiding . . 120
In the cross of Christ 203
Jesus, priceless 121
Redeemer of Israel 313
'Tis the blessed hour of . . . 83
What a friend we have . . 85, 86

Repentance (*see also* **Forgiveness, Grace, Mercy, Reconciliation, Sin**)

See numbers 103-119
Beneath the cross of Jesus . 428
Come thou fount of every . . 31
God of grace and God of . . 419
Here at the water's brink . . 354
More love to thee, O 411
My Jesus, I love thee 204
My Lord, I come this hour . 357
O God in heaven, we 356
O Jesus, thou art 385
O Lord of light and love . . 435
Pass me not, O gentle 149
Remembering thy Son, O . 341

Resignation (*see also* **Obedience**)

Father, when in love to . . . 116
He leadeth me; oh, blessed . 123
Master, speak! Thy 410

Responses (*see* **Prayer Responses**)

Rest

Come, thou long-expected . 201
"Come ye apart" 79
Come ye yourselves apart . . 84
Day is dying in the west 45
How gentle God's 130
I heard the voice of 134

It came upon the 256
Jesus, the very thought . . . 167
O God, in restless 177
O Love that wilt not let . . . 132
'Tis the blessed hour of 83

Restoration (*see also* **Church, Scriptures**)

Afar in old Judea 296
By revelation called of 366
Fountain of all Revelation . 298
Let us give praise to the . . . 398
Rejoice, ye Saints of 36
The Spirit of God like a 33
We thank thee, O God, for . 307

Resurrection (*see also* **Christ's Resurrection, Eternal Life**)

See numbers 271-274, 278-280
Go to dark Gethsemane . . . 266
My song is love unknown . 202
O Lord, grace our 1
O love of God, how . . 188, 189
Redeeming Grace has 351

Revelation (*see also* **Light, Scriptures, Truth**)

See numbers 296-309
Come now, sound the call . 386
Come, risen Lord 344
Father in thy mysterious . . 141
Forgive us, Lord, for 103
"Go, make of all 392
Great is thy faithfulness . . . 187
In Nature's voice we hear . 441
Let your heart be broken . . 377
Look for the beautiful 437
Lord, I was blind 178
Lord, speak to me 412
Master, speak! Thy 410
My children, "hear ye 205
Mysterious Presence, ... 169
Newborn of God, his 247
O love of God, how . . 188, 189
Open my eyes, O Lord . . . 454
Praise to the living God! . . . 47
Send forth thy light, O 317
Spirit divine, attend our . . 288
Teach me, God, to 176
Teach me, my God and . . . 439
The Spirit of God like a 33
Where cross the crowded . . 383
With a steadfast faith 497

Sabbath (*see* **Lord's Day**)

Sacraments (*see* **Baptism, Blessing of Children, Confirmation, Health and Healing, Lord's Supper, Marriage, Ordination**)

Safety (*see* **Protection, Refuge**)

TOPICAL

I heard the bells on 250
It came upon the 256
Leave we now the table of . 326
My life flows on in endless . 157
O come, O come, ... 211
O God of every nation 175
O Zion, haste 476
Pour down thy Spirit from . 165
Silent night 244
Sound over all waters 261
The Church's one 294
We've a story to tell to the . 477
While humble shepherds . . 236

Pentecost (see also Church, Holy Spirit)

See numbers 285-289
Come, O Creator Spirit . . . 283
Great and marvelous are . . . 48
He lives in us! Immortal . . . 199
O Christ, my Lord, create . 174
On this day earth shall . . . 245

People of God (see Children of God)

Perseverance (see Commitment, Strength)

Personal Worth (see Worth)

Petition (see Supplication)

Power (see Strength)

Praise (see also Thanks)

See numbers 18-72, 224-229, 252-258, 271-278
Again, dear Savior 494
Angels from the realms of . 231
Angels we have heard on . . 237
Be present at our table, . . . 336
Come, gracious Lord 492
For all the saints 480
For the beauty of the earth . 75
God of eternity 192
God of grace and God of . . 419
God of our fathers 191
God, the source of light . . . 406
God who gives to life its . . . 184
Great God our source 444
Great is Thy faithfulness . 187
Hail to the Brightness of . . 318
Heavenly Father, we 112
Holy Spirit, come with . . . 287
How can creation's voice . 300
In Christ there is no . . 448, 449
Jesus, the very thought of . . 167
Join with us in sweet 475
Let us break bread 342
Let us give praise to the . . . 398
Let us sing a world-wide . . 468

Lift high the cross 263
Lord, I was blind 178
Lord of the bronze-green . . 456
Lord, we come before thee . 10
Love divine, all loves 170
Make room within my 182
My God, how wonderful . . 193
My life flows on in 157
Mysterious Presence, ... 169
Now, on land and sea 501
O come, all ye faithful 238
O Lord, grace our 1
O Lord of heaven 77
O Lord of heaven 396
Of the Father's love 220
Once more before we part . 500
Sound over all waters 261
Sweet the time, exceeding . . . 4
Teach me, God, to 176
There's a spirit in the 214
This God is the God we . . . 481
Unto God, who knows our . 472
We are one in the Spirit . . . 466
We gather together 11
With thankful hearts we 3

Prayer (see also Meditation, Supplication)

See numbers 79-87
Awake! Ye saints of God . . 140
Draw thou my soul 168
Go to dark Gethsemane . . . 266
I need thee every hour 129
I sought the Lord 213
I would be true 404
Let us breathe one 482
Let us pray for one 312
More love to thee, O 411
O thou God, who hearest . . 105
Take time to be holy 180
Unto God, who knows our . 472
With eyes of faith 122
With thankful hearts we 3
You may sing of the beauty . . 8

Prayer Responses

See numbers 88-102
Be present at our table, . . . 336
Cast thy burden upon the . 133
Dear Master in whose life . 113
Grant us, Lord, the grace . 413
Heavenly Father, grant . . . 496
Hosanna to the Lamb 34
Let the words of my 461
Lord, here amidst the 427
My Jesus, I love thee 204
O thou who hearest every . . 16
O worship the Lord 15
Praise God, from whom . . . 43
Spirit of truth, of life, of . 426
The Lord bless you and . . . 483

Priesthood (see also Call, Commission, Ministry, Ordination)

According to the gifts 363
Lord, pour thy Spirit 364
Lord God, we meet 365
O God, send Heralds 429

Pride (see Humility)

Prophetic Ministry

See numbers 375-379
A charge to keep I have . . . 399
Awake! Ye saints of God . . 140
Beloved community of . . . 414
Brothers, sisters, let us 403
Christ for the world we . . . 478
Declare, O heavens, the . . . 21
Eternal God, whose 370
For all the saints 480
For the fruits of all creation . 73
For the healing of the 452
Forth in thy name, O 498
God send us saints whose . . 425
Hast thou heard it, O my . 390
Help us express your love . 415
In Nature's voice we hear . 441
Leave we now the table of . 326
Lord, speak to me 412
Lord, thy church on earth . 438
Lord, whose love through . . 17
Make us, O God, a church . 484
O Church of God, arise . . . 451
O Jesus Christ, to thee . 224
Prophetic Church, the 293
Savior, thy dying love 442
Send me forth, O blessed . 424
Shout the tidings of 469
The cause of Zion 314
The church's life is built . . 297
The voice of God is 394
Thou whose purpose is to . 111
We thank thee, O God, for . 307
When Holy Ghost shall . . . 471
When the church of Jesus . 445
Where cross the crowded . 383

Protection (see also Refuge)

Abide with me 128
Again, dear Savior 494
Amazing grace 104
Children of the heavenly . . 156
Come thou fount of every . . 31
Father almighty, grant to . . 81
God be with you till . . 488, 489
God is my strong 160, 161
God of grace and God of . . 419
God of our fathers 191
Great God, attend while . . 311
Guide us, O thou great . . . 311
He leadeth me; oh, blessed . 123
I sought the Lord 213
My faith looks up to thee . . 143

Let us sing of Easter..... 279
Lift your glad voices..... 271
Lord, thy church on earth. 438
Morning has broken...... 22
My life flows on in endless. 157
Now in this moment...... 58
Now let our hearts within. 495
Now let us from this table. 327
Now the green blade rises. 280
O, holy Dove of God..... 285
O Lord, grace our......... 1
O Lord of light and love. 435
Oh, for a thousand....... 19
Thank You for giving me... 74
The cause of Zion....... 314
The Lord's my shepherd.. 124
There is a balm in Gilead. 147
Thou whose purpose is to. 111

New Year

God is working his...... 324
Standing at the portal.... 144

Night

Abide with me.......... 128
Again, dear Savior...... 494
Day is dying in the west.... 45
Lord of all hopefulness... 185
Now, on land and sea.... 501
Rejoice, ye Saints of 36

Obedience (see also **Resignation**)

A charge to keep I have... 399
According to thy gracious. 325
Be with me, Lord....... 487
Behold thy sons and..... 361
Breathe on me, breath of.. 179
Church of Christ, in..... 291
Come down, O Love..... 289
From isles and..... 417, 418
God send us saints whose.. 425
He leadeth me; oh, blessed. 123
He lives in us! Immortal.. 199
Here at the water's brink.. 354
I need thee every hour.... 129
Jesus calls us o'er the..... 371
Jesus is calling......... 391
Jesus, mighty king in..... 353
Make room within my.... 182
Make us, O God, a...... 484
Master, speak! Thy...... 410
My Lord, I know that all.. 457
My song is love unknown. 202
O day of God, draw nigh. 319
O Jesus, I have promised. 463
O Jesus, our Lord, thy.... 229
O my people, saith the... 387
O son of God, thou...... 222
Obedient, Lord, to thy.... 359
Oh, for a closer walk with. 117
Our Father, who in heaven. 80

Send me forth, O blessed.. 424
Sovereign and.......... 12
Take my life and let it.... 408
The voice of God is...... 394
Touch me, Lord, with thy. 409
Unto the calmly gathered. 450
We thank thee, O God, for. 307
With a steadfast faith.... 497

Offering, Offertory (see also **Commitment, Gifts, Sharing**)

All things are thine...... 397
As saints of old........ 405
As with gladness men of.. 254
Brothers, sisters, let us.... 403
From thee all skill and..... 89
How shall we come before. 106
If suddenly upon the..... 389
Just as I am, thine own... 421
Lord, may our hearts be... 26
Lord, may thy will be..... 92
More love to thee, O..... 411
O help us, Lord, to keep.... 90
Praise God, from whom... 43
Savior, thy dying love.... 442
Sing to the Lord of....... 46
Source of all gifts....... 400
Take my life and let it.... 408
We give thee but thine.... 401
We plow the fields........ 76
We thank you, Lord, for... 78
When the church of Jesus. 445
With my substance I will.. 460

Opening of Service (see **Call to Worship, Gathering, Invocation**)

Ordinances (see **Baptism, Blessing of Children, Confirmation, Health and Healing, Lord's Supper, Marriage, Ordination**)

Ordination (see also **Priesthood**)
See numbers 362-366
O God, send Heralds..... 429

Outreach (see **Mission, Witness**)

Pain (see **Suffering**)

Palm Sunday (see also **Christ's Passion and Death**)
All glory, laud and honor.. 23
My song is love unknown. 202
Praise him, praise him!.... 68
Ride on, ride on in....... 268
When, his salvation...... 225

Pardon (see **Forgiveness, Grace, Mercy**)

Parents (see also **Children, Family, Youth**)
We bring our children,... 348
When God created human. 434

Patience (see also **Hope**)
Lord of the bronze-green.. 456
O Master, let me walk.... 462
Spirit of God, descend.... 181
Within the shelter of our... 9

Patriotism (see **Nations**)

Peace—Inner
Again, dear Savior...... 494
Away in a manger... 232, 233
Beyond the mist and..... 152
Break thou the bread of... 173
Breathe on me, breath.... 179
Come down, O Love..... 289
Come, gracious Lord..... 492
Come ye youselves apart... 84
Creator of sunrises...... 186
Dear Lord and God of.... 115
Father, in thy mysterious.. 141
From thee all skill and..... 89
Good news! Great joy to.. 243
Great God of all the...... 91
Great hills may tremble... 153
Holy Spirit, truth divine.. 281
How gentle God's....... 130
I need thee every hour.... 129
In the cross of Christ I.... 203
Jesus, priceless treasure... 121
Let us breathe one fervent. 482
Lord, let thy blessing rest.. 490
Lord, let thy Holy Spirit.. 346
Lord of all hopefulness... 185
My life flows on in endless. 157
Now, on land and sea.... 501
O God, in restless....... 177
O Master, let me walk.... 462
O thou joyful, O thou.... 235
Oh, for a closer walk with. 117
One hour with Jesus...... 82
The Lord bless you and... 483
We come, aware of sin... 334

Peace—National and World (see also **Kingdom of God, Nations, Unity, Zion**)
See numbers 314-323
Again, dear Savior...... 494
Come, thou, O King of... 206
Creator of sunrises...... 186
Declare, O heavens, the.... 21
For the beauty of the..... 75
For the healing of the.... 452
Good news! Great joy to.. 243
Great God our source.... 444
Great hills may tremble... 153
Hark, the herald angels... 252
Heir of all the waiting.... 253

Ministry (*see also* Servanthood, Service)

See numbers 412-424

A diligent and grateful. . .362
According to the gifts that.363
As saints of old. 405
Bear each other's burdens.369
Brothers and sisters of. . .388
For the fruits of all. 73
Help us accept each other.171
In Nature's voice we hear.441
Jesus' hands were kind. . . .443
Lord God, we meet in. . . .365
Lord, thy church on earth.438
Lord, whose love through. .17
Make us, O God, a church.484
O Church of God, arise. . .451
O Jesus Christ, to thee. . . .224
O Lord of light and love. .435
Send forth thy light, O. . . .317
The voice of God is. 394
There's a spirit in the air. .214
Thou must be true thyself.379
We thank thee, God, for. .465
Where cross the crowded.383

Mission (*see also* Call, Commission, Witness)

See numbers 291-294, 474-478

A charge to keep I have. . .399
As saints of old. 405
Bear each other's burdens.369
Come, labor on. 384
Come ye yourselves apart. .84
For bread before us. 340
Forth in thy name, O. 498
"Go, make of all. 392
Go now forth into the. . . .436
God is working his. 324
Hark! The voice of Jesus. .381
In Nature's voice we hear.441
Leave we now the table of.326
Lord, thy church on earth.438
Make us, O God, a church.484
Now let our hearts within.495
O Church of God, arise. . .451
O Master Workman of the.219
O may thy church build. .431
O my people, saith the. . . .387
Rise up O saints of. 378
Sent forth by God's. 493
Shout the tidings of. 469
The bread that giveth. . . .423
The church's life is built. .297
The Spirit of God like a. . . .33
The vision of a life to. . . .349
The voice of God is. 394
Though anxious and. 380
Thy love, O God, has all. .163
When the church of Jesus.445
Yesu, Yesu, fill us with. . .407
Your cause be mine. 420

Morning

Holy, holy, holy. 56
Lord of all hopefulness. . .185
Morning has broken. 22
Thank You for giving me. . .74
When morning gilds the. . .35

Motherhood (*see* Parents)

Music

Earth and all stars. 49
Hallelujah! Hallelujah!. . . .53
Let us sing a world-wide. .468
My life flows on in endless.157
Sing songs of joy. 241
These things shall be: a. . .323
This is my song. 315

Mystery

Amazing grace. 104
Beyond the mist and 152
Crown him with many. . .228
Father in thy mysterious. .141
Go to dark Gethsemane. . .266
God of earth and planets. .198
I wonder as I wander. 251
Immortal, invisible, God. . .32
Jesus, the very thought of. .167
My song is love unknown.202
Mysterious Presence,. 169
O Christ, my Lord, create.174
O Jesus, thou art. 385
O little town of. 248
O Lord, how can it be. . . .332
O love of God, how. . .188, 189
O Sacred Head, now. . . .262
Unto the calmly gathered.450
What wondrous love is. . .216
You satisfy the hungry. . . .345

Nations (*see also* Peace—National and World, World)

All hail the power of. . .70, 71
Faith of our fathers. 433
For the healing of the. . . .452
From all that dwell below. .50
God has spoken through. .306
God of our fathers. 191
God send us saints whose. .425
Join with us in sweet. 475
Let us pray for one. 312
Let us sing a world-wide. .468
Lord of all nations grant. .467
My soul, praise the Lord!. .61
O Church of God, arise. . .451
O come, O come. 211
O God of every nation. . . .175
O Zion, haste. 476
The church's life is built. .297
This is my song. 315
Thy kingdom come, O. . . .320
We gather together. 11
We've a story to tell to. . . .477

Nature (*see also* Beauty, God the Creator)

All creatures of our God. . .72
All things bright and. 18
Creator of sunrises. 186
Day is dying in the west. . . .45
Earth and all stars. 49
Earth with her ten. 194
Eternal Ruler of the. 458
Fairest Lord Jesus. 226
For the beauty of the. 75
God of creation. 395
God of earth and planets. .198
God of the earth, the sky. . .65
God, the source of light. . .406
God, who touchest earth. .172
Great is Thy faithfulness. .187
Heaven and earth and sea. .51
In Nature's voice we hear.441
Joyful, joyful, we adore. . . .20
Lord of the bronze-green. .456
Morning has broken. 22
My soul, praise the Lord!. .61
O sing the mighty power. . .42
Praise ye the Lord!. 62, 63
This is my Father's. 52
We thank thee, God for. . .465
When morning gilds the. . .35
With happy voices ringing.29

Neighbors (*see also* Community, Fellowship)

Brothers and sisters of. . . .388
For the fruits of all. 73
Help us accept each other.171
In Christ there is no. . .448, 449
Let us pray for one. 312
Let us sing a world-wide. .468
Lord of all nations. 467
O God of every nation. . . .175
O Jesus, Master, when. . . .422
O may thy church build. .431
Teach me God to wonder.176
The weight of past and. . .118
These things shall be. 323
We thank thee, God, for. .465
We thank you, Lord, for. . .78
Yesu, Yesu, fill us with. . .407

New Life

See numbers 170-174, 349-357

Angels roll the rock. 277
Beneath the forms of. 339
Father, when in love to. . .116
Forgive our sins as we. . . .108
Good Christian friends,. . .275
Hail to the Brightness of.318
Hark, the herald angels. . .252
Heir of all the waiting. . . .253
How can creation's voice.300
How shall we come before.106
Let God be God. 197
Let us give praise to the. . .398

Light (*see also* **Intellect, Knowledge, Revelation, Truth**)

Amazing grace 104
Come down, O Love 289
Come, Holy Ghost, our . . . 286
Dear Master in whose life . 113
God has spoken through . . . 306
God of smallness, God of . 164
God, the source of light . . 406
Great God our source 444
Holy Spirit, truth divine . . 281
I heard the voice of 134
Immortal, invisible, God . . . 32
In the cross of Christ I 203
Joyful, joyful, we adore 20
Look for the beautiful 437
Lord, in this hour 150
Lord, whose love through . . 17
My children, "hear ye . . . 205
My life flows on in endless . 157
O God, our Source of . 301, 302
O Love that wilt not let . . . 132
O Word of God incarnate . 305
Oh, for a closer walk with . 117
Open my eyes, O Lord 454
Send forth thy light, O . . . 317
Sometimes a light . . . 154, 155
Sovereign and 12
Spirit divine, attend our . . 288
Spirit of God, descend . . . 181
Walk in the light 303
We limit not the truth 309
Your cause be mine 420

Lord's Day

In God's most holy 5
Lord, may our hearts be . . . 26
O help us, Lord, to keep . . . 90
O thou who hearest every . . 16

Lord's Supper

See numbers 325-345
Break thou the bread of . . . 173
Come, ye disconsolate 166
Come, ye yourselves apart . . 84
My song is love unknown . 202
O Lord, around thine 7
O Lord, grace our 1
O thou, whose youthful . . . 207
Sent forth by God's 493
There's a spirit in the 214
What wondrous love is . . . 216
Word of God, come down . 227

Love (*see also* **God's Love, Christ's Love**)

See numbers 403-409, 447-452
Bear each other's burdens . 369
Beloved community of . . . 414
Beneath the forms of 339
Blest be the tie that 485
Breathe on me, breath of . . 179
Come, Holy Ghost, our . . . 286

Creator of sunrises 186
Every good and perfect . . . 151
Faith of our fathers 433
Father, bless thy word to . . 474
Father when in love to 116
For the beauty of the 75
God who gives to life its . . . 184
Gracious Spirit, dwell 284
Grant us, Lord, the grace . 413
Great God, as followers of . 13
Help us accept each other . 171
Help us express your love . 415
Hope of the world . . . 208, 209
If suddenly upon the 389
In God's most holy 5
Jesus calls us o'er the 371
Jesus, the very thought of . . 167
Joyful, joyful, we adore 20
Let us pray for one 312
Lord, I want to be a 464
Lord, let thy Holy Spirit . 346
Lord of all nations grant . . 467
Lord, thy church on earth . 438
Love divine, all loves 170
Make us, O God, a church . 484
Met in thy sacred name 2
More love to thee, O 411
My Jesus, I love thee 204
My Lord, I know that all . 457
My song is love unknown . 202
Now let us from this table . 327
O God, from whom 367
O God, whose presence . . . 14
O Jesus, Master, when . . . 422
O Lord of heaven and 396
O Lord, thy people 352
O Lord, we come in 455
O Love that wilt not let . . . 132
O Master, let me walk . . . 462
O may thy church build . . 431
O my people, saith the . . . 387
O thou joyful, O thou 235
O thou, whose youthful . . . 207
Pour down thy Spirit from . 165
Prophetic Church, the . . . 293
Savior, thy dying love 442
Send forth thy light, O . . . 317
Sing to the Lord a joyful . . 55
Source of all gifts 400
Spirit divine, attend our . . 288
Spirit of God, descend . . . 181
Teach me, God, to 176
The weight of past and . . . 118
Thou must be true thyself . 379
Unmoved by fear, my 131
Walk in the light 303
We are one in the Spirit . . . 466
We bring our children . . . 348
We thank you, Lord, for . . . 78
Where beauty, truth, and . 321
With eyes of faith 122
Your cause be mine 420

Loyalty (*see* **Commitment, Duty**)

Marriage (*see also* **Family**)

Behold thy sons and 361
O God, from whom 367
O Lord, around thine 7
O perfect love 368
With a steadfast faith 497

Maturation (*see* **Growth, Change**)

Maundy Thursday (*see* **Christ's Passion & Death**)

Meditation (*see also* **Prayer**)

"Come ye apart!" 79
Come ye yourselves apart . . 84
God himself is with us 39
Lord, let thy blessing rest . . 490
Nearer, my God, to . . 138, 139
O God, in restless living . . 177
One hour with Jesus 82
Sometimes a light . . . 154, 155
Sweet hour of prayer 87
Take time to be holy 180
Unto the calmly gathered . 450
With eyes of faith 122

Memorial Services (*see* **Eternal Life, Resurrection**)

Mercy (*see also* **Forgiveness, Grace, Repentance, Sin**)

Bread of the world 329
Cast thy burden upon the . 133
Come thou fount of every . . 31
Come ye disconsolate 166
Great is thy faithfulness . . . 187
I am trusting thee, Lord . . . 127
I know not what the 126
I lift my soul to thee 110
Lead on, O King Eternal . . 374
Let us break bread 342
Let us pray for one 312
Lord, thy mercy now 114
May we who know the 416
My God, how wonderful . . 193
O how blessed are the 322
O Jesus Christ, to thee . . . 224
O Master, let me walk 462
Pass me not, O gentle 149
The Lord's my shepherd . . 124
These things shall be: a . . . 323
We would see Jesus . . 217, 218
When Jesus wept 270
Where wilt thou put thy . . 148

Might (*see* **Strength**)

Mind (*see* **Intellect, Knowledge**)

TOPICAL

Intellect and Intelligence (see also **Knowledge, Light, Teaching**)

Beyond the mist and 152
Creation flows 69
God of smallness 164
God who gives to life its . . 184
He lives in us! 199
Mysterious Presence 169
Prophetic church, the 293

Invitation (see also **Call, Challenge, Supplication**)

See numbers 381-387
Awake! Ye saints of God . . 140
Behold the Savior at your . 372
Brothers, sisters, let us 403
"Come ye apart!" 79
Come, ye disconsolate 166
Come ye yourselves apart . . 84
Hast thou heard it, O my . . 390
I heard the voice of Jesus . . 134
Jesus calls us o'er the 371
Jesus is calling 391
Join with us in sweet 475
Lift high the cross 263
O come, O come 211
O, holy Dove of God 285
O little town of 248
O young and fearless 210
Shout the tidings of 469
We would see Jesus . . 217, 218
Within the shelter of our 9

Invocation (see also **Call to Worship, Gathering**)

See numbers 1-17
Almighty Father, hear our . . 88
Come, thou almighty 54
Come thou fount of every . . 31
Great God, attend while . . . 59
Heavenly Father, we 112
Let the words of my 461
May thy presence be ours . 102

Internationalism (see **World**)

Jesus (see **Christ** categories)

Joy

See numbers 235-238, 271-279
Angels from the realms of . 231
As with gladness men of . . 254
Christ for the world we . . . 478
Come, rejoice before your . . 44
Come, thou, O King of . . 206
Declare, O heavens, the . . . 21
Faith of our fathers 433
Father, who in Jesus 331
For the beauty of the 75
From all that dwell below . . 50
Go tell it on the 249
Good Christian friends . . . 260
Good news! Great joy to . 243

Great God, attend while . . 59
Hail to the brightness of . . 318
Hark, the herald angels . . . 252
Heir of all the waiting 253
Holy, holy, holy is the 57
Holy Spirit, truth divine . . 281
I would be true 404
If by your grace I choose . . 432
It came upon the 256
Jesus good above all other . 259
Jesus, the very thought of . . 167
Joy to the world! 258
Joyful, joyful, we adore . . . 20
Lord, let thy Holy Spirit . . 346
Lord of all hopefulness . . . 185
Lord, thy church on earth . 438
Morning has broken 22
My life flows on in endless . 157
O Jesus, the giver of all we . 64
O Lord, thy people 352
O Love that wilt not let . . . 132
Oh, for a thousand 19
Rejoice, ye Saints of 36
Sing songs of joy 241
Sing to the Lord a joyful . . 55
Sound over all waters 261
Teach me, God, to 176
The vision of a life to be . . 349
Though anxious and 380
When morning gilds the . . 35
With happy voices ringing . 29

Judgment (see also **Discernment, Law**)

Come, thou, O King of . . . 206
O day of God, draw nigh . . 319
The Lord Jehovah reigns . . . 25
The love of God is broad . . 107
Where cross the crowded . 383
Where restless crowds are . 373

Justice (see also **Law**)

Awake! Ye saints of God . . 140
For the healing of the 452
O day of God, draw nigh . . 319
O how blessed are the 322
Rise up O saints of God . . . 378
The Lord Jehovah reigns . . . 25
There's a spirit in the air . . 214
These things shall be: a . . . 323

King (see **God's Majesty and Power**)

Kingdom of God (see also **Peace—National and World, Unity—Zion**)

See numbers 310-324
Beloved community of . . . 414
By thy redeeming cross . . . 292
Christ for the world we . . . 478
Church of Christ, in latter . 291
Come, thou long-expected . 201
Draw thou my soul 168

Eternal God, whose 370
Forth in thy name, O 498
God of eternity 192
God of grace and God of . . 419
God of our fathers 191
God send us saints whose . . 425
God, the source of light . . 406
God who gives to life its . . 184
Heir of all the waiting . . . 253
Here, O my Lord, I see . . . 328
In God's most holy 5
In Nature's voice we hear . 441
It came upon the 256
Joy to the world! 258
Lead on, O King Eternal . . 374
Make room within my 182
Newborn of God, his 247
O Christ, my Lord, create . 174
O Son of God, thou 222
Our Father, who in 80
Pour down thy Spirit 165
Rise up O saints of God! . . 378
Sent forth by God's 493
Sing praise to God 40
"Still other sheep I have" . . 479
Teach me, God, to 176
The church's life is built . 297
The city is alive, O God . . 375
The Lord almighty spoke . 195
The Spirit of God like a . . 33
We've a story to tell to the . 477
When Holy Ghost shall . . 471
Where cross the crowded . 383
While humble shepherds . . 236
With my substance I will . . 460
Would you bless our 447

Knowledge (see also **Intelligence, Light, Science, Teaching, Wisdom**)

Come, Holy Ghost, our . . . 286
Fountain of all revelation . 298
Lord, lead me by your 183
May we who know the 416
O come, O come, ... 211
O God, our Source of . 301, 302
O Lord, thy benediction . . 486
We limit not the truth of . . 309

Labor (see **Work**)

Law (see also **Judgment, Justice**)

God of smallness, God of . . 164
Holy Spirit, truth divine . . 281
Praise to the living God! . . 47

Lent (see **Christ's Passion and Death**)

Liberty (see **Freedom**)

When Holy Ghost shall . . . 471
Within the shelter of our 9
You satisfy the hungry 345

Home (see **Children, Family, Marriage, Parents, Youth**)

Hope (see also **Faith, Trust**)
See numbers 244-258,
    291-296, 306-325
Angels from the realms of . 231
Angels we have heard on . . 237
Blest be the tie that 485
Brothers, sisters, let us 403
Come down, O Love 289
Come, labor on 384
Come now, sound the call . 386
Come, thou long-expected . 201
Come thou, O King of 206
Declare, O heavens, the 21
Eternal God whose power . 370
For the Book of Mormon's . 221
For the healing of the 452
Forth in thy name, O 498
God of eternity 192
God send us saints whose . . 425
Great God our source 444
Help us accept each other . 171
Here at thy table, Lord . . . 333
Here, O my Lord, I see . . . 328
Holy Spirit, come with . . . 287
Hope of the World . . . 208, 209
How can creation's voice . 300
I lift my soul to thee, ... 110
In Christ there is no . . 448, 449
In memory of the Savior's . 330
Jesus, the very thought . . . 167
Just as I am 119
Let us sing of Easter 279
Lord, I was blind 178
Lord of all hopefulness . . . 185
Lord, thy church on earth . 438
Lord, whose love through . . 17
Now let our hearts within . 495
O come, all ye faithful . . . 238
O come, O come, ... 211
O God of every nation 175
O God, our help in ages . . . 200
O Lord, grace our 1
O love of God, how . . 188, 189
O my people, saith the . . . 387
O Son of God, thou 222
O Zion, haste 476
Open my eyes, O Lord 454
Our Father, who in 80
Praise him, praise him! 68
Rejoice, ye Saints of 36
Rise up O saints of God! . . 378
Sound over all waters 261
Sovereign and 12
The bread that giveth 423
The city is alive, O God . . . 375

The vision of a life to 349
Thy love, O God, has all . . 163
'Twas on that dark, that . . 337
Unto God, who knows our . 472
Walk in the light 303
We are living, we are 376
We are one in the Spirit . . . 466
We've a story to tell to the . 477
What a friend we have . . 85, 86
When Holy Ghost shall . . . 471
Where cross the crowded . 383
Where restless crowds are . 373
Within the shelter of our 9

House of God (see also **Church**)
Creator God, creating still . 190
God himself is with us 39
Lord, thou hast brought 6
Within the shelter of our 9

Humanity and Humanness (see also **Worth**)
A mighty fortress 142
Creation flows 69
Declare, O heavens, the 21
Eternal God, whose 370
Father in thy mysterious . . 141
For the beauty of the 75
God of earth and planets . . 198
Great hills may tremble . . . 153
Help us accept each other . 171
Holy Spirit, come with . . . 287
I know not what the 126
I would be true 404
If by Your grace I choose . 432
In heavenly love abiding . . 120
Just as I am 119
Lord, in this hour 150
Lord, save your world 310
Lord, whose love through . . 17
My God, how wonderful . . 193
O God, our help in ages . . . 200
O may thy church build . . . 431
Praise, my soul, the King . . . 41
Tenderly, tenderly, lead . . 146
The city is alive, O God . . . 375
The Lord Jehovah reigns . . . 25
There's a church within . . 290
We limit not the truth of . . 309
When God created human . 434
Where restless crowds are . 373
Where wilt thou put thy . . 148
World around us, sky 135

Humility
A mighty fortress 142
According to the gifts that . 363
Be with me, Lord 487
Beneath the cross of 428
Beyond the mist and 152
Come, labor on 384
God of earth and planets . . 198

Great hills may tremble . . . 153
Here we have come, dear . . 109
How shall we come before . 106
I am trusting thee, Lord . . . 127
I know not what the 126
I sought the Lord 213
I would be true 404
Just as I am, thine own . . . 421
O God, in restless living . . 177
O how blessed are the 322
Unto God, who knows our . 472
With eyes of faith 122
Yesu, Yesu, fill us with . . . 407

Imagination and Originality (see **Creativity**)

Incarnation (see also **Christmas, Christ's Divinity**)
See numbers 230-261
Beneath the forms of 339
Christ is alive! Let 272
Creation flows 69
Dear Master, in whose 113
Eternal God, whose 370
For the Book of Mormon's . 221
Forth in thy name, O 498
"Go, make of all 392
God who spoke in the 308
Gracious Spirit, dwell 284
He lives in us! 199
How can creation's voice . 300
If suddenly upon the 389
In Nature's voice we hear . 441
Let your heart be broken . . 377
Lord, here amidst the 427
Lord, lead me by your 183
Lord, speak to me 412
Love divine, all loves 170
Make room within my 182
My song is love unknown . 202
Mysterious Presence 169
Now let our hearts within . 495
O Jesus, Master, when 422
O Word of God incarnate . 305
Send forth thy light, O . . . 317
Sweet the time, exceeding . . 4
Teach me, God, to 176
Teach me, my God and . . . 439
The city is alive, O God . . . 375
There's a church within . . 290
There's a spirit in the 214
Unto the calmly gathered . 450
Walk in the light 303
When God created human . 434

Integrity (see also **Trust**)
I would be true 404
Lord of the bronze-green . . 456
These things shall be: a . . . 323
Thou must be true 379

TOPICAL

Grace for Meal

Be present at our table,... 336
Praise God, from whom... 43

Gratitude (see **Praise, Thanks**)

Grief (see **Comfort, Suffering**)

Growth (see also **Change**)

Breathe on me, breath of.. 179
Come, O Creator Spirit... 283
Fountain of all revelation. 298
God has spoken through.. 306
Gracious Spirit, dwell... 284
Here we have come, dear.. 109
In heavenly love abiding.. 120
Let us pray for one...... 312
Lord, I want to be a...... 464
Lord, lead me by your.... 183
Lord, let thy Holy...... 346
Make room within my... 182
Make us, O God, a church. 484
My Lord, I come this..... 357
Now the green blade..... 280
O God, our Source of. 301, 302
O, holy Dove of God.... 285
Oh, for a closer walk with. 117
Once more before we part. 500
Onward to Zion,....... 316
Open my eyes, O Lord.... 454
Pour down thy Spirit..... 165
Savior, like a shepherd... 162
Sent forth by God's...... 493
Sovereign and.......... 12
Spirit of God, descend.... 181
The love of God is broad.. 107
The Spirit of God like a.. 33
The weight of past and... 118
There's a church within.. 290
We are living, we are..... 376
We limit not the truth of. 309
Within the shelter of our.... 9
Your cause be mine...... 420

Guidance

A mighty fortress........ 142
Abide with me.......... 128
Amazing grace......... 104
Be with me, Lord,...... 487
Behold thy sons and..... 361
Church of Christ in...... 291
Come down, O Love..... 289
Dear Master in whose life. 113
Eternal ruler of the...... 458
Father almighty, grant to.. 81
Father hear the prayer... 453
God be with you till.. 488, 489
God of creation........ 395
God of our fathers....... 191
Great God our source.... 444
Great is Thy faithfulness.. 187
Guide us, O thou great... 311
Hast thou heard it, O my. 390
He leadeth me; oh, blessed. 123

I am trusting thee, Lord... 127
Jesus good above all other. 259
Jesus, mighty king in Zion 353
Jesus, Savior, pilot me.... 145
Let us give praise to the... 398
Let us pray for one...... 312
Lord, as we rise to leave... 491
Lord, lead me by your.... 183
Lord, let thy Holy Spirit.. 346
Lord, thou hast brought.... 6
Master, speak! Thy...... 410
May thy presence be ours. 102
Met in thy sacred name, O.. 2
My faith looks up the thee. 143
Now in this moment...... 58
Now thank we all our God.. 60
O God of every nation.... 175
O God, our Source of. 301, 302
O God, the eternal Father. 335
O God, whose presence.... 14
O Jesus, I have promised.. 463
O Lord, around thine altar.. 7
O Lord, thy benediction.. 486
O Master, let me walk.... 462
O Word of God incarnate. 305
Oh, for a closer walk..... 117
Open my eyes, O Lord.... 454
Remembering thy Son, O. 341
Savior, like a shepherd... 162
Take time to be holy..... 180
Teach me, my God and... 439
Tenderly, tenderly, lead.. 146
The living Word of...... 299
The Lord's my shepherd.. 124
There's an old, old path... 158
Unto God, who knows our. 472
We gather together....... 11
Within the shelter of our.... 9
World around us, sky.... 135
Would you bless our..... 447

Harvest (see also **Thanks**)

As saints of old......... 405
Come, ye thankful..... 37, 38
Sing to the Lord of....... 46
We plow the fields........ 76

Health and Healing

A mighty fortress........ 142
Bear each other's burdens. 369
Beloved community of.... 414
Come, ye disconsolate.... 166
Deep were his wounds,... 269
For the healing of all..... 452
Gracious Spirit, dwell.... 284
Heir of all the waiting.... 253
Help us accept each other. 171
Here we have come, dear.. 109
Hope of the world... 208, 209
Jesus' hands were kind.... 443
Let God be God........ 197
Lord, I was blind........ 178
Lord, who views all..... 459

Make us, O God, a church. 484
O Jesus Christ, to thee.... 224
O Lord, grace our......... 1
O Lord, we come in...... 455
Rise up O saints of...... 378
Send forth thy light, O.... 317
Sometimes a light... 154, 155
The city is alive, O...... 375
The weight of past and... 118
There is a balm in....... 147
We would see Jesus 217, 218
Where cross the crowded. 383
Word of God, come down. 227

Heaven (see **Eternal Life**)

Holy Spirit

See numbers 281-289
All to Jesus I surrender... 430
Baptized in water....... 350
Behold thy sons and..... 361
Breathe on me, breath.... 179
Come, gracious Lord..... 492
Come, thou almighty..... 54
Creator God, creating.... 190
Descend, O Spirit....... 355
God has spoken through.. 306
Great and marvelous are... 48
He lives in us! Immortal.. 199
Heavenly Father, we..... 112
How can creation's voice. 300
If by Your grace I choose.. 432
Let God be God........ 197
Life of ages, richly....... 304
Lord, let thy Holy...... 346
Lord of all nations grant. 467
Lord, we come before thee.. 10
Love divine, all loves..... 170
Met in thy sacred name,.... 2
Mysterious Presence,..... 169
Now let our hearts within. 495
O God in heaven, we..... 356
O God, in restless living.. 177
O Jesus Christ, to thee.... 224
O Jesus, the giver of all.... 64
O Lord, grace our......... 1
O Lord, we come as..... 360
O my people, saith the.... 387
Obedient, Lord, to thy.... 359
Oh, for a closer walk..... 117
Praise to the living....... 47
Rejoice, ye Saints of..... 36
Sometimes a light... 154, 155
Sovereign and.......... 12
Spirit of God, descend.... 181
The Lord almighty spoke.. 195
The Spirit of God like a.. 33
There is a balm in....... 147
There's a spirit in the..... 214
Thou whose purpose is to. 111
Thy love, O God, has all.. 163
Touch me, Lord, with thy. 409
Walk in the light........ 303

God is working his......324
God of smallness, God of..164
God who gives to life its...184
God who spoke in the....308
Great and marvelous are...48
Great God, attend while...59
Great God our source....444
Holy, holy, holy is the.....57
Holy, holy, holy.........56
Immortal, invisible, God...32
Let us give praise to the...398
Lord of the bronze-green..456
My soul, praise the.......61
O God of every nation...175
O Lord of heaven and....396
O sing the mighty power...42
O worship the King....27, 28
Oh, for a thousand.......19
Praise the Lord, ye.......66
Praise to the Lord, the....67
Praise ye the Lord!.....62, 63
Sing praise to God.......40
Soldiers of Christ........393
The Lord Jehovah reigns...25
The Spirit of God like a....33
There's a spirit in the.....214
This God is the God we...481
This is my Father's.......52
Where wilt thou put thy..148

God the Sustainer (*see also* **Comfort, Refuge**)

See numbers 45-48, 73-78, 124-128, 140-144

A charge to keep I have...399
All things are thine......397
As saints of old.........405
Be with me, Lord,......487
Cast thy burden upon the.133
Come, thou fount of......31
Come, ye thankful.....37, 38
Creator God, creating....190
Father almighty, grant....81
Father, hear the prayer...453
Fountain of all revelation.298
From thee all skill and.....89
God be with you till..488, 489
God is my strong....160, 161
God is working his......324
God of earth and planets..198
God of eternity.........192
God of our fathers......191
God of the earth, the sky,..65
God, the source of light...406
God who spoke in the....308
Great God, attend while...59
Great hills may tremble..153
Great is Thy faithfulness.187
Hallelujah! Hallelujah!....53
He lives in us! Immortal..199
Holy Spirit, truth........281
How firm a foundation...136

How gentle God's.......130
I know that my.....273, 274
Immortal, invisible, God...32
Leave we now the table of.326
Let God be God.........197
Let us breathe one fervent.482
Lord, lead me by your....183
Lord, thou hast brought....6
Lord, we come before thee..10
Mysterious Presence.....169
Now in this moment......58
Now let our hearts within.495
Now thank we all our God..60
O God, our help in ages..200
O God, our Source of.301, 302
O Lord, grace our.........1
O Lord of heaven and....396
O thou God, who hearest..105
O thou who hearest every..16
O worship the King...27, 28
Our Father, who in......80
Pass me not, O gentle....149
Praise, my soul, the King...41
Praise to the Lord, the.....67
Redeemer of Israel......313
Sing to the Lord a joyful...55
We gather together.......11
Where wilt thou put thy..148
With happy voices ringing.29
With thankful hearts we....3
You satisfy the hungry....345

Good Friday (*see* **Christ's Passion**)

Gospel

See numbers 469-477

Afar in old Judea........296
Faith of our fathers......433
God forgave my sin in....382
I heard the voice of......134
I wonder as I wander.....251

Lord, save your world....310
Love divine, all loves.....170
May we who know the....416
My children, "hear ye....205
My life flows on in endless.157
My song is love unknown.202
Nearer, my God, to..138, 139
Newborn of God, his.....247
Now let us from this......327
O Church of God, arise...451
O love of God, how..188, 189
Praise him, praise him!....68
Send me forth, O blessed..424
Sometimes a light....154, 155
Sweet the time, exceeding...4
Tell me the story of......215
The Church's one.......294
There is a balm in Gilead.147
Thy love, O God, has all..163
We thank thee, O God,...307

Grace (*see also* **Forgiveness, Mercy, Reconciliation, Repentance, Salvation**)

A mighty fortress.......142
All hail the power of...70, 71
Amazing grace.........104
An upper room.........343
Beneath the cross of.....428
Beyond the mist and.....152
Children of the heavenly..156
Come down, O Love.....289
Come, gracious Lord,....492
Come thou fount of every..31
Come thou long-expected.201
Creator God, creating....190
Every good and perfect...151
Fairest Lord Jesus.......226
For the beauty of the.....75
Great God, attend while...59
Great is thy............187
Heavenly Father, grant...496
Help us express your love..415
Here at thy table, Lord...333
Here at thy table, Lord...338
Here, O my Lord, I see...328
Here we have come, dear..109
I am trusting thee, Lord...127
I know that my Redeemer.212
I know that my.....273, 274
I sought the Lord........213
If by Your grace I choose..432
In heavenly Love abiding.120
Jesus, the very thought of..167
Joyful, joyful, we adore....20
Leave we now the table of.326
Let your heart be broken..377
Lift your glad voices.....271
Look at this man, born of.230
Lord, I was blind........178
Lord, lead me by your....183
Lord, who views all.....459
My children, "hear ye....205
My faith looks up to.....143
My shepherd will supply..125
My song is love unknown.202
Now in this moment......58
Now let our hearts within.495
O God, whose presence....14
O Jesus, our Lord, thy....229
O Lord of heaven and.....77
O Sacred Head, now.....262
O thou joyful, O thou....235
Oh, for a thousand.......19
Pass me not, O gentle....149
Praise, my soul, the King...41
Redeeming Grace has....351
Sovereign and..........12
Spirit of truth, of life, of..426
The Lord bless you and...483
The Lord Jehovah reigns...25
There's a church within..290
'Tis the blessed hour of....83
When God created human.434

Let us break bread 342
O come, all ye faithful 238
Praise to the Lord, the 67
Rejoice, ye Saints of latter . . 36
Spirit of truth, of life, ... 426
"Still other sheep I have" . . 479
'Tis the blessed hour of 83
Would you bless our 447

Gifts of the Spirit (see **Spiritual Gifts**)

Gifts, Giving (see also **Offering, Sharing, Thanks**)

According to the gifts that . 363
All to Jesus I surrender . . . 430
Beloved community of . . . 414
For the fruits of all 73
God forgave my sin in 382
Grant us, Lord, the grace . 413
Help us express your love . 415
Let your heart be broken . . 377
Lord, pour thy Spirit from . 364
O Lord of heaven 77
O Lord of heaven 396
Savior, thy dying love 442
Sing to the Lord of 46
Source of all gifts 400
Spirit of truth, of life, of . . . 426
Teach us, O Lord, true . . . 440
The Lord our God alone . . . 196
The vision of a life to be . . 349
We give thee but thine 401
We thank thee, God, for . . 465
We thank you, Lord, for . . . 78
With my substance I will . . 460

God the Creator (see also **Beauty, Creation, Nature**)

See numbers 20-22, 50-53, 61-63

All creatures of our God . . . 72
All things bright and 18
Come, rejoice before your . 44
Creation flows 69
Creator God, creating 190
Creator of sunrises 186
Earth with her ten 194
For the beauty of the 75
For the fruits of all 73
God of creation 395
God of earth and planets . 198
God of the earth, the sky . . 65
God, the source of light . . . 406
God who spoke in the 308
God, who touchest earth . . 172
Great and marvelous are . . 48
Great God our source 444
Holy, holy, holy 56
Let us give praise to the . 398
Lord of the bronze-green . . 456
Mysterious Presence, ... 169
Now in this moment 58
Now, on land and sea 501

O sing the mighty power . 42
Praise the Lord, ye 66
Sing praise to God 40
Source of all gifts 400
The Lord almighty spoke . . 195
Thy love, O God, has all . 163
We plow the fields 76
When God created human . 434
When kindled by Thy 282
With happy voices ringing . 29
World around us, sky 135

God the Eternal

A mighty fortress 142
Abide with me 128
Creation flows unceasingly . 69
Eternal God, whose power . 370
For the Book of Mormon's . 221
From all that dwell below . . 50
God has spoken through . . 306
God of eternity 192
Great God our source 444
Great is Thy faithfulness . . 187
Heaven and earth and sea . . 51
Holy, holy, holy 56
If by your grace I choose . . 432
Immortal, invisible, ... 32
Lead on, O King 374
Let us give praise to the . . . 398
Now thank we all our 60
O God of every nation . . . 175
O God, our help in ages . . . 200
Praise, my soul, the King . . . 41
Praise to the living God! . . . 47
Standing at the portal 144
This God is the God we . . . 481
When kindled by Thy 282

God the Father

An upper room 343
Blest be thou, O God of . . . 24
Children of the heavenly . . 156
Dear Lord and God of 115
Father, bless thy word to . . 474
Praise, my soul, the King . . . 41
Standing at the portal 144
This is my Father's world . . 52
'Tis midnight, and on 264

God's Love (see also **Christ's Love**)

See numbers 40-42, 130-132, 163-166, 186-194

All things bright and 18
Awake! Ye saints of God . . 140
Beyond the mist and doubt . 152
Brothers, sisters, let us 403
Children of the heavenly . . 156
Come down, O Love 289
Come, gracious Lord, ... 492
Come, rejoice before your . . 44
Eternal God, whose power . 370
Father, in thy mysterious . . 141

Father, who in Jesus 331
For the fruits of all creation . 73
Fountain of all revelation . 298
God has spoken through . . 306
God in his love for us 402
God of earth and planets . . 198
God of the earth, the sky, . . 65
God, who touchest earth . . 172
Great and marvelous are . . 48
Great God our source 444
Help us express your love . . 415
Here at thy table, Lord . . . 333
Holy, holy, holy 56
Holy Spirit, truth divine . . 281
I know not what the future . 126
I lift my soul to thee, Lord . 110
I sought the Lord 213
In heavenly love abiding . . 120
Join with us in sweet 475
Joyful, joyful, we adore . . . 20
Let us breathe one fervent . 482
Let us sing a world-wide . . 468
Let us sing of Easter 279
Life of ages, richly 304
Look at this man, born of . 230
Lord, lead me by your 183
Lord, let thy blessing 490
Lord, who views all 459
My life flows on in endless . 157
My Lord, I come this hour . 357
My shepherd will supply . . 125
"My times are in thy 137
Newborn of God, his 247
Now in this moment 58
Now, on land and sea 501
Now thank we all our 60
O, holy Dove of God 285
O how blessed are the 322
O Lord, around thine altar . . 7
O Lord of heaven and 77
O Master, to all 347
O perfect love 368
O worship the King 27, 28
O Zion, haste 476
Praise to the living God! . . . 47
Praise ye the Lord! 62, 63
Redeeming Grace has 351
Tenderly, tenderly, lead . . 146
The city is alive, O God . . . 375
The love of God is broad . . 107
'Twas on that dark, that . . 337
Unto God, who knows our . 472
We bring our children, . . . 348
We thank you, Lord, for . . . 78
When God created human . 434

God's Majesty and Power

See numbers 188-198

A mighty fortress 142
All hail the power of . . . 70, 71
Blest be thou, O God of . . . 24
Come, gracious Lord, ... 492
Declare, O heavens, the . . . 21

Endowment (*see* **Gifts, Spiritual Gifts**)

Epiphany (*see* **Christmas**)

Eternal Life (*see also* **Resurrection**)

See numbers 271-280
Abide with me 128
Again, dear Savior 494
An upper room 343
Breathe on me, breath of . . 179
Creation flows 69
Day is dying in the 45
Deep were his wounds, . . . 269
Lord, in this hour 150
Love divine, all loves 170
O God, our help in ages . . . 200
O Love that wilt not let . . . 132
Praise to the living God! . . . 47
Sweet the time, exceeding . . . 4

Evangelism (*see* **Call, Invitation, Mission, Witness**)

Evening

Abide with me 128
Day is dying in the 45
Lord of all hopefulness . . . 185
Now, on land and sea 501

Excellence

Beloved community of . . . 414
Just as I am, thine own to . 421
O Son of God, thou 222

Expansion (*see* **Call, Invitation, Mission, Witness**)

Exploration (*see also* **Adventure**)

Come now, sound the call . 386
Hark! the voice of Jesus . . . 381
Hast thou heard it, O my . . 390
Open my eyes, O Lord 454
Prophetic Church, the 293

Faith (*see also* **Hope, Trust**)

See numbers 119-162
Amazing grace 104
Break thou the bread of . . . 173
Come now, sound the call . 386
Eternal Ruler of the 458
Faith of our fathers 433
God is working his 324
Hast thou heard it, O my . . 390
How can creation's voice . 300
I know that my Redeemer . 212
I know that my 273, 274
I would be true 404
In memory of the Savior's . 330
Lead on, O King Eternal . . 374
Let us sing of Easter 279
Lord, lead me by your 183
Now, on land and sea 501
O day of God, draw nigh . . 319

O God of every nation 175
O Master, let me walk 462
Obedient, Lord, to thy 359
Remembering thy Son, O . 341
Spirit of God, descend 181
The bread that giveth 423
The Spirit of God like a 33
This is my Father's world . . 52
Though anxious and 380
'Tis the blessed hour of . . . 83
We thank thee, O God, for . 307
With a steadfast faith 497

Family (*see also* **Children, Marriage, Parents, Youth**)

Baptized in water 350
Now let us from this table . 327
O thou, whose youthful . . . 207
When God created human . 434
Within the shelter of our 9
Would you bless our 447

Fatherhood (*see* **Parents**)

Fear (*see also* **Danger, Faith**)

For the healing of the 452
God is my strong 160, 161
"My times are in thy 137
O Jesus, I have promised . . 463
O Lord, around thine altar . . 7
Oh, for a faith that will . . . 159
Standing at the portal 144
The love of God is broad . . 107

Fellowship (*see also* **Children of God, Community, Unity**)

Beneath the forms of 339
Blest be the tie that binds . . 485
For all the saints 480
For the beauty of the 75
Great God of all the 91
Help us accept each other . 171
In Christ there is no . . 448, 449
Jesus loves the little 223
Let us break bread 342
Let us pray for one 312
Let us sing a world-wide . . 468
My Lord, I know that all . . 457
O Jesus, Master, when 422
O Lord, thy people 352
O may thy church build . . 431
O thou, whose youthful . . . 207
Sweet the time, exceeding . . . 4
There's an old, old path . . . 158
Walk in the light 303
With a steadfast faith 497
You may sing of the 8

Forgiveness (*see also* **Grace, Mercy, Reconciliation, Repentance, Sin**)

See numbers 103-119
A charge to keep I have . . . 399
Creator of sunrises 186

God forgave my sin in . . . .
Help us accept each . . . . . .
Here at the water's brink . . 3..
Lord of all nations grant . . 467
My God, how wonderful . . 193
O Christ, my Lord, create . 174
O God in heaven, we 356
O Lord, we come in 455
Our Father, who in 80
Pour down thy Spirit 165
Remembering thy Son, O . 341
We come, aware of sin . . . 334

Freedom

Creator of sunrises 186
Every good and perfect . . . 151
Faith of our fathers 433
For the healing of all 452
God of grace and God 419
Holy Spirit, truth divine . . 281
I know that my Redeemer . 212
In heavenly love abiding . . 120
Lord, I was blind 178
Lord, save your world 310
My Lord, I know that all . . 457
Prophetic Church, the 293
The love of God is broad . . 107
The weight of past and . . . 118
These things shall be: 323
We come, aware of sin . . . 334

Friendship (*see* **Fellowship, Love**)

Fruits of the Spirit (*see* **Faith, Humility, Love, Joy, Patience, Peace**)

Funerals (*see* **Resurrection, Eternal Life**)

Future

Angels from the realms of . 231
Father, in thy mysterious . . 141
Heir of all the waiting 253
I know not what the 126
It came upon the 256
Let us pray for one 312
Love divine, all loves 170
Newborn of God, his 247
Now in this moment 58
O come, O come, ... 211
The cause of Zion 314
The Church's one 294
These things shall be: a . . . 323
We limit not the truth 309

Gathering—Congregational, Fellowship, Zionic

See numbers 1-17
Come, rejoice before your . . 44
Come, thou Almighty 54
Earth and all stars 49
God has spoken through . . 306
Here we have come, dear . 109

Lord, I was blind 178
Lord, lead me by your 183
Lord, save your world 310
More love to thee, O Christ . 411
My God, how wonderful . . 193
O Lord, my Lord, create . . 174
O God of every nation . . . 175
O Jesus, I have promised . . 463
O Lord, how can it be 332
O Lord, we come in 455
O Sacred Head, now 262
Pass me not, O gentle 149
Thy love, O God, has all . . 163
Unto the calmly gathered . . 450
Where restless crowds are . . 373

Confidence (see **Faith, Hope, Trust**)

Confirmation
See numbers 358-361
Baptized in water 350
Descend, O Spirit 355
Lord, let thy Holy Spirit . . . 346

Consecration (see **Commitment, Duty**)

Contrition (see **Confession, Repentance**)

Convey (see also **Teaching**)
See numbers 468-479
Go now forth into the 436
O help us, Lord, to keep 90

Courage (see also **Strength**)
Awake! Ye saints of God . . . 140
Faith of our fathers 433
Father, hear the prayer we . 453
God is my strong 160, 161
He leadeth me; oh, blessed . 123
In heavenly love abiding . . 120
Jesus, Savior, pilot me 145
Lord, as we rise to leave . . . 491
Lord of all nations grant . . 467
Make us, O God, a church . 484
My shepherd will supply . . 125
Now let our hearts within . 495
Now let us from this table . 327
O Jesus Christ, to thee 224
O Jesus, I have 463
Oh, for a faith that will . . . 159
Tenderly, tenderly, lead . . 146
The vision of a life to be . . 349
There's an old, old path . . . 158
Thou whose purpose is to . 111
We are living, we are 376
Would you bless our 447

Covenant (see **Commitment**)

Creation (see also **Beauty, God the Creator, Nature**
Creation flows 69
Earth and all stars 49

God of earth and planets . . 198
How can creation's voice . 300
Morning has broken 22
O love of God, how . . 188, 189
Sing to the Lord of 46
This is my Father's world . . 52

Creativity (see also **Gifts, Stewardship**)
Come now, sound the call . 386
Earth and all stars 49
God who gives to life its . . . 184
Lord, as we rise to leave . . . 491

Creator (see **Creation, God the Creator**)

Cross (see also **Atonement, Christ's Passion and Death**)
See numbers 262-267
According to thy gracious . 325
Beneath the cross of Jesus . 428
By thy redeeming cross . . . 292
Deep were his wounds, . . . 269
Forgive our sins as we 108
Here at thy table, Lord, . . . 338
In the cross of Christ I 203
Jesus Christ is risen today . 278
Jesus good above all other . 259
Lord, whose love through . . 17
My song is love unknown . 202
Nearer, my God, to . . 138, 139
O God, the eternal Father . 335
O Love that wilt not let . . . 132
The Church's one 294

Crucifixion (see **Christ's Passion and Death**)

Danger (see also **Fear**)
Great God our source 444
Great hills may tremble . . . 153
He leadeth me; oh, blessed . 123
In heavenly love abiding . . 120
Jesus, Savior, pilot me 145
My shepherd will supply . . 125
Oh, for a faith that will . . . 159

Darkness (see **Night**)

Death (see **Eternal Life, Resurrection**)

Dedication (see **Commitment, Duty, Purity**)

Dedication of Buildings, etc.
Christ is the foundation . . . 295
Lord, thou hast brought us . . 6
The Lord our God alone is . 196

Dependability (see **Trust**)

Devotion (see **Commitment, Duty, Love, Purity**)

Direction (see **Guidance**)

Discernment (see also **Judgment**)
God of smallness, God of . . 164
How can creation's voice . 300
Let us pray for one 312
My Lord, I know that all . . 457
O Son of God, thou 222
Teach me, God, to 176
We thank thee, God, for . . 465
When kindled by thy 282

Discipleship (see **Servanthood, Service**)

Doctrine and Covenants (see also **Revelation, Scriptures**)
Afar in old Judea 296
God has spoken through . . 306
Praise to the living God 47
The living Word of 299
We limit not the truth of . . 309

Doxologies (see also **Praise**)
(St. 3) All praise and 60
Come rejoice before your . . 44
God himself is with us 39
Praise God from whom all . . 43
Praise to the living God 47

Duty (see also **Commitment**)
Brothers, sisters, let us 403
Father almighty, grant to . . 81
Go to dark Gethsemane . . . 266
God, the source of light . . . 406
In God's most holy 5
O Son of God, thou 222
Spirit divine, attend our . . 288

Earth (see also **World**)
Creator of sunrises 186
Earth and all stars 49
God in his love for us 402
God of creation 395
God of the earth and 198
God of the earth, the sky, . . 65
God who spoke in the 308
God who touchest earth . . 172
Heaven and earth and sea . . 51
Help us express your love . . 415
My soul, praise the Lord! . . 61
O sing the mighty power . . 42
Praise ye the Lord! 62, 63
This is my Father's 52
We plow the fields 76

Easter (see **Christ's Resurrection**)

Ecology (see **Nature, Stewardship**)

Education (see **Intellect, Knowledge, Teacher, and Teaching**)

O Christ, my Lord, create . 174
O Church of God, arise . . . 451
O God, send Heralds 429
O Lord, thy people 352
O may thy church build . 431
O Word of God incarnate . 305
Rejoice, ye Saints of latter . 36
The church's life is built . . 297
The city is alive, O God . . . 375
Thy love, O God, has all . . 163
When the church of Jesus . 445
You may sing of the 8

City

Earth and all stars 49
Lord of the bronze-green . . 456
Lord, thy church on earth . 438
O Jesus Christ, to thee 224
The city is alive, O God . . . 375
When the church of Jesus . 445
Where restless crowds are . 373

Close of Service (see Benediction, Sending Forth)

Comfort

See numbers 82-87
Blest be the tie that binds . . 485
Come. O Creator Spirit . . . 283
Come, ye disconsolate 166
Father, in thy mysterious . 141
Guide us, O Thou great . . . 311
Heir of all the waiting . . . 253
How gentle God's 130
Lord, we come before thee . . 10
O day of God, draw nigh . . 319
O how blessed are the 322
O Lord, around thine altar . . 7
Obedient, Lord, to thy 359
Sometimes a light . . . 154, 155
Sovereign and 12
Standing at the portal 144
'Tis midnight, and on 264
We thank thee, O God, for . 307

Commission (see also Call, Mission)

A charge to keep I have . . . 399
Come now, sound the call . 386
Creator of sunrises 186
"Go, make of all 392
Go now forth into the 436
God forgave my sin in 382
Jesus, mighty king in Zion . 353
Leave we now the table of . 326
Lord, thy church on earth . 438
Lord, who views all 459
Tell it! Tell it out with 470
The cause of Zion 314
The church's life is built . . 297
The voice of God is 394
When Holy Ghost shall . . . 471

Commitment (see also Baptism, Duty)

See numbers 403-467

A diligent and grateful . . . 362
All things are thine 397
As with gladness men of . . 254
Be with me, Lord 487
Behold the Savior at your . 372
Breathe on me, breath of . . 179
Brothers and sisters of 388
By thy redeeming cross . . . 292
Come down, O Love 289
Dear Lord and God of 115
Descend, O Spirit 355
Father, who in Jesus 331
Forth in thy name, O 498
God is working his 324
God of creation 395
God of our fathers 191
God who gives to life its . . . 184
God, who touchest earth . . 172
Gracious Spirit, dwell 284
Great God, as followers of . . 13
Hark! The voice of Jesus . . 381
Hast thou heard it, O my . . 390
He lives in us! Immortal . . 199
Here at the water's brink . . 354
Here we have come, dear . . 109
Hope of the world . . . 208, 209
How shall we come before . 106
I love to tell the story 473
In God's most holy 5
Jesus calls us o'er the 371
Jesus good above all other . 259
Jesus, priceless treasure . . . 121
Just as I am 119
Let us pray for one 312
Lord, I want to be a 464
Lord, may our hearts be . . . 26
Lord, save your world 310
Lord, thou hast brought us . . 6
Lord, thy mercy now 114
Lord, whose love through . . 17
Make room within my 182
My faith looks up to thee . . 143
My Jesus, I love thee 204
My shepherd will supply . . 125
Nearer, my God, to . . 138, 139
Now let us from this table . 327
O Jesus our Lord, thy 229
O Jesus the giver 64
O Jesus, thou art standing . 385
O Lord, thy benediction . . 486
O Love that wilt not let . . . 132
O Master Workman of the . 219
O Sacred Head, now 262
Oh, for a closer walk with . 117
Onward to Zion, faithful . 316
Redeeming Grace has 351
Remembering thy Son, O . 341
Rise up O saints of God! . . 378
Savior, like a Shepherd . . . 162

Source of all gifts 400
Take time to be holy 180
Tell it! Tell it out 470
Tenderly, tenderly, lead . . 146
The church's life is built . . 297
The voice of God is 394
There's a church within . . 290
This is my song 315
Unto God, who knows our . 472
Walk in the light 303
We are living, we are 376
We thank thee, O God, for . 307
We would see Jesus . . 217, 218
When, his salvation 225
When Holy Ghost shall . . . 471
Where beauty, truth, and . 321
Who will go forth and 499
You satisfy the hungry 345

Communion with God (see Meditation, Prayer)

Communion Service (see Lord's Supper)

Community (see also Children of God, Church, Fellowship, Unity)

All things are thine 397
Baptized in water 350
Bear each other's burdens . 369
Beloved community of . . . 414
Beneath the forms of 339
Brothers and sisters of 388
Christ is the foundation . . . 295
Come, risen Lord 344
For all the saints 480
Heavenly Father, grant . . . 496
Let us break bread 342
Let us pray for one 312
O God to us be present . . . 358
O Jesus, Master, when 422
O thou, whose youthful . . . 207
The vision of a life to be . . . 349
These things shall be: a . . . 323
Where beauty, truth, and . 321
Would you bless our 447
You satisfy the hungry 345

Compassion (see Forgiveness, Grace, Mercy, Reconciliation)

Confession (see also Repentance)

See numbers 103-119
All things are thine 397
Bread of the world 329
Brothers and sisters of 388
Come ye yourselves apart . . 84
Father almighty, grant to . . 81
Father in thy mysterious . . 141
Great God our source 444
I need thee every hour . . . 129
I sought the Lord 213
If suddenly upon the street . 389

O thou God, who hearest. . 105
Oh, for a closer walk with. 117
'Tis midnight, and on. . . . 264
'Twas on that dark, that. . 337

Christ the Redeemer

All creatures of our God. . . 72
All glory, laud and honor. . 23
Beneath the cross of Jesus. 428
Bread of the world. 329
Break thou the bread of. . . 173
By thy redeeming cross. . . 292
Christ for the world we. . . 478
Come, thou almighty King. 54
Come thou fount of every. . 31
Come, thou long-expected. 201
Come, thou, O King of. . 206
Come, ye disconsolate. . . . 166
Creator God, creating still. 190
Deep were his wounds. . . . 269
Draw thou my soul. 168
Good Christian friends. . . 260
Guide us, O Thou. 311
Hail to the brightness of. . 318
Heavenly Father, grant. . . 496
Heir of all the waiting. . . . 253
Here at thy table, Lord. . . 338
Hope of the world. . . 208, 209
I heard the voice of Jesus. . 134
I know that my Redeemer. 212
I know that my. 273, 274
I wonder as I wander. 251
In the cross of Christ I. . . . 203
Jesus Christ is risen today. 278
Life of ages, richly poured. 304
Look for the beautiful. . . . 437
Lord, save your world. . . . 310
Lord, we come before thee. . 10
Lord, whose love through. . 17
My Jesus, I love thee. . . . 204
My song is love unknown. 202
O Christ, my Lord, create. 174
O come, O come,. 211
Of the Father's love. 220
Oh, for a thousand. 19
On this day earth shall. . . 245
Once in royal David's city. 240
Pass me not, O gentle. . . . 149
Praise him, praise him!. . . . 68
Praise, my soul, the King. . . 41
Praise the Lord, ye. 66
Redeemer of Israel. 313
The Church's one. 294
The voice of God is. 394
Thou whose purpose is to. 111
We've a story to tell to the. 477
When, his salvation. 225
With eyes of faith. 122
Word of God, come down. 227

Christ the Shepherd

See numbers 81-86, 123-125
Afar in old Judea. 296

Come, ye disconsolate. . . . 166
God be with you till. . 488, 489
How can creation's voice. 300
How firm a foundation. . . 136
I sought the Lord. 213
In heavenly love abiding. . 120
Jesus good above all other. 259
Jesus, Savior, pilot me. . . . 145
Let us breathe one fervent. 482
Lord of all hopefulness. . . 185
My faith looks up to thee. . 143
Praise him, praise him!. . . . 68
Savior, like a shepherd. . . 162
"Still other sheep I have". 479
There's an old, old path. . . 158
Where restless crowds are. 373
With thankful hearts we. . . . 3
You satisfy the hungry. . . . 345

Christ the Son

God of eternity. 192
God who spoke in the. . . . 308
Lord God of Hosts. 446
Silent night. 244

Christ, the Universal

All hail the power of. . . 70, 71
Angels from the realms of. 231
Christ is alive! Let. 272
Come, thou O King of. . . . 206
Come, thou long-expected. 201
Eternal God, whose. 370
Fairest Lord Jesus. 226
Faith of our fathers. 433
For the Book of Mormon's. 221
Hark, the herald angels. . . 252
In Christ there is no. . 448, 449
In God's most holy. 5
Let us sing a world-wide. . 468
Life of ages, richly. 304
O God, whose presence. . . . 14
O Jesus Christ, to thee. . . . 224
"Still other sheep I have". 479
The Church's one. 294
While humble shepherds. . 236

Christ the Way

Away in a manger. . . 232, 233
Bear each other's burdens. 369
Dear Master, in whose life. 113
Draw thou my soul. 168
Eternal God, whose. 370
Forgive us, Lord, for. 103
Go to dark Gethsemane. . . 266
God of earth and planets. . 198
God, the source of light. . . 406
Great God, as followers of. . 13
Heir of all the waiting. . . . 253
Help us accept each other. 171
Hope of the world. . . 208, 209
I would be true. 404
Jesus' hands were kind. . . . 443
Jesus, mighty king in Zion. 353

Jesus, Savior, pilot me. . . . 145
Lord, I want to be a. 464
Lord, lead me by your. . . . 183
Make room within my. . . . 182
My children, "hear ye. . . . 205
Nearer, my God, to. . 138, 139
Newborn of God, his. 247
Now let our hearts within. 495
Now let us from this table. 327
O God, send Heralds. 429
O Master Workman of. . . 219
O Son of God, thou. 222
O young and fearless. 210
Once in royal David's city. 240
Silvery star, precious star. 239
Soldiers of Christ, arise. . . 393
Take time to be holy. 180
Tenderly, tenderly, lead. . 146
The bread that giveth. . . . 423
The city is alive, O God. . . 375
There's an old, old path. . . 158
Thou whose purpose is to. 111
Thy love, O God, has all. . 163
We would see Jesus. . 217, 218
When the church of Jesus. 445
Where restless crowds are. 373
With a steadfast faith. . . . 497
Yesu, Yesu, fill us with. . . 407

Christ the Word

Bread of the world. 329
Break thou the bread of. . . 173
Come, gracious Lord,. . . . 492
Declare, O heavens, the. . . . 21
For the Book of Mormon's. 221
Great God our source. . . . 444
How can creation's voice. 300
How firm a foundation. . . 136
Immortal, invisible, God. . . 32
Morning has broken. 22
My children, "hear ye. . . . 205
O Word of God incarnate. 305
The Lord almighty spoke. . 195
This God is the God we. . . 481
What child is this. 257
Where cross the crowded. 383
With thankful hearts we. . . . 3
Word of God, come down. 227

Church (see also **Community,
House of God, Restoration**)

See numbers 290-295
All hail the power of. . . 70, 71
Eternal ruler of the. 458
Father, who in Jesus. 331
For all the saints. 480
For the beauty of the earth. 75
God of grace and God of. . 419
Let all the world in every. . . 30
Lord, as we rise to leave. . . 491
Lord, thy church on earth. 438
Make us, O God, a church. 484

Look for the beautiful. . . . 437
Lord, here amidst the. . . . 427
Lord, I want to be a. 464
Lord, lead me by your. 183
Lord, speak to me. 412
Lord, whose love through. . 17
Make room within my. . . . 182
Make us, O God, a church. 484
Master, speak! Thy. 410
Now let us from this table. 327
O Jesus, Master, when. . . . 422
O Master, let me walk. . . . 462
O young and fearless. 210
Take time to be holy. 180
Teach me, my God and. . . 439
The bread that giveth. . . . 423
We give thee but thine. . . . 401
When the church of Jesus. 445
With a steadfast faith. . . . 497

Christmas

See numbers 231-261
Come thou long-expected. 201
O come, O come, ... 211
Of the Father's love. 220
Tell me the story of Jesus. 215
We would see Jesus. . 217, 218

Christ's Birth (see **Christmas**)

Christ's Divinity

Afar in old Judea. 296
All glory, laud, and honor. . 23
Angels from the realms of. 231
Come, thou long-expected. 201
Crown him with many. . . 228
Fairest Lord Jesus. 226
God of eternity. 192
God, the source of light. . . 406
God who spoke in the. . . . 308
Hark, the herald angels. . . 252
Joy to the world!. 258
Let God be God. 197
Love divine, all loves. 170
O love of God. 188. 189
Of the Father's love. 220
Once in royal David's city. 240
Praise him, praise him!. . . . 68
Ride on, ride on in. 268
Sweet the time, exceeding. . . 4
We would see Jesus. . 217, 218
What child is this. 257
When, his salvation. 225
When I survey the. 265
When morning gilds the. . . 35

Christ's Humanity

Angels from the realms of. 231
Away in a manger. . . 232, 233
Come thou long-expected. 201
"Come ye apart!". 79
Fairest Lord Jesus. 226
Go, tell it on the mountain. 249
God who spoke in the. . . . 308

Hark, the herald angels. . . 252
Look at this man, born of. 230
Lord of all hopefulness. . . 185
Newborn of God, his. . . . 247
O Master Workman of the. 219
O Son of God, thou. 222
O young and fearless. 210
Once in royal David's city. 240
Silent night. 244
Silvery star, precious star. 239
Sweet the time, exceeding. . . 4
'Tis midnight, and on. . . . 264
We would see Jesus. . 217, 218
What child is this. 257
When, his salvation. 225
When Jesus wept. 270

Christ's Life

Dear Lord and God of. . . . 115
Dear Master, in whose life. 113
For the Book of Mormon's. 221
Jesus' hands were kind. . . . 443
My song is love unknown. 202
Newborn of God, his. . . . 247
O Master Workman of the. 219
O Son of God, thou. 222
O thou, whose youthful. . . 207
O young and fearless. 210
Ride on, ride on in. 268
Silvery star, precious star. 239
Tell me the story of Jesus. 215
The first Nowell. 246
There's a spirit in the air. . 214
We would see Jesus. . 217, 218
When, his salvation. 225
Yesu, Yesu, fill us with. . . 407

Christ's Love (see also **God's Love**)

A mighty fortress. 142
All to Jesus I surrender. . . 430
As saints of old. 405
Behold the Savior at your. 372
Christ is alive! Let. 272
Crown him with many. . . 228
For the beauty of the earth. 75
Go to dark Gethsemane. . . 266
God forgave my sin in. . . . 382
Great God our source. . . . 444
Here at thy table, Lord, . . . 338
I know that my Redeemer. 212
I know that my. 273, 274
I love to tell the story. . . . 473
If suddenly upon the. 389
Jesus' hands were kind. . . . 443
Jesus is calling. 391
Jesus loves the little. 223
Jesus, the very thought of. . 167
Joy to the world!. 258
Just as I am, thine own to. 421
Lift high the cross. 263
Look at this man, born of. 230
Lord of all nations grant. . 467

Lord, whose love through. . 17
Love divine, all loves. 170
My song is love unknown. 202
Now let us from this table. 327
Now the green blade rises. 280
O Jesus Christ, to thee. . . 224
O Jesus, the giver of all we. . 64
O Jesus, thou art standing. 385
One hour with Jesus. 82
Praise him, praise him!. . . . 68
Savior, like a shepherd. . . 162
Savior, thy dying love. . . . 442
Sweet the time, exceeding. . . 4
Tell me the story of Jesus. 215
There's a spirit in the air. 214
'Tis the blessed hour of. . . . 83
What a friend we have. . 85, 86
What wondrous love is. . . 216
When, his salvation. 225
When I survey the. 265
Where cross the crowded. 383
Where restless crowds are. 373
Yesu, Yesu, fill us with. . . 407

Christ's Passion and Death (see also **Atonement, Cross, Palm Sunday**)

See numbers 262-270
According to thy gracious. 325
Look at this man, born of. 230
My song is love unknown. 202
Tell me the story of Jesus. 215
'Twas on that dark, that. . 337
What wondrous love is. . . 216

Christ's Resurrection (see also **Resurrection**)

See numbers 271-280
Crown him with many. . . 228
Go to dark Gethsemane. . . 266
Jesus good above all other. 259
Jesus loves the little. 223
Lift high the cross. 263
On this day earth shall. . . 245
Redeeming Grace has. . . . 351
Were you there. 267

Christ the Lamb

According to thy gracious. 325
Come thou fount of every. . 31
Crown him with many. . . 228
From isles and. 417, 418
Go to dark Gethsemane. . . 266
Here at thy table, Lord. . . 338
Hosanna to the Lamb. 34
In the cross of Christ I. . . . 203
Jesus, priceless treasure. . . 121
Just as I am. 119
My faith looks up to thee. . 143
O God, the eternal Father. 335
O Jesus, thou art standing. 385
O love that wilt not let me. 132
O Sacred Head, now. 262

TOPICAL

Ride on, ride on in majesty!. 268
What wondrous love is this. 216
When I survey the 265
With eyes of faith 122

Awe (*see* **Mystery**)

Baptism (*see also* **Commitment**)

See numbers 350-357
"Go, make of all disciples". 392
Just as I am 119
O Jesus, the giver of all we . . 64
O Lord, around thine altar . . 7

Beauty (*see also* **Nature**)

All things bright and 18
Eternal God, whose power . 370
For the beauty of the earth . . 75
God, the source of light . . . 406
God, who touchest earth . . 172
Look for the beautiful 437
Teach me, God, to wonder . 176
We thank thee, God, for . . . 465
Where beauty, truth, and . . 321

Benediction (*see also* **Sending Forth**)

See numbers 480-501
Father, bless thy word to . . 474
Leave we now the table of . 326
Lord, thank you for this 93
May we who know the 416
Praise God, from whom all . . 43

Bible (*see* **Scriptures**)

Blessing of Children

See numbers 346-349
When God created human . 434

Blessing of Food (*see* **Grace for Meal**)

Book of Mormon (*see also* **Revelation, Scriptures**)

Afar in old Judea 296
God has spoken through . . 306
"Still other sheep I have" . 479

Brotherhood (*see* **Children of God, Community, Fellowship, Neighbors, Unity**)

Call (*see also* **Commission, Invitation, Mission**)

A diligent and grateful . . . 362
According to the gifts 363
"Go, make of all 392
He lives in us! Immortal . . 199
Jesus is calling 391
Let God be God 197
Lord God, we meet in 365
Now let our hearts 495
O God, send Heralds 429

O Lord, we come as 360
Send forth thy light, O 317
The cause of Zion 314
The living Word of 299
The voice of God is 394
Touch me, Lord, with thy . 409
Who will go forth and 499

Call to Worship (*see also* **Gathering, Invocation**)

See numbers 1-17
All creatures of our God . . . 72
Come, rejoice before your . . 44
From all that dwell below . . 50
God himself is with us 39
Hosanna to the Lamb 34
I sought the Lord 213
Let all the world in every . . . 30
O sing the mighty power . . . 42
O worship the King 27, 28
Praise God, from whom all . 43
Praise the Lord, ye 66
Praise to the Lord, the 67
Praise ye the Lord! 62, 63
Sing praise to God 40
The Lord almighty spoke . . 195

Calm (*see* **Peace-Inner**)

Care

Bear each other's burdens . 369
For the fruits of all 73
For the healing of the 452
God be with you till . . 488, 489
Help us accept each other . 171
How gentle God's 130
I would be true 404
Let us pray for one 312
Let your heart be broken . . 377
Make us, O God, a church . 484
My Lord, I know that all . . 457
Now let us from this table . 327
O Church of God, arise . . 451
O Jesus Christ, to thee . . . 224
O Jesus, Master, when . . . 422
O Master, let me walk 462
The vision of a life to be . . 349
We bring our children, . . . 348
We thank thee, God, for . 465
When the church of Jesus . 445

Celebration (*see* **Joy**)

Challenge (*see also* **Invitation**)

See numbers 369-394
Awake! Ye saints of God . . 140
Brothers, sisters, let us . . . 403
God of grace and God of . 419
God who spoke in the . . . 308
Let us give praise to the . . 398
Let us pray for one 312
May we who know the . . . 416
Now let us from this table . 327
O young and fearless 210

Onward to Zion, faithful . . 316
Open my eyes, O Lord 454
Standing at the portal 144
Who will go forth and 499

Change (*see also* **Growth**)

Beyond the mist and 152
Come now, sound the call . 386
Creator God, creating 190
Father, in thy mysterious . . 141
God of grace and God of . . 419
God, who touchest earth . . 172
Help us accept each other . 171
Here we have come, dear . . 109
In heavenly love abiding . . 120
My Lord, I know that all . . 457
O Lord of light and love . . 435
These things shall be: a . . . 323
We are living, we are 376
We've a story to tell to the . 477
Where restless crowds are . 373

Children (*see also* **Blessing of Children, Family, Youth**)

Children of the heavenly . . 156
Jesus good above all 259
Jesus loves the little 223
Once in royal David's 240
We bring our children, . . . 348
When, his salvation 225

Children of God (*see also* **Kingdom of God, Unity, Zion**)

Behold thy sons and 361
Brothers and sisters of 388
Children of the heavenly . . 156
Come, rejoice before your . . 44
Come, thou, O King of . . . 206
Eternal ruler of the 458
From isles and 417, 418
God of earth and planets . . 198
Great God, as followers of . 13
If by your grace I choose . . 432
Join with us in sweet 475
Let all the world in every . . . 30
O Lord, thy people 352
O Lord, we come as 360
Redeemer of Israel 313
Thy love, O God, has all . . 163
Yesu, Yesu, fill us with . . . 407
You may sing of the 8
You satisfy the hungry 345

Christ-like Life

According to the gifts that . 363
As saints of old 405
Bear each other's 369
Behold the Savior at your . 372
"Come ye apart!" 79
Draw thou my soul 168
For the healing of the 452
If suddenly upon the 389
Jesus' hands were kind . . . 443
Let your heart be broken . . 377

16:3b-f 317, 459
16:4b, c 409
16:4e 317, 464
16:5d 105
17:4a, b 47, 61, 64,
69, 187, 411
17:5 . . . . . . 77, 200, 203,
207, 217, 240, 244,
254, 267, 350
17:7 357
17:18 . . . . 358, 360
17:19 . . . . 347, 348
17:21 . . . . 352, 354
17:22a 328, 335, 341,
342, 343
18:1a-c 142, 195
18:6 . . . . 14, 119, 283, 312
19:3a 265
22:9a, b 463
22:23 . . . . . . 19, 69, 190,
191, 219
26:1a-c 338
26:3d-g 393
28:2b 16
29:2d, c 5
32:3a, d, e 173
34:1 187
34:6 . . . . . 3, 121, 170, 318
474, 486
36:11b 264, 266
36:12e 227
38:2 . . . . . . 124, 218, 454
38:5 . . . . 458, 460
38:9a, c 498
39:1, 2, 5c 177, 351,
353, 385, 496
42:3a, b 206
42:5 221
43:8 . . . . 301, 302
45:1c-e 202

45:2 . . . . 477, 478
46:9 . . . . 37, 38, 405
49:5 . . . . 313, 323
50:8e-g 500
53:2a, b 359
58:1 130
58:6d 290
59:1 6,11
59:2 . . . . 8, 60, 90
59:3 336
59:4, 5a, b 18, 73, 76,
395, 402, 465
61:6c-e 129
62:2b 476
63:1a 372
63:7 134
64:2d, e 116,165
64:7a 229
65:1a-d 215, 261, 304,
315, 390
68:1d 380
68:4a-c 346, 348, 434
76:1, 2a, b . . 13, 27, 28, 62,
63, 150, 321, 483
76:3 . . . . 273, 274, 275
76:4g 205, 237, 272
77:4 482
81:4c . . 184, 316, 387, 437
83:7 . . . . 183, 285, 297
83:17c 31, 490
85:1 287
85:2 . . . . 36, 228
85:3 492
85:16, 17, 18 . . . . . . 7, 29,
32, 33, 58, 132, 138,
139, 168, 501
85:21a, b 486
85:36 . . . . 79, 87, 196
85:41 448
90:1 . . . . . . 190, 305, 406

90:3b, c 12
90:6d 434
95:3a 301, 302
97:4 . . . . 362, 424
98:4 311
98:5g-j . . 52, 137, 156, 177
100:7a 117
101:2b-f 395, 396, 397
101:2g 427
104:42 307
108:7c 42, 238
108:10a 473
115:1e 488
110:23a-c 225
111:2 367
117:13 91
119:2 9
119:6c 1
119:8b 151, 363, 365
119:9 455
122:17 . . . . 107, 497
128:8b, c 224
132:3, 4 . . . 392, 421, 442,
472
135:3 333
136:3c 386
137:6 . . . . 314, 398
138:3a, b 293
140:5c, d . . . 294, 314, 398
141:8 495
142:5 451
147:7 . . . . . 301, 302, 309
150:7 . . . . . 369, 402, 456
150:11a 118
150:12 . . . . 290, 292
151:8a, 9 . . . . . . 429, 432
153:9 . . . . . 209, 362, 377,
387, 394, 400, 425, 459
154:7 380

Topical Index

Accountability (*see* **Stewardship**)

Activity (*see* **Service**)

Adoration (*see* **Praise**)

Advent (*see* **Christmas**)

Adventure (*see also* **Exploration**)

Be with me, Lord, ... 487
Declare, O heavens, the 21
From isles and 417, 418
Jesus, Savior, pilot me 145
Let your heart be broken . . 377

Now in this moment 58
Now let us from this table . . 327
Sometimes a light 154, 155
Tenderly, tenderly, lead . . . 146
Thou whose purpose is to . . 111
We are living, we are 376
World around us, sky 135
Your cause be mine 420

Alienation (*see* **Reconciliation**)

Amen(*s*)

See numbers 95-101

Assurance (*see* **Faith, Hope, Trust**)

Atonement (*see also* **Christ's Passion and Death, Cross**)

Bread of the world 329
Here at thy table, Lord, we . 338
Jesus Christ is risen today . . 278
Jesus loves the little 223
Look at this man, born of . . 230
Now the green blade rises . . 280
O Sacred Head, now 262

3:30 . . .176, 180, 182, 437
3:31-36 . . . .110, 114, 135
3:42-56 . . . . .50, 113, 135
147, 166, 439
3:61-66 . . . . . .23, 89, 113,
127, 148, 154, 155,
157, 185
5:90, 91 29
6:41, 42 . . . . .14, 24
6:47, 48 356
6:61 196
6:103, 104 169
8:18-20 . . . . . .8, 174, 214
9:132-137 . . . . .19, 20, 30,
44, 75, 144, 324, 370
12:36, 37 . . . . . . .183, 221
12:56, 57 175
13:7-10, 15-17 . . .353, 361
13:22-26 . . . . . .286, 352
13:27-30 . . . . . .159, 171,
210, 311, 380, 384, 411
14:4-6 . . . . .385, 416
14:11, 12 . . . . . . .80, 408
15:10 303

Jacob
2:22-24 377
3:9-17 . . . . . .41, 65, 122,
150, 200
4:3-6 313

Enos
1:5 94

Jarom
1:9 82

Omni
1:46, 47 . . . . .56, 322

Mosiah
1:46-49 . . . .415, 417, 418
1:53, 54 463
1:97-103 . . . . . . .247, 252
1:115, 116 119
2:3 341
2:13, 14 61
2:18-27 . . . . .67, 181, 349,
360, 388, 397, 423, 465
2:28-36 . . . .103, 388, 396,
403, 423, 445
2:43 427
2:49 496
3:7-9 . . . . .351, 357
3:16, 17, 21 . . . . .2, 161,
197, 371, 462
7:77 436
8:28-35 220
8:47-52 441

8:67-69 307
9:51-55 364
11:139, 140 165

Alma
3:27-32 . . . .138, 139, 289,
464, 493
3:57-59 . . . . . .55, 83, 391,
394, 457
3:87, 88 258
5:17, 18 211
5:19 . . . . . .232, 233, 248
5:21, 22 189
5:38-41 . . . .111, 293, 327
5:44 . . . . .488, 489
10:19, 26 246
12:2-5 . . . . .366, 425
13:51 149
14:82, 96 . . . . .17, 392
14:88 . . . . .35, 59, 68
14:91 78
14:92-97 . . . .26, 321, 378
14:123-128 . . . . . .21, 130,
192, 193, 225, 315,
334, 467
15:60-61 382
16:178-182 141
16:198-200 178
16:219-222 . . . . . .9, 140
16:238 105
17:66-69 . . . . . .176, 376
18:9-11 494
18:14, 16, 17 430
19:78 . . . . .450, 484
21:2 40
22:20 434
30:2 117

Helaman
2:74, 75 . . . . . . .136, 145
2:111, 112 256
5:59, 66 239
5:97 497

III Nephi
4:43-45, 48 . . . . .226, 481
5:11-17 . . . .273, 274, 275
5:110-112 120
7:20 479
8:6-10 . . . . .217, 218
8:25, 26 33
8:33-39 . . . .325, 332, 335,
337, 340
9:14-16 359
9:40-45 333
12:26-28 265

IV Nephi
1:17, 19 449

Book of Mormon
4:77, 78 42
Ether
1:106-108 123
5:7-9 276
5:28 . . . . .183, 472
5:33, 34 . . . .132, 194, 317
5:41 500

Moroni
3:1-3 365
6:3-6 . . . . .85, 86, 330,
350, 358
7:3 . . . . .177, 490
7:11 . . . . .204, 409
7:24, 25 160
7:47, 48 143
7:50-52 . . . .108, 369, 466
8:18 . . . . .223, 347
8:19 47
10:5-7 285
10:29, 30 . . . . . . .12, 446

DOCTRINE AND
COVENANTS

1:3 . . . . .197, 450
1:4 . . .163, 214, 293, 310,
469, 471
1:5a-c 114
1:8 144
2:1 . . . . .324, 446
3:15e, 16-18 . . . .291, 356
4:1 . . . . . . .210, 222, 296,
378, 403, 417, 418
5:5b 159
6:1, 2 . . . . .381, 438
6:3 386
6:4 . . . . .440, 470
6:10 45
6:15, 16 . . . . . .2, 4, 112,
131, 167
8:3d, e 122
10:2 . . . . .420, 470
10:3 . . . . .10, 297
10:5 412
10:6, 7 . . . .127, 146, 148,
154, 155, 179, 282,
284, 416
10:11b, c, 12 208,
298, 410
11:2a, b 475
11:4, 5 . . . . .109, 331, 389
12:2 436
12:3 316
12:4a 181

I Corinthians
1:18 292
2:9-13 . . . . . 298, 382, 412
3:10, 11 . . . . 294, 295
6:19, 20 421
8:6 47
10:16, 17 . . . 339, 340, 345
10:31 498
11:23-29 . . . 327, 342, 343
12:27 291
13:1-7 . . . . 367, 466
13:8-12 . . . . 301, 302
13:13 151
15:3, 4 267
15:18-22 . . . . . . 275, 277
15:54-58 . . . . 11, 271, 419

II Corinthians
1:21, 22 493
5:14-21 . . . . 107, 135,
252, 399, 431, 493
7:8-10 116
8:9 460
9:7, 8 . . . . 400, 413
9:15 74
10:4, 5 393
13:4 199
13:11, 14 489

Galatians
2:20 . . . . 199, 272, 329
3:26-29 . . . . 458, 468
5:13, 14 388
5:22-25 . . . . 284, 464, 466
6:2 369
6:7-10 423
6:14 . . . . . . 203, 265, 428

Ephesians
1:1-12 . . . . . . 12, 169, 446
2:4-7 362
2:8-10 143
2:13-22 . . . . 107, 295, 355,
414, 431, 480
3:8-12 . . . . 188, 201
3:14-19 . . . 172, 186, 194,
411, 447
4:1-6 . . . . . . 405, 432, 451
4:11-16 . . . . 290, 366
4:30 287
5:8 303
5:25-28 368
6:10-17 419
6:23, 24 483

Philippians
1:9-11 . . . . 474, 482
2:1-4 377

2:5-12 . . . . . . 70, 182, 230,
420, 469
3:7-14 . . . . . 164, 454, 457
4:4-7 . . . . 7, 115, 487
4:8 . . . . 404, 437
4:10-13 . . . . 113, 199, 435
4:19, 20 . . . . 75, 127

Colossians
1:2-18 . . . 21, 32, 312, 481
3:1-4 166
3:11-17 . . . . 175, 331, 449,
496

I Thessalonians
2:19 14
3:11-13 485

I Timothy
1:5 . . . . 108, 416
1:15-17 54
2:4-6 276
3:16 41
4:12 404
6:11-14 . . 9, 399, 433, 472

II Timothy
1:6, 7 . . . . 164, 439
2:15 486
2:19-21 109
3:14-17 306

Titus
2:13, 14 68
3:3-7 . . . . 41, 104, 118,
202, 262, 355

Hebrews
1:1-3 . . . . . . 195, 220, 226,
308
1:6 236
2:14-17 . . . . 205, 428
5:4, 5, 10 364
10:22-24 168
11:1 497
11:13-16 . . . . 300, 320
12:1, 2 . . . . 143, 299, 384
13:6 463
13:14-16 . . . . 74, 383
13:20, 21 . . . . 163, 494

James
1:2-4 300
1:5 81
1:17, 18 . . . . . . 37, 38, 46,
151, 282
1:25-27 . . . . 379, 401

I Peter
1:3-5 . . . . 212, 269
1:7 303

1:8 204
2:9, 10 . . . . 363, 398
2:20-25 . . . . 165, 251, 442
3:8 91
5:1-3 364
5:6, 7 281

II Peter
1:4-8 . . . . 22, 443
1:19 319

I John
1:1-3 406
1:7-9 341
2:4-10 379
3:1-3 . . . . 152, 170, 240,
3:14-24 . . . . . 78, 339, 427,
452, 465, 485
4:7 102
4:16, 19 . . . . 171, 204
4:21 422
5:3 130
5:14 92

Jude
3 433
24, 25 102

Revelation
1:7, 8 220
3:20 . . . . 372, 385
5:12, 13 . . . . 35, 43, 71
19:1, 5, 6 . . . . 55, 480

BOOK OF MORMON

I Nephi
1:23 . . . . 310, 319
3:58, 62 . . . . 236, 255
3:66, 67 238
3:70, 82-87 . . . . . . 77, 216,
264, 268
3:187 . . . . . . 224, 429, 470
3:197, 198 . . . . . . 261, 467
5:5 158
5:59 . . . . . . 131, 229, 459,
491
5:126-131 . . . . . 25, 51, 72
6:38-41 . . . . 146, 374
7:56-59 . . . . 3, 81, 124,
162, 175

II Nephi
1:36-38 393
1:71-77 . . . . 104, 188, 228,
260, 269, 271
1:95 . . . . 62, 63
1:117-120 304
1:122, 123 355

Pittsfield......386, 459
Van Fleet..........306

8.7.8.7. Double with refrain
Story of Jesus.......215

8.7.8.7.4.4.4.7.7.
Bryn Calfaria.......44

8.7.8.7.6.6.6.6.7.
Ein' feste Burg.......142

8.7.8.7.8.6.
Vesper Hymn........501

8.7.8.7.8.7.
Irby...........240
Lauda Anima........41
New Malden........452
Picardy...........253
Siberia...........311
Unser Herrscher (Neander)
.............308

8.7.8.7.8.7.7.
Cwm Rhondda......419
Divinium mysterium..220

8.7.8.7.8.8.7.
Mit Freuden zart......40
Richmond Beach.297, 420
W zlobie lezy.......242

8.8.7.7.8.
The Church Within Us 290

8.8.8. with alleluias
Victory...........276

8.8.8. with refrain
Vulpius (Gelobt sei Gott)
.............275

8.8.8. Double
God Our Source......444
Melita.............6
Mozart...........389
Old 113th..........65

8.8.8.4.
Almsgiving......77, 396

8.8.8.6.
Just As I Am........421
Sydenham Street.....195

8.8.8.7.
Quem pastores...259, 331

8.8.8.8. (Long Meter, L.M.)
Adon olom.........169
Agincourt..........55
Alstone...........321

Ashland...........441
Belsize Square......418
Bishop...........487
Brookfield......222, 415
Canonbury.....412, 486
Craig.............122
Dedicare......188, 417
De Tar...........189
Deus tuorum militum
(Grenoble)....268, 293
Duke Street...50, 69, 140
Eisenach.....359, 498
Federal Street.......492
Germany (Gardiner)
.............383, 397
Gratefulness.....26, 349
Hamburg...165, 337, 364
Hebron.........13, 422
Hesperus.......348, 426
Hicks...........3, 365
Hursley.....14, 113, 352
Kedron...........310
Maryton....282, 347, 462
Melrose......425, 467
Mendon....355, 400, 432
Old Hundredth.......43
Olive's Brow........264
Praise.............62
Retreat........118, 174
Rimington..........63
Rockingham....205, 265
St. Crispin.....414, 431
St. Hylda..........434
Silver Hill......90, 109
Solothurn...178, 427, 450
Tallis' Canon........196
Truro......274, 323
Tryggare Kan ingen
vara...........156
Uxbridge.....59, 336
Veni Creator.......283
Waltham...........250
Wareham..........327
When Jesus Wept.....270
Woodworth.........119

8.8.8.8. (Long Meter) with alleluias
Lasst uns erfreuen....273
Whitefield.........272

8.8.8.8. (Long Meter) with refrain
He Leadeth Me......123
St. Catherine.......433
Sing of His Mighty Love.48
Veni Emmanuel.....211

8.8.8.8. Double (Long Meter Double, L.M.D.)
Sweet Hour of Prayer...87
Contrast (De Fleury)..481

8.8.8.8.6.
St. Margaret....132, 455

8.8.8.8.8.
Park Street.........131

8.8.8.8.8. with alleluias
Lasst uns erfreuen.....21

8.8.8.8.8.6. with refrain
Lasst uns erfreuen.....72

8.9.
Intercession (Refrain)...88

9.7.9.7. with refrain
Earth and All Stars....49

9.8.8.9.
God Be With You (Deus vobiscum).........326
Randolph.........489

9.8.8.9. with refrain
God Be With You (Deus vobiscum).........488

9.8.9.5.
Thank You..........74

9.8.9.6. with refrain
The Beatitudes.......322

9.8.9.8.
Folk Song.........343

9.8.9.8. Double
Prophet...........307
Rendez a Dieu.......329

9.9.9.6.
Lois..............285

9.9.9.9. with refrain
Freely, Freely.......382

9.10.9. Double with refrain
Saboath.............57

9.10.9.9. with refrain
Assurance...........58

9.10.9.10.
Zion..............316

10.4.6.6.6.6.10.4.
Livingston..........30

10.8.8.7.7. with refrain
Message...........477

10.8.10.7. with refrain
Jesus Is Calling Today . 391

10.8.10.10. with refrain
Consecration 472

10.9.10.9.9.
Russian Melody . . 102, 409

10.10. with refrain
Let Us Break Bread . . . 342

10.10.10. Double
Yorkshire 458

10.10.10.4.4.
Sine Nomine 480

10.10.10.6.
Peace 213

**10.10.10.10. (See also
6.4.6.4.D.)**
Carpenter . 367(E), 494(E^b)
Crucifier 263
Eventide 128
Langran 328
Livorno 423
Morecambe . 16(B^b), 181(C)
National Hymn 191
Penitentia 84
Sursum Corda 103,
344, 440
Toulon 247
Wiesbaden 150

10.10.10.10. Double
Tenderly Lead Thou Me
On 146

10.10.10.10.10.
Belden 437

10.10.11.11.
Hanover 28
Lyons 27
Paderborn 61

10.10.13.10.
Were You There 267

10.11.10.11.
Lyons 229

10.11.11.12.
Slane 185

10.11.11.11.12.11.10.11.
Trumpet 271

11.7.11.7.
Edwards 497

11.8.11.8.
Meditation (Beloved) . . 313

11.10.10.11.
Nöel Nouvelet 280

11.10.11.10.
Ancient of Days 208
Bergen må vika 153
Chisholm 79
City of God 224
Consolator 166
Cushman 217
Ecology 402
Mora Proctor 163, 218
O Perfect Love 368
Strength and Stay 141
Vicar 209
Welwyn 429, 446
Wesley 318, 398

11.10.11.10. with refrain
Faithfulness 187
Let God Be God 197
Tidings 476

11.10.11.10. Double
Star in the East 234

11.10.11.10.10.
Peek 404

11.10.11.10.11.10.
Finlandia . . . . 107(E^b),
315(F)

11.11.11.5.
Cloisters 491
Flemming 81

**11.11.11.11. (See also
6.5.6.5. D.)**
Cradle Song 233
Foundation 136
Gordon 204
Holiness 180
I Love Thee 186

Mine Are the Hungry . . 388
Mueller 232
O Jesus the Giver 64
One Hour with Jesus . . . 82
St. Denio 32, 261

11.12.12.10.
Nicaea 56

12.9.12.12.9.
Wondrous Love 216

12.10.11. with refrain
Adeste fideles 238

12.10.12.10.
Marnie 341

**12.10.12.10.11.10 with
refrain**
Praise Him, Praise
Him 68

12.11.11.12.
I Wonder as I Wander . 251

12.11.12.11.
Kremser 11

12.11.12.11. with refrain
Paraclete 33

12.12.12.12.
Fellowship 8
Leoni 47

13.8.
Porter 15

13.13.14. with refrain
St. Brendan's 466

14.11.6.11.
Lord, I Want to be a
Christian 464

14.14.4.7.8.
Lobe den Herren 67

15.11.15.12. with refrain
Master, Use Me 424

Irregular
Purpose 324

Irregular with refrain
The First Nowell 246

Scripture Index

Where Inspired Version versification differs from other versions, the I.V. verses are listed first with the others in parentheses.

BIBLE

Genesis
1:3, 12, 19, 20, 29. (9, 16-18, 26). 42

Exodus
13:21. . . . . .185, 313
20:8. 90

Leviticus
20:7, 8. . . . . .180, 356

Numbers
6:24-26 501

Deuteronomy
4:29. 140
30:14-16, 19, 20. 169

Joshua
24:14-16. . . . . . .376, 391

I Samuel
3:10. 410

I Chronicles
16:23-31. . . . . . .15, 18, 43, 49, 52, 141
29:10-14. . . . .24, 71, 192, 229, 401

II Chronicles
5:13. 53

Job
19:25. 212

Psalms
16:8, 9, 11. . . . . . .44, 133
18:1-3 3
19:1, 14. . . . .66, 180, 461
23. . . .124, 125, 158, 162
24:1-5 6
25:1-7, 20, 21. 110
25:4, 5. 129
27:7. 94
29:2. 15
29:11. 94
30:1-4. . . . . .19, 455
31:1-3, 5. 374
31:14, 15. 137
34:1, 3, 4, 7-9, 22. . . .138, 139, 492
37:3-4 390
43:3, 4. 317
46:1, 2, 7-10. 153
47:1-7 25

50:1-6. . . . . .4, 316
50:14, 15. . . . . . .74, 453
51:1, 10-12. . . . .172, 174, 182
51:15-17 106
52:9 88
55:16, 17. 87
55:22. 133
62:1, 2, 5-8. 22
65:1, 2 16
66:1, 2 40
69:34. 43
71:5. 148
71:22, 23 277
73:24-26, 28. . . .149, 426
84:10-12 59
86:5, 6 112
89:8, 9 145
90:1, 2 200
90:16, 17. 222
91:2. 142
92:1, 2 78
95:1-6. . . . . .29, 396, 500
96:1, 11-13. 184
96:7-9. . . . . .15, 26
97:1, 6, 9-12. . . .48, 57, 88
98:1-9 258
99:1-5 258
100 . . . . .44, 74
103:1-4. . . . . .46, 67, 68
104:1-5 45
104:31-33 51
107:1-6 60
116:12, 13. 332
117 50
118:24. 90
119:18. 454
119:57, 58. 114
119:108. 461
122:1. 8
135:1-3 31
139:7-14. . . . . . .65, 126
145:1-5 473
145:8-12. . . .27, 28, 193
147:12-19, 21. .1, 76, 319
148. . . . . .62, 63, 66, 72
149:1, 2 30
150. . . . . .20, 53

Proverbs
3:5, 6. . . . . .191, 198
3:9. . . . . .400, 460

Ecclesiastes
3:14. 196
5:19, 20. 64

Isaiah
1:26, 27. 320
2:2, 3. 323
6:1-5 56
6:5-8. .381, 394, 410, 424, 495, 499
7:14. 255
9:6, 7. 259
11:1, 2, 4, 5, 9. . . .70, 255, 324
12:2-6. . . . . .57, 250
26:3, 4. .10, 126, 185, 198
40:9-11. . . . . . . .318, 476
40:28-31. . . . . . .84, 125
41:6. 422
41:10. . .52, 121, 126, 136
42:16. 146
44:23. 66
48:17. 123
52:6, 7. . . . .157, 261, 456
53:2-5. . . . .122, 230, 276
53:5-7 262
53:12. 333
54:10. 153
58:13, 14. 5
60:1-3 36
61:1-3 206
61:10, 11. 49

Jeremiah
6:16. 158
8:22. 147
31:3. 193

Ezekiel
37:3-5 280

Daniel
12:3. 172

Joel
2:27-29 376
3:16, 17. 321

Amos
3:7. 307

Micah
5:2. 248
6:6-8. .103, 106, 117, 445, 450

SCRIPTURE

Habakkuk
2:20 39

Zechariah
2:13 39
9:9, 10 211

Matthew
2:1-6 (1:18-23) . . 234, 235, 253, 260
3:1-11 (2:1-11) . . 231, 241, 242, 243, 245, 246, 254, 257
3:40-43 (13-15) 350
3:45 (16) 354
4:19 (20) 371
5:2-11 322
5:15-18 (13-16) . . 111, 413, 444
6:9-15 (9-13) . 80, 174, 320
6:34 (30) 159
9:41, 42 (35, 36) . . . 452
9:43, 44 (37, 38) 73
10:34, 35, 38 (39, 40, 42) 383, 440, 443
11:29, 30 (28-30) . . . 1, 82, 83, 115, 128, 134, 334
17:4 (5) 296
18:20 2
19:4-6 . . . . 367, 368
19:13-15 349
20:26-28 . . . 207, 407, 436
21:5-7 (6-9) 225
21:7, 13 (9, 15) 34
21:19, 20 (21, 22) . . . 85, 86
23:37 375
25:41 (40) 401
26:22-27 (26-30) 326, 335, 337
26:35, 36 (38, 39) . . . 266
28:2-5 (2-7) 278
28:17-19 (18-20) . . . 353, 392, 438, 470, 475

Mark
4:30, 31 (37-39) 145
6:32-37 (31-37) 79, 84, 373
7:36 (37) 178
8:36-38 (34, 35) 409, 444, 462
10:11-14 (13-16) 223, 346, 347, 348
10:26 (27) 157
10:42-45 . . . . 17, 440
11:9-12 (9, 10) 23, 34
14:20-24 (22-24) 330
14:35-40 (31-36) 264
16:3-5 (4-7) 245

Luke
1:26-33 . . . 234, 241, 249
2:4-20 . . . . . 231, 232, 233, 235, 236, 237, 238, 239, 242, 243, 244, 245, 247, 248, 249, 250, 256, 257
2:25-32 . . . . 201, 211, 253
2:46-49 219
2:51, 52 . . . . 207, 240, 447
3:28, 29 285
4:16-21 . . . . 230, 369, 373, 429, 438, 451
6:36-38 388
10:1, 2 . . . . 424, 477
10:37, 38 407
10:39-43 207
11:14 (13) 288
12:29-35 (27-32) 125, 457
13:34, 35 224
18:13 149
18:26-30 111
19:36, 37 (37, 38) . . . 268
22:14-21 . . . . . . 325, 337, 338, 343
22:41, 42 270
24:12-31 (13-32) 128, 207, 336, 344, 495

John
1:1-4, 14 . . . . . . 195, 205, 305, 308
1:11, 12 280
1:17 227
1:29 216
2:1-11 207
3:14, 15 263
3:16, 17 . . . . . . 310, 375, 478
4:25, 26 (23, 24) 4, 54, 82, 426
5:40 (39) 299
6:32-35 . . . . 327, 334, 339, 345
6:37-40 259
6:47-51 . . . . 173, 329
6:56, 57 328
6:65-69 484
8:31, 32 . . . . 163, 227
9:25 178
10:4, 9 120
10:11, 13 147
10:15-18 . . . . 216, 479
10:27-29 . . . . 156, 162
11:25, 26 271
12:13 34

12:21-24 . . . . . . 217, 218, 263, 280
12:27, 31-33 270
13:34, 35 466
14:6-18 . . . . 215, 222, 283, 284, 286
14:21 389
14:26 361
14:27 . . . . 177, 494
15:1, 2, 4, 7 186
15:9-11 380
15:15, 16 . . . . . . 210, 213, 326, 365
16:12-14 . . . 227, 306, 309
16:32, 33 . . . . . . 208, 270
17:3 . . . . 176, 409, 471
20:19, 20 278
20:21, 22 179

Acts
1:7, 8 . . . . . 267, 471, 473
2:1-4 245
2:28 167
2:37-39 . . . . 357, 435
2:41-43, 46, 47 . . . . . 214, 344
4:31-33 279
5:30-32 . . . . . 77, 269, 378
8:14-17 359
10:34, 35 . . . . . 304, 315, 467, 468
20:28 . . . . 363, 499

Romans
1:16, 17 . . . 160, 161, 477
4:17, 20, 21 453
5:1-5 . . . . . . 58, 213, 281
5:6-11 . . . . 118, 152, 202, 251
6:3-14 . . . . 279, 351, 356, 360, 430, 442
8:14-19 . . . . . 13, 289, 314, 352, 358
8:22-28 . . . . . . 17, 89, 154, 155, 288
8:35-39 . . . 121, 132, 448
9:14-16 346
10:13-16 (13-17) 215, 476
11:33-36 . . . . 55, 150, 189, 370
12:1-21 . . . . 163, 209, 297, 403, 408, 414, 415, 445, 450, 455, 484, 487, 491
14:9, 17-19 . . . . 322, 323, 441, 490
16:25-27 48

7.7.7.7. with refrain
Dix 75
Gloria 237
Starlight and Song 239

7.7.7.7. Double
Benevento 37
Dancer 482
Hollingside 408
Invocation 10
Maidstone 51
Spanish Chant 116
St. George's Windsor . . . 38

7.7.7.7. Double with refrain
Mendelssohn 252

7.7.7.7.4. with refrain
Chautauqua 45

7.7.7.7.7.
Hendon 4, 474

7.7.7.7.8.8.8.7.
Join the Children of the Lord 475

7.7.9. with refrain
Chereponi 407

7.8.7.8.8.8.
Liebster Jesu 227

7.10.8.10.10.10.
The Lord Bless You and Keep You 483

8.4.8.4.8.8.
O Jesu 78

8.4.8.4.8.8.8.4.
East Acklam 73

8.5.8.5.
Bullinger 127
Sacred Rest 172

8.5.8.5. with refrain
Pass Me Not 149

8.6.6.8. with refrain
Diadem 70

8.6.8.6. (Common Meter, C.M.)
Arlington 7
Azmon 19
Belmont 292
Bradford 212
Bridgman 42
Communion 338
Confirmation 354, 361

Cooling 80, 193
Crimond 124
Detroit 243
Evan 159, 363
Hurst 199
Lloyd 286
McKee 448
Manoah . . . 2, 303, 366
Martyrdom 325
Morning Song 190
Naomi 117, 490
New Britain 104
Richmond 346
St. Agnes 167, 288
St. Anne 200
St. Columba 339, 362
St. Magnus 416
St. Peter . . 330(D), 449 (Eb)
Stracathro 106
Yarrington 89

8.6.8.6. (Common Meter) with refrain
The Savior at the Door 372
Gift of Finest Wheat . . 345

8.6.8.6. (Common Meter Double, C.M.D.)
Bethlehem (Seraph) . . . 435
Carol 256
Ellacombe 471
Forest Green 370, 484
Hills 309
Jerusalem 465
Kingsfold 182
Massachusetts . . . 300, 360
Materna 219
Norse Air (No Other Plea, or Landas) . . . . . 357(Ab), 405(G), 495(G)
Resignation 125
St. Matthew 314, 358
Saintly Praise 36
Vox dilecti 134

8.6.8.6. (Common Meter Double) with repeat
Thaxted 375

8.6.8.6.6.
Christmas 236
Dove of Peace . . . 108, 356

8.6.8.6.6.8.
Antioch 258

8.6.8.6.7.6.8.6.
St. Louis 248

8.6.8.6.8.6.
Brother James' Air 126, 350
Coronation 71
Morning Song 457

8.6.8.6.8.8.
O Jesu 207

8.6.8.8.6.
Lobt Gott, ihr Christen . . 9
Rest 115

8.6.11.6.6.7.6.7.5.
Birmingham 133

8.7.7.7.11.
Children 223

8.7.8.7.
Carter 410
Dominus regit me . . . 351
Galilee 371
Heavenly Dove 430
Hymn of Praise . . . 53, 164
Kingdom 114, 221
Norman 24
Omni die 112
Rathbun 203
Sardis 453, 460, 496
Stuttgart 353, 413

8.7.8.7. with refrain
Greensleeves 257
Proclamation 469
Regent Square 231
How Can I Keep from Singing 157

8.7.8.7. Double
Abbott's Leigh 184
All the Way 447
Austria 376, 468
Beach Spring 287
Blaenwern 85, 170
Bradbury 162
Decatur 312
Ebenezer 135
Ellesdie . . 381(Ab), 390(A)
Erie (Converse) 86
Geneva 403, 438
Holy Manna 279
Hyfrydol 17, 66, 201
Hymn to Joy . . . 20, 470
In Babilone 406
Ladue Chapel 111
Leslie 298
My Redeemer (Admonition) 387
Nettleton 31

6.4.6.4.6.6.4.
Wilmington 139

6.4.6.4.6.6.4.4.
More Love to Thee 411

6.4.6.4.6.6.6.4.
Bethany 138
God of Eternity 192
St. Edmund 168
Something for Jesus . . . 442

6.5.6.5. Double (See also 11.11.11.11.)
Bjorklund Major 377
Hermas 198
King's Weston 445
Noël Nouvelet 443
Penitence 295

6.5.6.5. Double with refrain
Hermas 144

6.5.9. with refrain
Teach Me God 176

6.6.4.6.6.6.4.
Italian Hymn 54, 478
Olivet 91, 143

6.6.5.6.6.5.7.8.6.
Jesu meine Freude 121

6.6.6. Double
Laudes Domini 35

6.6.6.6.
St. Cecilia 320

6.6.6.6. Double
Denby 451
Hawarden 479

6.6.6.6.4.4.4.4.
Love Unknown 202

6.6.6.6.6. with refrain
Personent hodie 245

6.6.6.6.8.8.
Marlee 269
Sutherland 25

6.6.6.6.8.8.8.
Lenox 206

6.6.7.7.7.8.5.5.
In dulci jubilo 260

6.6.8. Double with repeat
Olwen (Poverty) 369

6.6.8.6. (Short Meter, S.M.)
Boylston 399
Carlisle 439

Dennis 137, 485
Festal Song . . . . . . 302(A), 319(A), 378(B^b)
Ferguson 148
James 130
O'Kelley 499
St. Andrew 401
Trentham 179, 500

6.6.8.6. (Short Meter) with refrain
Vineyard Haven 301

6.6.8.6. Double (Short Meter Double, S.M.D.)
Diademata 228, 393
Terra beata 52

6.6.8.6.6.8.6.6.
Wunderbarer König (Arnsberg) 39

6.6.8.6.8.6.
Loyalty 379

6.6.8.8.6.6.
Walhof 152

6.6.8.9.6.6.
Stille Nacht 244

6.6.11. Double
Down Ampney 289

6.6.11.6.6.11. Double
Ash Grove 493

6.7.
Tandy 34

6.7.6.7.6.6.6.6.
Nun danket alle Gott 60, 334

6.8.6.
Kirtland 332

6.9.8.9.
In corde meo 461

7.6.7.5.7.6.7.6.
Doane II 83

7.6.7.6.
St. Alphege 335

7.6.7.6. Double
Aurelia 120, 160, 171, 294
Craigmillar 373
Ewing 5, 296, 340
Faithful 29
Holy Wings 1, 183
Lancashire . . 317, 374, 392

Mabune 230
Munich 305
Nyland 177
Passion Chorale 262
St. Hilda 385
St. Theodulph 23, 175
Springtime 154, 225
Vigil . . . . 110(A), 210(A^b), 299(A)
Watermouth 463
Webb 394
Wedlock 161
Wie lieblich ist der Maien 46
Zoan 456

7.6.7.6. with refrain
Balm in Gilead 147
Go Tell It 249
Royal Oak 18

7.6.7.6. Double with refrain
Hankey 473
Wir pflügen 76

7.6.7.6.6.7.6.
Es ist ein Ros' 255

7.6.7.6.7.6.7.5.
Rutherford 380

7.6.7.6.7.6.7.6.6.
Surprise 155

7.6.7.6.7.7.7.7.
Emerald 151, 436

7.6.8.6.8.6.8.6.
St. Christopher 428

7.7.7. Double
Ashburton 284
Dix 254
Faithful Guide 105
Gethsemane 266
Pilot 145
Toplady 194

7.7.7.7.
Elsworth 291
Gottschalk (Mercy) . . . 12
Harts 304
Holy Spirit Truth Divine 281
Lauds 214

7.7.7.7. with alleluias
Easter Hymn 277
Llanfair 278

Royal Oak 18
Russian Melody . . 102, 409
Rutherford 380

Sabaoth 57
Sacred Rest 172
St. Agnes 167, 288
St. Alphege 335
St. Andrew 401
St. Anne 200
St. Brendan's 466
St. Catherine 433
St. Cecelia 320
St. Christopher 428
St. Columba 339, 362
St. Crispin 414, 431
St. Denio 32, 261
St. Edmund 168
St. George's Windsor . . . 38
St. Hilda 385
St. Hylda 434
St. Louis 248
St. Magnus 416
St. Margaret 132, 455
St. Matthew 314, 358
St. Peter . . . . 330 (D),
449 (E^b)
St. Theodulph 23, 175
Saintly Praise 36
Sardis 453, 460, 496
Savage 92, 93
Schönster Herr Jesu . . . 226
Seraph 435
Siberia 311
Silver Hill 90, 109
Sine Nomine 480
Sing of His Mighty Love
. . . . 48
Slane 185
Solothurn . . . 178, 427, 450
Something for Jesus . . . 442
Songs of Joy 241

Spanish Chant 116
Springtime 154, 225
Star in the East 234
Starlight and Song 239
Stille Nacht 244
Story of Jesus 215
Stracathro 106
Strength and Stay 141
Stuttgart 353, 413
Surprise 155
Sursum Corda . . . 103, 344,
440
Sutherland 25
Sweet Hour of Prayer . . . 87
Sydenham Street 195

Tallis' Canon 196
Tandy 34
Teach Me God 176
Tenderly Lead Thou
Me On 146
Terra beata 52
Thank You 74
Thaxted 375
The Beatitudes 322
The Church Within
Us 290
The First Nowell 246
The Lord Bless You
and Keep You 483
The Old, Old Path . . . 158
The Savior at the
Door 372
Tidings 476
Toplady 194
Toulon 247
Trentham 179, 500
Trumpet 271
Truro 274, 323
Tryggare kan ingen
vara 156

Unser Herrscher 308
Uxbridge 59, 336

Van Fleet 306
Veni Creator 283
Veni Emmanuel 211
Vesper Hymn 501
Vicar 209
Victory 276
Vigil . . . . 110 (A), 210 (A^b),
299 (A)
Vineyard Haven 301
Vox dilecti 134
Vulpius 275

W zlobie lezy 242
Walhof 152
Waltham 250
Wareham 327
Watermouth 463
Webb 394
Wedlock 161
Welwyn 429, 446
Were You There? 267
Wesley 318, 398
When Jesus Wept 270
Whitefield 272
Wie lieblich ist der
Maien 46
Wiesbaden 150
Wilmington 139
Wir pflügen 76
Wondrous Love 216
Woodworth 119
Wunderbarer König . . . 39

Yarrington 89
Yorkshire 458

Zion 316
Zoan 456

Metric Index

S.M.—6.6.8.6.
C.M.—8.6.8.6.

L.M.—8.8.8.8.

4.5.4.4.5.
Songs of Joy 241

4.5.7.6.6.7.
O Sanctissima 235

4.10.10.10.4.
Ora labora 384

5.5.5.4. Double
Bunessan 22

5.5.5.5. with refrain
The Old, Old Path . . . 158

5.5.6.5.
After Prayer 94

5.6.8.5.5.8.
Schönster Herr Jesu . . . 226

5.7.8.5.8.5.8.5. with refrain
Judas Maccabeus 395

6.2.
Savage 92, 93

6.4.6.4. with refrain
Need 129

**6.4.6.4. Double (see also
10.10.10.10.)**
Bread of Life 173
333, 454

Hendon 4, 474
Hermas 144, 198
Hesperus 348, 426
Hicks 3, 365
Hills 309
Holiness 180
Hollingside 408
Holy Manna 279
Holy Spirit, Truth Divine
. . . . 281
Holy Wings 1, 183
How Can I Keep from
Singing 157
Hursley 14, 113, 352
Hurst 199
Hyfrydol 17, 66, 201
Hymn of Praise . . . 53, 164
Hymn to Joy 20, 470

I Love Thee 186
I Wonder As I Wander 251
In Babilone 406
In corde meo 461
In dulci jubilo 260
Intercession (Refrain) . . . 88
Invocation 10
Irby 240
Italian Hymn 54, 478

James 130
Jerusalem 465
Jesu, meine Freude 121
Jesus Is Calling Today . 391
Join the Children of the
Lord 475
Judas Maccabeus 395
Just as I Am 421

Kedron 310
Kingdom 114, 221
King's Weston 445
Kingsfold 182
Kirtland 332
Kremser 11

Ladue Chapel 111
Lancashire . . 317, 374, 392
Landas . . 357 (A^b), 405 (G),
495 (G)
Langran 328
Lasst uns erfreuen . . 21, 72,
273
Lauda Anima 41
Laudes Domini 35
Lauds 214
Lenox 206

Leoni 47
Leslie 298
Let God Be God 197
Let Us Break Bread . . . 342
Liebster Jesu 227
Livingston 30
Livorno 423
Llanfair 278
Lloyd 286
Lobe den Herren 67
Lobt Gott, ihr Christen . 9
Lois 285
Lord, I Want to Be . . . 464
Love Unknown 202
Loyalty 379
Lyons . . . . 27 (A^b), 229(G)

McKee 448
Mabune 230
Maidstone 51
Manoah 2, 303, 366
Marlee 269
Marnie 341
Martyrdom 325
Maryton 282, 347, 462
Massachusetts . . . 300, 360
Master, Use Me 424
Materna 219
Meditation 313
Melita 6
Melrose 425, 467
Mendelssohn 252
Mendon 355, 400, 432
Mercy 12
Message 477
Mine Are the Hungry . . 388
Mit Freuden zart 40
Mora Proctor 163, 218
Morecambe . 16 (B^b),181 (C)
More Love to Thee . . . 411
Morning Song . . . 190, 457
Mozart 389
Mueller 232
Munich 305
My Redeemer 387

Naomi 117, 490
National Hymn 191
Neander 308
Need 129
Nettleton 31
New Britain 104
New Malden 452
Nicaea 56
No Other Plea . . . 357 (A^b),
405 (G), 495 (G)

Noël Nouvelet . . . 280, 443
Norman 24
Norse Air . . . . . . 357 (A^b),
405 (G), 495 (G)
Nun danket alle Gott . . 60,
334
Nyland 177

O Jesu 78, 207
O Jesus, the Giver 64
O Perfect Love 368
O Sanctissima 235
O'Kelley 499
Old 100th 43
Old 113th 65
Olive's Brow 264
Olivet 91, 143
Olwen 369
Omni Die 112
One Hour with Jesus . . . 82
Ora labora 384

Paderborn 61
Paraclete 33
Park Street 131
Pass Me Not 149
Passion Chorale 262
Peace 213
Peek 404
Penitence 295
Penitentia 84
Personent hodie 245
Picardy 253
Pilot 145
Pittsfield 386, 459
Porter 15
Poverty 369
Praise 62
Praise Him, Praise Him! 68
Proclamation 469
Prophet 307
Purpose 324

Quem pastores . . . 259, 331

Randolph 489
Rathbun 203
Regent Square 231
Rendez à Dieu 329
Resignation 125
Rest 115
Retreat 118, 174
Richmond 346
Richmond Beach . 297, 420
Rimington 63
Rockingham 205, 265

Tune Index

Italicized listings are alternate names by which some tunes are known.

Abbott's Leigh 184
Adeste fideles 238
Admonition 387
Adon olom 169
After Prayer 94
Agincourt 55
All the Way 447
Almsgiving 77, 396
Alstone 321
Ancient of Days 208
Antioch 258
Arlington 7
Arnsberg 39
Ash Grove 493
Ashburton 284
Ashland 441
Assurance 58
Aurelia . 120, 160, 171, 294
Austria 376, 468
Azmon 19

Balm in Gilead 147
Beach Spring 287
Belden 437
Belmont 292
Beloved 313
Belsize Square 418
Benevento 37
Bergen må vika 153
Bethany 138
Bethlehem 435
Birmingham 133
Bishop 487
Bjorklund Major 377
Blaenwern 85, 170
Boylston 399
Bradbury 162
Bradford 212
Bread of Life 173, 333,
454
Bridgman 42
Brookfield 222, 415
Brother James' Air . . . 126,
350
Bryn Calfaria 44
Bullinger 127
Bunessan 22

Canonbury 412, 486
Carlisle 439
Carol 256
Carpenter . 367 (E), 494 (Eᵇ)

Carter 410
Chautauqua 45
Chereponi 407
Children 223
Chisholm 79
Christmas 236
City of God 224
Cloisters 491
Communion 338
Confirmation . . . 354, 361
Consecration 472
Consolator 166
Contrast 481
Converse 86
Cooling 80, 193
Coronation 71
Cradle Song 233
Craig 122
Craigmillar 373
Crimond 124
Crucifer 263
Cushman 217
Cwm Rhondda 419

Dancer 482
De Fleury 481
De Tar 189
Decatur 312
Dedicare 188, 417
Denby 451
Dennis 137, 485
Detroit 243
Deus tuorum militum . 268,
293
Deus vobiscum . . . 326, 488
Diadem 70
Diademata 228, 393
Divinum mysterium . . 220
Dix 75, 254
Doane II 83
Dominus regit me 351
Dove of Peace . . . 108, 356
Down Ampney 289
Duke Street . . . 50, 69, 140

Earth and All Stars 49
East Acklam 73
Easter Hymn 277
Ebenezer 135
Ecology 402
Edwards 497
Ein' feste Burg 142

Eisenach 359, 498
Ellacombe 471
Ellesdie . . . 381(Aᵇ), 390(A)
Elsworth 291
Emerald 151, 436
Erie 86
Es ist ein' Ros' 255
Evan 159, 363
Eventide 128
Ewing 5, 296, 340

Faithful 29
Faithful Guide 105
Faithfulness 187
Federal Street 492
Fellowship 8
Ferguson 148
Festal Song . . . . . 302 (A),
319 (A), 378 (Bᵇ)
Finlandia . 107 (Eᵇ), 315 (F)
Flemming 81
Folksong 343
Forest Green 370, 484
Foundation 136
Freely, Freely 382

Galilee 371
Gardiner 383, 397
Gelobt sei Gott 275
Geneva 403, 438
Germany 383, 397
Gethsemane 266
Gift of Finest Wheat . . 345
Gloria 237
Go Tell It 249
God Be with You . 326, 488
God of Eternity 192
God Our Source 444
Gordon 204
Gottschalk 12
Gratefulness 26, 349
Greensleeves 257
Grenoble 268, 293

Hamburg . . . 165, 337, 364
Hankey 473
Hanover 28
Harts 304
Hawarden 479
He Leadeth Me 123
Heavenly Dove 430
Hebron 13, 422

Rowlands, W. P. (1860-1937)..... 85, 170
Runyan, William M. (1870-1957).... 187
Russian Melody.............. 102, 409

Sacred Harp (1844)........... 161, 287
•Saints' Harmony (1889)............ 312
Sandys, William, Christmas Carols
  (1833) 246
Sankey, Ira Allan (1874-1915)....... 192
Sateren, Leland B. (1913-   )..... 269
•Savage, Ola Gunsolley (1895-1976). 92, 93
Schein, Johann H. (1586-1630)... 359, 498
Schlesische Volkslieder (1842)....... 226
Schneider, Kent E. (1946-   )..... 290
Schneider, Martin G............... 74
Scholtes, Peter (1938-   )........ 466
Schulz, Johann A. P. (1747-1800)...... 76
Schumann, Robert A. (1810-1856)412, 486
Scott-Gatty, Alfred (1847-1918).. 429, 446
Shaw, Geoffrey (1879-1943).... 106, 265
Shaw, Martin (1875-1958)
  .... 18, 200, 238, 324
Sheppard, Franklin L. (1852-1930).... 52
Sherwin, William F. (1826-1888)
  .... 45, 173, 333, 454
Sibelius, Jean (1865-1957)...... 107, 315
Silesian Folk Melody.............. 226
Six, Herbert (1909-   )........... 99
Smart, Henry (1813-1879)
  .... 231, 317, 374, 392
Smith, Alfred M. (1879-1971)
  .... 103, 344, 440
Smith, Henry Percy (1825-1898)
  .... 282, 347, 462
•Smith, Norman W. (1833-1917)
  .... 8, 146, 482
Southern Harmony (1835)
  .... 104, 125, 216, 279, 310
Southgate, Thomas B. (1814-1868)
  .... 222, 415
Stainer, John (1840-1901).......... 100
Stebbins, George Coles (1846-1945)
  .... 79, 180
Steurlein, Johann (1546-1613)........ 46
Stevenson, John A. (1761-1833)...... 501
Stralsund Gesangbuch (1665)........ 67
Strassburger Kirchenamt (1525)...... 65
Sullivan, Arthur Seymour (1842-1900)
  .... 168, 423
Supplement to Kentucky Harmony
  (1820) 243
Supplement to the New Version (1708)200
Swedish Folk Melody... 1, 110, 153, 154,
  156, 183, 210, 225, 299
Sweney, John R. (1837-1899)....... 215
Swiss Traditional Melody... 178, 427, 450

Tallis, Thomas (c. 1505-1585).... 97, 196
•Tandy, F. Phillip (1943-   )....... 34
Tattersall's Psalmody (1794)....... 235
Taylor, Cyril Vincent (1907-   ).... 184
Teschner, Melchior (1584-1635).. 23, 175
Thiman, Eric (1900-1959).......... 304
Tomer, W. G. (1832-1896)....... 326, 488
Turner, Herbert B. (1852-1927)..... 217

Urhan, Chretien (1790-1845)....... 380

Vaughan Williams, Ralph (1872-1958)
  ...... 21, 72, 178, 182, 259, 273, 289,
  331, 370, 427, 445, 450, 480, 484, 489
Venua, Frederick M. A. (1788-1872).. 131
Vulpius, Melchior (c. 1570-1615).... 275

Wade, John Francis (c. 1710-1786)... 238
Wagner, Richard (1813-1883)........ 95
Wainwright, John (1723-1768)...... 458
Walch, James (1837-1901).......... 476
Walker, William (early 19th c.)
  .... 104, 279, 310
Walter, William Henry (1825-1893)
  .... 302, 319, 378
Walton, James George (1821-1905)... 433
Ward, Samuel Augustus (1847-1903).. 219
Warren, George William (1828-1902) 191
Webb, George J. (1803-1887)....... 394
Webbe, Samuel (1740-1816)
  .... 37, 166, 346
•Weddle, Franklyn S. (1905-   ) . 30, 64,
  67, 98, 122, 188, 291, 298, 316, 417, 497
Wells, Marcus M. (1815-1895)....... 105
Welsh Carol..................... 369
Welsh Hymn Melody.......... 32, 261
Welsh Traditional Melody.......... 493
Wesley, Samuel Sebastian (1810-1876)
  .... 120, 160, 171, 294, 479
Wetzel, Richard D. (1935-   )..... 270
Whelpton, George (1847-1930)....... 94
Williams, Robert (c. 1781-1821)..... 278
Williams, Thomas J. (1869-1944)... 135
Willing, Christopher E. (1830-1904).. 321
Willis, Richard Storrs (1819-1900).. 256
Wilson, Hugh (1764-1825)......... 325
Wilson, John (1905-   )...... 214, 343
Witt, Christian F. (1660-1716)... 353, 413
Woodbury, Isaac Baker (1819-1858).. 271
Work, John W., III (1901-1967)...... 249
Wyeth, John (1770-1858)............ 31
Wyeth's Repository of Sacred Music,
  Part Second (1813).......... 190, 457

Yarrington, John................. 89
Young, Carlton R. (1926-   ).. 117, 490

COMPOSERS

Kremser, Edward (1838-1914)......11
Kreutz, Robert E. (1922-   )......345

Landis, Keith (1922-) 272, 367, 441, 494
Lane, Spencer (1843-1903)........295
Langran, James (1835-1909)........328
Leech, Jeffery (1931-   ).....285, 377
Lewis, Freeman (1780-1859).......313
•Lewis, Louise Hills (1887-1948)
..................309, 354, 361
Lockhart, Charles (1745-1815)......439
Lovelace, Austin C. (1919-   )
.............9, 108, 356, 402
Lowry, Robert (1826-1899). 129, 442, 447
Luther, Martin (1483-1546)........142
Lutkin, Peter Christian (1858-1931)..483
Lyon, Meyer (1751-1797)..........47
Lyra Davidica (1708).............277

Main, Hubert P. (1839-1926)....381, 390
Maker, Frederick Charles (1844-1927)
.........90, 109, 115, 425, 428, 467
Malan, H. A. C. (1787-1864)......4, 474
Mann, Arthur Henry (1850-1929)....463
Marsh, Donald (1923-   )........322
Marshall, Jane M. (1924-   )......155
Mason, Lowell (1792-1872) ...13, 19, 59,
    91, 137, 138, 143, 165, 258, 318, 336.
        337, 364, 398, 399, 422, 485
McCarthy, David (1931-   )......452
McCutchan, Robert Guy (1877-1958)..15
McGranahan, James (1840-1907)....387
Meiningen Gesangbuch (1693)......305
Mendelssohn, Felix (1809-1847)
...........88, 133, 252, 334
Milgrove, Benjamin (1731-1810).....304
Miller, Edward (1731-1807)....205, 265
Miller, W. Frederic...............226
•Mills, Arthur Hicks (1870-1943)
..................3, 130, 365
•Mills, Henry Richard (1844-1933)
..................386, 459
Moe, Daniel (1926-   )........224
Monk, William Henry (1823-1889)
.........14, 75, 128, 254, 276
Moore, William................279
•Morgan, John L. (1869-1913)........82
Mozart, Wolfgang Amadeus (1756-1791)
.................381, 389, 390
Murray, James R. (1841-1905).......232

Nägeli, Johann George (1768 or 1773-
1836)............117, 137, 485, 490
•Neal, Harold (1916-   ).......341
Neander, Joachim (1650-1680)...39, 308
Netherlands Traditional Melody......11

Nichol, Henry Ernest (1862-1928)....477
Nicholson, Sydney Hugo (1875-1947). 263
Niles, John Jacob (1892-   )......251
Noble, T. Tertius (1867-1953).......384
Norse Folk Melody........357, 405, 495
Norton, Caroline E. S. (1808-1877)...307

Obetz, John (1933-   )...223, 234, 443
O'Boyle, Kathryn Reese............246
•O'Kelley, Eleanor (1934-   ).....499
Old Tune....................10, 36
Oliver, Henry Kemble (1800-1885)...492
Owen, William (1814-1893)........44
Owens, Carol..................382

Paderborn Gesangbuch (1765).......61
Palestrina, Giovanni P. da(1525-1594)276
Peace, Albert (1844-1912)......132, 455
Peek, Joseph Yates (1843-1911)......404
Piae Cantiones (1582).........220, 245
Plainsong..........211, 220, 283, 364
Polish Carol..................242
Pond, Sylvanus Billings (1792-1871)..311
Praetorius, Michael (1571-1621).....225
Praxis Pietatis Melica (c. 1647).......60
Prichard, Rowland Hugh (1811-1887)
..................17, 66, 201
Psalmodia Sacra (1715)........353, 413
Purday, Charles H. (1799-1885).....465

Quaker Hymn..................157

Redhead, Richard (1820-1901)......266
Redner, Lewis Henry (1831-1908)....248
Reimann, Johann Balthasar (1702-1749)
..................78, 207
Reinagle, Alexander Robert (1799-1877)
..................330, 449
Responses for the Church Year.......89
Revivalist, The (1869).............213
Reynolds, William J. (1920-   ) 163, 218
Rickard, Jeffrey.............272, 441
•Rider, Dale (1948-   ).......150
Rimbault, Edward F. (1816-1876)....380
Roberts, Caradog (1879-1935).......369
Roberts, John, *Canaidau y Cyssegr*
    (1839).....................32, 261
•Robison, Pamela (1947-   ).......241
Robson, R. Walker.................281
Rockstro, William Smith (1823-1895). 112
Root, George F. (1820-1895).......223
Rosecrans, James H. (19th c.).......372
Rossini, Gioacchino A. (1792-1868)
..................2, 303, 366
Routley, Erik (1917-   )
..........139, 185, 367, 373, 494

English Traditional Melody. . . 18, 33, 52, 246, 257, 343, 370, 484
Evans, David (1874-1948). . . 22, 177, 278
Ewing, Alexander (1830-1895). 5, 296, 340

Fink, Gottfried Wilhelm (1783-1846). 435
Finnish Traditional Melody. 177
Fischer, William Gustavus(1835-1912)473
Flemming, Friedrich Ferdinand (1778-1813) 81
Fleury, Maria de. 481
•Forscutt, Mark H. (1834-1903)
. . . . 24, 151, 436
Franklin, Benjamin (1706-1790). 379
French Traditional Carol
. . . . 237, 253, 280, 443
•Fry, Charles (1872-1969). 332, 338
•Fry, Evan A. (1902-1959)
. . . . 188, 298, 417, 497

Gabriel, Charles H. (1856-1932). 48
Gaelic Melody. 22
Gardiner, William, *Sacred Melodies* (1815). 292, 383, 397
Gauntlett, Henry J. (1805-1876)
. . . . 240, 335, 353, 413
Geistliche Kirchengesäng, Cologne (1623). 21, 72, 255, 273
Genevan Psalter (1551) 43
German Carol. 259, 260, 331
German Traditional Melody
. . . . 311, 355, 400, 432
Gerovitch, Eliezer (1844-1914). 169
Gesangbuch der Herzogel, Wirtemburgischen Katholischen Hofkapelle (1784). 471
Ghana Folk Song. 407
Giardini, Felice de (1716-1796). . . 54, 478
Gilbert, Walter B. (1829-1910). 51
Gläser, Carl (1784-1839). 19
Gordon, Adoniram Judson (1836-1895)204
Goss, John (1800-1880). 41
Gottschalk, Louis Moreau (1829-1869). 12
Gould, John Edgar (1822-1875). 145
•Graves, William (1915-   ). 53, 164
Greatorex, Henry W., *Collection of Church Music* (1851). 2, 366
Gregorian Chant. 165, 337
Greiter, Matthäus (c. 1500-1552). 65
Grenoble Antiphoner (1753). . . . 268, 293
Gruber, Franz (1787-1863). 244
•Gustavus, Verna Schaar (1906-   ). . 472

Hampton, Calvin (1938-   ). 189
Handel, George F. (1685-1759)
. . . . 212, 236, 258, 395

Hassler, Hans Leo (1564-1612). 262
Hastings, Thomas (1784-1872)
. . . . 118, 174, 194
Hatton, John (? -1793). 50, 69, 140
Havergal, Frances Ridley (1836-1879)
. . . . 144, 198
Havergal, William Henry (1793-1870)
. . . . 159, 363, 456
Hawaiian Melody. 472
Haweis, Thomas (1734-1820). 346
Haydn, Franz Joseph (1732-1809)376, 468
Haydn, Johann Michael (1737-1806)
. . . . 27, 229
Hayne, Leighton George (1836-1883). 320
Hebrew Melody. 47
Helmore, Thomas (1811-1890). 211
Hemy, Henri F. (1818-1888). 433
Hermann, Nicolaus (c. 1485-1561). . . . 9
Herron, R. 234
Hirschberg Gesangbuch (1741). . . 78, 207
Hodges, Edward (1796-1867). . . . 20, 470
Hoffman, Elisha A. (1839-1929). 424
Holbrook, Joseph Perry (1822-1888). . 487
Holden, Oliver (1765-1844). 71
Holst, Gustav (1874-1934). 375
•Houston, Oliver, Jr. (1928-   ). 101
Howard, Cuthbert (1856-1927). 286
Hughes, John (1873-1932). 419
Husband, Edward (1843-1908). 385
Hutcheson, Charles *Christian Vespers*, Glasgow (1832). 106

Ireland, John (1879-1962). 202
Irish Traditional Melody. . . 185, 339, 362
Irvine, Jessie Seymour (1836-1887). . . 124

Jackisch, Frederick F. (1922-   ). . . 152
Jackson, Francis (1917-   ). 73
Jackson, Robert (1842-1914) 179, 284, 500
Jacob, Gordon (1895-   ). . . . 126, 350
Jeffery, J. Albert (1854-1929). 208
Johnson, David N. (1922-   ). 49, 157, 186
Jones, David H. (1900-   ). 242
Jude, William Herbert (1851-1922). . . 371

Katholisches Gesangbuch (Vienna, c. 1774). 113, 352
Kettring, Donald D. (1907-   ). 200, 228
Kingsley, George (1811-1884). . . . 42, 148
Kirkpatrick, William J. (1838-1921)
. . . . 233, 357, 405, 495
Klusmeier, Ron. 176
Knapp, Phoebe P. (1839-1908). 58
Knapp, William (1698-1768). 327
Knecht, Justin Heinrich (1752-1817). . 385
Kocher, Conrad (1786-1872). 75, 254

Composers, Arrangers, and Sources Index

Restoration composers' and arrangers' names are preceded by a dot (•).

Abbey, Alonzo J. (1825-1887)....80, 193
Abe, Seigi.....................230
"Agincourt Song" (15th c.)..........？.55
Ahle, Johann Rudolph (1625-1673)...227
Allen, Chester G. (1838-1878).......68
Allgemeines Katholisches Gesangbuch,
  Vienna (1774)..................14
American Folk Hymn..147, 267, 342, 464
American Folk Tune..108, 249, 356, 448
•Anderson, Mary Audentia (1872-
  1963).....................158, 239
Appalachian Folk Carol...........251
Appalachian Folk Hymn............234
Arnatt, Ronald (1930-   )......111
Arne, Thomas Augustine (1710-1778)...7
Atkinson, Frederick Cook (1841-
  1897)....................16, 181
Avery, Richard (1934-   ).......322

Bach, Johann Sebastian (1685-
  1750).....29, 121, 227, 262, 359, 498
Bain, James Leith Macbeth (c. 1840-
  1925)....................126, 350
Baker, Henry (1835-1910).....348, 426
Barnby, Joseph (1838-
  1896)....35, 368, 401, 421, 491
Baumbach, Adolph (1830-1880).....461
Beethoven, Ludwig van (1770-
  1827)......20, 42, 453, 460, 470, 496
Belden, Franklin E. (19th c.).......437
Billings, William (1746-1800).......270
Birkbeck, J. B. (1831-1917)........172
Blomquist, Joel (1840-1930).......430
Bock, Fred (1939-   ).............377
Bohemian Brethren's *Kirchengesange*
  (1566) 40
•Booth, Francis Hurst (1923-   )....199
Bortniansky, Dimitri (1751-1825)....501
Bourgeois, Louis (c. 1510-
  c. 1561)...............43, 247, 329
Bradbury, William B. (1816-1868)
  ....25, 57, 87, 119, 123, 162, 264, 469
Bradford Mary A. (1821-1902)...26, 349
Bradshaw, Ralph................64
Broadwood, Lucy (1858-1929)......182
Brumbaugh, Wilber E. (1931-1977)...388
Bullinger, Ethelbert W. (1837-1913)..127
Burleigh, Harry T. (1866-1949)......448
Burney, Charles (1726-1814)....274, 323
•Butler, William E. (1889-1967)......434

Caldwell, Mary E. (1909-   )......142
Calkin, John Baptiste (1827-1905)...250

Callcott, William H. (1807-1882).....88
Carlson, Gordon H.................197
Carr, Benjamin (1769-1831)........116
Carter, Edmund S. (1845-1923)......410
Cartford, Gerhard M. (1923-   )...444
Christensen, F...................475
Christian Harmony (1805).........186
•Church, Charles Fremont, Jr.
  (1904-   ) 306
Clark, Jeremiah (c. 1670-1707)......416
Clarke, Frederick R. C. (1931-   )..195
•Clothier, Louita (1936-   )....216, 418
Conkey, Ithamar (1815-1867).......203
Converse, Charles Crozat (1832-1918)..86
Copes, V. Earle (1921-   )
  ....65, 114, 209, 221
Corner's *Gesangbuch* (1631)........112
Croft, William (1678-
  1727).............28, 200, 314, 358
Crüger, Johann (1598-1662)..60, 121, 334
Curry, Lawrence (1906-   )....71, 238

Dale, Charles J...................451
Danish........................96
Davis, Katherine K. (1892-1980) 300, 360
Day, George Henry (1883-1966).403, 438
Dearle, Edward (1806-1891)........84
Dickey, Mark S. (1885-1961)......1, 183
Dirksen, Richard (1921-   )......301
Doane, William H. (1832-1915)
  ....83, 149, 411
Douglas, C. Winfred (1867-1944)....283
Duckworth, Francis (1862-1941)......63
Dutch Traditional Melody..........406
Dyer, Samuel (1785-1835)..355, 400, 432
Dykes, John Bacchus (1823-1876)...6, 56,
  77, 134, 141,167, 288, 351, 396, 408

Early American Melody........136, 481
Eckhardt, A. Royce (1937-   ) 297, 420
Edson, Lewis (1748-1820)..........206
Efimov, Alexander............102, 409
Ellor, James (1819-1899)...........70
•Elser, Rosalee (1925-   ) .46, 104, 118,
  125, 126, 136, 147,154, 161, 174, 176,
  190, 199, 209,213, 225, 233, 243, 245,
  251, 279,287, 310, 322, 341, 342, 350,
  384, 388, 391, 407, 430, 447, 456, 457,
                                464, 493
Elvey, George Job (1816-1893)
  ....38, 228, 393, 414, 431
Emerson, Luther Orlando (1820-1915)391

Robinson, Robert (1735-1790). . . . 31, 311
•Robison, Pamela (1947-   ). 241
Rogozin, P. 102, 409
Romanis, William (1824-1899). 165
Romanov, R. 102, 409
Rupp, Anne Neufeld (1932-   ). . . . 287
•Russell, Naomi (1921-   ). . . . 150, 164,
234, 334, 341, 350, 395

Sandell, Lina (Sandell-Berg,
Caroline V.) (1832-1903). 153, 156
•Savage, Ola Gunsolley (1895-1976). . . . 90
Schlesische Volkslieder (1842). 226
Schneider, Kent E. (1946-   ). 290
Schneider, Martin G. 74
Scholtes, Peter (1938-   ). 466
Schubring, Julius (1806-1889). 133
Schutz, Johann J. (1640-1690). 40
Scott, Robert Balgarnie Young
(1899-   ). 319
Scott, Thomas (1705-1775). 277
Scottish Psalter (1650). 124
Scriven, Joseph (1820-1886). 85, 86
Sears, Edmund H. (1810-1876). 256
•Selden, Eric L. (1925-   ). . . . 183, 386
Sherlock, Hugh (1905-   ). 438
Shurtleff, Earnest W. (1862-1917). . . . 374
Sidebotham, Mary A. (1833-1913). . . . 114
Sigourney, Lydia H. (1793-1865). . . . 148
•Smith, David H. (1844-1904). 8, 312
•Smith, Elbert A. (1871-1959). 239
•Smith, Emma, Sacred Hymns, collection
(1841) 354
•Smith, Frederick M. (1874-1946). . . . 316
•Smith, Joseph III (1832-1914). 131,
146, 482, 490
•Smith, Vida Elizabeth (1865-1945). . . 158
Smith, Walter Chalmers (1825-1908). . 32
•Snow, Eliza Roxey (1804-1887). 140
Spaeth, Harriet Krauth (1845-1925). . 255
Spannaus, Olive Wise (1916-   ). . . 467
•Spencer, Geoffrey F. (1927-   ). . . 1, 54,
106, 151, 230, 297, 299, 314, 349,
351, 358, 398, 495
Stennett, Samuel (1727-1795). 338
Stocking, Jay T. (1870-1936). 219
Stone, Lloyd (1912-   ). 315
Stone, Samuel J. (1839-1900). 294
Struther, Jan (1901-1953). 185
Swain, Joseph (1761-1796). 313
Symonds, John A. (1840-1893). 323

•Tandy, F. Phillip (1943-   ). 34
Tappan, William Bingham (1794-
1849) 264
Tarrant, William G. (1853-1928). 29

Tate, Nahum (1652-1715). 236
Tersteegen, Gerhard (1697-1769). . . . 39
Theodulph of Orleans (c. 760-821). . . . 23
Thomson, Mary Ann (1834-1923). . . . 476
Thring, Godfrey (1823-1903). 228
Thrupp, Dorothy A. (1779-1847). . . . 162
Trueblood, David Elton (1900-   ). . 111
•Tyree, Alan (1929-   ). . . . 110, 142,
205, 206, 297, 301, 302, 350, 360, 434
Tweedy, Henry Hallam (1868-1953). . 370

•Updike, L. Wayne (1916-   ). 497
Utech, George (1931-   ). 444

Van de Venter, Judson W. (1855-
1939). 430
Van Der Haas, Walter. 74
Van Dyke, Henry (1852-1933). 20
Van Lelyveld, Peter-Paul. 74
Veni Creator Spiritus. 283

Walford, William W. (1772-1850). . . . 87
Walter, Howard Arnold (1883-1918). . 404
Ware, Henry (1793-1843). 13, 271
Waring, Anna Laetitia (1820-1910)
. . . . 120, 457
Watson, Charles E. (1869-1942. 195
Watts, Isaac (1674-1748). 25, 42, 50,
59, 62, 63, 125, 200, 258, 265, 337, 492
•Webb, William F. (1928-   ). 357
Webster, Bradford Gray (1898-   ). 224
•Weddle, Franklyn S. (1905-   ). . . . 291
•Weldon, Clair (1928-   ). 221
Wesley, Charles (1707-1788). . 19, 54, 170,
201, 212, 252, 278, 286, 393, 399, 498
Westendorf, Omer (1916-   ). . 345, 493
Westwood, Horace (1884-1956). 426
Whittier, John Greenleaf (1807-1892)
. . . . 115, 126, 261, 427, 450
Williams, Peter (1722-1796). 311
Williams, William (1717-1791). 311
Willis, Love Maria (1824-1908). 453
Winchester, Caleb Thomas (1847-
1920). 196
Winkworth, Catherine (1827-1878). . . 60,
67, 121
Wolcott, Samuel (1813-1886). 478
Wordsworth, Christopher (1807-1885)
. . . . 77, 396
Work, John W., Jr. (1872-1925). 249
Wren, Brian (1936-   ). 214, 272

•Yamada, Hiroshi (1935-   ). 230
Yigdal of Daniel Ben Judah (14th c.). . . 47
Young, John Freeman (1820-1885). . . 244
Yuki, Ko (1896-   ). 230

Landsberg, Max (1845-1928) 47
Lane, Grace 456
Larcom, Lucy (1826-1893) 168
Lathbury, Mary Ann (1841-1913). 45, 173
Latin 211, 238, 259, 260, 276, 278
Leech, Bryan Jeffrey (1931-   )
. . . . 153, 182, 197, 285, 377, 420
Lennen, Elinor 9
•Lewis, William (1856-1919) 82
Littledale, Richard F. (1833-1890) . . . 289
Littlefield, Milton Smith (1864-1934). 222
Lloyd, William Freeman (1791-1853). 137
Longfellow, Henry W. (1807-1882) . . . 250
Longfellow, Samuel (1819-1892) 65,
281, 288, 501
Longstaff, William Dunn (1822-1894). 180
Lowry, Robert (1826-1899) 157
•Luff, Joseph (1852-1948) 387
Luther, Martin (1483-1546) 142
Lynch, Thomas T. (1818-1871) 284
Lyra Davidica (1708) 278
Lyte, Henry Francis (1793-1847). . 41, 128

Mann, Newton (1836-1926) 47
•Maples, Evelyn (1919-   ) 186,
346, 348, 431, 432
March, Daniel (1816-1909) 381
Marsh, Donald (1923-   ) 322
Matheson, Annie (1853-1924) 451
Matheson, George (1842-1906) 132
Matson, William Todd (1833-1899) . . . 178
Maurus, Hrabanus (776-856) 283
•McCullough, Albert (1901-1961) 472
•McLaughlin, Kenneth L. (1951-   )
. . . . 365, 436, 459
McWhood, Leonard B. (1870-1939) 91
Medley, Samuel (1738-1799) 273, 274
•Mills, Frank W. (1876-1963) 247
Milman, Henry H. (1791-1868) 268
Mohr, Joseph (1792-1848) 244
Monsell, John (1811-1875) . . . 46, 55, 295
Montgomery, James (1771-1854)
. . . . 160, 161, 231, 266, 325, 364
•Moon, Cleo Hanthorne (1904-   )
. . . . 109, 118, 326, 415, 455
Moore, Thomas (1779-1852) 166
Morse, Kenneth I. (1913-   ) 388
Münster Gesangbuch (1677) 226
Murray, Robert (1832-1910) 413

Neale, John M. (1818-1866) 23, 211,
220, 259, 260
Neander, Joachim (1650-1680) 51, 67
Netherlands Folk Song 11
Newbolt, Michael Robert (1874-1956) 263
Newhall, Charles S. (1842-1935) 422

Newton, John (1725-1807). 104, 216, 496
Nichol, H. Ernest (1862-1928) 477
Niles, John Jacob (1892-   ) 251
North, Frank Mason (1850-1935) 383
Numbers 6:24-26 483

Oakeley, Frederick (1802-1880) 238
•Oakman, Arthur A. (1905-1975) 292
Old Edition 36, 354
Olson, Ernest W. (1870-1958) 156
Onderdonk, Henry U. (1789-1858) 24
Owens, Carol 382
Oxenham, John (1852-1941) 448, 449

Palmer, Ray (1808-1887) 143
Park, John Edgar (1879-1956). . 217, 218
Pearson, E. Lincoln (1917-   ) 153
Perronet, Edward (1726-1792) 70, 71
Peters, Mary Bowly (1813-1856) 3
Phelps, Sylvanus Dryden (1816-1895). 442
•Phelps, W. W. (1792-1872) 33, 64,
194, 313
Piae Cantiones (1582) 245
Pierpoint, Folliot S. (1835-1917) 75
Pilgrim Hymnal, The (1904) 213
Polish 242
Pott, Francis (1832-1909) 276
•Pratt, Parley P. (1807-1857) 206, 356, 361
Prentiss, Elizabeth P. (1818-1878) 411
Psalm 19:14 461
Psalm 23 125
Psalm 25 110
Psalm 96:9 15
Psalm 98 258
Psalm 148 66
Psalter 496

Quinn, James 227

Rankin, Jeremiah Eames (1828-1904)
. . . . 488, 489
•Rawson, Don C. (1932-   ) 102, 409
Rawson, George (1807-1889) 309
Reed, Andrew (1787-1862) 288
Reed, Edith M. G. (1885-1933) 242
Reid, William Watkins, Jr. (1923-   )
. . . . 175, 198, 375
Reid, William Watkins, Sr. (1890-   )
. . . . 103, 207, 440
Richardson, Clarence F. (1879- ?) . . . 389
Rinkart, Martin (1586-1649) 60
Rippon, John, *Selection of Hymns*
(1787) 136
Roberts, Daniel C. (1841-1907) 191

Elliott, Charlotte (1789-1871)....... 119
•Elser, Rosalee (1925-   )...... 223, 380
English Traditional Carol.......... 246
European Edition (1840)....... 229, 416

Faber, Frederick W. (1814-1863)
.... 193, 433
Falk, Johannes D. (1768-1826)....... 235
Farjeon, Eleanor (1881-1965)....... 22
Farquharson, Walter Henry
(1936-   )........... 176, 184, 447
Fawcett, John (1739-1817)......... 485
Featherstone, William R. (1842-1878) .204
Fellows, John (? -1785)........... 353
•Ferris, Deam (1912-   )......... 298
Fitch, W. R.................. 423
Forness, Norman O. (1936-   ).... 378
•Forscutt, Mark H. (1834-1903).... 2, 112
Fosdick, Harry Emerson (1878-
1969)................... 177, 419
Foundling Hospital Collection (1796). .66
•Fowler, William (1830-1865)....... 307
Francis of Assisi (1182-1226)........ 72
Francis, Benjamin (1734-1799)...... 460
Franck, Johann (1618-1677)....... 121
French Traditional Carol.......... 237
Frostenson, Anders........ 107, 300
Frothingham, Nathaniel L. (1793-1870) .14
•Fry, Charles (1872-1969).......... 332
•Fry, Evan A. (1902-1959)..... 122, 306,
335, 359, 366, 417, 418, 471, 479

Gabriel, Charles H. (1856-1932)..... 391
Garriott, Jean (1918-   )........ 135
Gerhardt, Paul (1607-1676)........ 262
German..................... 35, 255
Gillman, F. J. (1866-1949).......... 425
Gilmore, Joseph H. (1834-1918)...... 123
Gladden, Washington (1836-1918)... 462
Grant, Robert (1785-1838).... 27, 28, 116
•Graves, William (1915-   )....... 53
Green, F. Pratt (1903-). .73, 343, 402, 445
•Gunn, Raymond (1925-   )...... 362
Gurney, Dorothy Blomfield (1858-1932). .368

Ham, Marion Franklin (1867-1956)
.... 253, 293
Hammond, William (1719-1783)..... 10
Hankey, Katherine (1834-1911)..... 473
Harkness, Georgia (1891-1974)..... 208,
209, 315, 470
Harlow, Samuel Ralph (1885-1972)
.... 210, 406
Harrington, Helen (1909-   )... 439
Hart, Joseph (1712-1768)...... 481, 500
Hart, Lucius................ 469

Hartshorne, Hugh............... 37, 38
Hastings, Thomas (1784-1872). .166, 318
Hatch, Edwin (1835-1889)........ 179
Havergal, Francis Ridley (1836-
1879)........... 127, 144, 408, 412
Hawks, Annie Sherwood (1835-1872) .129
Hearn, Marianne (1834-1909)...... 421
Heber, Reginald (1783-1826)..... 56, 329
Hedge, Frederick Henry (1805-1890)
.... 12, 142
Herbert, George (1593-1632..... 30, 439
Herklots, Rosamond E. (1905-   ). .108
•Higdon, Barbara McFarlane
(1930-   )............. 40, 69
Hill, Frances Thompson........ 279
Hoffman, Elisha A. (1839-1929).... 424
Holmes, John Haynes (1879-1964).... 394
Homer, Charlotte G............. 48
Hopper, Edward (1818-1888)...... 145
Hosmer, Frederick Lucian (1840-
1929)..................... 320
How, William Walsham (1823-1897)
.... 305, 385, 401, 480
•Howard, Barbara (1930-   )...... 58,
194, 339, 369, 380, 499
•Howard, Richard (1929-   ).... 58, 399
Hoyt, May P.................. 333
Huber, Jane Parker............. 190
Hughes, Donald Wynn (1911-1967)
.... 152
•Hunker, E. Y. (1899-1966)......... 282
Hunter, John (1848-1917).......... 113
Hymns for the Young (1836)....... 162

Isaiah 54:10.................. 153

Johnson, Samuel (1822-1882).... 141, 304
Johnson, William (1906-   )...... 269
•Jordan, Mildred (1918-   )...... 441
Joseph, Jane M. (c. 1894-1929)...... 245
Jubilee Harp.................. 80
•Judd, Peter (1943-   )......... 363

"K" in John Rippon's Selection of
Hymns (1787)................. 136
Kaan, Fred (1929-   )... 107, 171, 300,
308, 327, 331, 367, 452, 491
Kane, Victor (1906-   )......... 484
Katterjohn, Henry (1869-1931)..... 235
Kelly, Thomas (1769-1855)........ 474
Ken, Thomas (1637-1711)......... 43
Kethe, William (? -1594)........ 61
King, John (1789-1858)........... 225
Kingsley, Charles (1819-1875)...... 89
Kitchin, George William (1827-1912). 263
Knapp, Shepherd (1873-1946)...... 446

Authors, Translators, and Sources Index

Restoration authors' and translators' names are preceded by a dot (•).

Adams, Sara Flowers(1805-1848). 138, 139

Adkins, Leon M. (1896-   ). 392

Ainger, Arthur C. (1841-1919). 324

•Aldridge, Dennis (1934-   ). 6

Alexander, Cecil Frances (1818-1895)
. . . . .18, 240, 371

Alexander, James Waddell (1804-1859)
. . . . 262

Alford, Henry (1810-1871). 37, 38

Alington, Cyril Argentine (1872-1955) 275

American Folk Hymn. 147, 249,
267, 342, 464

Appalachian Folk Carol. 251

Armitage, Ella S. (1841-1931). 435

Armstrong, John (1813-1856). 486

Arnold, John, *Compleat Psalmodist*
(1749) 278

•Athey, Margaret (1936-   ). . . .336, 400

Aurelius Clemens Prudentius (348-413)
. . . . 220

Avery, Richard (1934-   ). 322

Babcock, Maltbie D. (1858-1901). 52

Bagby, W. H. (19th century). 372

Baker, Henry W. (1821-1877). 220

Baker, Theodore (1851-1934). . . . 11, 255

Bartholemew, William (1793-1867). . .133

Barton, Bernard (1784-1849). 303

Bateman, Henry (1802-1872). 403

Bathurst, William Hiley (1796- 1877) . 159

Baughen, Michael A. 44

Bayly, Albert F. (1901-). . .17, 163, 310

Beach, Seth Curtis (1837-1932). 169

Belden, Franklin E. (19th century). . . 437

Bernard of Clairvaux (1091-1153)
. . . . .167, 262

Berwick Hymnal (1886). 81

Bianco da Siena (d. 1434). 289

Bickersteth, Edward H. (1825-1906). . .84

Billings, William (1746-1800). 270

Blaisdell, James A. (1867-1957). 339

Bode, John E. (1816-1874). 463

Bonar, Horatius (1808-1889). 134,
188, 189, 328, 379

Borthwick, Jane Laurie (1813-1897). . 384

Bowring, John (1792-1872). 203

Brenner, Scott Francis (1903-   ). . .355

Bridges, Matthew (1800-1894). 228

Bridges, Robert (1844-1930). 283

Briggs, George Wallace (1875-1959) . 344

Brokering, Herbert (1926-   ). 49

Brooks, Phillips (1835-1893). 248

Brown, Jeanette Perkins (1887- 1960). 465

Burder, George (1752-1832). 4

Burrowes, Elisabeth (1883-   ). 429

Campbell, Jane M. (1817-1878). 76

Caswall, Edward (1814-1878). . . . 35, 167

Cennick, John (1718-1755). 336, 487

Chadwick, John White (1840-1904). . .458

•Cheville, Roy A. (1897-   ). 61, 64,
296, 317, 340, 347, 352, 390, 397, 410,
454, 468, 498

Chisholm, Thomas O. (1866-1960). . . .79,
187

Christensen, F. 475

Christierson, Frank von (1900-). 243, 405

Church Chorals and Choir Studies
(1850) 226

Clark, Thomas Curtis (1877-1953). . .373

Claudius, Matthias (1740-1815). 76

Clephane, Elizabeth C. (1830-1869). . 428

•Clothier, Richard (1937-   ). 480

Coffin, Henry S. (1877-1954). 211

•Coffman, Linda E. (1945-   ). 199

Colvin, Tom (1925 -   ). 407

Conder 105

Cotterill, Thomas (1779-1823). 330

Cowper, William (1731-1800). 117,
154, 155

Cox, Frances Elizabeth(1812-1897). 40, 51

Coxe, Arthur Cleveland (1818-1896). . 376

•Crayne, Mabel Williams (1880-1980). 346

Croly, George (1780-1860). 181

Cropper, Margaret (1886-1980). 443

Crosby, Fanny J. (1820-1915). 57, 58,
68, 83, 149, 192, 215

Crossman, Samuel (1624-1683). 202

Crum, J. M. C. (1872-1958). 280

Custer, Chester E. (1920-   ). 174

Davis, Robert (1881-1950). 78

Dearmer, Percy (1867-1936). 259

•Derry, Charles (1826-1921). 7, 26

Dix, William C. (1837-1898). . . . 254, 257

Doctrine and Covenants, Section 154. . 380

Doddridge, Philip (1702-1751). 130

Dodgshun, Ernest (1876-1944). 5,
321, 414

•Draper, Maurice (1918-   ). 312

Draper, William H. (1855-1933). 72

Edgar, Mary S. (1889-1973). 172

•Edwards, Alice (1899-1973). 408

Edwards, Robert Lansing (1915-   ). 21

Ellerton, John (1826-1893). 494

Now, on Land and Sea Descending

501

D. and C. 85:16a-e
Numbers 6:24-26

VESPER HYMN 8.7.8.7.8.6.

1. Now, on land and sea de-scend-ing, Brings the
night its peace pro-found; Let our ves-per
hymn be blend-ing With the ho-ly calm a-round.

2. Soon as dies the sun-set glo-ry, Stars of
heaven shine out a-bove, Tell-ing still the
an-cient sto-ry— Their Cre-a-tor's change-less love.

3. Now, our wants and bur-dens leav-ing To His
care who cares for all, Cease we fear-ing,
cease we griev-ing: At His touch our bur-dens fall.

4. As the dark-ness deep-ens o'er us, Lo! e-
ter-nal stars a-rise; Hope and faith and
love rise glo-rious, Shin-ing in the spir-it's skies.

*Ju-bi-la-te! Ju-bi-la-te! Ju-bi-la-te! A-men.

* "Jubilate" (ū-bĭ-lah-tā) means "Shout joyfully (to God)."

Text: Samuel Longfellow, 1819-1892; refrain added.
Tune: Dimitri Bortniansky, 1751-1825; arr. John A. Stevenson, 1761-1833.

499 Who Will Go Forth and Serve?

Isaiah 6:8
Acts 20:28

O'KELLEY S.M.

"Who will go forth and serve?" We speak, "O God, send us
To bring thy peace and heal-ing touch, We go now in thy name."

Text: Barbara Howard, 1930 - ; copyright 1980 Reorganized Church of Jesus Christ of Latter Day Saints.
Tune: Eleanor O'Kelley, 1934 - ; copyright 1980 by the composer. Used by permission.

500 Once More Before We Part

Ether 5:41
D. and C. 50:8e-g

TRENTHAM S.M.

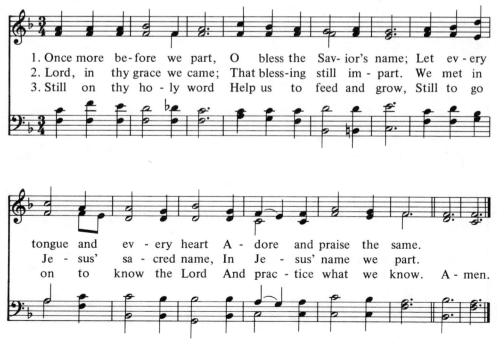

1. Once more be-fore we part, O bless the Sav-ior's name; Let ev-ery
2. Lord, in thy grace we came; That bless-ing still im - part. We met in
3. Still on thy ho-ly word Help us to feed and grow, Still to go

tongue and ev-ery heart A - dore and praise the same.
Je - sus' sa - cred name, In Je - sus' name we part.
on to know the Lord And prac - tice what we know. A - men.

Text: Joseph Hart, 1712-1768.
Tune: Robert Jackson, 1842-1914.

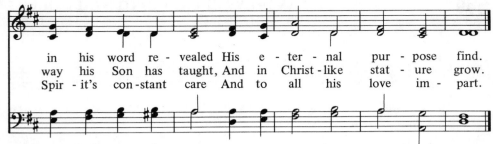

in his word re - vealed His e - ter - nal pur - pose find.
way his Son has taught, And in Christ - like stat - ure grow.
Spir - it's con - stant care And to all his love im - part.

Text: L. Wayne Updike, 1916 - ; alt.
Tune: Franklyn S. Weddle, 1905 - , and Evan A. Fry, 1902-1959; alt.
Text and tune copyright 1956 Herald Publishing House.

Forth in Thy Name, O Lord, We Go 498

D. and C. 38:9a, c
I Corinthians 10:31

EISENACH L.M.

1. Forth in thy name, O Lord, we go, Our dai - ly
2. The task thy wis - dom hath as - signed We long to -
3. Forth in thy name, O Lord, we go With gifts di -

la - bor to pur - sue; Thy mind, O Lord, we
geth - er to ful - fill, In all our works thy
verse, with hearts as one, That in our la - bors

long to know And serve in all we speak and do.
pres - ence find, And prove thy good and per - fect will.
we may grow In - to the king - dom of thy Son. A - men.

Text: Charles Wesley, 1707-1788; alt. by Roy A. Cheville, 1897 - .
Tune: Johann H. Schein, 1586-1630; harm. by Johann Sebastian Bach, 1685-1750.

496   Heavenly Father, Grant Thy Blessing

Mosiah 2:49
Colossians 3:15, 16

SARDIS 8.7.8.7.

1. Heaven-ly Fa-ther, grant thy bless-ing On the teach-ing of this day,
*2. May the grace of Christ, our Sav-ior, And the Fa-ther's bound-less love,
3. Thus may we a-bide in un-ion With each oth-er and the Lord,

That our hearts, thy fear pos-sess-ing, May from sin be turned a-way.
With the Ho-ly Spir-it's fa-vor, Rest up-on us from a-bove.
And pos-sess, in sweet com-mun-ion, Joys which earth can-not af-ford. A-men.

* Stanza 2 may be used as a response.

Text: John Newton, 1725-1807, and Psalter.
Tune: Ludwig van Beethoven, 1770-1827.

497   With a Steadfast Faith

Hebrews 11:1
Helaman 5:97

EDWARDS 11.7.11.7.

1. With a stead-fast faith to-geth-er let us walk
2. With a stead-fast faith to-geth-er let us walk
3. With a stead-fast faith to-geth-er let us walk,

As we seek our Fa-ther's mind; In our dai-ly task, and
That each one on earth may know The a-bun-dant life, the
Serv-ing with a com-mon heart, Shar-ing grate-ful-ly the

Now Let Our Hearts Within Us Burn

495

Isaiah 6:5-8
Luke 24:29-31 (30-32)

NORSE AIR (No Other Plea, or Landas) C.M.D.
See 357 for a higher setting.
Alternate tune: MASSACHUSETTS (360)

1. Now let our hearts with-in us burn As with a clean-sing fire.
2. As in an-oth-er time and place, A-long a for-lorn road,
3. How can we now de-ny that voice That calls us from with-in,

Your gra-cious Word has stirred in us A surge of new de-sire.
The Lord's re-new-ing grace pre-vailed Till new-born cour-age glowed;
Or blind-ly claim we need not bear An-oth-er's pain and sin?

Should vi-sion fail and cour-age yield To care-less com-pro-mise,
Our wor-ship here has lift-ed us From self-in-dul-gent care
In hearts that beat ex-ul-tant-ly Re-new your per-fect will;

Then re-di-rect our falt'-ring steps To brav-er en-ter-prise.
And strength-ened us to in-car-nate The price-less hope we share.
And send us forth, re-stored a-gain, Our mis-sion to ful-fill.

Text: Geoffrey F. Spencer, 1927 - ; copyright 1980 Reorganized Church of Jesus Christ of Latter Day Saints.
Tune: Norse Folk Melody; arr. William J. Kirkpatrick, 1838-1921.

494

Hebrews 13:20, 21
John 14:27

Again, Dear Savior

CARPENTER 10.10.10.10.
See 367 for a higher setting.

1. A - gain, dear Sav - ior to thy name we raise
2. Grant us thy peace, Lord, through the com - ing night;
3. Grant us thy peace through - out our earth - ly life;
4. Thy peace in life, the balm of ev - ery pain;

With one ac - cord our part - ing hymn of praise;
Turn thou for us its dark - ness in - to light;
Peace to thy Church from er - ror and from strife;
Thy peace in death, the hope to rise a - gain;

Guard thou the lips from sin, the hearts from shame,
From harm and dan - ger keep thy chil - dren free,
Peace to our land, the fruit of truth and love;
Then, when thy voice shall bid our con - flict cease,

That in this house have called up - on thy name.
For dark and light are both a - like to thee.
Peace in each heart, thy Spir - it from a - bove:
Share with us, Lord, thine ev - er - last - ing peace. A - men.

Text: John Ellerton, 1826-1893, alt.
Tune: Keith Landis, 1922 - ; harm. Erik Routley, 1917 - ; copyright 1977 Praise Publications, Inc.; used by permission.

The seed of his teach-ing, Re - cep - tive souls reach-ing,
With your feast you feed us, With your light now lead us;

Shall blos - som in ac - tion for God and for all.
U - nite us as one in this life that we share.

His grace did in - vite us; His love shall u - nite us
Then may all the liv - ing With praise and thanks-giv - ing

To work for God's king - dom and an - swer his call.
Give hon - or to Christ and his name that we bear.

Text: Omer Westendorf, 1916 - ; copyright 1964 World Library Publications; reprinted with permission.
Tune: Traditional Welsh Melody; harm. Rosalee Elser, 1925 - ; copyright 1980 Rosalee Elser; used by permission.

493

Sent Forth by God's Blessing

II Corinthians 5:14-21
II Corinthians 1:21, 22

ASH GROVE 6.6.11.6.6.11.D.

Unison (or harmony)

1. Sent forth by God's bless - ing, Our true faith con - fess - ing,
2. With praise and thanks-giv - ing To God ev - er - liv - ing,

The peo - ple of God from his dwell - ing take leave.
The tasks of our ev - 'ry - day life we will face.

The sup - per is end - ed. Oh, now be ex - tend - ed
Our faith ev - er shar - ing, In love ev - er car - ing,

The fruits of this ser - vice in all who be - lieve.
Em - brac - ing his chil - dren of each tribe and race.

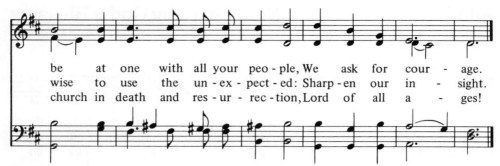

be   at   one with   all your peo - ple, We   ask   for   cour -   age.
wise   to   use   the   un - ex - pect - ed: Sharp - en   our   in   -   sight.
church   in   death and res - ur - rec - tion, Lord of   all   a   -   ges!

Text: Fred Kaan, 1929 - ; copyright © 1968 by Galliard Ltd. Sole U. S. agent: Galaxy Music Corp., N. Y. Used by permission.
Tune: Joseph Barnby, 1838-1896.

Come, Gracious Lord, Descend and Dwell   492

D. and C. 85:3   FEDERAL STREET L.M.
Psalm 34:8, 9

1. Come,   gra - cious Lord, de - scend and dwell   By   faith and
2. Come   fill   our hearts with   in - ward strength; Make our   a -
3. Now   to   the God whose power can   do   More than our

love   in   ev - ery breast; Then shall we know and   taste and
wak - ened souls pos - sess And learn the height and breadth and
thoughts and wish - es know, Be   ev - er - last - ing hon - or

feel   The   joys that can - not   be   ex - pressed.
length Of   thine e - ter - nal love and grace.
done   By   all   the church, through Christ, his   Son.   A - men.

Text: Isaac Watts, 1674-1748; alt.
Tune: H. K. Oliver, 1800-1885.

490

Moroni 7:3
Romans 14:19

Lord, Let Thy Blessing Rest

NAOMI C.M.

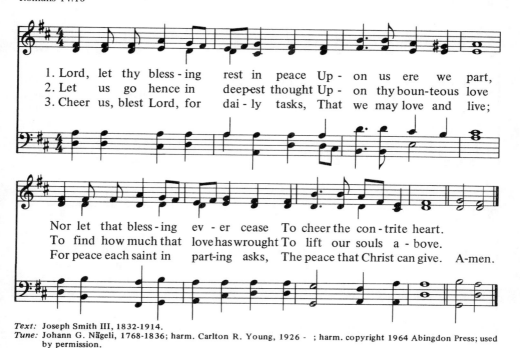

1. Lord, let thy bless-ing rest in peace Up-on us ere we part,
2. Let us go hence in deep-est thought Up-on thy boun-teous love
3. Cheer us, blest Lord, for dai-ly tasks, That we may love and live;

Nor let that bless-ing ev-er cease To cheer the con-trite heart.
To find how much that love has wrought To lift our souls a-bove.
For peace each saint in part-ing asks, The peace that Christ can give. A-men.

Text: Joseph Smith III, 1832-1914.
Tune: Johann G. Nägeli, 1768-1836; harm. Carlton R. Young, 1926- ; harm. copyright 1964 Abingdon Press; used by permission.

491

Romans 12:2
I Nephi 5:59

Lord, as We Rise to Leave

CLOISTERS 11.11.11.5.

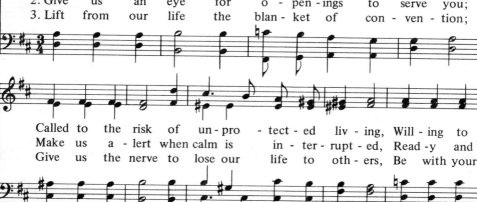

1. Lord, as we rise to leave the shell of wor-ship,
2. Give us an eye for o-pen-ings to serve you;
3. Lift from our life the blan-ket of con-ven-tion;

Called to the risk of un-pro-tect-ed liv-ing, Will-ing to
Make us a-lert when calm is in-ter-rupt-ed, Read-y and
Give us the nerve to lose our life to oth-ers, Be with your

God Be with You Till We Meet Again

489

II Corinthians 13:11, 14
Alma 5:44

RANDOLPH 9.8.8.9.
Alternate hymn: 488

1. God be with you till we meet a - gain;
2. God be with you till we meet a - gain;
3. God be with you till we meet a - gain;
4. God be with you till we meet a - gain;

By His coun - sels guide, up - hold you,
'Neath His wings se - cure - ly hide you,
When life's per - ils thick con - found you,
Keep love's ban - ner float - ing o'er you,

With His sheep se - cure - ly fold you:
Dai - ly man - na still pro - vide you:
Put His arms un - fail - ing round you:
Smite death's threat - 'ning wave be - fore you:

God be with you till we meet a - gain.

Text: Jeremiah E. Rankin, 1828-1904.
Tune: Ralph Vaughan Williams, 1872-1958; from *The English Hymnal* by permission of Oxford University Press; arr. alt. with permission.

488 God Be with You Till We Meet Again

D. and C. 115:1e
Alma 5:44

GOD BE WITH YOU (Deus vobiscum)
9.8.8.9. with refrain
Alternate hymn: 489

1. God be with you till we meet a-gain, By his coun-sels guide, up-hold you,
2. God be with you till we meet a-gain, Dai-ly man-na still pro-vide you,

With his sheep se-cure-ly fold you; God be with you till we meet a-gain.
Neath his wings pro-tect and hide you; God be with you till we meet a-gain.

Refrain

Till we meet, till we meet, Till we meet at Je-sus' feet;

Till we meet, till we meet a-gain, Till we meet,

Till we meet, till we meet, God be with you till we meet a-gain.

Till we meet, till we meet a-gain,

Text: Jeremiah E. Rankin, 1828-1904.
Tune: William G. Tomer, 1832-1896.

ho - lier live, And ev - ery lamp more bright - ly burn.
held se - cure Will bring a hope their stu - dents share.
low - liest here Far bet - ter than a king - dom find. A - men.

Text: John Armstrong, 1813-1856.
Tune: Robert A. Schumann, 1810-1856.

Be with Me, Lord, Where'er I Go

487

Philippians 4:4-7
Romans 12:9-18

BISHOP L.M.

1. Be with me, Lord, wher - e'er I go; Teach me what
2. Pre - vent me lest I har - bor pride, Lest I in
3. En - rich me al - ways with thy love; My kind pro -
4. Oh, may I ev - er do thy will, And thine and

thou wouldst have me do; Sug - gest what - e'er I think or
mine own strength con - fide. Show me my weak - ness; let me
tec - tor ev - er prove; Thy sig - net put up - on my
on - ly thine ful - fill; Let all my time and all my

say; Di - rect me in the nar - row way.
see I have my power, my all from thee.
breast, And let thy Spir - it on me rest.
ways Be spent and end - ed to thy praise. A - men.

Text: John Cennick, 1718-1755.
Tune: J. P. Holbrook, 1822-1888.

485
Blest Be the Tie that Binds

I Thessalonians 3:11-13
I John 3:14, 16

DENNIS S.M.

1. Blest be the tie that binds Our hearts in Chris-tian love;
2. Be-fore our Fa-ther's throne We pour our ar-dent prayers;
3. We share our mu-tual woes, Our mu-tual bur-dens bear,
4. When here our path-ways part We suf-fer mu-tual pain;

The fel-low-ship of kin-dred minds Is like to that a-bove.
Our fears, our hopes, our aims are one, Our com-forts and our cares.
And of-ten for each oth-er flows The sym-pa-thiz-ing tear.
Yet, one in Christ and one in heart, We hope to meet a-gain.

Text: John Fawcett, 1739-1817; alt.
Tune: Arr. from Johann G. Nägeli, 1773-1836, by Lowell Mason, 1792-1872.

486
O Lord, Thy Benediction Give

D. and C. 34:6
D. and C. 85:21a, b

CANONBURY L.M.

1. O Lord, thy ben-e-dic-tion give On all who
2. Give those who teach true hearts and pure, Clear minds and
3. Give those who learn the will-ing ear, The spir-it

teach, on all who learn, That so thy church may
strong, sur-charged with prayer; Give them a faith which
meek, the fruit-ful mind; Such gifts will help the

Make Us, O God, a Church That Shares

484

Alma 19:78
Romans 12:9-18

FOREST GREEN C.M.D.

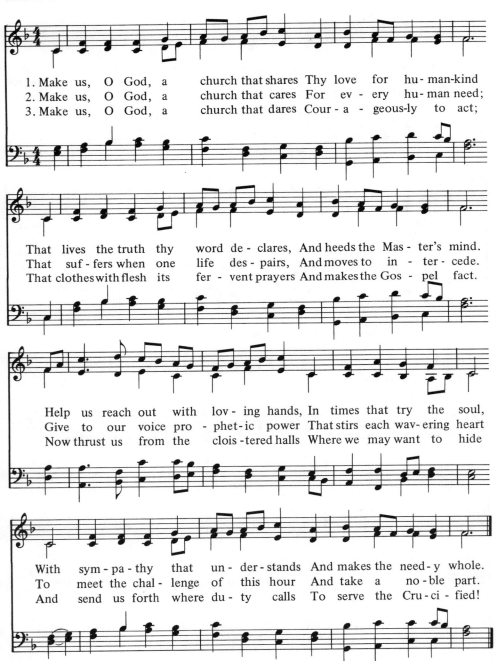

1. Make us, O God, a church that shares Thy love for hu-man-kind
2. Make us, O God, a church that cares For ev - ery hu-man need;
3. Make us, O God, a church that dares Cour - a - geous-ly to act;

That lives the truth thy word de - clares, And heeds the Mas - ter's mind.
That suf - fers when one life des - pairs, And moves to in - ter - cede.
That clothes with flesh its fer - vent prayers And makes the Gos - pel fact.

Help us reach out with lov - ing hands, In times that try the soul,
Give to our voice pro - phet-ic power That stirs each wav-ering heart
Now thrust us from the clois -tered halls Where we may want to hide

With sym - pa - thy that un - der-stands And makes the need-y whole.
To meet the chal - lenge of this hour And take a no - ble part.
And send us forth where du - ty calls To serve the Cru - ci - fied!

Text: Victor Kane, 1906 - ; alt. Copyright 1971 The Hymn Society of America. Used by permission.
Tune: English traditional melody, coll., adapt. and arr. by Ralph Vaughan Williams, 1872-1958. From *The English Hymnal* by permission of Oxford University Press.

483

The Lord Bless You and Keep You

D. and C. 76:2a
Ephesians 6:23, 24

THE LORD BLESS YOU AND KEEP YOU
7.10.8.10.10.10.

The Lord bless you and keep you; The Lord lift his coun-te-nance up-

on you, and give you peace, and give you peace; The
and give you peace,___ and give you peace,___ the Lord

Lord make his face to shine up - on you, and be gra - cious un - to
make his face and be gra-cious,

you, be gra-cious, The Lord be gra-cious, gra-cious un-to you. A - men.
and

Text: Numbers 6:24-26
Tune: Peter C. Lutkin, 1858-1931. By permission of The Parish Press, Fond du Lac, Wisconsin.

Let Us Breathe One Fervent Prayer

482

Philippians 1:9-11
D. and C. 77:4

DANCER 7.7.7.7.D

1. Let us breathe one fer-vent prayer, Ere from hence our foot-steps tend,
2. Go with rev - erent pur-pose hence, Strengthened, helped, by Spir - it's power;

To the Prince up - on whose care All our hopes and joys de - pend.
Christ is help - er, strength, de - fense; Bless him for this peace-ful hour.

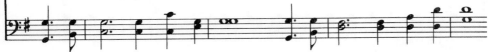

Look be - neath, a - round, a - bove— All is filled with bless - ed peace;
Look with chas-tened hearts be - fore; See, the clouds are sil - ver lined!

'Tis the gift of God's best love— Pray that love may still in - crease.
What as - sur - ance need we more? God is ev - er true and kind.

Text: Joseph Smith, III, 1832-1914, alt.
Tune: Norman W. Smith, 1833-1917.

481 · This God Is the God We Adore

Colossians 1:16-18
III Nephi 4:43-45, 48

CONTRAST (De Fleury) L.M.D.

This God is the God we a-dore, Our faith-ful, un-

change-a-ble friend Whose love is as large as his power And

knows not be-gin-ning nor end. 'Tis Je-sus, the first and the

last, Whose Spir-it will guide us safe home; We'll praise him for

all that is past, And trust him for all that's to come.

Text: Joseph Hart, 1712-1768.
Tune: Early American Melody, attr. to Maria de Fleury.

For All the Saints

480

Ephesians 2:19-22
Revelations 19:1, 5, 6

SINE NOMINE 10.10.10.4.4.

Unison

1. For all the saints who from their la - bors rest,
2. May we thy saints, thy ser - vants true and bold,
3. O blest com - mun - ion, fel - low-ship di - vine!
4. From earth's wide bounds, from o - cean's far - thest coast,

And for all liv - ing saints who thee con - fess,
Serve as the saints who no - bly lived of old,
Saints old and new joined in one grand de - sign;
From age to age re - sounds the count-less host,

Thy name, O Je - sus, be for - ev - er blest.
The world to win and with thy love en - fold.
For all are one in thee, and all are thine.
In praise to Fa - ther, Son, and Ho - ly Ghost.

Al - le - lu - ia, Al - le - lu - ia!

Text: William Walsham How, 1823-1897; rev. Richard Clothier, 1937 - .
Tune: Ralph Vaughan Williams, 1872-1958; from *The English Hymnal* by permission of Oxford University Press.

479

Still Other Sheep I Have

III Nephi 7:20
John 10:16

HAWARDEN 6.6.6.6.D.

1. "Still oth - er sheep I have," Said Christ in days of old;
2. "My voice to them shall speak, My law and gos - pel give;
3. He who is Is - rael's King Shall Is - rael ne'er for - get

"They, too, shall hear my voice And gath - er to one fold;
And Scrip - tures they shall write, Bear wit - ness that I live.
Un - til all scat - tered sheep In one great fold are met;

Of Is - rael's cho - sen seed, Through E - gypt's Jo - seph come—
Lost Is - rael, too, shall hear And write the words I speak;
One God o'er all the earth, One Christ, one king - dom, too!

In Jo - seph's land they wait For Is - rael's prom - ised One.
Then Scrip - tures, tribes, and laws Be gath - ered, one, com - plete."
The Book of Mor - mon bears This wit - ness that is true.

Text: Evan A. Fry, 1902-1959; copyright 1956 Herald Publishing House.
Tune: Samuel S. Wesley, 1810-1876.

And Christ's great king-dom shall come on earth, The king-dom of love and light.

Text and Tune: H. Ernest Nichol, 1862-1928.

Christ for the World We Sing 478

D. and C. 45:2a-d
John 3:16-17

ITALIAN HYMN 6.6.4.6.6.6.4.

1. Christ for the world we sing; The world to Christ we bring
2. Christ for the world we sing; The world to Christ we bring
3. Christ for the world we sing; The world to Christ we bring
4. Christ for the world we sing; The world to Christ we bring

With lov - ing zeal: The poor and them that mourn, The faint and
With fer - vent prayer: The way - ward and the lost, By rest - less
With one ac - cord, With us the work to share, With us re -
With joy - ful song: The new - born souls whose days, Re - claimed from

o - ver - borne, Sin - sick and sor - row - worn, Whom Christ doth heal.
pas - sions tossed, Re - deemed at count - less cost From dark de - spair.
proach to dare, With us the cross to bear For Christ, our Lord.
er - ror's ways, In - spired with hope and praise, To Christ be - long.

Text: Samuel Wolcott, 1813-1886.
Tune: Felice de Giardini, 1716-1796.

477
We've a Story to Tell to the Nations

D. and C. 45:2
Luke 10:1, 2

MESSAGE 10.8.8.7.7. with refrain

1. We've a sto-ry to tell to the na-tions That shall
2. We've a song to be sung to the na-tions That shall
3. We've a mes-sage to give to the na-tions That the
4. We've a Sav-ior to show to the na-tions, Who the

turn their hearts to the right, A sto-ry of truth and mer-cy,
lift their hearts to the Lord, A song that shall con-quer e-vil
Lord who reign-eth a-bove Hath sent us His Son to save us
path of sor-row has trod, That all of the world's great peo-ples

A sto-ry of peace and light, A sto-ry of peace and light.
And shat-ter the spear and sword, And shat-ter the spear and sword.
And show us that God is love, And show us that God is love.
Might come to the truth of God, Might come to the truth of God.

Refrain

For the dark-ness shall turn to dawn-ing, And the dawn-ing to noon-day bright,

O Zion, Haste

476

Romans 10:13-16 (13-15, 17)
D. and C. 62:2b

TIDINGS 11.10.11.10. with refrain

1. O Zi - on, haste, thy mis - sion high ful - fill - ing,
2. Be - hold how man - y thou - sands still are ly - ing
3. Pro - claim to ev - ery peo - ple, tongue, and na - tion

To tell to all the world that God is light, That he who
Bound in the dark-some pris - on-house of sin, With none to
That God, in whom they live and move, is love; Tell how he

made all na - tions is not will - ing One soul should per - ish,
tell them of the Sav - ior's dy - ing, Or of the life he
stooped to save his lost cre - a - tion And died on earth that

Refrain

lost in shades of night. Pub - lish glad ti - dings, ti - dings of
died for them to win.
all may live a - bove.

peace, Ti - dings of Je - sus, re - demp-tion and re - lease.

Text: Mary A. Thomson, 1834-1923.
Tune: James Walch, 1837-1901.

475

Join with Us in Sweet Accord

Matthew 28:18, 19 (19, 20)
D. and C. 11:2a, b

JOIN THE CHILDREN OF THE LORD
7.7.7.7.8.8.8.7.

1. Join with us in sweet ac-cord; Sing the prais-es of the Lord,
2. Tell the na-tions, all a-broad, Of the true and liv-ing God,

Praise un-to his ho-ly name; Ev-ery heart his love pro-claim,
Of his mer-cies, of his love, Of his com-ing from a-bove,

Send the news to ev-ery na-tion; Show the way un-to sal-va-tion;
Of his word by rev-e-la-tion, Of his works in all cre-a-tion;

Give to all this in-vi-ta-tion: Join to-geth-er in the Lord.
Give to all this in-vi-ta-tion: Join to-geth-er in the Lord.

Text: F. Christensen, alt.
Tune: F. Christensen.

Refrain

I love to tell the sto-ry; 'Twill be my theme in glo-ry,

To tell the old, old sto-ry Of Je-sus and his love.

Text: Katherine Hankey, 1834-1911.
Tune: William G. Fischer, 1835-1912.

Father, Bless Thy Word to All 474

D. and C. 34:6
Philippians 1:9-11

HENDON 7.7.7.7.7.

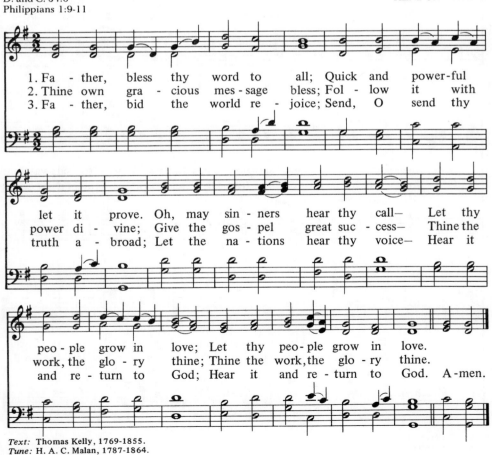

1. Fa - ther, bless thy word to all; Quick and power-ful
2. Thine own gra - cious mes - sage bless; Fol - low it with
3. Fa - ther, bid the world re - joice; Send, O send thy

let it prove. Oh, may sin - ners hear thy call— Let thy
power di - vine; Give the gos - pel great suc - cess— Thine the
truth a - broad; Let the na - tions hear thy voice— Hear it

peo - ple grow in love; Let thy peo - ple grow in love.
work, the glo - ry thine; Thine the work, the glo - ry thine.
and re - turn to God; Hear it and re - turn to God. A - men.

Text: Thomas Kelly, 1769-1855.
Tune: H. A. C. Malan, 1787-1864.

473 I Love to Tell the Story

D. and C. 108:10a

Acts 1:8

HANKEY 7.6.7.6.D. with refrain

Unto God, Who Knows Our Every Weakness   472

Ether 5:28
D. and C. 132:3b, 4

CONSECRATION 10.8.10.10. with refrain

1. Un - to God, who knows our ev - ery weak - ness, With faith we
2. Though the task be great that lies be - fore us, We trust in
3. Lord, ac - cept the hum - ble con - se - cra - tion Of our lives, our

lift our hearts in prayer, Ask - ing, in hu - mil - i - ty and meek-ness,
One di - vine - ly strong, Knowing well at last we'll be vic - to - rious;
tal - ents to thy cause, Till thy word is preached in ev - ery na - tion

Refrain

For his love, his di - rec - tion, and his care.
We will pray that the time will not be long. In these lat - ter days,
And each one has a knowl-edge of thy laws.

with songs of praise, We all must help to spread the gos- pel sto - ry,

Our ev - ery deed from sin be freed Till Zi - on we re - deem.

Text: Albert McCullough, 1901-1961.
Tune: Hawaiian Melody, arr. by Verna Schaar Gustavus, 1906 - .

471 When Holy Ghost Shall Come in Power

Acts 1:8
D. and C. 1:4

ELLACOMBE C.M.D.

1. "When Ho - ly Ghost shall come in power, With knowledge deep, pro-found,
2. A - pos - tles, proph-ets, mar - tyrs, saints Have known him, have con-fessed
3. We would not hide the gos - pel's light, But sens - ing our great need,

Ye shall be wit - ness - es of me To earth's re - mot - est bound.
That Je - sus Christ is King of Kings, God's Son, for - ev - er blessed.
We would be wit - ness - es of Christ In life, in word, in deed.

Pro - claim my words un - to the world, To hum - ble folk and kings;
Grant, Lord, we too may see and hear And know thee as did they,
Un - til thy king-dom comes on earth, We pledge our lives a - new;

Bear wit - ness of those things ye know, The peace my Spir - it brings."
Then send us forth to tes - ti - fy Of Christ, the liv - ing way.
Till out of Zi - on light shall shine In wit - ness strong and true.

Text: Evan A. Fry, 1902-1959; alt.; copyright 1956 Herald Publishing House.
Tune: From *Gesangbuch der Herzogel, Wirtemburgischen Katholischen Hofkapelle,* 1784.

Tell It! Tell It Out with Gladness

470

Matthew 28:17-19 (18-20)
D. and C. 6:4

HYMN TO JOY 8.7.8.7.D.

1. Tell it! Tell it out with glad-ness, God's good news on ev - ery hand,
2. Lord, we thank thee for the trea-sure Hid with - in the sa - cred page.
3. "Go and teach," thus spoke the Mas-ter, Ris - en vic - tor from the grave.

Sin for - giv - en, lives trans-fig - ured, All in God's great lov - ing plan.
We would be thy faith - ful her - alds To our deep - ly trou-bled age;
Still he gives this great com - mis - sion To his faith - ful ones, and brave.

In the scrip-tures find the wit-ness To God's might-y acts of yore;
We would pub-lish thy sal - va - tion, Ev - er on thy side to stand,
Let us know the gos - pel sto - ry Of what we through Christ can be.

Lis - ten, heed, o - bey, and serve him; Kneel be - fore him and a - dore.
Liv - ing, serv - ing, giv - ing, send-ing Life to quick-en ev - ery land.
Send it! Send it to the na - tions That God's love may set us free.

Text: Georgia Harkness, 1891-1974; alt.; copyright 1966 The Hymn Society of America. Used by permission.
Tune: Arr. from Ludwig van Beethoven, 1770-1827, by Edward Hodges, 1796-1867.

469 Shout the Tidings of Salvation

Philippians 2:8-11
D. and C. 1:4b-e

PROCLAMATION 8.7.8.7. with refrain

1. Shout the ti - dings of sal - va - tion To the a - ged and the young
2. Shout the ti - dings of sal - va - tion O'er the prai-ries of the West
3. Shout the ti - dings of sal - va - tion, Min - gling with the o - cean's roar,
4. Shout the ti - dings of sal - va - tion O'er the is -lands of the sea

Till the pre-cious in - vi - ta - tion Wak - ens ev - ery heart and tongue.
Till each gath-ering con-gre - ga - tion With the gos - pel sound is blest.
Till the ships of ev -ery na - tion Bear the news from shore to shore.
Till, in hum-ble ad - o - ra - tion, All to Christ shall bow the knee.

Refrain

Send the sound the earth a-round, From the ris -ing to the set-ting of the sun,

Till each gath-ering crowd Shall pro-claim a-loud, "The glo - rious work is done!"

Text: Lucius Hart.
Tune: William B. Bradbury, 1816-1868, alt.

Let Us Sing a Worldwide Anthem

468

Galatians 3:26-28
Acts 10:34, 35

AUSTRIA 8.7.8.7.D.

1. Let us sing a world-wide an-them, Ming-ling saints of ma-ny a land,
2. Let us have a world-wide chor-us, Ev- 'ry kin-dred, tribe, and tongue

In the gos-pel mo-tif join-ing, At the lead-ing of God's hand.
Sing-ing of God's love out-reach-ing, Of his min-is-try far-flung.

Though di-verse, we blend to-ge-ther In a sym-pho-ny di-vine,
Let us sing how ev-'ry per-son Can by love be well en-ticed,

As we vow un-to our Fa-ther, "We are one, for we are thine."
And be blend-ed by His Spir-it In the Church of Je-sus Christ.

Text: Roy Cheville, 1897 - . Copyright 1980 Reorganized Church of Jesus Christ of Latter Day Saints.
Tune: Franz Joseph Haydn, 1732-1809.

467

Acts 10:34, 35
I Nephi 3:197

Lord of All Nations

MELROSE L.M.

1. Lord of all na-tions, grant me grace To love all
2. Break down the wall that would di-vide Thy chil-dren,
3. For-give me, Lord, where I have erred By love-less
4. Give me thy cour-age, Lord, to speak When-ev-er
5. With thine own love may I be filled And by thy

peo - ple, ev - 'ry race, And in each per - son
Lord, on ev - 'ry side. My neigh-bor's good let
act and thought - less word. Make me to see the
strong op - press the weak. Should I my - self the
Ho - ly Spir - it willed, That all I touch, wher -

may I see My kin - dred loved, re - deemed by thee.
me pur - sue; Let Chris-tian love bind warm and true.
wrong I do Will cru - ci - fy my Lord a - new.
vic - tim be, Help me for - give, re - mem-b'ring thee.
e'er I be, May be di - vine - ly touched by thee.

Text: Olive Wise Spannaus, 1916 - ; from *The Worship Supplement*, copyright 1969 by Concordia Publishing House;
altered and used by permission.
Tune: Frederick C. Maker, 1844-1927.

We Are One in the Spirit

466

John 13:34, 35
Moroni 7:52

ST. BRENDAN'S 13.13.14. with refrain

Unison (or harmony) f

1. We are one in the Spir - it, we are one in the Lord;
2. We will walk with each oth - er, we will walk hand in hand;
3. We will work with each oth - er, we will work side by side;
4. All praise to the Fa - ther, from whom all things come,

We are one in the Spir - it, we are one in the Lord;
We will walk with each oth - er, we will walk hand in hand;
We will work with each oth - er, we will work side by side;
And all praise to Christ Je - sus, his on - ly Son,

And we pray that all u - ni - ty may one day be re - stored:
And to - geth - er we'll spread the news that God is in our land:
And we'll guard each one's dig - ni - ty and save each one's pride:
And all praise to the Spir - it, who makes us one:

Refrain

And they'll know we are Chris - tians by our love, by our

love; Yes, they'll know we are Chris - tians by our love.

465 We Thank Thee, God, for Eyes to See

D. and C. 59:4, 5a
I John 3:16-19

JERUSALEM C.M.D.

1. We thank thee, God, for eyes to see The beau-ty of the earth;
2. Help us re-mem-ber that to some The eye and ear and mind
3. O may our eyes be o-pen, Lord, To see our neigh-bor's need;

For ears to hear the words of love And hap-py sounds of mirth;
Bring sights and sounds of ug-li-ness And on-ly sad-ness find;
And may our ears be kept a-lert Their cries for help to heed;

For minds that find new thoughts to think, New won-ders to ex-plore;
Help us re-mem-ber that to them The world has seemed un-fair;
Make keen our minds to plan the best For one an-oth-er's good,

For health and free-dom to en-joy The good thou hast in store.
That we should strive to bring to them The beau-ty all may share.
That all the world may be at last One friend-ly neigh-bor-hood.

Text: Jeanette E. Perkins Brown, 1887-1960; copyright 1936 Sydney A. Weston; copyright renewed 1964 Elmer M.
Olsen. Used by permission of The Pilgrim Press.
Tune: Charles H. Purday, 1799-1885.

Lord, I Want to Be a Christian

464

Galatians 5:22, 23, 25
Alma 3:27-29

LORD, I WANT TO BE A CHRISTIAN 14.11.6.11.

1. Lord, I want to be a Chris-tian in my heart, in my heart;
2. Lord, I want to be more lov-ing in my heart, in my heart;
3. Lord, I want to be more ho-ly in my heart, in my heart;
4. Lord, I want to be like Je-sus in my heart, in my heart;

Lord, I want to be a Chris-tian in my heart.
Lord, I want to be more lov-ing in my heart.
Lord, I want to be more ho-ly in my heart.
Lord, I want to be like Je-sus in my heart.

In my heart, in my heart,
In my heart, in my heart,

Lord, I want to be a Chris-tian in my heart.
Lord, I want to be more lov-ing in my heart.
Lord, I want to be more ho-ly in my heart.
Lord, I want to be like Je-sus in my heart.

Text: American Folk Hymn.
Tune: American Folk Hymn; arr. Rosalee Elser, 1925 - . Copyright 1980 Rosalee Elser; used by permission.

463 O Jesus, I Have Promised

Hebrews 13:6
D. and C. 22:9a, b

WATERMOUTH 7.6.7.6.D.

1. O Je - sus, I have prom - ised To serve thee to the end;
2. O let me feel thee near me! The world is ev - er near;
3. O let me hear thee speak - ing In ac - cents clear and still,
4. O Je - sus, thou hast prom - ised To all who fol - low thee

Be thou for - ev - er near me, My Mas - ter and my Friend;
I see the sights that daz - zle; The tempt - ing sounds I hear;
A - bove the storms of pas - sion, The mur - murs of self - will!
That where thou art in glo - ry There shall thy serv - ant be;

I shall not fear the bat - tle If thou art by my side,
My foes are ev - er near me, A - round me and with - in,
O speak to re - as - sure me, To has - ten, or con - trol;
And, Je - sus, I have prom - ised To serve thee to the end;

Nor wan - der from the path-way If thou wilt be my Guide.
But, Je - sus, draw thou near - er And shield my soul from sin.
O speak and make me lis - ten, Thou Guard-ian of my soul!
O give me grace to fol - low My Mas - ter and my Friend. A-men.

Text: John E. Bode, 1816-1874.
Tune: Arthur H. Mann, 1850-1929.

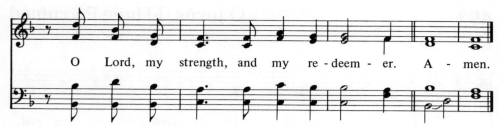

O Lord, my strength, and my re-deem-er. A - men.

Text: Psalm 19:14.
Tune: Adolph Baumbach, 1830-1880.

O Master, Let Me Walk with Thee

462

Mark 8:36 (34)
Mosiah 3:21

MARYTON L.M.

1. O Mas-ter, let me walk with thee In low-ly paths of ser-vice free; Tell me thy se-cret; help me bear The strain of toil, the fret of care.

2. Help me the slow of heart to move By some clear, win-ning word of love; Teach me the way-ward feet to stay, And guide them in the home-ward way.

3. Teach me thy pa-tience; still with thee In clos-er, dear-er com-pa-ny, In work that keeps faith sweet and strong, In trust that tri-umphs o-ver wrong,

4. In hope that sends a shin-ing ray Far down the fu-ture's broad-ening way, In peace that on-ly thou canst give; With thee, O Mas-ter, let me live. A - men.

Text: Washington Gladden, 1836-1918.
Tune: H. Percy Smith, 1825-1898.

460 With My Substance I Will Honor

Proverbs 3:9
D. and C. 38:5c, d

SARDIS 8.7.8.7.

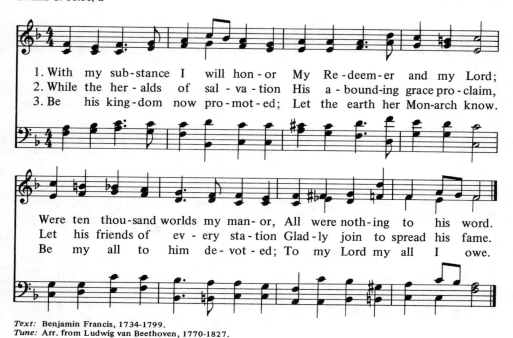

1. With my sub-stance I will hon-or My Re-deem-er and my Lord;
2. While the her-alds of sal-va-tion His a-bound-ing grace pro-claim,
3. Be his king-dom now pro-mot-ed; Let the earth her Mon-arch know.

Were ten thou-sand worlds my man-or, All were noth-ing to his word.
Let his friends of ev-ery sta-tion Glad-ly join to spread his fame.
Be my all to him de-vot-ed; To my Lord my all I owe.

Text: Benjamin Francis, 1734-1799.
Tune: Arr. from Ludwig van Beethoven, 1770-1827.

461 Let the Words of My Mouth

Psalm 19:14
Psalm 119:108

IN CORDE MEO 6.9.8.9.

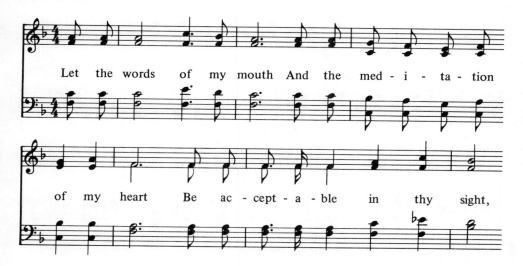

Let the words of my mouth And the med-i-ta-tion

of my heart Be ac-cept-a-ble in thy sight,

Lord, Who Views All People Precious 459

D. and C. 153:9
D. and C. 16:3b-f

PITTSFIELD 8.7.8.7.D.

1. Lord, who views all peo-ple pre-cious, Wor-thy, love - ly in your sight;
2. Heal the bruised and bro-ken-heart - ed, Those enmeshed in sin and strife;

Who, through mer - cy and com-pas - sion, Calls us for - ward in - to light,
By the Spir - it, grant your peo - ple Wholeness in this earth-ly life.

We ac - cept the great com-mis-sion. May we, strength-ened with your power,
God of re - con-cil - i - a -tion, We, your saints, give you the praise

Join with Christ in common pur-pose—Serv-ing no - bly in this hour.
For your grace and pa -tient gui-dance As this prayer, with joy, we raise. A-men.

Text: Kenneth L. McLaughlin, 1951 - ; copyright 1980 Reorganized Church of Jesus Christ of Latter Day Saints.
Tune: H. R. Mills, 1844-1933.

458 Eternal Ruler of the Ceaseless Round

D. and C. 38:5a-c
Galatians 3:26-29

YORKSHIRE 10.10.10.D.

1. E - ter - nal Rul - er of the cease-less round Of cir-cling plan-ets sing-ing on their way, Guide of the na-tions from the night pro - found In - to the glo - ry of the per - fect day, Rule in our hearts that we may ev - er be Guid - ed and strength-ened and up-held by thee.

2. We are of thee, the chil-dren of thy love, The fam -ily of thy well-be - lov - ed Son; De - scend, O Ho - ly Spir - it, like a dove In - to our hearts, that we may be as one— As one with thee, to whom we ev - er tend; As one with him, our broth-er and our friend.

3. We would be one in ha - tred of all wrong, One in our love of all things sweet and fair, One with the joy that break - eth in - to song, One with the grief that trem-bleth in - to prayer, One in the power that makes the chil -dren free To fol - low truth, and thus to fol -low thee. A - men.

Text: J. W. Chadwick, 1840-1904.
Tune: J. Wainwright, 1723-1768.

My Lord, I Know That All My Life

457

Luke 12:29-35 (27-32)
Alma 3:58

MORNING SONG 8.6.8.6.8.6.

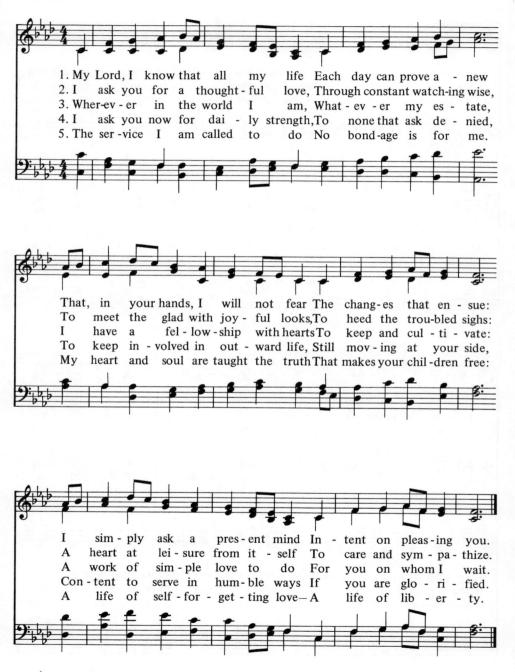

1. My Lord, I know that all my life Each day can prove a - new
2. I ask you for a thought - ful love, Through constant watch-ing wise,
3. Wher-ev - er in the world I am, What - ev - er my es - tate,
4. I ask you now for dai - ly strength, To none that ask de - nied,
5. The ser - vice I am called to do No bond-age is for me.

That, in your hands, I will not fear The chang-es that en - sue:
To meet the glad with joy - ful looks, To heed the trou-bled sighs:
I have a fel - low-ship with hearts To keep and cul - ti - vate:
To keep in - volved in out - ward life, Still mov - ing at your side,
My heart and soul are taught the truth That makes your chil -dren free:

I sim - ply ask a pres-ent mind In - tent on pleas-ing you.
A heart at lei - sure from it - self To care and sym - pa - thize.
A work of sim - ple love to do For you on whom I wait.
Con - tent to serve in hum-ble ways If you are glo - ri - fied.
A life of self - for - get - ting love— A life of lib - er - ty.

Text: Anna Laetitia Waring, 1820-1910, alt.
Tune: Wyeth's *Repository of Sacred Music, Part Second*, 1813; harm. Rosalee Elser, 1925 - ; copyright 1980 by Rosalee Elser; used by permission.

456

Lord of the Bronze-Green Prairies

D. and C. 150:7
Isaiah 52:7

ZOAN 7.6.7.6.D.

1. Lord of the bronze-green prai - ries, God of the pound-ing seas,
2. Give us clean hearts and val - iant, Firm wills to cher -ish all

Of shel -tered coves and ham - lets, Of or - chards, lakes and trees:
These gifts, so var - ied, splen - did. O hear us when we call

Your pulse beats in the cit - ies, Steel-ribbed and ris - ing high,
For self - con-trol and pa - tience, In - teg - ri - ty and power,

Your spir - it broods o'er moun-tains Whose stern peaks stab the sky.
That fu - ture gen - er - a - tions May know we served this hour. A -men.

Text: Grace Lane; from *The Hymn*, copyright 1972 The Hymn Society of America; used by permission.
Tune: William H. Havergal, 1793-1870; harm. Rosalee Elser, 1925 - . Copyright 1980 Rosalee Elser; used by permission.

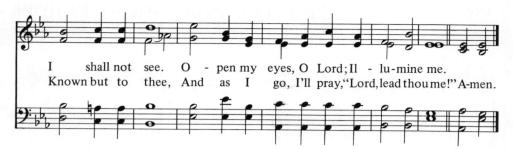

I shall not see. O - pen my eyes, O Lord; Il - lu-mine me.
Known but to thee, And as I go, I'll pray,"Lord, lead thou me!" A-men.

Text: Roy A. Cheville, 1897 - ; copyright 1950 Herald Publishing House.
Tune: William F Sherwin, 1826-1888.

O Lord, We Come in Gratitude 455

Psalm 30:1-4
Romans 12:1, 2

ST. MARGARET 8.8.8.8.6.

1. O Lord, we come in grat - i - tude For all the full and
2. O Lord, for - give our will - ful sins; For - give the sub - tle
3. O Lord, re - store, if this thy will, The health of bod - y,
4. In - spire a clear, en - dur - ing zeal, In all our ways with

boun-teous years. We bring our ser - vice, bring our hopes; We
sins of race. Thy bless - ing clear the coun - te - nance Where
mind, and soul. A cour - ier for thy cause re - store To
thee to stand, In life to serve, in death to yield, Rich

bring to thee our cares and fears; We bring our prayers to thee.
dwells thy love, and ra - di - ates A glow-ing love for thee.
ser - vice full and free and whole, In great - er love for thee.
in thy love and thy com - mand—This is our prayer to thee. A-men.

Text: Cleo Hanthorne Moon, 1904 - ; copyright 1956 Herald Publishing House.
Tune: Albert Peace, 1844-1912.

453 Father, Hear the Prayer We Offer

Psalm 50:14, 15
Romans 4:17, 20, 21

SARDIS 8.7.8.7.

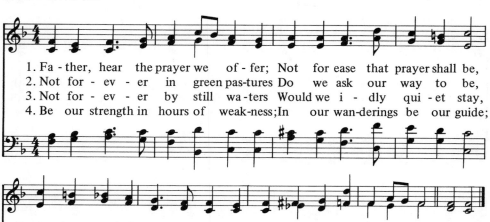

1. Fa - ther, hear the prayer we of - fer; Not for ease that prayer shall be,
2. Not for - ev - er in green pas-tures Do we ask our way to be,
3. Not for - ev - er by still wa-ters Would we i - dly qui - et stay,
4. Be our strength in hours of weak-ness; In our wan-derings be our guide;

But for strength that we may ev - er Live our lives cou - ra - geously.
But the steep and rug - ged path-way May we tread re - joic-ing - ly.
But would smite the liv - ing foun-tains From the rocks a - long the way.
Through en - deav - or, fail - ure, dan - ger, Fa - ther, be thou at our side. A-men.

Text: Love M. Willis, 1824-1908.
Tune: Arr. from Ludwig van Beethoven, 1770-1827.

454 Open My Eyes, O Lord

Psalm 119:18
D. and C. 38:2

BREAD OF LIFE 6.4.6.4.D.

1. O - pen my eyes, O Lord, That I may see What - ev - er
2. On - ward I go, O Lord, On Zi - on's way, Read - y to

glimpse of truth Thou hast for me. With - out thy guid - ing help
meet the call Of each new day. New fron-tiers beck - on me,

For the Healing of the Nations

452

Matthew 9:41, 42 (35, 36)
I John 3:14, 16-18

NEW MALDEN 8.7.8.7.8.7.

Unison (or harmony)

1. For the heal-ing of the na-tions, Lord, we pray with one ac-cord; For a just and e-qual shar-ing Of the things that earth af-fords. To a life of love in ac-tion Help us rise and pledge our word.

2. Lead us, Fa-ther, in-to free-dom; From de-spair your world re-lease, That re-deemed from war and ha-tred, Men may come and go in peace. Show us how through care and good-ness Fear will die and hope in-crease.

3. All that kills a-bun-dant liv-ing, Let it from the earth be banned: Pride of sta-tus, race, or school-ing, Dog-mas keep-ing man from man. In our com-mon quest for jus-tice May we hal-low life's brief span.

Text: Fred Kaan, 1929 - ; copyright © 1968 by Galliard Ltd. Sole U. S. agent: Galaxy Music Corp., N. Y. Used by permission.
Tune: David McCarthy, 1931 - ; copyright 1971 by the composer. Used by permission.

451

O Church of God, Arise

Ephesians 4:1-6
D. and C. 142:5

DENBY 6.6.6.6.D.

1. O Church of God, a-rise And take thy lamp of love,
2. Re-buke the dev-il's mart; The souls in prison re-lease;
3. In ev-ery dark-est place Let ra-diant warmth be shed

The light that nev-er dies On earth, in heaven a-bove!
Bind up the bro-ken heart; Give joy and mirth and peace.
Till in each drear-y face The joy of God is read.

With wis-dom and with truth Keep quick and straight the flame,
What-ev-er things are fair, What-ev-er things are just,
Tell all the souls on earth, The great-est and the least,

The light of love and youth, To save a world of shame.
Go, make them free as air And plen-teous as the dust!
Love calls us from our birth To share God's gra-cious peace.

Text: Annie Matheson, 1853-1924, alt.
Tune: Charles J. Dale; from the *Lutheran Hymnal.*

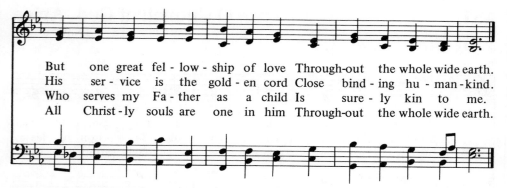

But one great fel-low-ship of love Through-out the whole wide earth.
His ser-vice is the gold-en cord Close bind-ing hu-man-kind.
Who serves my Fa-ther as a child Is sure-ly kin to me.
All Christ-ly souls are one in him Through-out the whole wide earth.

Text: John Oxenham, 1852-1941; alt.; used by permission of Desmond Dunkerley.
Tune: Alexander R. Reinagle, 1799-1877.

Unto the Calmly Gathered Thought 450

Micah 6:6-8
Alma 19:78

SOLOTHURN L.M.

Unison (or harmony)

1. Un - to the calm - ly gath - ered thought The in - ner-
2. That to be saved is on - ly this, Sal - va - tion
3. That wor - ship's deep - er mean - ing lies In mer - cy,

most of truth is taught, The mys - tery, dim - ly
from our self - ish - ness; From sin it - self, and
and not sac - ri - fice, Not proud hu - mil - i -

un - der - stood, That love of God is love of good;
not the pain That warns us of its chaf - ing chain;
ties of sense, But love's un - forced o - be - di - ence.

Text: John Greenleaf Whittier, 1807-1892.
Tune: Swiss Traditional Melody; arr. Ralph Vaughan Williams, 1872-1958; used by permission of Oxford University Press.

448 In Christ There Is No East or West

D. and C. 85:41
Romans 8:35-39

McKEE C.M.
Alternate hymn: 449

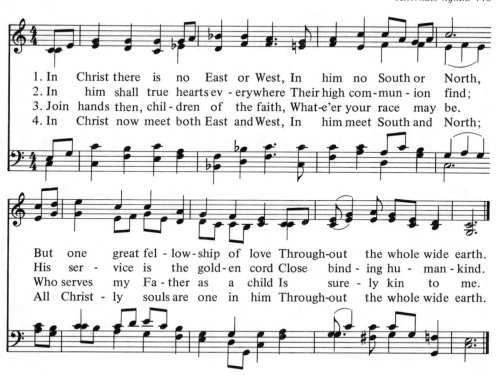

1. In Christ there is no East or West, In him no South or North,
2. In him shall true hearts ev-erywhere Their high com-mun-ion find;
3. Join hands then, chil-dren of the faith, What-e'er your race may be.
4. In Christ now meet both East and West, In him meet South and North;

But one great fel-low-ship of love Through-out the whole wide earth.
His ser-vice is the gold-en cord Close bind-ing hu-man-kind.
Who serves my Fa-ther as a child Is sure-ly kin to me.
All Christ-ly souls are one in him Through-out the whole wide earth.

Text: John Oxenham, 1852-1941; alt.; used by permission of Desmond Dunkerley.
Tune: American Folk Melody, adapted by Harry T. Burleigh, 1866-1949; copyright 1940 by Harry T. Burleigh. Used by cooperation of the Executor of the Estate of Harry T. Burleigh.

449 In Christ There Is No East or West

Colossians 3:11
IV Nephi 1:17, 19

ST. PETER C.M.
See 330 for a lower setting
Alternate hymn: 448

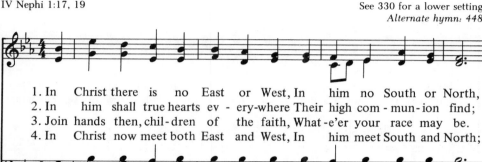

1. In Christ there is no East or West, In him no South or North,
2. In him shall true hearts ev-ery-where Their high com-mun-ion find;
3. Join hands then, chil-dren of the faith, What-e'er your race may be.
4. In Christ now meet both East and West, In him meet South and North;

Would You Bless Our Homes

447

Ephesians 3:14-19
Luke 2:51, 52

ALL THE WAY 8.7.8.7.D.
Alternate tune: NETTLETON (31)

1. Would you bless our homes and fam-ilies, Lord of life, who calls us here.
2. When our way is un-de-mand-ing, Let us use the time that's ours
3. From the homes in which we're nur-tured, With the love that shapes us there,

In our world of stress and ten - sion Teach us love that con-quers fear.
To de - light in sim - ple pleas-ures, Shar-ing joys in gen - tle hours.
Teach us, Lord, to claim as fam - ily Ev - ery-one whose life we share.

Help us learn to love each oth - er With a love that con-stant stays;
When our way is anx-ious walk -ing And a heav - y path we plod,
And through all that life may of - fer May we in your love re - main.

Teach us when we face our trou -bles Love's ex-pressed in man - y ways.
Teach us trust in one an - oth - er And in you, our gra - cious God.
May the love we share in fam -ilies Be a - live to praise your name.

Text: Walter Farquharson, 1936 - ; copyright 1977 The Frederick Harris Music Company; used by permission.
Tune: Robert Lowry, 1826-1899; alt. 1980 Rosalee Elser, 1925 - .

446

Lord God of Hosts

Ephesians 1:3, 9, 10
D. and C. 2:1

WELWYN 11.10.11.10.

1. Lord God of Hosts, whose pur-pose, nev-er swerv-ing,
2. Strong Son of God, whose work was his that sent thee,
3. Lord God, whose grace has called us to thy serv-ice,

Leads toward the day of Je-sus Christ, thy Son,
One with the Fa-ther, thought and deed and word,
How good thy thoughts toward us, how great their sum!

Grant us to march a-mong thy faith-ful le-gions,
One make us all, true com-rades in thy serv-ice,
We work with thee, we go where thou wilt lead us,

Armed with thy cour-age, till the world is won.
And make us one in thee with God, the Lord.
Un-til in all the earth thy king-dom come. A-men.

Text: Shepherd Knapp, 1873-1946.
Tune: Alfred Scott-Gatty, 1847-1918.

When the Church of Jesus

445

Micah 6:6-8
Mosiah 2:28, 29, 32, 36

KING'S WESTON 6.5.6.5.D.
Alternate tune: BJORKLUND MAJOR (377)

Unison (or harmony)

1. When the church of Je - sus Shuts its out - er door
2. If our hearts are lift - ed Where de - vo - tion soars
3. Lest the gifts we of - fer—Mon - ey, tal - ents, time—

Lest the roar of traf - fic Drown the voice of prayer:
High a - bove this hun - gry, Suf - f'ring world of ours:
Serve to salve our con - science To our se - cret shame:

May our prayers, Lord, make us E - ven more a - ware
Lest our hymns should drug us To for - get its needs,
Lord, re - prove, in - spire us By the way you give;

That the world we ban - ish is our Chris - tian care.
Forge our Chris - tian wor - ship in - to Chris - tian deeds.
Teach us, dy - ing Sa - vior, how true Chris - tians live.

Text: F. Pratt Green, 1903 - ; alt.; used by permission of Oxford University Press.
Tune: Ralph Vaughan Williams, 1872-1958. From *Enlarged Songs of Praise* by permission of Oxford University Press.

444

Matthew 5:15, 16
Mark 8:36-38 (34, 35)

Great God, Our Source

GOD OUR SOURCE 8.8.8.D.

Unison (or harmony) ♩ *remains constant*

1. Great God, our source and Lord of space, O Force of all by whose sheer power The pri-mal fires that flared and raged Were struck, blazed on, and still are made: Oh, save us, Lord, at this fierce hour From threat-'ning fires that we have laid.

2. Great God of fire, in - car - nate flame, Through Christ in whom your love has burned And burns the way for our dark pace On cos - mic routes with - in us turned: Lead us be - yond a tom - ic night; Guide, Lord, in hope our bro - ken race.

3. Lord of the at - om, we praise your might, Ex - pressed in ter - ri - fy - ing light; Be - fore us rise the flames as pyres, Or bursts of love— they blind our sight. Help us, our Lord, oh, help us see New forms of peace through suf - f'ring fires. A - men.

Jesus' Hands Were Kind Hands

443

Matthew 10:34, 35, 38 (39, 40, 42)
II Peter 1:5-8

NOËL NOUVELET 6.5.6.5.D

1. Je - sus' hands were kind hands, Do - ing good to all,
2. Take my hands, Lord Je - sus; Let them work for you,

Heal - ing pain and sick - ness, Bless - ing chil - dren small,
Make them strong and gen - tle, Kind in all I do.

Wash - ing tired feet, and Lift - ing those who fall:
Touch me with your Spir - it Till I'm gen - tle, too,

Je - sus' hands were kind hands, Do - ing good to all.
Till my hands are kind hands, Quick to work for you.

Text: Margaret B. Cropper, 1886-1980; alt.; used by permission of Anne Hopkinson, Executor of the Margaret B. Cropper Estate.
Tune: Traditional French Carol.

442

Savior, Thy Dying Love

D. and C. 132:3, 4
Romans 6:6-11

SOMETHING FOR JESUS 6.4.6.4.6.6.6.4.

1. Sav - ior, thy dy - ing love Thou gav - est me,
Nor should I aught with - hold, Dear Lord, from thee;
In love my soul would bow, My heart ful - fill its vow,
Some of - fering bring thee now, Some - thing for thee.

2. Give me a faith - ful heart, Like - ness to thee,
That each de - part - ing day Hence - forth may see
Some work of love be - gun, Some deed of kind - ness done,
Some wan - derer sought and won, Some - thing for thee.

3. All that I am and have, Thy gifts so free,
Ev - er in joy or grief, My Lord, for thee;
And when thy face I see, My ran - somed soul shall be
Through all e - ter - ni - ty Some - thing for thee. A - men.

Text: S. Dryden Phelps, 1816-1895.
Tune: Robert Lowry, 1826-1899.

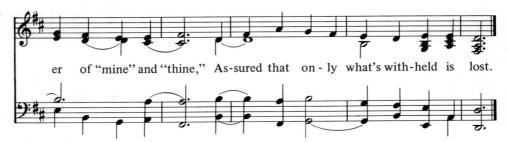

er of "mine" and "thine," As-sured that on - ly what's with-held is lost.

Text: William Watkins Reid, Sr., 1890 - ; copyright 1965 The Hymn Society of America; used by permission.
Tune: Alfred M. Smith, 1879-1971; copyright by composer. Used by permission of Mrs. Alfred M. Smith.

In Nature's Voice We Hear You, Lord 441

Mosiah 8:47-52
Romans 14:9, 17

ASHLAND L.M.

1. In Na - ture's voice we hear you, Lord. In rush - ing
2. In homes so rich or homes so poor, The cit - ies
3. Your voice we hear and an - swer, Lord; We'll ven - ture
4. New skills we'll learn, new arts we'll gain To help all

streams we hear you speak; In rum - bling clouds, in
large, the ham - lets small— Where - ev - er there is
forth to meet this need With hand and heart and
per - sons know their worth; With pur - pose strong, with

gen - tle rain, And in the tower - ing moun - tain peaks.
hu - man need We hear Your voice call out to all.
mind in - spired In thought and word and dai - ly deed.
faith re - newed To build Your king - dom here on earth.

Text: Mildred Jordan, 1918 - ; copyright 1980 Reorganized Church of Jesus Christ of Latter Day Saints.
Tune: Keith Landis, 1922 - ; harm. Jeffrey Rickard; alt.; copyright 1977 Praise Publications, Inc.; used by permission.

439 Teach Me, My God and King

II Nephi 3:48
II Timothy 1:6, 7

CARLISLE S.M.

1. Teach me, my God and King, In all things thee to see; Teach
me to be in ev-ery-thing All thou wouldst have me be.

2. In all I think or say, Lord, may I not of - fend. In
all I do, be thou the way; In all be thou the end.

3. Each task I un - der - take, Though weak and mean to me, If
un - der - tak - en for thy sake Draws strength and worth from thee.

4. Teach me, then, Lord, to bring To all that I may be, To
all I do, my God and King, A con - scious-ness of thee. A-men.

Text: George Herbert, 1593-1633; alt. by Helen Harrington, 1909 - .
Tune: Charles Lockhart 1745-1815.

440 Teach Us, O Lord, True Thankfulness

Mark 10:42-45
D. and C. 6:4

SURSUM CORDA 10.10.10.10.

Unison (or harmony)

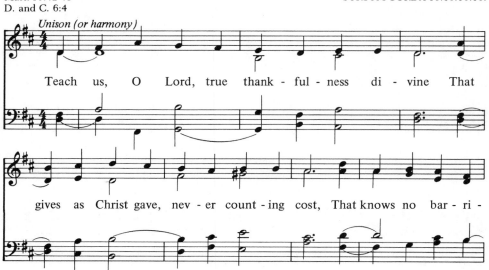

Teach us, O Lord, true thank - ful - ness di - vine That
gives as Christ gave, nev - er count - ing cost, That knows no bar - ri -

Lord, Thy Church on Earth Is Seeking

438

Matthew 28:17-19 (18-20)
D. and C. 6:1, 2a, b

GENEVA 8.7.8.7.D.

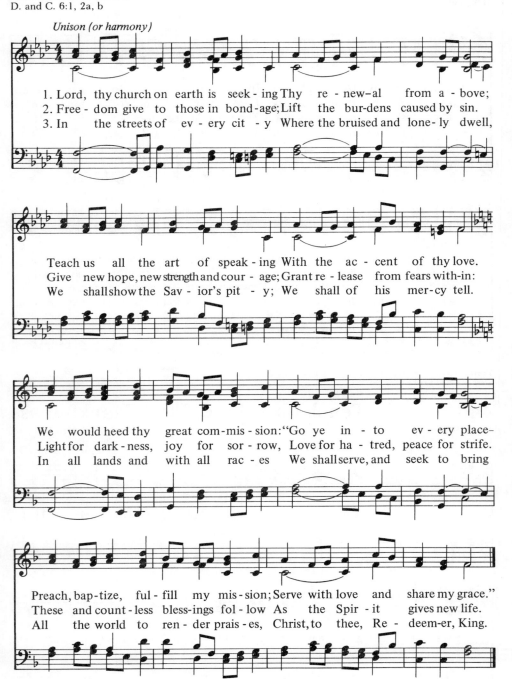

1. Lord, thy church on earth is seek-ing Thy re-new-al from a-bove;
2. Free-dom give to those in bond-age; Lift the bur-dens caused by sin.
3. In the streets of ev-ery cit-y Where the bruised and lone-ly dwell,

Teach us all the art of speak-ing With the ac-cent of thy love.
Give new hope, new strength and cour-age; Grant re-lease from fears with-in:
We shall show the Sav-ior's pit-y; We shall of his mer-cy tell.

We would heed thy great com-mis-sion: "Go ye in-to ev-ery place—
Light for dark-ness, joy for sor-row, Love for ha-tred, peace for strife.
In all lands and with all rac-es We shall serve, and seek to bring

Preach, bap-tize, ful-fill my mis-sion; Serve with love and share my grace."
These and count-less bless-ings fol-low As the Spir-it gives new life.
All the world to ren-der prais-es, Christ, to thee, Re-deem-er, King.

Text: Hugh Sherlock, 1905 - ; alt.; used by permission of the author.
Tune: George Henry Day, 1883-1966; copyright 1942 by The Church Pension Fund. Used by permission.

437

Look for the Beautiful

Philippians 4:8
D. and C. 81:4c

BELDEN 10.10.10.10.10.

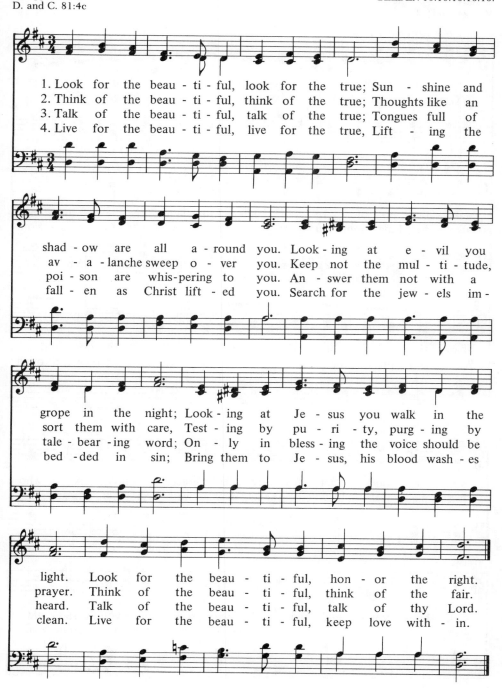

1. Look for the beau-ti-ful, look for the true; Sun - shine and shad - ow are all a - round you. Look-ing at e - vil you grope in the night; Look - ing at Je - sus you walk in the light. Look for the beau - ti - ful, hon - or the right.

2. Think of the beau-ti-ful, think of the true; Thoughts like an av - a - lanche sweep o - ver you. Keep not the mul - ti - tude, sort them with care, Test - ing by pu - ri - ty, purg - ing by prayer. Think of the beau - ti - ful, think of the fair.

3. Talk of the beau-ti-ful, talk of the true; Tongues full of poi - son are whis-pering to you. An - swer them not with a tale - bear - ing word; On - ly in bless - ing the voice should be heard. Talk of the beau - ti - ful, talk of thy Lord.

4. Live for the beau-ti-ful, live for the true, Lift - ing the fall - en as Christ lift - ed you. Search for the jew - els im - bed - ded in sin; Bring them to Je - sus, his blood wash - es clean. Live for the beau - ti - ful, keep love with - in.

Text and Tune: Franklin E. Belden, 19th century.

Go Now Forth into the World

436

D. and C. 12:2
Matthew 20:26-28

EMERALD 7.6.7.6.7.7.7.7.7.7.

1. Go now forth in-to the world; Of your-selves be giv - ing.
2. Grant us wis-dom for the task; Give us broad-er vi - sion

Make dis-ci-ples of all lands; Tell them Christ is liv - ing.
Of the king-dom-build-ing plan And the Great Com-mis-sion.

Share the news that Christ makes whole Bat-tered lives and
We give praise for lives that feel God's great power, through

wea-ry souls— That his lov-ing grace up-holds All who
Christ made real. In all acts, may we re-veal Hearts a-

seek him— young and old, All who seek him— young and old.
live with mis-sion zeal, Hearts a-live with mis-sion zeal.

Text: Kenneth L. McLaughlin, 1951 - ; copyright 1980 Reorganized Church of Jesus Christ of Latter Day Saints.
Tune: Mark H. Forscutt, 1834-1903.

435 O Lord of Light and Love and Power

Philippians 4:10-13
Acts 2:38, 39

BETHLEHEM (Seraph) C.M.D.

1. O Lord of light and love and power, How joy-ful life might be
If in thy serv-ice ev-ery hour We lived and moved with thee;
If we in all our zeal and might By thee were sanc-ti-fied
And ev-er found our chief de-light In work-ing at thy side!

2. 'Tis ne'er too late, while life shall last, A new life to be-gin;
'Tis ne'er too late to leave the past And break with self and sin;
And we this day, both old and young, Would ear-nest-ly as-pire
For hearts to no-bler pur-pose strung, And pur-ri-fied de-sire.

3. Not for our-selves a-lone we plead, But for all faith-ful souls
Who serve thy cause by word or deed, Whose names thy book en-rolls.
Oh, speed thy work, vic-to-rious King, And give the work-ers might,
That through the world thy truth may ring, And all may see thy light!

Text: Ella S. Armitage, 1841-1931, alt.
Tune: Gottfried W. Fink, 1783-1846.

When God Created Human Life

434

D. and C. 68:4a-c
D. and C. 90:6d

ST. HYLDA L.M.
Alternate tune: HESPERUS (348)

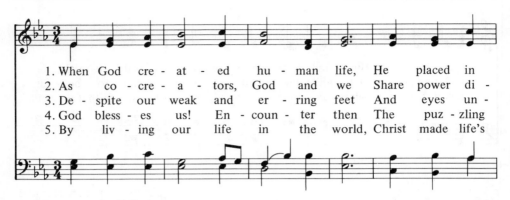

1. When God cre - at - ed hu - man life, He placed in
2. As co - cre - a - tors, God and we Share power di -
3. De - spite our weak and er - ring feet And eyes un -
4. God bless - es us! En - coun - ter then The puz - zling
5. By liv - ing our life in the world, Christ made life's

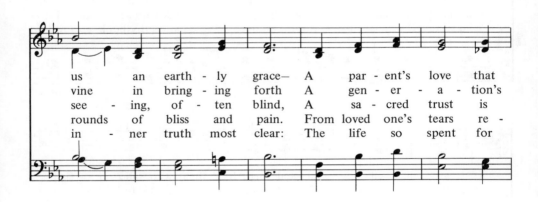

us an earth - ly grace— A par - ent's love that
vine in bring - ing forth A gen - er - a - tion's
see - ing, of - ten blind, A sa - cred trust is
rounds of bliss and pain. From loved one's tears re -
in - ner truth most clear: The life so spent for

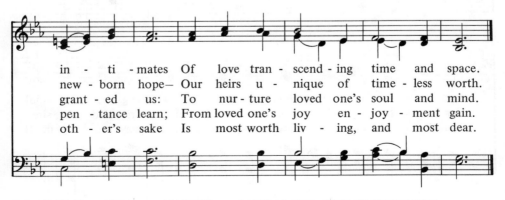

in - ti - mates Of love tran - scend - ing time and space.
new - born hope— Our heirs u - nique of time - less worth.
grant - ed us: To nur - ture loved one's soul and mind.
pen - tance learn; From loved one's joy en - joy - ment gain.
oth - er's sake Is most worth liv - ing, and most dear.

Text: Alan D. Tyree, 1929 - ; copyright 1980 Reorganized Church of Jesus Christ of Latter Day Saints.
Tune: William E. Butler, 1889-1967; copyright 1956 Herald Publishing House.

433

Faith of Our Fathers

I Timothy 6:12
Jude 3

ST. CATHERINE L.M. with refrain

1. Faith of our fa - thers, liv - ing still In spite of dun - geon,
2. The mar - tyrs, chained in pris - ons dark, Were still in heart and
3. Faith of our fa - thers! We will love Both friend and foe in

fire, and sword, Oh, how our hearts beat high with joy
con - science free; And blest would be their chil - dren's fate
all our strife; Pro - claim thee, too, as love knows how,

Refrain

When - e'er we hear that glo - rious word!
Though they, like them, should die for thee. Faith of our fa - thers,
By sav - ing Word and faith - ful life.

ho - ly faith, We will be true to thee till death.

Text: Frederick W. Faber, 1814-1863; alt.
Tune: Henri F. Hemy, 1818-1888; refrain, James G. Walton, 1821-1905.

pain That truth's dis-tor-tions still im-part.
each In spite of col-or, cult, or call.
love And Spir-it's pow-er lights the land. A-men.

Text: Evelyn Maples, 1919 - ; copyright 1980 Reorganized Church of Jesus Christ of Latter Day Saints.
Tune: George J. Elvey, 1816-1893.

If by Your Grace I Choose to Be 432

MENDON L.M.

Ephesians 4:1-6
D. and C. 151:8a, 9

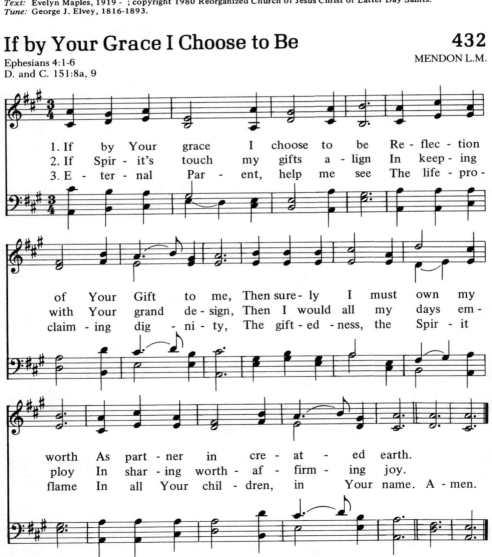

1. If by Your grace I choose to be Re-flec-tion
2. If Spir-it's touch my gifts a-lign In keep-ing
3. E-ter-nal Par-ent, help me see The life-pro-

of Your Gift to me, Then sure-ly I must own my
with Your grand de-sign, Then I would all my days em-
claim-ing dig-ni-ty, The gift-ed-ness, the Spir-it

worth As part-ner in cre-at-ed earth.
ploy In shar-ing worth-af-firm-ing joy.
flame In all Your chil-dren, in Your name. A-men.

Text: Evelyn Maples, 1919 - ; copyright 1980 Reorganized Church of Jesus Christ of Latter Day Saints.
Tune: Traditional German Melody, arr. by Samuel Dyer, 1785-1835.

430

Romans 6:8-14
Alma 18:14, 16, 17

All to Jesus I Surrender

HEAVENLY DOVE 8.7.8.7.

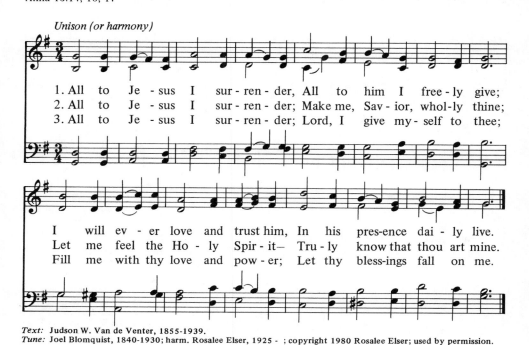

Unison (or harmony)

1. All to Je - sus I sur - ren - der, All to him I free - ly give;
2. All to Je - sus I sur - ren - der; Make me, Sav - ior, whol - ly thine;
3. All to Je - sus I sur - ren - der; Lord, I give my - self to thee;

I will ev - er love and trust him, In his pres-ence dai - ly live.
Let me feel the Ho - ly Spir - it— Tru - ly know that thou art mine.
Fill me with thy love and pow - er; Let thy bless-ings fall on me.

Text: Judson W. Van de Venter, 1855-1939.
Tune: Joel Blomquist, 1840-1930; harm. Rosalee Elser, 1925 - ; copyright 1980 Rosalee Elser; used by permission.

431

Ephesians 2:14, 18-22
II Corinthians 5:17-20

O May Thy Church Build Bridges

ST. CRISPIN L.M.

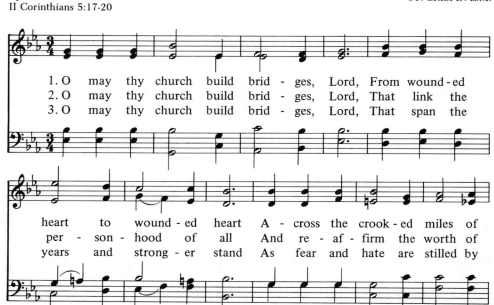

1. O may thy church build brid - ges, Lord, From wound - ed
2. O may thy church build brid - ges, Lord, That link the
3. O may thy church build brid - ges, Lord, That span the

heart to wound - ed heart A - cross the crook - ed miles of
per - son - hood of all And re - af - firm the worth of
years and strong - er stand As fear and hate are stilled by

O God, Send Heralds

429

Luke 4:18
D. and C. 151:9

WELWYN 11.10.11.10.
Alternate tune: CITY OF GOD (224)

1. O God, send her - alds who will nev - er fal - ter,
2. Not to be served but on - ly to be serv - ing,
3. Em - pires have come, have flour - ished and de - part - ed,
4. Send her - alds, then, in whom your heart re - joic - es;

Who dare to walk where Christ has set his feet,
To feed the hun - ger in the hu - man heart,
But still your Church, as wit - ness to your way,
Send those who hear the call that sets us free,

Who know the Church as bea - con and as al - tar
To know that love which comes with - out de - serv - ing,
Lives on in dark - ness, light of the true - heart - ed
With ea - ger hearts and ju - bi - lat - ing voic - es

Where hu - man need and your a - bun - dance meet.
That love which on - ly Je - sus can im - part.
And calls to ac - tion those whose feet would stay.
Each mak - ing an - swer, "Here am I! Send me." A-men.

Text: Elisabeth Burrowes, 1883 - ; alt.; from *Ten New Hymns on the Ministry*, copyright 1966 The Hymn Society of America, Wittenberg University, Springfield, OH 45501. Used by permission.
Tune: Alfred Scott-Gatty, 1847-1918.

428

Galatians 6:14
Hebrews 2:14-17

Beneath the Cross of Jesus

ST. CHRISTOPHER 7.6.8.6.8.6.8.6.

1. Be - neath the cross of Je - sus I fain would take my stand—
2. Up - on the cross of Je - sus Mine eye at times can see
3. I take, O cross, thy shad - ow For my a - bid -ing place.

The shad - ow of a might - y Rock With - in a wea - ry land;
The ver - y dy - ing form of One Who suf - fered there for me;
I ask no oth - er sun - shine than The sun - shine of his face;

A home with-in the wil - der - ness, A rest up - on the way,
And from my strick - en heart with tears Two won - ders I con - fess—
Con- tent to own no oth - er place, To know no gain nor loss,

From burn - ing of the noon- tide heat And bur - dens of the day.
The won - ders of re - deem - ing love, And my un -worth-i - ness.
My sin - ful self my on - ly shame, My glo - ry all, the cross.

Text: Elizabeth C. Clephane, 1830-1869.
Tune: Frederick C. Maker, 1844-1927.

selves as gifts to thee: Oh, bind our hearts this

sa - cred hour In faith and hope and char - i - ty.

Text: Horace Westwood, 1884-1956; copyright Beacon Press; used by permission.
Tune: Henry Baker, 1835-1910.

Lord, Here Amidst the Poor

427

SOLOTHURN L.M.

Mosiah 2:43
I John 3:16-18

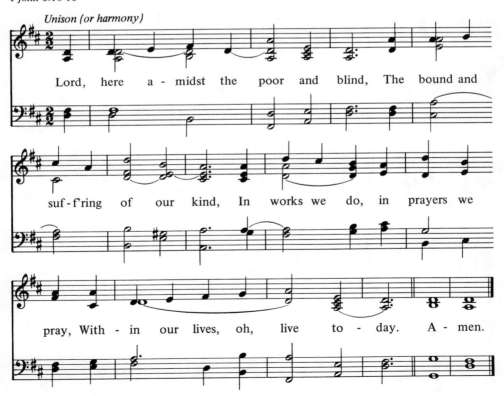

Unison (or harmony)

Lord, here a - midst the poor and blind, The bound and

suf - f'ring of our kind, In works we do, in prayers we

pray, With - in our lives, oh, live to - day. A - men.

Text: John Greenleaf Whittier, 1807-1892.
Tune: Swiss Traditional Melody; arr. Ralph Vaughan Williams, 1872-1958; used by permission of Oxford University Press.

425 — God Send Us Saints

Alma 12:4, 5
D. and C. 153:9

MELROSE L.M.

1. God send us saints whose aim 'twill be, Not to de-
2. God send us saints a - lert and quick His loft - y
3. God send us saints of stead - fast will, Pa - tient, cou-
4. God send us saints with hearts a - blaze, All truth to

fend some an - cient creed But to live out the
pre - cepts to trans - late Un - til the laws of
ra - geous, strong, and true, With vi - sion clear and
love, all wrong to hate; These are the pa - triots

laws of right In ev - ery thought and word and deed.
right be - come The laws and hab - its of the state.
mind e - quipped His will to learn, his work to do.
na - tions need; These are the bul - warks of the state.

Text: F. J. Gillman, 1866-1949, alt.
Tune: Frederick C. Maker, 1844-1927.

426 — Spirit of Truth, of Life, of Power

John 4:25, 26 (23, 24)
Psalm 73:25, 26, 28

HESPERUS L.M.

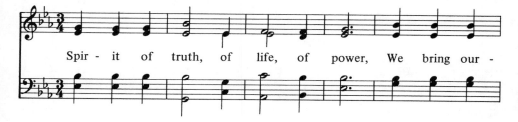

Spir - it of truth, of life, of power, We bring our -

take the bless - ed light of the gos - pel there.
take the bless - ed hope of the gos - pel there.
take the bless - ed joy of the gos - pel there.

Refrain

Call me forth to ac - tive ser - vice,
Call me forth, call me forth, to ac - tive ser - vice, call me forth,

And my prompt re - sponse shall be, "Here am I, send me!"

I am read - y to re - port for or - ders, Mas - ter, sum - mon

me; And I'll go on an - y er - rand of love for thee.

Text and Tune: Elisha A. Hoffman, 1839-1929.

424

Isaiah 6:8
Luke 10:2

Send Me Forth, O Blessed Master

MASTER, USE ME 15.11.15.12. with refrain

1. Send me forth, O bless-ed Mas-ter! There are souls in sor-row bowed; Send me forth to homes of want and homes of care, And with joy I will o-bey the call, and in thy bless-ed name I will

2. There are lives that may be bright-ened by a word of hope and cheer; There are souls with whom life's bless-ings I should share; There are hearts that may be light-ened of the bur-dens which they bear; Let me

3. There is work with-in the vine-yard; there is ser-vice to be done; There's a mes-sage of sal-va-tion to de-clare; In-to hearts that know not Je-sus I would speak the sav-ing Word; Let me

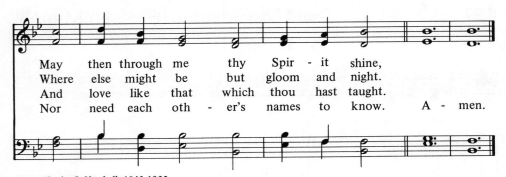

May then through me thy Spir - it shine,
Where else might be but gloom and night.
And love like that which thou hast taught.
Nor need each oth - er's names to know. A - men.

Text: Charles S. Newhall, 1842-1935.
Tune: Lowell Mason, 1792-1872.

The Bread That Giveth Strength 423

Mosiah 2:22-24, 28
Galatians 6:7-10

LIVORNO 10.10.10.10

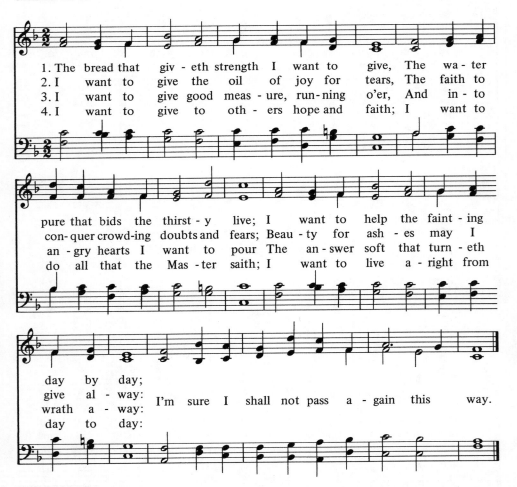

1. The bread that giv - eth strength I want to give, The wa - ter
2. I want to give the oil of joy for tears, The faith to
3. I want to give good meas - ure, run - ning o'er, And in - to
4. I want to give to oth - ers hope and faith; I want to

pure that bids the thirst - y live; I want to help the faint - ing
con - quer crowd - ing doubts and fears; Beau - ty for ash - es may I
an - gry hearts I want to pour The an - swer soft that turn - eth
do all that the Mas - ter saith; I want to live a - right from

day by day;
give al - way: I'm sure I shall not pass a - gain this way.
wrath a - way:
day to day:

Text: W. R. Fitch.
Tune: Arthur S. Sullivan, 1842-1900.

421

Just as I Am, Thine Own to Be

I Corinthians 6:19, 20
D. and C. 132:3, 4

JUST AS I AM 8.8.8.6.

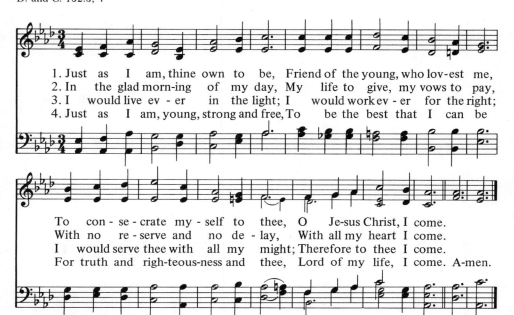

1. Just as I am, thine own to be, Friend of the young, who lov-est me,
2. In the glad morn-ing of my day, My life to give, my vows to pay,
3. I would live ev-er in the light; I would work ev-er for the right;
4. Just as I am, young, strong and free, To be the best that I can be

To con-se-crate my-self to thee, O Je-sus Christ, I come.
With no re-serve and no de-lay, With all my heart I come.
I would serve thee with all my might; Therefore to thee I come.
For truth and righ-teous-ness and thee, Lord of my life, I come. A-men.

Text: Marianne Hearn, 1834-1909.
Tune: Joseph Barnby, 1838-1896.

422

O Jesus, Master, When Today

I John 4:21
Isaiah 41:6

HEBRON L.M.

1. O Je-sus, Mas-ter, when to-day I meet a-long
2. To cheer them in their on-ward way Till eve-ning ends
3. Grant, too, that they my need may know As side by side
4. Then give our hands a touch di-vine And to our voic-

the crowd-ed way My bur-dened neigh-bors, mine and thine,
the var-ied day, To kin-dle so a grow-ing light
we on-ward go, An e-qual need of kind-ly thought
es tones like thine As side by side we on-ward go,

Your Cause Be Mine, Great Lord Divine 420

Philippians 2:5-12
D. and C. 10:2

RICHMOND BEACH 8.7.8.7.8.8.7.

Unison (or harmony*) ♩ *remains constant*

1. Your cause be mine, great Lord di - vine. Your aim be my am-
2. Your cause be mine, great Lord di - vine. This be my life's vo-
3. Your cause be mine, great Lord di - vine. The world's e - man - ci -

bi - tion: For wast - ed is my great-est strength Un - less it
ca - tion: To seek the prize when life is done— Your lov - ing
pa - tion: To let Your light in - vade the dark In ev - ery

find ex - pres-sion In love that gives it - self a - way, In life re -
ap - pro - ba - tion. Di - min - ish pride; in - crease my love. O may Your
sit - u - a - tion, To prove You in a thou-sand ways, To serve You

spon - sive to o - bey The terms of Your com - mis - sion.
Spir - it now re - move All self - ish mo - ti - va - tion.
well with zeal a - blaze Through life's un - known du - ra - tion.

*Tenors should read treble clef when necessary.

Text: Bryan Jeffery Leech, 1931 - .
Tune: A. Royce Eckhardt, 1937 - .
Text and tune copyright 1973 by Covenant Press; all rights reserved; used by permission.

419

God of Grace and God of Glory

I Corinthians 15:57, 58
Ephesians 6:10-17

CWM RHONDDA 8.7.8.7.8.7.7.

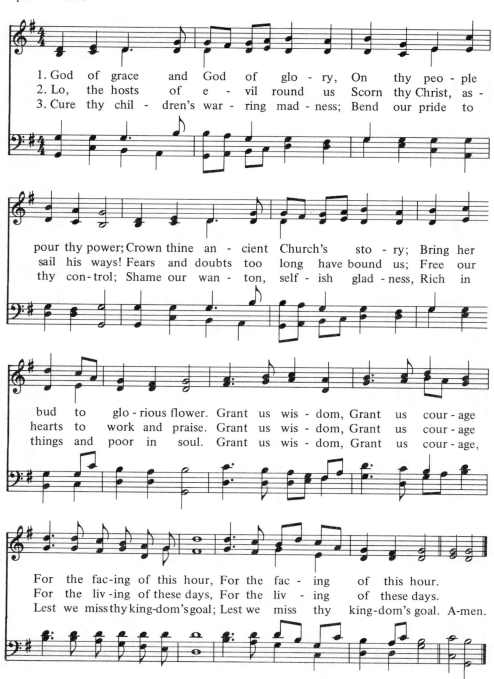

1. God of grace and God of glory, On thy people pour thy power; Crown thine an - cient Church's sto - ry; Bring her bud to glo - rious flower. Grant us wis - dom, Grant us cour - age For the fac-ing of this hour, For the fac - ing of this hour.

2. Lo, the hosts of e - vil round us Scorn thy Christ, as - sail his ways! Fears and doubts too long have bound us; Free our hearts to work and praise. Grant us wis - dom, Grant us cour - age For the liv -ing of these days, For the liv - ing of these days.

3. Cure thy chil - dren's war - ring mad - ness; Bend our pride to thy con - trol; Shame our wan - ton, self - ish glad - ness, Rich in things and poor in soul. Grant us wis - dom, Grant us cour - age, Lest we miss thy king-dom's goal; Lest we miss thy king-dom's goal. A-men.

Text: Harry Emerson Fosdick, 1878-1969. Used by permission of Elinor Fosdick Downs.
Tune: John Hughes, 1873-1932. Used by permission of Snell and Sons Ltd.

man - y climes, Thy chil - dren, Lord, now call to me.
courts of kings, They wait, all those for whom Christ died.
bid me go, I shall go glad - ly, in thy power.
count the cost, Thy peo - ple serve, wher - e'er they be.

Text: Evan A. Fry, 1902-1959; alt. Copyright 1956 Herald Publishing House.
Tune: Franklyn S. Weddle, 1905 - ; harm. Evan A. Fry, 1902-1959. Copyright 1956 Herald Publishing House.

From Isles and Continents Afar   418

Mosiah 1:46-49
D. and C. 4:1

BELSIZE SQUARE L.M.
Alternate hymn: 417

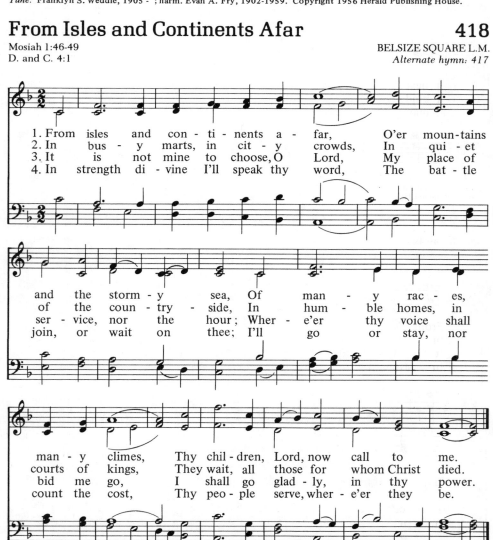

1. From isles and con - ti - nents a - far, O'er moun-tains
2. In bus - y marts, in cit - y crowds, In qui - et
3. It is not mine to choose, O Lord, My place of
4. In strength di - vine I'll speak thy word, The bat - tle

and the storm - y sea, Of man - y rac - es,
of the coun - try - side, In hum - ble homes, in
ser - vice, nor the hour; Wher - e'er thy voice shall
join, or wait on thee; I'll go or stay, nor

man - y climes, Thy chil - dren, Lord, now call to me.
courts of kings, They wait, all those for whom Christ died.
bid me go, I shall go glad - ly, in thy power.
count the cost, Thy peo - ple serve, wher - e'er they be.

Text: Evan A. Fry, 1902-1959; alt. Copyright 1956 Herald Publishing House.
Tune: Louita Clothier, 1936 - .

416 May We Who Know the Joyful Sound

I Timothy 1:5
II Nephi 14:4-6

ST. MAGNUS C.M.

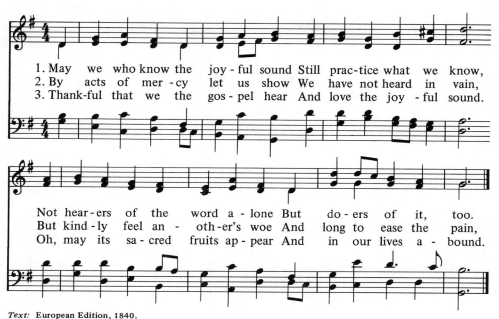

1. May we who know the joy-ful sound Still prac-tice what we know,
2. By acts of mer-cy let us show We have not heard in vain,
3. Thank-ful that we the gos-pel hear And love the joy-ful sound.

Not hear-ers of the word a-lone But do-ers of it, too.
But kind-ly feel an-oth-er's woe And long to ease the pain,
Oh, may its sa-cred fruits ap-pear And in our lives a-bound.

Text: European Edition, 1840.
Tune: Jeremiah Clark, c. 1670-1707.

417 From Isles and Continents Afar

Mosiah 1:46-49
D. and C. 4:1

DEDICARE L.M.
Alternate hymn: 418

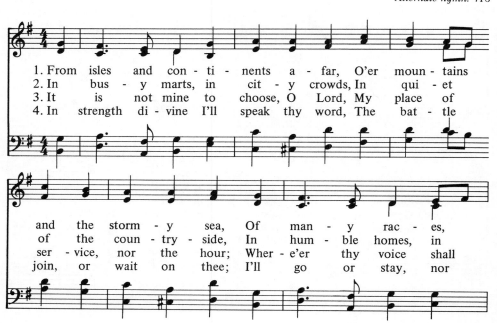

1. From isles and con-ti-nents a-far, O'er moun-tains
2. In bus-y marts, in cit-y crowds, In qui-et
3. It is not mine to choose, O Lord, My place of
4. In strength di-vine I'll speak thy word, The bat-tle

and the storm-y sea, Of man-y rac-es,
of the coun-try-side, In hum-ble homes, in
ser-vice, nor the hour; Wher-e'er thy voice shall
join, or wait on thee; I'll go or stay, nor

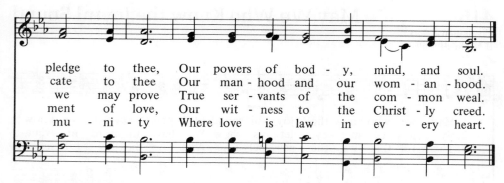

pledge to thee, Our powers of bod - y, mind, and soul.
cate to thee Our man - hood and our wom - an - hood.
we may prove True ser - vants of the com - mon weal.
ment of love, Our wit - ness to the Christ - ly creed.
mu - ni - ty Where love is law in ev - ery heart.

Text: Ernest Dodgshun, 1876-1944.
Tune: George J. Elvey, 1816-1893, alt.

Help Us Express Your Love

415

Mosiah 1:49
Romans 12:9, 10

BROOKFIELD L.M.

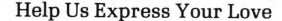

1. Help us ex - press your love, O Lord— Com - mit - ted
2. There is no sea - son when we dare With - hold our
3. The grace of God can flood the heart, Give love its

to one world in thee! A - bun - dant gifts en - hance our
love from hu - man - kind. Em - brac - ing earth's sup - port - ing
full - ness and its glow: Our un - con - fined and free de -

lives; Oh, free them for hu - man - i - ty!
strength, We match what - ev - er needs we find.
light Springs forth im - pelled by na - ture's flow. A - men.

Text: Cleo Hanthorne Moon, 1904 - ; copyright 1980 Reorganized Church of Jesus Christ of Latter Day Saints.
Tune: Thomas B. Southgate, 1814-1868.

413 Grant Us, Lord, the Grace of Giving

II Corinthians 9:7, 8
Matthew 5:18 (16)

STUTTGART 8.7.8.7.

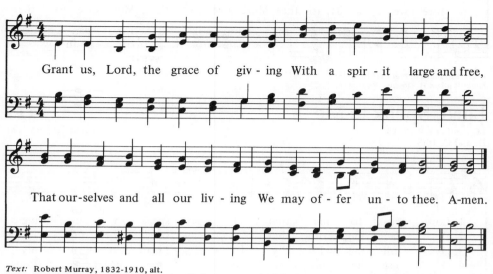

Grant us, Lord, the grace of giv-ing With a spir-it large and free,

That our-selves and all our liv-ing We may of-fer un-to thee. A-men.

Text: Robert Murray, 1832-1910, alt.
Tune: Christian F. Witt, 1660-1716, *Psalmodia Sacra*, 1715; adapt. by Henry J. Gauntlett, 1805-1876.

414 Beloved Community of God

Romans 12:1, 9-18
Ephesians 2:19-22

ST. CRISPIN L.M.

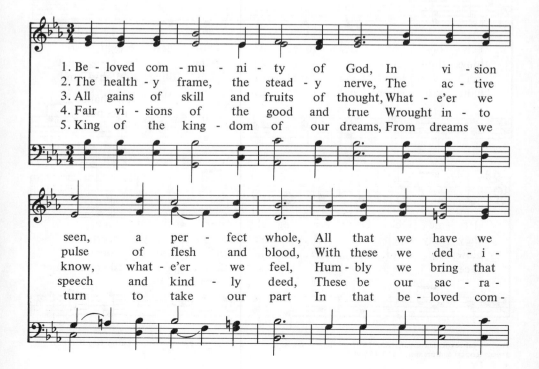

1. Be - loved com - mu - ni - ty of God, In vi - sion
2. The health - y frame, the stead - y nerve, The ac - tive
3. All gains of skill and fruits of thought, What - e'er we
4. Fair vi - sions of the good and true Wrought in - to
5. King of the king - dom of our dreams, From dreams we

seen, a per - fect whole, All that we have we
pulse of flesh and blood, With these we ded - i -
know, what - e'er we feel, Hum - bly we bring that
speech and kind - ly deed, These be our sac - ra -
turn to take our part In that be - loved com -

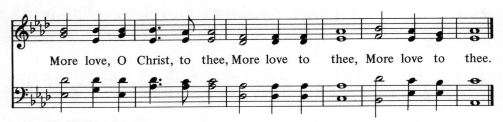

More love, O Christ, to thee, More love to thee, More love to thee.

Text: Elizabeth P. Prentiss, 1818-1878.
Tune: William H. Doane, 1832-1915.

Lord, Speak to Me

412

I Corinthians 2:12, 13
D. and C. 10:5

CANONBURY L.M.

1. Lord, speak to me that I may speak In living ech-oes of thy tone; As thou hast sought, so let me seek Thine err-ing chil-dren lost and lone.

2. O teach me, Lord, that I may teach The pre-cious things thou dost im-part, And wing my words that they may reach The hid-den depths of man-y a heart.

3. O fill me with thy full-ness, Lord, Un-til my ver-y heart o'er-flow In kin-dling thought and glow-ing word, Thy love to tell, thy praise to show.

4. O use me, Lord, use e-ven me, Just as thou wilt, and when and where, Un-til thy bless-ed face I see, Thy rest, thy joy, thy glo-ry share. A-men.

Text: Frances R. Havergal, 1836-1879.
Tune: Robert Schumann, 1810-1856.

410 Master, Speak! Thy Servant Heareth

Isaiah 6:8
I Samuel 3:10

CARTER 8.7.8.7.

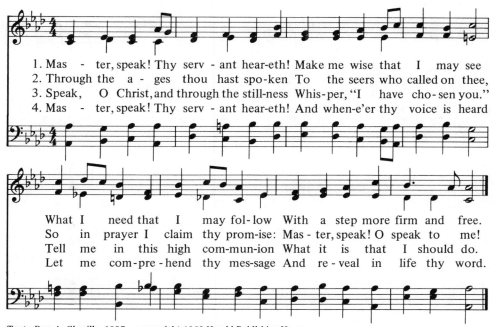

1. Mas - ter, speak! Thy serv - ant hear-eth! Make me wise that I may see
2. Through the a - ges thou hast spo-ken To the seers who called on thee,
3. Speak, O Christ, and through the still-ness Whis-per, "I have cho-sen you."
4. Mas - ter, speak! Thy serv - ant hear-eth! And when-e'er thy voice is heard

What I need that I may fol-low With a step more firm and free.
So in prayer I claim thy prom-ise: Mas - ter, speak! O speak to me!
Tell me in this high com-mun-ion What it is that I should do.
Let me com-pre - hend thy mes-sage And re - veal in life thy word.

Text: Roy A. Cheville, 1897 - ; copyright 1950 Herald Publishing House.
Tune: Edmund S. Carter, 1845-1923.

411 More Love to Thee, O Christ

Ephesians 3:19
II Nephi 13:29, 30

MORE LOVE TO THEE 6.4.6.4.6.6.4.4.

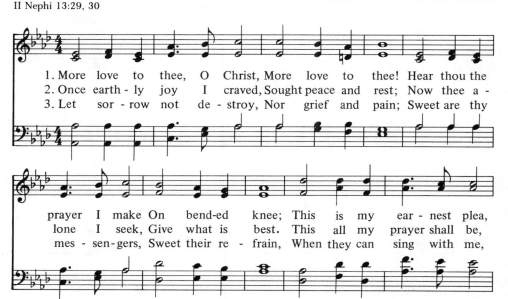

1. More love to thee, O Christ, More love to thee! Hear thou the
2. Once earth - ly joy I craved, Sought peace and rest; Now thee a -
3. Let sor - row not de - stroy, Nor grief and pain; Sweet are thy

prayer I make On bend-ed knee; This is my ear - nest plea,
lone I seek, Give what is best. This all my prayer shall be,
mes - sen-gers, Sweet their re - frain, When they can sing with me,

Touch Me, Lord, with Thy Spirit Eternal 409

John 17:3
D. and C. 16:4b, c

RUSSIAN MELODY 10.9.10.9.9.

1. Touch me, Lord, with thy Spir-it e-ter-nal;
2. Teach me, Lord, to walk hum-bly be-fore thee;
3. Fill me, Lord, with thine in-fi-nite pow-er;

Stir my soul to re-spond to thy call. Take my
May I has-ten thy will to o-bey. Make me
Make me firm, make me pure, make me whole. With thy

love, for I of-fer it free-ly; Hear my prayer as I
wise to see clear-ly thy pur-pose; Keep me true to my
Spir-it to strength-en and guide me, I shall serve thee with

thank thee for all. Hear my prayer as I thank thee for all.
call-ing, I pray. Keep me true to my call-ing, I pray.
all of my soul. I shall serve thee with all of my soul.

Text: R. Romanov or P. Rogozin; adapted from the Russian by Don C. Rawson, 1932 - ; alt.; adaptation copyright 1979 by Zionic Research Institute, Inc. All rights reserved. Used by permission.
Tune: Russian Melody arr. by Alexander Efimov.

408 Take My Life and Let It Be

Romans 12:8
II Nephi 14:12

HOLLINGSIDE 7.7.7.7.D.
Alternate tune: HENDON (4)*

1. Take my life and let it be Con - se - crat - ed, Lord, to thee;
2. Take my sil - ver and my gold; Naught of thine would I with - hold;

Take my mo - ments and my days; Let them flow in cease - less praise.
Take my heart, my mind, my will; Let them be thy serv - ants still.

Take my hands, my feet, my love; At thine im - pulse let them move;
Take my love; my Lord, I pour At thy feet its treas - ure store;

Take my voice and let me sing Al - ways, on - ly, for my King.
Take my - self, and I will be Ev - er, on - ly, all for thee. A - men.

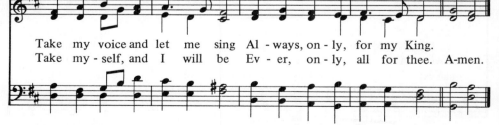

* With Alternate Tune HENDON, divide into 4 stanzas, repeating last line of each stanza.

Text: Frances Ridley Havergal, 1836-1879; alt. by Alice Edwards, 1899-1973.
Tune: John B. Dykes, 1823-1876.

Yesu, Yesu, Fill Us with Your Love

407

Matthew 20:26-28
Luke 10:37-38

CHEREPONI 7.7.9. with refrain

Refrain
Ye - su,* Ye - su, Fill us with your love.
Ye - su your love.
Ye - su

Show us how to serve the neigh-bors we have from you.
to serve we have from you.

Stanza
1. Kneels at the feet of His friends, Si - lent - ly wash - es their
2. Neigh-bors are rich folk and poor; Neigh-bors are black, brown and
3. These are the ones we should serve; These are the ones we should
4. Lov - ing puts us on our knees, Serv - ing as though we are

feet, Mas - ter who acts as a slave to them.
white; Neigh-bors are near - by and far a - way.
love. All these are neigh - bors to us and you.
slaves; This is the way we should live with you.

* "Ye-su" is pronounced "Yā-soo."

406 God, the Source of Light and Beauty

D. and C. 90:1a-e
I John 1:1-3

IN BABILONE 8.7.8.7.D.

1. God, the source of light and beau-ty, Grant re-sponse in sense and sight;
2. Great Mu - si - cian of the thun-der, Build - er of the moun-tain range,
3. Au - thor of cre - a - tion's be - ing, Thou hast shared our pain and loss;

Stir our minds to fol -low du -ty; Rouse our souls from earth-born night;
Paint - er of the sun -set's splen-dor, Plan - ner of the sea - son's change,
Through Christ's gal-lant life of serv-ice Shines the ra - diance of the cross.

Give us through our cloud-ed vi - sion Clear - er knowl-edge of thy will,
Help us fill our lives with beau - ty; Still the roar of guns and strife;
God, the source of light and beau - ty, Faith as - sures thy reign a - bove.

Till thine un - de -feat -ed pur-pose Through our lives thou shalt ful- fill.
Build thy king-dom of the fu -ture Here with-in our dai - ly life.
Here on earth we need thy pres-ence; Teach us how to walk in love. A-men.

Text: S. Ralph Harlow, 1885-1972.
Tune: Dutch Traditional Melody.

As Saints of Old Their Firstfruits Brought

405

D. and C. 46:9
Ephesians 4:1-6

NORSE AIR (No Other Plea, or Landas) C.M.D.
See 357 for a higher setting.

1. As saints of old their first-fruits brought Of or-chard, flock, and field
2. A world in need now sum-mons us To la-bor, love, and give;
3. In gra-ti-tude and hum-ble trust We bring our best to-day,

To God, the giv-er of all good, The source of boun-teous yield;
To make our life a sa-cri-fice That oth-er souls may live;
To serve your cause and share your love With all a-long life's way.

So we to-day first-fruits would bring, The wealth of this good land,
The church of Christ is call-ing us To make the dream come true:
O God, who gave your-self to us In Christ, your lov-ing Son,

Of farm and mar-ket, shop and home, Of mind and heart and hand.
A world re-deemed by Christ-like love, All life in Christ made new.
Teach us to give our-selves each day Un-til life's work is done. A-men.

Text: Frank von Christierson, 1900- ; alt.; from *Ten New Stewardship Hymns.* Copyright 1961 The Hymn Society of America. Used by permission.
Tune: Norse Folk Melody; arr. William J. Kirkpatrick, 1838-1921.

404

Philippians 4:8
I Timothy 4:12

I Would Be True

PEEK 11.10.11.10.10.

1. I would be true, for there are those who trust me; I would be pure, for there are those who care; I would be strong, for there is much to suffer; I would be brave, for there is much to dare; I would be brave, for there is much to dare.

2. I would be friend of all, the foe, the friendless; I would be giving, and forget the gift; I would be humble, for I know my weakness; I would look up and laugh and love and lift; I would look up and laugh and love and lift.

3. I would be prayerful through each busy moment; I would be constantly in touch with God; I would be tuned to hear his slightest whisper; I would have faith to keep the path Christ trod; I would have faith to keep the path Christ trod.

Text: Howard Arnold Walter, 1883-1918.
Tune: Joseph Yates Peek, 1843-1911.

Brothers, Sisters, Let Us Gladly

403

D. and C. 4:1
Romans 12:1

GENEVA 8.7.8.7.D.
Alternate tune: HYMN TO JOY (20)

Unison (or harmony)

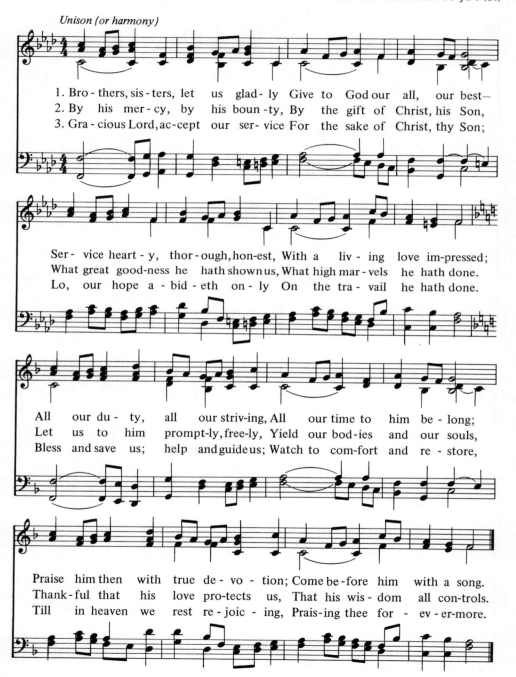

1. Bro-thers, sis-ters, let us glad-ly Give to God our all, our best—
2. By his mer-cy, by his boun-ty, By the gift of Christ, his Son,
3. Gra-cious Lord, ac-cept our ser-vice For the sake of Christ, thy Son;

Ser-vice heart-y, thor-ough, hon-est, With a liv-ing love im-pressed;
What great good-ness he hath shown us, What high mar-vels he hath done.
Lo, our hope a-bid-eth on-ly On the tra-vail he hath done.

All our du-ty, all our striv-ing, All our time to him be-long;
Let us to him prompt-ly, free-ly, Yield our bod-ies and our souls,
Bless and save us; help and guide us; Watch to com-fort and re-store,

Praise him then with true de-vo-tion; Come be-fore him with a song.
Thank-ful that his love pro-tects us, That his wis-dom all con-trols.
Till in heaven we rest re-joic-ing, Prais-ing thee for-ev-er-more.

Text: Henry Bateman, 1802-1872, alt.
Tune: George Henry Day, 1883-1966. Copyright 1942 by the Church Pension Fund. Used by permission.

402

D. and C. 150:7
D. and C. 59:4, 5a, b

God in His Love for Us

ECOLOGY 11.10.11.10.

Unison (or harmony)

1. God in his love for us lent us this plan - et,
2. Thanks be to God for its boun - ty and beau - ty,
3. Long have our tra - gic wars ruined our har - vest;
4. Cas - ual de - spoil - ers, or high priests of Mam - mon

Gave it a pur - pose in time and in space;
Life that sus - tains us in bod - y and mind:
Long has Earth bowed to the ter - ror of force.
Sell - ing the fu - ture for pre - sent re - wards,

Small as a spark from the fire of cre - a - tion,
Plen - ty for all, if we learn how to share it,
Now we pol - lute it, in cyn - i - cal si - lence:
Care - less of life and con - temp - tuous of beau - ty:

Cra - dle of life and the home of our race.
Rich - es un - dreamed of to fath - om and find.
Poi - son the foun - tain of life at its source.
Bid us re - mem - ber, the Earth is the Lord's!

F♯ on last stanza only.

Text: F. Pratt Green, 1903 - ; alt.; from *Sixteen Stewardship Hymns of the Environment*, copyright 1973 by the Hymn Society of America. Used by permission.
Tune: Austin C. Lovelace, 1919 - ; copyright 1974 Augsburg Publishing House. Used by permission.

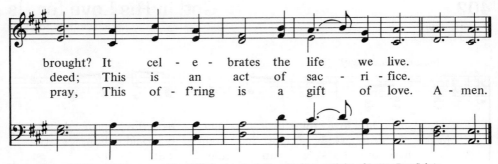

brought? It cel - e - brates the life we live.
deed; This is an act of sac - ri - fice.
pray, This of - f'ring is a gift of love. A - men.

Text: Margaret Athey, 1936 - ; copyright 1980 Reorganized Church of Jesus Christ of Latter Day Saints.
Tune: Traditional German Melody; arr. by Samuel Dyer, 1785-1835.

We Give Thee But Thine Own 401

Matthew 25:41 (40)
I Chronicles 29:14

ST. ANDREW S.M.

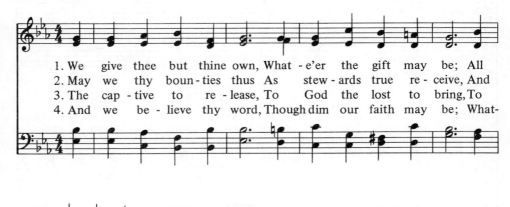

1. We give thee but thine own, What - e'er the gift may be; All
2. May we thy boun - ties thus As stew - ards true re - ceive, And
3. The cap - tive to re - lease, To God the lost to bring, To
4. And we be - lieve thy word, Though dim our faith may be; What-

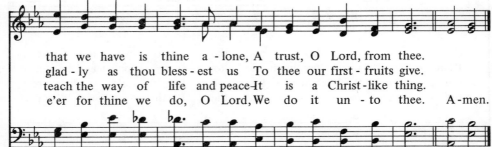

that we have is thine a - lone, A trust, O Lord, from thee.
glad - ly as thou bless - est us To thee our first - fruits give.
teach the way of life and peace—It is a Christ - like thing.
e'er for thine we do, O Lord, We do it un - to thee. A - men.

Text: William Walsham How, 1823-1897.
Tune: Joseph Barnby, 1838-1896.

399

I Timothy 6:11-14
II Corinthians 5:16-18

A Charge to Keep I Have

BOYLSTON S.M.

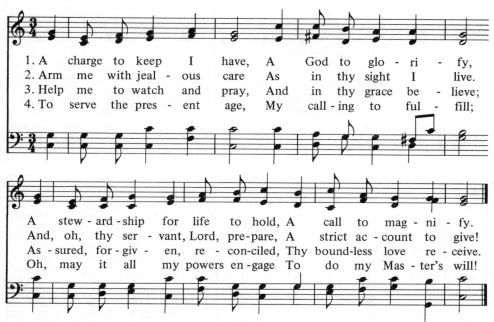

1. A charge to keep I have, A God to glo - ri - fy,
2. Arm me with jeal - ous care As in thy sight I live.
3. Help me to watch and pray, And in thy grace be - lieve;
4. To serve the pres - ent age, My call - ing to ful - fill;

A stew - ard - ship for life to hold, A call to mag - ni - fy.
And, oh, thy ser - vant, Lord, pre - pare, A strict ac - count to give!
As - sured, for - giv - en, re - con - ciled, Thy bound-less love re - ceive.
Oh, may it all my powers en - gage To do my Mas - ter's will!

Text: Charles Wesley, 1707-1788, alt.; St. 3 alt. by Richard Howard, 1929 - .
Tune: Lowell Mason, 1792-1872.

400

II Corinthians 9:7, 8
Proverbs 3:9

Source of All Gifts

MENDON L.M.

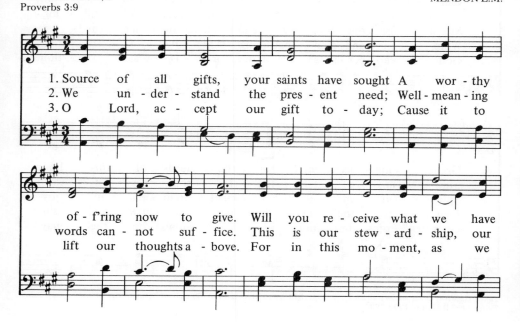

1. Source of all gifts, your saints have sought A wor - thy
2. We un - der - stand the pres - ent need; Well - mean - ing
3. O Lord, ac - cept our gift to - day; Cause it to

of - f'ring now to give. Will you re - ceive what we have
words can - not suf - fice. This is our stew - ard - ship, our
lift our thoughts a - bove. For in this mo - ment, as we

Let Us Give Praise to the God of Creation

398

D. and C. 137:6
D. and C. 140:5c, d

WESLEY 11.10.11.10.

1. Let us give praise to the God of cre - a - tion,
2. Per - sons are a - gents by God's gra - cious will - ing,
3. All things are sa - cred, for use with thanks - giv - ing,
4. Gift - ed - ness flows from the fount of cre - a - tion;
5. Now let the saints hail so rich a foun - da - tion,

Lord of all his - tory and source of all power,
Blessed with as - sur - ance of ul - ti - mate worth.
Bound - less re - sour - ces for each to em - ploy;
Truth from all sour - ces de - mands dis - ci - pline;
Forged in our her - i - tage, liv - ing to - day;

Call - ing us now to the world's re - stor - a - tion;
Power is with - in us for his - tory's ful - fill - ing,
Strength for the bod - y and soul's ful - ler liv - ing;
Wom - en and men shar - ing skill's ded - i - ca - tion,
God who per - sists in the prom - ised sal - va - tion

Grant - ing us strength for the needs of this hour.
Stew - ards of all the re - sour - ces of earth.
Spir - it and el - e - ment bond - ed in joy.
Bear - ing the bur - dens of sor - row and sin.
Goes on be - fore us and shows us the way.

Text: Geoffrey F. Spencer, 1927 - . Copyright 1980 Reorganized Church of Jesus Christ of Latter Day Saints.
Tune: Lowell Mason, 1792-1872.

397

D. and C. 101:2b-e
Mosiah 2:19-23

All Things Are Thine

GERMANY (Gardiner) L.M.

1. All things are thine, O Lord of life! Thou hast or-
2. Thou hast e - nough for all thy saints, In field, in
3. To work to - geth - er, Lord, with thee, We own to
4. Yet word a - lone will not suf - fice For stew - ard -

dained these gifts a - bove That we may build on earth with
mine, in sea, in air, If we shall learn to dwell as
be our com - mon call, To build a blest com - mu - ni -
ship of farm or mart; This mind, this hand must im - ple -

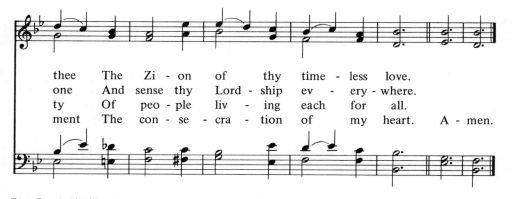

thee The Zi - on of thy time - less love.
one And sense thy Lord - ship ev - ery - where.
ty Of peo - ple liv - ing each for all.
ment The con - se - cra - tion of my heart. A - men.

Text: Roy A. Cheville, 1897 - ; alt.; copyright 1950 Herald Publishing House.
Tune: William Gardiner's *Sacred Melodies*, 1815.

Refrain

God of cre - a - tion, we would be cre - a - tors too,

Bless our ef - forts us - ing wise - ly all that comes from you. A - men.

Text: Naomi Russell, 1921 - ; copyright 1980 Reorganized Church of Jesus Christ of Latter Day Saints.
Tune: George Friedrich Handel, 1685-1759.

O Lord of Heaven and Earth and Sea   396

Mosiah 2:36
Psalm 95:3-6

ALMSGIVING 8.8.8.4.

1. O Lord of heaven and earth and sea, To thee all praise and glo - ry
2. We lose what on our - selves we spend; We have as treas - ure with-out
3. What-ev - er, Lord, we yield to thee Re-paid a thou -sand-fold will
4. To thee from whom we all de - rive Our life, our gifts, our power to

be! How shall we show our love to thee, Who giv-est all?
end What-ev - er, Lord, to thee we lend, Who giv-est all.
be; Then glad-ly will we give to thee, Who giv-est all—
give. Oh, may we ev - er with thee live, Who giv-est all! A - men.

Text: Christopher Wordsworth, 1807-1885.
Tune: John B. Dykes, 1823-1876.

395

D. and C. 59:4, 5a, b
D. and C. 101:2b-f

God of Creation

JUDAS MACCABEUS
5.7.8.5.8.5.8.5. with refrain

1. God of cre - a - tion, help us each to un - der - stand
2. Earth's stores of rich - es, like life - giv - ing rain and sun
3. Grant us di - rec - tion as we seek for bet - ter ways

How to use the vast re - sourc - es of both sea and land.
Are your gen - er - ous pro - vi - sions meant for ev - ery - one.
To pro - vide for our well - be - ing and pro - long our days.

Teach us how to plant and har - vest— not for graft or greed
May we use them as in - tend - ed— nev - er waste - ful - ly—
Field and for -est, air and wa - ter— may we ev - er share

But that there may be suf - fi - cient for a world in need.
Not just for this gen - er - a - tion but those yet to be.
As stew -ards in pro - tect - ing, us - ing them with care.

The Voice of God Is Calling

394

Alma 3:57-59
Isaiah 6:8

WEBB 7.6.7.6.D.

1. The voice of God is call-ing Its sum-mons un-to men
2. I hear my peo-ple cry-ing In cot and mine and slum;
3. We heed, O Lord, thy sum-mons, And an-swer, "Here are we!"

As once he spoke in Zi-on, So now he speaks a-gain:
No field or mart is si-lent; No cit-y street is dumb.
Send us up-on thine er-rand; Let us thy serv-ants be.

Whom shall I send to suc-cor My peo-ple in their need?
I see my peo-ple fall-ing In dark-ness and de-spair;
Our strength is dust and ash-es, Our years a pass-ing hour—

Whom shall I send to loos-en The bonds of lust and greed?
Whom shall I send to shat-ter The fet-ters which they bear?
But thou canst use our weak-ness To mag-ni-fy thy power. A-men.

Text: John Haynes Holmes, 1879-1964; used by permission of Roger W. Holmes.
Tune: George J. Webb, 1803-1887.

393

II Nephi 1:36-38
D. and C. 26:3d-g

Soldiers of Christ, Arise

DIADEMATA S.M.D.

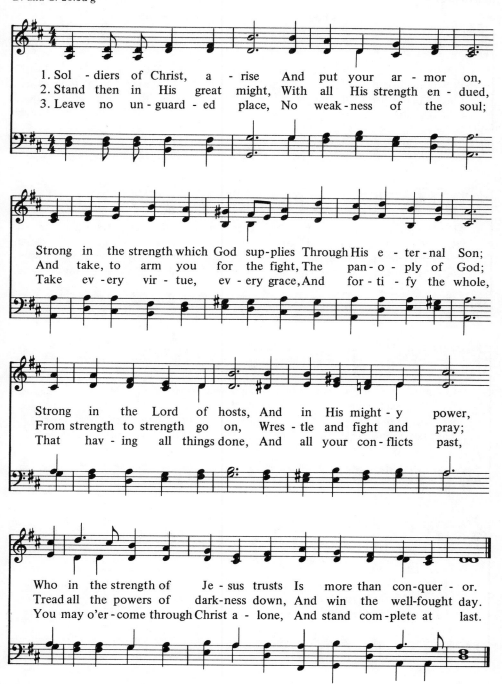

1. Sol - diers of Christ, a - rise And put your ar - mor on,
2. Stand then in His great might, With all His strength en - dued,
3. Leave no un - guard - ed place, No weak - ness of the soul;

Strong in the strength which God sup-plies Through His e - ter - nal Son;
And take, to arm you for the fight, The pan - o - ply of God;
Take ev - ery vir - tue, ev - ery grace, And for - ti - fy the whole,

Strong in the Lord of hosts, And in His might - y power,
From strength to strength go on, Wres - tle and fight and pray;
That hav - ing all things done, And all your con - flicts past,

Who in the strength of Je - sus trusts Is more than con-quer - or.
Tread all the powers of dark-ness down, And win the well-fought day.
You may o'er - come through Christ a - lone, And stand com-plete at last.

Text: Charles Wesley, 1707-1788, alt.
Tune: George J. Elvey, 1816-1893.

Go, Make of All Disciples

392

Matthew 28:17-19 (18-20)
Alma 14:82, 96

LANCASHIRE 7.6.7.6.D.

1. "Go, make of all dis - ci - ples." We hear the call, O Lord,
2. "Go, make of all dis - ci - ples," bap - tiz - ing in the name
3. "Go, make of all dis - ci - ples." We at thy feet would stay
4. "Go, make of all dis - ci - ples." We wel - come thy com - mand.

That comes from thee, our Fa - ther, In thine e - ter - nal Word.
Of Fa - ther, Son, and Spir - it, From age to age the same.
Un - til each life's vo - ca - tion Ac - cents thy ho - ly way.
"Lo, I am with you al - way." We take thy guid - ing hand.

In - spire our ways of learn - ing Through ear - nest, fer - vent prayer,
We call each new dis - ci - ple To fol - low thee, O Lord,
We cul - ti - vate the na - ture God plants in ev - ery heart,
The task looms large be - fore us; We fol - low with - out fear,

And let our dai - ly liv - ing Re - veal thee ev - ery - where.
Re - deem - ing soul and bod - y By wa - ter and the Word.
Re - veal - ing in our wit - ness The Mas - ter Teach-er's art.
In heaven and earth thy pow - er Shall bring God's king - dom here.

Text: Leon M. Adkins, 1896 - ; copyright 1955, 1964 Abingdon Press; used by permission.
Tune: Henry Smart, 1813-1879.

391

Joshua 24:15
Alma 3:57, 58

Jesus Is Calling

JESUS IS CALLING TODAY 10.8.10.7. with refrain

1. Je-sus is call-ing! O hear him to-day, Call-ing for you,
2. Je-sus is call-ing! Your ser-vice he needs, Call-ing for you,
3. Je-sus is call-ing! He stands at the door, Call-ing for you,

Call-ing for you. Will you not quick-ly the sum-mons o-bey?
Call-ing for you. Ten-der-ly, pa-tient-ly with you he pleads;
Call-ing for you. O-pen your heart, and his mer-cy im-plore;

Refrain

Je-sus is call-ing for you! Call-ing for you;

Call-ing for you! Hear him to-day; do not

turn him a-way! Je-sus is call-ing for you!

Text: Charles H. Gabriel, 1856-1932.
Tune: Luther O. Emerson, 1820-1915, alt. by Rosalee Elser, 1925 - .

Hast Thou Heard It, O My Brother

390

D. and C. 65:1a
Psalm 37:3-4

ELLESDIE 8.7.8.7.D.
See 381 for a lower setting.

1. Hast thou heard it, O my broth-er, God's e - ter - nal voice to thee,
2. Wilt thou an - swer, O my sis - ter, Doubt-ing not the beck-oning star
3. Hast thou heard it, O my neigh-bor, Like pro-phet - ic souls of yore?

Soft - ly call - ing toward the out-land Where his Zi - on yet shall be?
Like a bea - con guid - ing for-ward Where the fron - tier coun-tries are?
When the com-mon mind was list-less, They God's vi - tal mes - sage bore.

"Some-thing for you; go and find it. Brave the broad un-chart-ed sea,
Hear God's whis-per in the still-ness,"Go, my child, I bid you go.
Search the stores of earth and heav-en; Watch the skies for guid -ing ray;

Where be - yond the seen ho - ri - zon Lies the land of prom-ise free."
When you move in faith, my Spir - it Shall with-in your spir - it glow."
Trust in God and in each oth - er For the light of each newday.

Text: Roy A. Cheville, 1897 - , alt. Copyright 1950 Herald Publishing House.
Tune: Wolfgang Amadeus Mozart, 1756-1791, arr. by Hubert P. Main, 1839-1926.

389

John 14:21
D. and C. 11:4, 5

If Suddenly upon the Street

MOZART 8.8.8.D.

1. If sud-den-ly up-on the street My gra-cious Sav-ior
2. His eye would pierce my out-ward show; His thought my in-most
3. If on the day or in the place Where-in he met me

I should meet, And he should say, "As I love thee,
thought would know; And if I said, "I love thee, Lord,"
face to face My life could show some kind-ness done,

What love hast thou to of-fer me?" Then what could this poor
He would not heed my spo-ken word Un-less my dai-ly
Some pur-pose formed, some work be-gun For his dear sake, then

heart of mine Dare of-fer to that heart di-vine?
life should tell That ver-i-ly I loved him well.
were it meet Love's gift to lay at Je-sus' feet.

Text: Clarence F. Richardson, 1879 - ?
Tune: Wolfgang Amadeus Mozart, 1756-1791.

Brothers and Sisters of Mine

388

Luke 6:36-38
Mosiah 2:22, 24, 28

MINE ARE THE HUNGRY 11.11.11.11.

1. Broth - ers and sis - ters of mine are the hun - gry Who
2. Stran - gers and neigh - bors, they claim my at - ten - tion; They
3. Peo - ple are they, men and wom - en and chil - dren; And
4. God of all liv - ing, we make our con - fes - sion: Too

sigh in their sor - row and weep in their pain.
sleep by my door - step, they sit by my bed.
each has a heart keep - ing time with my own.
long we have wast - ed the wealth of our lands.

Sis - ters and broth - ers of mine are the home-less Who
Neigh - bors and stran - gers, their an - guish con - cerns me, And
Peo - ple are they, per - sons made in God's im - age; So
God of all lov - ing, re - new our com - pas - sion And

wait with - out shel - ter from wind and from rain.
I must not feast till the hun - gry are fed.
what shall I of - fer them, bread or a stone?
o - pen our hearts while we reach out our hands.

Text: Kenneth I. Morse, 1913 - .
Tune: Wilbur E. Brumbaugh, 1931-1977.
Text and tune copyright 1974 by The Brethren Press, Elgin, IL; harm. alt. by Rosalee Elser, 1925 - ; used by permission.

387

D. and C. 153:9
D. and C. 81:4c

O My People, Saith the Spirit

MY REDEEMER (Admonition) 8.7.8.7.D.

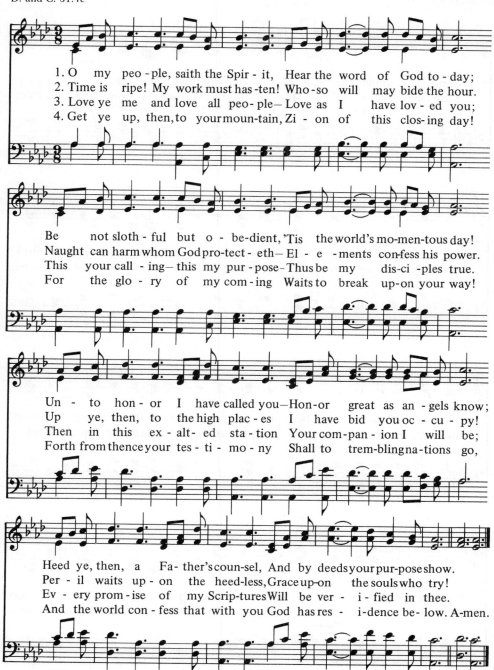

1. O my peo-ple, saith the Spir-it, Hear the word of God to-day;
2. Time is ripe! My work must has-ten! Who-so will may bide the hour.
3. Love ye me and love all peo-ple— Love as I have lov-ed you;
4. Get ye up, then, to your moun-tain, Zi-on of this clos-ing day!

Be not sloth-ful but o-be-dient, 'Tis the world's mo-men-tous day!
Naught can harm whom God pro-tect-eth— El-e-ments con-fess his power.
This your call-ing— this my pur-pose— Thus be my dis-ci-ples true.
For the glo-ry of my com-ing Waits to break up-on your way!

Un-to hon-or I have called you— Hon-or great as an-gels know;
Up ye, then, to the high plac-es I have bid you oc-cu-py!
Then in this ex-alt-ed sta-tion Your com-pan-ion I will be;
Forth from thence your tes-ti-mo-ny Shall to trem-bling na-tions go,

Heed ye, then, a Fa-ther's coun-sel, And by deeds your pur-pose show.
Per-il waits up-on the heed-less, Grace up-on the souls who try!
Ev-ery prom-ise of my Scrip-tures Will be ver-i-fied in thee.
And the world con-fess that with you God has res-i-dence be-low. A-men.

Text: Joseph Luff, 1852-1948.
Tune: James McGranahan, 1840-1907, alt.

Come Now, Sound the Call of Zion

386

D. and C. 136:3c
D. and C. 6:3

PITTSFIELD 8.7.8.7.D.

1. Come now, sound the call of Zi - on! Share with peo-ple of the earth.
2. Saints with vi - sion of the fu - ture Need foun - da - tions strong and true;

All are called to be dis - ci - ples; Now's the time for world re - birth.
As they seek new rev - e - la - tion, God's in - tent is born a - new.

Dare we search for new hor - i - zons? Is our faith a hope-less dream?
Jour-ney forth to high ad - ven-ture, Bring-ing faith and hope to all.

Or by faith shall we be build - ers And with God the world re - deem?
Each in - vest - ment made in oth - ers Is re - sponse to Zi - on's call.

385

Revelation 3:20
II Nephi 14:4, 5

O Jesus, Thou Art Standing

ST. HILDA 7.6.7.6.D.

1. O Je - sus, thou art stand - ing Out - side the fast-closed door,
2. O Je - sus, thou art knock - ing, And, lo, thy hand is scarred,
3. O Je - sus, thou art plead - ing In ac - cents meek and low,

In low - ly pa - tience wait - ing To pass the thresh-old o'er.
And thorns thy brow en - cir - cle, And tears thy face have marred.
"I died for you, my chil - dren, And will ye treat me so?"

We bear the name of Chris - tians, His name and sign we bear;
O love that pass - eth knowl - edge, So pa - tient - ly to wait!
O Lord, with shame and sor - row, We o - pen now the door;

O shame, thrice shame up - on us To keep him stand - ing there!
O sin that hath no e - qual, So fast to bar the gate!
Dear Sav - ior, en - ter, en - ter, And leave us nev - er - more! A - men.

Text: William Walsham How, 1823-1897.
Tune: Justin H. Knecht, 1752-1817, and Edward Husband, 1843-1908.

Come, Labor On

384

II Nephi 13:28-30
Hebrews 12:1-2

ORA LABORA 4.10.10.10.4.

Unison (or harmony)

1. Come, la-bor on. Who dares stand i-dle on the har-vest plain, While all a-round us waves the gold-en grain? And to each ser-vant does the Mas-ter say, "Go work to-day."

2. Come, la-bor on. Claim the high call-ing an-gels can-not share— To young and old the gos-pel glad-ness bear; Re-deem the time; its hours too swift-ly fly. The night draws nigh.

3. Come, la-bor on. A-way with gloom-y doubts and faith-less fear! No arm so weak but may do serv-ice here: By fee-blest a-gents may our God ful-fill His righ-teous will.

4. Come, la-bor on. No time for rest till glows the west-ern sky, Till the long shad-ows o'er our path-way lie, And a glad sound comes with the set-ting sun, "Well done, well done!"

Text: Jane Laurie Borthwick, 1813-1897.
Tune: T. Tertius Noble, 1867-1953; arr. Rosalee Elser, 1925 - ; copyright 1980 Rosalee Elser; used by permission.

383 Where Cross the Crowded Ways of Life

Matthew 10:38 (42)
Hebrews 13:14, 16

GERMANY (Gardiner) L.M.

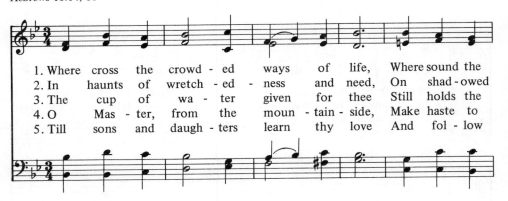

1. Where cross the crowd - ed ways of life, Where sound the
2. In haunts of wretch - ed - ness and need, On shad - owed
3. The cup of wa - ter given for thee Still holds the
4. O Mas - ter, from the moun - tain - side, Make haste to
5. Till sons and daugh - ters learn thy love And fol - low

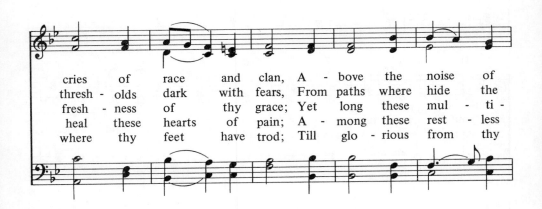

cries of race and clan, A - bove the noise of
thresh - olds dark with fears, From paths where hide the
fresh - ness of thy grace; Yet long these mul - ti -
heal these hearts of pain; A - mong these rest - less
where thy feet have trod; Till glo - rious from thy

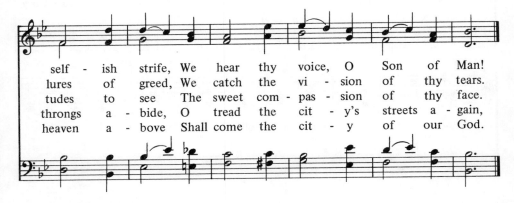

self - ish strife, We hear thy voice, O Son of Man!
lures of greed, We catch the vi - sion of thy tears.
tudes to see The sweet com - pas - sion of thy face.
throngs a - bide, O tread the cit - y's streets a - gain,
heaven a - bove Shall come the cit - y of our God.

Text: Frank Mason North, 1850-1935, alt.
Tune: William Gardiner's *Sacred Melodies*, 1815.

God Forgave My Sin in Jesus' Name

382

Alma 15:60, 61
I Corinthians 2:9-12

FREELY, FREELY
9.9.9.9. with refrain

Unison

1. God for - gave my sin in Je - sus' name; I've been born a -
2. All power is given in Je - sus' name, In earth and

gain in Je - sus' name; And in Je - sus' name I come to
heaven in Je - sus' name; And in Je - sus' name I come to

Refrain

you To share his love as he told me to. He said, "Free - ly,
you To share his power as he told me to.

free - ly you have re - ceived: Free - ly, free - ly give. Go in my

name, and, be - cause you be - lieve, Oth - ers will know that I live."

381

Hark! The Voice of Jesus Calling

D. and C. 6:2
Isaiah 6:8

ELLESDIE 8.7.8.7.D.
See 390 for a higher setting.

1. Hark! The voice of Je - sus call-ing, "Who will go and work to - day?
2. If you can - not cross the o - cean And far mis - sion lands ex - plore,
3. Let none hear you i - dly say-ing, "There is noth-ing I can do,"

Fields are white and har - vests wait-ing; Who will bear the sheaves a - way?"
You can find the need - y near-er; You can help them at your door.
While so ma - ny souls are dy - ing, And the Mas-ter calls for you.

Ear - nest-ly the Mas - ter call - eth; Rich re - ward he of - fers free;
If you can - not give your thou-sands, You can serve with will - ing might,
Take the task he gives you glad - ly; Let his work your pleas-ure be;

Who will an - swer, glad - ly say-ing, "Here am I, O Lord, send me."
And what-e'er you do for Je - sus Will be pre - cious in his sight.
An - swer quick-ly when he call - eth, "Here am I, O Lord, send me."

Text: Daniel March, 1816-1909, alt.
Tune: Wolfgang Amadeus Mozart, 1756-1791; arr. by Hubert P. Main, 1839-1926.

It needs the o-ver-flow of heart To give the lips full speech.
Live tru-ly, and thy life shall be A great and no-ble creed.

Text: Horatius Bonar, 1808-1889, alt.
Tune: Attr. to Benjamin Franklin, 1706-1790.

Though Anxious and Disheartened 380

D. and C. 68:1d
II Nephi 13:29

RUTHERFORD 7.6.7.6.7.6.7.5.

Though anx-ious and dis-heart-ened, Be peo-ple of good cheer.

Move out in faith em-pow-ered, My Spir-it will be there.

In love sup-port each oth-er With un-der-stand-ing hearts.

Move out, pro-claim my gos-pel; I have gone be-fore.

Text: Arr. from *D. and C.* 154 by Barbara Howard, 1930 - , and Rosalee Elser, 1925 - ; copyright 1980 Reorganized Church of Jesus Christ of Latter Day Saints.
Tune: Adapted from Chrétien Urhan, 1790-1845, by Edward F. Rimbault, 1816-1876.

378

D. and C. 4:1
Alma 14:92-96

Rise Up, O Saints of God

FESTAL SONG S.M.
See 319 for a lower setting.

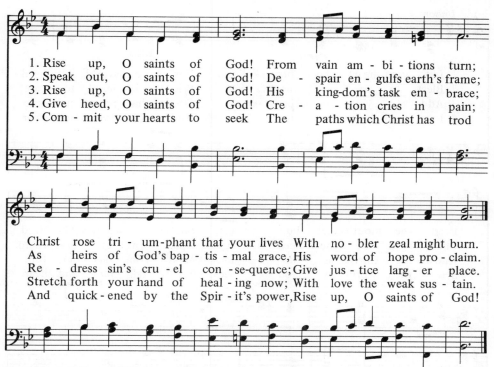

1. Rise up, O saints of God! From vain am-bi-tions turn;
2. Speak out, O saints of God! De - spair en-gulfs earth's frame;
3. Rise up, O saints of God! His king-dom's task em - brace;
4. Give heed, O saints of God! Cre - a - tion cries in pain;
5. Com - mit your hearts to seek The paths which Christ has trod

Christ rose tri - um-phant that your lives With no - bler zeal might burn.
As heirs of God's bap - tis - mal grace, His word of hope pro - claim.
Re - dress sin's cru - el con - se-quence; Give jus-tice larg - er place.
Stretch forth your hand of heal - ing now; With love the weak sus - tain.
And quick - ened by the Spir - it's power, Rise up, O saints of God!

Text: Norman O. Forness, 1936 - ; copyright 1978 from *Lutheran Book of Worship*; used by permission of Augsburg
Publishing House representing the publishers and copyright holders.
Tune: William H. Walter, 1825-1893.

379

James 1:25-27
I John 2:4-10

Thou Must Be True Thyself

LOYALTY 6.6.8.6.8.6.

1. Thou must be true thy - self If thou the truth would teach;
2. Think tru - ly, and thy thoughts The starv - ing world shall feed;

Thy soul must o - ver - flow if thou An - oth - er's soul would reach;
Speak tru - ly, and each word of thine Shall be a fruit - ful seed;

Let Your Heart Be Broken

377

D. and C. 153:9
Jacob 2:22-24

BJORKLUND MAJOR 6.5.6.5.D.

1. Let your heart be bro - ken For a world in need:
2. Blest to be a bless - ing, Priv - i - leged to care,
3. Add to your be - liev - ing Deeds that prove it true.
4. Let your heart be ten - der And your vi - sion clear;

Feed the mouths that hun - ger, Soothe the wounds that bleed,
Chal - lenged by the need— Ap - par - ent ev - ery - where.
Know - ing Christ as Sav - ior, Make Him Mas - ter, too.
See the world as God sees, Serve all far and near.

Give the cup of wa - ter And the loaf of bread—
Where the world is want - ing, Fill the va - cant place.
Fol - low in His foot - steps, Go where He has trod;
Let your heart be bro - ken By an - oth - er's pain;

Be the hands of Je - sus, Serv - ing in His stead.
Be the means through which the Lord re - veals His grace.
In the world's great trou - ble Risk your - self for God.
Share your rich re - sourc - es, Give and give a - gain.

Text and Tune: Bryan Jeffery Leech, 1931 - ; copyright 1975 by The Evangelical Covenant Church of America; alt.
Tune arr. Fred Bock, 1939 - ; arr. copyright 1976 by Fred Bock Music Company; alt; all rights
reserved. Used by permission.

376

We Are Living, We Are Dwelling

Joel 2:27-29
Joshua 24:14-16

AUSTRIA 8.7.8.7.D.

1. We are liv-ing, we are dwell-ing In a grand and awe-ful time
2. Worlds are chang-ing, old forms crum-bling; Souls of cour-age times de-mand;

When each hour some fate is tell-ing: To be liv-ing is sub-lime.
Those who see the way as proph-ets Lead on toward the prom-ised land.

Rise, O saints, in all thy vig-or; Stand e-rect on ho-ly sod;
Rise, O saints, in all thy vi-sion, Let thy voice be heard a-broad.

Turn from aim-less in-de-ci-sion, Rise up in the strength of God.
Speak! let all thy faith and wis-dom Count for Zi-on, count for God.

Text: A. Cleveland Coxe, 1818-1896, alt.
Tune: Franz Joseph Haydn, 1732-1809.

The City Is Alive, O God

John 3:16, 17
Matthew 23:37

THAXTED C.M.D. with repeat

Unison

1. The cit-y is a-live, O God, With sound of rush-ing feet,
2. O God, in-spire your church to-day To take Christ's ser-vant role,

With flash-ing lights and ra-pid change That pulse through ev-ery street.
To love the world, to hear its claims, To sense its yearn-ing soul;

But oft there's in-hu-man-i-ty Be-hind the bright fa-cade,
To live with-in the mar-ket-place, To serve both weak and strong,

And emp-ty souls with hun-gry hearts Cry out for help, O God.
To lose her-self, to share her dream, To give the world her song!

And emp-ty souls with hun-gry hearts Cry out for help, O God.
To lose her-self, to share her dream, To give the world her song.

Text: William Watkins Reid, Jr., 1923 - ; alt.; copyright 1969 The Hymn Society of America; used by permission.
Tune: Gustav Holst, 1874-1934, adapted from *The Planets*; copyright 1921 Goodwin & Tabb; used by permission of G. Schirmer, Inc.

374

Psalm 31:1-3, 5
I Nephi 6:38-41

Lead On, O King Eternal

LANCASHIRE 7.6.7.6.D.

1. Lead on, O King E - ter - nal. The day of march has come;
2. Lead on, O King E - ter - nal, Till sin's fierce war shall cease,
3. Lead on, O King E - ter - nal. We fol - low, not with fears,

Hence-forth in fields of con - quest Thy tents shall be our home.
And ho - li - ness shall whis - per The sweet a - men of peace;
For glad-ness breaks like morn - ing Wher-e'er thy face ap - pears.

Through days of prep - a - ra - tion Thy grace has made us strong,
For not with swords' loud clash - ing Nor roll of stir - ring drums—
Thy cross is lift - ed o'er us, We jour - ney in its light;

And now, O King E - ter - nal, We lift our bat - tle song.
With deeds of love and mer - cy The heaven - ly king-dom comes.
The crown a - waits the con - quest; Lead on, O God of might. A-men.

Text: Ernest W. Shurtleff, 1862-1917.
Tune: Henry Smart, 1813-1879.

Where Restless Crowds Are Thronging 373

Luke 4:18, 19
Mark 6:33-37 (32-37)

CRAIGMILLAR 7.6.7.6.D.

1. Where rest-less crowds are throng-ing A-long the cit-y ways,
2. In scenes of want and sor-row And haunts of fla-grant wrong,
3. O Christ, be-hold thy peo-ple— They press on ev-'ry hand!

Where pride and greed and tur-moil Con-sume the fe-vered days,
In homes where kind-ness fal-ters And strife and fear are strong,
Bring light to all the cit-ies Of our be-lov-ed land.

Where vain am-bi-tions ban-ish All thoughts of praise and prayer,
In bus-y street of bar-ter, In lone-ly thor-ough-fare,
May all our bit-ter striv-ing Give way to vi-sions fair

The peo-ple's spir-its wa-ver: But thou, O Christ, art there.
The peo-ple's spir-its lan-guish: But thou, O Christ, art there.
Of right-eous-ness and jus-tice: For thou, O Christ, art there.

Text: Thomas Curtis Clark, 1877-1953; alt.; from *Five City Hymns,* copyright 1954 The Hymn Society of America;
used by permission.
Tune: Erik Routley, 1917 - ; from *Eternal Light* by Erik Routley; copyright 1971 Carl Fischer, Inc., New York.
International copyright secured. All rights reserved. Used by permission.

372
Behold the Savior at Your Door

Revelation 3:20
D. and C. 63:1a

THE SAVIOR AT THE DOOR C.M. with refrain

1. Be-hold the Sav-ior at your door, Your kind - est, tru - est friend,
2. Oh, yes, the bless-ed Son of God, Though Lord of all a - bove,
3. "If an - y - one will hear my voice And o - pen un - to me,

Is seek - ing en-trance to your heart, Your life with his to blend.
Now paus-es at your low - ly door And speaks in tones of love.
I'll sup with him and he with me, And friends we'll al - ways be."

Refrain

The Sav - ior's knock-ing at your door, And ask - ing en - trance in;

He's knock - ing, ask - ing o'er and o'er; O o - pen un - to him!

Text: W. H. Bagby, 19th century, U. S.
Tune: James H. Rosecrans, 19th century, U. S.

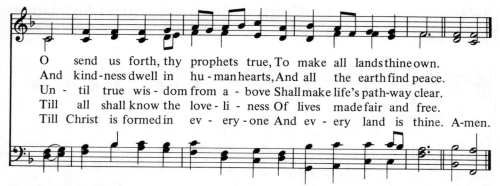

O send us forth, thy prophets true, To make all lands thine own.
And kind-ness dwell in hu-man hearts, And all the earth find peace.
Un - til true wis - dom from a - bove Shall make life's path-way clear.
Till all shall know the love - li - ness Of lives made fair and free.
Till Christ is formed in ev - ery - one And ev - ery land is thine. A-men.

Text: Henry H. Tweedy, 1868-1953.
Tune: English Traditional Melody; coll., adapt. and arr. by Ralph Vaughan Williams, 1872-1958; from *The English Hymnal* by permission of Oxford University Press.

Jesus Calls Us O'er the Tumult 371

Matthew 4:19 (20)
Mosiah 3:16, 17

GALILEE 8.7.8.7.

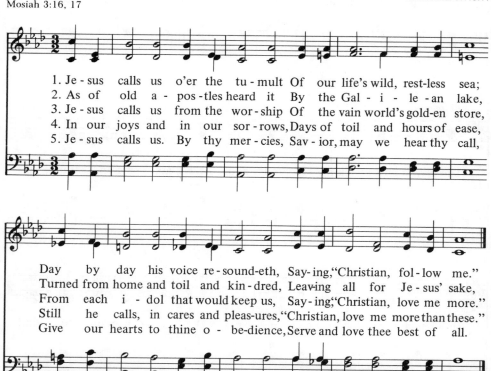

1. Je - sus calls us o'er the tu - mult Of our life's wild, rest-less sea;
2. As of old a - pos -tles heard it By the Gal - i - le - an lake,
3. Je - sus calls us from the wor - ship Of the vain world's gold-en store,
4. In our joys and in our sor - rows, Days of toil and hours of ease,
5. Je - sus calls us. By thy mer - cies, Sav - ior, may we hear thy call,

Day by day his voice re-sound-eth, Say-ing, "Christian, fol-low me."
Turned from home and toil and kin-dred, Leav-ing all for Je - sus' sake,
From each i - dol that would keep us, Say-ing, "Christian, love me more."
Still he calls, in cares and pleas-ures, "Christian, love me more than these."
Give our hearts to thine o - be-dience, Serve and love thee best of all.

Text: Cecil F. Alexander, 1818-1895, alt.
Tune: William H. Jude, 1851-1922.

370   Eternal God, Whose Power Upholds

II Nephi 9:133-137
Romans 11:33, 34, 36

FOREST GREEN C.M.D.

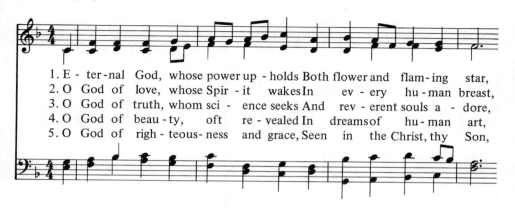

1. E - ter-nal God, whose power up - holds Both flower and flam-ing star,
2. O God of love, whose Spir - it wakes In ev - ery hu-man breast,
3. O God of truth, whom sci - ence seeks And rev - erent souls a - dore,
4. O God of beau-ty, oft re - vealed In dreams of hu - man art,
5. O God of righ - teous-ness and grace, Seen in the Christ, thy Son,

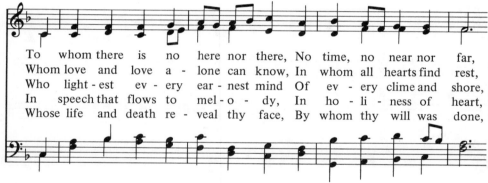

To whom there is no here nor there, No time, no near nor far,
Whom love and love a - lone can know, In whom all hearts find rest,
Who light-est ev - ery ear - nest mind Of ev - ery clime and shore,
In speech that flows to mel - o - dy, In ho - li - ness of heart,
Whose life and death re - veal thy face, By whom thy will was done,

No a - lien race, no for - eign shore, No child un-sought, un - known,
Help us to spread thy gra - cious reign Till greed and hate shall cease,
Dis - pel the gloom of er - ror's night, Of ig - nor-ance and fear,
Teach us to shun all ug - li - ness That blinds our eyes to thee,
In - spire thy her - alds of good news To live thy life di - vine,

Bear Each Other's Burdens

369

Galatians 6:2
D. and C. 150:7

OLWEN (Poverty)
6.6.8.D. with repeat

1. Bear each oth-er's bur-dens, Share each oth-er's suf-f'ring,
And love as the Sav-ior has shown. The strength of our
car-ing Heals pain souls are bear-ing And we are no
long-er a - lone. Bear each oth-er's bur-dens, Share
each oth-er's suf-f'ring, And love as the Sav-ior has shown.

2. God calls us to heal-ing, Di - vine love re - veal-ing,
Wher-ev-er we meet hu - man need. In times so mo -
men-tous, Ex - pect-ant, por - ten-tous, The world suf-fers
an - guish and greed. God calls us to heal-ing, Divine love re - veal - ing, Wher-ev-er we meet hu - man need.

Text: Barbara Howard, 1930 - ; copyright 1980 Reorganized Church of Jesus Christ of Latter Day Saints.
Tune: Welsh Carol; arr. Caradog Roberts, 1879-1935; used by permission of the Union of Welsh Independents, Swansea, Wales.

Commission and Commitment

Challenge 369-394

Stewardship 395-402

Service and Commitment 403-467

Witness 468-479

Benediction and Sending Forth 480-501

368

O Perfect Love

Matthew 19:4-6
Ephesians 5:25-28

O PERFECT LOVE 11.10.11.10.

1. O per-fect Love, all hu-man thought tran-scend-ing,
2. O per-fect Life, be thou their full as-sur-ance
3. Grant them the joy which bright-ens earth-ly sor-row;

Low-ly we kneel in prayer be-fore thy throne,
Of ten-der char-i-ty and stead-fast faith,
Grant them the peace which calms all earth-ly strife,

That theirs may be the love which knows no end-ing
Of pa-tient hope and qui-et, brave en-dur-ance,
And to life's day the glo-rious un-known mor-row

Whom thou for-ev-er-more dost join in one.
With child-like trust that fears nor pain nor death.
That dawns up-on e-ter-nal love and life. A-men.

Text: Dorothy Frances Blomfield Gurney, 1858-1932. Used by permission of Oxford University Press.
Tune: Arr. from Joseph Barnby, 1838-1896.

O God, from Whom Mankind Derives Its Name 367

D. and C. 111:2
I Corinthians 13:1-7

CARPENTER 10.10.10.10.
See 494 for a lower setting.

1. O God, from whom man - kind de - rives its name,
2. May through their un - ion oth - er lives be blessed,
3. Pre - serve their days from in - ward - ness of heart;
4. From stage to stage on life's un - fold - ing way
5. Lord, bless us all to whom this day brings joy.

Whose cov - e - nant of grace re - mains the same,
Their door be wide to stran - ger and to guest.
To each the gift of truth - ful speech im - part.
Bring to their minds the vows they make this day.
Let no e - vents our u - ni - ty de - stroy,

Be with these two who now be - fore you wait;
Give them the un - der - stand - ing that is kind;
Their bond be strong a - gainst all strain and strife
Your Spir - it be their guide in ev - ery move,
And help us, till all sense of time is lost,

Grant them the bless - ing of an o - pen mind.
En - large the love they come to con - se - crate.
A - mid the chang - es of this earth - ly life.
Their faith in Christ the ba - sis of their love.
To live in love and not to count the cost. A - men.

Text: Fred Kaan, 1929 - ; copyright © 1968 by Galliard Ltd. Sole U. S. agent: Galaxy Music Corp., N. Y. Used by permission.
Tune: Keith Landis, 1922 - ; harm. Erik Routley, 1917 - ; copyright 1977 Praise Publications, Inc.; used by permission.

366 By Revelation Called of God

Alma 12:2-5
Ephesians 4:11-13

MANOAH C.M.

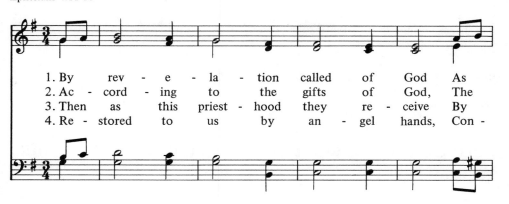

1. By rev - e - la - tion called of God As
2. Ac - cord - ing to the gifts of God, The
3. Then as this priest - hood they re - ceive By
4. Re - stored to us by an - gel hands, Con -

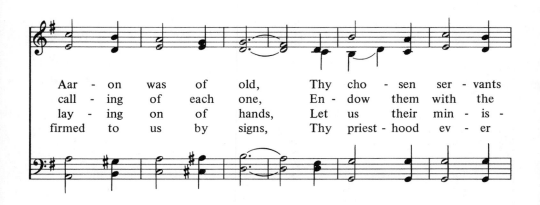

Aar - on was of old, Thy cho - sen ser - vants
call - ing of each one, En - dow them with the
lay - ing on of hands, Let us their min - is -
firmed to us by signs, Thy priest - hood ev - er

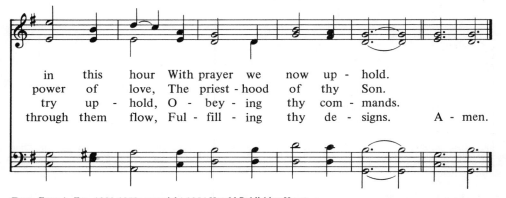

in this hour With prayer we now up - hold.
power of love, The priest - hood of thy Son.
try up - hold, O - bey - ing thy com - mands.
through them flow, Ful - fill - ing thy de - signs. A - men.

Text: Evan A. Fry, 1902-1959; copyright 1956 Herald Publishing House.
Tune: Arr. from Gioacchino A. Rossini, 1792-1868, in Henry W. Greatorex's *Collection of Church Music*, 1851.

ply,   And clothe   thy   priests with   righ - teous - ness.
heart, And   love   the   souls whom   thou   dost   love.   A - men.

Text: James Montgomery, 1771-1854.
Tune: Plainsong, Mode I, arr. Lowell Mason, 1792-1872.

Lord God, We Meet in Jesus' Name

365

John 15:15, 16
Moroni 3:1-3

HICKS L.M.

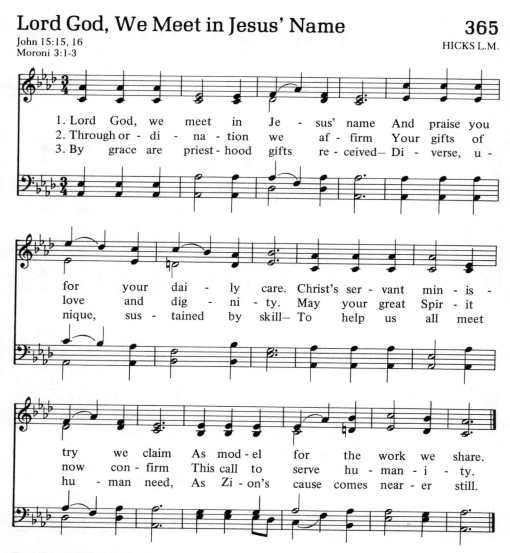

1. Lord   God,   we   meet   in   Je - sus' name   And   praise you
2. Through or - di - na - tion   we   af - firm   Your   gifts of
3. By   grace   are   priest - hood   gifts   re - ceived—   Di - verse, u -

for   your   dai - ly   care. Christ's ser - vant   min - is -
love   and   dig - ni - ty. May   your   great   Spir - it
nique,   sus - tained   by   skill—   To   help   us   all   meet

try   we   claim   As   mod - el   for   the   work   we   share.
now   con - firm   This   call   to   serve   hu - man - i - ty.
hu - man   need,   As   Zi - on's   cause   comes   near - er   still.

Text: Kenneth L. McLaughlin, 1951 - ; copyright 1980 Reorganized Church of Jesus Christ of Latter Day Saints.
Tune: Arthur H. Mills, 1870-1943.

363 According to the Gifts That God

D. and C. 119:8b
I Peter 2:9

EVAN C.M.

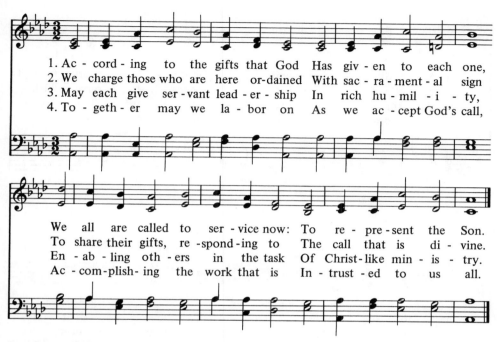

1. Ac - cord - ing to the gifts that God Has giv - en to each one,
2. We charge those who are here or - dained With sac - ra - ment - al sign
3. May each give ser - vant lead - er - ship In rich hu - mil - i - ty,
4. To - geth - er may we la - bor on As we ac - cept God's call,

We all are called to ser - vice now: To re - pre - sent the Son.
To share their gifts, re - spond - ing to The call that is di - vine.
En - ab - ling oth - ers in the task Of Christ - like min - is - try.
Ac - com - plish - ing the work that is In - trust - ed to us all.

Text: Peter A. Judd, 1943 - ; copyright 1980 Reorganized Church of Jesus Christ of Latter Day Saints.
Tune: William H. Havergal, 1793-1870.

364 Lord, Pour Thy Spirit from on High

Mosiah 9:51-55
I Peter 5:1-3

HAMBURG L.M.

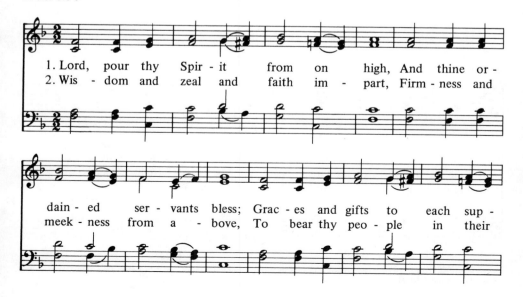

1. Lord, pour thy Spir - it from on high, And thine or -
2. Wis - dom and zeal and faith im - part, Firm - ness and

dain - ed ser - vants bless; Grac - es and gifts to each sup -
meek - ness from a - bove, To bear thy peo - ple in their

A Diligent and Grateful Heart

362

D. and C. 97:4c, d
D. and C. 153:9b

ST. COLUMBA C.M.

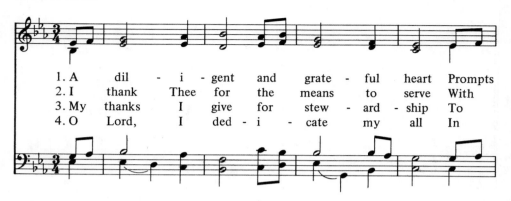

1. A dil - i - gent and grate - ful heart Prompts
2. I thank Thee for the means to serve With
3. My thanks I give for stew - ard - ship To
4. O Lord, I ded - i - cate my all In

me to sing thy praise. Thy love and mer - cies
tal - ents and with tithes, For shar - ing brings the
min - is - ter through deeds, To serve and share with
this re - sponse to thee. Help me to mag - ni-

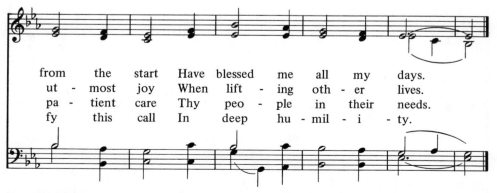

from the start Have blessed me all my days.
ut - most joy When lift - ing oth - er lives.
pa - tient care Thy peo - ple in their needs.
fy this call In deep hu - mil - i - ty.

Text: Raymond Gunn, 1925 - ; copyright 1980 Reorganized Church of Jesus Christ of Latter Day Saints.
Tune: Traditional Irish Melody.

361 Behold Thy Sons and Daughters, Lord

John 14:26
II Nephi 13:10, 15-17

CONFIRMATION C.M.

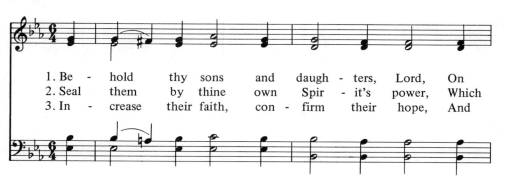

1. Be - hold thy sons and daugh - ters, Lord, On
2. Seal them by thine own Spir - it's power, Which
3. In - crease their faith, con - firm their hope, And

whom we lay our hands; They have ful - filled the
pu - ri - fies from sin, And may they find from
guide them in the way; With com - fort bear their

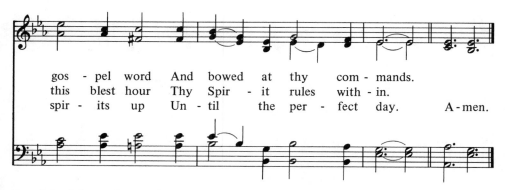

gos - pel word And bowed at thy com - mands.
this blest hour Thy Spir - it rules with - in.
spir - its up Un - til the per - fect day. A - men.

Text: Parley P. Pratt, 1807-1857; alt.
Tune: Louise Hills Lewis, 1887-1948.

O Lord, We Come As Children All

360

Romans 6:3-5
Mosiah 2:18-22

MASSACHUSETTS C.M.D.

Unison (or harmony *)

1. O Lord, we come as chil-dren all Be - fore thy gra - cious face,
2. In con - fir - ma - tion's sac - ra - ment, We can per - ceive thy hand
3. The sym - bol of this sa - cred rite Has mean-ing for us all

And pray thy Ho - ly Spir - it now May per - me - ate this place.
Placed there with those that now con - firm—Oh, lead us by that hand!
As new - born Saints join el - der ones In an - swer to God's call.

While in bap - ti - sm's cleans-ing stream, We con - se - crat - ed there
As we em - brace thy prom-ised grace, A - like both young and old,
Lord Je - sus Christ, em - pow'r us now With Ho - ly Spir - it's might

Our heart, our soul, our mind's in - tent To serve with lov - ing care.
We pray thy Spir - it to sus - tain Our lives, with love en - fold.
To serve thy cause un - flinch-ing - ly, Find fa - vor in thy sight.

* Tenors should read treble clef when necessary.

Text: Alan D. Tyree, 1929 - ; copyright 1980 Reorganized Church of Jesus Christ of Latter Day Saints.
Tune: Katherine K. Davis, 1892-1980; copyright 1964 Abingdon Press. Used with permission.

359 Obedient, Lord, to Thy Command

Acts 8:14-17
D. and C. 53:2a, b

EISENACH L.M.

1. O - be - dient, Lord, to thy com - mand,
2. Bap - tize them with the Ho - ly Ghost,
3. May Spir - it's light and truth and power,

Bap - tized in wa - ter in thy name,
That Spir - it which is teach - er, guide,
Its knowl - edge, wis - dom, joy, and peace,

These now thy prom - ised bless - ing seek,
That in their hearts pre - pared by faith
Its tes - ti - mo - ny of thy Son

The seal of their a - dop - tion claim.
The Com - fort - er may now a - bide.
Bring life that nev - er - more shall cease. A - men.

Text: Evan A. Fry, 1902-1959; copyright 1956 Herald Publishing House.
Tune: Johann H. Schein, 1586-1630; harm. Johann Sebastian Bach, 1685-1750.

O God, to Us Be Present Here

358

D. and C. 17:18b, c
Romans 8:14-16

ST. MATTHEW C.M.D.

1. O God, to us be pres-ent here, In lay-ing on of hands,
2. We claim the blest re - la-tion-ship, Em - pow-ered by your Son,
3. We do not claim the Spir-it's gifts For priv - i - lege or gain;

Sym - bol - ic of the Spir-it's pow-er That ser-vant-hood de-mands.
That shat-ters ev - ery bar-ri - er And makes of man-y one.
Who - ev - er knows the ser-vant's joy Must bear the ser-vant's pain.

This sac - ra - men-tal act con-firms Bap-ti - sm's call to life,
The new com - mu - ni - ty in Christ Is giv - en from a - bove;
Yet we would ask for strength to share The suf-fering Lord's tra -vail,

That fash-ions pur - pose from de - spair And har-mo - ny from strife.
The Spir - it bonds the Saints of God In u - ni - ty and love.
For grace to keep the faith un - til Your king-dom shall pre - vail.

Text: Geoffrey F. Spencer, 1927 - ; copyright 1980 Reorganized Church of Jesus Christ of Latter Day Saints.
Tune: William Croft, 1678-1727.

357 My Lord, I Come This Hour to Make

Mosiah 3:8, 9
Acts 2:37-39

NORSE AIR (No Other Plea, or Landas) C.M.D.
See 405 for a lower setting.

1. My Lord, I come this hour to make My cov-e-nant with thee.
2. A life-long prom-ise I would make: Thee on-ly will I serve.

Re-veal-ing truth and bound-less grace, Thy love has won my heart.
I seek for-give-ness now of thee; I come to be re-born.

I have no oth-er gift for thee Ex-cept the life I bring.
En-dow my life with love and power To grow and live for thee.

I give my-self, so let me be A hum-ble child of thine.
Help me re-flect thy won-drous love As oth-ers have for me.

Text: William F. Webb, 1928 - . Copyright 1980 Reorganized Church of Jesus Christ of Latter Day Saints.
Tune: Norse Folk Melody; arr. William J. Kirkpatrick, 1838-1921.

doubt; Seal us as Christ's, with - in, with - out.
win New life, new hope, re - lease from sin.
Lord; Bap - tize all na - tions with your Word. A - men.

Text: Scott Francis Brenner, 1903 - ; copyright 1972 The Westminster Press; from *The Worshipbook—Services and Hymns*; used and altered by permission.
Tune: Traditional German Melody, arr. by Samuel Dyer, 1785-1835.

O God in Heaven, We Believe

356

DOVE OF PEACE 8.6.8.6.6.

D. and C. 3:16-18
Leviticus 20:7, 8

Unison

1. O God in heav - en, we be - lieve The prom - ise we have read; Thy word with meek - ness we re - ceive, And fol - low Christ, our head, And fol - low Christ, our head.
2. When we re - pent of all our sins And come with bro - ken heart, We to thy cov - e - nant en - ter in And choose the bet - ter part, And choose the bet - ter part.
3. As we are bur - ied in the stream, In Je - sus' bless - ed name, Oh, may thy light up - on us beam, The Spir - it's heav - en - ly flame, The Spir - it's heav - en - ly flame.
4. O Lord, ac - cept our hum - ble prayer, And all our sins for - give; New life im - part from this good hour And grant that we may live, And grant that we may live. A - men.

Text: Parley P. Pratt, 1807-1857.
Tune: American Folk Tune; arr. Austin C. Lovelace, 1919 - ; copyright 1977 by Agape, Carol Stream, IL 60187; international copyright secured; all rights reserved; used by permission.

354 Here at the Water's Brink We Stand

Matthew 3:45 (16)
D. and C. 17:21

CONFIRMATION C.M.

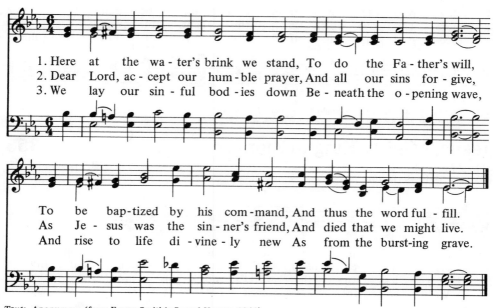

1. Here at the wa-ter's brink we stand, To do the Fa-ther's will,
2. Dear Lord, ac-cept our hum-ble prayer, And all our sins for-give,
3. We lay our sin-ful bod-ies down Be-neath the o-pening wave,

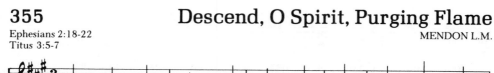

To be bap-tized by his com-mand, And thus the word ful-fill.
As Je-sus was the sin-ner's friend, And died that we might live.
And rise to life di-vine-ly new As from the burst-ing grave.

Text: Anonymous (from Emma Smith's *Sacred Hymns*, 1841).
Tune: Louise Hills Lewis, 1887-1948.

355 Descend, O Spirit, Purging Flame

Ephesians 2:18-22
Titus 3:5-7

MENDON L.M.

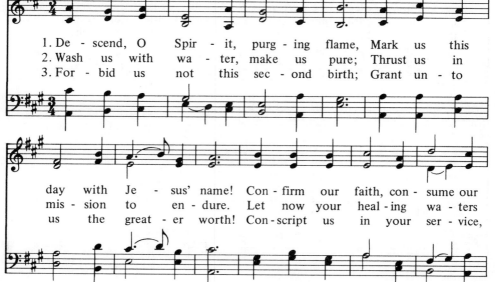

1. De-scend, O Spir-it, purg-ing flame, Mark us this
2. Wash us with wa-ter, make us pure; Thrust us in
3. For-bid us not this sec-ond birth; Grant un-to

day with Je-sus' name! Con-firm our faith, con-sume our
mis-sion to en-dure. Let now your heal-ing wa-ters
us the great-er worth! Con-script us in your ser-vice,

day New life in thee, with thine be - gun.
more— Thy love which is the light, the way.
thee, And in bap - ti - sm seal it now. A - men.

Text: Roy A. Cheville, 1897 - ; copyright 1956 Herald Publishing House.
Tune: Adapted from *Katholisches Gesangbuch*, Vienna, c. 1774.

Jesus, Mighty King in Zion 353

STUTTGART 8.7.8.7.

II Nephi 13:7-10
Matthew 28:17-19 (18-20)

1. Je - sus, might - y King in Zi - on, Thou a -
2. As an em - blem of thy pas - sion, And thy
3. Fear - less of the world's de - spis - ing, We the
4. We will fol - low none but Je - sus, Je - sus

lone our Guide shalt be; Thy com - mis - sion we re -
vic - tory o'er the grave, We who seek the great sal -
an - cient path pur - sue, Bur - ied with our Lord, and
is the Life, the Way; This the path in which he

ly on, We will fol - low none but thee.
va - tion Are bap - tized be - neath the wave.
ris - ing To a life di - vine - ly new.
leads us, This the gate to end - less day. A - men.

Text: John Fellows, ?-1785.
Tune: Christian F. Witt, 1660-1716, *Psalmodia Sacra*, 1715; adapt. by Henry J. Gauntlett, 1805-1876.

351   Redeeming Grace Has Touched Our Lives

Romans 6:3, 4
D. and C. 39:2

DOMINUS REGIT ME 8.7.8.7.

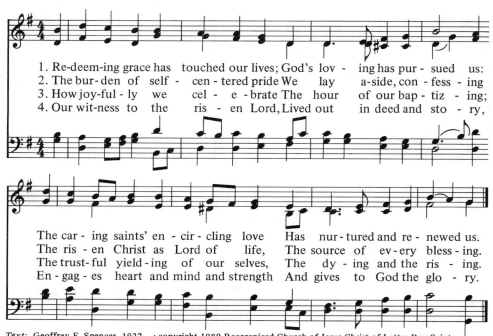

1. Re-deem-ing grace has touched our lives; God's lov - ing has pur - sued us:
2. The bur - den of self - cen - tered pride We lay a-side, con - fess - ing
3. How joy-ful - ly we cel - e -brate The hour of our bap - tiz - ing;
4. Our wit-ness to the ris - en Lord, Lived out in deed and sto - ry,

The car - ing saints' en - cir - cling love Has nur-tured and re - newed us.
The ris - en Christ as Lord of life, The source of ev - ery bless - ing.
The trust-ful yield-ing of our selves, The dy - ing and the ris - ing.
En - gag - es heart and mind and strength And gives to God the glo - ry.

Text: Geoffrey F. Spencer, 1927 - ; copyright 1980 Reorganized Church of Jesus Christ of Latter Day Saints.
Tune: John B. Dykes, 1823-1876.

352   O Lord, Thy People Gathered Here

Romans 8:16-17
II Nephi 13:22-26

HURSLEY L.M.

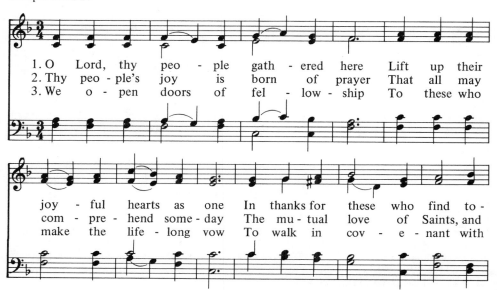

1. O Lord, thy peo - ple gath - ered here Lift up their
2. Thy peo - ple's joy is born of prayer That all may
3. We o - pen doors of fel - low-ship To these who

joy - ful hearts as one In thanks for these who find to -
com - pre - hend some-day The mu - tual love of Saints, and
make the life - long vow To walk in cov - e - nant with

Baptized in Water

350

Moroni 6:3-5
Matthew 3:40-43 (13-15)

BROTHER JAMES' AIR 8.6.8.6.8.6.

1. Bap - tized in wa - ter, you be - came a per - son born
2. To some it comes as burst - ing light in this, your spe -
3. You now share mem - ber - ship with - in a larg - er fam -

a - new. You made a cov - e - nant, and now God
cial hour; It may come slow - ly, and in time, as
i - ly. Each time you take the bread and wine, you'll

adds his prom - ise, too: His Ho - ly Spir - it
an un - fold - ing flower. How - ev - er it may
know that you will be A - mong the man - y

can be yours to - day and all life through.
come to you, you'll feel God's love and power.
car - ing Saints in world com - mu - ni - ty.

Text: Naomi Russell, 1921 - ; alt. by Alan D. Tyree, 1929 - ; copyright 1980 Reorganized Church of Jesus Christ of Latter Day Saints.
Tune: James Leith Macbeth Bain, c. 1840-1925; harm. Gordon Jacob, 1895 - ; adapted by Rosalee Elser, 1925 - ; by permission of Oxford University Press.

349

Mosiah 2:25, 27
Matthew 19:13-15

The Vision of a Life to Be

GRATEFULNESS L.M.

1. The vi - sion of a life to be, The joy and
2. What gifts in bless - ing can we share? A home of
3. We do not pray for shel - tered ease Where risk and
4. Not for one child our prayers re - sound, But for the

hope of all the race, The price - less gift of
true com - mu - ni - ty, A con - gre - ga - tion's
strug - gle have no part, But for - ti - tude for
chil - dren of the earth May joy in - crease and

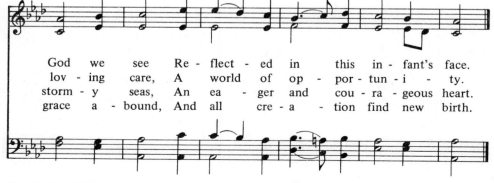

God we see Re - flect - ed in this in - fant's face.
lov - ing care, A world of op - por - tun - i - ty.
storm - y seas, An ea - ger and cou - ra - geous heart.
grace a - bound, And all cre - a - tion find new birth.

Text: Geoffrey F. Spencer, 1927 - ; copyright 1980 Reorganized Church of Jesus Christ of Latter Day Saints.
Tune: Mary A. Bradford, 1821-1902.

fess,   And   ev - ery   child   you   long   to   bless.
prayer For   par - ents' faith, for   church's   care.
ate   To   bless this   life   we   con - se - crate.   A - men.

Text: Roy A. Cheville, 1897 - ; alt.; copyright 1956 Herald Publishing House.
Tune: H. Percy Smith, 1825-1898.

We Bring Our Children, Lord, to Thee   348

Mark 10:11-14 (13-16)   HESPERUS L.M.
D. and C. 68:4a-c

1. We   bring   our   chil - dren, Lord, to   thee   Be - fore this
2. Teach us   to   know   our   chil - dren's worth, To   cel - e -
3. We   thank thee for   each   pre - cious life   Born in - to

loved com - mu - ni - ty,   Con - firm - ing   pres - ence
brate their gifts   from birth. Let   each   be   par - ent,
beau - ty,   in - to   strife. Let   each   child   feel   thy

of   thy   grace   As   lit - tle   ones   en - rich   this place.
lov - ing   all,   Re - spond-ing gent - ly   to   each call.
time - less   care,   Un - ceas - ing, lov - ing, ev - ery - where.

Text: Evelyn Maples, 1919 - ; copyright 1980 Reorganized Church of Jesus Christ of Latter Day Saints.
Tune: Henry Baker, 1835-1910.

346 Lord, Let Thy Holy Spirit Come

Romans 9:14-16
D. and C. 68:4a-c

RICHMOND C.M.

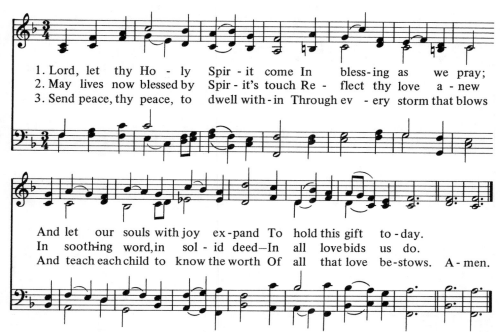

1. Lord, let thy Ho - ly Spir - it come In bless-ing as we pray;
2. May lives now blessed by Spir - it's touch Re - flect thy love a - new
3. Send peace, thy peace, to dwell with - in Through ev - ery storm that blows

And let our souls with joy ex-pand To hold this gift to - day.
In sooth-ing word, in sol - id deed—In all love bids us do.
And teach each child to know the worth Of all that love be-stows. A - men.

Text: Mabel Williams Crayne, 1880-1980; rev. Evelyn Maples, 1919 - ; copyright 1980 Reorganized Church of Jesus Christ of Latter Day Saints.
Tune: Thomas Haweis, 1734-1820; abr. by Samuel Webbe, Jr., 1770-1843.

347 O Master to All Children Dear

Moroni 8:18
D. and C. 17:19

MARYTON L.M.

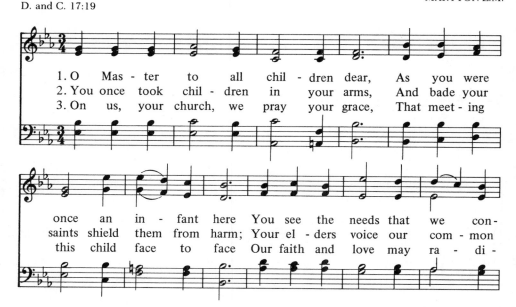

1. O Mas - ter to all chil - dren dear, As you were
2. You once took chil - dren in your arms, And bade your
3. On us, your church, we pray your grace, That meet - ing

once an in - fant here You see the needs that we con-
saints shield them from harm; Your el - ders voice our com - mon
this child face to face Our faith and love may ra - di-

You Satisfy the Hungry Heart

345

John 6:32-34
I Corinthians 10:16, 17

GIFT OF FINEST WHEAT
C.M. with refrain

Unison (or harmony)

Refrain

You sat-is-fy the hun-gry heart With gift of fin-est wheat;

Manuals only

Come give to us, O sav-ing Lord, The bread of life to eat. *Fine*

Pedal

1. As when the shep-herd calls his sheep, They know and heed his voice,
2. With joy-ful lips we sing to you Our praise and grat-i-tude,
3. Here is the cup we bless and share The blood of Christ out-poured;
4. The mys-t'ry of your pres-ence, Lord, No mor-tal tongue can tell:
5. You give your-self to us, O Lord; Then self-less let us be,

Manuals only   *Pedal*

Repeat Refrain

So when you call your fam-'ly, Lord, We fol-low and re-joice.
That you should count us wor-thy, Lord, To share this heav'n-ly food.
And here one cup, one loaf, de-clare Our one-ness in the Lord.
Whom all the world can-not con-tain Comes in our hearts to dwell.
To serve each oth-er in your name In truth and char-i-ty.

Text: Omer Westendorf, 1916 - .
Tune: Robert E. Kreutz, 1922 - .
Text and tune copyright 1976 Board of Governors, 41st International Eucharistic Congress, Inc. Used by permission of the Archdiocesan Music Office, Philadelphia, PA.

344

Luke 24:29-31 (30-32)
Acts 2:46, 47

Come, Risen Lord

SURSUM CORDA 10.10.10.10.

Unison (or harmony)

1. Come, ris - en Lord, and deign to be our guest;
2. We meet, as in that up - per room they met,
3. One bod - y we, one bod - y who par - take,
4. One with each oth - er, Lord, for one in thee,

Nay, let us be thy guests— the feast is thine;
Thou at the ta - ble, bless - ing, yet dost stand;
One church u - nit - ed in com - mun - ion blest;
Who art one Sav - ior and one liv - ing Head;

Thy - self at thine own board make man - i - fest
"This is my bod - y;" so thou giv - est yet:
One name we bear, one bread of life we break,
Then o - pen thou our eyes, that we may see;

In this our sac - ra - ment of bread and wine.
Faith still re - ceives the cup as from thy hand.
With all thy saints on earth and saints at rest.
Be known to us in break - ing of the bread. A - men.

Text: George Wallace Briggs, 1875-1959; from *Enlarged Songs of Praise* by permission of Oxford University Press.
Tune: Alfred M. Smith, 1879-1971; copyright by composer. Used by permission of Mrs. Alfred M. Smith.

face to the ris-ing sun, O Lord, have mer-cy on me. A-men.

Text: American Folk Hymn.
Tune: American Folk Hymn; harm. by Rosalee Elser, 1925 - ; copyright 1980 Rosalee Elser; used by permission.

An Upper Room Did Our Lord Prepare   343

D. and C. 17:22a
I Corinthians 11:23-26

FOLKSONG 9.8.9.8.

Unison

1. An Up-per Room did our Lord pre-pare for those he
loved un-til the end: and his dis-ci-ples still gath-er
there, to cel-e-brate their Ris-en Friend.

2. A last-ing gift Je-sus gave his own: to share his
bread, his lov-ing cup. What-ev-er bur-dens may bow us
down, he by his Cross shall lift us up.

3. And af-ter Sup-per he washed their feet, for ser-vice,
too, is sac-ra-ment. In him our joy shall be made complete— sent out to serve, as he was sent.

4. No end there is! We de-part in peace. He loves beyond our ut-ter-most: in ev-ery room in our Fa-ther's
house he will be there, as Lord and Host.

Text: F. Pratt Green, 1903 - ; used by permission of Oxford University Press.
Tune: English Traditional Melody; arr. John Wilson, 1905 - ; by permission of Oxford University Press.

342

Let Us Break Bread Together

D. and C. 17:22a
I Corinthians 11:26-29

LET US BREAK BREAD 10.10. with refrain

1. Let us break bread to-geth-er on our knees; Let us break bread to-geth-er on our knees. When I fall on my knees, with my face to the ris-ing sun, O Lord, have mer-cy on me.

2. Let us drink wine to-geth-er on our knees; Let us drink wine to-geth-er on our knees.

3. Let us praise God to-geth-er on our knees. Let us praise God to-geth-er on our knees. When I fall on my knees with my

Remembering Thy Son, O God

341

I John 1:7-9
Mosiah 2:3

MARNIE 12.10.12.10.

1. Re - mem - ber - ing thy Son, O God, to thee we come
2. Christ gives us in his stead this blest me - mo - rial bread
3. Di - rect us in thy way; be with us ev - 'ry day.

A - ware of sins from which we seek re - lease.
That we may eat of it, and drink the wine;
Lord, touch our eyes that we may clear - ly see

For - give our er - ring ways on this thy ho - ly day;
As we par - take, dear Lord, in keep - ing with thy word,
The plan thou hast de - signed for us and hu - man - kind;

For - give us, Lord, we pray, and grant thy peace.
Touch ev - 'ry heart and make it tru - ly thine.
O may we ev - er find our faith in thee.

Text: Naomi Russell, 1921 - ; copyright 1980 Reorganized Church of Jesus Christ of Latter Day Saints.
Tune: Harold Neal, 1916 - ; arr. Rosalee Elser, 1925 - ; copyright 1980 Reorganized Church of Latter Day Saints.

340

For Bread Before Us Broken

I Corinthians 10:16, 17
III Nephi 8:33-39

EWING 7.6.7.6.D.

1. For bread be-fore us bro-ken, For wine be-fore us poured,
2. We join in sol-emn prom-ise Here at this ho-ly board

For words which thou hast spo-ken, We give thee thanks, O Lord.
That we may be more wor-thy To have thy Spir-it, Lord.

In prayer that we'll be strength-ened, And be a-gain re-stored,
For serv-ice now en-dow us, As-sured of watch and ward,

In faith that thou wilt aid us, We seek thy ta-ble, Lord.
And send us forth u-nit-ed To build thy king-dom, Lord. A-men.

Text: Roy A. Cheville, 1897 - . Copyright 1956 by Herald Publishing House.
Tune: Alexander Ewing, 1830-1895.

Beneath the Forms of Outward Rite

339

John 6:33, 34
I Corinthians 10:16, 17

ST. COLUMBA C.M.

1. Be - neath the forms of out - ward rite Thy
2. The bread is al - ways sa - cred bread Which
3. The bless - ed cup is on - ly passed In
4. Oh, Mas - ter, through these sym - bols shared, Re -

sup - per, Lord, is spread In ev - ery qui - et
feeds our com - mon need, And when we bear each
mem - o - ry of Thee, For life a - new pours
store us, in this hour, To be Thy bod - y

up - per room Where faint - ing souls are fed.
oth - er's pain We feast with thee in - deed.
out its wine In love that sets us free.
here on earth With sac - ra - men - tal power.

Text: James A. Blaisdell, 1867-1957; alt. by Barbara Howard, 1930 - ; copyright 1980 Reorganized Church of Jesus Christ of Latter Day Saints.
Tune: Traditional Irish Melody.

338

Here at Thy Table, Lord, We Meet

Luke 22:19, 20
D. and C. 26:1a-c

COMMUNION C.M.

1. Here at thy ta - ble, Lord, we meet To feed on
2. He who pre - pares this rich re - past Him - self comes
3. Here peace and par - don sweet - ly flow, Oh, what de -
4. Deep was the suf - fering he en - dured Up - on the ac -
5. Sure there was nev - er love so free, Dear Sav - ior,

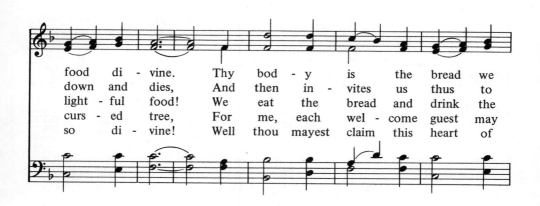

food di - vine. Thy bod - y is the bread we
down and dies, And then in - vites us thus to
light - ful food! We eat the bread and drink the
curs - ed tree, For me, each wel - come guest may
so di - vine! Well thou mayest claim this heart of

eat, Thy pre - cious blood the wine.
feast Up - on the sac - ri - fice.
wine But think on no - bler good.
say, 'Twas all en - dured for me.
me, Which owes so much to thine. A - men.

Text: Samuel Stennett, 1727-1795.
Tune: Charles Fry, 1872-1969.

we May find com-mun-ion here with thee. A-men.

Text: John Cennick, 1718-1755; alt. Margaret Athey, 1936 - .
Tune: Lowell Mason, 1792-1872.

'Twas on That Dark, That Solemn Night   337

III Nephi 8:33, 36
Luke 22:19-21

HAMBURG L.M.

1. 'Twas on that dark, that sol-emn night, When powers of
2. Be-fore the mourn-ful scene be-gan, He took the
3. "This is my bod-y bro-ken for sin; Re-ceive and
4. "Do this," he said, "till time shall end, In mem-ory

earth and hell a-rose A-gainst the Son, e'en
bread and blessed and broke; What love through all his
eat the liv-ing food." He took the cup, and
of your dy-ing friend; Meet at my ta-ble

God's de-light, His friends be-trayed him to his foes.
ac-tions ran! What won-drous words of grace he spoke!
blessed the wine,"'Tis the new cov-'nant in my blood."
and re-cord The love of your de-part-ed Lord."

Text: Isaac Watts, 1674-1748.
Tune: Gregorian Chant, arr. Lowell Mason, 1792-1872.

335

Matthew 26:24, 26 (28, 29)
III Nephi 8:33, 36

O God, the Eternal Father

ST. ALPHEGE 7.6.7.6.

1. O God, the e - ter - nal Fa - ther, Bless to our souls this bread
2. We eat in true re - mem-brance Of sa - cred blood once shed,
3. The name of Christ our Sav - ior We take on us a - new,
4. As we keep his com-mand-ments, Re - mem-bering him each hour,

As we par-take in mem - ory Of Christ, our liv - ing head.
Of Je - sus' bro - ken bod - y, His ris - ing from the dead.
And cov - e - nant be - fore him His will in all to do.
His Spir - it will be with us In guid - ing love and power.

Text: Evan A. Fry 1902-1959; copyright 1956 Herald Publishing House.
Tune: H J. Gauntlett, 1805-1876.

336

Luke 24:29, 30 (30, 31)
D. and C. 59:3

Be Present at Our Table, Lord

UXBRIDGE L.M.

Be pres - ent at our ta - ble, Lord; Be here and

ev - ery-where a - dored; Thy chil - dren bless; and grant that

We Come, Aware of Sin

334

Alma 14:124, 128
Matthew 11:29, 30

NUN DANKET ALLE GOTT 6.7.6.7.6.6.6.6.

1. We come, a-ware of sin with-in us and a-round us,
2. You give us, in your stead, this bread that we may eat it
3. Your rec-on-cil-ing love has freed us in this hour.

To seek for-give-ness, Lord, for wrongs that long have bound us.
And have your Spir-it near to guide us as we need it.
We go re-newed, re-stored, through your re-deeming pow-er.

Help us to find re-lease through your per-vad-ing peace
Through this sym-bol-ic wine, you grant us strength di-vine;
As dark-ness leaves with dawn, our bur-dens now are gone,

And fill our com-ing days with grat-i-tude and praise.
We drink and feel our souls a-gain be-com-ing whole.
Each crush-ing care e-rased by mir-a-cle of grace.

Text: Naomi Russell, 1921 - ; copyright 1980 Reorganized Church of Jesus Christ of Latter Day Saints.
Tune: Johann Cruger, 1598-1662; harm. Felix Mendelssohn, 1809-1847.

333

III Nephi 9:40-45
D. and C. 135:3

Here at Thy Table, Lord

BREAD OF LIFE 6.4.6.4.D.

1. Here at thy ta - ble, Lord, This sa - cred hour,
2. Sit at our feast, dear Lord; Break thou the bread;
3. So shall our life of faith Be full, be sweet,
4. Come then, O ho - ly Christ; Feed us, we pray;

O let us feel thee near In lov - ing power,
Fill thou the cup that brings Life to the dead,
And we shall find our strength For each day meet.
Touch with thy pierc - ed hand Each com - mon day,

Call - ing our thoughts a - way From self and sin
That we may find in thee Par - don and peace,
Fed by thy liv - ing bread, All hun - ger past,
Mak - ing this earth - ly life Full of thy grace

As to thy ban - quet hall We en - ter in.
And from all bond - age win A full re - lease.
We shall be sat - is - fied And saved at last.
Till in the home of heaven We find our place. A - men.

Text: May P. Hoyt.
Tune: William F. Sherwin, 1826-1888.

new un-bound us, keep our hearts with joy a-flame.
lives re-mak-ing, young and old, we praise your name.
make us a-ble; bless-ing on our work we claim.
ser-vice fit-ted, let us now your love pro-claim.

Text: Fred Kaan, 1929 - ; copyright 1968 by Galliard Ltd. Sole U. S. agent: Galaxy Music Corp., N. Y. Used by permission.

Tune: 14th Century German Carol Melody; arr. Ralph Vaughan Williams, 1872-1958; from *The English Hymnal*; used by permission of Oxford University Press.

O Lord, How Can It Be

Psalm 116:12, 13
III Nephi 8:33-39

332

KIRTLAND 6.8.6.

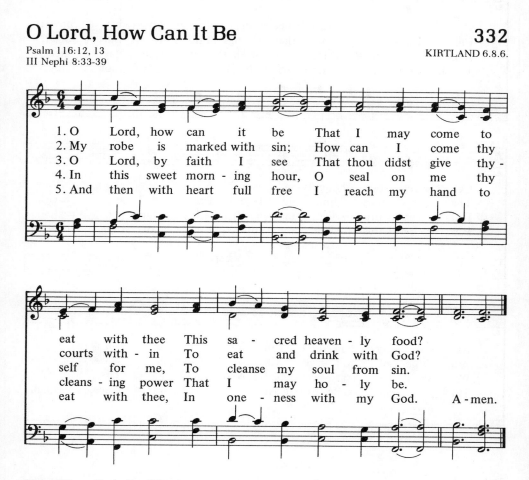

1. O Lord, how can it be That I may come to
2. My robe is marked with sin; How can I come thy
3. O Lord, by faith I see That thou didst give thy-
4. In this sweet morn-ing hour, O seal on me thy
5. And then with heart full free I reach my hand to

eat with thee This sa-cred heaven-ly food?
courts with-in To eat and drink with God?
self for me, To cleanse my soul from sin.
cleans-ing power That I may ho-ly be.
eat with thee, In one-ness with my God. A-men.

Text and Tune: Charles Fry, 1872-1969.

330

In Memory of the Savior's Love

Moroni 6:5, 6
Mark 14:20-24 (22-24)

ST. PETER C.M.

1. In mem-ory of the Sav-ior's love We keep the sa-cred feast,
2. By faith we take the bread of life With which our souls are fed,
3. Be-neath his ban-ner thus we sing The won-ders of his love,

Where each who bears the Sav-ior's name Is made a wel-come guest.
The cup in to-ken of his blood That was for sin-ners shed.
And thus an-tic-i-pate by faith The heaven-ly feast a-bove.

Text: Thomas Cotterill, 1779-1823.
Tune: Alexander R. Reinagle, 1799-1877.

331

Father, Who in Jesus Found Us

D. and C. 11:4, 5
Colossians 3:11-17

QUEM PASTORES 8.8.8.7.

1. Fa - ther, who in Je - sus found us, God whose
2. For the sac - ra - men - tal break - ing, for the
3. For the ser - vice of this ta - ble, lead us
4. Through our call - ing close - ly knit - ted, dai - ly

love is all a - round us, who to free - dom
hon - or of par - tak - ing, for your life our
to a life more sta - ble, for our wit - ness
to your praise com - mit - ted, for a life of

Bread of the World

John 6:47-51
Galatians 2:20

RENDEZ A DIEU 9.8.9.8.D.

remains constant

Bread of the world, in mer-cy bro-ken, Wine of the
soul, in mer-cy shed, By whom the words of life are spo-ken,
And in whose death our sins are dead, Look on the heart by sor-row
bro-ken, Look on the tears by sin-ners shed, And be Thy
feast to us the to-ken That by Thy grace our souls are fed.

Text: Reginald Heber, 1783-1826.
Tune: Attr. to Louis Bourgeois, c. 1510-c. 1561.

328

John 6:56, 57
D. and C. 17:22a

Here, O My Lord

LANGRAN 10.10.10.10.

1. Here, O my Lord, I see thee face to face;
2. Here would I feed up-on the bread of God,
3. This is the hour of ban-quet and of song;

Here would I touch and han-dle things un-seen;
Here drink with thee the roy-al wine of heaven;
This is the heaven-ly ta-ble spread for me.

Here grasp with firm-er hand the e-ter-nal grace,
Here would I lay a-side each earth-ly load,
Here let me feast, and feast-ing still pro-long

And all my wea-ri-ness up-on thee lean.
Here taste a-fresh the calm of sin for-given.
The brief, bright hour of fel-low-ship with thee. A-men.

Text: Horatius Bonar, 1808-1889.
Tune: James Langran, 1835-1909.

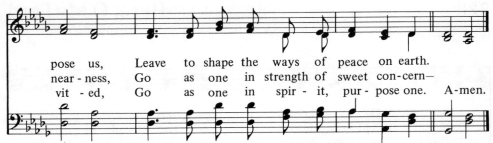

pose us, Leave to shape the ways of peace on earth.
near - ness, Go as one in strength of sweet con-cern—
vit - ed, Go as one in spir - it, pur - pose one. A-men.

Text: Cleo Hanthorne Moon, 1904 - ; copyright 1980 Reorganized Church of Jesus Christ of Latter Day Saints.
Tune: W. G. Tomer, 1832-1896.

Now Let Us from This Table Rise 327

I Corinthians 11:26
John 6:35

WAREHAM L.M.

1. Now let us from this ta - ble rise Re - newed in
2. With minds a - lert up - held by grace, To spread the
3. To fill each hu - man house with love, It is the
4. Then give us cour - age, Fa - ther - God, To choose a -

bod - y, mind, and soul; With Christ we die and
Word in speech and deed, We fol - low in the
sac - ra - ment of care; The work that Christ be -
gain the pil - grim way, And help us to ac -

live a - gain, His self - less love has made us whole.
steps of Christ At one with man in hope and need.
gan to do We hum - bly pledge our - selves to share.
cept with joy The chal - lenge of to - mor - row's day.

Text: Fred Kaan, 1929 - ; copyright 1968 by Galliard Ltd. Sole U. S. agent: Galaxy Music Corp., N. Y. Used
by permission.
Tune: William Knapp, 1698-1768.

325
According to Thy Gracious Word

Luke 22:17-20
III Nephi 8:33-36

MARTYRDOM C.M.

1. Ac - cord - ing to thy gra - cious word, In meek hu - mil - i - ty,
2. Thy bod - y, bro - ken for my sake, My bread from heaven shall be;
3. Geth - sem - a - ne, can I for - get? Or there thy con - flict see,
4. When to the cross I turn mine eyes, And rest on Cal - va - ry,

This will I do, my dy - ing Lord, I will re - mem - ber thee.
The cup, thy pre - cious blood I take, And thus re - mem - ber thee.
Thine ag - o - ny and blood - y sweat, And not re - mem - ber thee?
O Lamb of God, my sac - ri - fice, I must re - mem - ber thee. A - men.

Text: James Montgomery, 1771-1854.
Tune: Hugh Wilson, 1764-1825.

326
Leave We Now the Table of Our Lord

Matthew 26:25-27 (29, 30)
John 15:15, 16

GOD BE WITH YOU 9.8.8.9.
Alternate tune: Randolph (489)

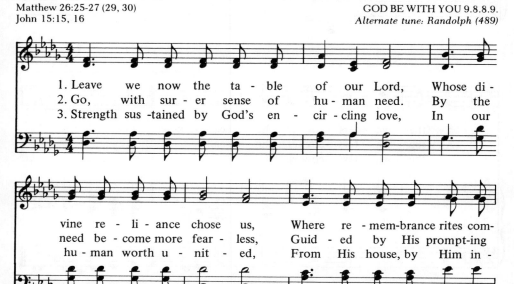

1. Leave we now the ta - ble of our Lord, Whose di -
2. Go, with sur - er sense of hu - man need. By the
3. Strength sus - tained by God's en - cir - cling love, In our

vine re - li - ance chose us, Where re - mem - brance rites com -
need be - come more fear - less, Guid - ed by His prompt - ing
hu - man worth u - nit - ed, From His house, by Him in -

do to   has-ten the time, The   time that shall sure - ly   be,
fight with   sor-row and sin To   set the   cap-tives free,
near - er   draws the time, The   time that shall sure - ly   be,

When the   earth shall be   filled with the   glo - ry of God
That the   earth may be   filled with the   glo - ry of God
When the   earth shall be   filled with the   glo - ry of God

As the   wa - ters cov-er the   sea? *(2. From)*
As the   wa - ters cov-er the   sea."
As the   wa - ters cov-er the   sea.

Text: Arthur C. Ainger, 1841-1919.
Tune: Martin Shaw, 1875-1958; from *Enlarged Songs of Praise* by permission of Oxford University Press.

324

God Is Working His Purpose Out

D. and C. 2:1a-c
II Nephi 9:133-137

PURPOSE Irregular

1. God is work-ing his pur-pose out As year suc-ceeds to year; God is work-ing his pur-pose out, And the time is draw-ing near; What can we

2. From ut-most east to ut-most west, Where hu-man feet have trod, By the mouth of man-y mes-sen-gers Goes forth the voice of God: "Fight ye the

3. All we can do is noth-ing worth Un-less God bless-es the deed; Vain-ly we hope for the har-vest-tide Till God gives life to the seed; Yet near-er and

com - ing— watch and see: the King-dom of the Lord!

Text and Tune: Richard K. Avery, 1934 - , and Donald S. Marsh, 1923 - ; alt. by Rosalee Elser, 1925 - ; copyright 1979 Hope Publishing Co., Carol Stream, IL; used by permission.

These Things Shall Be: A Loftier Race

323

D. and C. 49:5a, b
Isaiah 2:2, 3

TRURO L.M.

1. These things shall be: a loft - ier race Than e'er the
2. They shall be gen - tle, brave, and strong And spill no
3. Na - tion with na - tion, land with land, In trust shall
4. New arts shall bloom of loft - ier mold, And grand - er

world hath known shall rise With flame of free - dom
drop of blood but dare All that may plant Christ's
live as com - rades free; In ev - ery heart and
mu - sic thrill the skies, And ev - ery life shall

in their souls, And light of knowl-edge in their eyes.
lord - ship firm On earth and fire and sea and air.
brain shall throb The pulse of one com - mun - i - ty.
be a song, When all the earth is par - a - dise.

Text: John A. Symonds, 1840-1893, alt.
Tune: Charles Burney, 1726-1814.

322 O How Blessed Are the Poor in Spirit

Matthew 5:2-11
Romans 14:17-19

THE BEATITUDES 9.8.9.6. with refrain

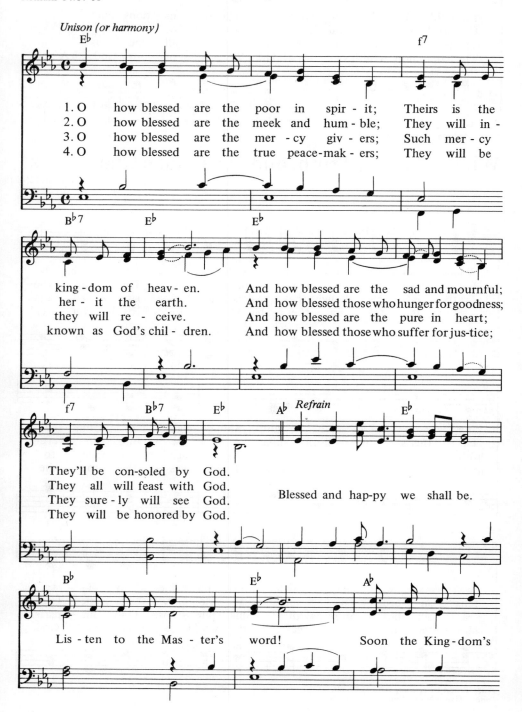

Unison (or harmony)

1. O how blessed are the poor in spir - it; Theirs is the king - dom of heav - en. And how blessed are the sad and mournful; They'll be con-soled by God.
2. O how blessed are the meek and hum - ble; They will in - her - it the earth. And how blessed those who hunger for goodness; They all will feast with God.
3. O how blessed are the mer - cy giv - ers; Such mer - cy they will re - ceive. And how blessed are the pure in heart; They sure - ly will see God.
4. O how blessed are the true peace-mak - ers; They will be known as God's chil - dren. And how blessed those who suffer for jus-tice; They will be honored by God.

Refrain

Blessed and hap-py we shall be. Lis - ten to the Mas - ter's word! Soon the King - dom's

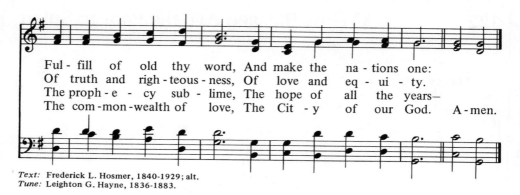

Ful - fill of old thy word, And make the na - tions one:
Of truth and righ - teous - ness, Of love and eq - ui - ty.
The proph - e - cy sub - lime, The hope of all the years—
The com - mon - wealth of love, The Cit - y of our God. A - men.

Text: Frederick L. Hosmer, 1840-1929; alt.
Tune: Leighton G. Hayne, 1836-1883.

Where Beauty, Truth, and Love Make One   321

Alma 14:96, 97
Joel 3:16, 17

ALSTONE L.M.

1. Where beau - ty, truth, and love make one, The heaven - ly
2. For beau - ty is the smile di - vine That in the
3. Truth is his thought that makes us free, Un - veil - ing
4. Love is the Fa - ther's heart that knows His chil - dren's

king - dom is be - gun; Shine, light of God, that
Fa - ther's face doth shine, And na - ture an - swering
life's re - al - i - ty, As age by age to
joys, his chil - dren's woes; This was the way the

we may see On earth this no - ble trin - i - ty.
tells a - broad The ver - y glo - ry of the Lord.
ea - ger hearts More of his pur - pose God im - parts.
Mas - ter trod Who gave the world a Sav - ior God.

Text: Ernest Dodgshun, 1876-1944, alt.
Tune: Christopher E. Willing, 1830-1904.

319

Psalm 145:17-19
I Nephi 1:23

O Day of God, Draw Nigh

FESTAL SONG S.M.
See 378 for a higher setting.

1. O day of God, draw nigh In beau - ty and in power;
2. Bring to our trou - bled minds, Un - cer - tain and a - fraid,
3. Bring jus - tice to our land That all may dwell se - cure,
4. Bring to our world of strife Thy sov - ereign word of peace,
5. O day of God, draw nigh As at cre - a - tion's birth.

Come with thy time-less judg-ment now To match our pres - ent hour.
The qui - et of a stead-fast faith, Calm of a call o - beyed.
And fine - ly build for days to come Foun-da - tions that en - dure.
That war may haunt the earth no more And des - o - la - tions cease.
Let there be light a - gain, and set Thy judg-ments on the earth.

Text: R. B. Y. Scott, 1899 - ; used by permission of the author.
Tune: William H. Walter, 1825-1893.

320

Matthew 6:11
Isaiah 1:26, 27

Thy Kingdom Come, O Lord

ST. CECILIA 6.6.6.6.

1. Thy king - dom come, O Lord, Wide - cir - cling as the sun;
2. One in the bond of peace, Of ser - vice glad and free,
3. Speed, speed the longed - for time Fore - told by rap - tured seers—
4. Till rise at last, to span Its firm foun - da - tions broad,

Hail to the Brightness

318

Isaiah 40:9-11
D. and C. 34:6

WESLEY 11.10.11.10.

1. Hail to the bright-ness of Zi - on's glad morn - ing!
2. Hail to the bright-ness of Zi - on's glad morn - ing,
3. See, from all lands, from the isles of the o - cean,

Joy to the lands that in dark - ness have lain!
Long by the proph - ets of Is - rael fore - told;
Praise to Je - ho - vah as - cend - ing on high;

Hushed be the ac - cents of sor - row and mourn - ing;
Hail to the mil - lions from bond - age re - turn - ing;
Fall - en the en - gines of war and com - mo - tion;

Zi - on in tri - umph be - gins her mild reign.
Gen - tiles and Jews the blest vi - sion be - hold.
Shouts of sal - va - tion are rend - ing the sky.

Text: Thomas Hastings, 1784-1872.
Tune: Lowell Mason, 1792-1872.

317

Send Forth Thy Light, O Zion

Psalm 43:3, 4
D. and C. 16:3c, 4e

LANCASHIRE 7.6.7.6.D.

1. Send forth thy light, O Zi - on! Out from thy towers shall go
2. Send forth thy love, O Zi - on! Thy call is from a - bove,
3. Send forth thy life, O Zi - on! Not for thy - self a - lone

The ra - diant beams a peo - ple In tune with God can know.
To make on earth in - car - nate Christ's sac - ri - fi - cial love.
Have come life - giv - ing pow - ers By which the soul has grown.

Up - borne by high - er con - cepts Of God's e - ter - nal call,
For by the saints out - reach - ing To those their lives can bless
Thy prom - ise builds a peo - ple Well-skilled in mind and hand.

Let shine a - far the guide-lights, Re - veal - ing God to all.
Shall come Zi - on - ic wit - ness To heal earth's bro - ken - ness.
Thy life is like a leav - en Of hope in ev - ery land.

Text: Roy A. Cheville, 1897 - , alt.; copyright 1956 Herald Publishing House.
Tune: Henry Smart, 1813-1879.

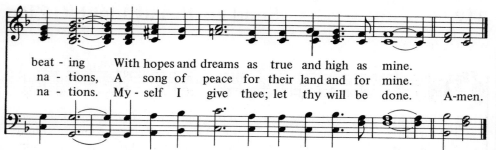

beat - ing With hopes and dreams as true and high as mine.
na - tions, A song of peace for their land and for mine.
na - tions. My-self I give thee; let thy will be done. A-men.

Text: Lloyd Stone, 1912 - , sts. 1, 2 (alt.), Georgia Harkness, 1891-1974, st. 3 (alt.); copyright 1980 by Lorenz Publishing Company; used by permission.
Tune: Jean Sibelius, 1865-1957; arr. copyright, 1933, by Presbyterian Board of Christian Education; renewed, 1961; from *The Hymnbook*. Used by permission of The Westminster Press. Melody is public domain in U. S. A.; outside U. S. A., original melody copyright by Breitkopf & Härtel, Wiesbaden. Used by permission.

Onward to Zion

D. and C. 81:4c
Psalm 50:1-5

316

ZION 9.10.9.10.

1. On - ward to Zi - on, faith-ful and strong, Zi - on the
2. On - ward to Zi - on, to Christ we be - long, Serv - ice the
3. We have the prom - ise that Je - sus will come, Zi - on the
4. Je - sus the Sav - ior, meet - ing the throng, Oh, may his

beau - ti - ful beck - ons us on, On - ward and up - ward
watch - word we fight a - gainst wrong! On - ward to Zi - on,
beau - ti - ful beck - ons us on, Let us be faith - ful,
com - ing be not de - layed long; To God the glo - ry,

bat - tle a - long,
march with a song, Zi - on the beau - ti - ful beck - ons us on.
his will be done,
to him the song,

Text: Frederick M. Smith, 1874-1946; copyright 1950 Herald Publishing House.
Tune: Franklyn S. Weddle, 1905 - ; copyright 1950 Herald Publishing House.

315

Acts 10:34, 35
Alma 14:127, 128

This Is My Song

FINLANDIA 11.10.11.10.11.10.
See 107 for a lower setting.

1. This is my song, O God of all the na - tions,
2. My coun-try's skies are blu - er than the o - cean,
3. This is my prayer, O Lord of all earth's king - doms,

A song of peace for lands a - far and mine. My land is
And sun - light beams on clo - ver-leaf and pine. But oth - er
Thy king-dom come; on earth thy will be done. Let Christ be

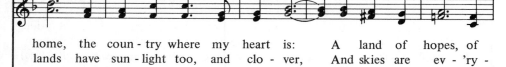

home, the coun - try where my heart is: A land of hopes, of
lands have sun - light too, and clo - ver, And skies are ev - 'ry -
lift - ed up till all shall serve him, And hearts u - nit - ed

dreams, of grand de - sign; But oth - er hearts in oth - er lands are
where as blue as mine. Oh, hear my song, thou God of all the
learn to live as one. Oh, hear my prayer, thou God of all the

The Cause of Zion Summons Us

314

D. and C. 140:5c, d
D. and C. 137:6a

ST. MATTHEW C.M.D.
Alternate tune: ELLACOMBE (471)

1. The cause of Zi-on sum-mons us To claim a dis-tant dream:
2. The cause of Zi-on cel-e-brates The vic-to-ry o-ver fear,
3. The cause of Zi-on proph-e-sies The fu-ture yet to be,

The love of God in ev-ery place, The will of God su-preme.
The wit-ness of the king-dom's pow-er, New life al-read-y here.
When men and wom-en ev-ery-where Shall walk in dig-ni-ty.

The vi-sion calls us to our task. For-sak-ing self and pride,
Al-though ful-fill-ment seems re-mote, The jour-ney just be-gun,
We now an-ti-ci-pate the day When pain and tears shall cease,

We love and re-con-cile with Christ The world for which he died.
The King-dom has al-read-y come; The vic-tor-y is won.
When hu-man-kind shall live as one In right-eous-ness and peace.

Text: Geoffrey F. Spencer, 1927 - . Copyright 1980 Reorganized Church of Jesus Christ of Latter Day Saints.
Tune: William Croft, 1678-1727.

313
Redeemer of Israel

Jacob 4:3-6
Exodus 13:21

MEDITATION (Beloved) 11.8.11.8.

1. Re - deem - er of Is - rael, our on - ly de - light,
2. We know he is com - ing to gath - er his sheep
3. How long we have wan - dered as stran - gers in sin
4. As chil - dren of Zi - on, good ti - dings for us,

On whom for a bless - ing we call,
And plant them in Zi - on in love;
And cried in the des - ert for thee!
The to - kens al - read - y ap - pear;

Our shad - ow by day, and our pil - lar by night,
For why in the val - ley of death should they weep
Our foes have re - joiced when our sor - rows they've seen,
Fear not and be just, for the king - dom is ours,

Our King, our Com - pan - ion, our All!
Or a - lone in the wil - der - ness rove?
But Is - rael will short - ly be free.
And the hour of re - demp - tion is near.

Text: W. W. Phelps, 1792-1872; arr. from Joseph Swain, 1761-1796.
Tune: Freeman Lewis, 1780-1859.

Let Us Pray for One Another

312

Colossians 1:9, 10
D. and C. 18:6a

DECATUR 8.7.8.7.D.

1. Let us pray for one an-oth-er That our minds and hearts may blend
2. We are walk-ing down time's vis-ta; Zi-on's ban-ner now un-furled
3. O'er the world the day is dawn-ing Through the Spir-it's light and power

As we grow in love and mer-cy, Day by day, till life shall end.
Calls to stew-ard-ship of car-ing And re-demp-tion of the world.
When the peo-ple of all na-tions Sense the chal-lenge of this hour.

We can see how oth-ers need us; May we al-so dare to say
Let us pray that we may ev-er Sense God's guid-ance in the way;
That our lives may now be giv-en To each oth-er in His way,

That in love we'll share to-geth-er; For each oth-er let us pray.
As we try to live for oth-ers, For each oth-er let us pray.
In the name of Christ the Sav-ior, For each oth-er let us pray.

Text: Maurice L. Draper, 1918 - , based on David H. Smith, 1844-1904. Copyright 1980 Reorganized Church of Jesus Christ of Latter Day Saints.
Tune: Revised from *Saints' Harmony*, 1889.

311 Guide Us, O Thou Great Jehovah

D. and C. 98:4d-f
II Nephi 13:27-30

SIBERIA 8.7.8.7.8.7.
Alternate tune: CWM RHONDDA (419)

1. Guide us, O thou great Je-ho-vah, Saints un-to the prom-ised land; We are weak, but thou art a-ble; Hold us with thy pow-er-ful hand. Ho-ly Spir-it, Ho-ly Spir-it, Feed us till the Sav-ior comes.

2. O-pen, Je-sus, Zi-on's foun-tains; Let her rich-est bless-ings come; Let the fi-er-y, cloud-y pil-lar Guard us to that ho-ly home. Great Re-deem-er, Great Re-deem-er, Bring, O bring the wel-come day!

3. When the earth be-gins to trem-ble, Bid our fear-ful thoughts be still; When thy judg-ments spread de-struc-tion, Keep us safe on Zi-on's hill, Sing-ing prais-es, Sing-ing prais-es, Songs of glo-ry un-to thee. A-men.

Text: William Williams, 1717-1791; tr. by Peter Williams, 1722-1796; rev. by Robert Robinson, 1735-1790.
Tune: German Melody, attr. to S. B. Pond, 1792-1871.

Lord, Save Your World

310

John 3:16, 17
I Nephi 1:23

KEDRON L.M.

1. Lord, save your world; in bit-ter need To
2. Lord, save your world; our souls are bound In
3. Lord, save your world; we strive in vain To
4. Lord, save your world, since you have sent The
5. Then save us now, by Je-sus' power, And

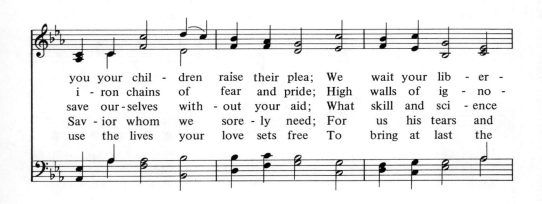

you your chil - dren raise their plea; We wait your lib - er -
i - ron chains of fear and pride; High walls of ig - no -
save our-selves with - out your aid; What skill and sci - ence
Sav - ior whom we sore - ly need; For us his tears and
use the lives your love sets free To bring at last the

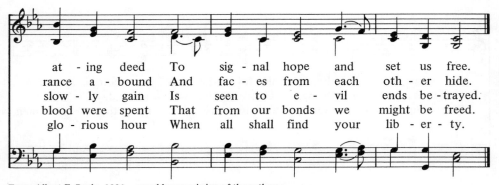

at - ing deed To sig - nal hope and set us free.
rance a - bound And fac - es from each oth - er hide.
slow - ly gain Is seen to e - vil ends be-trayed.
blood were spent That from our bonds we might be freed.
glo - rious hour When all shall find your lib - er - ty.

Text: Albert F. Bayly, 1901 - ; used by permission of the author.
Tune: William Walker's *Southern Harmony*, 1835; arr. Rosalee Elser, 1925 - ; copyright 1980 Rosalee Elser; used by permission.

309

We Limit Not the Truth of God

John 16:12-14
D. and C. 147:7

HILLS C.M.D.

1. We lim - it not the truth of God To our poor reach of mind
2. Who dares to bind to their dull sense The or - a - cles of heaven
3. O Fa - ther, Son and Spir - it, send Us in - crease from a - bove;

By no - tions of our day and sect, Crude, par - tial, and con - fined.
For all the na - tions, tongues, and climes, And all the a - ges given?
En - large, ex - pand all Chris - tian souls To com - pre - hend thy love,

No, let a new and bet - ter hope With - in our hearts be stirred—
That u - ni - verse, how much un - known! That o - cean un - ex - plored!
And make us all go on to know, With no - bler powers con - ferred,

The Lord hath yet more light and truth To break forth from his word.

Text: George Rawson, 1807-1889.
Tune: Louise Hills Lewis, 1887-1948.

God Who Spoke in the Beginning

John 1:1-4, 14
Hebrews 1:1-3

UNSER HERRSCHER
(Neander) 8.7.8.7.8.7.

1. God who spoke in the be - gin - ning, Form - ing rock and
2. God who spoke through peo - ple, na - tions, Through e - vents long
3. God whose speech be - comes in - car - nate— Christ is ser - vant,

shap - ing spar, Set all life and growth in mo - tion,
past and gone, Show - ing still to - day his pur - pose,
Christ is Lord!— Calls us to a life of ser - vice,

Earth - ly world and dis - tant star; He who calls the
Speaks su - preme - ly through his Son; He who calls the
Heart and will to ac - tion stirred; He who us - es

earth to or - der Is the ground of what we are.
earth to or - der Gives his word and it is done.
our o - be - dience, Has the first and fi - nal word.

Text: Fred Kaan, 1929 - ; alt. by permission; copyright 1968 by Galliard Ltd. Sole U. S. agent: Galaxy Music Corp., N. Y. Used by permission.
Tune: Joachim Neander, 1650-1680.

307   # We Thank Thee, O God, for a Prophet

Mosiah 8:67-69   PROPHET 9.8.9.8.D.
Amos 3:7

1. We thank thee, O God, for a proph-et To guide us in
2. When dark clouds of trou-ble hang o'er us And threat-en our

these lat-ter days; We thank thee for send-ing the gos-pel To
peace to de-stroy, There is hope smil-ing bright-ly be-fore us, And we

light-en our minds with its rays; We thank thee for ev-er-y
know that de-liv-erance is nigh. We doubt not the Lord nor his

bless-ing Be-stowed by thy boun-te-ous hands; We feel it a
good-ness; We've proved him in days that are past; The Saints who will

pleas-ure to serve thee, And love to o-bey thy com-mands.
la-bor for Zi-on Will sure-ly be bless-ed at last. A-men.

Text: William Fowler, 1830-1865, alt.
Tune: Caroline E. S. Norton, 1808-1877; alt.

God Has Spoken Through the Ages 306

John 16:12-14
II Timothy 3:14-17

VAN FLEET 8.7.8.7.D.

1. God has spo-ken through the a-ges, Giv-ing light and truth for all.
2. Through the pag-es of the Scrip-tures, God's e-ter-nal truths are shown,
3. While we thank thee for thy Scrip-tures, For thy word re-vealed of old,
4. Speed the day of Zi-on's wit-ness, When all peo-ples of the earth

If our minds are tuned to hear him, Can we not dis-cern his call?
But in fi-nite words and phras-es God him-self can-not be known;
Lead us, Lord, to new re-veal-ment; Still to us new truths un-fold.
Who have writ-ten sa-cred Scrip-tures Shall per-ceive each Scrip-ture's worth.

God, whose works are nev-er end-ed, And whose words shall nev-er cease,
For the In-fi-nite is broad-er Than our minds can ev-er know;
As our in-tel-lect in-creas-es, As our spir-its grow toward thee,
Then all na-tions which have writ-ten Shall each oth-er's Scrip-tures know.

Of those words will give his chil-dren, And his Scrip-tures still in-crease.
God's un-bound-ed store of wis-dom Waits our read-i-ness to grow.
Lord, with Ho-ly Spir-it quick-en; Make us know and hear and see.
Give one wit-ness of the Sav-ior, Which to ev-ery tribe shall go. A-men.

Text: Evan A. Fry, 1902-1959. Copyright 1956 Herald Publishing House.
Tune: Charles F. Church, Jr., 1904 - . Copyright 1956 Herald Publishing House.

305

O Word of God Incarnate

D. and C. 90:1
John 1:1, 14

MUNICH 7.6.7.6.D.

1. O Word of God in-car-nate, O wis-dom from on high,
2. The Church from her dear Mas-ter Re-ceived the gift di-vine,

O truth un-changed, un-chang-ing, O light of our dark sky,
And still that light she lift-eth O'er all the earth to shine.

We praise thee for the ra-diance That from the hal-lowed page,
It is the chart and com-pass That o'er life's surg-ing sea,

A lan-tern to our foot-steps, Shines on from age to age.
'Mid mists and rocks and dark-ness, Still guides, O Christ to thee.

Text: William Walsham How, 1823-1897.
Tune: Meiningen Gesangbuch, 1693.

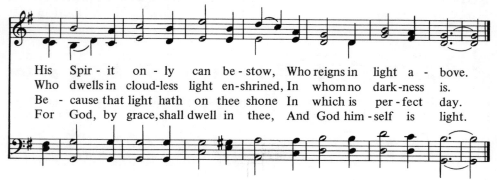

Text: Bernard Barton, 1784-1849.
Tune: Arr. from Gioacchino A. Rossini, 1792-1868.

Life of Ages, Richly Poured

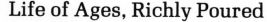

304

II Nephi 1:117-120
Acts 10:34, 35

HARTS 7.7.7.7.

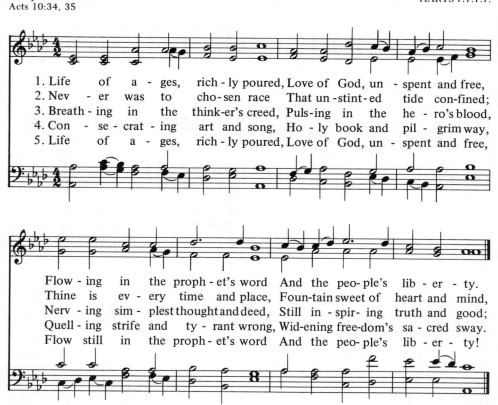

1. Life of a-ges, rich-ly poured, Love of God, un-spent and free,
2. Nev-er was to cho-sen race That un-stint-ed tide con-fined;
3. Breath-ing in the think-er's creed, Puls-ing in the he-ro's blood,
4. Con-se-crat-ing art and song, Ho-ly book and pil-grim way,
5. Life of a-ges, rich-ly poured, Love of God, un-spent and free,

Flow-ing in the proph-et's word And the peo-ple's lib-er-ty.
Thine is ev-ery time and place, Foun-tain sweet of heart and mind,
Nerv-ing sim-plest thought and deed, Still in-spir-ing truth and good;
Quell-ing strife and ty-rant wrong, Wid-ening free-dom's sa-cred sway.
Flow still in the proph-et's word And the peo-ple's lib-er-ty!

Text: Samuel Johnson, 1822-1882.
Tune: Benjamin Milgrove, 1731-1810; harm. Eric Thiman, 1900-1959; used by permission of the United Reformed Church, London.

302 O God, Our Source of Truth

I Corinthians 13:8-12
D. and C. 95:3a

FESTAL SONG S.M.
See 378 for a higher setting
Alternate hymn: 301

1. O God, our Source of truth By whom we find our way,
2. We treas - ure what we have Of truth, an am - ple ray;
3. At best, we know in part, Which lim - its what we say.
4. When as a child we spoke And un - der-stood and thought,
5. For a - dult days, the truth Through dark - ened glass is shown.

Re - veal the knowl-edge that we seek Suf - fi - cient for our day.
We brief - ly hold that cher-ished light—It van - ish - es a - way.
But when the per - fect light is come, The part is done a - way.
A child - ish faith and sim - ple joy Were all we craved or sought.
Still yearn we for the prom-ised day: To know as we are known.

Text: Alan D. Tyree, 1929 - ; copyright 1980 Reorganized Church of Jesus Christ of Latter Day Saints.
Tune: William H. Walter, 1825-1893.

303 Walk in the Light

Ephesians 5:8
II Nephi 15:10

MANOAH C.M.

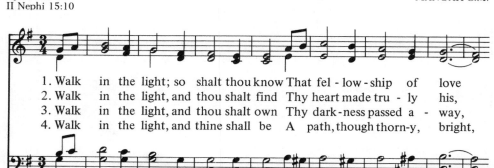

1. Walk in the light; so shalt thou know That fel - low - ship of love
2. Walk in the light, and thou shalt find Thy heart made tru - ly his,
3. Walk in the light, and thou shalt own Thy dark-ness passed a - way,
4. Walk in the light, and thine shall be A path, though thorn-y, bright,

O God, Our Source of Truth

301

I Corinthians 13:8-12
D. and C. 95:3a

VINEYARD HAVEN S.M. with refrain
Alternate hymn: 302

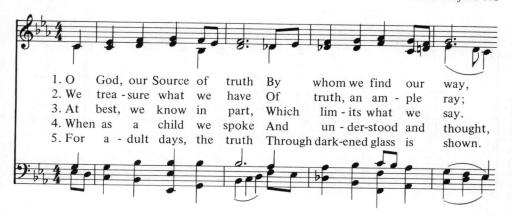

1. O God, our Source of truth By whom we find our way,
2. We trea - sure what we have Of truth, an am - ple ray;
3. At best, we know in part, Which lim - its what we say.
4. When as a child we spoke And un - der-stood and thought,
5. For a - dult days, the truth Through dark-ened glass is shown.

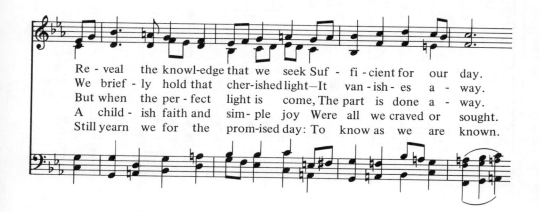

Re - veal the knowl-edge that we seek Suf - fi - cient for our day.
We brief - ly hold that cher-ished light—It van - ish - es a - way.
But when the per - fect light is come, The part is done a - way.
A child - ish faith and sim - ple joy Were all we craved or sought.
Still yearn we for the prom-ised day: To know as we are known.

Refrain

Lord, guide us, di - rect us, Shine light up - on our way.

\> = marcato accent — marked, stressed.
− = tenuto — held; sustained to full value.

Text: Alan D. Tyree, 1929 - ; copyright 1980 Reorganized Church of Jesus Christ of Latter Day Saints.
Tune: Richard Dirksen, 1921 - ; © copyright 1974 Harold Flammer, Inc.; sole selling agent; Shawnee Press, Inc., Delaware Water Gap PA 18327; international copyright secured; all rights reserved; reprinted with permission.

300

How Can Creation's Voice Be Still

Hebrews 11:13-16
James 1:2-4

MASSACHUSETTS C.M.D.
Alternate tune: RESIGNATION (125)

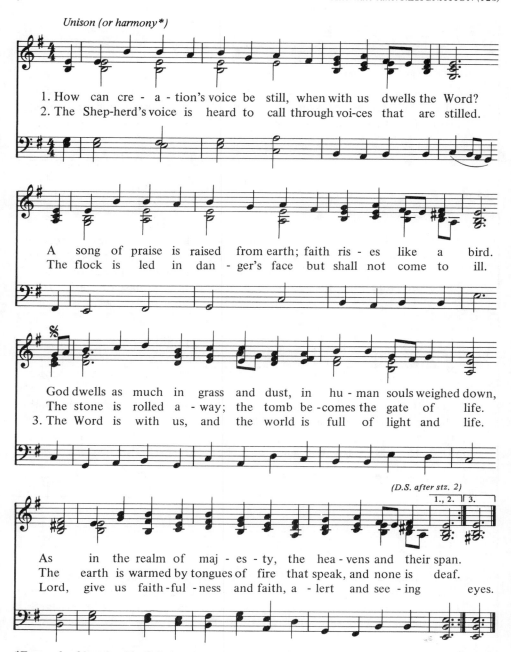

Unison (or harmony*)

1. How can cre - a - tion's voice be still, when with us dwells the Word?
2. The Shep-herd's voice is heard to call through voi-ces that are stilled.

A song of praise is raised from earth; faith ris - es like a bird.
The flock is led in dan - ger's face but shall not come to ill.

God dwells as much in grass and dust, in hu - man souls weighed down,
The stone is rolled a - way; the tomb be - comes the gate of life.
3. The Word is with us, and the world is full of light and life.

(D.S. after stz. 2)

1., 2. ‖ 3.

As in the realm of maj - es - ty, the hea - vens and their span.
The earth is warmed by tongues of fire that speak, and none is deaf.
Lord, give us faith - ful - ness and faith, a - lert and see - ing eyes.

*Tenors should read treble clef when necessary.

Text: Anders Frostenson, trans. Fred Kaan, 1929 - ; trans. copyright 1976 Stainer & Bell Ltd. Sole U. S. agent: Galaxy Music Corp., N. Y. Used with permission.
Tune: Katherine K. Davis, 1892-1980; copyright 1964 Abingdon Press. Used with permission.

The Living Word of Scripture

299

John 5:40 (39)
Hebrews 12:1

VIGIL 7.6.7.6.D.
See 210 for a lower setting.

1. The liv-ing Word of scrip-ture Pro-vides the guide and source
2. A proph-et on the moun-tain, A child with-in the womb,
3. De-liv-erance in the des-ert, A pil-lar's guid-ing ray,
4. Our bro-thers and our sis-ters, True saints of ev-ery age

For saints in search of wis-dom And light to chart their course.
A youth in ear-nest search-ing, The wo-men at the tomb;
The grove's re-stor-ing vi-sion, Pro-phet-ic power to-day;
Who share with us their sto-ry, Speak out from ev-ery page.

The stran-gers and the pil-grims Who owned the cause sub-lime
How glo-ri-ous a com-pany Reach out their hands to ours;
In all the gen-er-a-tions Of his-tory's broad ex-panse,
That sto-ry is not end-ed, For still God's voice is heard

Have glimpsed the rev-e-la-tion, And an-swered in their time.
Their faith a vi-brant wit-ness To God's re-deem-ing powers.
The Word has proved suf-fi-cient For ev-ery cir-cum-stance.
Through all who bear the call-ing To be the liv-ing Word.

Text: Geoffrey F. Spencer, 1927 - ; copyright 1980 Reorganized Church of Jesus Christ of Latter Day Saints.
Tune: Swedish Folk Melody.

298   Fountain of All Revelation

D. and C. 10:11b, c, 12
I Corinthians 2:9-13

LESLIE 8.7.8.7.D.

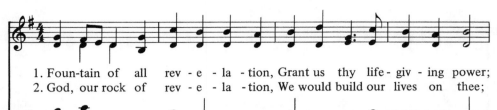

1. Foun-tain of all rev - e - la - tion, Grant us thy life - giv - ing power;
2. God, our rock of rev - e - la - tion, We would build our lives on thee;

With - out thee no sure sal - va - tion Will de - liv - er us this hour.
For with-out thy sure foun - da - tion None can find sta - bil - i - ty.

May no veil of our tra - di - tion Mask the light that comes from thee!
We will or - der not thy wis-dom To some cher-ished form or mold,

Let not pride nor low am-bi - tion Waste the strength that sets us free.
But will search for truths now hid-den As we live by those we hold. A-men.

Text: Deam Ferris, 1912 - . Copyright 1956 by Herald Publishing House.
Tune: Franklyn S. Weddle, 1905 - . Alt. by Evan A. Fry, 1902-1959. Copyright 1956 by Herald Publishing House.

The Church's Life

297

D. and C. 83:7b-e
Romans 12:3-8

RICHMOND BEACH 8.7.8.7.8.8.7.

Unison (or harmony*) ♩ *remains constant*

1. The church's life is built up-on The rock of rev-e-
2. A church which seeks the king-dom's goal Re-sponds with con-se-
3. We do not dare to rest con-tent In face of our con-

la-tion. Our joy-ful hearts are nur-tured by Pro-phet-ic in-spi-
cra-tion. God's light is not our own do-main— His word is for the
di-tion; Through com-mon mind, our full con-sent Will bet-ter serve our

ra-tion. No pri-vate creed shall dull our mind Nor sel-fish
na-tions. Pro-phet-ic fire con-sumes the whole: All mem-bers
mis-sion. To those who seek to know His mind, Ex-pand-ing

pride un-du-ly bind The Spir-it's val-i-da-tion.
share pro-phet-ic role; God's will is our sal-va-tion.
gift of truth to find, The Lord grants his com-mis-sion.

* Tenors should read the treble clef when necessary.

Text: Geoffrey F. Spencer, 1927 - , and Alan D. Tyree, 1929 - . Copyright 1980 Reorganized Church of Jesus
Christ of Latter Day Saints.
Tune: A. Royce Eckhardt, 1937 - ; copyright 1973 Covenant Press; used by permission.

296

Afar in Old Judea

Matthew 17:4 (5)
D. and C. 4:1a-c

EWING 7.6.7.6.D.

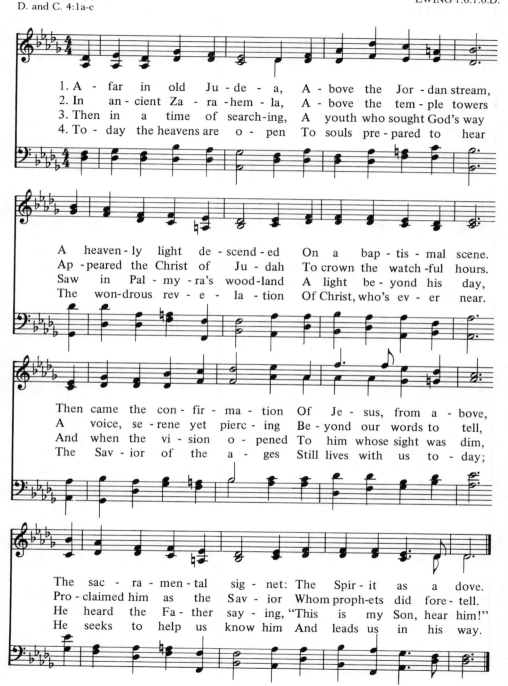

1. A - far in old Ju - de - a, A - bove the Jor - dan stream,
2. In an - cient Za - ra - hem - la, A - bove the tem - ple towers
3. Then in a time of search - ing, A youth who sought God's way
4. To - day the heavens are o - pen To souls pre - pared to hear

A heaven - ly light de - scend - ed On a bap - tis - mal scene.
Ap - peared the Christ of Ju - dah To crown the watch - ful hours.
Saw in Pal - my - ra's wood - land A light be - yond his day,
The won - drous rev - e - la - tion Of Christ, who's ev - er near.

Then came the con - fir - ma - tion Of Je - sus, from a - bove,
A voice, se - rene yet pierc - ing Be - yond our words to tell,
And when the vi - sion o - pened To him whose sight was dim,
The Sav - ior of the a - ges Still lives with us to - day;

The sac - ra - men - tal sig - net: The Spir - it as a dove.
Pro - claimed him as the Sav - ior Whom proph - ets did fore - tell.
He heard the Fa - ther say - ing, "This is my Son, hear him!"
He seeks to help us know him And leads us in his way.

Text: Roy A. Cheville, 1897 - , alt. Copyright 1956 Herald Publishing House.
Tune: Alexander Ewing, 1830-1895.

Christ Is the Foundation

295

Ephesians 2:19-21
I Corinthians 3:10, 11

PENITENCE 6.5.6.5.D.

1. Christ is the foun-da-tion Of the house we raise;
   Be its walls sal-va-tion, And its gate-ways praise;
   May its thresh-old low-ly To the Lord be dear;
   May the hearts be ho-ly That shall wor-ship here.

2. Here may vows be seal-ed By thy Spir-it, Lord;
   Here the sick be heal-ed, And the lost re-stored;
   Here the bro-ken-heart-ed Thy for-give-ness prove;
   Here the friends long part-ed Be re-stored to love.

3. Here may ev-ery to-ken Of thy pres-ence be;
   Here may chains be bro-ken, Pris-oners here set free;
   Here may light il-lu-mine Ev-ery soul of thine,
   Lift-ing up the hu-man In-to the di-vine.

4. Here may God the Fa-ther, Christ the Sav-ior, Son,
   With the Ho-ly Spir-it, Be a-dored as one
   Till the whole cre-a-tion At thy foot-stool fall,
   And in ad-o-ra-tion Own thee Lord of all.

Text: John Samuel Bewley Monsell, 1811-1875.
Tune: Spencer Lane, 1843-1903.

294

The Church's One Foundation

D. and C. 140:5c, d
I Corinthians 3:10, 11

AURELIA 7.6.7.6.D.

1. The Church's one foun-da - tion Is Je-sus Christ, her Lord;
2. E - lect from ev-ery na - tion, Yet one o'er all the earth,
3. 'Mid toil and trib-u - la - tion And tu-mult of her war,
4. Yet she on earth hath un - ion With God, the Three in One,

She is his new cre - a - tion By wa-ter and the word;
Her char-ter of sal-va - tion—One Lord, one faith, one birth;
She waits the con-sum-ma - tion Of peace for-ev-er-more,
And mys-tic sweet com-mun - ion With those whose rest is won.

From heaven he came and sought her To be his ho-ly bride;
One ho-ly name she bless - es, Par-takes one ho-ly food,
Till with the vi-sion glo - rious Her long-ing eyes are blest,
Oh, hap-py ones and ho - ly! Lord, give us grace that we,

With his own blood he bought her, And for her life he died.
And to one hope she press - es With ev-ery grace en - dued.
And the great church vic-to - rious Shall be the church at rest.
Like them, the meek and low - ly, On high may dwell with thee.

Text: Samuel J. Stone, 1839-1900.
Tune: Samuel S. Wesley, 1810-1876.

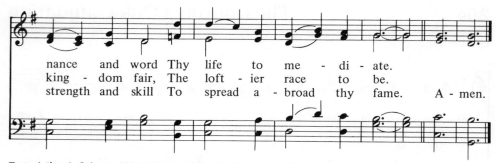

nance and word Thy life to me - di - ate.
king - dom fair, The loft - ier race to be.
strength and skill To spread a - broad thy fame. A - men.

Text: Arthur A. Oakman, 1905-1975; copyright 1956 Herald Publishing House.
Tune: William Gardiner's *Sacred Melodies*, 1812.

Prophetic Church, the Future Waits 293

Alma 5:38-41
D. and C. 138:3a, b

DEUS TUORUM MILITUM (Grenoble) L.M.

1. Pro - phet - ic Church, the fu - ture waits Thy li - ber -
2. Free from the bonds that bind the mind To nar - row
3. A free - dom that re - veres the past, But trusts the

at - ing min - is - try; Go for - ward in the
thought and life - less creed; Free from a so - cial
dawn - ing fu - ture more; And bids the soul, in

power of love, Pro - claim the truth that makes us free.
code that fails To serve the cause of hu - man need;
search of truth, Ad - ven - ture bold - ly and ex - plore.

Text: Marion Franklin Ham, 1867-1956, alt.; copyright Beacon Press; used by permission.
Tune: Melody from the *Grenoble Antiphoner*, 1753.

291 Church of Christ, in Latter Days

D. and C. 3:15e, 16, 17
I Corinthians 12:27

ELSWORTH 7.7.7.7.

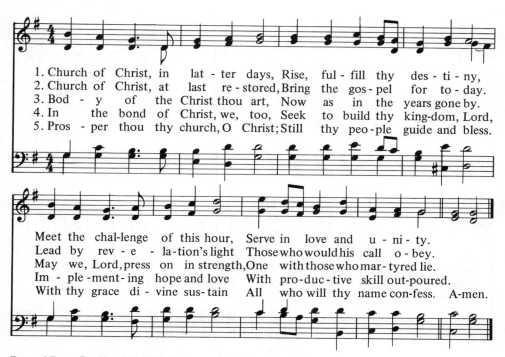

1. Church of Christ, in lat-ter days, Rise, ful-fill thy des-ti-ny,
2. Church of Christ, at last re-stored, Bring the gos-pel for to-day.
3. Bod-y of the Christ thou art, Now as in the years gone by.
4. In the bond of Christ, we, too, Seek to build thy king-dom, Lord,
5. Pros-per thou thy church, O Christ; Still thy peo-ple guide and bless.

Meet the chal-lenge of this hour, Serve in love and u-ni-ty.
Lead by rev-e-la-tion's light Those who would his call o-bey.
May we, Lord, press on in strength, One with those who mar-tyred lie.
Im-ple-ment-ing hope and love With pro-duc-tive skill out-poured.
With thy grace di-vine sus-tain All who will thy name con-fess. A-men.

Text and Tune: Franklyn S. Weddle, 1905 - ; copyright 1956 Herald Publishing House.

292 By Thy Redeeming Cross, O Lord

I Corinthians 1:18
D. and C. 150:12

BELMONT C.M.

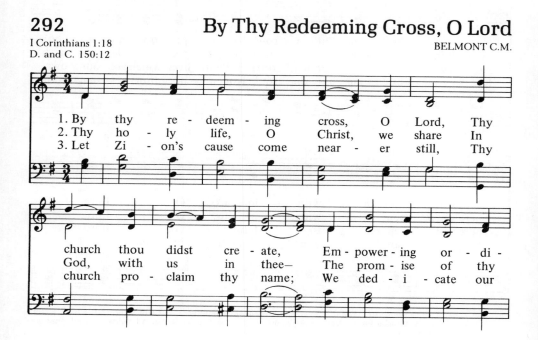

1. By thy re-deem-ing cross, O Lord, Thy
2. Thy ho-ly life, O Christ, we share In
3. Let Zi-on's cause come near-er still, Thy

church thou didst cre-ate, Em-power-ing or-di-
God, with us in thee— The prom-ise of thy
church pro-claim thy name; We ded-i-cate our

There's a Church Within Us

290

Ephesians 4:11-16
D. and C. 150:12

THE CHURCH WITHIN US 8.8.7.7.8.

1. There's a church with - in us, O Lord,
2. There's po - ten - tial with - in us, O Lord,
3. There's some build - ing to be done, O Lord,
4. There's the church with - in us, O Lord,

There's a church with - in us, O Lord.
Some - thing's stir - ring with - in us, O Lord.
There's some build - ing to be done, O Lord.
There's the church with - in us, O Lord.

Not a build - ing but a soul, Not a por - tion but a whole,
Some - thing's strain - ing to have birth, To be vis - i - ble on earth;
Not with steel, not with stone, But with lives which are our own
Not a build - ing but one soul, Not a por - tion but one whole,

There's a church with - in us, O Lord.
There's po - ten - tial with - in us, O Lord.
There's the church to be built, O Lord.
We are your Church in the world.

289

Alma 3:27-29
Romans 8:14-16

Come Down, O Love Divine

DOWN AMPNEY 6.6.11.D.

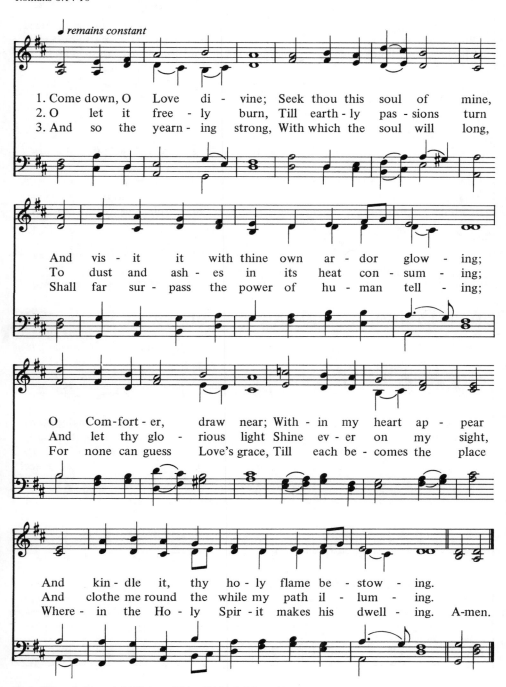

♩ *remains constant*

1. Come down, O Love di - vine; Seek thou this soul of mine,
2. O let it free - ly burn, Till earth - ly pas - sions turn
3. And so the yearn - ing strong, With which the soul will long,

And vis - it it with thine own ar - dor glow - ing;
To dust and ash - es in its heat con - sum - ing;
Shall far sur - pass the power of hu - man tell - ing;

O Com-fort - er, draw near; With - in my heart ap - pear
And let thy glo - rious light Shine ev - er on my sight,
For none can guess Love's grace, Till each be - comes the place

And kin - dle it, thy ho - ly flame be - stow - ing.
And clothe me round the while my path il - lum - ing.
Where - in the Ho - ly Spir - it makes his dwell - ing. A-men.

Text: Bianco da Siena, d. 1434; trans. Richard F. Littledale, 1833-1890.
Tune: Ralph Vaughan Williams, 1872-1958. From *The English Hymnal* by permission of Oxford University Press.

We are joy - ful, we are ea - ger, Yearn-ing for your gra - cious deed;
Burn a - way our wast-ed sad - ness And en - flame us with your love;
Teach us love and trust-ing kind-ness; Bare our arms to those who hurt;

Rest up - on your con-gre - ga - tion; Give us power of God, we plead.
Burst up - on our con-gre - ga - tion. Give us glad - ness from a - bove.
Breathe up - on our con-gre - ga - tion And in - spire us with your Word.

Text: Ann Neufeld Rupp, 1932 - .
Tune: The Sacred Harp, 1844; harm. Rosalee Elser, 1925 - ; copyright 1980 Rosalee Elser; used by permission.

Spirit Divine, Attend Our Prayer 288

Luke 11:14 (13)
Romans 8:26, 27

ST. AGNES C.M.
Alternate tune: Richmond (346)

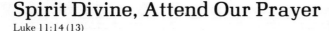

1. Spir - it di - vine, at - tend our prayer, And make our hearts thy home;
2. Come as the light! To us re - veal The truth we long to know.
3. Come as the fire, and purge our hearts Like sac - ri - fi - cial flame
4. Come as the wind, O breath of God! O pen - te - cos - tal grace!

De - scend with all thy gra - cious power; Come, Ho - ly Spir - it, come.
Re - veal the nar - row path of right, The way of du - ty show.
Till our whole souls an of - fering be In love's re - deem - ing name.
Come, make thy great sal - va - tion known Wide as the hu - man race.

Text: Andrew Reed, 1787-1862; adapted by Samuel Longfellow, 1819-1892.
Tune: John B. Dykes, 1823-1876.

286 Come, Holy Ghost, Our Hearts Inspire

John 14:16-18
II Nephi 13:26

LLOYD C.M.

1. Come, Ho - ly Ghost, our hearts in - spire; Let us thine in - fluence prove;
2. Come, Ho - ly Ghost, for moved by thee The proph - ets wrote and spoke;
3. Ex - pand thy wings, ce - les - tial dove; Brood o'er our na - tures' night;
4. God, through thine aid we then shall know If thou with - in us shine,

Source of the old pro - phet - ic fire, Fountain of light and love!
Un - lock the truth, thy - self the key; Un - seal the sa - cred book.
On our dis - or - dered spir - its move, And let there now be light.
And sound with all thy saints be - low The depth of love di - vine. A - men.

Text: Charles Wesley, 1707-1788.
Tune: Cuthbert Howard, 1856-1927.

287 Holy Spirit, Come with Power

Ephesians 4:30
D. and C. 85:1

BEACH SPRING 8.7.8.7.D.

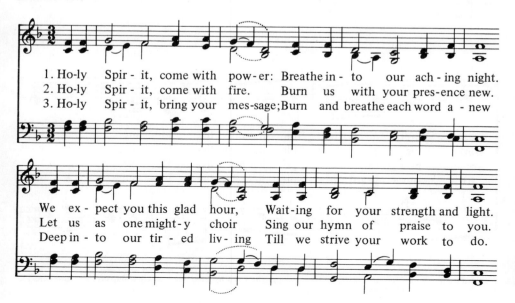

1. Ho - ly Spir - it, come with pow - er: Breathe in - to our ach - ing night.
2. Ho - ly Spir - it, come with fire. Burn us with your pres - ence new.
3. Ho - ly Spir - it, bring your mes - sage; Burn and breathe each word a - new

We ex - pect you this glad hour, Wait - ing for your strength and light.
Let us as one might - y choir Sing our hymn of praise to you.
Deep in - to our tir - ed liv - ing Till we strive your work to do.

O Holy Dove of God Descending

Luke 3:28, 29
Moroni 10:5-7

LOIS 9.9.9.6.

Unison (or harmony)

1. O ho-ly Dove of God de-scend-ing, You are the
2. O ho-ly Wind of God now blow-ing, You are the
3. O ho-ly Rain of God now fall-ing, You make the
4. O ho-ly Flame of God now burn-ing, You are the

love that knows no end-ing. All of our shat-tered
seed that God is sow-ing. You are the life that
Word of God en-thrall-ing, You are that in-ner
power of Christ re-turn-ing. You are the an-swer

dreams You're mend-ing: Spir-it, now live in me.
starts us grow-ing: Spir-it, now live in me.
voice now call-ing: Spir-it, now live in me.
to our yearn-ing: Spir-it, now live in me. A-men.

284 Gracious Spirit, Dwell with Me

Galatians 5:22-25
D. and C. 10:6, 7

ASHBURTON 7.7.7.D.

1. Gra - cious Spir - it, dwell with me, I my - self would
2. Truth - ful Spir - it, dwell with me, I my - self would
3. Ho - ly Spir - it, dwell with me, I my - self would

gra - cious be; And with words that help and heal
truth - ful be; And with wis - dom kind and clear
ho - ly be; Cleansed and freed from sin, I would

Would thy life in mine re - veal; And with ac - tions
Let thy life in mine ap - pear; And with ac - tions
Choose and cher - ish all things good; And what - ev - er

bold but meek Would for Christ, my Sav - ior, speak.
neigh - bor - ly Speak my Lord's sin - cer - i - ty.
I can be, Give to God who gave me thee. A - men.

Text: Thomas T. Lynch, 1818-1871, alt.
Tune: Robert Jackson, 1842-1914.

is De - rives, E - ter - nal One, from Thee. A - men.

Text: E. Y. Hunker, 1899-1966; copyright 1980 Reorganized Church of Jesus Christ of Latter Day Saints.
Tune: H Percy Smith, 1825-1898.

Come, O Creator Spirit 283

John 14:6, 10, 16, 17
D. and C. 18:6

VENI CREATOR L.M.

Unison — ♪ remains constant

1. Come, O Cre - a - tor Spir - it, come, And make with - in our
2. O Com - fort - er, that name is thine, Of God most high the
3. Our sens - es with thy light in - flame, Our hearts to heaven - ly
4. May we by thee the Fa - ther learn, And know the Son, and

hearts thy home; To us thy grace ce - les - tial give,
gift di - vine; The well of life, the fire of love,
love re - claim; Our bod - ies' poor in - fir - mi - ty
thee dis - cern, Who art of both; and so a - dore

Who of thy breath - ing move and live.
Our souls' a - noint - ing from a - bove.
With strength per - pet - ual for - ti - fy.
In per - fect faith for - ev - er - more. A - men.

Text: Veni Creator Spiritus attr. Hrabanus Maurus, 776-856; trans. Robert Bridges, 1844-1930.
Tune: Sarum plainsong Mode VIII; harm. Winfred Douglas, 1867-1944.

281 Holy Spirit, Truth Divine

Romans 5:5
I Peter 5:6, 7

HOLY SPIRIT, TRUTH DIVINE 7.7.7.7.

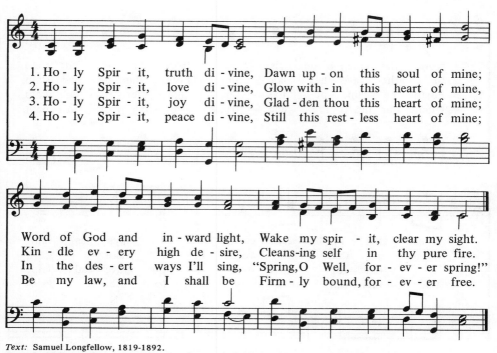

1. Ho - ly Spir - it, truth di - vine, Dawn up - on this soul of mine;
2. Ho - ly Spir - it, love di - vine, Glow with - in this heart of mine,
3. Ho - ly Spir - it, joy di - vine, Glad - den thou this heart of mine;
4. Ho - ly Spir - it, peace di - vine, Still this rest - less heart of mine;

Word of God and in - ward light, Wake my spir - it, clear my sight.
Kin - dle ev - ery high de - sire, Cleans-ing self in thy pure fire.
In the des - ert ways I'll sing, "Spring, O Well, for - ev - er spring!"
Be my law, and I shall be Firm - ly bound, for - ev - er free.

Text: Samuel Longfellow, 1819-1892.
Tune: R. Walker Robson, copyright 1936 Paterson's Publications, Ltd.; used by permission.

282 When Kindled by Thy Spirit's Light

James 1:17
D. and C. 10:7a

MARYTON L.M.

When kin - dled by Thy Spir - it's light, Our minds, il -

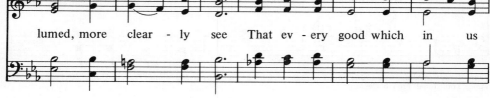

lumed, more clear - ly see That ev - ery good which in us

Now the Green Blade Rises

Ezekiel 37:3-5
John 1:11, 12

280

NOËL NOUVELET 11.10.10.11.

1. Now the green blade ris - es from the bur - ied grain,
2. In the grave they laid him, Love whom sin had slain,
3. Forth he came at Eas - ter, like the ris - en grain,
4. When our hearts are win - try, griev - ing, or in pain,

Wheat that in dark earth man - y days has lain;
Think - ing that he would nev - er wake a - gain,
He that for three days in the grave had lain;
Your touch can call us back to life a - gain,

Love lives a - gain, that with the dead has been:
Laid in the earth like grain that sleeps un - seen:
Raised from the dead my liv - ing Lord is seen:
Fields of our hearts that dead and bare have been:

Love is come a - gain like wheat a - ris - ing green.

Text: J. M. C. Crum, 1872-1958; from *The Oxford Book of Carols* by permission of Oxford University Press.
Tune: Traditional French Carol.

279
Let Us Sing of Easter Gladness

Acts 4:31-33
Romans 6:4-8

HOLY MANNA 8.7.8.7.D.

1. Let us sing of Eas-ter glad-ness That re-joic-es ev-ery day,
2. When we touch Truth's heal-ing gar-ment And be-hold life's pu-ri-ty,
3. Liv-ing meek-ly as the Mas-ter, Who of God was glo-ri-fied,

Sing of hope and faith up-lift-ed; Love has rolled the stone a-way.
When we find in Love the ref-uge That is man's se-cu-ri-ty,
Look-ing ev-er to the ra-diance Of his won-drous Eas-ter-tide;

Lo, the prom-ise and ful-fill-ment, Lo, the Man whom God hath made,
When we turn from earth to Spir-it, And from self have won re-lease,
Freed of fear, of pain, and sor-row, Giv-ing God the hon-or due,

Seen in glo-ry of an Eas-ter Crowned with light that can-not fade.
Then we see the ris-en Sav-ior, Then we know his prom-ised peace.
Ev-ery day will be an Eas-ter Filled with ben-e-dic-tions new.

Text: Frances Thompson Hill; copyright 1932, renewed 1960, The Christian Science Board of Directors. All rights reserved Used by permission.
Tune: William Moore in William Walker's *Southern Harmony*, 1835; harm. Rosalee Elser, 1925 - ; copyright 1980 Rosalee Elser; used by permission.

Jesus Christ Is Risen Today

278

John 20:19, 20
Matthew 28:2-5 (2-7)

LLANFAIR 7.7.7.7. with alleluias
Alternate tune: EASTER HYMN (277)

1. Je - sus Christ is risen to - day,
2. Hymns of praise then let us sing, Al - le - lu - ia!
3. Sing we to our God a - bove,

Our tri - um -phant ho - ly day,
Un - to Christ, our heaven - ly King, Al - le - lu - ia!
Praise e - ter - nal as His love;

Who did once, up - on the cross,
Who en -dured the cross and grave, Al - le - lu - ia!
Praise Him, all ye heaven-ly host,

Suf - fer to re -deem our loss.
Sin - ners to re -deem and save. Al - le - lu - ia!
Fa - ther, Son, and Ho - ly Ghost.

Text: Latin, 14th Century; trans. in *Lyra Davidica*, 1708; stanza 2, John Arnold's *Compleat Psalmodist*, 1749; stanza 3, Charles Wesley, 1707-1788.
Tune: Robert Williams, c. 1781-1821; harm. David Evans, 1874-1948. From *The Revised Church Hymnary* by permission of Oxford University Press.

277 Angels, Roll the Rock Away

I Corinthians 15:18-22
Psalm 71:22, 23

EASTER HYMN 7.7.7.7. with alleluias
Alternate tune: LLANFAIR (278)

1. An - gels, roll the rock a - way!
2. 'Tis the Sav - ior! Ser - aphs, raise, Al - le - lu - ia!
3. Praise him, all ye heaven-ly choirs!

Death, yield up thy might - y prey!
Your tri - um - phant shout of praise, Al - le - lu - ia!
Praise him, sweep your gold - en lyres!

See, he ris - es from the tomb,
Let the earth's re - mot - est bound, Al - le - lu - ia!
Praise him in the no - blest songs,

Ris - es with im - mor - tal bloom,
Hear the joy - in - spir - ing sound, Al - le - lu - ia!
Praise him with ten thou - sand tongues!

Text: Thomas Scott, 1705-1775.
Tune: Lyra Davidica, 1708.

Al - le - lu - ia! Al - le - lu - ia! Al - le - lu - ia!

Text: Cyril A. Alington, 1872-1955, alt.; used by permission of Hymns Ancient and Modern Ltd.
Tune: Melchior Vulpius, c. 1570-1615.

The Strife Is O'er

276

Ether 5:7-9
I Timothy 2:4-6

VICTORY 8.8.8. with alleluias

Al - le - lu - ia! Al - le - lu - ia! Al - le - lu - ia!

1. The strife is o'er, the bat - tle done; Now is the vic - tor's
2. Death's might - iest pow'rs have done their worst, And Je - sus has his
3. On the third morn, he rose a - gain, Glo - rious in maj - es -
4. Lord, by the stripes that wounded thee From death's dread sting thy

tri - umph won; O let the song of praise be sung:
foes dis - persed; Let shouts of praise and joy out - burst:
ty to reign; O let us swell the joy - ful strain:
serv - ants free That we may live and sing to thee:

Al - le - lu - ia!

Text: From 17th Century Latin, trans. Francis Pott, 1832-1909.
Tune: Giovanni P. da Palestrina, 1525-1594; arr. William H. Monk, 1823-1889.

274   I Know That My Redeemer Lives

D. and C. 76:3a, f, h
III Nephi 5:11-17

TRURO L.M.
Alternate hymn: 273

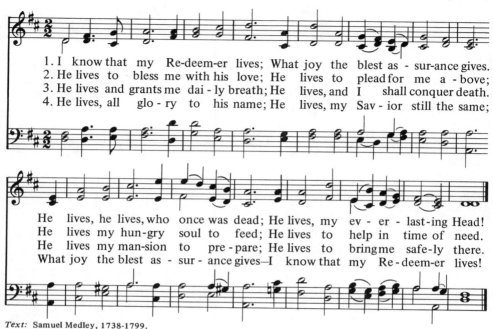

1. I know that my Re-deem-er lives; What joy the blest as-sur-ance gives.
2. He lives to bless me with his love; He lives to plead for me a-bove;
3. He lives and grants me dai-ly breath; He lives, and I shall conquer death.
4. He lives, all glo-ry to his name; He lives, my Sav-ior still the same;

He lives, he lives, who once was dead; He lives, my ev-er-last-ing Head!
He lives my hun-gry soul to feed; He lives to help in time of need.
He lives my man-sion to pre-pare; He lives to bring me safe-ly there.
What joy the blest as-sur-ance gives—I know that my Re-deem-er lives!

Text: Samuel Medley, 1738-1799.
Tune: Charles Burney, 1726-1814.

275   Good Christian Friends, Rejoice and Sing

I Corinthians 15:20-22
D. and C. 76:3f, g

VULPIUS (Gelobt Sei Gott) 8.8.8. with refrain

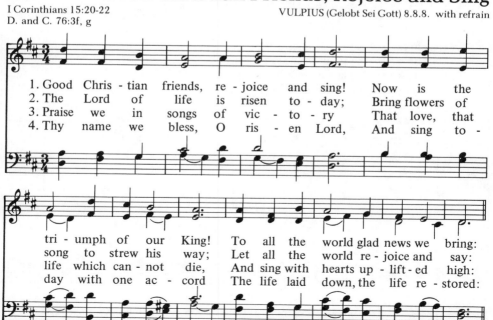

1. Good Chris-tian friends, re-joice and sing! Now is the
2. The Lord of life is risen to-day; Bring flowers of
3. Praise we in songs of vic-to-ry That love, that
4. Thy name we bless, O ris-en Lord, And sing to-

tri-umph of our King! To all the world glad news we bring:
song to strew his way; Let all the world re-joice and say:
life which can-not die, And sing with hearts up-lift-ed high:
day with one ac-cord The life laid down, the life re-stored:

I Know That My Redeemer Lives

273

D. and C. 76:3a, f, h
III Nephi 5:11-17

LASST UNS ERFREUEN L.M. with alleluias
Alternate hymn: 274

1. I know that my Re-deem-er lives; What joy the blest as-sur-ance gives.
2. He lives to bless me with his love; He lives to plead for me a-bove;
3. He lives and grants me dai-ly breath; He lives, and I shall con-quer death.
4. He lives, all glo-ry to his name; He lives, my Sav-ior still the same;

Al-le-lu - ia! Al-le-lu - ia!

He lives, he lives, who once was dead;
He lives my hun-gry soul to feed;
He lives my man-sion to pre-pare;
What joy the blest as-sur-ance gives—

He lives, my ev-er-last-ing Head!
He lives to help in time of need.
He lives to bring me safe-ly there.
I know that my Re-deem-er lives!

Al-le-lu - ia! Al-le-lu - ia!

Al-le-lu - ia! Al-le-lu - ia! Al-le-lu - ia!

Text: Samuel Medley, 1738-1799.
Tune: Melody from *Geistliche Kirchengesäng*, Cologne, 1623; arr. & harm. Ralph Vaughan Williams, 1872-1958.
From *The English Hymnal* by permission of Oxford University Press.

272

Christ Is Alive

D. and C. 76:4g
Galatians 2:20

WHITEFIELD L.M. with alleluias

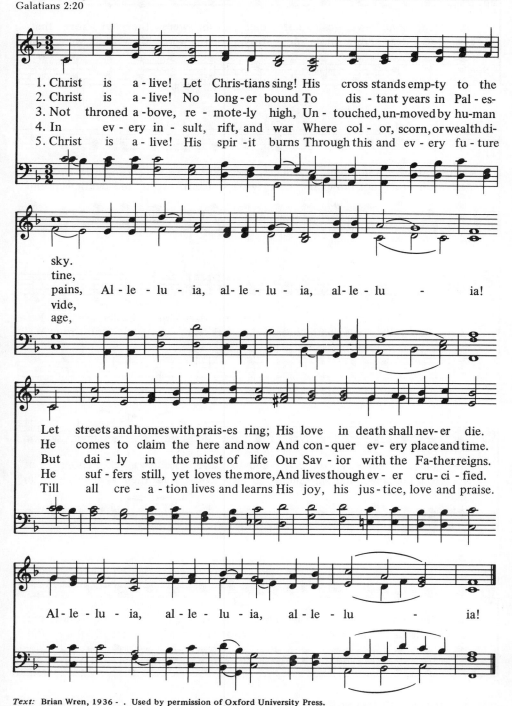

1. Christ is a-live! Let Chris-tians sing! His cross stands emp-ty to the
2. Christ is a-live! No long-er bound To dis-tant years in Pal-es-
3. Not throned a-bove, re-mote-ly high, Un-touched, un-moved by hu-man
4. In ev-ery in-sult, rift, and war Where col-or, scorn, or wealth di-
5. Christ is a-live! His spir-it burns Through this and ev-ery fu-ture

sky.
tine,
pains, Al-le-lu-ia, al-le-lu-ia, al-le-lu - ia!
vide,
age,

Let streets and homes with prais-es ring; His love in death shall nev-er die.
He comes to claim the here and now And con-quer ev-ery place and time.
But dai-ly in the midst of life Our Sav-ior with the Fa-ther reigns.
He suf-fers still, yet loves them more, And lives though ev-er cru-ci-fied.
Till all cre-a-tion lives and learns His joy, his jus-tice, love and praise.

Al-le-lu - ia, al-le-lu - ia, al-le-lu - ia!

Text: Brian Wren, 1936 - . Used by permission of Oxford University Press.
Tune: Keith Landis, 1922 - ; harm. Jeffrey Rickard; copyright 1977 Praise Publications, Inc. Used by permission.

ris-en, and we can-not die. Vain were the ter-rors that
gave us death can-not de-stroy. Sad were the life we must

gath-ered a-round him, And short the do-min-ion of death and the
part with to-mor-row If tears were our birth-right and death were our

grave; He burst from the fet-ters of dark-ness that bound him, Re-
end; But Je-sus hath cheered the dark val-ley of sor-row; We'll

splen-dent in glo-ry, to live and to save. Loud was the cho-rus of
rise from the dead and im-mor-tal as-cend. Lift then your voic-es in

an-gels on high; The Sav-ior hath ris-en, and we shall not die.
tri-umph on high, For Je-sus hath ris-en, and we shall not die.

Text: Henry Ware, Jr., 1794-1843, alt.
Tune: Isaac B. Woodbury, 1819-1858.

270

John 16:32, 33
Luke 22:41, 42

When Jesus Wept

WHEN JESUS WEPT L.M.

Unison

(1)* When Je - sus wept, the fall - ing tear

(2) In mer - cy flowed be - yond all bound;

(3) When Je - sus groaned, a trem - bling fear

(4) Seized all the guilt - y world a - round.

* May be used as a four part canon unaccompanied.
Text: William Billings, 1746-1800.
Tune: William Billings, 1746-1800; harm. by Richard D. Wetzel, 1935 - ; copyright 1972 by The Westminster Press.
Used by permission.

271

John 11:25, 26
I Corinthians 15:54-57

Lift Your Glad Voices

TRUMPET 10.11.11.11.12.11.10.11.

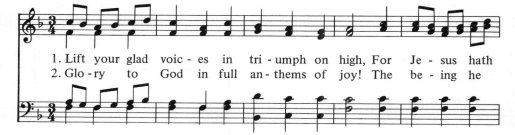

1. Lift your glad voic - es in tri - umph on high, For Je - sus hath

2. Glo - ry to God in full an - thems of joy! The be - ing he

Deep Were His Wounds

269

II Nephi 1:71-75
Acts 5:30-32

MARLEE 6.6.6.6.8.8.

1. Deep were his wounds, and red, On cru - el
Cal - va - ry, As on the cross he bled In
bit - ter ag - o - ny. But they, whom sin has
wound - ed sore, Find heal - ing in the wounds he bore.

2. He suf - fered shame and scorn, And wretch - ed,
dire dis - grace; For - sak - en and for - lorn, He
hung there in our place. But all who would from
sin be free Look to his cross for vic - to - ry.

3. His life, his all, he gave When he was
cru - ci - fied; Our bur - dened souls to save, What
fear - ful death he died! But each of us, though
dead in sin, Through him e - ter - nal life may win.

Text: William Johnson, 1906 - .
Tune: Leland B. Sateren, 1913 - .
Text and tune copyright 1958 the Lutheran *Service Book and Hymnal*; used by permission.

268

Ride On, Ride On in Majesty

Luke 19:36, 37 (37, 38)
I Nephi 3:82-86

DEUS TUORUM MILITUM L.M.

Unison (or harmony)

1. Ride on, ride on in maj - es - ty! Hark, all the
2. Ride on, ride on in maj - es - ty! In low - ly
3. Ride on, ride on in maj - es - ty! As all the
4. Ride on, ride on in maj - es - ty! In low - ly

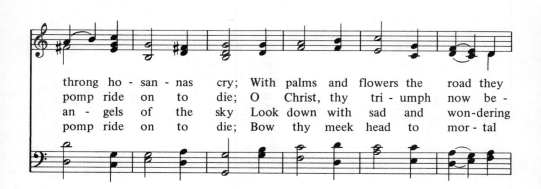

throng ho - san - nas cry; With palms and flowers the road they
pomp ride on to die; O Christ, thy tri - umph now be -
an - gels of the sky Look down with sad and won-dering
pomp ride on to die; Bow thy meek head to mor - tal

strew, With Christ his des - tined way pur - sue.
gin O'er cap - tive death and con - quered sin.
eyes To see the ap - proach-ing sac - ri - fice.
pain, Then take, O God, thy power and reign. A - men.

Text: Henry H. Milman, 1791-1868, alt.
Tune: From *Grenoble Antiphoner*, 1753.

Were You There

I Corinthians 15:3, 4
D. and C. 17:5a-d

WERE YOU THERE 10.10.13.10.

1. Were you there when they cru - ci - fied my Lord? Were you
2. Were you there when they nailed him to the tree? Were you
3. Were you there when they laid him in the tomb? Were you
4. Were you there when the sun re - fused to shine? Were you
5. Were you there when God raised him from the tomb? Were you

there when they cru - ci - fied my Lord?
there when they nailed him to the tree?
there when they laid him in the tomb? Oh!_____
there when the sun re - fused to shine?
there when God raised him from the tomb?

Some-times it caus - es me to trem - ble, trem - ble, trem - ble.

Were you there when they cru - ci - fied my Lord?
Were you there when they nailed him to the tree?
Were you there when they laid him in the tomb?
Were you there when the sun re - fused to shine?
Were you there when God raised him from the tomb?

Text: American Folk Hymn.
Tune: American Folk Hymn.

266 Go to Dark Gethsemane

Matthew 26:35, 36 (38, 39)
D. and C. 36:11b

GETHSEMANE 7.7.7.D.

1. Go to dark Gethsemane, Ye who feel the
2. See him at the judgment hall, Beaten, bound, re-
3. Calvary's mournful mountain climb; There adoring
4. Early hasten to the tomb Where they laid his

tempter's power; Your Redeemer's conflict see;
viled, arraigned; See him meekly bearing all;
at his feet, Mark that miracle of time,
breathless clay; All is solitude and gloom.

Watch with him one bitter hour; Turn not from his
Love for us his soul sustained. Shun not suffering,
God's own sacrifice complete. "It is finished!"
Who has taken him away? Christ is ris'n! He

griefs away; Learn of Jesus Christ to pray.
shame, nor loss; Learn of Christ to bear the cross.
hear him cry; Learn of Jesus Christ to die.
meets our eyes. Savior, cause us so to rise.

Text: James Montgomery, 1771-1854.
Tune: Richard Redhead, 1820-1901.

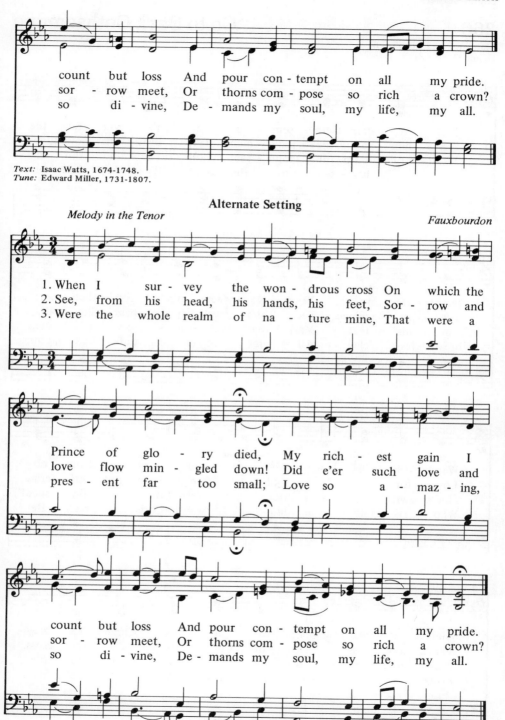

count but loss And pour con - tempt on all my pride.
sor - row meet, Or thorns com - pose so rich a crown?
so di - vine, De - mands my soul, my life, my all.

Text: Isaac Watts, 1674-1748.
Tune: Edward Miller, 1731-1807.

Alternate Setting

Melody in the Tenor   *Fauxbourdon*

1. When I sur - vey the won - drous cross On which the
2. See, from his head, his hands, his feet, Sor - row and
3. Were the whole realm of na - ture mine, That were a

Prince of glo - ry died, My rich - est gain I
love flow min - gled down! Did e'er such love and
pres - ent far too small; Love so a - maz - ing,

count but loss And pour con - tempt on all my pride.
sor - row meet, Or thorns com - pose so rich a crown?
so di - vine, De - mands my soul, my life, my all.

Setting: Geoffrey Shaw, 1879-1943; used by permission of Faith Press Ltd.

264 'Tis Midnight, and on Olive's Brow

D. and C. 36:11b
Mark 14:35-40 (31-36)

OLIVE'S BROW L.M.

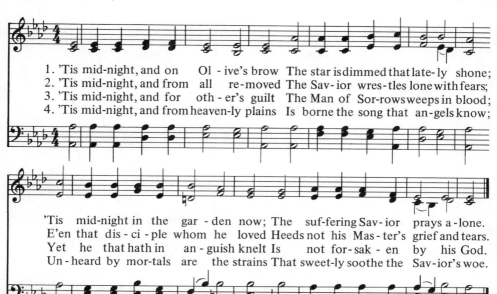

1. 'Tis mid-night, and on   Ol - ive's brow The star is dimmed that late-ly shone;
2. 'Tis mid-night, and from   all re-moved The Sav-ior wres-tles lone with fears;
3. 'Tis mid-night, and for   oth-er's guilt The Man of Sor-rows weeps in blood;
4. 'Tis mid-night, and from heaven-ly plains Is borne the song that an-gels know;

'Tis mid-night in the gar-den now; The suf-fering Sav-ior prays a-lone.
E'en that dis-ci-ple whom he loved Heeds not his Mas-ter's grief and tears.
Yet he that hath in an-guish knelt Is not for-sak-en by his God.
Un-heard by mor-tals are the strains That sweet-ly soothe the Sav-ior's woe.

Text: William B. Tappan, 1794-1849.
Tune: William B. Bradbury, 1816-1868.

265 When I Survey the Wondrous Cross

D. and C. 19:3a
Galatians 6:14

ROCKINGHAM L.M.

1. When   I   sur - vey   the   won - drous   cross   On   which   the
2. See,   from   his   head,   his   hands,   his   feet,   Sor - row   and
3. Were   the   whole realm   of   na - ture   mine,   That   were   a

Prince   of   glo - ry   died,   My   rich - est   gain   I
love   flow   min - gled   down!   Did   e'er   such   love   and
pres - ent   far   too   small;   Love   so   a - maz - ing,

Lift High the Cross

John 3:14, 15
John 12:23, 24

CRUCIFIER 10.10.10.10.

Unison

Lift high the cross, the love of Christ pro - claim

Fine

till all the world a - dore his sa - cred name.

Harmony

1. Come, Chris - tian, fol - low where our Sav - ior trod,
2. O Lord, once lift - ed high on Cal - va - ry,
3. O may our song of tri - umph ev - er be

D. C.

O love vic - to - rious, Christ the Son of God.
As thou hast prom - ised, draw us un - to thee.
Praise to the Cru - ci - fied for vic - to - ry.

accomp.

Text: George William Kitchin, 1827-1912; Michael Robert Newbolt, 1874-1956; alt.; used by permission of the proprietors of *Hymns Ancient and Modern.*
Tune: Sydney Hugo Nicholson, 1875-1947; used by permission of the proprietors of *Hymns Ancient and Modern.*

262
O Sacred Head, Now Wounded

Isaiah 53:5-7
Titus 3:3-7

PASSION CHORALE 7.6.7.6.D.

1. O sa-cred Head, now wound-ed, With grief and shame weighed down;
2. What thou, my Lord, hast suf-fered Was all for sin-ners' gain;
3. What lan-guage shall I bor-row To thank thee, dear-est Friend,

Now scorn-ful-ly sur-round-ed With thorns, thine on-ly crown;
Mine, mine was the trans-gres-sion, But thine the dead-ly pain.
For this thy dy-ing sor-row, Thy pit-y with-out end?

O sa-cred Head, what glo-ry, What bliss till now was thine!
Lo, here I fall, my Sav-ior; 'Tis I de-serve thy place.
O make me thine for-ev-er; And should I faint-ing be,

Yet though de-spised and go-ry, I joy to call thee mine.
Look on me with thy fa-vor; Vouch-safe to me thy grace.
Lord, let me nev-er, nev-er Out-live my love to thee. A-men.

Text: Attr. to Bernard of Clairvaux, 1091 - 1153; tr. (German) by Paul Gerhardt, 1607 - 1676; tr. (English) by James
W. Alexander, 1804 - 1859.
Tune: Hans Leo Hassler, 1564 - 1612; harm. by J. S. Bach, 1685 - 1750.

Sound over All Waters

261

Isaiah 52:6, 7
I Nephi 3:197, 198

ST. DENIO 11.11.11.11.

1. Sound o-ver all wa-ters, reach out from all lands,
2. Blow, bu-gles of bat-tle, the march-es of peace,
3. With glad ju-bi-la-tions, bring hope to the world;

The chor-us of voic-es, the clasp-ing of hands;
East, west, north and south, let the long quar-rel cease;
The dark night is end-ing, and dawn has un-furled;

Sing hymns that were sung by the stars of the morn;
O sing ye the song an-gels sang at the birth;
Rise, hope of the a-ges, a-rise like the sun;

Sing songs of the an-gels when Je-sus was born.
Sing glo-ry to God and good-will on the earth.
All speech flow to mu-sic; all hearts beat as one!

Text: John Greenleaf Whittier, 1807-1892; alt.
Tune: Welsh Hymn Melody; John Robert's *Canaidau y Cyssegr*, 1839.

260 Good Christian Friends, Rejoice

Matthew 2:3, 4 (1:20, 21)
II Nephi 1:73, 74

IN DULCI JUBILO 6.6.7.7.7.8.5.5.

1. Good Chris - tian friends, re - joice With heart and soul and voice;
2. Good Chris - tian friends, re - joice With heart and soul and voice;
3. Good Chris - tian friends, re - joice With heart and soul and voice;

Give ye heed to what we say: Je - sus Christ is born to - day;
Now ye hear of end - less bliss: Je - sus Christ was born for this!
Now ye need not fear the grave; Je - sus Christ was born to save!

Ox and ass be - fore him bow, And he is in the man - ger now.
He has o - pened heav - en's door, And we are blest for - ev - er - more.
Calls you one and calls you all To gain his ev - er - last - ing hall.

Christ is born to - day! Christ is born to - day!
Christ was born for this! Christ was born for this!
Christ was born to save! Christ was born to save!

Text: Medieval Latin Carol; tr. John M. Neale, 1818-1866, alt.
Tune: German carol, 14th century.

Jesus, Good Above All Other

Isaiah 9:6, 7
John 6:37-40

QUEM PASTORES 8.8.8.7.

1. Je - sus, good a - bove all oth - er,
2. Je - sus, cra - dled in a man - ger,
3. Je - sus, for thy peo - ple dy - ing,
4. Lord, in all our do - ings guide us;

Gen - tle child of gen - tle moth - er,
For us fac - ing ev - ery dan - ger,
Ris - en Mas - ter, death de - fy - ing,
Pride and hate shall ne'er di - vide us;

In a sta - ble born our broth - er,
Liv - ing as a home - less stran - ger,
Lord, in heaven thy grace sup - ply - ing,
We'll go on with thee be - side us,

Give us grace to per - se - vere.
Make we thee our King most dear.
Keep us to thy pres - ence near.
And with joy we'll per - se - vere!

Text: Percy Dearmer, 1867-1936; sts. 1 & 2 borrowed from 12th century Latin, tr. John Mason Neale, 1818-1866;
from *The English Hymnal* by permission of Oxford University Press.
Tune: 14th Century German Carol Melody; arr. Ralph Vaughan Williams, 1872-1958; from *The English Hymnal*; used
by permission of Oxford University Press.

258

Joy to the World!

Alma 3:87, 88
Psalm 98:1-9

ANTIOCH 8.6.8.6.6.8.

1. Joy to the world! The Lord is come; Let earth re - ceive its King;
2. Joy to the world; The Sav - ior reigns; Let all their songs em - ploy
3. No more let sin and sor - row grow, Nor thorns in - fest the ground;
4. He rules the world with truth and grace, And makes the na - tions prove

Let ev - ery heart pre - pare him room,
While fields and floods, rocks, hills, and plains
He comes to make his bless - ings flow
The glo - ries of his righ - teous - ness

And heaven and na - ture sing, And heaven and na - ture sing,
Re - peat the sound-ing joy, Re - peat the sound-ing joy,
Far as the curse is found, Far as the curse is found,
And won - ders of his love, And won - ders of his love,

And heaven and na-ture sing,

And heaven and na-ture sing, And heaven and na-

And heaven, and heaven and na - ture sing.
Re - peat, re - peat the sound - ing joy.
Far as, far as the curse is found.
And won - ders, won - ders of his love.

ture sing.

Text: Based on Psalm 98, by Isaac Watts, 1674-1748.
Tune: George F. Handel, 1685-1759; arr. by Lowell Mason, 1792-1872.

What Child Is This

257

Matthew 3:9-11 (2:9-11)
Luke 2:6-18

GREENSLEEVES 8.7.8.7. with refrain

Unison (or harmony)

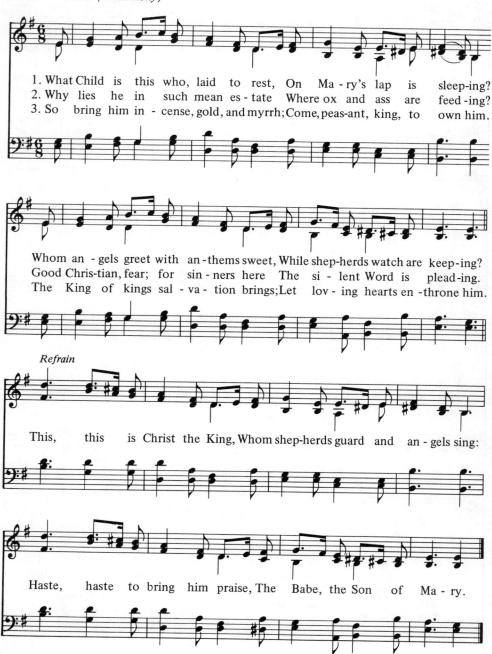

1. What Child is this who, laid to rest, On Ma - ry's lap is sleep-ing?
2. Why lies he in such mean es - tate Where ox and ass are feed-ing?
3. So bring him in - cense, gold, and myrrh; Come, peas-ant, king, to own him.

Whom an - gels greet with an - thems sweet, While shep-herds watch are keep-ing?
Good Chris-tian, fear; for sin - ners here The si - lent Word is plead-ing.
The King of kings sal - va - tion brings; Let lov - ing hearts en -throne him.

Refrain

This, this is Christ the King, Whom shep-herds guard and an - gels sing:

Haste, haste to bring him praise, The Babe, the Son of Ma - ry.

Text: William Chatterton Dix, 1837-1898.
Tune: 16th Century English Tune.

256 It Came Upon the Midnight Clear

Helaman 2:111, 112
Luke 2:8-14

CAROL C.M.D.

1. It came up-on the mid-night clear, That glo-rious song of old,
2. Still through the clo-ven skies they come, With peace-ful wings un-furled;
3. O ye, be-neath life's crush-ing load, Whose forms are bend-ing low,
4. For lo, the days are has-tening on, By proph-et bards fore-told,

From an-gels bend-ing near the earth To touch their harps of gold:
And still ce-les-tial mu-sic floats O'er all the wea-ry world;
Who toil a-long the climb-ing way With pain-ful steps and slow,
When with the ev-er cir-cling years Comes round the age of gold;

"Peace to the earth, good will to men, From heaven's all gra-cious King!"
A-bove its sad and low-ly plains They bend on heaven-ly wing,
Look up, for glad and gold-en hours Come swift-ly on the wing;
When peace shall o-ver all the earth Its fi-nal splen-dors fling,

The earth in sol-emn still-ness lay To hear the an-gels sing.
And ev-er o'er its ba-bel sounds The bless-ed an-gels sing.
O rest be-side the wea-ry road, And hear the an-gels sing!
And the whole world send back the song Which now the an-gels sing!

Text: Edmund H. Sears, 1810-1876.
Tune: Richard S. Willis, 1819-1900.

Lo, How a Rose E'er Blooming

255

Isaiah 11:1, 2
I Nephi 3:58-62

ES IST EIN ROS' 7.6.7.6.6.7.6.

♩ remains constant

1. Lo, how a rose e'er bloom-ing From ten-der stem hath
2. I-sai-ah 'twas fore-told it, The rose I have in
3. This flower, whose fra-grance ten-der With sweet-ness fills the

sprung! Of Jes-se's lin-eage com-ing As those of old have
mind; With Ma-ry we be-hold it, The vir-gin moth-er
air, Dis-pels with glo-rious splen-dor The dark-ness ev-ery-

sung. It came a flow-er bright, A-mid the
kind. To show God's love a-right Of her was
where. True man, yet ver-y God, From sin and

cold of win-ter, When half-spent was the night.
born a Sav-ior, When half-spent was the night.
death He saves us And light-ens ev-ery load.

Text: German, 16th century, tr. Theodore Baker, 1851-1934, Sts. 1, 2, alt.; tr. Harriet Krauth Spaeth, 1845-1925, St. 3.
Tune: Geistliche Kirchengesäng, Cologne, 1599; harm. Michael Praetorius, 1571-1621.

254

As with Gladness Men of Old

Matthew 3:9, 10 (2:9, 10)
D. and C. 17:5a-g

DIX 7.7.7.D.

1. As with glad - ness men of old Did the guid - ing
2. As with joy - ful steps they sped To that low - ly
3. As they of - fered gifts most rare At that man - ger
4. Ho - ly Je - sus, ev - ery day Keep us in the

star be - hold, As with joy they hailed its light
man - ger bed, There to bend the knee be - fore
rude and bare, So may we with ho - ly joy,
nar - row way; And when earth - ly things are past,

Lead - ing on - ward, beam - ing bright, So, most gra - cious
Him whom heaven and earth a - dore, So may we with
Pure and free from sin's al - loy, All our cost - liest
Bring our ran - somed souls at last Where they need no

Lord, may we Ev - er - more be led to thee.
will - ing feet Ev - er seek thy mer - cy seat.
treas - ures bring, Christ, to thee, our heaven - ly King.
star to guide, Where no clouds thy glo - ry hide.

Text: William C. Dix, 1837-1898.
Tune: Arr. from Conrad Kocher, 1786-1872, by W. H. Monk, 1823-1889.

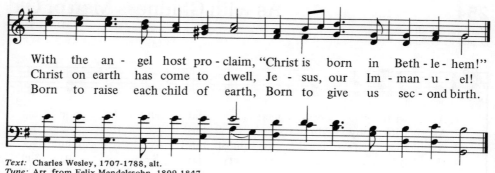

With the an - gel host pro - claim, "Christ is born in Beth - le - hem!"
Christ on earth has come to dwell, Je - sus, our Im - man - u - el!
Born to raise each child of earth, Born to give us sec - ond birth.

Text: Charles Wesley, 1707-1788, alt.
Tune: Arr. from Felix Mendelssohn, 1809-1847.

Heir of All the Waiting Ages

253

Matthew 2:3-6 (1:20-23)
Luke 2:25-32

PICARDY 8.7.8.7.8.7.

Unison

1. Heir of all the wait - ing a - ges, Hope of a - ges yet to be,
2. Thou shalt be the great phy - si - cian For the ills of hu - man - kind;
3. An - gel voic - es in the heav - ens Joy - ful - ly pro - claim thy birth,

Light to those that sit in dark - ness, Liv - ing truth to make us free:
Thou shalt heal the wound - ed spir - it, And give vi - sion to the blind—
Sing - ing of a prom - ised king - dom, Reign of right - teous - ness and worth—

Strick - en souls shall know the com - fort Of thy gra - cious min - is - try.
Larg - er life for all who seek it In the child - like heart and mind.
Songs of proph - e - cy and prom - ise, Peace, good - will have come to earth.

Text: Marion Franklin Ham, 1867-1956; alt.; copyright Beacon Press. Used by permission.
Tune: Traditional French Carol.

252

Hark, the Herald Angels Sing

Mosiah 1:102, 103
II Corinthians 5:17, 18, 21

MENDELSSOHN 7.7.7.7.D. with repeat

1. Hark, the her-ald an-gels sing, "Glo-ry to the new-born King,
2. Christ, by high-est heaven a-dored, Christ, the ev-er-last-ing Lord,
3. Hail, the heaven-born Prince of Peace! Hail, the Son of Righ-teous-ness!

Peace on earth, and mer-cy mild, God and sin-ners rec-on-ciled."
In the man-ger born a King, While a-dor-ing an-gels sing,
Life and light to all he brings, Risen with heal-ing in his wings;

Joy-ful, all ye na-tions, rise, Join the tri-umph of the skies;
"Peace on earth, to men good-will;" Bid the trem-bling soul be still;
Mild he lays his glo-ry by, Born that we no more may die,

With the an-gel host pro-claim, "Christ is born in Beth-le-hem!"
Christ on earth has come to dwell, Je-sus, our Im-man-u-el!
Born to raise each child of earth, Born to give us sec-ond birth;

I Wonder as I Wander

251

Romans 5:6-8
I Peter 2:21-24

I WONDER AS I WANDER 12.11.11.12.

1. I won-der as I wan-der, out un-der the sky, How
2. When Ma-ry birthed Je-sus, 'twas in a cow's stall, With
3. If Je-sus had want-ed for an-y wee thing, A
4. I won-der as I wan-der, out un-der the sky, How

Je - sus the Sav - ior did come for to die For
wise men and farm-ers and shep-herds and all; But
star in the sky or a bird on the wing, Or
Je - sus the Sav - ior did come for to die For

poor or-nery peo-ple like you and like I; I
high from God's heav-en a star's light did fall, And the
all of God's an-gels in heav'n for to sing, He
poor or-nery peo-ple like you and like I; I

won-der as I wan-der, out un-der the sky.
prom-ise of a - ges it then did re-call.
sure-ly could have had it, 'cause he was the King.
won-der as I wan-der, out un-der the sky.

Text and Tune: Appalachian Folk Carol collected and adapted by John Jacob Niles, 1892 - ; copyright 1934, 1944
G. Schirmer, Inc. Arr. 1980 Rosalee Elser, 1925 - ; used by permission.

250 I Heard the Bells on Christmas Day

Luke 2:14
Isaiah 12:2

WALTHAM L.M.

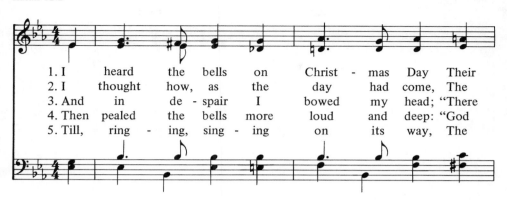

1. I heard the bells on Christ - mas Day Their
2. I thought how, as the day had come, The
3. And in de - spair I bowed my head; "There
4. Then pealed the bells more loud and deep: "God
5. Till, ring - ing, sing - ing on its way, The

old fa - mil - iar car - ols play, And wild and sweet the
bel - fries of all Chris - ten - dom Had rolled a - long the un-
is no peace on earth," I said, "For hate is strong and
is not dead, nor doth he sleep; The wrong shall fail, the
world re - volved from night to day, A voice, a chime, a

words re - peat Of peace on earth, good - will to men.
bro - ken song Of peace on earth, good - will to men,
mocks the song Of peace on earth, good - will to men."
right pre - vail, With peace on earth, good - will to men."
chant sub - lime Of peace on earth, good - will to men!

Text: Henry W. Longfellow, 1807-1882.
Tune: J. Baptiste Calkin, 1827-1905.

Go, Tell It on the Mountain

249

Luke 1:30-33
Luke 2:7-11

GO TELL IT 7.6.7.6. with refrain

Unison

Go, tell it on the moun - tain, O - ver the hills and ev - 'ry-where;

Fine

Go, tell it on the moun - tain That Je - sus Christ is born!

Harmony

1. While shep - herds kept their watch-ing O'er si - lent flocks by night,
2. The shep - herds feared and trem - bled When lo! a - bove the earth
3. Down in a low - ly man - ger The hum - ble Christ was born,

D. C.

Be - hold through-out the heav-ens There shone a ho - ly light.
Rang out the an - gel cho - rus That hailed our Sav - ior's birth.
And God sent us sal - va - tion That bless - ed Christ-mas morn.

Text: American Folk Hymn; stanzas by John W. Work, Jr., 1872-1925.
Tune: American Folk Melody, harm. by John W. Work, III, 1901-1967.
Text and tune from *American Negro Songs and Spirituals.* Used by permission of Mrs. John W. Work, III.

248

O Little Town of Bethlehem

Alma 5:19
Micah 5:2

ST. LOUIS 8.6.8.6.7.6.8.6.
Alternate tune: FOREST GREEN (484)

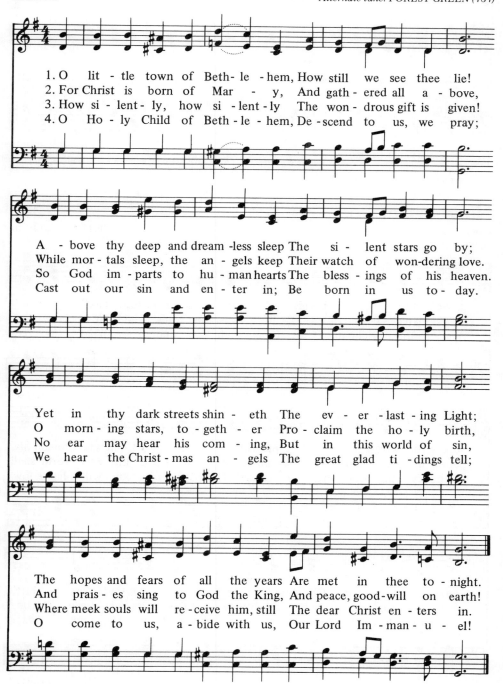

1. O lit- tle town of Beth- le -hem, How still we see thee lie!
2. For Christ is born of Mar - y, And gath- ered all a - bove,
3. How si - lent- ly, how si -lent -ly The won- drous gift is given!
4. O Ho - ly Child of Beth - le -hem, De -scend to us, we pray;

A - bove thy deep and dream -less sleep The si - lent stars go by;
While mor -tals sleep, the an - gels keep Their watch of won-dering love.
So God im -parts to hu - man hearts The bless - ings of his heaven.
Cast out our sin and en -ter in; Be born in us to - day.

Yet in thy dark streets shin - eth The ev - er -last- ing Light;
O morn - ing stars, to -geth - er Pro - claim the ho - ly birth,
No ear may hear his com - ing, But in this world of sin,
We hear the Christ -mas an - gels The great glad ti -dings tell;

The hopes and fears of all the years Are met in thee to - night.
And prais - es sing to God the King, And peace, good-will on earth!
Where meek souls will re -ceive him, still The dear Christ en - ters in.
O come to us, a -bide with us, Our Lord Im -man - u - el!

Text: Phillips Brooks, 1835-1893.
Tune: Lewis H. Redner, 1831-1908.

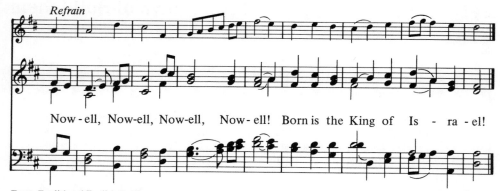

Now - ell, Now-ell, Now-ell, Now-ell! Born is the King of Is - ra - el!

Text: Traditional English Carol.
Tune: Traditional English Melody in W. Sandys' *Christmas Carols*, 1833; descant by Kathryn Reese O'Boyle, copyright
1941 by the Presbyterian Board of Christian Education; renewed 1969; from *The Hymnal for Youth*; used by
permission of The Westminster Press.

Newborn of God 247

Mosiah 1:97-102
Luke 2:16-19

TOULON 10.10.10.10.

1. New - born of God, his glo - ry man - i - fest, God's gift of
2. The fresh - ness of God's life was in this child. He grew in
3. If one bright day can bring such love and peace, What glo - ry

love so won - drous - ly ex - pressed! The Ho - ly Child who brought his
youth, in man - hood, ho - ly, mild. A no - bler life this world shall
when his king - dom shall in - crease! Then Christ - mas joy will hal - low

gift to earth At Christ - mas time in true hearts finds re - birth.
nev - er see; By him we know what God with us can be.
all our days, And thoughts of him en - light - en all our ways!

Text: Frank W. Mills, 1876-1963; alt.; copyright 1956 Herald Publishing House.
Tune: Louis Bourgeois, c. 1510-c. 1561.

246

Matthew 3:1, 9-11 (2:1, 9-11)
Alma 10:19, 26

The First Nowell

THE FIRST NOWELL   Irregular with refrain

Descant

1. The first Now-ell the an-gel did say Was to cer-tain poor
2. They look-ed up and saw a star Shin-ing in the
3. And by the light of that same star, Three Wise Men
4. This star drew nigh to the north-west, O'er Beth-le-hem
5. Then en-tered in those Wise Men three; Full rev-er-ent-

shep-herds in fields as they lay, In fields where they lay a -
east be - yond them far, And to the earth it
came from a coun-try a - far; To seek for a king was
then it took its rest, And there it did both
ly up - on the knee, They of - fered there, in

keep-ing their sheep, On a cold win-ter's night that was so deep.
gave great light, And so it con - tin-ued both day and night.
their in - tent, And to fol-low the star wher - ev - er it went.
stop and stay Right o - ver the place where Je - sus lay.
his pres - ence, Their gold and myrrh and frank - in - cense.

On This Day Earth Shall Ring

245

Luke 2:15-20
Matthew 3:1-11 (2:1-11)

PERSONENT HODIE
6.6.6.6.6. with refrain

Unison (or harmony)

1. On this day earth shall ring With the song chil-dren sing
2. God's bright star o'er his head, Wise men three to him led;
3. On this day an-gels sing; With their song earth shall ring,

To the Lord, Christ our King, Born on earth to save us;
Kneel they low by his bed, Lay their gifts be-fore him,
Prais-ing Christ, Heav-en's King, Born on earth to save us;

Refrain

Him the Fa-ther gave us.
Praise him and a-dore him. *Id - e - o - o - o, Id - e - o -
Peace and love he gave us.

o - o, Id - e - o glo-ri - a in ex-cel-sis De - o!

* Ideo is pronounced Ē - dā - o. The refrain means "Therefore give glory to God in the highest."

Special stanza for Easter:

4. For our kind he was slain,
Deep in grave he hath lain;
And he rose yet again
Swift to reign in glory.
This the Easter Story.

Special stanza for Pentecost:

5. Now at God's Pentecost,
Thee we praise, Holy Ghost;
Losing thee, we are lost.
May thy grace amending
Give us peace unending.

Text: Piae Cantiones, 1582; tr. Jane M. Joseph, c. 1894-1929; copyright 1924 J. Curwen & Sons, Ltd.; used by permission of G. Schirmer, Inc.
Tune: Piae Cantiones, 1582; harm. Rosalee Elser, 1925 - ; copyright 1980 Rosalee Elser; used by permission.

244

Silent Night! Holy Night!

Luke 2:8, 13, 14, 16
D. and C. 17:5a-d

STILLE NACHT 6.6.8.9.6.6.

1. Si - lent night! Ho - ly night! All is calm, all is bright Round yon
2. Si - lent night! Ho - ly night! Shep-herds quake at the sight! Glo - ries
3. Si - lent night! Ho - ly night! Son of God, love's pure light Ra - diant

vir - gin moth - er and child! Ho - ly In - fant, so ten-der and mild,
stream from heav - en a - far, Heaven-ly hosts sing Al - le - lu - ia,
beams from thy ho - ly face With the dawn of re - deem - ing grace,

Sleep in heav - en - ly peace;___ Sleep in heav - en - ly peace.
Christ, the Sav - ior, is born;___ Christ, the Sav - ior, is born!
Je - sus, Lord, at thy birth;___ Je - sus, Lord, at thy birth.

Text: Joseph Mohr, 1792-1848; tr. John Freeman Young, 1820-1885.
Tune: Franz Gruber, 1787-1863.

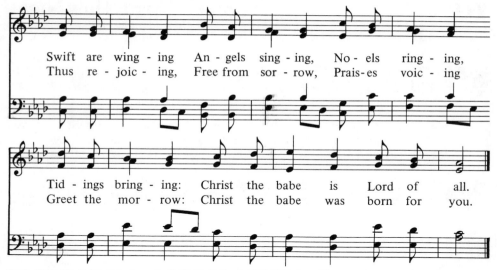

Swift are wing-ing An-gels sing-ing, No-els ring-ing,
Thus re - joic - ing, Free from sor - row, Prais-es voic - ing

Tid - ings bring - ing: Christ the babe is Lord of all.
Greet the mor - row: Christ the babe was born for you.

Text: From the Polish; paraphrase by Edith M. G. Reed, 1885-1933; from *Kingsway Carol Book*; used by permission of Evans Bros. Ltd.
Tune: Polish Carol; harm. David H. Jones, 1900 - ; copyright 1955 by John Ribble, from *The Hymnbook*, used by permission of the Westminster Press.

Good News! Great Joy to All the Earth 243

Luke 2:7-20
Matthew 3:10, 11 (2:10, 11)

DETROIT C.M.

Unison (or harmony)

1. Good news! Great joy to all the earth–The Prince of Peace is born!
2. Re - joice in hope! Cast out all fear! God's love in - cludes us all.
3. Rise up for peace! Let ev - ery life Re - spond with heart and hand:
4. Re - joice! Give thanks! The Christ has come: Re - ceive his life; be free!

God's peace he brings to hu - man hearts By fear and con - flict torn.
In Christ God calls us all to peace: Now heed that trum - pet call!
Cast out the bit - ter - ness and strife In ours and ev - ery land.
Let all the world be whole in him Who brings God's lib - er - ty!

Text: Frank von Christierson, 1900 - ; copyright 1976 The Hymn Society of America; used by permission.
Tune: *Supplement to Kentucky Harmony*, 1820; harm. Rosalee Elser, 1925 - ; copyright 1980 Rosalee Elser; used by permission.

241

Matthew 3:1, 2 (2:1, 2)
Luke 1:26-33

Sing Songs of Joy

SONGS OF JOY 4.5.4.4.5.

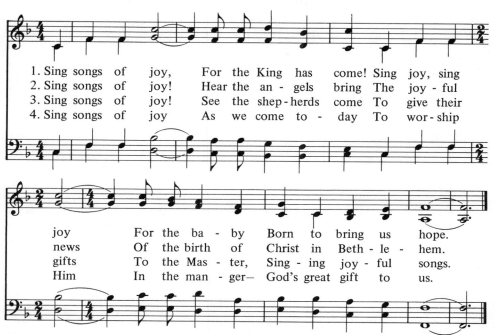

1. Sing songs of joy, For the King has come! Sing joy, sing
2. Sing songs of joy! Hear the an - gels bring The joy - ful
3. Sing songs of joy! See the shep - herds come To give their
4. Sing songs of joy As we come to - day To wor - ship

joy For the ba - by Born to bring us hope.
news Of the birth of Christ in Beth - le - hem.
gifts To the Mas - ter, Sing - ing joy - ful songs.
Him In the man - ger— God's great gift to us.

Text and Tune: Pamela Robison, 1947 - ; copyright 1980 Reorganized Church of Jesus Christ of Latter Day Saints.

242

Luke 2:7-20
Matthew 3:10, 11, (2:10, 11)

Infant Holy, Infant Lowly

W ZLOBIE LEZY 8.7.8.7.8.8.7.

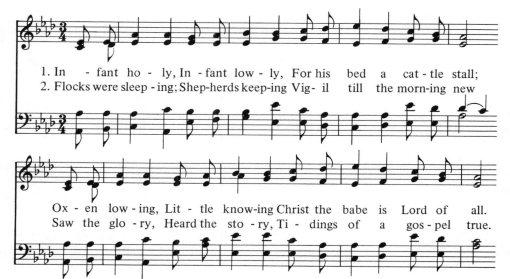

1. In - fant ho - ly, In - fant low - ly, For his bed a cat - tle stall;
2. Flocks were sleep - ing; Shep - herds keep - ing Vig - il till the morn - ing new

Ox - en low - ing, Lit - tle know - ing Christ the babe is Lord of all.
Saw the glo - ry, Heard the sto - ry, Ti - dings of a gos - pel true.

Once in Royal David's City

240

Luke 2:52
I John 3:2

IRBY 8.7.8.7.8.7.

1. Once in roy - al Da - vid's cit - y Stood a low - ly
2. He came down to earth from heav - en Who is God and
3. For he is our child - hood's pat - tern; Day by day like
4. And our eyes at last shall see him, Through his own re -

cat - tle shed, Where a moth - er laid her ba - by
Lord of all, And his shel - ter was a sta - ble,
us he grew; He was lit - tle, weak, and help - less;
deem - ing love; For that child so dear and gen - tle

In a man - ger for his bed: Mar - y was that
And his cra - dle was a stall: With the poor, and
Tears and smiles like us he knew: And he feel - eth
Is our Lord in heaven a - bove, And he leads his

moth - er mild, Je - sus Christ her lit - tle child.
mean, and low - ly Lived on earth our Sav - ior ho - ly.
for our sad - ness, And he shar - eth all our glad - ness.
chil - dren on To the place where he is gone.

Text: Cecil Frances Alexander, 1818-1895; alt.
Tune: Henry J. Gauntlett, 1805-1876

239

Luke 2:8-16
Helaman 5:59, 66

Silvery Star, Precious Star

STARLIGHT AND SONG 7.7.7.7. with refrain

1. Sil-ver-y star, pre-cious star, Shin-ing o-ver Beth-le-hem,
2. Beau-ti-ful song, won-drous song Kneel-ing shep-herds wept to hear,
3. Ba-by Sa-vior, born at night In the a-ges long a-go,
4. Lo, we hear the song o'er-head! Lo, we see the star a-rise!

Guid-ing Wise Men from a-far, In the still night lead-ing them.
Chant-ed by God's ho-ly throng, Sing-ing peace and joy and cheer.
An-gels sang and stars gave light For thy hum-ble home be-low.
Like the Wise Men we are led In the still night un-to Christ.

Refrain

Star-light and song All the night long,

Her-alds of morn; Je-sus is born.

Text: Elbert A. Smith, 1871-1959.
Tune: Audentia Anderson, 1872-1963. Text and tune copyright 1950 Herald Publishing House.

dore

come, let us a - dore him, O come, let us a - dore him, Christ, the Lord!

Text: Anonymous, Latin, 18th Century; trans. Frederick Oakeley, 1802-1880, and others.
Tune: John F. Wade, c. 1710-1786; descant by Lawrence Curry, 1906 - ; copyright 1941 by the Presbyterian Board of
Christian Education; renewed 1969; from *The Hymnal for Youth*; used by permission of The Westminster Press.

Alternate Setting: Stanza 2

Melody in the Tenor　　　　　　　　　　　　　　　　　　　　　　　　　　*Fauxbourdon*

2. O sing, choirs of an - gels, sing in ex - ul - ta - tion, Sing,

all ye cit - i - zens of heaven a - bove! Glo - ry to God, all

O come, let us a - dore him, O

glo - ry in the high - est;　　　O come, let us a -

O come, let us a - dore him, O

come, let us a - dore him,

dore him, a dore him, O come, let us a - dore him, Christ, the Lord!

come, let us a - dore him,

Setting: Arr. by Martin Shaw, 1875-1958; copyright 1924 Martin Shaw; used by permission of G. Schirmer, Inc.

238

D. and C. 108:7c
I Nephi 3:66, 67

O Come, All Ye Faithful

ADESTE FIDELES 12.10.11. with refrain

Descant (stanza 3)

1. O come, all ye faith-ful, joy-ful and tri - um-phant, O come
2. O sing, choirs of an - gels, sing in ex-ul - ta - tion, O sing,
3. All hail! Lord, we greet thee, born this hap-py morn-ing, O Je -

ye, O come ye to Beth - le - hem; Come and be-hold him,
all ye cit - i - zens of heaven a - bove! Glo - ry to God, all
sus, to thee be all glo - ry given; Word of the Fa - ther,

Refrain

O come a -

born the King of an - gels;
glo - ry in the high - est; O come, let us a - dore him, O
now in flesh ap - pear - ing;

Angels We Have Heard on High

237

Luke 2:8-14
D. and C. 76:4g

GLORIA 7.7.7.7. with refrain

1. An - gels   we have heard   on high Sweet - ly sing - ing o'er   the plains,
2. Shep-herds, why this   ju -   bi - lee? Why   your joy - ous songs pro - long?
3. Come to Beth - le - hem   and see   Him whose birth the   an - gels sing;

And   the moun - tains in   re - ply   Ech - o - ing their joy - ous strains.
What   the glad - some ti - dings be   Which in - spire your heaven - ly song?
Come a - dore,   on bend - ed knee,   Christ the Lord, our new - born King.

Refrain

Glo - - - ri - a   in ex - cel - sis De - o,

Glo - - - ri - a   in ex - cel - sis De - o.

Text: Traditional French Carol.
Tune: Traditional French Carol.

236 While Humble Shepherds

Hebrews 1:6
I Nephi 3:58, 62

CHRISTMAS 8.6.8.6.6.

1. While hum-ble shep-herds watched their flocks In Beth-lehem's
2. "Fear not," he said, for sud - den dread Had seized each
3. "To you, in Beth - le - hem this day Is born of
4. Thus spake the an - gel; and forth-with Ap - peared a
5. "All glo - ry be to God on high, And to the

fields by night, An an - gel sent from heaven ap-peared And
trou - bled mind; "Glad ti - dings of great joy I bring To
Da - vid's line The Sav - ior, who is Christ the Lord; Be -
shin - ing throng Of an - gels prais - ing God, and thus Ad -
earth be peace; Good - will is shown by heaven to all, And

filled the field with light; And filled the field with light.
you and hu - man - kind; To you and hu - man - kind.
hold in heaven his sign; Be - hold in heaven his sign!"
dressed their joy - ful song, Ad - dressed their joy - ful song:
nev - er - more shall cease; And nev - er - more shall cease."

Text: Nahum Tate, 1652-1715.
Tune: George F. Handel, 1685-1759.

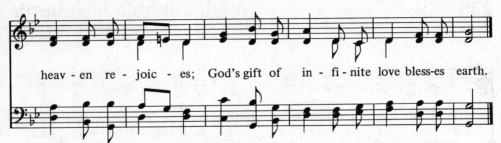

heav - en re - joic - es; God's gift of in - fi - nite love bless-es earth.

Text: Naomi Russell, 1921 - ; copyright 1980 Reorganized Church of Jesus Christ of Latter Day Saints.
Tune: Appalachian Folk Hymn attr. to R. Herron; harm. John Obetz, 1933 - ; copyright 1980 Reorganized Church of Jesus Christ of Latter Day Saints.

O Thou Joyful, O Thou Wonderful 235

Matthew 2:1-6 (1:18-23)
Luke 2:4-11

O SANCTISSIMA 4.5.7.6.6.7.

1. O thou joy - ful, O thou won-der-ful Grace re - veal - ing
2. O thou joy - ful, O thou won-der-ful Love re - veal - ing
3. O thou joy - ful, O thou won-der-ful Peace re - veal - ing

Christ-mas - tide! Je - sus came to win us From all sin with-
Christ-mas - tide! Loud ho - san - nas sing - ing And all prais - es
Christ-mas - tide! Dark - ness dis - ap - pear - eth, God's own light now

in us: Glo - ri - fy the ho - ly child!
bring - ing: May thy love with us a - bide.
near - eth: Peace and joy to all be - tide.

Text: Johannes D. Falk, 1768-1826, St. 1; Anonymous, Sts. 2, 3; trans. Henry Katterjohn, 1869-1931.
Tune: Tattersall's Psalmody, 1794.

234

Luke 1:26-30
Matthew 2:3, 4 (1:20, 21)

Joseph, Kind Joseph

STAR IN THE EAST 11.10.11.10.D.

1. Jo - seph, kind Jo - seph, look down in the man - ger; look on this
2. Ma - ry, brave Ma - ry, look down at your first - born; cra - dle him
3. Je - sus, dear Je - sus, look out at the hill - side; see how the

child to be known as your son. Care for him ten - der - ly
close to you now while you may. Treas - ure these mo - ments so
night is made bright by your star. On - ly the faith - ful will

un - til his Fa - ther calls him to do what no oth - er has done.
they will sus - tain you when he must go to show oth - ers the way.
fol - low its guid - ing; on - ly the wise see the Light that you are.

Refrain

An - gels in cho - rus sing glad hal - le - lu - jahs; hills ech - o

back the good news of the birth. Beth - le - hem sleeps but all

Away in a Manger

233

Luke 2:6, 7
Alma 5:19

CRADLE SONG 11.11.11.11.
Alternate hymn: 232

1. A-way in a man-ger, no crib for his bed,
2. The cat-tle are low-ing, the poor ba-by wakes,
3. Be near me, Lord Je-sus; I ask thee to stay

The lit-tle Lord Je-sus laid down his sweet head;
But lit-tle Lord Je-sus, no cry-ing he makes.
Close by me for-ev-er, and love me, I pray.

The stars in the bright sky looked down where he lay,
I love thee, Lord Je-sus; look down from the sky
Bless all the dear chil-dren in thy ten-der care,

The lit-tle Lord Je-sus, a-sleep on the hay.
And stay by my cra-dle till morn-ing is nigh.
And fit us for heav-en to live with thee there.

Text: Anonymous.
Tune: Melody by W. J. Kirkpatrick, 1838-1921; harm. by Rosalee Elser, 1925 - . Copyright 1980 by Rosalee Elser. Used by permission.

232

Away in a Manger

Luke 2:11, 12
Alma 5:19

MUELLER 11.11.11.11.
Alternate hymn: 233

1. A - way in a man - ger, no crib for his bed,
2. The cat - tle are low - ing; the poor ba - by wakes,
3. Be near me, Lord Je - sus; I ask thee to stay

The lit - tle Lord Je - sus laid down his sweet head;
But lit - tle Lord Je - sus, no cry - ing he makes.
Close by me for - ev - er, and love me, I pray.

The stars in the sky looked down where he lay,
I love thee, Lord Je - sus; look down from the sky
Bless all the dear chil - dren in thy ten - der care,

The lit - tle Lord Je - sus, a - sleep on the hay.
And stay by my cra - dle till morn - ing is nigh.
And fit us for heav - en to live with thee there.

Text: Anonymous.
Tune: James R. Murray, 1841-1905.

Angels from the Realms of Glory

231

Matthew 3:1, 2, 10, 11 (2:1, 2, 10, 11)
Luke 2:8-14

REGENT SQUARE 8.7.8.7. with refrain

1. An - gels from the realms of glo - ry, Wing your flight o'er
2. Shep - herds in the fields a - bid - ing, Watch - ing o'er your
3. Sag - es, leave your con - tem - pla - tions, Bright - er vi - sions
4. Saints be - fore the al - tar bend - ing, Watch - ing long in

all the earth; Ye who sang cre - a - tion's sto - ry
flocks by night, God with us is now re - sid - ing,
beam a - far. Seek the great De - sire of na - tions—
hope and fear. Sud - den - ly the Lord, de - scend - ing,

Refrain

Now pro - claim Mes - si - ah's birth:
Yon - der shines the in - fant light;
Ye have seen his na - tal star;
In his tem - ple shall ap - pear;

Come and wor - ship,

Come and wor - ship, Wor - ship Christ, the new - born King.

Text: James Montgomery, 1771-1854.
Tune: Henry Smart, 1813-1879.

230 Look at This Man, Born of God

Philippians 2:5-11
Luke 4:16-21

MABUNE 7.6.7.6.D

1. Look at this man, born of God In a low-ly man-ger.
2. Look at this man, born of God One with the af-flict-ed.
3. Look at this man, born of God, To-tal-ly self-giv-ing;

Man of sor-row and tra-vail, Nor to grief a stran-ger.
Nev-er such a-maz-ing grace In our race de-pict-ed.
No re-ward but cru-el death, E-ven then for-giv-ing.

Bro-ken-heart-ed for the poor, His own good un-heed-ing;
Bear-ing hu-man pain and sin, Poor and sick be-friend-ing;
Lift-ed up up-on the cross, End-less love in him re-vealed;

Look at this man, love of God, All our loves ex-ceed-ing.
Look at this man, sent of God; God's own life ex-tend-ing.
Look at this man, Son of God, By whose suff'-ring we are healed.

Text: Ko Yuki, 1896 - ; by permission of the Hymnal Committee, United Church of Christ in Japan. Trans. Hiroshi Yamada, 1935 - ; arr. Geoffrey F. Spencer, 1927 - ; copyright 1980 Reorganized Church of Jesus Christ of Latter Day Saints.
Tune: Seigi Abe; used by permission of the Hymnal Committee, United Church of Christ in Japan.

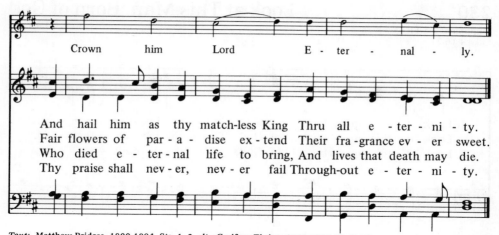

Crown him Lord E - ter - nal - ly.

And hail him as thy match-less King Thru all e - ter - ni - ty.
Fair flowers of par - a - dise ex - tend Their fra - grance ev - er sweet.
Who died e - ter - nal life to bring, And lives that death may die.
Thy praise shall nev - er, nev - er fail Through-out e - ter - ni - ty.

Text: Matthew Bridges, 1800-1894, Sts. 1, 2, alt.; Godfrey Thring, 1823-1903, St. 3, alt.
Tune: George J. Elvey, 1816-1893; descant by Donald D. Kettring, 1907 - ; copyright 1941 by the Presbyterian Board of Christian Education; renewed 1969; from *The Hymnal for Youth*; used by permission of The Westminster Press.

O Jesus, Our Lord

229

D. and C. 64:7a
I Nephi 5:59

LYONS 10.11.10.11.

1. O Je - sus, our Lord, thy name be a - dored For all the rich
2. Thrice hap - py are they who hear and o - bey And share in the

bless-ings con - veyed in thy word; Be - liev - ing, we trace thy won-ders
bless-ings of this gos-pel day; That bless-ing be mine, through fa - vor

of grace And cheer - ful - ly join in a con - cert of praise.
di - vine, And, O my Re - deem - er, the glo - ry be thine. A - men.

Text: European Edition, 1840.
Tune: Adapted from Johann Michael Haydn, 1737-1806.

228 Crown Him with Many Crowns

D. and C. 85:2
II Nephi 1:71-73

DIADEMATA S.M.D.

Descant (stanza 4 only)

4. Crown him Lord, The Po - ten - tate of time;

1. Crown him with man - y crowns, The Lamb up - on his throne:
2. Crown him the Lord of love: Be - hold his hands and side,
3. Crown him the Lord of life: Who tri - umphed o'er the grave,
4. Crown him the Lord of years: The po - ten - tate of time,

Crown him Lord, In - ef - fa - bly sub - lime.

Hark! how the heav'n-ly an - them drowns All mu - sic but its own!
Rich wounds, yet vis - i - ble a - bove, In beau - ty glo - ri - fied;
And rose vic - to - rious in the strife For those he came to save;
Cre - a - tor of the roll - ing spheres, In - ef - fa - bly sub - lime.

Crown him Lord, Crown him Lord,

A - wake, my soul, and sing Of him who died for thee;
His reign shall know no end, And 'round his pierc - ed feet
His glo - ries now we sing, Who died and rose on high,
All hail, Re - deem - er, hail! For thou hast died for me;

Word of God, Come Down on Earth

227

John 16:13, 14
John 1:17

LIEBSTER JESU 7.8.7.8.8.8.

1. Word of God, come down on earth, Living rain from heav'n descending; Touch our hearts and bring to birth Faith and hope and love unending. Word almighty, we revere you; Word made flesh, we long to hear you.

2. Word eternal, throned on high, Word that brought to life creation, Word that came from heav'n to die, Crucified for our salvation, Saving Word, the world restoring, Speak to us, your love outpouring.

3. Word that caused blind eyes to see, Speak and heal our mortal blindness; Deaf we are: our healer be; Loose our tongues to tell your kindness. Be our Word in pity spoken; Heal the world, by our sin broken.

4. Word that speaks your Father's love, One with him beyond all telling, Word that sends us from above God the Spirit, with us dwelling, Word of truth, to all truth lead us, Word of life, with one Bread feed us. A-men.

Text: James Quinn, copyright © 1969 Geoffrey Chapman, a division of Cassell Ltd., London; used by permission.
Tune: Johann Rudolph Ahle, 1625-1673; arr. Johann Sebastian Bach, 1685-1750.

226

Fairest Lord Jesus

III Nephi 4:44, 45, 48
Hebrews 1:1-3

SCHÖNSTER HERR JESU 5.6.8.5.5.8.

Text: Münster Gesangbuch, 1677; Schlesische Volkslieder, 1842; tr. Church Chorals and Choir Studies, 1850.
Tune: Silesian Folk Melody in Schlesische Volkslieder, 1842; descant by W. Frederic Miller, copyright 1941 the Presbyterian Board of Christian Education; renewed 1969; from The Hymnal for Youth; used by permission of The Westminster Press.

When, His Salvation Bringing

225

Matthew 21:5-7 (6-9)
D. and C. 110:23a-c

SPRINGTIME 7.6.7.6.D.

1. When, his sal - va - tion bring - ing, To Zi - on Je - sus came,
2. And since the Lord re - tain - eth His love for chil - dren still,
3. For should we fail pro - claim - ing Our great Re - deem - er's praise,

The chil - dren all stood sing - ing Ho - san - na to his name;
Though now as King he reign - eth On Zi - on's heaven - ly hill,
The stones, our si - lence sham - ing, Would their ho - san - nas raise.

Nor did their zeal of - fend him, But as he rode a - long
We'll flock a - round his ban - ner Who sits up - on his throne,
But shall we on - ly ren - der The trib - ute of our words?

He let them still at - tend him, And smiled to hear their song.
And cry a - loud, "Ho - san - na To Dav - id's roy - al Son!"
No, while our hearts are ten - der, They, too, shall be the Lord's.

Text: John King, 1789-1858.
Tune: Swedish Folk Melody; harm. Rosalee Elser, 1925 - ; harm. copyright 1980 by Rosalee Elser. Used by permission.

224 O Jesus Christ, to Thee May Hymns Be Rising

Luke 13:34, 35
I Nephi 3:187

CITY OF GOD 11.10.11.10

1. O Jesus Christ, to thee may hymns be ris - ing
2. Grant us new cour - age, sac - ri - fi - cial, hum - ble,
3. Show us thy Spir - it, brood - ing o'er each cit - y,

In ev - 'ry cit - y for thy love and care;
Strong in thy strength to ven - ture and to dare;
As thou didst weep a - bove Je - ru - sa - lem.

In - spire our wor - ship; grant the glad sur - pris - ing
To lift the fall - en, guide the feet that stum - ble,
Seek - ing to gath - er all in love and pit - y,

That thy blest Spir - it brings us ev - 'ry - where.
Seek out the lone - ly and God's mer - cy share.
And heal - ing those who touch thy gar - ment's hem.

The hymn may be concluded by repeating the first stanza.

Text: Bradford Gray Webster, 1898 - ; alt.; from *Five New Hymns on the City*, copyright 1954 The Hymn Society of America; used by permission.
Tune: Daniel Moe, 1926 - ; copyright 1957 Augsburg Publishing House; reprinted by permission.

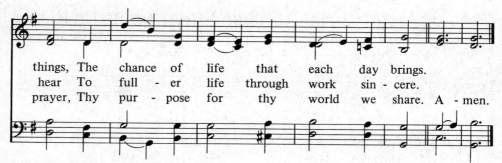

things, The chance of life that each day brings.
hear To full - er life through work sin - cere.
prayer, Thy pur - pose for thy world we share. A - men.

Text: Milton S. Littlefield, 1864-1934.
Tune: Thomas B. Southgate, 1814-1868.

Jesus Loves the Little Children

Mark 10:11-14 (13-16)
Moroni 8:18

223

CHILDREN 8.7.7.7.11.

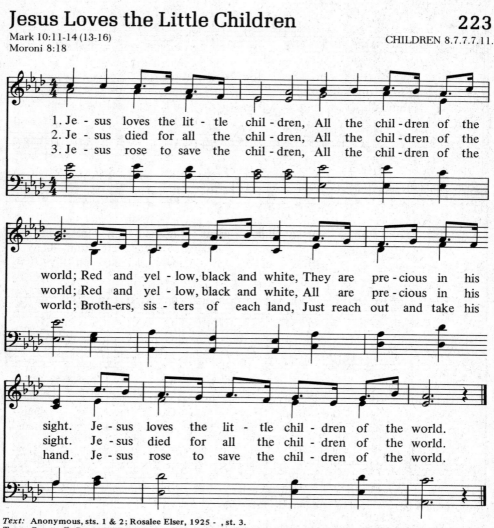

1. Je - sus loves the lit - tle chil - dren, All the chil - dren of the
2. Je - sus died for all the chil - dren, All the chil - dren of the
3. Je - sus rose to save the chil - dren, All the chil - dren of the

world; Red and yel - low, black and white, They are pre - cious in his
world; Red and yel - low, black and white, All are pre - cious in his
world; Broth-ers, sis - ters of each land, Just reach out and take his

sight. Je - sus loves the lit - tle chil - dren of the world.
sight. Je - sus died for all the chil - dren of the world.
hand. Je - sus rose to save the chil - dren of the world.

Text: Anonymous, sts. 1 & 2; Rosalee Elser, 1925 - , st. 3.
Tune: George F. Root, 1820-1895; arr. John Obetz, 1933 - ; copyright 1980 Reorganized Church of Jesus Christ of
Latter Day Saints.

221   For the Book of Mormon's Witness

D. and C. 42:5
II Nephi 12:37

KINGDOM 8.7.8.7.

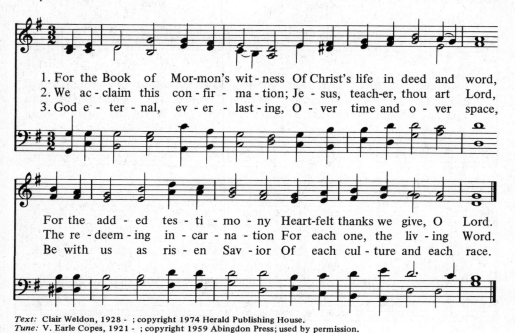

1. For the Book of Mor-mon's wit-ness Of Christ's life in deed and word,
2. We ac-claim this con-fir-ma-tion; Je-sus, teach-er, thou art Lord,
3. God e-ter-nal, ev-er-last-ing, O-ver time and o-ver space,

For the add-ed tes-ti-mo-ny Heart-felt thanks we give, O Lord.
The re-deem-ing in-car-na-tion For each one, the liv-ing Word.
Be with us as ris-en Sav-ior Of each cul-ture and each race.

Text: Clair Weldon, 1928 - ; copyright 1974 Herald Publishing House.
Tune: V. Earle Copes, 1921 - ; copyright 1959 Abingdon Press; used by permission.

222   O Son of God, Thou Madest Known

D. and C. 4:1
Psalm 90:16, 17

BROOKFIELD L.M.

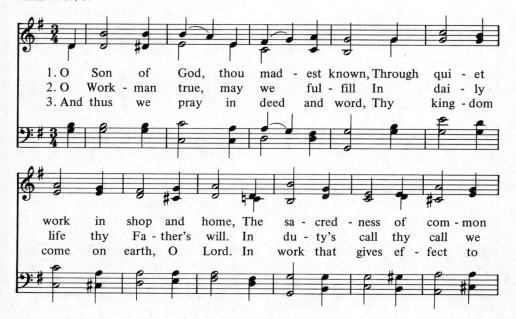

1. O Son of God, thou mad-est known, Through qui-et
2. O Work-man true, may we ful-fill In dai-ly
3. And thus we pray in deed and word, Thy king-dom

work in shop and home, The sa-cred-ness of com-mon
life thy Fa-ther's will. In du-ty's call thy call we
come on earth, O Lord. In work that gives ef-fect to

Of the Father's Love Begotten

Revelation 1:7, 8
Mosiah 8:28-35

DIVINUM MYSTERIUM 8.7.8.7.8.7.7.

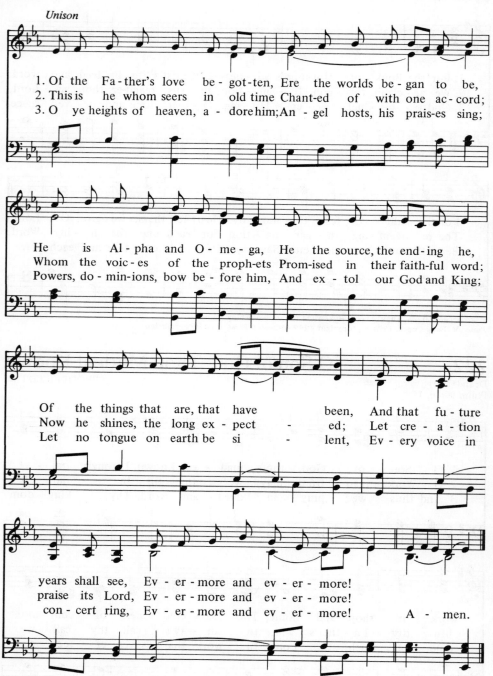

Unison

1. Of the Fa-ther's love be-got-ten, Ere the worlds be-gan to be,
2. This is he whom seers in old time Chant-ed of with one ac-cord;
3. O ye heights of heaven, a-dore him; An-gel hosts, his prais-es sing;

He is Al-pha and O-me-ga, He the source, the end-ing he,
Whom the voic-es of the proph-ets Prom-ised in their faith-ful word;
Powers, do-min-ions, bow be-fore him, And ex-tol our God and King;

Of the things that are, that have been, And that fu-ture
Now he shines, the long ex-pect - ed; Let cre-a-tion
Let no tongue on earth be si - lent, Ev-ery voice in

years shall see, Ev-er-more and ev-er-more!
praise its Lord, Ev-er-more and ev-er-more!
con-cert ring, Ev-er-more and ev-er-more! A-men.

Text: Aurelius Clemens Prudentius, 348-413; tr. John M. Neale, 1818-1866, and Henry W. Baker, 1821-1877.
Tune: 13th Century Plainsong, Mode V, published in *Piae Cantiones*, 1582.

219 — O Master Workman of the Race

D. and C. 22:23b
Luke 2:46-49

MATERNA C.M.D.

1. O Mas - ter Work-man of the race, Thou man of Gal - li - lee
2. O Car - pen - ter of Naz - a - reth, Build-er of life di - vine,
3. O thou who dost the vi - sion send And gives to each a task,

Who with the eyes of ear - ly youth E - ter - nal things did see,
Who shap - est us to God's own law, Thy-self the fair de - sign,
And with the task suf - fi-cient strength, Show us thy will, we ask;

We thank thee for thy boy - hood faith That shone thy whole life through:
Build us a tower of Christ-like height That we the land may view,
Give us a con-science bold and good, Give us a pur - pose true,

"Did ye not know it is my work My Fa - ther's work to do?"
And see like thee our no - blest work Our Fa - ther's work to do.
That it may be our high - est joy Our Fa - ther's work to do.

Text: Jay T. Stocking, 1870-1936.
Tune: Samuel A. Ward, 1847-1903.

We Would See Jesus

John 12:21-23
D. and C. 38:2

MORA PROCTOR 11.10.11.10.
Alternate hymn: 217

Unison

1. We would see Je - sus! Lo, his star is shin - ing
2. We would see Je - sus on the moun-tain teach - ing,
3. We would see Je - sus in his work of heal - ing
4. We would see Je - sus; in the ear - ly morn - ing

A - bove the sta - ble while the an - gels sing;
With all the lis - tening peo - ple gath - ered round,
At e - ven - tide be - fore the sun was set;
Still as of old he calls us, "Fol - low me;"

There in a man - ger on the hay re - clin - ing;
While birds and flow-ers and sky a - bove are preach-ing
Di - vine and hu - man, in his deep re - veal - ing
Let us a - rise, all less - er ser - vice scorn - ing.

Haste, let us lay our gifts be - fore the King.
The bless - ed - ness which sim - ple trust has found.
Of God and hu - man-kind in ser - vice met.
Lord, we are thine, we give our - selves to thee!

Text: J. Edgar Park, 1879-1956.
Tune: William J. Reynolds, 1920 - ; copyright 1975 Broadman Press. All rights reserved. Used by permission.

217   We Would See Jesus

John 12:21-23
D. and C. 17:5a-d

CUSHMAN 11.10.11.10.
Alternate hymn: 218

1. We would see Je-sus! Lo, his star is shin-ing
2. We would see Je-sus on the moun-tain teach-ing,
3. We would see Je-sus in his work of heal-ing
4. We would see Je-sus; in the ear-ly morn-ing

A-bove the sta-ble while the an-gels sing;
With all the lis-tening peo-ple gath-ered round,
At e-ven-tide be-fore the sun was set;
Still as of old he calls us, "Fol-low me;"

There in a man-ger on the hay re-clin-ing;
While birds and flowers and sky a-bove are preach-ing
Di-vine and hu-man, in his deep re-veal-ing
Let us a-rise, all less-er serv-ice scorn-ing.

Haste, let us lay our gifts be-fore the King.
The bless-ed-ness which sim-ple trust has found.
Of God and hu-man-kind in serv-ice met.
Lord, we are thine, we give our-selves to thee!

Text: J. Edgar Park, 1879-1956.
Tune: Herbert B. Turner, 1852-1927.

What Wondrous Love Is This

I Nephi 3:70, 86, 87
John 1:29

WONDROUS LOVE 12.9.12.12.9.

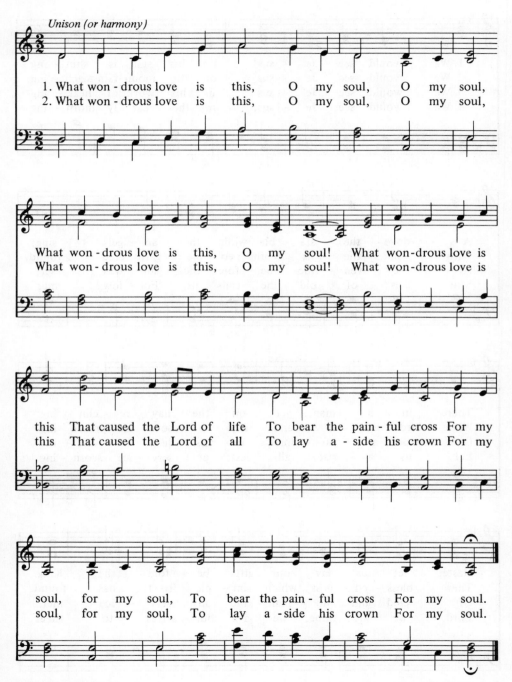

Unison (or harmony)

1. What won-drous love is this, O my soul, O my soul,
2. What won-drous love is this, O my soul, O my soul,

What won-drous love is this, O my soul! What won-drous love is
What won-drous love is this, O my soul! What won-drous love is

this That caused the Lord of life To bear the pain-ful cross For my
this That caused the Lord of all To lay a-side his crown For my

soul, for my soul, To bear the pain-ful cross For my soul.
soul, for my soul, To lay a-side his crown For my soul.

Text: John Newton, 1725-1807.
Tune: From *Southern Harmony*, 1835. Harm. by Louita Clothier, 1936 - ; copyright 1974 Herald Publishing House.

215

Tell Me the Story of Jesus

Romans 10:13-16 (13-17)
D. and C. 65:1a, d

STORY OF JESUS 8.7.8.7.D. with refrain

1. Tell me the sto - ry of Je - sus, Write on my heart ev - ery word,
2. Fast - ing a - lone in the des - ert, Tell of the days that he passed,
3. Tell of the cross where they nailed him, Writh - ing in an - guish and pain;

Refrain: Tell me the sto - ry of Je - sus, Write on my heart ev - ery word,

Fine

Tell me the sto - ry most pre - cious, Sweet-est that ev - er was heard;
How for our sins he was tempt - ed, Yet was tri - um - phant at last;
Tell of the grave where they laid him; Tell how he liv - eth a - gain;

Tell me the sto - ry most pre - cious, Sweet-est that ev - er was heard.

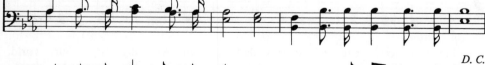

Tell how the an - gels, in cho - rus, Sang as they wel-comed his birth,
Tell of the years of his la - bor, Tell of the sor - row he bore;
Love in that sto - ry so ten - der, Clear - er than ev - er I see;

D. C.

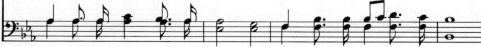

"Glo - ry to God in the high - est! Peace and good ti - dings to earth."
He was de-spised and af - flict - ed, Home-less, re - ject-ed and poor.
Stay, let me weep while you whis - per, Love paid the ran-som for me.

Text: Fanny J. Crosby, 1820-1915.
Tune: John R. Sweney, 1837-1899.

I that found, O Sav - ior true; No; I was found of thee.
much that I on thee took hold As thou, dear Lord, on me.
long be - fore - hand with my soul: Al - ways thou didst love me.

Text: Anonymous, 1880; rev. in *The Pilgrim Hymnal,* 1904.
Tune: The Revivalist, 1868; adapt. by Rosalee Elser, 1925 - ; copyright 1980 by Rosalee Elser; used by permission.

There's a Spirit in the Air   **214**

D. and C. 1:4b-e
Acts 2:41-43, 46, 47

LAUDS 7.7.7.7.

remains constant. Unison. The small notes are for the accompanist.

1. There's a spir - it in the air, call - ing peo - ple ev - ery - where:
2. Lose your shy - ness, find your tongue; tell the world what God has done:
3. When be - liev - ers break the bread, when a hun - gry child is fed:
4. Still his Spir - it leads the fight, see - ing wrong and set - ting right:
5. When a stran - ger's not a - lone, where the home - less find a home:
6. May his Spir - it fill our praise, guide our thoughts and change our ways.

Praise the love that Christ re - vealed, liv - ing, work - ing in our world.
God in Christ has come to stay. We can see his power to - day.
Praise the love that Christ re - vealed, liv - ing, work - ing in our world.
God in Christ has come to stay. We can see his power to - day.
Praise the love that Christ re - vealed, liv - ing, work - ing in our world.
God in Christ has come to stay. We can see his power to - day.

Text: Brian Wren, 1936 - ; copyright Oxford University Press; used by permission.
Tune: John Wilson, 1905 - ; copyright Oxford University Press; used by permission.

212   I Know That My Redeemer Lives

Job 19:25
I Peter 1:3-5

BRADFORD C.M.

1. I know that my Re - deem-er lives And ev - er prays for me;
2. I find him lift - ing up my head; He brings sal - va - tion near;
3. He wills that I should ho - ly be; What can with-stand his will?
4. Je - sus, I hang up - on thy word; I stead - fast -ly be -lieve

A to - ken of his love he gives, A pledge of lib - er - ty.
His pres - ence makes me free in - deed, And he will soon ap- pear.
The coun - sel of his grace in me He sure - ly shall ful - fill.
Thou wilt re - turn and claim me, Lord, And to thy - self re -ceive.

Text: Charles Wesley, 1707-1788.
Tune: George F. Handel, 1685-1759.

213   I Sought the Lord

John 15:16
Romans 5:1, 2

PEACE 10.10.10.6.

1. I sought the Lord, and af - ter- ward I knew He
2. Thou didst reach forth thy hand and mine en - fold; I
3. I find, I walk, I love, but oh, the whole Of

moved my soul to seek him, seek - ing me; It was not
walked and sank not on the storm-vexed sea; 'Twas not so
love is but my an- swer, Lord, to thee! For thou were

O Come, O Come, Emmanuel

211

Zechariah 9:9, 10
Alma 5:17, 18

VENI EMMANUEL L.M. with refrain

Unison (or harmony)

1. O come, O come, Em - man - u - el, And ran - som cap - tive
2. O come, thou Wis - dom from on high, And or - der all things
3. O come, De - sire of na - tions, bind All peo - ples in one

Is - ra - el, That mourns in lone - ly ex - ile
far and nigh; To us the path of knowl - edge
heart and mind; Bid en - vy, strife, and quar - rels

Refrain

here, Un - til the Son of God ap - pear.
show, And cause us in its ways to go. Re - joice! Re -
cease, Fill the whole world with heav - en's peace.

joice! Em - man - u - el Shall come to thee, O Is - ra - el!

Text: Latin, c. 9th century; tr. John M. Neale, 1818-1866, St. 1, alt.; tr. Henry S. Coffin, 1877-1954, Sts. 2, 3, alt.
Tune: Adapted from Plainsong, Mode I, by Thomas Helmore, 1811-1890; alt.

210 O Young and Fearless Prophet

D. and C. 4:1
II Nephi 13:29, 30

VIGIL 7.6.7.6.D.
See 110 for a higher setting.

1. O young and fear-less Proph-et of an-cient Gal-i-lee,
2. We mar-vel at the pur-pose that held thee to thy course
3. Cre-ate in us the splen-dor that dawns when hearts are kind,
4. O young and fear-less Proph-et, we need thy pres-ence here,

Thy life is still a sum-mons to serve hu-man-i-ty,
While ev-er on the hill-top be-fore thee loomed the cross,
That knows not race nor sta-tion as bound-aries of the mind,
A-mid our pride and glo-ry to see thy face ap-pear,

To make our thoughts and ac-tions less prone to please the crowd,
Thy stead-fast face set for-ward where love and du-ty shone,
That learns to val-ue beau-ty in heart or brain or soul,
Once more to hear thy chal-lenge a-bove our noi-sy day,

To stand with hum-ble cour-age for truth with strength en-dowed.
While we be-tray so quick-ly and leave thee there a-lone.
And longs to bind God's chil-dren in-to one per-fect whole.
A-gain to lead us for-ward a-long God's ho-ly way.

Text: S. Ralph Harlow, 1885-1972; alt.
Tune: Swedish Folk Melody.

Hope of the World

209

D. and C. 153:9
Romans 12:1, 2

VICAR 11.10.11.10.
Alternate hymn: 208

Unison (or Harmony) The small notes are for the accompanist.

1. Hope of the world, thou Christ of great com - pas - sion,
2. Hope of the world, God's gift from high - est heav - en,
3. Hope of the world, a - foot on dust - y high - ways,
4. Hope of the world, who by thy cross didst save us

Speak to our fear - ful hearts by con - flict rent.
Bring - ing to hun - gry souls the bread of life,
Show - ing to wan - dering souls the path of light,
From death and dark de - spair, from sin and guilt,

Save us, thy peo - ple, from con - sum - ing pas - sion,
Still let thy spir - it un - to us be giv - en
Walk thou be - side us lest the tempt - ing by - ways
We ren - der back the love thy mer - cy gave us;

Who by our own false hopes and aims are spent.
To heal earth's wounds and end her bit - ter strife.
Lure us a - way from thee to end - less night.
Take thou our lives, and use them as thou wilt. A - men.

Text: Georgia Harkness, 1891-1974. From *Eleven Ecumenical Hymns*, copyright 1954 by The Hymn Society of America. Used by permission.
Tune: V. Earle Copes, 1921 - ; copyright 1963 Abingdon Press; altered by Rosalee Elser, 1925 - . Used by permission.

208

John 16:33
D. and C. 10:12

Hope of the World

ANCIENT OF DAYS 11.10.11.10.
Alternate hymn: 209

1. Hope of the world, thou Christ of great com - pas - sion,
2. Hope of the world, God's gift from high - est heav - en,
3. Hope of the world, a - foot on dust - y high - ways,
4. Hope of the world, who by thy cross didst save us

Speak to our fear - ful hearts by con - flict rent.
Bring - ing to hun - gry souls the bread of life,
Show - ing to wan - dering souls the path of light,
From death and dark de - spair, from sin and guilt,

Save us, thy peo - ple, from con - sum - ing pas - sion,
Still let thy spir - it un - to us be giv - en
Walk thou be - side us lest the tempt - ing by - ways
We ren - der back the love thy mer - cy gave us;

Who by our own false hopes and aims are spent.
To heal earth's wounds and end her bit - ter strife.
Lure us a - way from thee to end - less night.
Take thou our lives and use them as thou wilt. A - men.

Text: Georgia Harkness, 1891-1974. From *Eleven Ecumenical Hymns*, copyright 1954 by The Hymn Society of America. Used by permission.
Tune: J. Albert Jeffery, 1854-1929.

O Thou, Whose Youthful Years Were Spent   207

Matthew 20:26-28
Luke 2:51, 52

O JESU 8.6.8.6.8.8.

1. O thou, whose youth-ful years were spent In Naz-a-reth's
qui-et ways Where home and shop were tem-ples blest
With sim-ple faith and praise, Grant, Lord, that mid the
world's mad press Our homes re-flect thy ho-li-ness.

2. Thou hon-ored guest at Ca-na's feast, For thee were
ta-bles spread; O wel-come, wel-come to our house,
Par-take of love and bread; May we thy ben-e-
dic-tion know As hearth-side joys and friend-ships grow.

3. The friend-ly home of Laz-a-rus Shared love and
peace with thee; Make now our home thy dwel-ling place
And us thy fam-i-ly; Give ear to Ma-ry's
eag-er quest; May Mar-tha's house-hold skills be blest.

4. Thou, who didst walk Em-ma-us road And talk with
anx-ious men, Whose pre-sence graced their cot-tage board,
Made dull hearts glow a-gain: Lo, here's our path, and
here's our gate; Come, sup with us; the night grows late.

Text: William Watkins Reid, Sr., 1890 - . Copyright 1961 by The Hymn Society of America; used by permission.
Tune: *Hirschberg Gesangbuch*, 1741; attr. to Johann Balthasar Reimann, 1702-1749; alt.

206

Come, Thou, O King of Kings

Isaiah 61:1-3
D. and C. 42:3a, b

LENOX 6.6.6.6.8.8.8.8.

1. Come, Thou, O King of kings! We've wait-ed long for thee,
2. Ho - san - nas now shall sound From all the ran - somed throng,
3. Hail! Prince of life and peace! Thrice wel - come to thy throne!

With heal - ing in thy wings, To set thy peo - ple free.
And glo - ry ech - o round A new tri - um - phal song.
While saints of ev - 'ry race Their Lord and Sav - ior own.

Come, thou de - sire of na - tions, come; Come, thou de - sire of
With songs of joy, a hap - pier strain, With songs of joy, a
The thank - ful na - tions bow the knee; The thank - ful na - tions

na - tions, come; Let Is - rael now be gath - ered home.
hap - pier strain, We wel - come in thy peace - ful reign.
bow the knee, And ev - ery tongue gives praise to thee. A - men.

Text: Parley P. Pratt, 1807-1857; alt. Alan D. Tyree, 1929 - .
Tune: Lewis Edson, 1748-1820.

ior art thou; If ev - er I loved thee, my Je - sus, 'tis now. A - men.

Text: William R. Featherstone, 1842-1878.
Tune: Adoniram J. Gordon, 1836-1895.

My Children, "Hear Ye Him," My Word   205

D. and C. 76:4g
John 1:14

ROCKINGHAM L.M.

1. My chil - dren, "hear ye him," my Word: In Je - sus
2. All words are to - kens, sym - bols still, With - out the
3. For rev - e - la - tion's light is dim Un - less in
4. The gos - pel was in Christ him - self, A liv - ing

is the gos - pel found; The gos - pel is the Life
mean - ing I in - tend Un - til it comes through life -
life it is re - vealed; Ex - pe - rience on - ly can
mes - sage all could see; That Life is light for all

ex - pressed; The Life is light and can't be bound.
e - vent: By liv - ing it you com - pre - hend.
re - lease My clear - est mes - sage, till then sealed.
the world: "My grace in your life, full and free."

Text: Alan D. Tyree, 1929 - ; copyright 1980 Reorganized Church of Jesus Christ of Latter Day Saints.
Tune: Edward Miller, 1731-1807.

203 In the Cross of Christ I Glory

D. and C. 17:5a-d
Galatians 6:14

RATHBUN 8.7.8.7.

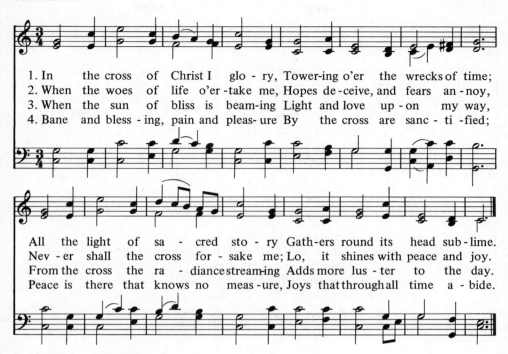

1. In the cross of Christ I glo - ry, Tower-ing o'er the wrecks of time;
2. When the woes of life o'er-take me, Hopes de -ceive, and fears an -noy,
3. When the sun of bliss is beam-ing Light and love up - on my way,
4. Bane and bless - ing, pain and pleas- ure By the cross are sanc - ti -fied;

All the light of sa - cred sto - ry Gath-ers round its head sub -lime.
Nev - er shall the cross for - sake me; Lo, it shines with peace and joy.
From the cross the ra - diance stream-ing Adds more lus - ter to the day.
Peace is there that knows no meas -ure, Joys that through all time a - bide.

Text: John Bowring, 1792-1872.
Tune: Ithamar Conkey, 1815-1867.

204 My Jesus, I Love Thee

Moroni 7:11
I Peter 1:8

GORDON 11.11.11.11.

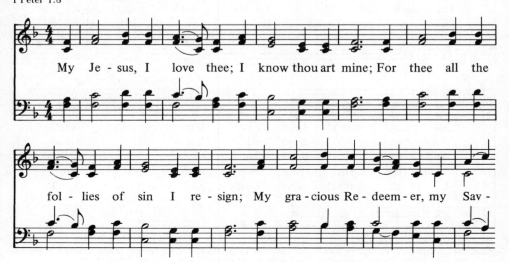

My Je - sus, I love thee; I know thou art mine; For thee all the

fol - lies of sin I re - sign; My gra - cious Re - deem - er, my Sav -

My Song Is Love Unknown

Romans 5:6-11
Titus 3:3-7

202

LOVE UNKNOWN 6.6.6.6.4.4.4.4.

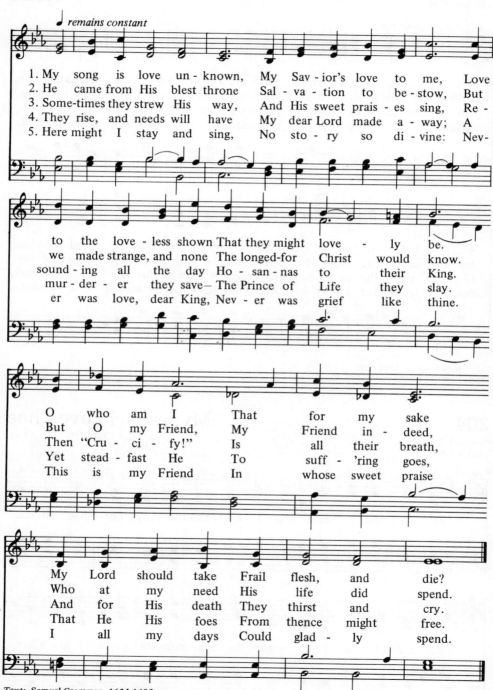

♩ remains constant

1. My song is love un-known, My Sav-ior's love to me, Love
2. He came from His blest throne Sal-va-tion to be-stow, But
3. Some-times they strew His way, And His sweet prais-es sing, Re-
4. They rise, and needs will have My dear Lord made a-way; A
5. Here might I stay and sing, No sto-ry so di-vine: Nev-

to the love-less shown That they might love-ly be.
we made strange, and none The longed-for Christ would know.
sound-ing all the day Ho-san-nas to their King.
mur-der-er they save— The Prince of Life they slay.
er was love, dear King, Nev-er was grief like thine.

O who am I That for my sake
But O my Friend, My Friend in-deed,
Then "Cru-ci-fy!" Is all their breath,
Yet stead-fast He To suff-'ring goes,
This is my Friend In whose sweet praise

My Lord should take Frail flesh, and die?
Who at my need His life did spend.
And for His death They thirst and cry.
That He His foes From thence might free.
I all my days Could glad-ly spend.

Text: Samuel Crossman, 1624-1683
Tune: John Ireland, 1879-1962; copyright and reprinted by permission of Mrs. Norah Kirby, successor to the late
Dr. John Ireland. Duplication is prohibited without written permission of the copyright owner.

201 Come, Thou Long-expected Jesus

Luke 2:25-31
Ephesians 3:8-12

HYFRYDOL 8.7.8.7.D.

1. Come, thou long-expected Jesus, Born to set all people free;
2. Born all people to deliver, Born a child and yet a King,

From our fears and sins release us; Let us find our rest in thee.
Born to reign in us forever, Now thy gracious kingdom bring.

Be our strength and consolation; Hope of all the earth thou art;
By thine own eternal Spirit Rule in all our hearts alone;

Dear desire of every nation, Joy of every longing heart.
By thine all-sufficient merit Raise us to thy glorious throne. A-men.

Text: Charles Wesley, 1707-1788.
Tune: Rowland Hugh Prichard, 1811-1887.

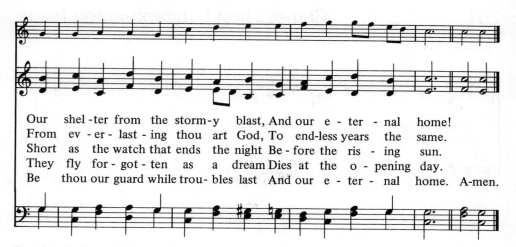

Our shel-ter from the storm-y blast, And our e-ter-nal home!
From ev-er-last-ing thou art God, To end-less years the same.
Short as the watch that ends the night Be-fore the ris-ing sun.
They fly for-got-ten as a dream Dies at the o-pening day.
Be thou our guard while trou-bles last And our e-ter-nal home. A-men.

Text: Isaac Watts, 1674-1748.
Tune: Melody from *Supplement to the New Version*, 1708, probably by William Croft, 1678-1727. Descant by Donald D. Kettring, 1907 - ; copyright 1941 by the Presbyterian Board of Christian Education; renewed 1969; from *The Hymnal for Youth*; used by permission of The Westminster Press.

Alternate Setting

Melody in the Tenor　　　　　　　　　　　　　　　　　　　　*Fauxbourdon*

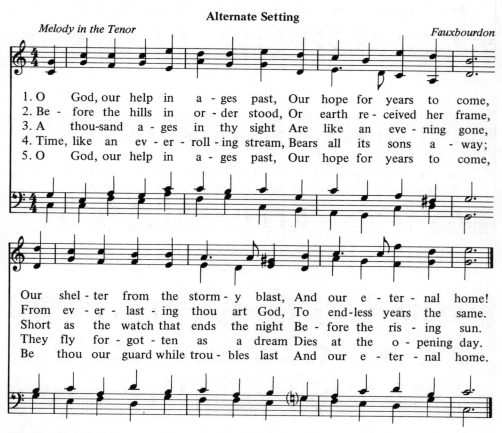

1. O God, our help in a-ges past, Our hope for years to come,
2. Be-fore the hills in or-der stood, Or earth re-ceived her frame,
3. A thou-sand a-ges in thy sight Are like an eve-ning gone,
4. Time, like an ev-er-roll-ing stream, Bears all its sons a-way;
5. O God, our help in a-ges past, Our hope for years to come,

Our shel-ter from the storm-y blast, And our e-ter-nal home!
From ev-er-last-ing thou art God, To end-less years the same.
Short as the watch that ends the night Be-fore the ris-ing sun.
They fly for-got-ten as a dream Dies at the o-pening day.
Be thou our guard while trou-bles last And our e-ter-nal home.

Text: Isaac Watts, 1674-1748.
Tune: Arr. by Martin Shaw, 1875-1958; copyright J. Curwen & Sons, Ltd.; used by permission of G. Schirmer, Inc.

199

He Lives in Us! Immortal King!

II Corinthians 13:4
Galatians 2:20

HURST C.M.

1. He lives in us! Im - mor - tal King! Cre - a - tion bows to Him.
2. He lives for us! What joy is ours! He light - ens ev - ery mind.
3. He lives through us! How great our task! What prom - ise we ful - fill!

He breathed in us the breath of life To make us one with Him.
He quick - ens us to know our worth; We sense His grand de - sign.
O - be - dient to His Spir - it's call, We im - ple - ment His will.

Text: Linda E. Coffman, 1945 - ; copyright 1980 Reorganized Church of Jesus Christ of Latter Day Saints.
Tune: Frances H. Booth, 1923 - ; harm. alt. by Rosalee Elser, 1925 - ; copyright 1956 Herald Publishing House.

200

O God, Our Help in Ages Past

Jacob 3:9-14
Psalm 90:1, 2

ST. ANNE C.M.

Descant

1. O God, our help in a - ges past, Our hope for years to come,
2. Be - fore the hills in or - der stood, Or earth re - ceived her frame,
3. A thou - sand a - ges in thy sight Are like an eve - ning gone,
4. Time, like an ev - er - roll - ing stream, Bears all its sons a - way;
5. O God, our help in a - ges past, Our hope for years to come,

God of Earth and Planets

198

Proverbs 3:5, 6
Isaiah 26:3, 4

HERMAS 6.5.6.5.D.

1. God of earth and plan - ets Rang - ing out - er space:
2. God of flower and o - cean— Fra - grance, beau - ty, power:

We in si - lent won - der Glimpse thy might and grace.
Of thy love and boun - ty Share we ev - ery hour.

God of worlds and a - toms, Each a mas - ter - piece:
God who sent us Je - sus— Teach - er, Friend, and Guide:

Deep - est probes of sci - ence Awe and faith in - crease.
We who are thy chil - dren In thy care a - bide.

Text: William Watkins Reid, Jr., 1923 - ; alt.; copyright 1965 Hymn Society of America; used by permission.
Tune: Frances Ridley Havergal, 1836-1879.

197

Let God Be God

Mosiah 3:16, 21
D. and C. 1:3

LET GOD BE GOD 11.10.11.10. with refrain

Unison (or harmony)

1. Let God be God, in this our pres-ent mo-ment, Let God be
2. Let God be God, or we shall nev-er fin-ish The task to
3. Let Christ be Lord, in all His ris-en pow-er; His gra-cious

Mas-ter, hold-ing in con-trol All parts of life as
which He calls us ev-'ry day; Lest err-ing, we in
Spir-it, un-sup-pressed and free; Our Fa-ther, re - cre -

gifts of His be-stow-ment, For mak-ing us now bro-ken,
un-be-lief di-min-ish The force, the pow'r He wish-es
ate us for this hour In - to the ones you wish for

strong and whole.
to dis-play. Let God be God, let Christ be Lord!
us to be.

Text: Bryan Jeffery Leech, 1931 - ; alt.; copyright 1972 by Fred Bock Music Company; all rights reserved; used by permission.
Tune: Gordon H. Carlson; copyright 1973 by the composer; used by permission.

Alternate Setting: to be sung as a canon (round).

The four-part setting can be used to accompany this canon by repeating the last four chords before the Amen.

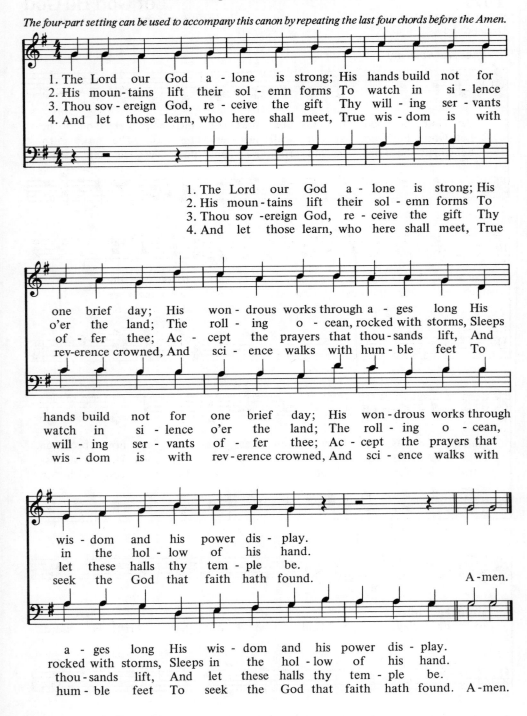

1. The Lord our God a-lone is strong; His hands build not for
2. His moun-tains lift their sol-emn forms To watch in si-lence
3. Thou sov-ereign God, re-ceive the gift Thy will-ing ser-vants
4. And let those learn, who here shall meet, True wis-dom is with

1. The Lord our God a-lone is strong; His
2. His moun-tains lift their sol-emn forms To
3. Thou sov-ereign God, re-ceive the gift Thy
4. And let those learn, who here shall meet, True

one brief day; His won-drous works through a-ges long His
o'er the land; The roll-ing o-cean, rocked with storms, Sleeps
of-fer thee; Ac-cept the prayers that thou-sands lift, And
rev-erence crowned, And sci-ence walks with hum-ble feet To

hands build not for one brief day; His won-drous works through
watch in si-lence o'er the land; The roll-ing o-cean,
will-ing ser-vants of-fer thee; Ac-cept the prayers that
wis-dom is with rev-erence crowned, And sci-ence walks with

wis-dom and his power dis-play.
in the hol-low of his hand.
let these halls thy tem-ple be.
seek the God that faith hath found.   A-men.

a-ges long His wis-dom and his power dis-play.
rocked with storms, Sleeps in the hol-low of his hand.
thou-sands lift, And let these halls thy tem-ple be.
hum-ble feet To seek the God that faith hath found. A-men.

Text: Caleb T. Winchester, 1847-1920.
Tune: Thomas Tallis, c. 1505-1585.

196
The Lord Our God Alone Is Strong

Ecclesiastes 3:14
D. and C. 85:36

TALLIS' CANON L.M.

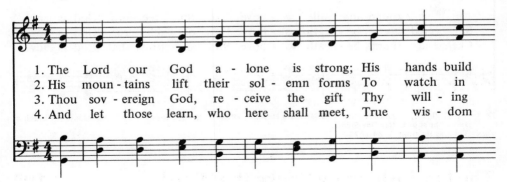

1. The Lord our God a - lone is strong; His hands build
2. His moun - tains lift their sol - emn forms To watch in
3. Thou sov - ereign God, re - ceive the gift Thy will - ing
4. And let those learn, who here shall meet, True wis - dom

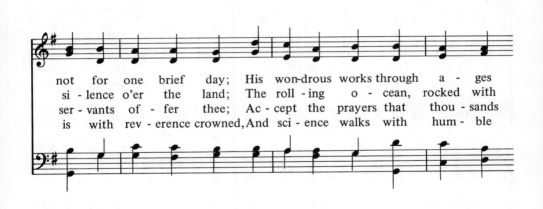

not for one brief day; His won-drous works through a - ges
si - lence o'er the land; The roll - ing o - cean, rocked with
ser - vants of - fer thee; Ac - cept the prayers that thou - sands
is with rev - erence crowned, And sci - ence walks with hum - ble

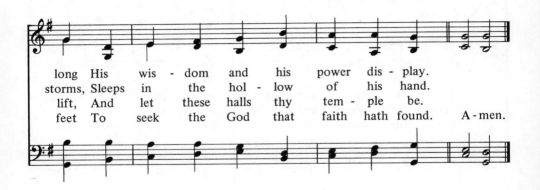

long His wis - dom and his power dis - play.
storms, Sleeps in the hol - low of his hand.
lift, And let these halls thy tem - ple be.
feet To seek the God that faith hath found. A - men.

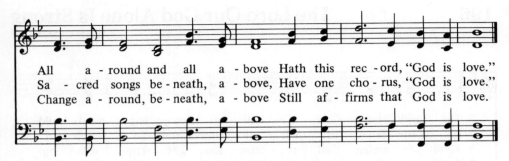

All   a - round and all a - bove Hath this rec - ord, "God is love."
Sa - cred songs be - neath, a - bove, Have one cho - rus, "God is love."
Change a - round, be - neath, a - bove Still af - firms that God is love.

Text: W. W. Phelps, 1792-1872, Sts. 1, 2; Barbara Howard, 1930 - , St. 3, copyright 1980 Reorganized Church of Jesus Christ of Latter Day Saints.
Tune: Thomas Hastings 1784-1872.

The Lord Almighty Spoke the Word 195

John 1:1-4
Hebrews 1:1-3

SYDENHAM STREET 8.8.8.6.
Alternate tune: JUST AS I AM (421)

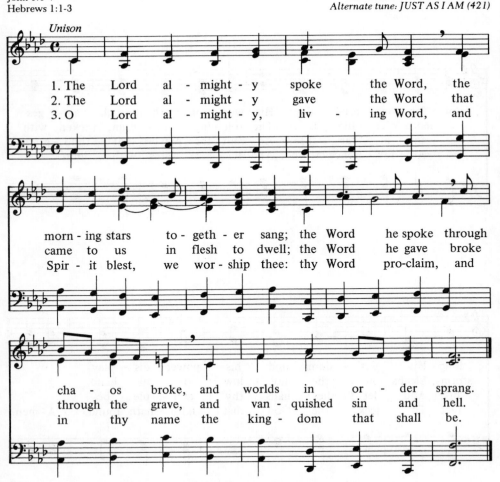

Unison

1. The Lord al - might - y spoke the Word, the
2. The Lord al - might - y gave the Word that
3. O Lord al - might - y, liv - ing Word, and

morn - ing stars to - geth - er sang; the Word he spoke through
came to us in flesh to dwell; the Word he gave broke
Spir - it blest, we wor - ship thee: thy Word pro-claim, and

cha - os broke, and worlds in or - der sprang.
through the grave, and van - quished sin and hell.
in thy name the king - dom that shall be.

Text: Charles E. Watson, 1869-1942; copyright Rodborough Tabernacle Church; used by permission.
Tune: Frederick R. C. Clarke, 1931 - ; copyright by the composer; used by permission.

193 My God, How Wonderful Thou Art

Psalm 145:8-12
Jeremiah 31:3

COOLING C.M.

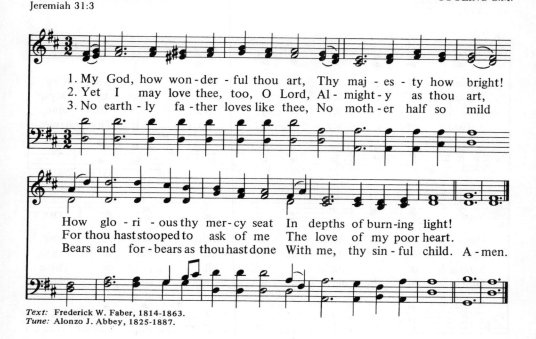

1. My God, how won-der-ful thou art, Thy maj-es-ty how bright!
2. Yet I may love thee, too, O Lord, Al-might-y as thou art,
3. No earth-ly fa-ther loves like thee, No moth-er half so mild

How glo-ri-ous thy mer-cy seat In depths of burn-ing light!
For thou hast stooped to ask of me The love of my poor heart.
Bears and for-bears as thou hast done With me, thy sin-ful child. A-men.

Text: Frederick W. Faber, 1814-1863.
Tune: Alonzo J. Abbey, 1825-1887.

194 Earth with Her Ten Thousand Flowers

Ephesians 3:14-19
Ether 5:33, 34

TOPLADY 7.7.7.D.

1. Earth with her ten thou-sand flowers, Air with all its beams and showers,
2. Sounds a-mong the vales and hills, In the woods, and by the rills,
3. Na-ture speaks of joy and pain; Floods may come from spring-time rain.

Heav-en's in-fi-nite ex-panse, O-cean's lus-trous coun-te-nance—
Of the breeze and of the bird, Of the gen-tle mur-mur stirred—
While we know de-light and strife, Christ is hope for all our life.

God of Eternity

192

I Chronicles 29:11-13
Alma 14:124, 125

GOD OF ETERNITY 6.4.6.4.6.6.6.4.

1. God of e-ter-ni-ty, Sav-ior and King,
2. God of e-ter-ni-ty, An-cient of Days,
3. God of e-ter-ni-ty, Rul-er di-vine,
4. God of e-ter-ni-ty, Love is Thy name;

Help us to hon-or Thee, Help while we sing;
Glo-rious in maj-es-ty, Au-thor of Praise;
Strength of the might-y hills, All power is Thine;
God of the earth and sea, Thee we pro-claim;

Now may the clouds of night Break in-to splen-dor bright,
Hear Thou our ear-nest call, While at thy feet we fall,
Bound-less Thy reign shall be, Won-drous Thy vic-to-ry,
Love through Thine on-ly Son Thy work of grace hath done;

Je-sus, our life and light, Our Lord and King!
Je-sus, our all in all, Our Lord and King!
Earth shall be fill'd with Thee, Our Lord and King!
O bless-ed Three in One, Our Lord and King! A-men.

Text: Fanny J. Crosby, 1820-1915.
Tune: Ira Allan Sankey, 1874-1915.

191 God of Our Fathers

Proverbs 3:5, 6
D. and C. 22:23

NATIONAL HYMN 10.10.10.10.

Fanfare optional

1. God of our fa - thers, whose al - might - y hand
2. Thy love di - vine hath led us in the past;
3. From war's a - larms, from dead - ly pes - ti - lence,
4. Re - fresh thy peo - ple on their toil - some way;

Leads forth in beau - ty all the star - ry band
In this free land by thee our lot is cast;
Be thy strong arm our ev - er sure de - fense;
Lead us from night to nev - er - end - ing day;

Of shin - ing worlds in splen - dor through the skies,
Be thou our Rul - er, Guard - ian, Guide, and Stay,
Thy true re - li - gion in our hearts in - crease;
Fill all our lives with love and grace di - vine,

Our grate - ful songs be - fore thy throne a - rise.
Thy word our law, thy paths our cho - sen way.
Thy boun - teous good - ness nour - ish us in peace.
And glo - ry, laud, and praise be ev - er thine. A - men.

Text: Daniel C. Roberts, 1841-1907.
Tune: George William Warren, 1828-1902.

thought.
flow.
die.
might,

2. O wide em- brac - ing, wondrous
3. We read thee best   in Christ who
4. We read thy power to bless and

thy   might.

Text: Horatius Bonar, 1808-1889.
Tune: Calvin Hampton, 1938 - ; copyright 1973 Concordia Publishing House; used by permission.

Creator God, Creating Still

190

D. and C. 22:23
D. and C. 90:1e-g

MORNING SONG C.M.

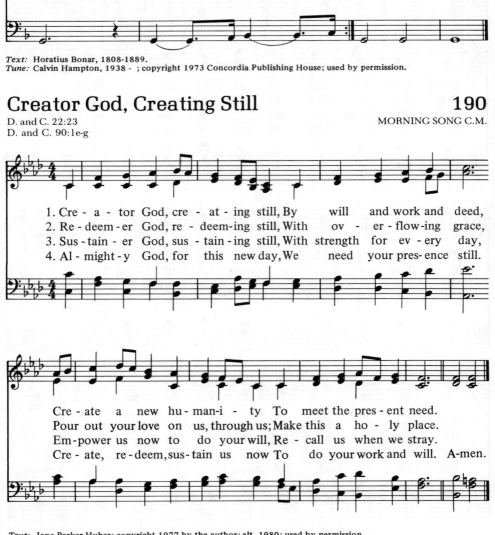

1. Cre - a - tor God, cre - at - ing still, By   will   and work and deed,
2. Re - deem - er God, re - deem-ing still, With   ov - er - flow-ing grace,
3. Sus - tain - er God, sus - tain-ing still, With strength for ev - er - y   day,
4. Al - might - y God, for this new day, We   need your pres-ence still.

Cre - ate   a   new hu - man-i - ty To   meet the pres-ent need.
Pour out your love on us, through us; Make this a ho - ly place.
Em-power us now to   do your will, Re - call us when we stray.
Cre - ate, re - deem, sus-tain us now To   do your work and will. A-men.

Text: Jane Parker Huber; copyright 1977 by the author; alt. 1980; used by permission.
Tune: Wyeth's *Repository of Sacred Music, Part Second*, 1813; harm. Rosalee Elser, 1925 - ; copyright 1980 by
     Rosalee Elser; used by permission.

189
O Love of God, How Strong and True

Romans 11:33-36
Alma 5:21, 22

DE TAR L.M.
Alternate hymn: 188

(obligato)

1. O love of God, how strong and true, Eternal
   love, We read thee
   came To bear for
   save Even in the

and yet ever new; Uncomprehended and un-
in the sky above; We read thee in the earth be-
us the cross of shame, Sent by the Father from on
darkness of the grave; Still more in resurrection

bought, Beyond all knowledge and all
low, In seas that swell and streams that
high Our life to live, our death to
light We read the fullness of thy

* Options: (a) Using the text, the obligato may be sung by high voices.
  (b) Melody and obligato lines may be sung *a cappella*.
  (c) Once the melody is familiar, the accompanist need not play the melody and obligato parts with the singers.

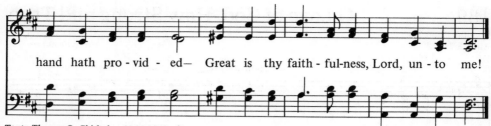

hand hath pro - vid - ed— Great is thy faith - ful-ness, Lord, un - to me!

Text: Thomas O. Chisholm, 1866-1960, alt.
Tune: William M. Runyan, 1870-1957.
Text and tune copyright 1923; renewal 1951 extended by Hope Publishing Company, Carol Stream, IL 60187; all rights reserved; used by permission.

O Love of God, How Strong and True 188

II Nephi 1:72-75
Ephesians 3:8-12

DEDICARE L.M.
Alternate hymn: 189

1. O love of God, how strong and true, E - ter - nal
2. O wide em - brac - ing, won - drous love, We read thee
3. We read thee best in Christ who came To bear for
4. We read thy power to bless and save In dark - ness

and yet ev - er new; Un - com - pre - hend - ed
in the sky a - bove; We read thee in the
us the cross of shame, Sent by the Fa - ther
e - ven of the grave; Still more in res - ur -

and un - bought, Be - yond all knowl-edge and all thought.
earth be - low, In seas that swell and streams that flow.
from on high Our life to live, our death to die.
rec - tion light We read the full - ness of thy might.

Text: Horatius Bonar, 1808-1889.
Tune: Franklyn S. Weddle, 1905 - ; harm. Evan A. Fry, 1902-1959; copyright 1956 Herald Publishing House.

187
Great Is Thy Faithfulness

D. and C. 17:4a, b
D. and C. 34:1

FAITHFULNESS 11.10.11.10. with refrain

1. Great is thy faith-ful-ness, O God my Fa-ther; There is no
2. Sum-mer and win-ter and spring-time and har-vest, Sun, moon, and
3. Par-don for sin and a peace that en-dur-eth, Thy own dear

shad-ow of turn-ing with thee; Thou chang-est not, thy com-
stars in their cours-es a-bove Join with all na-ture in
pres-ence to cheer and to guide; Strength for to-day and bright

pas-sions, they fail not; As thou hast been thou for-ev-er wilt be.
man-i-fold wit-ness To thy great faith-ful-ness, mer-cy, and love.
hope for to-mor-row, Bless-ings all mine, with ten thou-sand be-side!

Refrain

Great is thy faith-ful-ness! Great is thy faith-ful-ness! Morn-ing by

morn-ing new mer-cies I see; All of my bless-ings thy

Creator of Sunrises

186

John 15:1, 2, 4, 7
Ephesians 3:14-19

I LOVE THEE 11.11.11.11.

1. Cre - a - tor of sun - ri - ses, com - ets, and trees
2. For - give us the will - ful ex - ces - ses of greed
3. For - give us the wreck - age of ha - tred and war

Whose sam - pler of love is much grand - er than these,
That screen from un - car - ing eyes those who have need.
That sad - den our souls and the in - no - cent scar.

Call forth from thy chil - dren the col - ors of life
Though shar - ing be knowl - edge or serv - ice or bread,
Re - store us to or - der of sun - rise and trees

That free us for laugh - ter, that free us from strife.
E - quip us with faith as in truth we are led.
And love that can make the earth grand - er than these.

Text: Evelyn Maples, 1919 - ; copyright 1980 Reorganized Church of Jesus Christ of Latter Day Saints.
Tune: Christian Harmony, 1805, alt.; harm. David N. Johnson, 1922 - . Harm. copyright 1977 Praise Publications, Inc. Used by permission.

God's
Word for Us

God 199-200
Christ 201-230
Christ's birth 231-261
Christ's death 262-270
Christ's resurrection 271-280
Holy Spirit 281-289
The Church 290-295
Revelation 296-309
Zion and the Kingdom 310-324
Lord's Supper 325-345
Blessing 346-349
Baptism 350-353
Confirmation 354-361
Ordination 362-364
Marriage 407-408

God's Word for Us

God 186-200

Christ 201-230

Christ's birth 231-261

Christ's death 262-270

Christ's resurrection 271-280

Holy Spirit 281-289

The Church 290-295

Revelation 296-309

Zion and the Kingdom 310-324

Lord's Supper 325-345

Blessing 346-349

Baptism 350-357

Confirmation 358-361

Ordination 362-366

Marriage 367-368

Lord of All Hopefulness

Exodus 13:21
II Nephi 3:61

185

SLANE 10.11.11.12.

1. Lord of all hope-ful-ness, Lord of all joy,
2. Lord of all ea-ger-ness, Lord of all faith,
3. Lord of all kind-li-ness, Lord of all grace,
4. Lord of all gen-tle-ness, Lord of all calm,

Whose trust, ev-er child-like, no cares could de-stroy,
Whose strong hands were skilled at the plane and the lathe,
Your hands swift to wel-come, your arms to em-brace,
Whose voice is con-tent-ment, whose pre-sence is balm,

Be there at our wak-ing, and give us, we pray, Your
Be there at our la-bors, and give us, we pray, Your
Be there at our hom-ing, and give us, we pray, Your
Be there at our sleep-ing, and give us, we pray, Your

bliss in our hearts, Lord, at the break of the day.
strength in our hearts, Lord, at the noon of the day.
love in our hearts, Lord, at the eve of the day.
peace in our hearts, Lord, at the end of the day. A-men.

Text: Jan Struther, 1901-1953; from *Enlarged Songs of Praise* by permission of Oxford University Press.
Tune: Irish Traditional Melody; harm. Erik Routley, 1917 - ; used by permission of Erik Routley.

184 God Who Gives to Life Its Goodness

Psalm 96:1, 11-13
D. and C. 81:4c

ABBOT'S LEIGH 8.7.8.7.D.

1. God who gives to life its good-ness, God, cre-a - tor of all joy,
2. God who fills the earth with beau-ty, God who binds each friend to friend,

God who gives to us our free-dom, God who bless - es tool and toy:
God who names us co - cre - a - tors, God who wills that cha - os end:

Teach us how to laugh and praise you, deep with-in, your prais-es sing,
Grant us now cre - a - tive spir - its, minds re - spon-sive to your mind,

Till the whole cre - a - tion dan-ces for the good-ness of its King.
Hearts and wills your rule ex -tend-ing, all our acts by love re - fined.

Text: Walter Henry Farquharson, 1936 - ; alt.; used by permission of the author.
Tune: Cyril Vincent Taylor, 1907 - ; from *The BBC Hymn Book*; used by permission of Oxford University Press.

Lord, Lead Me by Your Spirit

183

D. and C. 83:7a-d
Ether 5:28

HOLY WINGS 7.6.7.6.D.

1. Lord, lead me by your Spir-it in-to a bet-ter light,
2. You're ev-er true and faith-ful in meet-ing all my need.
3. In end-less care and pres-ence, you give to ev-er-y life

In truth and un-der-stand-ing and knowl-edge of your will.
I bare-ly com-pre-hend you; I of-ten am a-fraid.
Com-pas-sion o-ver-flow-ing and love that's deep and wise.

I con-fess my sin be-fore you, con-fess my lack of love.
En-a-ble me to seek you with all my heart and mind,
Grant that I in glad re-spond-ing may sure-ly find the strength

Will you bring to life my vi-sion, my sense of awe, my faith.
And to find the re-as-sur-ance in the mys-ter-y you are.
To share the Christ with oth-ers, lov-ing free-ly, bear-ing grace.

Text: Eric L. Selden, 1925 - ; alt.; copyright 1980 Reorganized Church of Jesus Christ of Latter Day Saints.
Tune: Swedish Folk Melody; harm. Mark S. Dickey, 1885- 1961; alt.

182 Make Room Within My Heart, O God

Philippians 2:5-11
Psalm 51:1, 10-12

KINGSFOLD C.M.D.
Alternate tune: MASSACHUSETTS (300)

1. Make room with-in my heart, O God, That you may form in me
2. Di - rect my will, O King of kings; Sub - ject it to your own,

The im - age you have shown in Christ, My ver - y life to be.
That ev - ery im - pulse, ac - tion, word May make your king-dom known.

In - spire my thought, O loft - y One, To reach the high-est plane,
Ef - fect my prayer, great Trin - i - ty, E - ter - nal Three-in - One;

That I may know the mind of Christ, And him as great-est gain.
Com - bine each part of me to praise The Fa -ther, Spir - it, Son.

Text: Bryan Jeffery Leech, 1931 - ; copyright 1973 by Fred Bock Music Company. All rights reserved. Used by permission.
Tune: Melody coll. Lucy Broadwood, 1858-1929; harm. and arr. Ralph Vaughan Williams, 1872-1958; from the *English Hymnal* by permission of Oxford University Press.

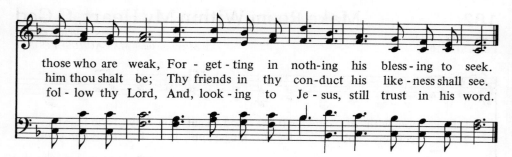

those who are weak, For - get - ting in noth-ing his bless - ing to seek.
him thou shalt be; Thy friends in thy con-duct his like - ness shall see.
fol - low thy Lord, And, look - ing to Je - sus, still trust in his word.

Text: William D. Longstaff, 1822-1894, alt.
Tune: George Coles Stebbins, 1846-1945.

Spirit of God, Descend upon My Heart 181

Mosiah 2:20-23
D. and C. 12:4a

MORECAMBE 10.10.10.10.

1. Spir - it of God, de - scend up - on my heart; Wean it from earth,
2. I ask no dream, no proph-et ec - sta - sies, No sud - den rend-
3. Teach me to feel that thou art al - ways nigh; Teach me the strug-
4. Teach me to love thee as thine an - gels love, One ho - ly pas-

through all its pul - ses move; Stoop to my weak - ness, might - y
ing of the veil of clay, No an - gel vis - it - ant, no
gles of the soul to bear, To check the ris - ing doubt, the
sion fill - ing all my frame, Bap - tis - m of the heaven-de-

as thou art, And make me love thee as I ought to love.
o - pening skies, But take the dim - ness of my soul a - way.
reb - el sigh; Teach me the pa - tience of un - an-swered prayer.
scend-ed Dove, My heart an al - tar, and thy love the flame. A-men.

Text: George Croly, 1780-1860.
Tune: Frederick Cook Atkinson, 1841-1897.

179 Breathe on Me, Breath of God

John 20:21, 22
D. and C. 10:6, 7

TRENTHAM S.M.

1. Breathe on me, Breath of God; Fill me with life a - new That I may love what thou dost love And do what thou wouldst do.
2. Breathe on me, Breath of God, Un - til my heart is pure, Un - til with thee I will one will— To do and to en - dure.
3. Breathe on me, Breath of God, Till I am whol - ly thine, Un - til this earth - ly part of me Glows with thy fire di - vine.
4. Breathe on me, Breath of God; So shall I nev - er die But live with thee the per - fect life Of thine e - ter - ni - ty. A - men.

Text: Edwin Hatch, 1835-1889.
Tune: Robert Jackson, 1842-1914.

180 Take Time to Be Holy

Leviticus 20:7, 8
II Nephi 3:30

HOLINESS 11.11.11.11.

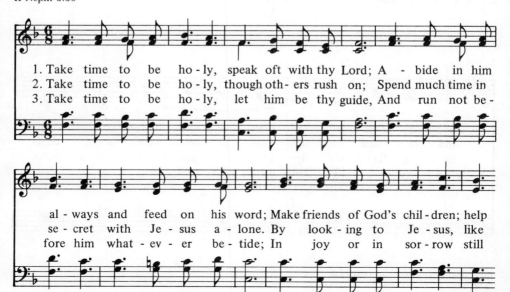

1. Take time to be ho - ly, speak oft with thy Lord; A - bide in him al - ways and feed on his word; Make friends of God's chil - dren; help
2. Take time to be ho - ly, though oth - ers rush on; Spend much time in se - cret with Je - sus a - lone. By look - ing to Je - sus, like
3. Take time to be ho - ly, let him be thy guide, And run not be - fore him what - ev - er be - tide; In joy or in sor - row still

Lord, I Was Blind: I Could Not See

178

John 9:25
Alma 16:198-200

SOLOTHURN L.M.

Unison (or harmony)

1. Lord, I was blind: I could not see In Thy marred vis - age an - y grace; But now the beau - ty of Thy face In ra - diant vi - sion dawns on me.
2. Lord, I was deaf: I could not hear The thrill - ing mu - sic of Thy voice; But now I hear Thee and re - joice, And all Thine ut - tered words are dear.
3. Lord, I was mute: I could not speak The grace and glo - ry of Thy name; But now, as touched with liv - ing flame, My lips Thine ea - ger prais - es wake.
4. Lord, I was dead: I could not stir My life - less soul to come to Thee; But now, since Thou hast quick - ened me, I rise from sin's dark sep - ul - cher.
5. Lord, Thou hast made the blind to see, The deaf to hear, the mute to speak, The dead to live; and lo, I break The chains of my cap - tiv - i - ty.

Text: William Todd Matson, 1833-1899.
Tune: Swiss Traditional Melody; arr. Ralph Vaughan Williams, 1872-1958; used by permission of Oxford University Press.

177 O God, in Restless Living

John 14:27
Moroni 7:3

NYLAND 7.6.7.6.D.

1. O God, in rest-less liv-ing We lose our spir-its' peace.
2. Teach us, be-yond our striv-ing, The rich re-wards of rest.
3. Re-cep-tive make our spir-its, Our need is to be still;

Calm our un-wise con-fu-sion, Bid thou our clam-or cease.
Who does not live se-rene-ly Is nev-er deep-ly blest.
As dawn fades flick-ering can-dle So dim our anx-ious will.

Let anx-ious hearts grow qui-et, Like pools at eve-ning still,
O tran-quil, ra-diant Sun-light, Bring thou our lives to flower,
Re-veal thy ra-diance through us, Thine am-ple strength re-lease.

Till thy re-flect-ed heav-ens All our spir-its fill.
Less wear-ied with our ef-fort, More a-ware of power.
Not ours but thine the tri-umph In the power of peace.

Text: Harry Emerson Fosdick, 1878-1969; used by permission of Elinor F. Downs.
Tune: Traditional Finnish Melody; harm. David Evans, 1874-1948; from the *Revised Church Hymnary 1927* by permission of Oxford University Press.

Teach Me, God, to Wonder

176

Alma 17:69
John 17:3

TEACH ME GOD 6.5.9. with refrain

Unison (or harmony)

1. Teach me God to won - der. Teach me God to see.
2. Let me God be o - pen, Let me lov - ing be.
3. Let me God be read - y, Let me be a - wake—
4. Teach me God to know you, Hear you when you speak—

Let your world of beau - ty cap - ture me.
Let your world of peo - ple speak to me.
In your pres - ent king - dom my place take.
See you in my neigh - bor when we meet.

Refrain

Praise to you be giv - en; Love for you be lived.

Life be cel - e - brat - ed; Joy you give.

Text: Walter Farquharson, 1936 - ; copyright 1977 The Frederick Harris Music Company; used by permission.
Tune: Ron Klusmeier; copyright 1977 The Frederick Harris Music Company; harm. 1980 Rosalee Elser, 1925 - ; used by permission.

175   O God of Every Nation

I Nephi 7:56-59
Colossians 3:11-14

ST. THEODULPH 7.6.7.6.D.

1. O God of ev-ery na - tion, of ev-ery race and land,
2. From lust for wealth and pow - er, from scorn of truth and right,
3. When hope and cour-age fal - ter, let thy still voice be heard;

Re - deem thy whole cre - a - tion with thine al - might - y hand.
From trust in bombs that show - er de - struc-tion through the night,
With faith that none can al - ter, thy ser - vants un - der - gird.

Where hate and fear di - vide us and bit - ter threats are hurled,
From pride of race and sta - tion and blind-ness to thy way,
Keep bright in us the vi - sion of days when war shall cease,

In love and mer - cy guide us, and heal our strife-torn world.
De - liv - er ev - ery na - tion, E - ter - nal God, we pray.
When ha - tred and di - vi - sion give way to love and peace.

Text: William Watkins Reid, Jr., 1923 - ; alt.; copyright 1958 The Hymn Society of America; used by permission.
Tune: Melchior Teschner, 1584-1635.

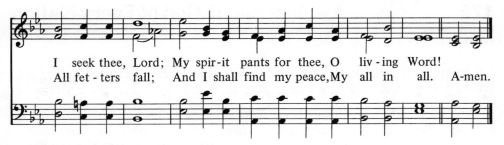

I seek thee, Lord; My spir-it pants for thee, O liv-ing Word!

All fet-ters fall; And I shall find my peace, My all in all. A-men.

Text: Mary A. Lathbury, 1841-1913.
Tune: William F. Sherwin, 1826-1888.

O Christ, My Lord, Create in Me 174

Matthew 6:10, 11 (9, 10)
II Nephi 8:18, 20

RETREAT L.M.

1. O Christ, my Lord, cre-ate in me The per-son I am meant to be. My soul es-tranged, I'm prone to sin; Re-deem my life, with-out, with-in.

2. O Lord, may ev-ery soul em-brace The won-ders of your match-less grace. From guilt and fear each one set free; Cre-ate a new hu-man-i-ty.

3. O Christ, make vis-i-ble your Church, As all for life and mean-ing search. Your will be done! O set a-flame That fel-low-ship which bears your name.

4. Em-man-u-el, O Prince of Peace, To ev-ery na-tion bring re-lease. Beat from each sword a plow-share strong; Your king-dom come: my prayer, my song. A-men.

Text: Chester E. Custer, 1920 - ; alt.; copyright 1972 by the author; used by permission.
Tune: Thomas Hastings, 1784-1872; arr. Rosalee Elser, 1925 - ; copyright 1980 Rosalee Elser; used by permission.

172 God, Who Touchest Earth with Beauty

Psalm 51:10-12
Daniel 12:3

SACRED REST 8.5.8.5.

1. God, who touch-est earth with beau-ty, Make my heart a-new;
2. Like thy springs and run-ning wa-ters Make me crys-tal pure;
3. Like thy danc-ing waves in sun-light Make me glad and free;
4. Like the arch-ing of the heav-ens Lift my thoughts a-bove;
5. God, who touch-est earth with beau-ty, Make my heart a-new;

With thy Spir-it re-cre-ate me, Pure and strong and true.
Like thy rocks of tower-ing gran-deur Make me strong and sure.
Like the straight-ness of the pine trees Let me up-right be.
Turn my dreams to no-ble ac-tion—Min-is-tries of love.
Keep me ev-er, by thy Spir-it, Pure and strong and true. A-men.

Text: Mary S. Edgar, 1889-1973; from *Under Open Skies*, copyright 1955 by Clarke, Irwin and Co. Ltd. Used by permission.
Tune: J. B. Birkbeck, 1831-1917.

173 Break Thou the Bread of Life

John 6:47-49
D. and C. 32:3a, d, e

BREAD OF LIFE 6.4.6.4.D.

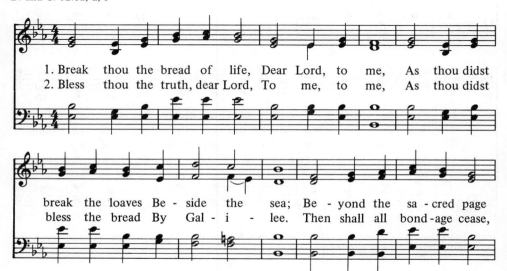

1. Break thou the bread of life, Dear Lord, to me, As thou didst
2. Bless thou the truth, dear Lord, To me, to me, As thou didst

break the loaves Be-side the sea; Be-yond the sa-cred page
bless the bread By Gal-i-lee. Then shall all bond-age cease,

Help Us Accept Each Other

171

II Nephi 13:29
I John 4:16, 19

AURELIA 7.6.7.6.D.
Alternate tune: THAXTED (375)

1. Help us ac-cept each oth-er as Christ ac-cept-ed us;
2. Teach us, O Lord, your les-sons, as in our dai-ly life
3. Let your ac-cept-ance change us, so that we may be moved
4. Lord, for to-day's en-coun-ters with all who are in need,

Teach us as sis-ter, bro-ther each per-son to em-brace.
We strug-gle to be hu-man and search for hope and faith.
In liv-ing sit-u-a-tions to do the truth in love;
Who hun-ger for ac-cept-ance, for righ-teous-ness and bread,

Be pres-ent, Lord, a-mong us and bring us to be-lieve
Teach us to care for peo-ple, for all— not just for some,
To prac-tice your ac-cept-ance un-til we know by heart
We need new eyes for see-ing, new hands for hold-ing on:

We are our-selves ac-cept-ed and meant to love and live.
To love them as we find them and as they may be-come.
The ta-ble of for-give-ness and laugh-ter's heal-ing art.
Re-new us with your Spir-it; Lord free us, make us one!

170 Love Divine, All Loves Excelling

I John 3:1-3
D. and C. 34:6

BLAENWERN 8.7.8.7.D.

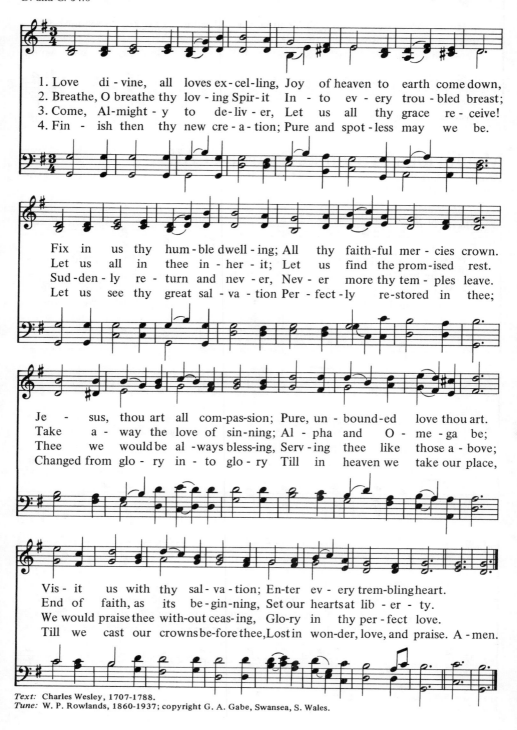

1. Love di-vine, all loves ex-cel-ling, Joy of heaven to earth come down,
2. Breathe, O breathe thy lov-ing Spir-it In-to ev-ery trou-bled breast;
3. Come, Al-might-y to de-liv-er, Let us all thy grace re-ceive!
4. Fin-ish then thy new cre-a-tion; Pure and spot-less may we be.

Fix in us thy hum-ble dwell-ing; All thy faith-ful mer-cies crown.
Let us all in thee in-her-it; Let us find the prom-ised rest.
Sud-den-ly re-turn and nev-er, Nev-er more thy tem-ples leave.
Let us see thy great sal-va-tion Per-fect-ly re-stored in thee;

Je-sus, thou art all com-pas-sion; Pure, un-bound-ed love thou art.
Take a-way the love of sin-ning; Al-pha and O-me-ga be;
Thee we would be al-ways bless-ing, Serv-ing thee like those a-bove;
Changed from glo-ry in-to glo-ry Till in heaven we take our place,

Vis-it us with thy sal-va-tion; En-ter ev-ery trem-bling heart.
End of faith, as its be-gin-ning, Set our hearts at lib-er-ty.
We would praise thee with-out ceas-ing, Glo-ry in thy per-fect love.
Till we cast our crowns be-fore thee, Lost in won-der, love, and praise. A-men.

Text: Charles Wesley, 1707-1788.
Tune: W. P. Rowlands, 1860-1937; copyright G. A. Gabe, Swansea, S. Wales.

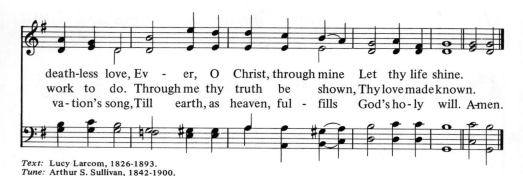

death-less love, Ev - er, O Christ, through mine Let thy life shine.
work to do. Through me thy truth be shown, Thy love made known.
va - tion's song, Till earth, as heaven, ful - fills God's ho - ly will. A - men.

Text: Lucy Larcom, 1826-1893.
Tune: Arthur S. Sullivan, 1842-1900.

Mysterious Presence, Source of All 169

II Nephi 6:103, 104
Deuteronomy 30:14-16, 19, 20

ADON OLOM L.M.

Moderato

1. Mys - te - rious Pres - ence, source of all— The world with -
2. Your breath is in the rush - ing wind; Your spir - it
3. Your hand un - seen to ac - cents clear A - woke the
4. That touch di - vine still, Lord, im - part; Still give the

out, the soul with - in— O fount of life, now
stirs in leaf and flower; Nor will you from the
psalm - ist's trem - bling lyre, And touched the lips of
proph - et's burn - ing word; And vo - cal in each

hear our call, And pour your liv - ing wa - ters in.
ea - ger mind With-hold your love and light and power.
ho - ly seer With flame from your own al - tar fire.
wait - ing heart Let liv - ing psalms of praise be heard.

Text: Seth Curtis Beach, 1837-1932, alt.
Tune: Eliezer Gerovitch, 1844-1914.

167
Jesus, the Very Thought of Thee

Acts 2:28
D. and C. 6:16

ST. AGNES C.M.

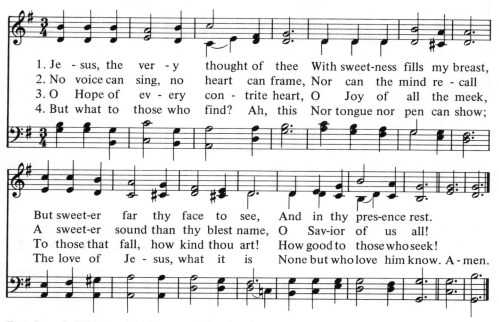

1. Je - sus, the ver - y thought of thee With sweet-ness fills my breast,
2. No voice can sing, no heart can frame, Nor can the mind re - call
3. O Hope of ev - ery con - trite heart, O Joy of all the meek,
4. But what to those who find? Ah, this Nor tongue nor pen can show;

But sweet-er far thy face to see, And in thy pres-ence rest.
A sweet-er sound than thy blest name, O Sav-ior of us all!
To those that fall, how kind thou art! How good to those who seek!
The love of Je - sus, what it is None but who love him know. A - men.

Text: Bernard of Clairvaux, 1091-1153; trans. Edward Caswall, 1814-1878; alt.
Tune: John B. Dykes, 1823-1876.

168
Draw Thou My Soul, O Christ

Hebrews 10:22-24
D. and C. 85:16

ST. EDMUND 6.4.6.4.6.6.6.4.

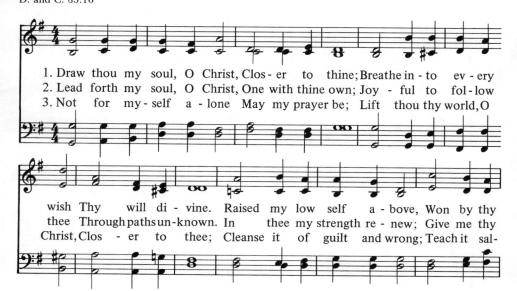

1. Draw thou my soul, O Christ, Clos - er to thine; Breathe in - to ev - ery
2. Lead forth my soul, O Christ, One with thine own; Joy - ful to fol - low
3. Not for my - self a - lone May my prayer be; Lift thou thy world, O

wish Thy will di - vine. Raised my low self a - bove, Won by thy
thee Through paths un-known. In thee my strength re - new; Give me thy
Christ, Clos - er to thee; Cleanse it of guilt and wrong; Teach it sal-

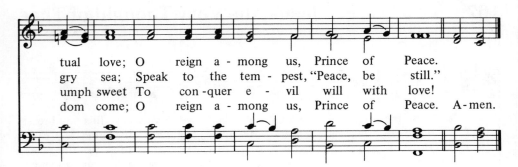

tual love; O reign a - mong us, Prince of Peace.
gry sea; Speak to the tem - pest, "Peace, be still."
umph sweet To con -quer e - vil will with love!
dom come; O reign a - mong us, Prince of Peace. A-men.

Text: William Romanis, 1824-1899.
Tune: Gregorian Chant, arr. Lowell Mason, 1792-1872.

Come, Ye Disconsolate 166

II Nephi 3:42, 47, 50
Colossians 3:1-4

CONSOLATOR 11.10.11.10.

1. Come, ye dis - con - so - late, wher - e'er ye lan - guish, Come to the
2. Joy of the des - o - late, light of the stray - ing, Hope of the
3. Here take the Bread of Life; drink wa - ters flow - ing Forth from the

mer - cy seat, fer - vent - ly kneel; Here bring your wound - ed hearts,
pen - i - tent, fade - less and pure! Here speaks the Com - fort - er,
throne of God, pure from a - bove: Come to the feast of love;

here tell your an - guish: Earth has no sor - row that God can-not heal.
ten - der - ly say - ing, "Earth has no sor - row that God can-not cure."
come, ev - er know -ing Earth has no sor - row God can -not re - move.

Text: Thomas Moore, 1779-1852, sts. 1, 2, alt.; Thomas Hastings, 1784-1872, st. 3, alt.
Tune: Samuel Webbe, 1740-1816.

164 God of Smallness, God of Greatness

Philippians 3:12-14
II Timothy 1:6, 7

HYMN OF PRAISE 8.7.8.7.

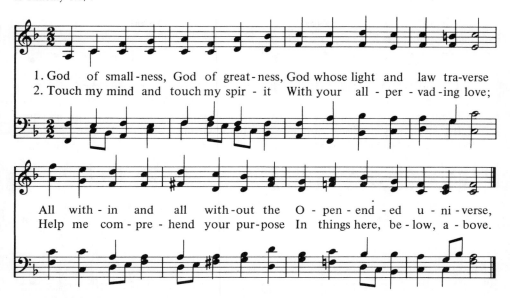

1. God of small-ness, God of great-ness, God whose light and law tra-verse
2. Touch my mind and touch my spir - it With your all - per - vad-ing love;

All with - in and all with-out the O - pen - end - ed u - ni - verse,
Help me com - pre - hend your pur-pose In things here, be - low, a - bove.

Text: Naomi Russell, 1921 - ; copyright 1980 Reorganized Church of Jesus Christ of Latter Day Saints.
Tune: William Graves, 1915 - ; alt.; copyright 1956 Herald Publishing House.

165 Pour Down Thy Spirit from Above

D. and C. 64:2d, e
Mosiah 11:139, 140

HAMBURG L.M.

1. Pour down thy Spir - it from a - bove And bid all
2. If in the souls where love should be, A - rise the
3. When - e'er in this wide world we meet Un - kind - ly
4. In ev - ery land, in ev - ery home, In ev - ery

strife and dis - cord cease; Join heart to heart in mu -
storm of fierce self - will, Calm thou the trou - bled, an -
deeds that an - ger move, Teach us for - give - ness; tri -
heart let love in - crease; Let love pro - claim thy king -

Thy Love, O God

Romans 12:1, 2
Hebrews 13:20, 21

MORA PROCTOR 11.10.11.10.

Unison

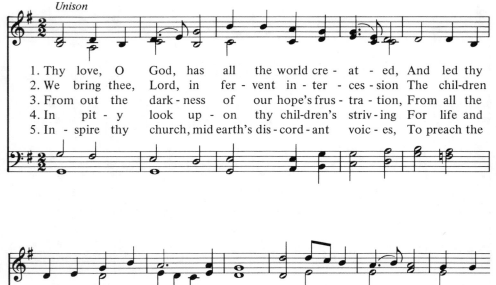

1. Thy love, O God, has all the world cre - at - ed, And led thy
2. We bring thee, Lord, in fer - vent in - ter - ces - sion The chil - dren
3. From out the dark - ness of our hope's frus - tra - tion, From all the
4. In pit - y look up - on thy chil - dren's striv - ing For life and
5. In - spire thy church, mid earth's dis - cord - ant voic - es, To preach the

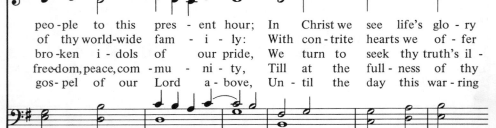

peo - ple to this pres - ent hour; In Christ we see life's glo - ry
of thy world-wide fam - i - ly: With con - trite hearts we of - fer
bro - ken i - dols of our pride, We turn to seek thy truth's il -
free - dom, peace, com - mu - ni - ty, Till at the full - ness of thy
gos - pel of our Lord a - bove, Un - til the day this war - ring

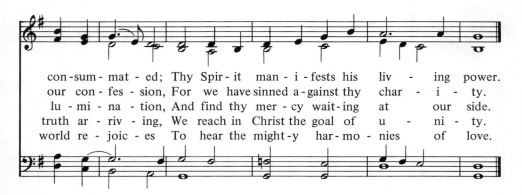

con - sum - mat - ed; Thy Spir - it man - i - fests his liv - ing power.
our con - fes - sion, For we have sinned a - gainst thy char - i - ty.
lu - mi - na - tion, And find thy mer - cy wait - ing at our side.
truth ar - riv - ing, We reach in Christ the goal of u - ni - ty.
world re - joic - es To hear the might - y har - mo - nies of love.

Text: Albert F. Bayly, 1901 - ; alt.; used by permission of the author.
Tune: William J. Reynolds, 1920 - ; copyright 1975 Broadman Press; all rights reserved; used by permission.

162 Savior, Like a Shepherd Lead Us

John 10:27, 29
I Nephi 7:56-59

BRADBURY 8.7.8.7.D.

1. Sav - ior, like a shep-herd lead us; Much we need thy ten - der care;
2. We are thine, do thou be - friend us; Be the guard-ian of our way;
3. Ear - ly let us seek thy fa - vor; Ear - ly let us do thy will;

In thy pleas-ant pas-tures feed us; For our use thy folds pre - pare.
Keep thy flock, from sin de - fend us; Seek us when we go a - stray.
Bless-ed Lord and on-ly Sav - ior, With thy love our bos-oms fill.

Bless - ed Je - sus, bless - ed Je - sus, Thou hast bought us, thine we are;
Bless - ed Je - sus, bless - ed Je - sus, Hear thy chil-dren when they pray:
Bless - ed Je - sus, bless - ed Je - sus, Thou hast loved us, love us still;

Bless - ed Je - sus, bless - ed Je - sus, Thou hast bought us, thine we are.
Bless - ed Je - sus, bless - ed Je - sus, Hear thy chil-dren when they pray.
Bless - ed Je - sus, bless - ed Je - sus, Thou hast loved us, love us still.

Text: From *Hymns for the Young,* 1836. Attr. to Dorothy A. Thrupp, 1779-1847.
Tune: William B. Bradbury, 1816-1868. Harm. alt. by Rosalee Elser, 1925 - .

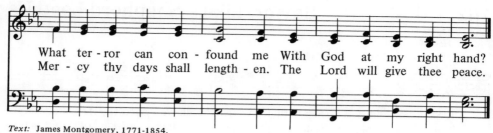

What ter-ror can con-found me With God at my right hand?
Mer-cy thy days shall length-en. The Lord will give thee peace.

Text: James Montgomery, 1771-1854.
Tune: Samuel S. Wesley, 1810-1876.

God Is My Strong Salvation

161

Romans 1:16, 17
Mosiah 3:21

WEDLOCK 7.6.7.6.D.
Alternate Hymn: 160

Unison

1. God is my strong sal - va - tion; What foe have I to fear?
2. Place on the Lord re - li - ance; My soul, with cour - age wait;

In dark - ness and temp - ta - tion, My light, my help is near.
His truth be thine af - fi - ance When faint and des - o - late.

Though hosts en - camp a - round me, Firm to the fight I stand.
His might thy heart shall strength - en, His love thy joy in - crease;

St. 1. St. 2.

What ter - ror can con - found me With God at my right hand?
Mer - cy thy days shall length - en. The Lord will give thee peace.

Text: James Montgomery, 1771-1854.
Tune: The Sacred Harp, 1844; arr. by Rosalee Elser, 1925 - ; copyright 1980 Rosalee Elser. Used by permission.

159   # Oh, for a Faith That Will Not Shrink

II Nephi 13:27-30
D. and C. 5:5b

EVAN C.M.

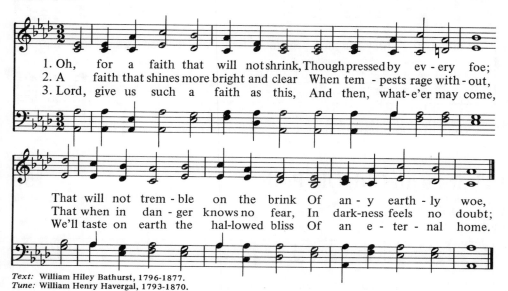

1. Oh, for a faith that will not shrink, Though pressed by ev-ery foe;
2. A faith that shines more bright and clear When tem - pests rage with-out,
3. Lord, give us such a faith as this, And then, what-e'er may come,

That will not trem - ble on the brink Of an - y earth - ly woe,
That when in dan - ger knows no fear, In dark-ness feels no doubt;
We'll taste on earth the hal-lowed bliss Of an e - ter - nal home.

Text: William Hiley Bathurst, 1796-1877.
Tune: William Henry Havergal, 1793-1870.

160   # God Is My Strong Salvation

Romans 1:16, 17
Moroni 7:24, 25

AURELIA 7.6.7.6.D.
Alternate hymn: 161

1. God is my strong sal - va - tion; What foe have I to fear?
2. Place on the Lord re - li - ance; My soul, with cour - age wait;

In dark - ness and temp - ta - tion, My light, my help is near.
His truth be thine af - fi - ance When faint and des - o - late.

Though hosts en - camp a - round me, Firm to the fight I stand.
His might thy heart shall strength - en, His love thy joy in - crease.

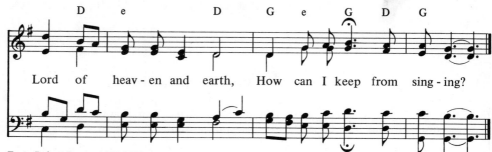

D	e		D	G	e	G	D	G

Lord of heav-en and earth, How can I keep from sing-ing?

Text: Robert Lowry, 1826-1899.
Tune: Quaker Hymn; harm. David N. Johnson, 1922 - ; copyright 1977 Praise Publications, Inc.; used by permission.

There's an Old, Old Path 158

Jeremiah 6:16
I Nephi 5:5

THE OLD, OLD PATH 5.5.5.5. with refrain

1. There's an old, old path Where the sun shines through Life's
2. Find the old, old path; 'Twill be ev-er new, For the
3. In this old, old path Are my friends most dear, And I
4. 'Tis an old, old path, Shad-owed vales be-tween, Yet I

dark storm clouds From its home of blue,
Sav-ior walks All the way with you,
walk with them, With the an-gels near,
fear-less walk With the Naz-a-rene,

In this old, old

path made strange-ly sweet By the touch di-vine of his bless-ed feet.

Text: Vida E. Smith, 1865-1945.
Tune: M. Audentia Anderson, 1872-1963.

157 My Life Flows On in Endless Song

Isaiah 52:7
II Nephi 3:61, 65, 66

HOW CAN I KEEP FROM SINGING 8.7.8.7. with refrain

rain,   To   cheer it af - ter rain.
may,   Bring   with it what   it may.
joice,   I   can - not but   re - joice.

Text: William Cowper, 1731-1800; alt.
Tune: Jane M. Marshall, 1924 - ; copyright 1974 Carl Fischer, Inc., New York; international copyright secured; all rights reserved; used by permission.

Children of the Heavenly Father   156

D. and C. 98:5h-j   TRYGGARE KAN INGEN VARA L.M.
John 10:27, 28

1. Chil - dren of the heaven - ly Fa - ther Safe - ly
2. Nei - ther life nor death shall ev - er From the
3. More se - cure is no one ev - er Than the

in his arms they gath - er; Nest - ling bird nor star in
Lord his chil - dren sev - er; Un - to them his grace he
loved ones of the Sav - ior; Not yon star on high a -

heav - en Such a ref - uge e'er was giv - en.
show - eth, And their sor - rows all he know - eth.
bid - ing Nor the bird in home - nest hid - ing.

Text: Caroline V. Sandell-Berg, 1832-1903; tr. Ernest W. Olson, 1870-1958; alt.; copyright Board of Publication, Lutheran Church in America.
Tune: Traditional Swedish Melody.

155

Sometimes a Light Surprises

II Nephi 3:61, 64, 65
D. and C. 10:6

SURPRISE 7.6.7.6.7.6.7.6.6.
Alternate hymn: 154

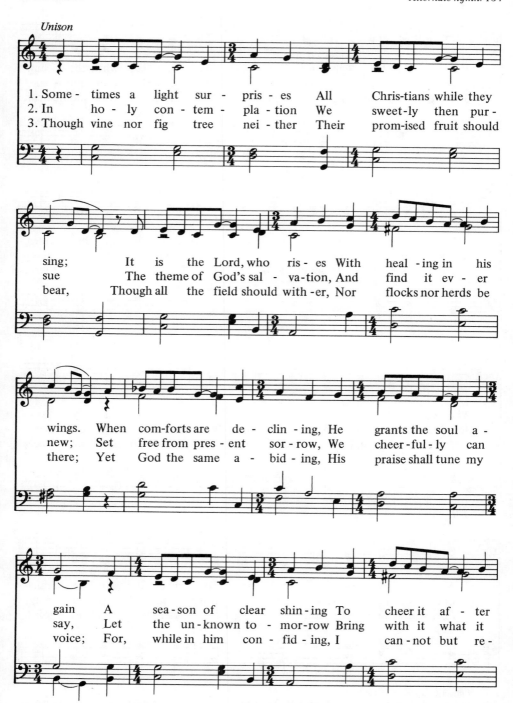

Unison

1. Some-times a light sur-pris-es All Chris-tians while they sing; It is the Lord, who ris-es With heal-ing in his wings. When com-forts are de-clin-ing, He grants the soul a-gain A sea-son of clear shin-ing To cheer it af-ter

2. In ho-ly con-tem-pla-tion We sweet-ly then pur-sue The theme of God's sal-va-tion, And find it ev-er new; Set free from pres-ent sor-row, We cheer-ful-ly can say, Let the un-known to-mor-row Bring with it what it

3. Though vine nor fig tree nei-ther Their prom-ised fruit should bear, Though all the field should with-er, Nor flocks nor herds be there; Yet God the same a-bid-ing, His praise shall tune my voice; For, while in him con-fid-ing, I can-not but re-

Sometimes a Light Surprises

154

II Nephi 3:61, 64, 65
D. and C. 10:6

SPRINGTIME 7.6.7.6.D.
Alternate hymn: 155

1. Some - times a light sur - pris - es All Chris-tians while they sing;
2. In ho - ly con - tem - pla - tion We sweet-ly then pur - sue
3. Though vine nor fig tree nei - ther Their prom-ised fruit should bear,

It is the Lord, who ris - es With heal - ing in his wings.
The theme of God's sal - va - tion, And find it ev - er new;
Though all the field should with - er, Nor flocks nor herds be there;

When com - forts are de - clin - ing, He grants the soul a - gain
Set free from pres - ent sor - row, We cheer - ful - ly can say,
Yet God the same a - bid - ing, His praise shall tune my voice;

A sea - son of clear shin - ing To cheer it af - ter rain.
Let the un - known to - mor - row Bring with it what it may,
For, while in him con - fid - ing, I can - not but re - joice.

Text: William Cowper, 1731-1800; alt.
Tune: Swedish Folk Melody; harm. Rosalee Elser, 1925 - ; harm. copyright 1980 by Rosalee Elser. Used by permission.

153

Great Hills May Tremble

Isaiah 54:10
Psalm 46:1, 2, 7, 9, 10

BERGEN MA VIKA 11.10.11.10.

1. Great hills may trem - ble and moun - tains may crum - ble,
2. Though peace be shat - tered by war's ag - i - ta - tion,
3. Strong to pre - serve us in mo - ments of dan - ger,

God's lov - ing - kind - ness con - tin - ues se - cure;
Though change and ten - sion give birth to great fears,
Strong when frus - tra - tion and frail - ty in - crease;

Peace He will give to the con - trite and hum - ble:
God still re - mains an un - shak - en foun - da - tion,
Strong to e - quip us for lov - ing the stran - ger,

Thus saith the Lord— His prom - ise is sure.
Strong to sup - port us through tur - bu - lent years;
Strong where our hu - man re - sourc - es may cease.

Text: Based on Isaiah 54:10 by Lina Sandell, 1832-1903; tr. E. Lincoln Pearson, 1917 - , st. 1, alt.; Bryan Jeffery
Leech, 1931 - , st. 2, 3. Copyright 1950, 1973 Covenant Press. All rights reserved. Used by permission.
Tune: Source Unknown.

da - tion nev - er fails, Faith's foun - da - tion nev - er fails.
soars on wings of hope, Free - dom soars on wings of hope.
great - est gift of all, Love, the great - est gift of all.

Text: Geoffrey F. Spencer, 1927 - ; copyright 1980 Reorganized Church of Jesus Christ of Latter Day Saints.
Tune: Mark H. Forscutt, 1834-1903.

Beyond the Mist and Doubt

I John 3:1, 2
Romans 5:8-11

152

WALHOF 6.6.8.8.6.6.

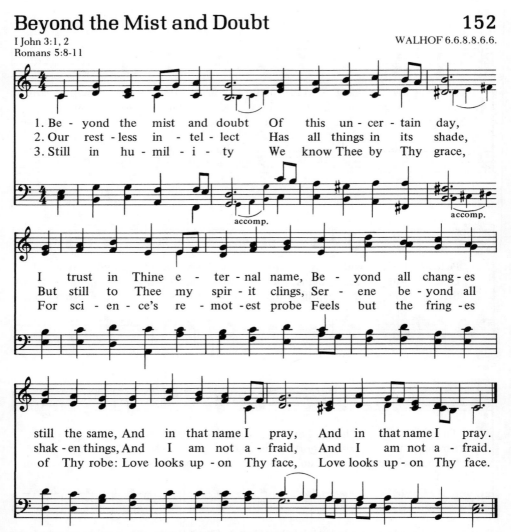

1. Be - yond the mist and doubt Of this un - cer - tain day,
2. Our rest - less in - tel - lect Has all things in its shade,
3. Still in hu - mil - i - ty We know Thee by Thy grace,

I trust in Thine e - ter - nal name, Be - yond all chang - es
But still to Thee my spir - it clings, Ser - ene be - yond all
For sci - en - ce's re - mot - est probe Feels but the fring - es

still the same, And in that name I pray, And in that name I pray.
shak - en things, And I am not a - fraid, And I am not a - fraid.
of Thy robe: Love looks up - on Thy face, Love looks up - on Thy face.

Text: Donald Wynn Hughes, 1911-1967; used by permission of J. D. P. Hughes.
Tune: Frederick F. Jackisch, 1922 - ; alt.; copyright 1978; from *Lutheran Book of Worship*; used by permission of
Augsburg Publishing House.

151 Every Good and Perfect Gift

James 1:17, 18
I Corinthians 13:13

EMERALD 7.6.7.6.7.7.7.7.7.

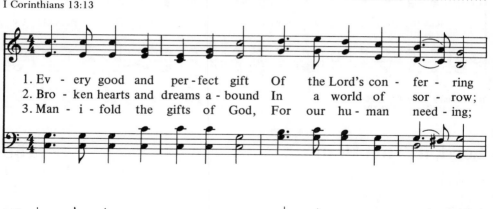

1. Ev - ery good and per - fect gift Of the Lord's con - fer - ring
2. Bro - ken hearts and dreams a - bound In a world of sor - row;
3. Man - i - fold the gifts of God, For our hu - man need - ing;

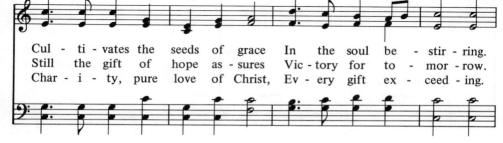

Cul - ti - vates the seeds of grace In the soul be - stir - ring.
Still the gift of hope as - sures Vic - tory for to - mor - row.
Char - i - ty, pure love of Christ, Ev - ery gift ex - ceed - ing.

Faith pro - claims a ris - en Lord, Cel - e - brates new
Hope to o - ver - come de - spair, Throw a - side the
In com - pas - sion's ten - der vein, Bread for hun - ger,

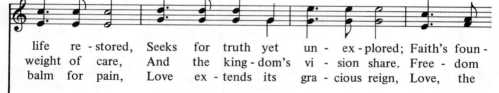

life re - stored, Seeks for truth yet un - ex - plored; Faith's foun -
weight of care, And the king - dom's vi - sion share. Free - dom
balm for pain, Love ex - tends its gra - cious reign, Love, the

hear my hum-ble cry; While on oth-ers thou art call-ing, Do not pass me by.

Text: Fanny J. Crosby, 1820-1915.
Tune: W. H. Doane, 1832-1915.

Lord, in This Hour

150

D. and C. 76:1, 2a, b
Romans 11:33, 34, 36

WIESBADEN 10.10.10.10.

Unison (or harmony)

1. Lord, in this hour en-a-ble us to see The breadth and
2. Earth-bound, we mark our days from dawn to night; We know that
3. We count a life from in-fan-cy's first cry Till death has

depth of thine e-ter-ni-ty. A thou-sand years to
dark-ness ev-er fol-lows light. Yet, though we can-not
stilled the last un-an-swered "Why?" But life and light go

thee are as a day. Help us to gain this view of time, we pray.
see, we know somewhere Be-yond our shad-owed sphere the sun is there.
on un-end-ing-ly— One bright mo-sa-ic known a-lone to thee.

Text: Naomi Russell, 1921 - ; copyright 1980 Reorganized Church of Jesus Christ of Latter Day Saints.
Tune: Dale G. Rider, 1948 - ; copyright 1974 White Harvest Music Corporation; used by permission.

148 Where Wilt Thou Put Thy Trust?

Psalm 71:5
II Nephi 3:61-66

FERGUSON S.M.

1. Where wilt thou put thy trust? In a frail form of clay
2. Where wilt thou cast thy care? Up-on an err-ing heart
3. No! Place thy trust a-bove This shad-owed realm of night,
4. His mer-cies will en-dure When skies and stars grow dim;

That to its el-e-ment of dust Must soon re-solve a-way?
Which hath its own sore ills to bear, And shrinks from sor-row's dart?
In Him whose bound-less power and love Thy con-fi-dence in-vite.
His change-less prom-ise stand-eth sure; Go cast thy care on Him.

Text: Lydia H. Sigourney, 1793-1865.
Tune: George Kingsley, 1811-1884.

149 Pass Me Not, O Gentle Savior

Alma 13:51
Luke 18:13

PASS ME NOT 8.5.8.5. with refrain

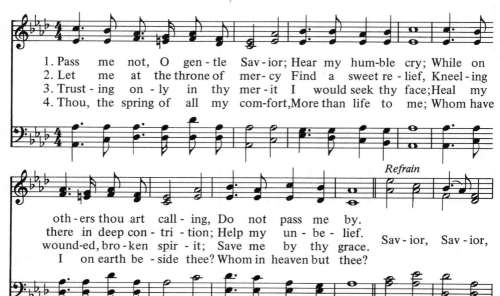

1. Pass me not, O gen-tle Sav-ior; Hear my hum-ble cry; While on
2. Let me at the throne of mer-cy Find a sweet re-lief, Kneel-ing
3. Trust-ing on-ly in thy mer-it I would seek thy face; Heal my
4. Thou, the spring of all my com-fort, More than life to me; Whom have

Refrain

oth-ers thou art call-ing, Do not pass me by.
there in deep con-tri-tion; Help my un-be-lief.
wound-ed, bro-ken spir-it; Save me by thy grace.
I on earth be-side thee? Whom in heaven but thee?

Sav-ior, Sav-ior,

There Is a Balm in Gilead

147

John 10:11, 13
II Nephi 3:44, 47, 50, 56

BALM IN GILEAD 7.6.7.6. with refrain

There is a balm in Gil - e - ad To make the wound - ed whole;

There is a balm in Gil - e - ad To heal the sin - sick soul.

1. Some-times I feel dis - cour-aged, And think my work's in vain, But
2. If you can't preach like Pe - ter, If you can't pray like Paul, Just

then the Ho - ly Spir - it Re - vives my soul a - gain. There is a
tell the love of Je - sus And say he died for all. There is a

Text: American Folk Hymn.
Tune: American Folk Hymn; arr. Rosalee Elser, 1925 - ; copyright 1980 Rosalee Elser; used by permission.

146 Tenderly, Tenderly, Lead Thou Me On

Isaiah 42:16
I Nephi 6:40

TENDERLY LEAD THOU ME ON 10.10.10.10.D.

1. Ten-der-ly, ten-der-ly, lead thou me on, On o'er the way where my
2. Faith-ful-ly, faith-ful-ly, hold-ing my hand, On the rough, slip-pery heights

Sav-ior hath gone; Bright on his path-way the sun-light hath shone;
safe-ly I stand, Look-ing a-way to the heav-en-ly strand;

Ten-der-ly, ten-der-ly, lead thou me on. Close to his hand I so
Ten-der-ly, ten-der-ly, he leads me on. Now has my weak heart grown

trem-bling-ly clung; Faint were the songs I so doubt-ing-ly sung, Bro-ken-ly
trust-ing-ly strong; Ways have grown short that seemed once to be long; Glad-ly I

fall-ing from fal-ter-ing tongue; Ten-der-ly, ten-der-ly, lead thou me on.
join in the tri-um-phant song, Ten-der-ly, ten-der-ly, lead-ing me on. A-men.

Text: Joseph Smith III, 1832-1914.
Tune: Norman W. Smith, 1833-1917.

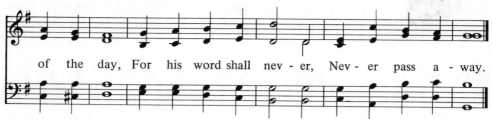

of the day, For his word shall nev - er, Nev - er pass a - way.

Text and Tune: Frances Ridley Havergal, 1836-1879.

Jesus, Savior, Pilot Me 145

Mark 4:30, 31 (37-39)
Psalm 89:8, 9

PILOT 7.7.7.D.

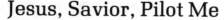

1. Je - sus, Sav - ior, pi - lot me O - ver life's tem - pes-tuous sea;
2. As a moth - er stills her child, Thou canst hush the o - cean wild;
3. When at last I near the shore, And the fear - ful break-ers roar

Un - known waves be-fore me roll, Hid - ing rock and treacherous shoal;
Bois - terous waves o - bey thy will When thou sayest to them, "Be still."
'Twixt me and the peace-ful rest, Then, while lean - ing on thy breast,

Chart and com - pass come from thee; Je - sus, Sav - ior, pi-lot me.
Won - drous Sov - ereign of the sea, Je - sus, Sav - ior, pi-lot me.
May I hear thee say to me, "Fear not; I will pi-lot thee." A - men.

Text: Edward Hopper, 1818-1888.
Tune: John E. Gould, 1822-1875.

144 Standing at the Portal

D. and C. 1:8
II Nephi 9:133-137

HERMAS 6.5.6.5.D. with refrain

1. Stand-ing at the por-tal Of the open-ing year, Words of
2. "I, the Lord, am with thee; Be thou not a-fraid! I will
3. He will nev-er fail us; He will not for-sake. His e-

com-fort meet us Hush-ing ev-ery fear, Spo-ken through the
help and strength-en; Be thou not dis-mayed! Yea, I will up-
ter-nal cov-enant He will nev-er break. Rest-ing on his

si-lence By our Fa-ther's voice, Ten-der, strong, and faith-ful,
hold thee With my own right hand; Thou art called and cho-sen
prom-ise, What have we to fear? God is all suf-fi-cient

Refrain

Mak-ing us re-joice:
In my sight to stand." On-ward then and fear not, Chil-dren
For the com-ing year.

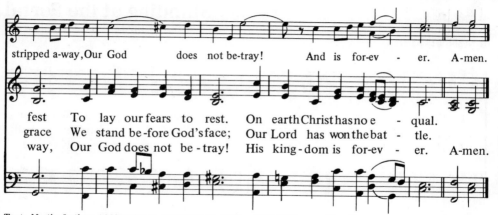

stripped a-way, Our God does not be-tray! And is for-ev - er. A-men.

fest   To   lay our fears to rest.   On earth Christ has no e - qual.
grace We stand be-fore God's face; Our Lord has won the bat - tle.
way,   Our God does not be - tray!   His king-dom is for-ev - er. A-men.

Text: Martin Luther, 1483-1546; tr. Frederick H. Hedge, 1805-1890; rev. Alan Tyree, 1929 - ; copyright 1980 Reorganized Church of Jesus Christ of Latter Day Saints.
Tune: Martin Luther, 1483-1546; descant by Mary E. Caldwell, 1909 - ; descant copyright 1976 by Paragon Associates, Inc.; all rights reserved; used by permission of The Benson Company, Inc., Nashville.

My Faith Looks Up to Thee

143

Moroni 7:47, 48
Hebrews 12:1, 2

OLIVET 6.6.4.6.6.6.4.

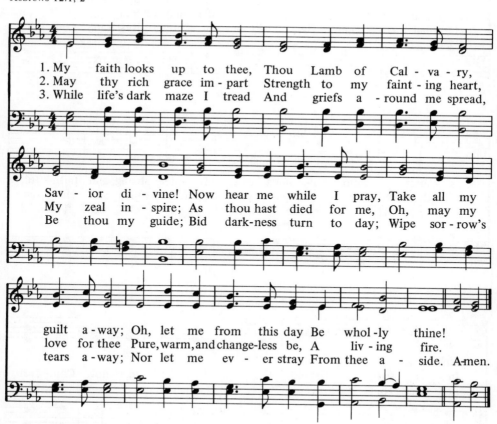

1. My   faith looks   up   to thee, Thou Lamb of   Cal - va - ry,
2. May   thy rich   grace im - part Strength to   my   faint - ing heart,
3. While life's dark maze I tread And   griefs a - round me spread,

Sav - ior di - vine! Now hear me while I pray, Take all my
My   zeal in - spire; As   thou hast died for me, Oh, may my
Be   thou my guide; Bid dark-ness turn to day; Wipe sor - row's

guilt a - way; Oh, let me from this day Be whol-ly thine!
love for thee Pure,warm,and change-less be, A   liv - ing fire.
tears a - way; Nor let me ev - er stray From thee a - side. A-men.

Text: Ray Palmer, 1808-1887.
Tune: Lowell Mason, 1792-1872.

142 A Mighty Fortress Is Our God

Psalm 91:2
D. and C. 18:1a-c

EIN' FESTE BURG 8.7.8.7.6.6.6.6.7.

Descant third stanza

3. That Word a - bove___ all, a - bid - eth;

1. A might-y for-tress is our God, A bul-wark nev-er fail - ing;
2. Did we in our own strength con-fide, Our striv-ing would be los - ing.
3. That Word a-bove all earth - ly powers, No thanks to them, a - bid - eth;

The gifts___ are ours, Who with us sid - eth.

Our help-er He a - mid the flood Of mor-tal ills pre-vail - ing.
Were not the right Man on our side, The Man of God's own choos - ing.
The Spir-it and the gifts are ours Through Him who with us sid - eth.

If all we love and claim—Our loved ones, wealth, and fame— Were from us

We have no foe to fear— Our strength, our help is near. Whose power is man-i-
Such love does Christ re-veal That all our wounds can heal; By his un-bound-ed
If all we love and claim— Our loved ones, wealth, and fame—Were from us stripped a-

Father, in Thy Mysterious Presence 141

I Chronicles 16:28-31
Alma 16:178-182

STRENGTH AND STAY 11.10.11.10.

1. Fa - ther, in thy mys - te - rious pres - ence kneel - ing,
2. Lord, we have wan - dered forth through doubt and sor - row,
3. Now, Fa - ther, now in thy dear pres - ence kneel - ing,

Oh, that our souls feel all thy kin - dling love!
And thou hast made each step an on - ward one;
Our spir - its yearn to feel thy kin - dling love;

For we are weak and need some deep re - veal - ing
So we will ev - er trust each un - known mor - row;
Now make us strong; we need thy deep re - veal - ing

Of trust and strength and calm-ness from a - bove.
Thou wilt sus - tain us till its work is done.
Of trust and strength and calm-ness from a - bove. A - men.

Text: Samuel Johnson, 1822-1882.
Tune: John B. Dykes, 1823-1876. Harm. alt. by Rosalee Elser, 1925 - .

140 Awake! Ye Saints of God, Awake

Deuteronomy 4:29
Alma 16:219-222

DUKE STREET L.M.

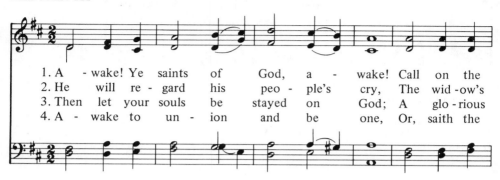

1. A - wake! Ye saints of God, a - wake! Call on the
2. He will re - gard his peo - ple's cry, The wid -ow's
3. Then let your souls be stayed on God; A glo - rious
4. A - wake to un - ion and be one, Or, saith the

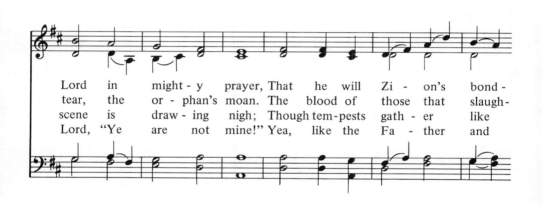

Lord in might - y prayer, That he will Zi - on's bond -
tear, the or - phan's moan. The blood of those that slaugh-
scene is draw - ing nigh; Though tem - pests gath - er like
Lord, "Ye are not mine!" Yea, like the Fa - ther and

age break, And bring to naught the fowl -er's snare.
tered lie Pleads not in vain be - fore his throne.
a flood, The storm, though fierce, will soon pass by.
the Son, Let all the saints in un -ion join. A - men.

Text: Eliza R. Snow, 1804-1887.
Tune: John C. Hatton, (?)-1793.

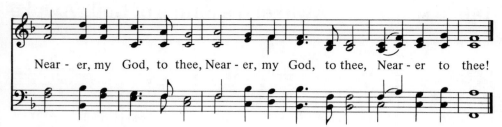

Text: Sarah F. Adams, 1805-1848.
Tune: Lowell Mason, 1792-1872.

Nearer, My God, to Thee 139

D. and C. 85:16
Psalm 34:1, 3, 4, 7-9, 22

WILMINGTON 6.4.6.4.6.6.4.
Alternate hymn: 138

1. Near - er, my God, to thee, Near - er to thee! E'en though it be a cross That rais - eth me, Still all my song shall be, Near - er, my God, to thee, near - er to thee!
2. Though like the wan - der - er, The sun gone down, Dark - ness be o - ver me, My rest a stone, Yet in my dreams I'd be Near - er, my God, to thee, near - er to thee!
3. There let the way ap - pear On - ward to heaven—All that thou send - est me In mer - cy given— An - gels to beck - on me Near - er, my God, to thee, near - er to thee!
4. Then, with my wak - ing thoughts Bright with thy praise; Out of my ston - y griefs Beth - el I'll raise, So by my woes to be Near - er, my God, to thee, near - er to thee!

Text: Sarah F. Adams, 1805-1848.
Tune: Erik Routley, 1917 - ; used by permission of the composer.

137 My Times Are in Thy Hand

Psalm 31:14, 15
D. and C. 98:5g-j

DENNIS S.M.

1. "My times are in thy hand!" My God, I wish them there;
2. "My times are in thy hand," What-ev-er they may be,
3. "My times are in thy hand!" Why should I doubt or fear?

My life, my friends, my soul I leave En-trust-ed to thy care.
If pleas-ing, pain-ful, dark, or bright, As best may seem to thee.
My Fa-ther's hand will nev-er cause His child a need-less tear. A-men.

Text: William Freeman Lloyd, 1791-1853; alt.
Tune: Johann G. Nägeli, 1773-1836; arr. Lowell Mason, 1792-1872.

138 Nearer, My God, to Thee

D. and C. 85:16
Psalm 34:1, 3, 4, 7-9, 22

BETHANY 6.4.6.4.6.6.6.4.
Alternate hymn: 139

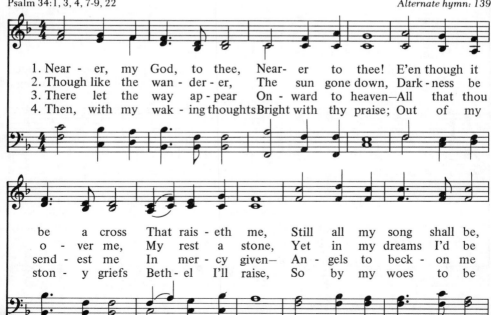

1. Near-er, my God, to thee, Near-er to thee! E'en though it
2. Though like the wan-der-er, The sun gone down, Dark-ness be
3. There let the way ap-pear On-ward to heaven—All that thou
4. Then, with my wak-ing thoughts Bright with thy praise; Out of my

be a cross That rais-eth me, Still all my song shall be,
o-ver me, My rest a stone, Yet in my dreams I'd be
send-est me In mer-cy given— An-gels to beck-on me
ston-y griefs Beth-el I'll raise, So by my woes to be

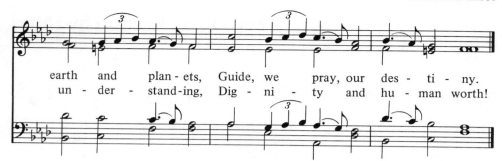

earth and plan - ets, Guide, we pray, our des - ti - ny.
un - der - stand - ing, Dig - ni - ty and hu - man worth!

Text: Jean E. Garriott, 1918 - ; alt.; copyright 1970 Hymn Society of America; used by permission.
Tune: Thomas J. Williams, 1869-1944; used by permission of Dilys A. Evans and Eluned Crump.

How Firm a Foundation

136

Helaman 2:74, 75
Isaiah 41:10

FOUNDATION 11.11.11.11.

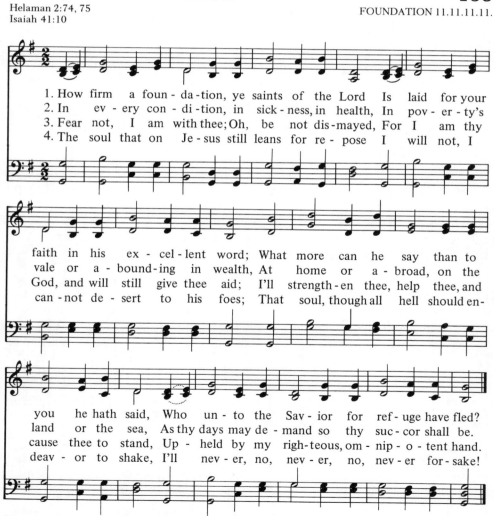

1. How firm a foun - da - tion, ye saints of the Lord Is laid for your
2. In ev - ery con - di - tion, in sick - ness, in health, In pov - er - ty's
3. Fear not, I am with thee; Oh, be not dis - mayed, For I am thy
4. The soul that on Je - sus still leans for re - pose I will not, I

faith in his ex - cel - lent word; What more can he say than to
vale or a - bound - ing in wealth, At home or a - broad, on the
God, and will still give thee aid; I'll strength - en thee, help thee, and
can - not de - sert to his foes; That soul, though all hell should en -

you he hath said, Who un - to the Sav - ior for ref - uge have fled?
land or the sea, As thy days may de - mand so thy suc - cor shall be.
cause thee to stand, Up - held by my right - eous, om - nip - o - tent hand.
deav - or to shake, I'll nev - er, no, nev - er, no, nev - er for - sake!

Text: "K" in John Rippon's *Selection of Hymns*, 1787.
Tune: Early American Melody; harm. Rosalee Elser, 1925 - ; copyright 1980 Rosalee Elser; used by permission.

135 World Around Us, Sky Above Us

II Corinthians 5:16, 17
II Nephi 3:34-36, 42

EBENEZER 8.7.8.7.D.

1. World a - round us, sky a - bove us, Framed our lives from
2. Winds of prom - ise swirl a - round us, Driv - ing us from

in - fan - cy; Lone - ly, we have climbed the moun - tains, Searching
pole to pole; Gold - en i - dols, crim - son al - tars, Lure us

for i - den - ti - ty; Low - ly sta - tions, pain - ful
on, far from our goal. Grant us time to write a

bar - riers, Blur our view and bruise our soul; You, who shape the
chap - ter In our ven - ture on this earth, Teach - ing trust and

I Heard the Voice of Jesus Say

134

Matthew 11:29, 30 (28-30)
D. and C. 63:7

VOX DILECTI C.M.D.

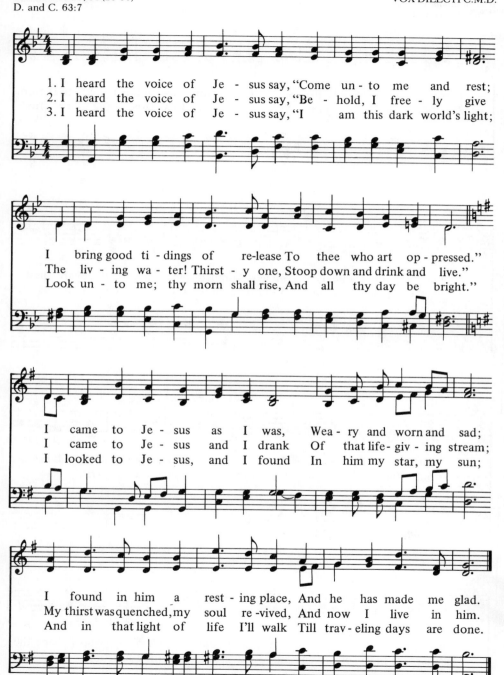

1. I heard the voice of Je - sus say, "Come un - to me and rest;
2. I heard the voice of Je - sus say, "Be - hold, I free - ly give
3. I heard the voice of Je - sus say, "I am this dark world's light;

I bring good ti - dings of re-lease To thee who art op - pressed."
The liv - ing wa - ter! Thirst - y one, Stoop down and drink and live."
Look un - to me; thy morn shall rise, And all thy day be bright."

I came to Je - sus as I was, Wea - ry and worn and sad;
I came to Je - sus and I drank Of that life- giv - ing stream;
I looked to Je - sus, and I found In him my star, my sun;

I found in him a rest - ing place, And he has made me glad.
My thirst was quenched, my soul re -vived, And now I live in him.
And in that light of life I'll walk Till trav - eling days are done.

Text: Horatius Bonar, 1808-1889, alt.
Tune: John B. Dykes, 1823-1876.

133 Cast Thy Burden upon the Lord

Psalm 55:22
Psalm 16:8, 9

BIRMINGHAM 8.6.11.6.6.6.7.5.

Cast thy bur-den up-on the Lord, And he shall sus-tain thee.

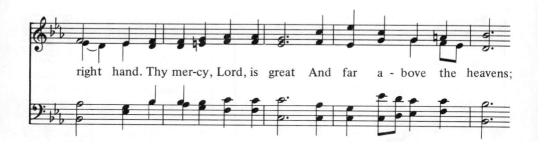

He nev-er will suf-fer the righ-teous to fall; He is at thy

right hand. Thy mer-cy, Lord, is great And far a-bove the heavens;

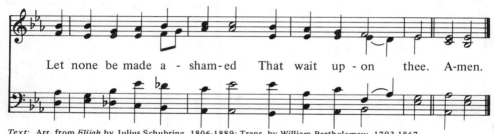

Let none be made a-sham-ed That wait up-on thee. A-men.

Text: Arr. from *Elijah* by Julius Schubring, 1806-1889; Trans. by William Bartholemew, 1793-1867.
Tune: Felix Mendelssohn, 1809-1847.

heard and my com-plaints; My prayers are heard and my com-plaints.
gift hath taught it me; Thy love's best gift hath taught it me.
Sav - ior, I de - pend; On thee, my Sav - ior, I de-pend!" A-men.

Text: Joseph Smith III, 1832-1914.
Tune: Frederick M. A. Venua, 1788-1872.

O Love That Wilt Not Let Me Go   132

Ether 5:33, 34
Romans 8:38, 39

ST. MARGARET 8.8.8.8.6.

1. O Love that wilt not let me go, I rest my wea - ry
2. O Light that fol - lowest all my way, I yield my flick - ering
3. O Joy that seek - est me through pain, I can - not close my
4. O Cross that lift - est up my head, I dare not ask to

soul in thee; I give thee back the life I owe That
torch to thee; My heart re - stores its bor - rowed ray That
heart to thee; I trace the rain - bow through the rain And
fly from thee; I lay in dust life's glo - ry dead, And

in thine o - cean depths its flow May rich - er, full - er be.
in thy sun - shine's blaze its day May bright-er, fair - er be.
feel the prom - ise is not vain That morn shall tear - less be.
from the ground there blos - soms red Life that shall end - less be.

Text: George Matheson, 1842-1906.
Tune: Albert Peace, 1844-1912.

130 How Gentle God's Command

I John 5:3
Alma 14:124

JAMES S.M.

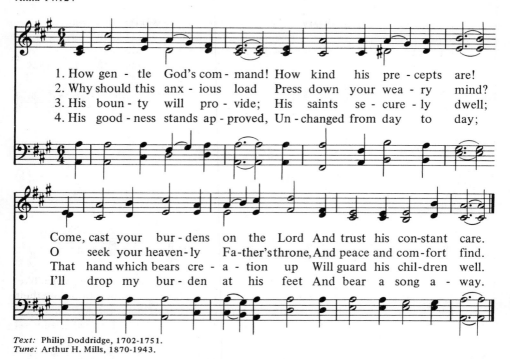

1. How gen - tle God's com - mand! How kind his pre - cepts are!
2. Why should this anx - ious load Press down your wea - ry mind?
3. His boun - ty will pro - vide; His saints se - cure - ly dwell;
4. His good - ness stands ap - proved, Un - changed from day to day;

Come, cast your bur - dens on the Lord And trust his con - stant care.
O seek your heaven - ly Fa - ther's throne, And peace and com - fort find.
That hand which bears cre - a - tion up Will guard his chil - dren well.
I'll drop my bur - den at his feet And bear a song a - way.

Text: Philip Doddridge, 1702-1751.
Tune: Arthur H. Mills, 1870-1943.

131 Unmoved by Fear, My Praise Is Due

I Nephi 5:59
D. and C. 6:15a, b

PARK STREET 8.8.8.8.8.8.

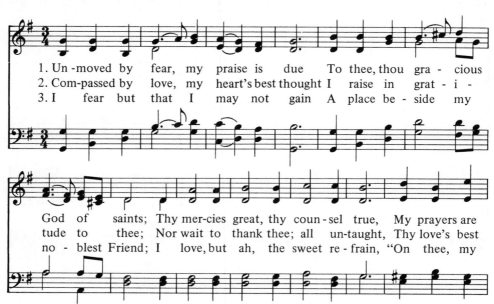

1. Un - moved by fear, my praise is due To thee, thou gra - cious
2. Com - passed by love, my heart's best thought I raise in grat - i -
3. I fear but that I may not gain A place be - side my

God of saints; Thy mer - cies great, thy coun - sel true, My prayers are
tude to thee; Nor wait to thank thee; all un - taught, Thy love's best
no - blest Friend; I love, but ah, the sweet re - frain, "On thee, my

com-forts flee, Help   of the help-less, O   a - bide with me.
round I   see; O   thou who chang-est not, a - bide with me.
stay can   be? Through cloud and sun-shine, Lord, a - bide with me.
vic - to - ry? I   tri-umph still if thou a - bide with me. A-men.

Text: Henry Francis Lyte, 1793-1847.
Tune: William Henry Monk, 1823-1889.

I Need Thee Every Hour   129

Psalm 25:4, 5   NEED 6.4.6.4. with refrain
D. and C. 61:6c-e

1. I need thee ev-ery hour, Most gra - cious Lord; No   ten - der voice like
2. I need thee ev-ery hour; Stay thou near - by; Temp-ta - tions lose their
3. I need thee ev-ery hour, In   joy   or   pain; Come quick-ly and a -
4. I need thee ev-ery hour; Teach me thy   will, And thy rich prom-is -

Refrain

thine Can   peace af - ford.
power When thou art nigh.   I need thee, oh, I need thee; Ev- ery hour I
bide, Or   life is vain.
es   In   me ful - fill.

need thee; Oh, bless me now, my Sav - ior; I come to thee. A - men.

Text: Annie S. Hawks, 1835-1872.
Tune: Robert Lowry, 1826-1899.

127 · I Am Trusting Thee, Lord Jesus

D. and C. 10:6
II Nephi 3:61

BULLINGER 8.5.8.5.

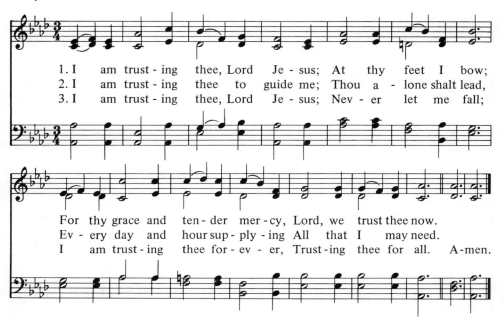

1. I am trust-ing thee, Lord Je-sus; At thy feet I bow;
2. I am trust-ing thee to guide me; Thou a-lone shalt lead,
3. I am trust-ing thee, Lord Je-sus; Nev-er let me fall;

For thy grace and ten-der mer-cy, Lord, we trust thee now.
Ev-ery day and hour sup-ply-ing All that I may need.
I am trust-ing thee for-ev-er, Trust-ing thee for all. A-men.

Text: Frances Ridley Havergal, 1836-1879.
Tune: Ethelbert W. Bullinger, 1837-1913.

128 · Abide with Me

Luke 24:28 (29)
Matthew 11:29, 30 (28-30)

EVENTIDE 10.10.10.10.

1. A - bide with me; fast falls the e - ven-tide. The dark-ness
2. Swift to its close ebbs out life's lit-tle day; Earth's joys grow
3. I need thy Spir-it ev-ery pass-ing hour; What but thy
4. I fear no foe with thee at hand to bless; Ills have no

deep-ens; Lord, with me a-bide. When oth-er help-ers fail, and
dim, its glo-ries pass a-way; Change and de-cay in all a-
grace can foil the tempt-er's power? Who like thy-self my guide and
weight, and tears no bit-ter-ness. Where is death's sting? Where, grave, thy

I Know Not What the Future Hath

126

Psalm 139:7-14
Isaiah 41:10

BROTHER JAMES' AIR 8.6.8.6.8.6.

1. I know not what the fu-ture hath Of mar-vel or sur-
2. And if my heart and flesh are weak To bear an un-tried
3. I know not where God's is-lands lift Their frond-ed palms in

prise; I on-ly know that life and death God's
pain, The frail-est reed God will not break, But
air; I on-ly know I can-not drift Be -

mer-cy un-der-lies. I on-ly know that
strength-en and sus-tain. The frail-est reed God
yond God's love and care. I on-ly know I

life and death God's mer-cy un-der-lies.
will not break, But strength-en and sus-tain.
can-not drift Be-yond God's love and care.

Text: John Greenleaf Whittier, 1807-1892; alt.
Tune: James Leith Macbeth Bain, c. 1840-1925; harm. Gordon Jacob, 1895 - ; adapted by Rosalee Elser, 1925 - ,
by permission of Oxford University Press.

125 My Shepherd Will Supply My Need

Psalm 23
Luke 12:29-35 (27-32)

RESIGNATION C.M.D.
Alternate tunes: *CRIMOND (124), NEW BRITAIN (104)*

Unison (or harmony)

1. My shep-herd will sup-ply my need; Je-ho-vah is his name:
2. When I walk through the shades of death his pres-ence is my stay;
3. The sure pro-vi-sions of my God At-tend me all my days;

In pas-tures fresh he makes me feed, Be-side the liv-ing stream.
One word of his sup-port-ing breath Drives all my fears a-way.
O may his house be my a-bode, And all my work be praise.

He brings my wan-dering spir-it back When I for-sake his ways;
His hand, in sight of all my foes, Doth still my ta-ble spread;
There will I find re-viv-ing rest, And free-ly go and come;

And leads me, for his mer-cy's sake, In paths of truth and grace.
My cup with bless-ings o-ver-flows, His oil a-noints my head.
No more a stran-ger, or a guest, But like a child at home.

Text: Psalm 23, para. by Isaac Watts, 1674-1748; alt.
Tune: Southern Harmony, 1835; harm. Rosalee Elser, 1925- ; harm. copyright 1980 Rosalee Elser.

Refrain

He lead-eth me, he lead-eth me, By his own hand he lead-eth me.

His faith-ful fol-lower I would be, For by his hand he lead-eth me.

Text: Joseph H. Gilmore, 1834-1918.
Tune: William B. Bradbury, 1816-1868.

The Lord's My Shepherd

124

Psalm 23
I Nephi 7:56-59

CRIMOND C.M.
Alternate tunes: NEW BRITAIN (104).
BROTHER JAMES' AIR * (126)

1. The Lord's my shep-herd; I'll not want. He makes me down to lie
2. My soul he doth re-store a-gain, And me to walk doth make
3. Yea, though I walk in death's dark vale, Yet will I fear no ill,
4. My ta-ble thou hast fur-nish-ed In pres-ence of my foes;
5. Good-ness and mer-cy all my life Shall sure-ly fol-low me;

In pas-tures green. He lead-eth me The qui-et wa-ters by.
With-in the paths of right-eous-ness, E'en for his own name's sake.
For thou art with me; and thy rod And staff me com-fort still.
My head thou dost with oil a-noint, And my cup o-ver-flows.
And in God's house for-ev-er-more My dwell-ing place shall be.

Text: Scottish Psalter, 1650.
Tune: Jessie Seymour Irvine, 1836-1887.

* Repeat last line in each stanza.

122 With Eyes of Faith

Isaiah 53:4, 5
Jacob 3:16, 17

CRAIG L.M.

1. With eyes of faith and heart of love I lift my mind and soul a-bove
2. In striv-ings oft I fight 'gainst sin But find scant righ-teous-ness with-in;
3. Per - fec-tion still doth God re - quire; We stum-ble oft, though we as - pire;
4. By faith I draw my dai - ly breath; By faith, through him, I con-quer death;

To him who full a - tone-ment made For all whose sins on him are laid.
Temp-ta-tions still as - sail my heart In which per - fec-tion finds small part.
The sin-less Christ's a - tone-ment free By faith per - fec-tion works in me.
By faith, my sin he doth for - give; By faith, his life in me doth live.

Text: Evan A. Fry, 1902-1959; copyright 1956 Herald Publishing House.
Tune: Franklyn S. Weddle, 1905 - ; copyright 1956 Herald Publishing House.

123 He Leadeth Me

Ether 1:106-108
Isaiah 48:17

HE LEADETH ME L.M. with refrain

1. He lead - eth me; oh, bless-ed thought! Oh, words with heaven-ly com-fort fraught!
2. Some-times mid scenes of deep-est gloom, Some-times where E-den's bow-ers bloom,
3. Lord, I would clasp thy hand in mine, Nor ev - er mur - mur nor re - pine,

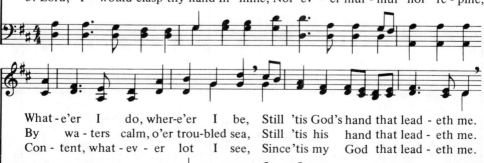

What-e'er I do, wher-e'er I be, Still 'tis God's hand that lead - eth me.
By wa - ters calm, o'er trou-bled sea, Still 'tis his hand that lead - eth me.
Con - tent, what-ev - er lot I see, Since 'tis my God that lead - eth me.

Jesus, Priceless Treasure

121

Isaiah 41:10
D. and C. 34:6

JESU, MEINE FREUDE 6.6.5.6.6.5.7.8.6.

1. Je - sus, price - less trea - sure, Source of pur - est plea - sure,
2. In thine arm I rest me; Foes who would mo - lest me
3. Hence, all thoughts of sad - ness! For the Lord of glad - ness,

Tru - est friend to me; Long my heart hath pant - ed Till it well-nigh
Can-not reach me here. Though the earth be shak - ing, Ev - ery heart be
Je - sus, en - ters in; Those who love the Fa - ther, Though the storms may

faint - ed, Thirst-ing af - ter thee. Thine I am, O spot-less Lamb;
quak - ing, God dis-pels our fear; Sin and hell in con-flict fell
gath - er, Still have peace with-in; Yea, what-e'er we here must bear,

I will suf - fer naught to hide thee, Ask for naught be - side thee.
With their heav - iest storms as - sail us: Je - sus will not fail us.
Still in thee lies pur - est plea - sure, Je - sus, price - less trea - sure!

Text: Johann Franck, 1618-1677; trans. Catherine Winkworth, 1827-1878; alt.
Tune: Johann Crüger, 1598-1662; harm. J. S. Bach, 1685-1750.

120

In Heavenly Love Abiding

III Nephi 5:110-112
John 10:4, 9

AURELIA 7.6.7.6.D

1. In heaven - ly love a - bid - ing, No change my heart shall fear;
2. Wher - ev - er he may guide me, No want shall turn me back;
3. Green pas - tures are be - fore me Which yet I have not seen;

And safe is such con - fid - ing, For noth - ing chang - es here.
My Shep - herd is be - side me, And noth - ing can I lack.
Bright skies will soon be o'er me Where dark - est clouds have been.

The storm may roar with - out me; My heart may low be laid,
His wis - dom ev - er wak - eth; His sight is nev - er dim;
My hope I can - not meas - ure; My path to life is free;

But God is round a - bout me, And I am not dis - mayed.
He knows the way he tak - eth, And I will walk with him.
My Sav - ior has my treas - ure, And he will walk with me.

Text: Anna L. Waring, 1823-1910.
Tune: Samuel S. Wesley, 1810-1876.

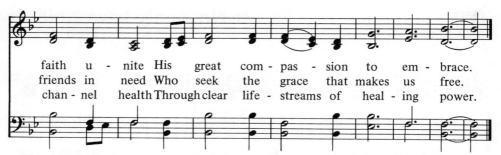

faith u - nite His great com - pas - sion to em - brace.
friends in need Who seek the grace that makes us free.
chan - nel health Through clear life - streams of heal - ing power.

Text: Cleo Hanthorne Moon, 1904 - ; copyright 1980 Reorganized Church of Jesus Christ of Latter Day Saints.
Tune: Thomas Hastings, 1784-1872; harm. Rosalee Elser, 1925 - ; harm. copyright 1980 Rosalee Elser.

Just as I Am, Without One Plea 119

D. and C. 18:6
Mosiah 1:115, 116

WOODWORTH L.M.

1. Just as I am, with - out one plea, But that thy
2. Just as I am, though tossed a - bout With ma - ny a
3. Just as I am, poor, wretch-ed, blind; Sight, rich - es,
4. Just as I am, thou wilt re - ceive, Wilt wel - come,

blood was shed for me, And that thou bid-dest me come to
con - flict, ma - ny a doubt; With strife and fears with - in, with -
heal - ing of the mind, Yea, all I need, in thee to
par - don, cleanse, re - lieve, Be - cause thy prom - ise I be -

thee, O Lamb of God, I come, I come.
out, O Lamb of God, I come, I come.
find, O Lamb of God, I come, I come.
lieve, O Lamb of God, I come, I come. A - men.

Text: Charlotte Elliott, 1789-1871; alt.
Tune: William B. Bradbury, 1816-1868.

117 Oh, for a Closer Walk with God

Alma 30:2
D. and C. 100:7a

NAOMI C.M.

Unison (or harmony)

1. Oh, for a clos-er walk with God, A calm and heaven-ly frame,
2. Re-turn, O ho-ly dove, re-turn, Sweet mes-sen-ger of rest!
3. The dear-est i-dol I have known, What-e'er that i-dol be,
4. So shall my walk be close with God, Calm and se-rene my frame;

A light to shine up-on the road That leads me to the Lamb!
I hate the sins that made thee mourn And drove thee from my breast.
Help me to tear it from thy throne And wor-ship on-ly thee.
So pur-er light shall mark the road That leads me to the Lamb.

Text: William Cowper, 1731-1800.
Tune: Johann G. Nägeli, 1768-1836; harm. Carlton R. Young, 1926 - ; harm. copyright 1964 Abingdon Press. Used by permission.

118 The Weight of Past and Fruitless Guilt

Romans 5:6-11
D. and C. 150:11a

RETREAT L.M.

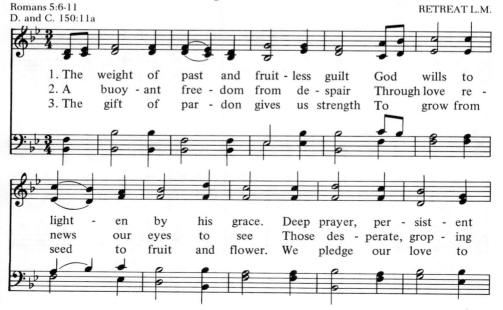

1. The weight of past and fruit-less guilt God wills to
2. A buoy-ant free-dom from de-spair Through love re-
3. The gift of par-don gives us strength To grow from

light-en by his grace. Deep prayer, per-sist-ent
news our eyes to see Those des-perate, grop-ing
seed to fruit and flower. We pledge our love to

Father, When in Love to Thee

116

II Corinthians 7:8-10
D. and C. 64:2d, e

SPANISH CHANT 7.7.7.7.D.

1. Fa - ther, when in love to thee Low we bow the a - dor -ing knee,
2. We re - pent the times we've stood For the things of less - er good,
3. Fa - ther, while we look to thee, Low - ly on the bend -ed knee,

When re - pent - ant to the skies Scarce - ly do we lift our eyes,
And for stew - ard - ship of time We have spent un - linked with thine.
And in pen - i -tence we turn, For thy par - don now we yearn.

Then, O hear us as we plead For thy help in time of need;
In the midst of sin and strife, Teach us how to live a life
Rec - on - cile us by thy love; Lift our souls to things a - bove;

On thy mer - cy we re - ly; Hear, for - give us when we cry.
Marked by grac - es of new birth, Wor - thy of thy saints on earth.
As we hum - bly now draw nigh, Hear, for - give us when we cry. A - men.

Text: Robert Grant, 1785-1838, Alt.
Tune: Arr. by Benjamin Carr, 1769-1831.

115   Dear Lord and God of Humankind

Philippians 4:4-7
Matthew 11:29, 30 (28-30)

REST 8.6.8.8.6.

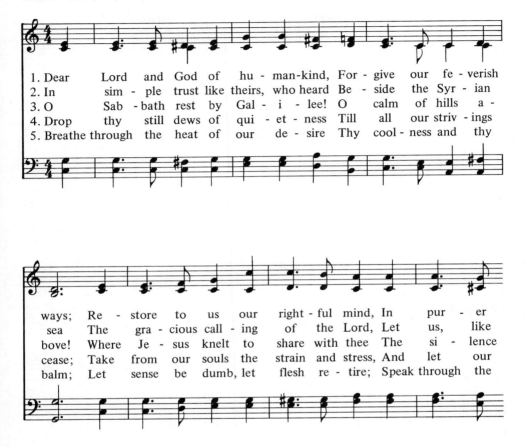

1. Dear Lord and God of hu - man-kind, For - give our fe - verish
2. In sim - ple trust like theirs, who heard Be - side the Syr - ian
3. O Sab - bath rest by Gal - i - lee! O calm of hills a -
4. Drop thy still dews of qui - et - ness Till all our striv - ings
5. Breathe through the heat of our de - sire Thy cool - ness and thy

ways; Re - store to us our right - ful mind, In pur - er
sea The gra - cious call - ing of the Lord, Let us, like
bove! Where Je - sus knelt to share with thee The si - lence
cease; Take from our souls the strain and stress, And let our
balm; Let sense be dumb, let flesh re - tire; Speak through the

lives thy ways to find, In deep - er rev - erence, praise.
them, with - out a word, Rise up and fol - low thee.
of e - ter - ni - ty, In - ter - pret - ed by love.
or - dered lives con - fess The beau - ty of thy peace.
earth - quake, wind, and fire, O still small voice of calm! A - men.

Text: John Greenleaf Whittier, 1807-1892; alt.
Tune: Frederick C. Maker, 1844-1927

shine To shame and guide this life of mine.
done, O thou, whose deeds and dreams were one! A - men.

Text: John Hunter, 1848-1917.
Tune: Adapted from *Katholisches Gesangbuch*, Vienna, c. 1774.

Lord, Thy Mercy Now Entreating 114

Psalm 119:57, 58
II Nephi 3:34-36

KINGDOM 8.7.8.7.

1. Lord, thy mer - cy now en - treat - ing, Low be -
2. Sin - ful thoughts and words un - lov - ing Rise a -
3. Hearts that far from thee were stray - ing While in
4. Pre - cious mo - ments i - dly wast - ed, Pre - cious
5. Lord, thy mer - cy still en - treat - ing, We with

fore thy throne we fall; Our mis - deeds to thee con -
gainst us one by one— Acts un - worth - y, deeds un -
prayer we bowed the knee, Lips that while thy prais - es
hours in fol - ly spent, Chris - tian vow and fight un -
shame our sins would own; From hence - forth, the time re -

fess - ing, On thy name we hum - bly call.
think - ing, Good that we have left un - done;
sound - ing Lift - ed not the soul to thee;
heed - ed, Scarce a thought to wis - dom lent—
deem - ing, May we live to thee a - lone. A - men.

Text: Mary A. Sidebotham, 1833-1913.
Tune: V. Earle Copes, 1921 - ; copyright 1959 Abingdon Press. Used by permission.

112 Heavenly Father, We Adore Thee

Psalm 86:5, 6
D. and C. 6:15, 16a

OMNI DIE 8.7.8.7.

1. Heaven-ly Fa-ther, we a - dore thee! At thy feet we hum-bly bow,
2. Thou art gra-cious, Lord; for - give us Ev - ery wrong that we have done;
3. In the name of Christ, our Sav - ior, Draw our minds from world-ly care;

Met to wor-ship, Lord, be - fore thee; Grant us each a bless-ing now.
Let no spir - it false de - ceive us; Bid thy Spir-it make us one.
Grant us each thy spe - cial fa - vor; Hear our ear-nest, fer-vent prayer. A - men.

Text: Mark H. Forscutt, 1834-1903.
Tune: Corner's *Gesangbuch*, 1631; arr. by William Smith Rockstro, 1823-1895.

113 Dear Master, in Whose Life I See

II Nephi 3:56, 61
Philippians 4:13

HURSLEY L.M.

1. Dear Mas - ter, in whose life I see All that I
2. Though what I dream and what I do In my weak

would, but fail to be, Let thy clear light for - ev - er
days are al - ways two, Help me, op - pressed by things un-

O - ver - come___ our sin - ful calm - ness; Rouse us with___
Teach us cour - age as we strug - gle In all lib -
Save us now___ from sat - is - fac - tion, When we pri -

___ re - demp - tive shame; Bap - tize with___ thy fier - y
er - at - ing strife; Lift the small - ness of our
vate - ly are free, Yet are un - dis - turbed in

Spir - it; Crown our lives___ with tongues of flame.
vi - sion By thine own___ a - bun - dant life.
spir - it By an - oth - ther's mis - er - y.

Text: "Baptism by Fire" in *The Incendiary Fellowship* by David Elton Trueblood, 1900 - ; copyright 1967 by David
Elton Trueblood; used by permission of Harper & Row, Publishers, Inc.
Tune: Ronald Arnatt, 1930 - ; copyright 1971 by Walton Music Corp.; international copyright secured; all rights
reserved; used by permission.

111
Thou Whose Purpose Is to Kindle

Alma 5:38-41
Matthew 5:15-18 (13-16)

LADUE CHAPEL 8.7.8.7.D.
Alternate tune: AUSTRIA (376)

1. Thou whose pur-pose is to kin-dle Now ig-nite us with thy fire; While the earth a-waits thy burn-ing, With thy pas-sion us in-spire.

2. Thou who, in thy ho-ly gos-pel, Wills that all should tru-ly live, Help us sense our share of fail-ure, Our tran-quil-li-ty for-give.

3. Lord, who still a sword de-liv-ers Rath-er than a plac-id peace, With thy sharp-ened word dis-turb us, From com-pla-cen-cy re-lease!

I Lift My Soul to Thee, Lord

110

Psalm 25:1-7, 20, 21
II Nephi 3:31-34

VIGIL 7.6.7.6.D.*
Alternate tune: HOLY WINGS (1)

1. I lift my soul to thee, Lord; My God, I trust in thee.
2. Re - mem - ber, Lord, thy mer - cies For they have been of old.
3. Turn thou to me; be gra - cious; Bring me from my dis - tress.

May I not be a - sham - ed: Let none ex - ult o'er me.
Re - mem - ber not trans - gres - sions From sin - ful days un - told.
Con - sid - er mine af - flic - tion, My sin which I con - fess.

Let none that wait up - on thee Be put to shame, O Lord,
Ac - cord - ing to thy mer - cy, Re - mem - ber now thy word;
My guilt is great! Oh, par - don For thy name's sake, I pray!

For thou art their sal - va - tion, Their goal and their re - ward.
For thy name's sake, re - mem - ber With stead - fast love, O Lord.
O God, re - deem thy peo - ple: In - struct them in the way.

Text: Arranged from Psalm 25 by Alan D. Tyree, 1929 - ; copyright 1980 Reorganized Church of Jesus Christ of Latter Day Saints.
Tune: Swedish Folk Melody.

*See 210 for a lower setting.

109 Here We Have Come, Dear Lord, to Thee

II Timothy 2:19-21
D. and C. 11:4

SILVER HILL L.M.

1. Here we have come, dear Lord, to thee, Of thy trans-
2. We bring to thee no glo - rious gift, No gift that
3. We turn to thee from sin we've served, That we have
4. Ac - cept our true re - pent - ance, Lord. All that we

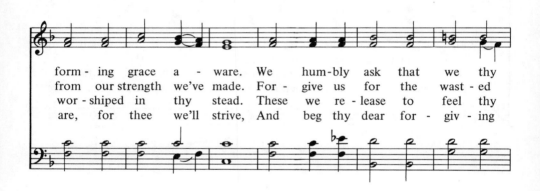

form - ing grace a - ware. We hum-bly ask that we thy
from our strength we've made. For - give us for the wast - ed
wor - shiped in thy stead. These we re - lease to feel thy
are, for thee we'll strive, And beg thy dear for - giv - ing

love, Thy work, thy joy hence - forth may share.
years, A - far from thee, a - lone, a - fraid.
warmth, Thy heal - ing hand up - on each head.
grace To touch our wast - ed gifts a - live. A-men.

Text: Cleo Hanthorne Moon, 1904 - ; copyright 1956 Herald Publishing House.
Tune: Frederick C. Maker, 1844-1927.

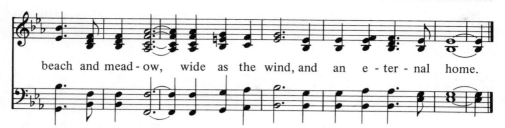

beach and mead-ow, wide as the wind, and an e-ter-nal home.

Text: Anders Frostenson; trans. Fred Kaan, 1929 - ; trans. copyright 1976 Stainer & Bell Ltd. Sole U. S. agent: Galaxy Music Corp., N. Y. Used with permission.
Tune: Jean Sibelius, 1865-1957; arr. copyright, 1933, by Presbyterian Board of Christian Education; renewed, 1961; from *The Hymnbook.* Used by permission of The Westminster Press. Melody is public domain in U.S.A.; outside U.S.A., original melody copyright by Breitkopf & Härtel, Wiesbaden. Used by permission.

Forgive Our Sins as We Forgive 108

I Timothy 1:5
Moroni 7:50-52

DOVE OF PEACE 8.6.8.6.6.

Unison (or harmony)

1. "For - give our sins as we for - give," you taught us,
2. How can your par - don reach and bless the un - for -
3. In blaz - ing light your cross re - veals the truth we
4. Lord, cleanse the depths with - in our souls, and bid re -

Lord, to pray; But you a - lone can grant us grace to
giv - ing heart That broods on wrongs and will not let old
dim - ly know; How small the debts men owe to us; how
sent - ment cease; Then, rec - on - ciled to God and man, our

live the words we say. To live the words we say.
bit - ter - ness de - part? Old bit - ter - ness de - part?
great our debt to you. How great our debt to you.
lives will spread your peace. Our lives will spread your peace.

Text: Rosamond E. Herklots, 1905 - ; used by permission of Oxford University Press.
Tune: American Folk Tune; arr. Austin C. Lovelace, 1919 - ; copyright 1977 by Agape, Carol Stream, IL 60187. International copyright secured. All rights reserved. Used by permission.

107

The Love of God

Ephesians 2:13-22
D. and C. 122:17

FINLANDIA 11.10.11.10.11.10.
See 315 for a higher setting.

Maintain a fairly quick tempo

1. The love of God is broad like beach and mead-ow,
2. We long for free-dom where our tru-est be-ing
3. But there are walls that keep us all di-vid-ed;
4. Oh, judge us, Lord, and in your judg-ment free us,

wide as the wind, and an e-ter-nal home. God leaves us
is giv-en hope and cour-age to un-fold. We seek in
we fence each oth-er in with hate and war. Fear is the
and set our feet in free-dom's o-pen space; Take us as

free to seek him or re-ject him; he gives us room to
free-dom space and scope for dream-ing, and look for ground where
bricks and mor-tar of our pris-on, our pride of self the
far as your com-pas-sion wan-ders a-mong the chil-dren

Refrain

an-swer "yes" or "no."
trees and plants can grow. The love of God is broad like
pris-on coat we wear.
of the hu-man race.

On - ly hide not now thy face, God of all - suf - fi - cient grace.
Each for - giv - en as thy child, Ran-somed, par-doned, rec - on - ciled. A-men.

Text: Attr. to Conder.
Tune: Marcus M. Wells, 1815-1895.

How Shall We Come Before You Now

106

Micah 6:6, 8
Psalm 51:15-17

STRACATHRO C.M.

1. How shall we come be - fore you now In
2. Such mea - ger vir - tues as we claim Are
3. So much re - solved, so lit - tle done; So
4. A bro - ken and a con - trite heart Has

this rich hour of praise? Shall righ - teous - ness or
your own gifts of grace; What can we bring of
quick to judge or blame; En - am - ored with our
brought us to this hour; And from the on - ly

mer - it prompt The joy - ful psalms we raise?
our own strength To of - fer in this place?
fool - ish pride, What mer - it can we claim?
gift we bring, New life springs in - to flower.

Text: Geoffrey F. Spencer, 1927 - ; copyright 1980 Reorganized Church of Jesus Christ of Latter Day Saints.
Tune: Melody from Charles Hutcheson's *Christian Vespers*, Glasgow, 1832; harm. Geoffrey Shaw, 1879-1943; alt.;
   from *Songs of Praise*, Enlarged Edition; used by permission of Oxford University Press.

104 — Amazing Grace

Titus 3:3-7
II Nephi 1:73-77

NEW BRITAIN C.M.

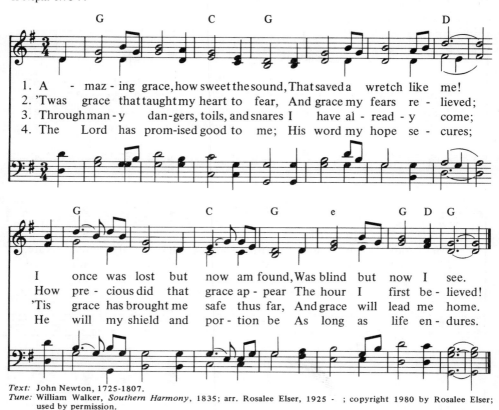

1. A - maz - ing grace, how sweet the sound, That saved a wretch like me!
2. 'Twas grace that taught my heart to fear, And grace my fears re - lieved;
3. Through man - y dan - gers, toils, and snares I have al - read - y come;
4. The Lord has prom-ised good to me; His word my hope se - cures;

I once was lost but now am found, Was blind but now I see.
How pre - cious did that grace ap - pear The hour I first be - lieved!
'Tis grace has brought me safe thus far, And grace will lead me home.
He will my shield and por - tion be As long as life en - dures.

Text: John Newton, 1725-1807.
Tune: William Walker, *Southern Harmony*, 1835; arr. Rosalee Elser, 1925 - ; copyright 1980 by Rosalee Elser; used by permission.

105 — O Thou God, Who Hearest Prayer

D. and C. 16:5d
Alma 16:238

FAITHFUL GUIDE 7.7.7.D.

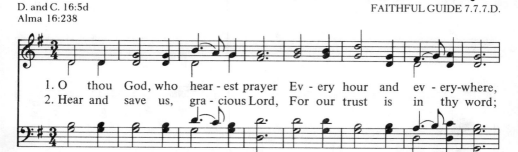

1. O thou God, who hear - est prayer Ev - ery hour and ev - ery-where,
2. Hear and save us, gra - cious Lord, For our trust is in thy word;

For His sake, whose blood we plead, Hear us in our hour of need;
Cleanse us from the stain of sin That thy peace may rule with - in;

Forgive Us, Lord

103

Micah 6:6, 8
Mosiah 2:28-32

SURSUM CORDA 10.10.10.10.

Unison (or harmony)

1. For - give us, Lord, for shal - low thank - ful - ness,
2. For - give us, Lord, for self - ish thanks and praise,
3. For - give us, Lord, for feast that knows not fast,
4. O - pen our eyes to glimpse thy love's in - tent,

For dull con - tent with warmth and shel - tered care,
For word that speaks at var - i - ance with deed.
For joy in things the while we starve the soul,
Our minds and hearts to plumb its depth and height.

For songs of praise for food and har - vest press,
For - give our thanks for walk - ing pleas - ant ways
For walls and wars that hide thy mer - cies vast
May thank - ful - ness be days in ser - vice spent,

While of thy rich - er gifts we're un - a - ware.
Un - mind - ful of a bro - ken neigh-bor's need.
And mar our vi - sion of the king - dom goal.
Re - flec - tion of Christ's life and love and light. A - men.

Text: William Watkins Reid, Sr., 1890 - ; alt. from *My God Is There, Controlling*; copyright 1965 The Hymn Society of America; used by permission.
Tune: Alfred M. Smith, 1879-1971; copyright by composer. Used by permission of Mrs. Alfred M. Smith.

101 **Threefold Amen**

A - men, A - men, A - men.

Tune: Oliver Houston, Jr., 1928 - ; copyright 1956 Herald Publishing House.

102 **May Thy Presence Be Ours**

Jude 24, 25
I John 4:7
RUSSIAN MELODY 10.9.10.9.9.

May thy pres - ence be ours in full meas - ure. Let thy

Spir - it a - bide with-out end. With thy love as our

hearts' great - est treas - ure, We will praise thee, our Lord

and our friend. We will praise thee, our Lord and our friend.

Tune: Russian Melody arr. by Alexander Efimov.

Sixfold Amen 99

Tune: Herbert Six, 1909 - ; copyright 1956 Herald Publishing House.

Sevenfold Amen 100

Tune: John Stainer, 1840-1901.

95 Dresden Amen

96 Threefold Amen

A -men, A - men.

A-men, A-men, A - men.

Tune: Richard Wagner, 1813-1883.

Tune: Danish.

97 Twofold Amen

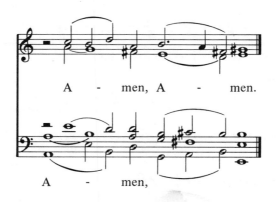

A - men, A - men.

A - men,

Tune: From Thomas Tallis, c. 1505-1585.

98 Fourfold Amen

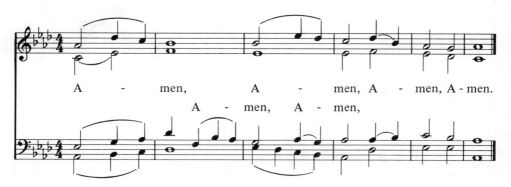

A - men, A - men, A - men, A-men.

A - men, A - men,

Tune: Franklyn S. Weddle, 1905 - ; copyright 1956 Herald Publishing House.

Lord, May Thy Will Be Done

92

SAVAGE 6.2.

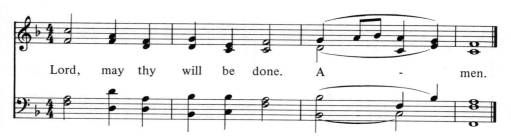

Lord, may thy will be done. A - men.

Tune: Ola Gunsolley Savage, 1895-1976; copyright 1956 Herald Publishing House.

Lord, Thank You for This Hour

93

SAVAGE 6.2.

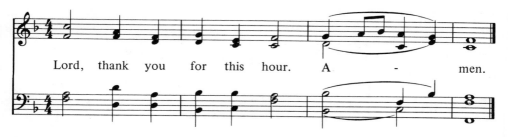

Lord, thank you for this hour. A - men.

Tune: Ola Gunsolley Savage, 1895-1976; copyright 1956 Herald Publishing House.

Hear Our Prayer, O Lord

94

Psalm 27:7
Enos 1:5

AFTER PRAYER 5.5.6.5.

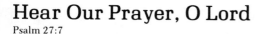

Hear our prayer, O Lord; Hear our prayer, O Lord;

In - cline thine ear to us, And grant us thy peace. A - men.

Tune: George Whelpton, 1847-1930.

90 O Help Us, Lord, to Keep This Day

Psalm 118:24
Exodus 20:8

SILVER HILL L.M.

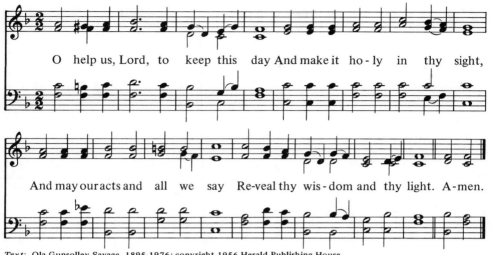

O help us, Lord, to keep this day And make it ho-ly in thy sight,

And may our acts and all we say Re-veal thy wis-dom and thy light. A-men.

Text: Ola Gunsolley Savage, 1895-1976; copyright 1956 Herald Publishing House.
Tune: Frederick C. Maker, 1844-1927.

91 Great God of All the Earth

I Peter 3:8
D. and C. 117:13

OLIVET 6.6.4.6.6.6.4.

Great God of all the earth, Lead us to know the worth

Of sym-pa-thy; May fel-low-ship in-crease, May all con-

ten-tion cease, O may we dwell in peace And u-ni-ty. A-men.

Text: Leonard B. McWhood, 1870-1939; copyright 1933 by the author. Used by permission of Stuart McWhood.
Tune: Lowell Mason, 1792-1872.

Almighty Father, Hear Our Prayer

88

Psalm 52:9
Psalm 97:10-12

INTERCESSION (Refrain) 8.9.

Al - might-y Fa - ther, hear our prayer And
bless all souls that wait be - fore thee. A - men.

Tune: Arr. from Felix Mendelssohn, 1809-1847 by William H. Callcott, 1807-1882.

From Thee All Skill and Science Flow

89

Romans 8:28
II Nephi 3:65

YARRINGTON C.M.

From Thee all skill and sci - ence flow, all pit - y, care, and love,
all calm and cour - age, faith and hope; O pour them from a - bove.

Text: Charles Kingsley, 1819-1875.
Tune: From *Responses for the Church Year* by John Yarrington, by permission of Chantry Music Press, Inc.

87

Sweet Hour of Prayer

D. and C. 85:36
Psalm 55:16, 17

SWEET HOUR OF PRAYER L.M.D.

1. Sweet hour of prayer, sweet hour of prayer, That calls me from a world of care,
2. Sweet hour of prayer, sweet hour of prayer, Thy wings shall my pe - ti - tion bear

And bids me at my Fa - ther's throne Make all my wants and wish - es known!
To Him, whose truth and faith - ful - ness En - gage the wait - ing soul to bless.

In sea - sons of dis - tress and grief My soul has oft - en found re - lief,
And since he bids me seek his face, Be - lieve his word, and trust his grace,

And oft es - caped the tempt - er's snare By thy re - turn, sweet hour of prayer.
I'll cast on him my ev - ery care And wait for thee, sweet hour of prayer.

Text: William W. Walford, 1772-1850.
Tune: William B. Bradbury, 1816-1868.

What a Friend We Have in Jesus

86

Matthew 21:19, 20 (21, 22)
Moroni 6:5

ERIE (Converse) 8.7.8.7.D.
Alternate hymn: 85

1. What a friend we have in Je - sus, All our sins and griefs to bear;
2. Have we tri - als and temp - ta - tions? Is there trou-ble an - y - where?
3. Are we weak and heav-y - la - den, Cum - bered with a load of care?

What a priv - i - lege to car - ry Ev - ery-thing to God in prayer!
We should nev - er be dis - cour - aged; Take it to the Lord in prayer!
Still the Sav - ior is our ref - uge; Take it to the Lord in prayer!

Oh, what peace we oft - en for - feit; Oh, what need-less pain we bear
Can we find a friend so faith - ful, Who will all our sor-rows share?
Do thy friends de-spise, for - sake thee? Take it to the Lord in prayer!

All be - cause we do not car - ry Ev - ery-thing to God in prayer.
Je - sus knows our ev - ery weak - ness; Take it to the Lord in prayer!
In his arms he'll take and shield thee; Thou wilt find a sol - ace there.

Text: Joseph Scriven, 1820-1886.
Tune: Charles C. Converse, 1832-1918.

85   What a Friend We Have in Jesus

Matthew 21:19, 20 (21, 22)
Moroni 6:5

BLAENWERN 8.7.8.7.D.
Alternate hymn: 86

1. What a friend we have in Je-sus, All our sins and griefs to bear;
2. Have we tri-als and temp-ta-tions? Is there trou-ble an-y-where?
3. Are we weak and heav-y-la-den, Cum-bered with a load of care?

What a priv-i-lege to car-ry Ev-ery-thing to God in prayer!
We should nev-er be dis-cour-aged; Take it to the Lord in prayer!
Still the Sav-ior is our ref-uge; Take it to the Lord in prayer!

Oh, what peace we of-ten for-feit; Oh, what need-less pain we bear
Can we find a friend so faith-ful, Who will all our sor-rows share?
Do thy friends de-spise, for-sake thee? Take it to the Lord in prayer!

All be-cause we do not car-ry Ev-ery-thing to God in prayer.
Je-sus knows our ev-ery weak-ness; Take it to the Lord in prayer!
In his arms he'll take and shield thee; Thou wilt find a sol-ace there.

Text: Joseph Scriven, 1820-1886.
Tune: W. P. Rowlands, 1860-1937; copyright G. A. Gabe, Swansea, S. Wales.

Come Ye Yourselves Apart

Mark 6:32-35 (31-34)
Isaiah 40:28, 29, 31

PENITENTIA 10.10.10.10.

1. Come ye your-selves a - part and rest a - while;
2. Come tell me all that ye have said and done,
3. Come ye and rest; the jour - ney is too great,
4. Then, fresh from con - verse with your Lord, re - turn

Wea - ry, I know it, of the press and throng,
Your vic - to - ries and fail - ures, hopes and fears.
And ye will faint be - side the way and sink;
And work till day - light soft - ens in - to even;

Wipe from your brow the sweat and dust of toil,
I know how hard - ly souls are wooed and won;
The bread of life is here for you to eat,
The brief hours are not lost in which ye learn

And in my qui - et strength a - gain be strong.
My choic - est wreaths are al - ways wet with tears.
And here for you the wine of love to drink.
More of your Mas - ter and his peace in heaven.

Text: Edward H. Bickersteth, 1825-1906.
Tune: Edward Dearle, 1806-1891.

83   'Tis the Blessed Hour of Prayer

Matthew 11:29, 30 (28-30)
Alma 3:57, 58

DOANE II 7.6.7.5.7.6.7.6.

1. 'Tis the bless-ed hour of prayer when our hearts low-ly bend,
2. 'Tis the bless-ed hour of prayer when the Sav-ior draws near
3. 'Tis the bless-ed hour of prayer when the tempt-ed and tried
4. At the bless-ed hour of prayer, trust-ing him, we be-lieve

And we gath-er to Je-sus, our Sav-ior and Friend;
With a ten-der com-pas-sion his chil-dren to hear;
To the Sav-ior who loves them their sor-rows con-fide;
That the bless-ings we're need-ing we'll sure-ly re-ceive;

If we come to him in faith his pro-tec-tion to share,
When he tells us we may cast at his feet ev-ery care,
With a sym-pa-thiz-ing heart he re-moves ev-ery care;
In the full-ness of this trust we shall lose ev-ery care;

What a balm for the wea-ry! Oh, how sweet to be there!

Text: Fanny J. Crosby, 1820-1915.
Tune: W. H. Doane, 1832-1915.

spo - ken and un - spo - ken; Hear us, our Fa - ther.
ways of cheer -ful du - ty, Lead us, Good Shep - herd.
save us from our e - vil, In - fi - nite Spir - it. A-men.

Text: Berwick Hymnal, 1886.
Tune: Friedrich F. Flemming, 1778-1813.

One Hour with Jesus 82

John 4:25, 26
Matthew 11:29, 30 (28-30)

ONE HOUR WITH JESUS 11.11.11.11.

1. One hour with Je-sus, the Shep-herd of the fold, I es -teem of more
2. The world and its fol-ly, I bid them all a-dieu; I find there no
3. One hour with Je-sus, a grand feast to my soul; His bur - dens are

val - ue than sil - ver or gold; The peace-ful com -mun-ion sent
com - fort that's last - ing and true; One hour with Je - sus, that
light and his yoke eas -ily borne; Though hard - ships and tri - als I

down from a - bove Makes clear to my vi - sion his mis - sion of love.
no - ble true friend, Brings peace to my soul that will nev - er - more end.
may have to meet, The Spir - it bears wit - ness the end will be sweet.

Text: William Lewis, 1856-1919.
Tune: John L. Morgan, 1869-1913.

80 Our Father, Who in Heaven Doth Dwell

Matthew 6:9-15 (9-13)
II Nephi 14:11, 12

COOLING C.M.

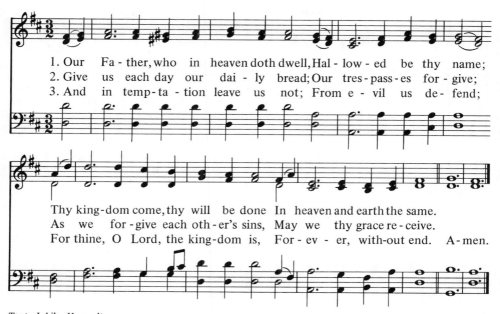

1. Our Fa - ther, who in heaven doth dwell, Hal - low - ed be thy name;
2. Give us each day our dai - ly bread; Our tres - pass - es for - give;
3. And in temp - ta - tion leave us not; From e - vil us de - fend;

Thy king-dom come, thy will be done In heaven and earth the same.
As we for - give each oth - er's sins, May we thy grace re - ceive.
For thine, O Lord, the king-dom is, For - ev - er, with-out end. A - men.

Text: Jubilee Harp; alt.
Tune: Alonzo J. Abbey, 1825-1887.

81 Father Almighty, Grant to Us Thy Blessing

James 1:5
I Nephi 7:56-59

FLEMMING 11.11.11.5.

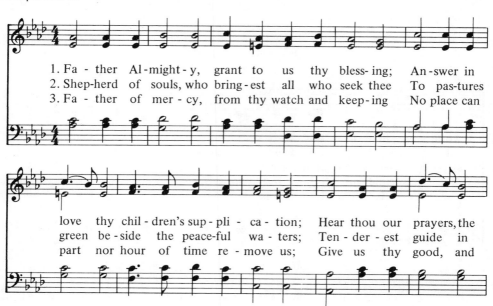

1. Fa - ther Al - might - y, grant to us thy bless - ing; An - swer in
2. Shep-herd of souls, who bring-est all who seek thee To pas-tures
3. Fa - ther of mer - cy, from thy watch and keep-ing No place can

love thy chil - dren's sup - pli - ca - tion; Hear thou our prayers, the
green be - side the peace-ful wa - ters; Ten - der - est guide in
part nor hour of time re - move us; Give us thy good, and

Come Ye Apart

D. and C. 85:36
Mark 6:32, 33 (31, 32)

CHISHOLM 11.10.11.10.

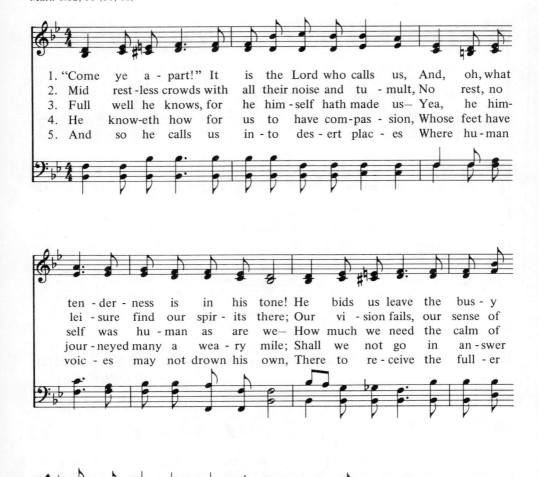

1. "Come ye a - part!" It is the Lord who calls us, And, oh, what
2. Mid rest - less crowds with all their noise and tu - mult, No rest, no
3. Full well he knows, for he him - self hath made us— Yea, he him-
4. He know - eth how for us to have com - pas - sion, Whose feet have
5. And so he calls us in - to des - ert plac - es Where hu - man

ten - der - ness is in his tone! He bids us leave the bus - y
lei - sure find our spir - its there; Our vi - sion fails, our sense of
self was hu - man as are we— How much we need the calm of
jour - neyed many a wea - ry mile; Shall we not go in an - swer
voic - es may not drown his own, There to re - ceive the full - er

world be - hind us And draw a - part a - while with him a - lone.
life's pro - por - tion, Un - less we seek the qui - et place of prayer.
sweet com - mun - ion New strength to gain for bat - tles yet to be.
to his bid - ding, "Come ye your - selves a - part and rest a - while"?
rev - e - la - tion He makes to those who wait with him a - lone.

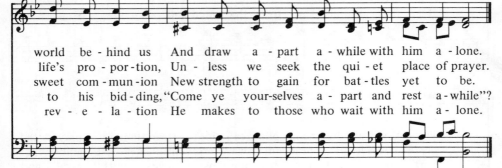

Text: Thomas O. Chisholm, 1866-1960.
Tune: George C. Stebbins, 1846-1945.

Contemplation and Renewal

Prayer 79-87

Prayer Responses 88-102

Repentance and Forgiveness 103-119

Faith and Trust 120-162

Renewal 163-185

78 We Thank You, Lord, for Strength of Arm

I John 3:16-18
Psalm 92:1, 2

O JESU 8.4.8.4.8.8.

1. We thank you, Lord, for strength of arm To
2. We thank you, Lord, for shel - tered home In
3. We thank you, Lord, for lav - ish love On

win our bread, And that, be - yond our need, is meat
cold and storm, And that, be - yond our need, is room
us be-stowed, E - nough to share with love - less folk

For friends un - fed: We thank you much for
For friends for - lorn: We thank you much for
To ease their load: Your love to us we

bread to live; We thank you more for bread to give.
place to rest, But more for shel - ter for our guest.
ill could spare, Yet dear - er is your love we share. A - men.

Text: Robert Davis, 1881-1950; alt.
Tune: Hirschberg Gesangbuch, 1741; Attr. to Johann Balthasar Reimann, 1702-1749; alt.

Refrain

All good gifts a-round us Are sent from heaven a-bove;

Then thank the Lord, O thank the Lord For all his love. A-men.

Text: Matthias Claudius, 1740-1815; tr. Jane M. Campbell, 1817-1878.
Tune: Johann A. P. Schulz, 1747-1800.

O Lord of Heaven and Earth and Sea   77

Acts 5:30, 31
D. and C. 17:5

ALMSGIVING 8.8.8.4.

1. O Lord of heaven and earth and sea, To thee all praise and glo-
2. Thou didst not spare thine on-ly Son, But gavest him for a world
3. For souls re-deemed, for sins for-given, For means of grace and hopes

ry be! How shall we show our love to thee, Who giv-est all?
un-done, And free-ly with that bless-ed One Thou giv-est all.
of heaven, What can to thee, O Lord, be given, Who giv-est all? A-men.

Text: Christopher Wordsworth, 1807-1885.
Tune: John B. Dykes, 1823-1876.

76

We Plow the Fields and Scatter

Psalm 147:12-19
D. and C. 59:4

WIR PFLÜGEN 7.6.7.6.D with refrain

1. We plow the fields and scat-ter The good seed on the land,
2. He on-ly is the Mak-er Of all things near and far;
3. We thank thee then, O Fa-ther, For all things bright and good:

But it is fed and wa-tered By God's al-might-y hand.
He paints the way-side flow-er, He lights the eve-ning star.
The seed-time and the har-vest, Our life, our health, our food.

He sends the snow in win-ter, The warmth to swell the grain,
The winds and waves o-bey him, By him the birds are fed;
No gifts have we to of-fer For all thy love im-parts,

The breez-es and the sun-shine, And soft, re-fresh-ing rain.
Much more to us, his chil-dren, He gives our dai-ly bread.
But that which thou de-sir-est, Our hum-ble, thank-ful hearts.

Thank You be-cause You love all peo-ple, Those both far and near.
Thank You, O Lord—You came a-mong us Bread and wine to share.
Thank You— You made me feel so glad And thank-ful as I do.

Text: Martin G. Schneider; English words by Walter Van Der Haas and Peter-Paul Van Lelyveld.
Tune: Martin G. Schneider.

For the Beauty of the Earth 75

II Nephi 9:135-137
Philippians 4:19, 20

DIX 7.7.7.7. with refrain

1. For the beau-ty of the earth, For the glo-ry of the skies,
2. For the joy of hu-man love, Broth-er, sis-ter, par-ent, child,
3. For thy church that ev-er-more Lift-eth ho-ly hands a-bove,
4. For thy-self, best Gift Di-vine To our race so free-ly given,

For the love which from our birth O-ver and a-round us lies:
Friends on earth and friends a-bove, For all gen-tle thoughts and mild:
Of-fering up on ev-ery shore Her pure sac-ri-fice of love:
For that great, great love of thine, Peace on earth, and joy in heaven:

Refrain

Lord of all, to thee we raise This our hymn of grate-ful praise. A-men.

Text: Folliot S. Pierpoint, 1835-1917.
Tune: Arr. from Conrad Kocher, 1786-1872, by W. H. Monk, 1823-1889.

74 Thank You for Giving Me the Morning

II Corinthians 9:15
Hebrews 13:15

THANK YOU 9.8.9.5.

After stanza 1, any number and order of stanzas is appropriate.

1. Thank You for giv-ing me the morn-ing; Thank You for ev-ery
2. Thank You— I have my oc-cu-pa-tion; Thank You for ev-ery
3. Thank You for man-y lit-tle sor-rows; Thank You for ev-ery

day that's new; Thank You that I can know my wor-ries
pleas-ure small; Thank You for mu-sic, light, and glad-ness;
kind-ly word; Thank You that ev-ery-where Your gui-dance

Can be cast on You.
Thank You for them all.
Reach-es ev-ery land.

4. Thank You— I see Your
5. Thank You, O Lord--You
6. Thank You, O Lord—Your

Word has mean-ing; Thank You— I know Your Spir-it here;
spoke un-to us; Thank You that for our words You care;
love is bound-less; Thank You that I am full of You;

For the Fruits of All Creation

73

D. and C. 59:4
Matthew 9:43, 44 (37, 38)

EAST ACKLAM 8.4.8.4.8.8.8.4.

Unison (or harmony)

1. For the fruits of all cre - a - tion, thanks be to God;
2. In the just re - ward of la - bor, God's will is done;
3. For the har - vests of the Spir - it, thanks be to God;

For these gifts to ev - ery na - tion, thanks be to God;
In the help we give our neigh - bor, God's will is done;
For the good we all in - her - it, thanks be to God;

For the plough - ing, sow - ing, reap - ing, Si - lent growth while we are sleep - ing,
In our world - wide task of car - ing For the hun - gry and de - spair - ing,
For the won - ders that as - tound us, For the truths that still con - found us,

Fu - ture needs in earth's safe - keep - ing, thanks be to God!
In the har - vests we are shar - ing, God's will is done.
Most of all, that love has found us, thanks be to God!

Text: F. Pratt Green, 1903 - ; alt.; used by permission of Oxford University Press.
Tune: Francis Jackson, 1917 - ; used by permission of the composer.

72 All Creatures of Our God and King

Psalm 148
I Nephi 5:127, 128, 130, 131

LASST UNS ERFREUEN 8.8.8.8.8.8. with refrain

1. All crea-tures of our God and King, Lift up your voic-es, with us sing,
2. Dear moth-er earth, who day by day Un - fold-est bless-ings on our way,
3. Let all things their Cre-a-tor bless And wor-ship him in hum-ble-ness.

Al - le - lu - ia! Al - le - lu - ia! Thou burn-ing sun with gold-en beam,
O praise him! Al - le - lu - ia! The flowers and fruits that in thee grow,
O praise him! Al - le - lu - ia! Praise, praise the Fa - ther, praise the Son,

Thou sil - ver moon with soft-er gleam,
Let them his glo - ry al - so show! O praise him, O praise him!
And praise the Spir - it, Three in One!

Al - le - lu - ia! Al - le - lu - ia! Al - le - lu - ia!

Text: St. Francis of Assisi, 1182-1226; tr. William H. Draper, 1855-1933. Copyright J. Curwen & Sons. Used by permission of G. Schirmer, Inc.
Tune: Melody from *Geistliche Kirchengesäng*, Cologne, 1623; arr. & harm. Ralph Vaughan Williams, 1872-1958. From *The English Hymnal* by permission of Oxford University Press.

All Hail the Power of Jesus' Name

71

Revelation 5:12, 13
I Chronicles 29:11-13

CORONATION 8.6.8.6.8.6.
Alternate hymn: 70

1. All hail the power of Jesus' name! Let angels prostrate fall!
2. Crown him, ye martyrs of our God, Who from his altar call;
3. Ye chosen seed of Israel's race, Ye remnant weak and small,
4. Let every kindred, every tribe On this terrestrial ball
5. Oh, that with yonder sacred throng We at his feet may fall!

Descant, stanzas 4 and 5

4. To him all majesty ascribe And crown him Lord of all;
5. We'll join the everlasting song And crown him Lord of all;

Bring forth the royal diadem And crown him Lord of all;
Extol the stem of Jesse's rod And crown him Lord of all;
Hail him who saves you by his grace And crown him Lord of all;
To him all majesty ascribe And crown him Lord of all;
We'll join the everlasting song And crown him Lord of all;

To him all majesty ascribe And crown him Lord of all.
We'll join the everlasting song And crown him Lord of all.

Bring forth the royal diadem And crown him Lord of all.
Extol the stem of Jesse's rod And crown him Lord of all.
Hail him who saves you by his grace And crown him Lord of all.
To him all majesty ascribe And crown him Lord of all.
We'll join the everlasting song And crown him Lord of all.

Text: Edward Perronet, 1726-1792.
Tune: Oliver Holden, 1765-1844; descant by Lawrence Curry, 1906 - ; descant copyright, 1941, by the Presbyterian Board of Christian Education; renewed, 1969; from *The Hymnal for Youth.* Used by permission of The Westminster Press.

70 All Hail the Power of Jesus' Name

Isaiah 11:1, 2
Philippians 2:9-11

DIADEM 8.6.6.8. with refrain
Alternate hymn: 71

1. All hail the power of Je - sus' name! Let an-gels pros-trate
2. Crown him, ye mar - tyrs of our God, Who from his al -tar
3. Ye cho - sen seed of Is - rael's race, Ye rem-nant weak and
4. Let ev - ery kin - dred, ev - ery tribe On this ter-res-trial
5. Oh, that with yon - der sa - cred throng We at his feet may

fall; Let an - gels pros - trate fall; Bring forth the roy - al
call; Who from his al - tar call; Ex - tol the stem of
small, Ye rem - nant weak and small, Hail him who saves you
ball, On this ter - res - trial ball, To him all maj -es-
fall! We at his feet may fall! We'll join the ev - er-

di - a - dem
Jes - se's rod
by his grace } And crown_____ him,
ty as - cribe
last - ing song } And crown him, crown him, crown him, crown him,

crown_____

crown him, crown him, crown him, And crown him Lord of all.

_____him.

Text: Edward Perronet, 1726-1792.
Tune: James Ellor, 1819-1899.

Tell of his ex-cel-lent great-ness; Praise him, praise him, ev-er in joy-ful song.

Text: Fanny J. Crosby, 1820-1915.
Tune: Chester G. Allen, 1838-1878; alt.

Creation Flows Unceasingly 69

D. and C. 17:4a, b
D. and C. 22:23

DUKE STREET L.M.
Alternate tune: BELSIZE SQUARE (418)

1. Cre - a - tion flows un - ceas - ing - ly Out of the
2. The morn - ing stars lift up their song; And all cre -
3. From God's own im - age be - ing comes, In hu - man
4. Spir - it and el - e - ment u - nite In the in -

time - less mind of God. Its pow - er moves up -
a - tion shouts for joy. The ebb and flow of
form fe - male and male; One in the glo - ry
tel - li - gence di - vine; God's work of im - mor -

on the deep And end - less reach - es of the void.
count - less forms Pro - claim di - vine ac - tiv - i - ty.
of the light, One in the like - ness of their Lord.
tal - i - ty With - out be - gin - ning, with - out end.

Text: Barbara McFarlane Higdon, 1930 - ; copyright 1980 Reorganized Church of Jesus Christ of Latter Day Saints.
Tune: John C. Hatton, ?-1793.

68 Praise Him, Praise Him

Psalm 103:1, 2
Titus 2:13, 14

PRAISE HIM, PRAISE HIM 12.10.12.10.11.10. with refrain

Unison (or harmony)

1. Praise him, praise him! Je-sus, our bless-ed Re-deem-er! Sing, O Earth, his
2. Praise him, praise him! Je-sus, our bless-ed Re-deem-er! For our sins he
3. Praise him, praise him! Je-sus, our bless-ed Re-deem-er! Heaven-ly por-tals

won-der-ful love pro-claim! Hail him, hail him! High-est arch-an-gels in glo-ry!
suf-fered and bled and died; He our Rock, our hope of e-ter-nal sal-va-tion.
loud with ho-san-nas ring! Je-sus, Sav-ior, reign-eth for-ev-er and ev-er;

Strength and hon-or give to his ho-ly name! Like a shep-herd, Je-sus will
Hail him, hail him! Je-sus, the Cru-ci-fied. Sound his prais-es, Jesus who
Crown him, crown him! Proph-et, and Priest, and King! Christ is com-ing, o-ver the

Refrain

guard his chil-dren; In his arms he car-ries them all day long.
bore our sor-rows, Love un-bound-ed, wonderful, deep, and strong. Praise him, praise him!
world vic-to-rious, Power and glo-ry un-to the Lord be-long.

Praise to the Lord, the Almighty

67

Psalm 103:1, 2
Mosiah 2:18-20

LOBE DEN HERREN 14.14.4.7.8.

1. Praise to the Lord, the Al-might-y, the King of cre-
a - tion! O my soul, praise him, for he is thy
health and sal - va - tion! All ye who hear, Now to his
tem - ple draw near, Praise him in glad ad - o - ra - tion!

2. Praise to the Lord, who doth pros - per thy work and defend thee; Sure - ly his good - ness and mer - cy here
dai - ly at - tend thee! Pon - der a - new What the Al-
might - y can do, If with his love he be - friend thee!

3. Praise to the Lord! O let all that is in me a-
dore him! All that hath life and breath, come now with
prais - es be - fore him! Let the A - men Sound from his
peo - ple a - gain: Glad - ly for - ev - er a - dore him.

Text: Joachim Neander, 1650-1680; trans. by Catherine Winkworth, 1827-1878.
Tune: Stralsund Gesangbuch, 1665; harm. by F. S. Weddle, 1905 - , alt. Harm. copyright 1956 by Herald Publishing House.

66 Praise the Lord, Ye Heavens, Adore Him

Psalm 19:1, 14
Isaiah 44:23

HYFRYDOL 8.7.8.7.D.

1. Praise the Lord, ye heavens, a - dore him; Praise him, an - gels, in the height;
2. Praise the Lord, for he is glo - rious; Nev - er shall his prom - ise fail:

Sun and moon, re - joice be - fore him; Praise him, all ye stars and light.
God hath made his saints vic - to - rious; Sin and death shall not pre - vail.

Praise the Lord, for he hath spo - ken; Worlds his might - y voice o - beyed;
Praise the God of our sal - va - tion; Hosts on high, his power pro - claim;

Laws which nev - er shall be bro - ken For their guid - ance hath he made.
Heaven and earth and all cre - a - tion Laud and mag - ni - fy his name.

Text: From Psalm 148. Foundling Hospital Collection, 1796.
Tune: Rowland Hugh Prichard, 1811-1887.

God of the Earth, the Sky, the Sea

65

Jacob 3:11-14
Psalm 139:7-10, 14

OLD 113th 8.8.8.D.

1. God of the earth, the sky, the sea! Mak - er of all
2. Thy love is in the sun - shine's glow; Thy life is in
3. We feel thy calm at eve - ning's hour, Thy gran - deur in

a - bove, be - low! Cre - a - tion lives and moves in thee;
the quick-ening air; When light - nings flash and storm winds blow,
the march of night; And when thy morn - ing breaks in power,

Thy pres - ent life through all doth flow.
There is thy power; thy law is there. We give thee thanks,
We hear thy word, "Let there be light."

Thy name we sing, Al - might - y Fa - ther, heaven-ly King. A - men.

Text: Samuel Longfellow, 1819-1892.
Tune: Strassburger Kirchenamt, 1525; probably by Matthäus Greiter, c. 1500-1552; harm. V. Earle Copes, 1921 - .
Harm. copyright 1964 Abingdon Press. Used by permission.

64 O Jesus, the Giver of All We Enjoy

Ecclesiastes 5:19, 20
D. and C. 17:4a, b

O JESUS, THE GIVER 11.11.11.11.

1. O Jesus, the giv-er of all we en-joy,
2. With joy we re-mem-ber the dawn of that day
3. We now are en-list-ed in Je-sus' blest cause,

Our lives to thy hon-or we wish to em-ploy;
When, led by the Spir-it the truth to o-bey,
Di-vine-ly as-sist-ed to con-quer his foes;

With prais-es un-ceas-ing we'll sing of thy name,
The light dawned up-on us and filled us with love,
His grace will sup-port us, his good-ness we'll prove

Thy good-ness ne'er ceas-ing, thy love we'll pro-claim.
The Spir-it's sure wit-ness sent down from a-bove.
In Zi-on's re-demp-tion through la-bors of love.

Text: W. W. Phelps, 1792-1872; stanza 3 adapted by Roy Cheville, 1897- .
Tune: Ralph Bradshaw. Copyright 1927 by the Corporation of the President of the Church of Jesus Christ of Latter
Day Saints. Adapted by Franklyn S. Weddle, 1905 - . Used by permission.

Praise Ye the Lord

63

Psalm 148
II Nephi 1:95

RIMINGTON L.M.
Alternate hymn: 62

1. Praise ye the Lord! 'Tis good to raise Your hearts and
2. He formed the stars, those heaven - ly flames; He counts their
3. Sing to the Lord! Ex - tol him high Who spreads his
4. He makes the grass the hills a - dorn, And clothes the
5. His saints are love - ly in his sight; He views his

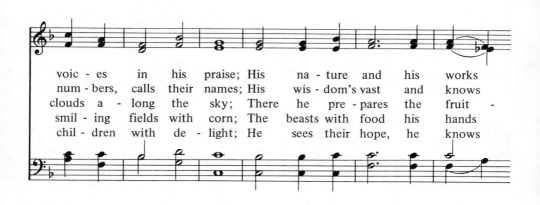

voic - es in his praise; His na - ture and his works
num - bers, calls their names; His wis - dom's vast and knows
clouds a - long the sky; There he pre - pares the fruit -
smil - ing fields with corn; The beasts with food his hands
chil - dren with de - light; He sees their hope, he knows

u - nite To make this du - ty your de - light.
no bound, A deep where all our thoughts are drowned.
ful rain, Nor lets the drops de - scend in vain.
sup - ply, And the young ra - vens, when they cry.
their fear, And looks and loves his im - age here.

Text: Isaac Watts, 1674-1748.
Tune: Francis Duckworth, 1862-1941; copyright; used by permission of Mrs. B. A. Duckworth.

62 Praise Ye the Lord

Psalm 148
II Nephi 1:95

PRAISE L.M.
Alternate hymn: 63

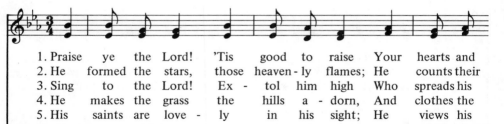

1. Praise ye the Lord! 'Tis good to raise Your hearts and
2. He formed the stars, those heaven-ly flames; He counts their
3. Sing to the Lord! Ex-tol him high Who spreads his
4. He makes the grass the hills a-dorn, And clothes the
5. His saints are love-ly in his sight; He views his

voic-es in his praise; His na-ture and his
num-bers, calls their names; His wis-dom's vast and
clouds a-long the sky; There he pre-pares the
smil-ing fields with corn; The beasts with food his
chil-dren with de-light; He sees their hope, he

works u-nite To make this du-ty your de-light.
knows no bound, A deep where all our thoughts are drowned.
fruit-ful rain, Nor lets the drops de-scend in vain.
hands sup-ply, And the young ra-vens, when they cry.
knows their fear, And looks and loves his im-age here.

Text: Isaac Watts, 1674-1748.
Tune: Anonymous.

My Soul, Praise the Lord

61

D. and C. 17:4a
Mosiah 2:13, 14

PADERBORN 10.10.11.11.

1. My soul, praise the Lord! O God, thou art great;
2. The earth where we dwell That jour - neys through space
3. O God, thou art great! My plea - sure shall be

The earth and all things Thy - self didst cre - ate.
Turns coun - tries a - round To see the sun's face;
To muse on the good And great - ness I see.

Thou laidst the foun - da - tion Of seas and of lands,
And high o'er the moun-tains The clouds gath - er rain
My full a - dor - a - tion I glad - ly shall give.

And stretched out the heav - ens As works of thy hand.
To drop o'er the val - leys In bless - ings a - gain.
My soul, praise the Lord now And long as I live.

Text: William Kethe, d. 1594. Alt. by Roy A. Cheville, 1897 - .
Tune: Paderborn 'Gesangbuch' 1765.

60 Now Thank We All Our God

Psalm 107:1-6
D. and C. 59:2d-h

NUN DANKET ALLE GOTT 6.7.6.7.6.6.6.6.

1. Now thank we all our God With heart and hands and voic - es,
2. Oh, may this boun -teous God Through all our life be near us,
3. All praise and thanks to God, The Fa - ther, now be giv - en,

Who won-drous things hath done, In whom his world re - joic - es;
With ev - er joy - ful hearts And bless- ed peace to cheer us;
The Son, and him who reigns With them in high - est heav - en,

Who from our moth - ers' arms Hath blessed us on our way
And keep us in his grace, And guide us when per - plexed,
The one e - ter - nal God, Whom earth and heaven a - dore;

With count - less gifts of love, And still is ours to - day.
And free us from all ills In this world and the next.
For thus it was, is now, And shall be ev - er - more.

Text: Martin Rinkart, 1586-1649; trans. by Catherine Winkworth, 1827-1878.
Tune: From *Praxis Pietatis Melica*, c. 1647, by Johann Crüger, 1598-1662.

this is our song, Prais-ing our Sav - ior all the day long.

Text: Stanzas by Richard P. Howard, 1929 - , and Barbara Howard, 1930 - ; copyright 1980 Reorganized Church of Jesus Christ of Latter Day Saints. Refrain by Fanny J. Crosby, 1820-1915.
Tune: Phoebe P. Knapp, 1839-1908.

Great God, Attend While Zion Sings 59

Alma 14:88
Psalm 84:10-12

UXBRIDGE L.M.

1. Great God, at - tend while Zi - on sings The joy that
2. God is our sun; he makes our day. God is our
3. All need - ful grace will God be - stow, And crown that
4. O God, our King, whose sov - ereign sway The glo - rious

from thy pres - ence springs; To spend one day with thee
shield; he guards our way From all the as-saults of hell
grace with glo - ry, too; He gives us all things, and
host of heaven o - bey, Whose gra - cious gift has made

on earth Ex - ceeds a thou-sand days of mirth.
and sin, From foes with - out and fears with - in.
with - holds No re - al good from up - right souls.
us free, Blest are the souls who trust in thee. A - men.

Text: Isaac Watts, 1674-1748; alt.
Tune: Lowell Mason, 1792-1872.

58

Now in This Moment

Romans 5:1-5
D. and C. 85:16a-e

ASSURANCE 9.10.9.9 with refrain

Joyously

1. Now in this mo - ment, now in this day, God is cre -
2. Past, pre - sent, fu - ture, joy, sor - row, hope, We write the

at - ing and lead - ing the way; Life is be - hind us,
sto - ry, and life is its scope. God's love as - sures us

life is be - fore; We write the sto - ry not heard be - fore.
through the un - known, God's grace sus - tains us, we're not a - lone.

Refrain

This is our sto - ry, this is our song, Prais - ing our

Sav - ior all the day long. This is our sto - ry,

Holy, Holy, Holy Is the Lord

57

Isaiah 12:2-6
Psalm 97:1, 6, 9, 11, 12

SABAOTH 9.10.9.D. with refrain

1. Ho - ly, ho - ly, ho - ly is the Lord! Sing, O ye peo - ple,
2. Praise him, praise him! Shout a - loud for joy! Chil - dren of Zi - on,

glad - ly a - dore him; Let the moun - tains trem - ble at his word;
her - ald the sto - ry; Sin and death his king - dom shall de - stroy;

Let the hills be joy - ful be - fore him. Might - y in wis - dom,
All the earth shall sing of his glo - ry. Praise him, ye an - gels,

bound - less in mer - cy, Great is Je - ho - vah, king o - ver all.
ye who be - hold him Robed in his splen - dor, match - less, di - vine.

Refrain   *a tempo*

Ho - ly, ho - ly, ho - ly is the Lord! Let the hills be joy - ful be - fore him.

Text: Fanny J. Crosby, 1820-1915, alt.
Tune: William B. Bradbury, 1816-1868.

56 Holy, Holy, Holy! Lord God Almighty

Isaiah 6:1-5
Omni 1:46, 47

NICAEA 11.12.12.10.

1. Ho-ly, ho-ly, ho-ly! Lord God Al-might-y!
Ear-ly in the morn-ing our song shall rise to thee;
Ho-ly, ho-ly, ho-ly, mer-ci-ful and might-y!
God in Three Per-sons, bless-ed Trin-i-ty!

2. Ho-ly, ho-ly, ho-ly! All the saints a-dore thee,
Cast-ing down their gold-en crowns a-round the glass-y sea;
Cher-u-bim and ser-a-phim fall-ing down be-fore thee,
Which wert and art and ev-er-more shalt be.

3. Ho-ly, ho-ly, ho-ly! Though dark-ness hide thee,
Though the eye made blind by sin thy glo-ry may not see,
On-ly thou art ho-ly, there is none be-side thee,
Per-fect in power, in love, and pu-ri-ty.

4. Ho-ly, ho-ly, ho-ly! Lord God Al-might-y!
All thy works shall praise thy name in earth and sky and sea;
Ho-ly, ho-ly, ho-ly, mer-ci-ful and might-y!
God in Three Per-sons, bless-ed Trin-i-ty! A-men.

Text: Reginald Heber, 1783-1826, alt.
Tune: John B. Dykes, 1823-1876.

to - ri - ous, Come and reign o - ver us, Al - pha of Days!
ev - ery place Till all cre - a - tion's face Hon - ors its Lord.
ev - ery heart, And ne'er from us de - part, Spir - it of power.

Text: Ascribed to Charles Wesley, 1707-1788, Sts. 1, 3; Geoffrey F. Spencer, 1927 - , St. 2, copyright 1980 Reorganized Church of Jesus Christ of Latter Day Saints.
Tune: Felice de Giardini, 1716-1796.

Sing to the Lord a Joyful Song 55

Revelation 19:1, 5, 6
Romans 11:33-36

AGINCOURT L.M.

Unison

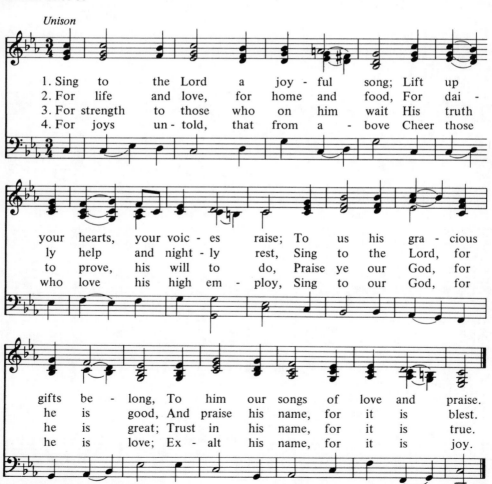

1. Sing to the Lord a joy - ful song; Lift up
2. For life and love, for home and food, For dai -
3. For strength to those who on him wait His truth
4. For joys un - told, that from a - bove Cheer those

your hearts, your voic - es raise; To us his gra - cious
ly help and night - ly rest, Sing to the Lord, for
to prove, his will to do, Praise ye our God, for
who love his high em - ploy, Sing to our God, for

gifts be - long, To him our songs of love and praise.
he is good, And praise his name, for it is blest.
he is great; Trust in his name, for it is true.
he is love; Ex - alt his name, for it is joy.

Text: John S. B. Monsell, 1811-1875.
Tune: "The Agincourt Song," 15th Century.

53 Hallelujah! Hallelujah!

Psalm 150
II Chronicles 5:13

HYMN OF PRAISE 8.7.8.7.

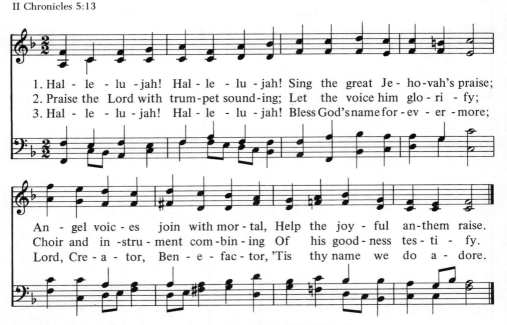

1. Hal - le - lu - jah! Hal - le - lu - jah! Sing the great Je - ho-vah's praise;
2. Praise the Lord with trum-pet sound-ing; Let the voice him glo - ri - fy;
3. Hal - le - lu - jah! Hal - le - lu - jah! Bless God's name for - ev - er - more;

An - gel voic - es join with mor - tal, Help the joy - ful an-them raise.
Choir and in -stru - ment com-bin - ing Of his good - ness tes - ti - fy.
Lord, Cre - a - tor, Ben - e - fac - tor, 'Tis thy name we do a - dore.

Text and Tune: William Graves, 1915 - ; alt.; copyright 1956 Herald Publishing House.

54 Come, Thou Almighty King

I Timothy 1:15-17
John 4:25, 26 (23, 24)

ITALIAN HYMN 6.6.4.6.6.6.4.

1. Come, thou Al - might - y King, Help us thy name to sing,
2. Je - sus, our Lord, come near; In ris - en glo - ry ap - pear.
3. Come, Ho - ly Com - fort - er, Thy sa - cred wit - ness bear

Help us to praise! Fa - ther all glo - ri - ous, O'er all vic -
With sweet ac - cord May thy re - deem - ing grace Be known in
In this glad hour; Thou who Al - might - y art, Now rule in

This Is My Father's World

Isaiah 41:10
D. and C. 98:5j

52

TERRA BEATA S.M.D.

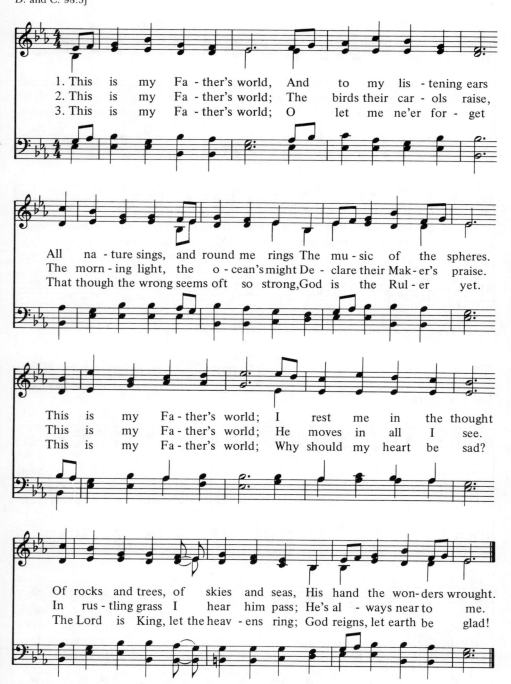

1. This is my Fa-ther's world, And to my lis-tening ears
2. This is my Fa-ther's world; The birds their car-ols raise,
3. This is my Fa-ther's world; O let me ne'er for-get

All na-ture sings, and round me rings The mu-sic of the spheres.
The morn-ing light, the o-cean's might De-clare their Mak-er's praise.
That though the wrong seems oft so strong, God is the Rul-er yet.

This is my Fa-ther's world; I rest me in the thought
This is my Fa-ther's world; He moves in all I see.
This is my Fa-ther's world; Why should my heart be sad?

Of rocks and trees, of skies and seas, His hand the won-ders wrought.
In rus-tling grass I hear him pass; He's al-ways near to me.
The Lord is King, let the heav-ens ring; God reigns, let earth be glad!

Text: Maltbie D. Babcock, 1858-1901.
Tune: Traditional English Melody, adapted by Franklin L. Sheppard, 1852-1930.

51
Heaven and Earth and Sea and Air

Psalm 104:31-33
I Nephi 5:126, 130, 131

MAIDSTONE 7.7.7.7.D.

1. Heaven and earth and sea and air God's e - ter - nal praise de - clare;
2. See how earth, with beau - ty decked, Tells a heaven-ly Arch - i - tect;
3. See the bil - lows tum-bling o'er, Chaf-ing with in - ces -sant roar;

Up, my soul, a - wake and raise Grate - ful hymns and songs of praise.
Woods and fields, with low - ing kine, Show their Mak - er all di - vine.
Hear them as they sink and swell Loud their Mak - er's prais-es tell.

See the sun with glo - rious ray Pierce the clouds at open - ing day;
See the birds, how, pair by pair, Swift they cleave the yield - ing air;
Through the world, great God, I trace Won - ders of thy power and grace.

Moon and stars in splen-dor bright Praise their God through si - lent night.
Thun - der, light - ning, storm, and wind God doth at his will un - bind.
Write more deep - ly on my heart What I am, and what thou art.

Text: From Psalm 19 by Joachim Neander, 1650-1680; tr. by Frances Elizabeth Cox, 1812-1897.
Tune: Walter B. Gilbert, 1829-1910.

I, too, will praise him with a new song!

Text: Herbert Brokering, 1926 - .
Tune: David N. Johnson, 1922 - .
Text and tune from *Twelve Folksongs and Spirituals,* copyright 1968 Augsburg Publishing House; used with permission.

From All That Dwell Below the Skies 50

Psalm 117
II Nephi 3:50

DUKE STREET L.M.

1. From all that dwell be - low the skies, Let the Cre -
2. E - ter - nal are thy mer - cies, Lord; E - ter - nal
3. Your loft - y themes, ye mor - tals, bring; Your songs of
4. In ev - ery land be - gin the song; To ev - ery

a - tor's praise a - rise; Let the Re - deem - er's
truth at - tends thy word: Thy praise shall sound from
praise di - vine - ly sing; The great sal - va - tion
land the strains be - long; In cheer - ful sound all

name be sung Through ev - ery land, by ev - ery tongue.
shore to shore, Till suns shall rise and set no more.
loud pro - claim, And shout for joy the Sav - ior's name.
voic - es raise, And fill the world with loud - est praise.

Text: Isaac Watts, 1674-1748, Sts. 1, 2; Sts. 3, 4 Anonymous.
Tune: John Hatton, (?)-1793.

49

I Chronicles 16:23-29
Isaiah 61:10, 11

Earth and All Stars

EARTH AND ALL STARS 9.7.9.7. with refrain

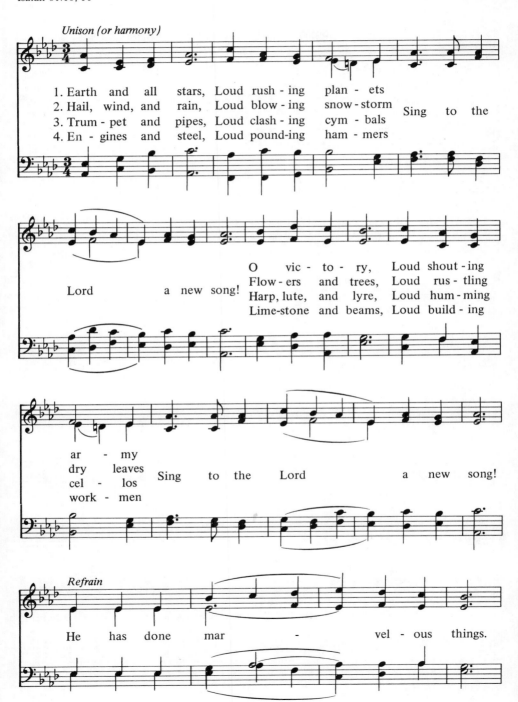

Unison (or harmony)

1. Earth and all stars, Loud rush - ing plan - ets
2. Hail, wind, and rain, Loud blow - ing snow - storm
3. Trum - pet and pipes, Loud clash - ing cym - bals
4. En - gines and steel, Loud pound-ing ham - mers

Sing to the

Lord a new song!

O vic - to - ry, Loud shout - ing
Flow - ers and trees, Loud rus - tling
Harp, lute, and lyre, Loud hum - ming
Lime-stone and beams, Loud build - ing

ar - my
dry leaves Sing to the Lord a new song!
cel - los
work - men

Refrain

He has done mar - vel - ous things.

Great and Marvelous Are Thy Works

48

Psalm 97:1, 6, 12
Romans 16:25-27

SING OF HIS MIGHTY LOVE L.M. with refrain

Unison (or harmony)

1. Great and mar-vel-ous are thy works, O Lord of hosts, al-might-y One!
2. Thou hast fash-ioned with thine own hand The earth be-low, the heavens a-bove;
3. O thou in-fi-nite, liv-ing God, Up-on us now thy Spir-it pour;

Earth and fir-ma-ment speak thy praise, Thy name is writ-ten in the sun.
Oh, how won-der-ful is thy power, And yet how ten-der is thy love.
We would wor-ship thee, laud and praise Thy ho-ly name for-ev-er - more.

Refrain

Sing of his might-y love, for it is won-der-ful;

Let his praise through all the earth re-sound; Hon-or and maj-es-ty

now and for-ev-er be Un-to God whose love and mer-cy have no bound.

Text: Charlotte G. Homer.
Tune: Charles H. Gabriel, 1856-1932.

47

Praise to the Living God

Moroni 8:19
I Corinthians 8:6

LEONI 12.12.12.12.

1. Praise to the liv - ing God! All prais - ed be thy name
2. Thy Spir - it flow - eth free, high surg - ing where it will,
3. E - ter - nal life hast thou im - plant - ed in the soul;

Who e'er hast been and e'er shalt be, and still the same.
In proph-et's word re - vealed of old and liv - ing still.
Thy love shall be our strength and stay while a - ges roll.

The one e - ter - nal God ere aught that now ap - pears:
Es - tab - lished is thy law, and change-less it shall stand,
Praise to the liv - ing God, all prais - ed be thy name

The first, the last, be - yond all thought through time - less years!
Deep writ up - on the hu - man heart, on sea or land.
Who e'er hast been and e'er shalt be, and still the same.

Text: Based on the Yigdal of Daniel Ben Judah, 14th century; tr. Max Landsberg, 1845-1928, and Newton Mann, 1836-1926; alt.; used with permission of the Ecumenical Women's Center, Chicago, IL, *Because We Are One People.*
Tune: Hebrew Melody; arr. Meyer Lyon, 1751-1797.

Sing to the Lord of Harvest

James 1:17
Psalm 103:1-4

WIE LIEBLICH IST DER MAIEN 7.6.7.6.D.

1. Sing to the Lord of har - vest, Sing songs of love and praise;
2. God makes the clouds bring fresh - ness, The des - erts bloom and spring,
3. Bring to this sa - cred al - tar The gifts his good - ness gave,

With joy - ful hearts and voic - es Our al - le - lu - ias raise.
The hills leap up in glad - ness, The val - leys laugh and sing.
The gold - en sheaves of har - vest, The souls Christ died to save.

By him the roll - ing sea - sons In fruit - ful or - der move;
God fills them with his full - ness, All things with large in - crease;
Our hearts lay down be - fore him When at his feet we fall,

Sing to the Lord of har - vest A joy - ous song of love.
He crowns the year with good - ness, With plen - ty and with peace.
And with our lives a - dore him Who gave his life for all.

Text: John S. B. Monsell, 1811-1875, alt.
Tune: Johann Steurlein, 1546-1613; arr. Rosalee Elser, 1925 - ; copyright 1980 Rosalee Elser; used by permission.

45

D. and C. 6:10
Psalm 104:1-5

Day Is Dying in the West

CHAUTAUQUA 7.7.7.7.4. with refrain

1. Day is dy - ing in the west; Heaven is touch - ing
2. Lord of life, be - neath the dome Of the u - ni -
3. While the deepen - ing sha - dows fall, Heart of Love, en -

earth with rest; Wait and wor - ship while the night
verse, thy home, Gath - er us who seek thy face
fold - ing all, Through the glo - ry and the grace

Sets the eve - ning lamps a - light Through all the sky.
To the fold of thine em - brace, For thou art nigh.
Of the stars that veil thy face, Our hearts as - cend.

Refrain

Ho - ly, ho - ly, ho - ly, Lord God of hosts! Heaven and earth are

full of thee! Heaven and earth are prais - ing thee, O Lord most high!

Text: Mary A. Lathbury, 1841-1913.
Tune: William F. Sherwin, 1826-1888.

Come, Rejoice Before Your Maker

44

II Nephi 9:133-137
Psalm 16:8, 9, 11

BRYN CALFARIA 8.7.8.7.4.4.4.7.7.
Alternate tune: HYMN OF PRAISE* (53)

1. Come, re-joice be-fore your Mak-er, All you peo-ples of the earth;
2. Know for cer-tain that Je-ho-vah Is the true and on-ly God;
3. Come with grate-ful hearts be-fore Him; En-ter now His courts with praise;
4. For the Lord our God is gra-cious—Ev-er-last-ing in His love.

Serve the Lord your God with glad-ness; Come be-fore Him with a song!
We are His, for He has made us— We are sheep with-in His fold.
Show your thank-ful-ness to-ward Him; Give due hon-or to His name.
And to ev-ery gen-er-a-tion His great faith-ful-ness en-dures.

Al-le-lu-ia, Al-le-lu-ia, Al-le-lu-ia!
Come be-
We are
Give due
His great

fore Him with a song, Come be-fore Him with a song!
sheep with-in His fold, We are sheep with-in His fold.
hon-or to His name, Give due hon-or to His name.
faith-ful-ness en-dures, His great faith-ful-ness en-dures.

Text: Michael A. Baughen; copyright 1973 Church Pastoral Aid Society, England; GIA Publ., Inc., U. S. Agent.
Used by permission.
Tune: William Owen, 1814-1893.

* Sing first two lines only.

42 — O Sing the Mighty Power of God

Genesis 1:3, 12, 19, 20, 29 (9, 16-18, 26)
Mormon 4:77, 78

BRIDGMAN C.M.

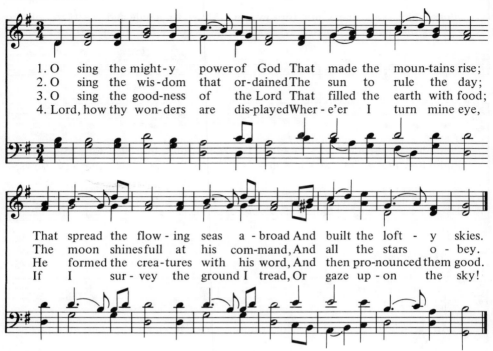

1. O sing the might-y power of God That made the moun-tains rise;
2. O sing the wis-dom that or-dained The sun to rule the day;
3. O sing the good-ness of the Lord That filled the earth with food;
4. Lord, how thy won-ders are dis-played Wher-e'er I turn mine eye,

That spread the flow-ing seas a-broad And built the loft-y skies.
The moon shines full at his com-mand, And all the stars o-bey.
He formed the crea-tures with his word, And then pro-nounced them good.
If I sur-vey the ground I tread, Or gaze up-on the sky!

Text: Isaac Watts, 1674-1748.
Tune: Ludwig van Beethoven, 1770-1827; arr. George Kingsley, 1811-1884.

43 — Praise God, from Whom All Blessings Flow

Psalm 69:34
I Chronicles 16:31

OLD HUNDREDTH L.M.

Praise God, from whom all bless-ings flow; Praise him, all crea-tures here be-low;

Praise him a-bove, ye heav'n-ly host; Praise Fa-ther, Son, and Ho-ly Ghost. A-men.

Text: Thomas Ken, 1637-1711.
Tune: Genevan Psalter, 1551, attr. to Louis Bourgeois, c. 1510-1561.

Praise him, still the same for - ev - er, Slow to chide and swift to bless;
In his hands he gent - ly bears us, Res - cues us from all our foes:

Praise him, praise him, al - le - lu - ia, Glo - rious in his faith - ful - ness.
Praise him, praise him, al - le - lu - ia, Wide -ly as his mer - cy flows.

Third setting

4. An - gels, help us to a - dore him: Ye be - hold him face to face;

Sun and moon bow down be - fore him: Dwell-ers all in time and space,

Praise him, praise him, al - le - lu - ia, Praise with us the God of grace.

Text: Henry Francis Lyte, 1793-1847.
Tune: John Goss, 1800-1880.

41

Titus 3:3-7
Jacob 3:9-16

Praise, My Soul, the King of Heaven

LAUDA ANIMA 8.7.8.7.8.7.

This hymn has three settings. The second (four-part) setting may be used for all stanzas.

First setting: Unison

1. Praise, my soul, the King of heav-en; To his feet thy trib-ute bring;

Ran-somed, healed, re-stored, for-giv-en, Who like thee his praise should sing?

Praise him, praise him, al-le-lu-ia, Praise the ev-er-last-ing King.

Second setting: Harmony

2. Praise him for his grace and fa-vor To our fa-thers in dis-tress;
3. Ten-der-ly he shields and spares us; Well our fee-ble frame he knows;

Sing Praise to God, Who Reigns Supreme

40

Alma 21:2
Psalm 66:1,2

MIT FREUDEN ZART 8.7.8.7.8.8.7.

This hymn is most effectively sung at a steady tempo and in a stately manner.

1. Sing praise to God, who reigns su-preme, the au-thor of cre - a - tion,
2. All you who name Christ's ho-ly name, give God all praise and glo - ry;

The God of power, the God of love, the God of our sal - va - tion;
All you who own his power pro-claim a - loud the won - drous sto - ry!

With - in the king - dom of his might All things are just and
Cast each false i - dol from its throne; The Lord is God, the

good and right: To God all praise and glo - ry.
Lord a - lone: To God all praise and glo - ry. A - men.

Text: Johann J. Schutz, 1640-1690; trans. F. E. Cox, 1812-1897; rev. Barbara McFarlane Higdon, 1930 -; Copyright 1980 Reorganized Church of Jesus Christ of Latter Day Saints.
Tune: Bohemian Brethren's *Kirchengesänge,* 1566.

39
God Himself Is with Us

Zechariah 2:13
Habakkuk 2:20

WUNDERBARER KÖNIG (Arnsberg) 6.6.8.6.6.8.6.6.6.

God him-self is with us: Let us now a-dore him,

And with awe ap-pear be-fore him. God is in his

tem - ple: All with-in keep si - lence, And be-fore him

bow with rev - erence. Him a-lone, God we own; To our

Lord and Sav - ior Prais-es sing for-ev - er.

Text: Gerhard Tersteegen, 1697-1769; tr. composite.
Tune: Joachim Neander, 1650-1680.

Come, Ye Thankful People, Come

38

D. and C. 46:9
James 1:17

ST. GEORGE'S WINDSOR 7.7.7.7.D.
Alternate hymn: 37

1. Come, ye thank-ful peo-ple, come, Raise the song of har-vest home.
2. All the bless-ings of the field, All the stores the gar-dens yield,
3. These to thee, our God, we owe, Source whence all our bless-ings flow,

All is safe-ly gath-ered in Ere the win-ter storms be-gin;
All the fruits in full sup-ply, Rip-ened 'neath the sum-mer sky,
And for these our souls shall raise Grate-ful vows and sol-emn praise.

God, our Ma-ker, doth pro-vide For our wants to be sup-plied;
All that spring with boun-teous hand Scat-ters o'er the smil-ing land,
Come, then, thank-ful peo-ple, come, Raise the song of har-vest home;

Come to God's own tem-ple, come, Raise the song of har-vest home.
All that lib-eral au-tumn pours From her rich o'er-flow-ing stores—
Come to God's own tem-ple, come, Raise the song of har-vest home.

Text: Henry Alford, 1810-1871; alt. by Hugh Hartshorne, 1915.
Tune: George J. Elvey, 1816-1893.

37

Come, Ye Thankful People, Come

D. and C. 46:9
James 1:17

BENEVENTO 7.7.7.7.D.
Alternate hymn:38

1. Come, ye thank-ful peo - ple, come, Raise the song of har -vest home.
2. All the bless-ings of the field, All the stores the gar - dens yield,
3. These to thee, our God, we owe, Source whence all our bless-ings flow,

All is safe-ly gath-ered in Ere the win - ter storms be - gin;
All the fruits in full sup-ply, Rip-ened 'neath the sum-mer sky,
And for these our souls shall raise Grate-ful vows and sol - emn praise.

God, our Mak - er, doth pro-vide For our wants to be sup-plied;
All that spring with boun - teous hand Scat -ters o'er the smil - ing land,
Come, then, thank-ful peo - ple, come, Raise the song of har - vest home;

Come to God's own tem - ple, come, Raise the song of har - vest home.
All that lib - eral au-tumn pours From her rich o'er- flow- ing stores—
Come to God's own tem - ple, come, Raise the song of har - vest home.

Text: Henry Alford, 1810-1871; alt. by Hugh Hartshorne, 1915.
Tune: Samuel Webbe, 1740-1816.

Rejoice, Ye Saints of Latter Days

36

Isaiah 60:1-3
D. and C. 85:2

SAINTLY PRAISE C.M.D.

1. Re - joice, ye Saints of lat - ter days, Lift up your heads and sing!
2. The Ho - ly Spir - it is sent down As in the days of old

With one ac - cord u - nite to praise Your ev - er - last - ing King.
To bring to mind things that are past And things to come un - fold.

No more in dark - ness need you walk, Nor tread in er - ror's night,
Oh, may it rest up - on us now While we're as - sem - bled here,

Refrain after second stanza only.
Oh, may it ev - er guide our feet In ways of right-eous - ness

For the Most High a - gain has called The dark - ness in - to light.
Bring con - so - la - tion to our souls, Our droop - ing spir - its cheer.

That we may be ac - count-ed meet To dwell in bless-ed - ness.

Text: Old Edition.
Tune: Old Tune.

34 Hosanna to the Lamb

Matthew 21:7, 13 (9, 15)
Mark 11:10

TANDY 6.7.

Ho-san-na to the Lamb, Al-le - lu-i-a,_____ A - men.

Text and Tune: F. Phillip Tandy, 1943 - ; copyright 1980 Reorganized Church of Jesus Christ of Latter Day Saints.

35 When Morning Gilds the Skies

Alma 14:88
Revelation 5:13

LAUDES DOMINI 6.6.6.D.

1. When morn-ing gilds the skies, My heart a-wak-ing cries,
2. Let earth's wide cir-cle round In joy-ful notes re-sound,
3. Be this, while life is mine, My can-ti-cle di-vine,

May Je-sus Christ be praised; A-like at work and prayer
May Je-sus Christ be praised! Let air and sea and sky
May Je-sus Christ be praised; Be this the e-ter-nal song

To Je-sus I re-pair; May Je-sus Christ be praised!
From depth to height re-ply, May Je-sus Christ be praised!
Through all the a-ges long, May Je-sus Christ be praised!

Text: From the German, 19th century; trans. Edward Caswall, 1814-1878.
Tune: Joseph Barnby, 1838-1896.

Refrain

We'll sing and we'll shout with the ar - mies of heav - en,

"Ho - san - nah, ho - san - nah to God and the Lamb!" Let

glo - ry to them in the high - est be giv - en

Hence - forth and for - ev - er! A - men, and a - men!

Text: W. W. Phelps, 1792-1872.
Tune: English Tune.

Sung at the dedication of Kirtland Temple.

33 The Spirit of God Like a Fire Is Burning

III Nephi 8:25, 26
D. and C. 85:18

PARACLETE 12.11.12.11. with refrain

1. The Spir - it of God like a fire is burn - ing;
2. The Lord is ex - tend - ing his saints' un - der - stand - ing,
3. We call in our sol - emn as - sem - blies, in spir - it,

The lat - ter-day glo - ry be - gins to come forth;
Re - stor - ing their judg - es and all as at first;
To spread forth the king - dom of heav - en a - broad,

The vi - sions and bless - ings of old are re - turn - ing;
The knowl - edge and pow - er of God are ex - pand - ing;
That we through our faith may be - gin to in - her - it

The an - gels are com - ing to vis - it the earth.
The veil o'er the earth is be - gin - ning to burst.
The vi - sions and bless - ings and glo - ries of God.

Immortal, Invisible, God Only Wise

32

Colossians 1:2, 14-17
D. and C. 85:16, 18

ST. DENIO 11.11.11.11.

1. Im - mor - tal, in - vis - i - ble, God on - ly wise,
2. Un - rest - ing, un - hast - ing, and si - lent as light,
3. To all, life thou giv - est— to both great and small;
4. Thou dwell - est in glo - ry, thou reign - est in light;

In light in - ac - ces - si - ble hid from our eyes,
Nor want - ing, nor wast - ing, thou rul - est in might,
In all life thou liv - est, the true life of all;
Thine an - gels a - dore thee, all veil - ing their sight;

Most bless - ed, most glo - rious, the An - cient of Days,
Thy jus - tice like moun - tains high soar - ing a - bove
We blos - som and flour - ish as leaves on the tree,
All praise we should ren - der; O help us to see

Al - might - y, vic - to - rious, thy great name we praise.
Thy clouds which are foun - tains of good - ness and love.
And with - er and per - ish— but naught chang - eth thee.
'Tis on - ly the splen - dor of light hid - eth thee!

Text: Walter Chalmers Smith, 1825-1908, alt.
Tune: Welsh Hymn Melody, John Roberts' *Canaidau y Cyssegr*, 1839.

31 Come Thou Fount of Every Blessing

D. and C. 83:17c
Psalm 135:1-3

NETTLETON 8.7.8.7.D.

1. Come thou Fount of ev-ery bless-ing, Tune my heart to sing thy grace;
2. Here I raise mine Eb-en-e-zer; Hith-er by thy help I'm come;
3. Oh, to grace how great a debt-or Dai-ly I'm con-strained to be!

Streams of mer-cy, nev-er ceas-ing, Call for songs of loud-est praise.
And I hope, by thy good pleas-ure, Safe-ly to ar-rive at home.
Let thy good-ness like a fet-ter Bind my wan-dering heart to thee.

Teach me some me-lo-dious son-net Sung by flam-ing tongues a-bove;
Je-sus sought me when a stran-ger, Wan-dering from the fold of God;
Prone to wan-der, Lord, I feel it, Prone to leave the God I love;

Praise the mount-I'm fixed up-on it—Mount of thy re-deem-ing love.
He, to res-cue me from dan-ger, In-ter-posed his pre-cious blood.
Here's my heart, O take and seal it, Seal it for thy courts a-bove. A-men.

Text: Robert Robinson, 1735-1790.
Tune: John Wyeth, 1770-1858.

Let All the World in Every Corner Sing

30

Psalm 149:1, 2
II Nephi 9:136, 137

LIVINGSTON 10.4.6.6.6.6.10.4.

1. Let all the world in ev-ery cor-ner sing, My God and King!
2. Let all the world in ev-ery cor-ner sing, My God and King!

The heavens are not too high, His praise may thith-er fly;
The Church with psalms must shout; No door can keep them out,

The earth is not too low, His prais-es there may grow.
But, a-bove all, the heart Must bear the long-est part.

Let all the world in ev-ery cor-ner sing, My God and King!
Let all the world in ev-ery cor-ner sing, My God and King!

Text: George Herbert, 1593-1632.
Tune: Franklyn S. Weddle, 1905- . Copyright 1956 by Herald Publishing House.

29 With Happy Voices Ringing

D. and C. 85:17, 18
II Nephi 5:90, 91

FAITHFUL 7.6.7.6.D.

1. With hap - py voic - es ring - ing, Thy chil - dren, Lord, ap - pear,
2. What though no eye be - holds thee, No hand thy touch may feel,
3. And shall we not a - dore thee With more than joy - ous song,

Their joy - ous prais - es bring - ing In an - thems full and clear.
Thy u - ni - verse un - folds thee, Thy star - ry heavens re - veal.
And live in truth be - fore thee, All beau - ti - ful and strong?

For skies of gold - en splen - dor, For az - ure roll - ing sea,
The earth and all its glo - ry, Our homes and all we love,
Lord, bless our souls' en - deav - or Thy ser - vants true to be,

For blos - soms sweet and ten - der, O Lord, we wor - ship thee.
Tell forth the won - drous sto - ry Of One who reigns a - bove.
And through all life, for - ev - er, To live our praise to thee. A - men.

Text: William G. Tarrant, 1853-1928.
Tune: Johann Sebastian Bach, 1685-1750.

O Worship the King

28

Psalm 145:9, 10
D. and C. 76:1

HANOVER 10.10.11.11.
Alternate hymn: 27

1. O wor - ship the King, all glo - rious a - bove,
2. His boun - ti - ful care what tongue can re - cite?
3. O tell of his might, O sing of his grace,

O grate - ful - ly sing his power and his love;
It breathes in the air, it shines in the light,
Whose robe is the light, whose can - o - py, space;

Our Shield and De - fend - er, the An - cient of Days,
It streams from the hills, it de - scends to the plain,
His mer - cies how ten - der, how firm to the end;

Pa - vil - ioned in splen - dor and gird - ed with praise.
And sweet - ly dis - tills in the dew and the rain.
Our Mak - er, De - fend - er, Re - deem - er and Friend!

Text: Robert Grant, 1785-1838, alt.
Tune: William Croft, 1678-1727.

27

O Worship the King

Psalm 145:9, 10
D. and C. 76:1

LYONS 10.10.11.11.
Alternate hymn: 28

1. O wor - ship the King, all glo - rious a - bove,
2. His boun - ti - ful care what tongue can re - cite?
3. O tell of his might, O sing of his grace,

O grate - ful - ly sing his power and his love;
It breathes in the air, it shines in the light,
Whose robe is the light, whose can - o - py, space;

Our Shield and De - fend - er, the An - cient of Days,
It streams from the hills, it de - scends to the plain,
His mer - cies how ten - der, how firm to the end;

Pa - vil - ioned in splen - dor and gird - ed with praise.
And sweet - ly dis - tills in the dew and the rain.
Our Mak - er, De - fend - er, Re - deem - er, and Friend!

Text: Robert Grant, 1785-1838, alt.
Tune: J. Michael Haydn, 1737-1806.

shine with beams so bright No mor-tal eye can bear the sight.
arm, and shall ful-fill His great de-crees and sov-ereign will.
name; I love his word; Join all my powers to praise the Lord!

Text: Isaac Watts, 1674-1748.
Tune: William B. Bradbury, 1816-1868.

Lord, May Our Hearts Be Tuned to Sing 26

Psalm 96:7-9
Alma 14:97

GRATEFULNESS L.M.

1. Lord, may our hearts be tuned to sing Thy great and
2. Great God, thy good-ness we a-dore; Help us to
3. Our sa-cred vows we now re-new, Our lives a-

ev-er-last-ing praise, Our will-ing hands an of-fering
sing thy bound-less love, Own thee as God for-ev-er-
fresh to thee de-vote; Help us to keep each prom-ise

bring To thee on this the chief of days.
more, And swell thy praise in realms a-bove.
true, And seek thy glo-ry to pro-mote. A-men.

Text: Charles Derry, 1826-1921.
Tune: Mary A. Bradford, 1821-1902.

24   Blest Be Thou, O God of Israel

I Chronicles 29:10, 11
II Nephi 6:41, 42

NORMAN 8.7.8.7.

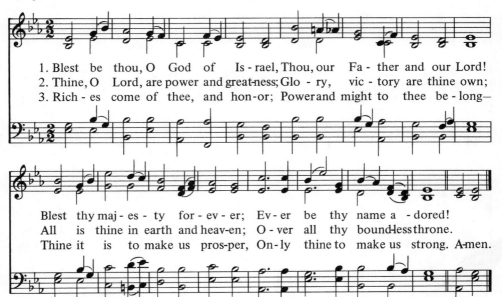

1. Blest be thou, O God of Is-rael, Thou, our Fa-ther and our Lord!
2. Thine, O Lord, are power and great-ness; Glo - ry, vic-tory are thine own;
3. Rich - es come of thee, and hon-or; Power and might to thee be-long—

Blest thy maj - es - ty for - ev - er; Ev - er be thy name a - dored!
All is thine in earth and heav-en; O - ver all thy bound-less throne.
Thine it is to make us pros-per, On - ly thine to make us strong. A-men.

Text: Attr. to Henry U. Onderdonk, 1789-1858.
Tune: Mark H. Forscutt, 1834-1903.

25   The Lord Jehovah Reigns

Psalm 47:1-7
I Nephi 5:126, 127, 130

SUTHERLAND 6.6.6.6.6.8.8.

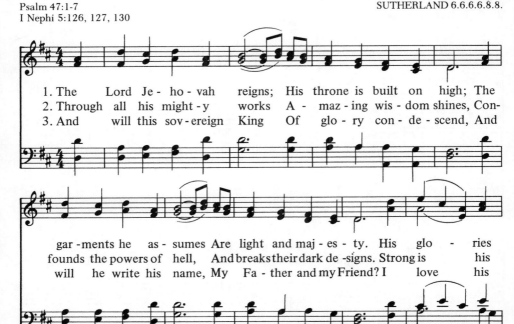

1. The Lord Je - ho - vah reigns; His throne is built on high; The
2. Through all his might - y works A - maz - ing wis - dom shines, Con-
3. And will this sov - ereign King Of glo - ry con - de - scend, And

gar - ments he as - sumes Are light and maj - es - ty. His glo - ries
founds the powers of hell, And breaks their dark de -signs. Strong is his
will he write his name, My Fa - ther and my Friend? I love his

All Glory, Laud, and Honor

23

Mark 11:9-12 (9, 10)
II Nephi 3:61, 65, 66

ST. THEODULPH 7.6.7.6.D.

1. All glo - ry, laud, and hon - or To thee, Re - deem - er, King,
2. The com - pa - ny of an - gels Are prais - ing thee on high,
3. To thee, be - fore thy pas - sion, They sang their hymns of praise;

To whom the lips of chil - dren Made sweet ho - san - nas ring.
Cre - a - tion and all mor - tals In cho - rus make re - ply.
To thee, now high ex - alt - ed, Our mel - o - dy we raise.

Thou art the King of Is - rael, Thou Da - vid's roy - al Son,
The mul - ti - tude of peo - ple With palms be - fore thee went;
Thou didst ac - cept their prais - es; Ac - cept the praise we bring,

Who in the Lord's name com - est, The King and Bless - ed One.
Our praise and prayer and an - thems Be - fore thee we pre - sent.
Who in all good de - light - est, Thou good and gra - cious King.

Text: Theodulph of Orleans, c. 760-821; trans. by John M. Neale, 1818-1866, alt.
Tune: Melchior Teschner, 1584-1635.

22 Morning Has Broken

II Peter 1:4-8
Psalm 62:1, 2, 5-8

BUNESSAN 5.5.5.4.D.

1. Morn-ing has bro - ken Like the first morn - ing; Black-bird has
2. Sweet the rain's new fall Sun - lit from heav - en, Like the first
3. Mine is the sun - light! Mine is the morn - ing Born of the

spo - ken Like the first bird. Praise for the sing - ing!
dew fall On the first grass. Praise for the sweet - ness
one light E - den saw play! Praise with e - la - tion,

Praise for the morn - ing! Praise for them, spring-ing Fresh from the Word!
Of the wet gar - den, Sprung in com-plete-ness Where his feet pass.
Praise ev -ery morn - ing, God's re - cre - a - tion Of the new day!

Text: Eleanor Farjeon, 1881-1965. Used by permission of David Higham Associates Ltd.
Tune: Gaelic melody; harm. by David Evans, 1874-1948; from *The Revised Church Hymnary* by permission of Oxford University Press.

Declare, O Heavens, the Lord of Space

21

Colossians 1:16-18
Alma 14:124, 125

LASST UNS ERFREUEN
8.8.8.8.8. with alleluias

1. De -clare, O heavens, the Lord of space; Re - ply broad lands in ev - ery place;
2. Launch forth in faith and bold-ly rise; Be - yond our plan-et pierce the skies,
3. Yet see this world with prob-lems filled; Earth longs for life the Mas-ter willed;
4. O Lord, whose power all space ex-tols, Draw near our lives, en-large our souls,

Tell his splen-dor! Al-le - lu - ia! New realms we find he first hath made;
Bound-less ven - ture! Al-le - lu - ia! No soar-ing flight can e'er out-run
Light its dark-ness! Al-le - lu - ia! Reach out all bro-ken lives to mend;
Dwell with-in us! Al-le - lu - ia! Stir deeds of grace to serve thy plan;

All be - ing is his power dis - played;
Truth God has shown us in his Son;
In Christ win peace no war will end; Al-le - lu - ia! Al-le - lu - ia!
Wake joy the morn-ing stars be - gan;

Al - le - lu - ia! Al - le - lu - ia! Al - le - lu - ia!

Text: Robert Lansing Edwards, 1915 - ; alt.; Copyright 1962 The Hymn Society of America. Used by permission.
Tune: Geistliche Kirchengesäng, Cologne, 1623; arr. Ralph Vaughan Williams, 1872-1958. From *The English Hymnal* by permission of Oxford University Press.

20   Joyful, Joyful, We Adore Thee

II Nephi 9:133-137
Psalm 150

HYMN TO JOY 8.7.8.7.D.

1. Joy - ful, joy - ful, we a - dore thee, God of glo - ry, Lord of love;
2. All thy works with joy sur-round thee; Earth and heaven re -flect thy rays.
3. Thou art giv - ing and for - giv - ing, Ev - er bless - ing, ev - er blest,

Hearts un - fold like flowers be - fore thee, Hail thee as the sun a - bove.
Stars and an - gels sing a -round thee, Cen - ter of un - bro - ken praise;
Well- spring of the joy of liv - ing, O - cean depth of hap - py rest!

Melt the clouds of sin and sad - ness; Drive the dark of doubt a-way;
Field and for - est, vale and moun-tain, Blos - soming mead-ow, flash-ing sea,
Thou our Fa - ther, Christ our broth-er, All who live in love are thine;

Giv - er of im - mor - tal glad-ness, Fill us with the light of day!
Chant-ing bird and flow-ing foun-tain Call us to re -joice in thee.
Teach us how to love each oth - er; Lift us to the joy di-vine. A-men.

Repeat Refrain

He made their glow-ing col-ors, He made their ti-ny wings.
The sun-set, and the morn-ing That bright-ens up the sky,
The ripe fruits in the gar-den, He made them ev-'ry one.
How great is God Al-might-y, Who has made all things well.

Text: Cecil Frances Alexander, 1818-1895.
Tune: Traditional English Melody adapted by Martin Shaw, 1875-1958; used by permission of J. Curwen and Sons;
G. Schirmer, Inc., U. S. agent.

Oh, for a Thousand Tongues to Sing   19

D. and C. 22:23   AZMON C.M.
Psalm 30:1-4

1. Oh, for a thou-sand tongues to sing My dear Re-deem-er's praise,
2. My gra-cious Mas-ter and my God, As-sist me to pro-claim,
3. Je-sus, the name that calms our fears, That bids our sor-rows cease;
4. He breaks the power of can-celed sin; He sets the pris-oner free;
5. He speaks, and, lis-tening to his voice, New life the dead re-ceive;

The glo-ries of my God and King, The tri-umphs of his grace!
To spread through all the earth a-broad, The hon-ors of thy name.
'Tis mu-sic in the sin-ner's ears, 'Tis life and health and peace.
His blood can make the foul-est clean; His love a-vails for me.
The mourn-ful, bro-ken hearts re-joice; The hum-ble poor be-lieve.

Text: Charles Wesley, 1707-1788.
Tune: Carl G. Gläser, 1784-1839; arr. Lowell Mason, 1792-1872.

18 All Things Bright and Beautiful

I Chronicles 16:23-29
D. and C. 59:4

ROYAL OAK 7.6.7.6. with refrain

Refrain

All things bright and beau-ti-ful, All crea-tures great and small,

All things wise and won-der-ful, The Lord God made them all.

Fine

1. Each lit-tle flower that o-pens, Each lit-tle bird that sings,
2. The pur-ple-head-ed moun-tain, The riv-er run-ning by,
3. The cold wind in the win-ter, The pleas-ant sum-mer sun,
4. He gave us eyes to see them, And lips that we might tell

Lord, Whose Love Through Humble Service   17

Mark 10:42-45
Alma 14:82, 96

HYFRYDOL 8.7.8.7.D.

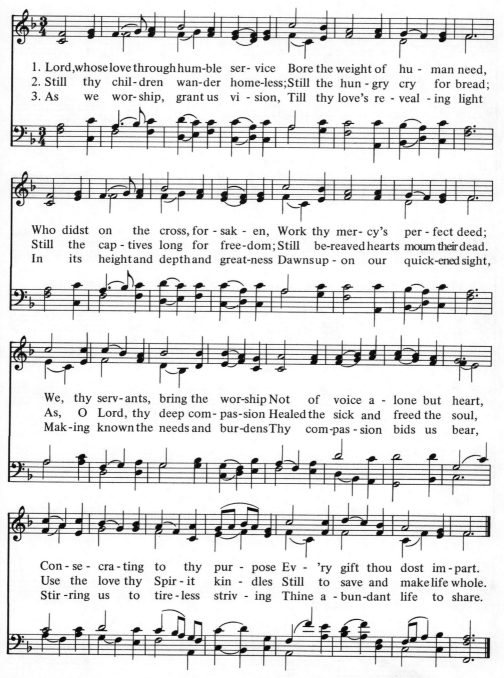

1. Lord, whose love through hum-ble ser-vice Bore the weight of hu-man need,
2. Still thy chil-dren wan-der home-less; Still the hun-gry cry for bread;
3. As we wor-ship, grant us vi-sion, Till thy love's re-veal-ing light

Who didst on the cross, for-sak-en, Work thy mer-cy's per-fect deed;
Still the cap-tives long for free-dom; Still be-reaved hearts mourn their dead.
In its height and depth and great-ness Dawns up-on our quick-ened sight,

We, thy serv-ants, bring the wor-ship Not of voice a-lone but heart,
As, O Lord, thy deep com-pas-sion Healed the sick and freed the soul,
Mak-ing known the needs and bur-dens Thy com-pas-sion bids us bear,

Con-se-cra-ting to thy pur-pose Ev-'ry gift thou dost im-part.
Use the love thy Spir-it kin-dles Still to save and make life whole.
Stir-ring us to tire-less striv-ing Thine a-bun-dant life to share.

Text: Albert F. Bayly, 1901 - ; alt. by author, 1975. Copyright 1961 by Albert F. Bayly; used by permission.
Tune: Rowland Hugh Prichard, 1811-1887.

15   O Worship the Lord

Psalm 96:9
I Chronicles 16:29

PORTER 13.8.

O wor-ship the Lord in the beau-ty of ho-li-ness;

Serve him with glad-ness, all the earth. A-men.

Text: Adapted from Psalm 96:9.
Tune: Robert Guy McCutchan, 1877-1958.

16   O Thou Who Hearest

Psalm 65:1, 2
D. and C. 28:2b

MORECAMBE 10.10.10.10.
See 181 for a higher setting.

O thou who hear-est ev-ery heart-felt prayer, With thy rich

grace, Lord, all our hearts pre-pare; Thou art our life, thou art our

love and light; O let this Sab-bath hour with thee be bright. A-men.

Text: Unknown.
Tune: Frederick Cook Atkinson, 1841-1897.

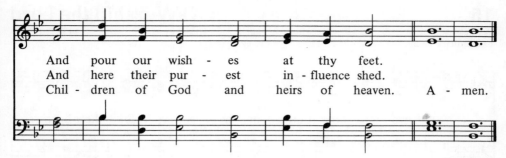

And pour our wish - es at thy feet.
And here their pur - est in - fluence shed.
Chil - dren of God and heirs of heaven. A - men.

Text: Henry Ware, 1793-1843.
Tune: Lowell Mason, 1792-1872.

O God, Whose Presence Glows in All — 14

I Thessalonians 2:19
D. and C. 18:6

HURSLEY L.M.

1. O God, whose pres - ence glows in all— With - in, a -
2. Thy truth be with the heart be - lieved By all who
3. Thy love its ho - ly in - fluence pour To keep us
4. Send down its an - gels to our side; Send in its

round us, and a - bove— Thy word we bless, thy name we
seek this sa - cred place; With power pro - claimed, in peace re -
meek and make us free, And throw its bind - ing bless - ing
calm up - on each breast; For we would know no oth - er

call, Whose word is Truth, whose name is Love.
ceived, Our spir - its' light thy Spir - it's grace.
more Round each with all, and all with thee.
guide, And we can need no oth - er rest. A - men.

Text: Nathaniel L. Frothingham, 1793-1870.
Tune: Allgemeines Katholisches Gesangbuch, Vienna, 1774; arr. William Henry Monk, 1823-1889.

12

Sovereign and Transforming Grace

Moroni 10:29, 30
D. and C. 90:3b, c

GOTTSCHALK (Mercy) 7.7.7.7.

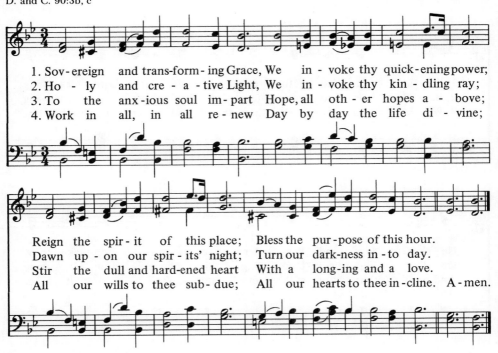

1. Sov-ereign and trans-form-ing Grace, We in-voke thy quick-ening power;
2. Ho - ly and cre-a-tive Light, We in-voke thy kin-dling ray;
3. To the anx-ious soul im-part Hope, all oth-er hopes a - bove;
4. Work in all, in all re-new Day by day the life di - vine;

Reign the spir-it of this place; Bless the pur-pose of this hour.
Dawn up-on our spir-its' night; Turn our dark-ness in-to day.
Stir the dull and hard-ened heart With a long-ing and a love.
All our wills to thee sub-due; All our hearts to thee in-cline. A-men.

Text: Frederick Henry Hedge, 1805-1890.
Tune: Arr. from Louis M. Gottschalk, 1829-1869.

13

Great God, as Followers of Thy Son

D. and C. 76:2a, b
Romans 8:16, 17

HEBRON L.M.

1. Great God, as fol-lowers of thy Son We bow be-fore
2. We seek the truth which Je-sus brought; His path of light
3. May faith and hope and love a-bound, Our sins and er -

thy mer-cy seat To wor-ship thee, the Ho-ly One,
we long to tread; Here be his ho-ly doc-trines taught,
rors be for-given, And we from day to day be found

We Gather Together

I Corinthians 15:57, 58
D. and C. 59:1

KREMSER 12.11.12.11.

1. We gath - er to - geth - er to ask the Lord's bless - ing;
2. Be - side us to guide us, our God with us join - ing,
3. We all do ex - tol thee, thou lead - er tri - umph - ant,

He chas - tens and has - tens his will to make known;
Or - dain - ing, main - tain - ing his king - dom di - vine;
And pray that thou still our de - fend - er wilt be.

The wick - ed op - press - ing cease them from dis - tress - ing.
So from the be - gin - ning the fight we were win - ning;
Let thy con - gre - ga - tion es - cape trib - u - la - tion.

Sing prais - es to his name; he for - gets not his own.
Thou, Lord, wast at our side; the glo - ry be thine!
Thy name be ev - er praised! O Lord, make us free! A - men.

Text: Netherlands Folk Song; trans. by Theodore Baker, 1851-1934.
Tune: Traditional Netherlands Melody, publ. 1625; arr. by Edward Kremser, 1838-1914.

10 — Lord, We Come Before Thee Now

D. and C. 10:3
Isaiah 26:3, 4

INVOCATION 7.7.7.7.D.

1. Lord, we come be-fore thee now; At thy feet we hum-bly bow.
2. Send some mes-sage from thy word That may joy and peace af-ford.

Fill our hearts with thy rich grace; Tune our lips to sing thy praise.
Com-fort those who weep and mourn; Let the time of joy re-turn.

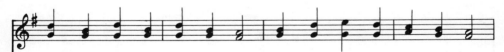

Lord, on thee our souls de-pend; In com-pas-sion now de-scend.
Heal the sick; the cap-tive free; Let us all re-joice in thee.

Lord, from here we would not go Till a bless-ing thou be-stow.
Let thy Spir-it now im-part Full sal-va-tion to each heart. A-men.

Text: William Hammond, 1719-1783, alt.
Tune: Old Tune.

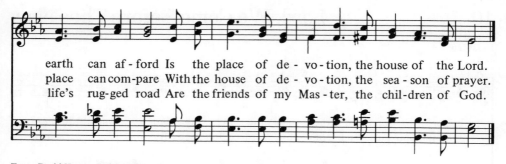

earth can af-ford Is the place of de-vo-tion, the house of the Lord.
place can com-pare With the house of de-vo-tion, the sea-son of prayer.
life's rug-ged road Are the friends of my Mas-ter, the chil-dren of God.

Text: David Hyrum Smith, 1844-1904.
Tune: Ascribed to Norman W. Smith, 1833-1917.

Within the Shelter of Our Walls 9

Alma 16:219-222
D. and C. 119:2

LOBT GOTT, IHR CHRISTEN
8.6.8.8.6.

1. With - in the shel - ter of our walls, Be pres - ent, Lord, to
2. Trans-form our spir - its as we learn Thy lov - ing dis - ci -
3. Make dai - ly bread a sac - ra - ment Which Thou, O Lord, might

guide. Where work is planned, where plea - sure calls, Where hearts keep
pline. When tasks are hard or du - ty stern, Give us the
share. Give con - ver - sa - tion high in - tent; Our dai - ly

ho - ly fes - ti - vals, Find wel - come, and a - bide.
wis - dom to dis - cern Thy com - rade - ship with - in.
strength for thee be spent With thought and lov - ing care. A - men.

Text: Elinor Lennen; copyright 1961 Hymn Society of America; used by permission.
Tune: Nicolaus Hermann, c. 1485-1561; harm. Austin C. Lovelace, 1919 - ; harm. copyright 1965 Abingdon Press.
   Used by permission.

7 O Lord, Around Thine Altar Now

D. and C. 85:16b-e
Philippians 4:6, 7

ARLINGTON C.M.

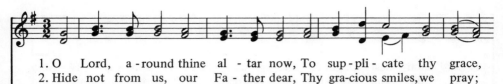

1. O Lord, a-round thine al-tar now, To sup-pli-cate thy grace,
2. Hide not from us, our Fa-ther dear, Thy gra-cious smiles, we pray;
3. Let thy great light il-lume our souls And guide our err-ing feet;
4. Then, gra-cious God, ac-cept us now, From thy great throne a-bove;

As chil-dren we would hum-bly bow And seek our Fa-ther's face.
But let thy love dis-pel our fear And draw us near to thee.
Thy Spir-it o'er us hold con-trol And keep us from de-ceit.
Help us to keep our sa-cred vow, And fill us with thy love. A-men.

Text: Charles Derry, 1826-1921.
Tune: Thomas A. Arne, 1710-1778.

8 You May Sing of the Beauty

II Nephi 8:19
Psalm 122:1

FELLOWSHIP 12.12.12.12.

1. You may sing of the beau-ty of moun-tain and dale, Of the sil-ver-y
2. You may boast of the sweet-ness of day's ear-ly dawn, Of the skies' soft-ening
3. You may val-ue the friend-ship of youth and of age, And se-lect for your

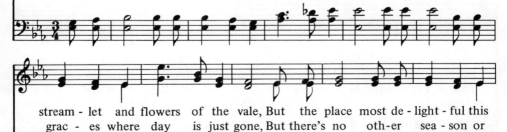

stream-let and flowers of the vale, But the place most de-light-ful this
grac-es where day is just gone, But there's no oth-er sea-son or
com-rades the no-ble and sage, But the friends that most cheer me on

Lord, Thou Hast Brought Us to This Place

6

D. and C. 59:1a, b
Psalm 24:1-5

MELITA 8.8.8.D.

1. Lord, thou hast brought us to this place As sure-ly as thy cho-sen race Was led to Is-rael's prom-ised land, Where bless-ings flowed on ev-ery hand. Al-might-y God, we dare to pray That thou wilt bless thy house this day.

2. Be still and won-der at God's grace That he for us did choose this place, And here in love he deigns to share His peace— and joys be-yond com-pare. Al-might-y God, we praise thy name, Thy won-drous prov-i-dence ac-claim.

3. The streams and wood-lands, flowers and trees, High hills and sun-shine, cool-ing breeze—Thou mad-est all— A set-ting fine For this thy house is tru-ly thine. Al-might-y God, for this place fair Ac-cept our hum-ble, thank-ful prayer.

4. We can-not give thee what is thine, So sim-ply pray that light may shine From out this place, that all may see Thy love for us and ours for thee. Al-might-y God, with strength en-dow Thy chil-dren for their wit-ness now. A-men.

Text: Dennis Aldridge, 1934 - ; copyright 1980 Reorganized Church of Jesus Christ of Latter Day Saints.
Tune: John B. Dykes, 1823-1876.

5 In God's Most Holy Presence

Isaiah 58:13, 14
D. and C. 29:2d, e

EWING 7.6.7.6.D.

1. In God's most ho - ly pres - ence We meet with one ac - cord
2. Our wor - ship will be fruit - less, And all our prayers be vain,
3. If we but love Thee tru - ly, Our love is not con - fined

To grasp the hand of friend - ship And learn of Christ, our Lord.
If, hold - ing this day sa - cred, We make the week pro - fane.
To Thee but grows ex - pan - sive, Em - brac - ing hu - man - kind.

We leave the week be - hind us, With all its toil and strain,
In ev - ery dai - ly du - ty High pur - pose we must show,
Help us in mu - tual ser - vice For all, a - broad, at home,

With grate - ful hearts to wel - come The Sab - bath once a - gain.
And as we hope for heav - en Make earth a heaven be - low.
To share the con - quering tra - vail That makes Thy king - dom come.

Text: Ernest Dodgshun, 1876-1944.
Tune: Alexander Ewing, 1830-1895.

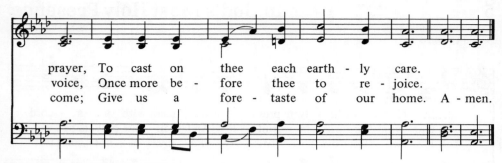

prayer, To cast on thee each earth - ly care.
voice, Once more be - fore thee to re - joice.
come; Give us a fore - taste of our home. A - men.

Text: Mary Bowly Peters, 1813-1856.
Tune: Arthur H. Mills, 1870-1943.

Sweet the Time, Exceeding Sweet 4

Psalm 50:5, 6
John 4:25, 26 (23-24)

HENDON 7.7.7.7.7.

1. Sweet the time, ex - ceed-ing sweet, When the Saints to -
2. Sing the Son's a - maz - ing love— How he left the
3. Sweet the place, ex - ceed-ing sweet, Where the Saints in

geth - er meet, When the Sav - ior is the theme, When they
realms a - bove, Took our na - ture and our place, Lived and
glo - ry meet, Where the Sav - ior's still the theme, Where they

joy to sing of him; When they joy to sing of him.
died to save our race; Lived and died to save our race.
see and sing of him; Where they see and sing of him.

Text: George Burder, 1752-1832.
Tune: Henri Abraham César Malan, 1787-1864.

2   Met in Thy Sacred Name, O Lord

D. and C. 6:15, 16a
Matthew 18:20

MANOAH C.M.

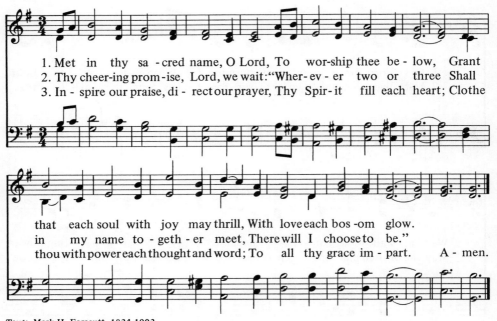

1. Met in thy sa-cred name, O Lord, To wor-ship thee be-low, Grant
2. Thy cheer-ing prom-ise, Lord, we wait:"Wher-ev-er two or three Shall
3. In-spire our praise, di-rect our prayer, Thy Spir-it fill each heart; Clothe

that each soul with joy may thrill, With love each bos-om glow.
in my name to-geth-er meet, There will I choose to be."
thou with power each thought and word; To all thy grace im-part. A-men.

Text: Mark H. Forscutt, 1834-1903.
Tune: Arr. from Gioacchino A. Rossini, 1792-1868, in Henry W. Greatorex's *Collection of Church Music*, 1851.

3   With Thankful Hearts We Meet, O Lord

I Nephi 7:56-59
D. and C. 34:6

HICKS L.M.

1. With thank-ful hearts we meet, O Lord, To sing thy
2. Dear Shep-herd of thy cho-sen flock, Thy peo-ple's
3. Thy pres-ence, Sav-ior, now we seek; Con-firm the

praise, to hear thy word, To seek thy face in ear-nest
shield, their shad-ow-ing rock, Once more we meet to hear thy
strong, sus-tain the weak; Way-worn and tired we hith-er

O Lord, Grace Our Communion

1

Matthew 11:29, 30
D. and C. 119:6c

HOLY WINGS 7.6.7.6.D.

1. O Lord, grace our com-mun-ion In the prom-ise of this hour.
2. In-to lives weighed down by sor-row Let thy Spir-it gent-ly flow;

We a-wait some con-fir-ma-tion Of thy lib-er-a-ting power.
May the bruised and bro-ken-heart-ed, Re-sur-rec-tion sure-ly know.

E-ven though thy Saints here gath-ered The hu-man bur-den share,
And so, re-newed in spir-it, With new-born hearts a-flame,

In the warmth of thy com-pas-sion, How can our hearts de-spair?
Let this wait-ing con-gre-ga-tion Rise up and praise thy name.

Text: Geoffrey F. Spencer, 1927 - ; copyright 1980 Reorganized Church of Jesus Christ of Latter Day Saints.
Tune: Swedish Folk Melody; harm. Mark S. Dickey, 1885-1961; alt.

Praise and Thanksgiving

Gathering for Worship 1-17

Praise 18-72

Thanksgiving 73-78

Acknowledgments

The work of production of the hymnal was coordinated by Peter Judd and Roger A. Revell. Carol Cavin prepared the copy for typesetting and handled the copyright and permissions arrangements. The engraving (typesetting) of the words and music on the hymn pages was done by the following employees of White Harvest Music Corporation: Dale G. Rider, Twila Hidy Rider, Doris Harding Criss, Edward Grove Mason, and William T. Stewart. Proofreading was by Norma Smith Coberly, Blake West, John Davies, Patricia Ballinger, and Marsha Morgan. Cover design and non-hymnic layout was prepared by the Office of Graphic Arts at the Auditorium. Hymn titles, indexes, and other non-hymnic text was set by Herald House, which also printed and published the hymnal. Others assisting in the project include Nadine Woods, Barbara Bryant Thatcher, Evelyn Maples, Bethany Andrews, Stephen Goff, David C. Hawley, Delores Fitzpatrick, and Mary Fincham.

but separate numbers. The other hymn is listed immediately below the tune name and meter as an alternate hymn. When it is suggested that a tune found elsewhere in the hymnal may be used appropriately with a particular text, this tune name and number is listed as an alternate tune.

When a tune is found elsewhere in the hymnal at a higher or lower setting (key), a note to this effect is included. A few hymns have descant, faux bourdon (melody in the tenor), or canon (round) settings in addition to the regular arrangement. These are provided to enhance the musical possibilities in the hymnal.

6. *Guitar chords* have been provided above the staff lines of some hymns. These do *not* apply to keyboard accompaniment, and it is not anticipated that keyboard instruments will be used simultaneously with guitars. Capital (upper case) letters are used to designate major chords. Small (lower case) letters are used to designate minor chords.

7. *Time signatures* are included in most hymns according to conventional notation and use. A few hymns have no time signature because the measures (bars) are of unequal length. In most of these cases an instructional note appears immediately above the top staff line of the hymn.

8. *Amens* are placed at the end of certain prayer hymns, and with those whose melodic and harmonic structures indicate the use of amens. The responsibility of deciding when the use of an amen is appropriate rests with the persons planning the worship service.

9. *Credit lines* appear below each hymn. Complete information is included regarding the sources of texts and tunes.

Copyrighted hymns include the words "copyright," "by permission," or the equivalent. Some of these copyrighted hymns may be reproduced for one-time use in worship bulletins. Others may not be reproduced without specific permission from the copyright holder. *A list of hymns that may not be reproduced without further permission appears on the copyright page at the front of this hymnal. Unauthorized reproduction of hymn texts or tunes for any purpose can result in legal action by the owners of the material.* For up-to-date information on the copyright status of a specific hymn contact the Music Office, the Auditorium, Independence, MO 64051.

The following abbreviations are used in the credit lines:

Abr.	- Abbreviated
Adapt.	- Adapted
Alt.	- Altered
Arr.	- Arranged
Attr.	- Attributed to
C.	- Circa
Coll.	- Collected
Harm.	- Harmonized
Rev.	- Revised
Tr., Trans.	- Translated or Translator

Additional information on the content and use of *Hymns of the Saints* can be found in the paperback book *Hymns in Worship: A Guide to "Hymns of the Saints"* by Roger A. Revell, Herald House 1981.

Harold Neal, Chairman, 1981 Hymnal Committee
Peter A. Judd, Director, Worship Office
Roger A. Revell, Director, Music Office

adequately express the church's best current understanding of the gospel. In some cases, an infrequently used hymn was thought to express important concepts and so was matched with a new tune. Some hymns from *The Hymnal* (1956) were retained with text changes. In some cases only a word or two was changed. In other cases major rewriting was necessary to make the hymn reflect adequately the best thinking of the church theologically and linguistically. The hymn texts generally reflect the "Policy of Inclusive Language" for church publications approved by the First Presidency in 1978.

Hymns of the Saints contains no identifiable children's or youth hymns. The committee has sought diligently for hymns that are representative of the expressions of all ages—hymns which can have meaning and be sung joyfully by all worshipers regardless of chronological age.

The image of the church as a world organization has been enhanced by the inclusion of a number of hymns from other than English-speaking countries. For practical purposes these texts have been translated into English. The committee also intentionally tried to include hymns that are meaningful to the Saints in all English-speaking countries where the hymnal will be used. It is recognized, however, that church members as they gather for worship in various places may wish to supplement this hymnal with hymns of their own choosing from other sources.

The hymnal offers new hymns in the traditional style, some in an unfamiliar setting, some folk and modern gospel hymns, and some in the contemporary classical style. Within this rich variety, a sense of unity can be felt by using hymns that express diversity of need and cultural background. As the Saints share in this pluralism of musical and poetic ministry, they may find their spiritual awareness enlarged and enriched.

The intent of the committee was to assemble a body of hymnody that can have wide usage throughout the church without trying to include all the hymns that the various jurisdictions of the church in various places may wish to use.

Every effort has been made to keep the hymns as simple to sing as possible, consistent with music's integrity as an art. Some who enjoy part singing (alto, tenor, bass) may encounter difficulty with some new tunes at first. The desire to provide music of warmth and vitality has resulted in the use of slightly complex rhythms, moving harmonies, and lyric-style melodies, some of which are intended to be sung in unison. However, as many of these "unison" tunes as possible have been given four-part settings.

The editors of the hymnal have arranged the page layout for maximum readability. The following features appear on the hymn pages:

1. The broad *category* in which the hymn is found appears at the top outside corner of the page. For maximum flexibility in the use of hymns, make regular use of the topical index when choosing hymns.

2. The hymn *number* appears immediately below the category designation.

3. The hymn *title* (first line) appears at the top of the hymn opposite the number, on the inside of the page.

4. Two *scriptures* are listed at the top left of each hymn. Where Inspired Version versification differs from that of other versions, *the I.V. verses are listed first, with those for other versions in parentheses.* See also scripture index.

5. The *tune name and meter* are listed at the top right of each hymn. When the same text is set to two different tunes, the hymns have adjacent

In 1971 a Committee on Congregational Music was established to study the need for a new hymnal. This committee superseded an earlier standing committee of the Music Department which had been evaluating hymn texts and tunes that were brought to its attention. The 1971 committee was formed in response to many written and verbal requests to consider the publication of a new official hymnal for the church.

The early 1970s saw considerable ferment, even turmoil, in contemporary hymn-writing and usage. The committee monitored and studied these phenomena while directing its efforts toward the production of two supplements to *The Hymnal* (1956). Published in 1974 and 1976, these supplements contained a total of twenty-five new hymns, some of a contemporary style. The response of the church was such that the First Presidency approved plans to publish an entirely new hymnal. The committee's name was then changed to the 1981 Hymnal Committee.

The task of hymn selection has been a formidable one. The committee recognized that since the early 1960s organized religion, including our own church, has passed through a sort of crucible characterized by changing theological concepts, the searching eye of historical research, shifting modes of expression, and increased sensitivity to the sanctity of personhood. The committee was also very much aware that the range of musical taste in the church had widened considerably during the past two decades. That the committee faced its task unflinchingly and brought it to fruition is a testimony of the members' individual and collective devotion and endurance. Theirs is an accomplishment that exacted virtually years of dedicated and ofttimes heart-rending service.

Hymns of the Saints contains a total of 501 hymns. These are organized in four major sections: Praise and Thanksgiving (78 hymns), Contemplation and Renewal (107 hymns), God's Word for Us (183 hymns), and Commission and Commitment (133 hymns). Each section is divided into categories for the purpose of ordering the hymns in the hymnal. Users of the hymnal are advised, however, to make frequent use of the topical index rather than to rely solely on the category designations that appear at the top of each hymn page. The topical index is extensive, and each hymn is included under several topics in addition to the category on the page. Regular use of this index will increase the versatility and usefulness of the entire hymnal and each individual hymn.

Of the 501 hymns, 292 were included in *The Hymnal* (1956). Four hymns were in the 1933 *Saints Hymnal* but not in *The Hymnal* (1956) or its supplements. Twenty-one appeared in the First and Second Supplements. One hundred and eighty-four are entirely new hymns not previously appearing in RLDS hymnals.

In total, 127 hymns have texts written in whole or in part by RLDS authors, and 88 hymn tunes were written, harmonized, or adapted by RLDS composers.

Criteria for hymn text selection focused on the extent to which texts expressed the faith of the Saints as best understood by the committee. Most hymns in *The Hymnal* (1956) that were not chosen for inclusion in this hymnal were omitted because they are seldom used, or because the text does not

Elementary School Music in Independence, Missouri. She served on the Board of Trustees of Graceland College from 1974 to 1980.

Roger A. Revell served as administrative assistant in the Music Department from 1971 to 1978, when he was named Director of the Music Office. His background in music education, youth ministries, management, and copyright law enabled him to make valuable contributions to the committee.

Ammon Roberson, a music educator, has served the church for many years as a choir director. In 1978 he received the Distinguished Music Alumnus Award from the Central Missouri State University, and retired in 1980 from their music department with the rank of Professor Emeritus. He brought a viewpoint to the committee that combined traditional RLDS sentiments with universal concepts.

Geoffrey Spencer has served the church as an appointee minister in many capacities. He is now President of the High Priest's Quorum and of the Temple School. His keen theological and historical insights were invaluable to the committee's work. One of the exciting aspects of the work of the committee was the discovery and stimulation of Brother Spencer's talent as hymn writer.

John Thumm, a former high school music teacher, is currently an appointee seventy. His musical background and field experience enabled him to make an important contribution to the process.

For many years Alta Topham has been a piano teacher, organist, and music director for the Shenandoah, Iowa, congregation. Her utter devotion and loyal support were an inspiration to the rest of the committee. Her practical experience, participation, and influence were characterized by a graciousness and gentleness of spirit that helped immeasurably.

Alan Tyree as a linguist, hymn-writer, theologian, and musician has made many contributions to the work of the committee. As a member of the Quorum of Twelve Apostles since 1966, his considerable contact with the church membership helped raise the committee's awareness of the worldwide needs of the church.

Richard Clothier and Kenneth Cooper both served on the committee between 1971 and 1975 while on the Graceland Music Faculty.

John Obetz, Auditorium organist, assisted the committee as a member of the music subcommittee. Doris Harding Criss served as the principal accompanist for the committee. From 1978 to 1980 Carol Cavin served as the committee's executive secretary.

Other persons and groups assisting in this project are named in the acknowledgments.

We express our appreciation to these people for their efforts and commend this hymnal to the church. May we indeed "sing to the Lord a new song" as we use *Hymns of the Saints* in our corporate worship.

The First Presidency

Wallace B. Smith
Duane E. Couey
Howard S. Sheehy, Jr.

May 1981

Foreword

It is with considerable pleasure that we present *Hymns of the Saints* to the church.

The publication of a new hymnal is a major event and has potential for enormous impact on the membership. A hymnal stands alongside the scriptures as a vital resource for the church's worship. Hymn singing is the principal form, or in some places the only form, by which we speak our faith together. It is a means whereby Saints around the world can experience a sense of unity as we sing the well-loved hymns of the church.

In order to express appropriately our best understanding and experience of the gospel it is necessary on occasion to revise our hymnal—introducing new hymns and discarding some old ones. By producing a new hymnal at this time we are responding to the invitation "Sing unto the Lord a new song" (Isaiah 42:10).

This hymnal is the culmination of many years of intensive work involving hymn selection and production of the book itself. The hymn selection committee was chaired by Harold Neal who from 1969 to 1978 served as Director of the Music Department (now Music Office). In 1978 Brother Neal was named Director of Ensembles and Fine Arts Consultant for the church. One of his continuing responsibilities has been to conduct the annual performance of *Messiah,* broadcasts of which are heard around the world. His previous musical experience includes membership in the London, Ontario, Symphony Orchestra, various conducting and choral responsibilities in church and community, and fifteen years on the Graceland College faculty. Brother Neal ably facilitated the work of the committee throughout its tenure.

The following persons served as members of the committee under Brother Neal's competent leadership:

Rosalee Elser is an accomplished organist and music theorist. Her natural talents and professional training have been enhanced by industrious application. As a result many hymns are richer in sound because of her skill as a harmonizer and arranger.

Barbara Higdon has taught English at Graceland College and other institutions of higher education. She is presently Vice President/Dean of Academic Affairs at Park College in Parkville, Missouri. Her skills in the use of the English language greatly facilitated the work of the committee.

Barbara Howard, a Herald House editor, made an imaginative and stimulating contribution to the theological integrity and poetic quality of hymn texts. She was one whose hymn-writing talents blossomed in response to need.

In the fall of 1975 Peter Judd was invited to join the committee by virtue of his appointment as Director of the Worship Office. His inquiring mind and mediating spirit strengthened the work of the committee.

The effectiveness of Aleta Runkle Page's contribution was consistent with her lifelong service in many areas of the church. She was a staff member on numerous occasions between 1956 and 1969 at music camps sponsored by the Music Department. She was employed for a number of years as Supervisor of

Lord's Prayer

Our Father who art in heaven, Hallowed be thy name. Thy kingdom come. Thy will be done on earth, as it is done in heaven. Give us this day, our daily bread. And forgive us our trespasses, as we forgive those who trespass against us. And suffer us not to be led into temptation, but deliver us from evil. For thine is the kingdom, and the power, and the glory, forever and ever, Amen.

—*Matthew 6:10-15 (Inspired Version)*

Communion Prayers

BREAD

O God, the eternal Father, we ask thee in the name of thy Son Jesus Christ, to bless and sanctify this bread to the souls of all those who partake of it, that they may eat in remembrance of the body of thy Son, and witness unto thee, O God, the eternal Father, that they are willing to take upon them the name of thy Son, and always remember him and keep his commandments which he has given them, that they may always have his Spirit to be with them. Amen.

—*Doctrine and Covenants 17:22d*

WINE

O God, the eternal Father, we ask thee in the name of thy Son Jesus Christ, to bless and sanctify this wine to the souls of all those who drink of it, that they may do it in remembrance of the blood of thy Son which was shed for them, that they may witness unto thee, O God, the eternal Father, that they do always remember him, that they may have his Spirit to be with them. Amen.

—*Doctrine and Covenants 17:23b*

Contents

Lord's Prayer and Communion Prayers
Foreword
Preface
Acknowledgments

SECTION 1 Praise and Thanksgiving

Gathering for Worship
Praise
Thanksgiving

SECTION 2 Contemplation and Renewal

Prayer
Prayer Responses
Repentance and Forgiveness

Faith and Trust
Renewal

SECTION 3 God's Word for Us

God
Christ
Christ's birth
Christ's death
Christ's resurrection
Holy Spirit
The Church
Revelation

Zion and the Kingdom
Lord's Supper
Blessing
Baptism
Confirmation
Ordination
Marriage

SECTION 4 Commission and Commitment

Challenge
Stewardship
Service and Commitment

Witness
Benediction and Sending Forth

INDEXES

Reprint Restrictions

Most hymns in this hymnal may be reproduced for onetime use only (e.g., in worship service bulletins). Following is a list of hymns that **cannot** be reproduced without specific written permission from the copyright holders:

Text: 44, 107, 153, 156, 171, 182, 197, 227, 300, 308, 315, 327, 331, 367, 452, 491, 493
Tune: 85, 108, 111, 163, 170, 202, 218, 297, 301, 356; (descant) 142
Both: 74, 79, 187, 285, 290, 322, 377, 382, 388, 420, 466

Please send two (2) copies of all reproduced hymns to Music Office, the Auditorium, Independence, MO 64051. Extensive efforts have been made to contact and acknowledge copyright owners. Errors or omissions, sent to the above address, will be corrected in subsequent printings.

Copyright © 1981   Corrected printing, 1982.

Herald Publishing House
Independence, Missouri

ISBN 0-8309-0326-7
Printed in the United States of America

Hymns of the Saints

Reorganized Church of Jesus Christ
of Latter Day Saints

Hymns
of the
Saints